# Introductory Business
# Statistics

**Senior Contributing Authors**

Alexander Holmes, The University Of Oklahoma
Barbara Illowsky, De Anza College
Susan Dean, De Anza College

# Table of Contents

# PREFACE

Welcome to *Introductory Business Statistics*, an OpenStax resource. This textbook was written to increase student access to high-quality learning materials, maintaining highest standards of academic rigor at little to no cost.

## About OpenStax

OpenStax is a nonprofit based at Rice University, and it's our mission to improve student access to education. Our first openly licensed college textbook was published in 2012, and our library has since scaled to over 25 books for college and AP® courses used by hundreds of thousands of students. OpenStax Tutor, our low-cost personalized learning tool, is being used in college courses throughout the country. Through our partnerships with philanthropic foundations and our alliance with other educational resource organizations, OpenStax is breaking down the most common barriers to learning and empowering students and instructors to succeed.

## About OpenStax Resources
### Customization

*Introductory Business Statistics* is licensed under a Creative Commons Attribution 4.0 International (CC BY) license, which means that you can distribute, remix, and build upon the content, as long as you provide attribution to OpenStax and its content contributors.

Because our books are openly licensed, you are free to use the entire book or pick and choose the sections that are most relevant to the needs of your course. Feel free to remix the content by assigning your students certain chapters and sections in your syllabus, in the order that you prefer. You can even provide a direct link in your syllabus to the sections in the web view of your book.

Instructors also have the option of creating a customized version of their OpenStax book. The custom version can be made available to students in low-cost print or digital form through their campus bookstore. Visit the Instructor Resources section of your book page on openstax.org for more information.

### Errata

All OpenStax textbooks undergo a rigorous review process. However, like any professional-grade textbook, errors sometimes occur. Since our books are web based, we can make updates periodically when deemed pedagogically necessary. If you have a correction to suggest, submit it through the link on your book page on openstax.org. Subject matter experts review all errata suggestions. OpenStax is committed to remaining transparent about all updates, so you will also find a list of past errata changes on your book page on openstax.org.

### Format

You can access this textbook for free in web view or PDF through openstax.org, and for a low cost in print.

## About *Introductory Business Statistics*

*Introductory Business Statistics* is designed to meet the scope and sequence requirements of the one-semester statistics course for business, economics, and related majors. Core statistical concepts and skills have been augmented with practical business examples, scenarios, and exercises. The result is a meaningful understanding of the discipline, which will serve students in their business careers and real-world experiences.

### Coverage and Scope

*Introductory Business Statistics* began as a customized version of OpenStax Introductory Statistics by Barbara Illowsky and Susan Dean. Statistics faculty at The University of Oklahoma used the business statistics version for several years, and the author has continually refined it based on student success and faculty feedback.

The book is structured in a similar manner to most traditional statistics textbooks. The most significant topical changes occur the latter chapters on regression analysis. Discrete probability density functions have been reordered to provide a logical progression from simple counting formulas to more complex continuous distributions. Many additional homework assignments have been added, as well as new, more mathematical examples.

*Introductory Business Statistics* places a significant emphasis on the development and practical application of formulas, so that students have a deeper understanding of their interpretation and application of data. To achieve this unique approach, the author included a wealth of additional material and purposely deemphasized the use of the scientific calculator. Specific changes regarding formula use include:

- Expanded discussions of the combinatorial formulas, factorials, and sigma notation
- Adjustments to explanations of the acceptance/rejection rule for hypothesis testing, as well as a focus on terminology regarding confidence intervals
- Deep reliance on statistical tables for the process of finding probabilities (which would not be required if probabilities relied on scientific calculators)
- Continual and emphasized links to the Central Limit Theorem throughout the book. *Introductory Business Statistics* consistently links each test statistic back to this fundamental theorem in inferential statistics.

Another fundamental focus of the book is the link between statistical inference and the scientific method. Business and economics models are fundamentally grounded in assumed relationships of cause and effect. They are developed to both test hypotheses and to predict from such models. This comes from the belief that statistics is the gatekeeper that allows some theories to remain and others to be cast aside for a new perspective of the world around us. This philosophical view is presented in detail throughout and informs the method of presenting the regression model, in particular.

The correlation and regression chapter includes confidence intervals for predictions, alternative mathematical forms to allow for testing categorical variables, and the presentation of the multiple regression model.

## Pedagogical Features

- **Examples** are placed strategically throughout the text to show students the step-by-step process of interpreting and solving statistical problems. To keep the text relevant for students, the examples are drawn from a broad spectrum of practical topics; these include examples about college life and learning, health and medicine, retail and business, and sports and entertainment.
- **Practice, Homework, and Bringing It Together** problems give the students problems at various degrees of difficulty while also including real-world scenarios to engage students.

## Additional Resources
### Student and instructor resources

We've compiled additional resources for both students and instructors, including Getting Started Guides, [other resources dependent on book]. Instructor resources require a verified instructor account, which you can apply for when you log in or create your account on openstax.org. Take advantage of these resources to supplement your OpenStax book.

### Community Hubs

OpenStax partners with the Institute for the Study of Knowledge Management in Education (ISKME) to offer Community Hubs on OER Commons – a platform for instructors to share community-created resources that support OpenStax books, free of charge. Through our Community Hubs, instructors can upload their own materials or download resources to use in their own courses, including additional ancillaries, teaching material, multimedia, and relevant course content. We encourage instructors to join the hubs for the subjects most relevant to your teaching and research as an opportunity both to enrich your courses and to engage with other faculty.

To reach the Community Hubs, visit www.oercommons.org/hubs/OpenStax.

### Technology partners

As allies in making high-quality learning materials accessible, our technology partners offer optional low-cost tools that are integrated with OpenStax books. To access the technology options for your text, visit your book page on openstax.org.

## About the authors
### Senior contributing authors

**Alexander Holmes, The University of Oklahoma**

**Barbara Illowsky, DeAnza College**

**Susan Dean, DeAnza College**

### Contributing authors

Kevin Hadley, Analyst, Federal Reserve Bank of Kansas City

### Reviewers

Birgit Aquilonius, West Valley College
Charles Ashbacher, Upper Iowa University, Cedar Rapids
Abraham Biggs, Broward Community College
Daniel Birmajer, Nazareth College

Roberta Bloom, De Anza College
Bryan Blount, Kentucky Wesleyan College
Ernest Bonat, Portland Community College
Sarah Boslaugh, Kennesaw State University
David Bosworth, Hutchinson Community College
Sheri Boyd, Rollins College
George Bratton, University of Central Arkansas
Franny Chan, Mt. San Antonio College
Jing Chang, College of Saint Mary
Laurel Chiappetta, University of Pittsburgh
Lenore Desilets, De Anza College
Matthew Einsohn, Prescott College
Ann Flanigan, Kapiolani Community College
David French, Tidewater Community College
Mo Geraghty, De Anza College
Larry Green, Lake Tahoe Community College
Michael Greenwich, College of Southern Nevada
Inna Grushko, De Anza College
Valier Hauber, De Anza College
Janice Hector, De Anza College
Jim Helmreich, Marist College
Robert Henderson, Stephen F. Austin State University
Mel Jacobsen, Snow College
Mary Jo Kane, De Anza College
John Kagochi, University of Houston--Victoria
Lynette Kenyon, Collin County Community College
Charles Klein, De Anza College
Alexander Kolovos
Sheldon Lee, Viterbo University
Sara Lenhart, Christopher Newport University
Wendy Lightheart, Lane Community College
Vladimir Logvenenko, De Anza College
Jim Lucas, De Anza College
Suman Majumdar, University of Connecticut
Lisa Markus, De Anza College
Miriam Masullo, SUNY Purchase
Diane Mathios, De Anza College
Robert McDevitt, Germanna Community College
John Migliaccio, Fordham University
Mark Mills, Central College
Cindy Moss, Skyline College
Nydia Nelson, St. Petersburg College
Benjamin Ngwudike, Jackson State University
Jonathan Oaks, Macomb Community College
Carol Olmstead, De Anza College
Barbara A. Osyk, The University of Akron
Adam Pennell, Greensboro College
Kathy Plum, De Anza College
Lisa Rosenberg, Elon University
Sudipta Roy, Kankakee Community College
Javier Rueda, De Anza College
Yvonne Sandoval, Pima Community College
Rupinder Sekhon, De Anza College
Travis Short, St. Petersburg College
Frank Snow, De Anza College
Abdulhamid Sukar, Cameron University
Jeffery Taub, Maine Maritime Academy
Mary Teegarden, San Diego Mesa College
John Thomas, College of Lake County

Philip J. Verrecchia, York College of Pennsylvania
Dennis Walsh, Middle Tennessee State University
Cheryl Wartman, University of Prince Edward Island
Carol Weideman, St. Petersburg College
Kyle S. Wells, Dixie State University
Andrew Wiesner, Pennsylvania State University

# 1 | SAMPLING AND DATA

**Figure 1.1** We encounter statistics in our daily lives more often than we probably realize and from many different sources, like the news. (credit: David Sim)

## Introduction

You are probably asking yourself the question, "When and where will I use statistics?" If you read any newspaper, watch television, or use the Internet, you will see statistical information. There are statistics about crime, sports, education, politics, and real estate. Typically, when you read a newspaper article or watch a television news program, you are given sample information. With this information, you may make a decision about the correctness of a statement, claim, or "fact." Statistical methods can help you make the "best educated guess."

Since you will undoubtedly be given statistical information at some point in your life, you need to know some techniques for analyzing the information thoughtfully. Think about buying a house or managing a budget. Think about your chosen profession. The fields of economics, business, psychology, education, biology, law, computer science, police science, and early childhood development require at least one course in statistics.

Included in this chapter are the basic ideas and words of probability and statistics. You will soon understand that statistics and probability work together. You will also learn how data are gathered and what "good" data can be distinguished from "bad."

## 1.1 | Definitions of Statistics, Probability, and Key Terms

The science of **statistics** deals with the collection, analysis, interpretation, and presentation of **data**. We see and use data in our everyday lives.

In this course, you will learn how to organize and summarize data. Organizing and summarizing data is called **descriptive statistics**. Two ways to summarize data are by graphing and by using numbers (for example, finding an average). After you have studied probability and probability distributions, you will use formal methods for drawing conclusions from "good" data. The formal methods are called **inferential statistics**. Statistical inference uses probability to determine how confident we can be that our conclusions are correct.

Effective interpretation of data (inference) is based on good procedures for producing data and thoughtful examination of the data. You will encounter what will seem to be too many mathematical formulas for interpreting data. The goal of statistics is not to perform numerous calculations using the formulas, but to gain an understanding of your data. The calculations can be done using a calculator or a computer. The understanding must come from you. If you can thoroughly grasp the basics of statistics, you can be more confident in the decisions you make in life.

## Probability

**Probability** is a mathematical tool used to study randomness. It deals with the chance (the likelihood) of an event occurring. For example, if you toss a **fair** coin four times, the outcomes may not be two heads and two tails. However, if you toss the same coin 4,000 times, the outcomes will be close to half heads and half tails. The expected theoretical probability of heads in any one toss is $\frac{1}{2}$ or 0.5. Even though the outcomes of a few repetitions are uncertain, there is a regular pattern of outcomes when there are many repetitions. After reading about the English statistician Karl **Pearson** who tossed a coin 24,000 times with a result of 12,012 heads, one of the authors tossed a coin 2,000 times. The results were 996 heads. The fraction $\frac{996}{2000}$ is equal to 0.498 which is very close to 0.5, the expected probability.

The theory of probability began with the study of games of chance such as poker. Predictions take the form of probabilities. To predict the likelihood of an earthquake, of rain, or whether you will get an A in this course, we use probabilities. Doctors use probability to determine the chance of a vaccination causing the disease the vaccination is supposed to prevent. A stockbroker uses probability to determine the rate of return on a client's investments. You might use probability to decide to buy a lottery ticket or not. In your study of statistics, you will use the power of mathematics through probability calculations to analyze and interpret your data.

## Key Terms

In statistics, we generally want to study a **population**. You can think of a population as a collection of persons, things, or objects under study. To study the population, we select a **sample**. The idea of **sampling** is to select a portion (or subset) of the larger population and study that portion (the sample) to gain information about the population. Data are the result of sampling from a population.

Because it takes a lot of time and money to examine an entire population, sampling is a very practical technique. If you wished to compute the overall grade point average at your school, it would make sense to select a sample of students who attend the school. The data collected from the sample would be the students' grade point averages. In presidential elections, opinion poll samples of 1,000–2,000 people are taken. The opinion poll is supposed to represent the views of the people in the entire country. Manufacturers of canned carbonated drinks take samples to determine if a 16 ounce can contains 16 ounces of carbonated drink.

From the sample data, we can calculate a statistic. A **statistic** is a number that represents a property of the sample. For example, if we consider one math class to be a sample of the population of all math classes, then the average number of points earned by students in that one math class at the end of the term is an example of a statistic. The statistic is an estimate of a population parameter, in this case the mean. A **parameter** is a numerical characteristic of the whole population that can be estimated by a statistic. Since we considered all math classes to be the population, then the average number of points earned per student over all the math classes is an example of a parameter.

One of the main concerns in the field of statistics is how accurately a statistic estimates a parameter. The accuracy really depends on how well the sample represents the population. The sample must contain the characteristics of the population in order to be a **representative sample**. We are interested in both the sample statistic and the population parameter in inferential statistics. In a later chapter, we will use the sample statistic to test the validity of the established population parameter.

A **variable**, or random variable, usually notated by capital letters such as $X$ and $Y$, is a characteristic or measurement that can be determined for each member of a population. Variables may be **numerical** or **categorical**. **Numerical variables** take on values with equal units such as weight in pounds and time in hours. **Categorical variables** place the person or thing into a category. If we let $X$ equal the number of points earned by one math student at the end of a term, then $X$ is a numerical variable. If we let $Y$ be a person's party affiliation, then some examples of $Y$ include Republican, Democrat, and Independent. $Y$ is a categorical variable. We could do some math with values of $X$ (calculate the average number of points earned, for example), but it makes no sense to do math with values of $Y$ (calculating an average party affiliation makes no sense).

**Data** are the actual values of the variable. They may be numbers or they may be words. **Datum** is a single value.

Two words that come up often in statistics are **mean** and **proportion**. If you were to take three exams in your math classes and obtain scores of 86, 75, and 92, you would calculate your mean score by adding the three exam scores and dividing by three (your mean score would be 84.3 to one decimal place). If, in your math class, there are 40 students and 22 are men and 18 are women, then the proportion of men students is $\frac{22}{40}$ and the proportion of women students is $\frac{18}{40}$. Mean and proportion are discussed in more detail in later chapters.

### NOTE

The words "**mean**" and "**average**" are often used interchangeably. The substitution of one word for the other is common practice. The technical term is "arithmetic mean," and "average" is technically a center location. However, in practice among non-statisticians, "average" is commonly accepted for "arithmetic mean."

## Example 1.1

Determine what the key terms refer to in the following study. We want to know the average (mean) amount of money first year college students spend at ABC College on school supplies that do not include books. We randomly surveyed 100 first year students at the college. Three of those students spent $150, $200, and $225, respectively.

### Solution 1.1

The **population** is all first year students attending ABC College this term.

The **sample** could be all students enrolled in one section of a beginning statistics course at ABC College (although this sample may not represent the entire population).

The **parameter** is the average (mean) amount of money spent (excluding books) by first year college students at ABC College this term: the population mean.

The **statistic** is the average (mean) amount of money spent (excluding books) by first year college students in the sample.

The **variable** could be the amount of money spent (excluding books) by one first year student. Let $X$ = the amount of money spent (excluding books) by one first year student attending ABC College.

The **data** are the dollar amounts spent by the first year students. Examples of the data are $150, $200, and $225.

## Try It Σ

**1.1** Determine what the key terms refer to in the following study. We want to know the average (mean) amount of money spent on school uniforms each year by families with children at Knoll Academy. We randomly survey 100 families with children in the school. Three of the families spent $65, $75, and $95, respectively.

## Example 1.2

Determine what the key terms refer to in the following study.

A study was conducted at a local college to analyze the average cumulative GPA's of students who graduated last year. Fill in the letter of the phrase that best describes each of the items below.

1. Population _f_  2. Statistic _g_  3. Parameter _e_  4. Sample _d_  5. Variable _b_  6. Data _c_

a) all students who attended the college last year

b) the cumulative GPA of one student who graduated from the college last year

c) 3.65, 2.80, 1.50, 3.90

d) a group of students who graduated from the college last year, randomly selected

e) the average cumulative GPA of students who graduated from the college last year

f) all students who graduated from the college last year

g) the average cumulative GPA of students in the study who graduated from the college last year

**Solution 1.2**
1. f; 2. g; 3. e; 4. d; 5. b; 6. c

## Example 1.3

Determine what the key terms refer to in the following study.

As part of a study designed to test the safety of automobiles, the National Transportation Safety Board collected and reviewed data about the effects of an automobile crash on test dummies. Here is the criterion they used:

| Speed at which Cars Crashed | Location of "drive" (i.e. dummies) |
|---|---|
| 35 miles/hour | Front Seat |

Table 1.1

Cars with dummies in the front seats were crashed into a wall at a speed of 35 miles per hour. We want to know the proportion of dummies in the driver's seat that would have had head injuries, if they had been actual drivers. We start with a simple random sample of 75 cars.

**Solution 1.3**

The **population** is all cars containing dummies in the front seat.

The **sample** is the 75 cars, selected by a simple random sample.

The **parameter** is the proportion of driver dummies (if they had been real people) who would have suffered head injuries in the population.

The **statistic** is proportion of driver dummies (if they had been real people) who would have suffered head injuries in the sample.

The **variable** $X$ = the number of driver dummies (if they had been real people) who would have suffered head injuries.

The **data** are either: yes, had head injury, or no, did not.

## Example 1.4

Determine what the key terms refer to in the following study.

An insurance company would like to determine the proportion of all medical doctors who have been involved in one or more malpractice lawsuits. The company selects 500 doctors at random from a professional directory and determines the number in the sample who have been involved in a malpractice lawsuit.

**Solution 1.4**

The **population** is all medical doctors listed in the professional directory.

The **parameter** is the proportion of medical doctors who have been involved in one or more malpractice suits in the population.

The **sample** is the 500 doctors selected at random from the professional directory.

The **statistic** is the proportion of medical doctors who have been involved in one or more malpractice suits in the sample.

The **variable** $X$ = the number of medical doctors who have been involved in one or more malpractice suits.

The **data** are either: yes, was involved in one or more malpractice lawsuits, or no, was not.

# 1.2 | Data, Sampling, and Variation in Data and Sampling

Data may come from a population or from a sample. Lowercase letters like $x$ or $y$ generally are used to represent data values. Most data can be put into the following categories:

- Qualitative
- Quantitative

**Qualitative data** are the result of categorizing or describing attributes of a population. **Qualitative data** are also often called categorical data. Hair color, blood type, ethnic group, the car a person drives, and the street a person lives on are examples of qualitative(categorical) data. Qualitative(categorical) data are generally described by words or letters. For instance, hair color might be black, dark brown, light brown, blonde, gray, or red. Blood type might be AB+, O-, or B+. Researchers often prefer to use quantitative data over qualitative(categorical) data because it lends itself more easily to mathematical analysis. For example, it does not make sense to find an average hair color or blood type.

**Quantitative data** are always numbers. Quantitative data are the result of **counting** or **measuring** attributes of a population. Amount of money, pulse rate, weight, number of people living in your town, and number of students who take statistics are examples of quantitative data. Quantitative data may be either **discrete** or **continuous**.

All data that are the result of counting are called **quantitative discrete data**. These data take on only certain numerical values. If you count the number of phone calls you receive for each day of the week, you might get values such as zero, one, two, or three.

Data that are not only made up of counting numbers, but that may include fractions, decimals, or irrational numbers, are called **quantitative continuous data**. Continuous data are often the results of measurements like lengths, weights, or times. A list of the lengths in minutes for all the phone calls that you make in a week, with numbers like 2.4, 7.5, or 11.0, would be quantitative continuous data.

## Example 1.5 Data Sample of Quantitative Discrete Data

The data are the number of books students carry in their backpacks. You sample five students. Two students carry three books, one student carries four books, one student carries two books, and one student carries one book. The numbers of books (three, four, two, and one) are the quantitative discrete data.

**1.5** The data are the number of machines in a gym. You sample five gyms. One gym has 12 machines, one gym has 15 machines, one gym has ten machines, one gym has 22 machines, and the other gym has 20 machines. What type of data is this?

## Example 1.6 Data Sample of Quantitative Continuous Data

The data are the weights of backpacks with books in them. You sample the same five students. The weights (in pounds) of their backpacks are 6.2, 7, 6.8, 9.1, 4.3. Notice that backpacks carrying three books can have different weights. Weights are quantitative continuous data.

**1.6** The data are the areas of lawns in square feet. You sample five houses. The areas of the lawns are 144 sq. feet, 160 sq. feet, 190 sq. feet, 180 sq. feet, and 210 sq. feet. What type of data is this?

## Example 1.7

You go to the supermarket and purchase three cans of soup (19 ounces) tomato bisque, 14.1 ounces lentil, and 19 ounces Italian wedding), two packages of nuts (walnuts and peanuts), four different kinds of vegetable (broccoli, cauliflower, spinach, and carrots), and two desserts (16 ounces pistachio ice cream and 32 ounces chocolate chip cookies).

Name data sets that are quantitative discrete, quantitative continuous, and qualitative(categorical).

**Solution 1.7**

One Possible Solution:

- The three cans of soup, two packages of nuts, four kinds of vegetables and two desserts are quantitative discrete data because you count them.

- The weights of the soups (19 ounces, 14.1 ounces, 19 ounces) are quantitative continuous data because you measure weights as precisely as possible.

- Types of soups, nuts, vegetables and desserts are qualitative(categorical) data because they are categorical.

Try to identify additional data sets in this example.

## Example 1.8

The data are the colors of backpacks. Again, you sample the same five students. One student has a red backpack, two students have black backpacks, one student has a green backpack, and one student has a gray backpack. The colors red, black, black, green, and gray are qualitative(categorical) data.

**1.8** The data are the colors of houses. You sample five houses. The colors of the houses are white, yellow, white, red, and white. What type of data is this?

### NOTE

You may collect data as numbers and report it categorically. For example, the quiz scores for each student are recorded throughout the term. At the end of the term, the quiz scores are reported as A, B, C, D, or F.

### Example 1.9

Work collaboratively to determine the correct data type (quantitative or qualitative). Indicate whether quantitative data are continuous or discrete. Hint: Data that are discrete often start with the words "the number of."

a. the number of pairs of shoes you own

b. the type of car you drive

c. the distance from your home to the nearest grocery store

d. the number of classes you take per school year

e. the type of calculator you use

f. weights of sumo wrestlers

g. number of correct answers on a quiz

h. IQ scores (This may cause some discussion.)

**Solution 1.9**
Items a, d, and g are quantitative discrete; items c, f, and h are quantitative continuous; items b and e are qualitative, or categorical.

**1.9** Determine the correct data type (quantitative or qualitative) for the number of cars in a parking lot. Indicate whether quantitative data are continuous or discrete.

### Example 1.10

A statistics professor collects information about the classification of her students as freshmen, sophomores, juniors, or seniors. The data she collects are summarized in the pie chart Figure 1.1. What type of data does this graph show?

## Classification of Statistics Students

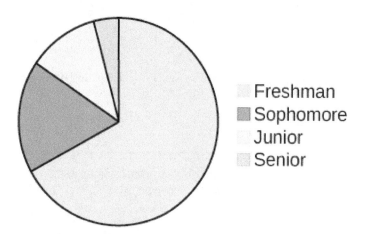

Figure 1.2

### Solution 1.10

This pie chart shows the students in each year, which is **qualitative (or categorical) data**.

## Try It Σ

**1.10** The registrar at State University keeps records of the number of credit hours students complete each semester. The data he collects are summarized in the histogram. The class boundaries are 10 to less than 13, 13 to less than 16, 16 to less than 19, 19 to less than 22, and 22 to less than 25.

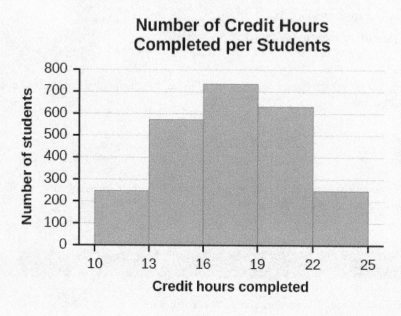

Figure 1.3

What type of data does this graph show?

## Qualitative Data Discussion

Below are tables comparing the number of part-time and full-time students at De Anza College and Foothill College enrolled for the spring 2010 quarter. The tables display counts (frequencies) and percentages or proportions (relative frequencies). The percent columns make comparing the same categories in the colleges easier. Displaying percentages along with the numbers is often helpful, but it is particularly important when comparing sets of data that do not have the same totals, such as the total enrollments for both colleges in this example. Notice how much larger the percentage for part-time students at Foothill College is compared to De Anza College.

| De Anza College | | | | Foothill College | | |
|---|---|---|---|---|---|---|
| | Number | Percent | | | Number | Percent |
| Full-time | 9,200 | 40.9% | | Full-time | 4,059 | 28.6% |
| Part-time | 13,296 | 59.1% | | Part-time | 10,124 | 71.4% |
| Total | 22,496 | 100% | | Total | 14,183 | 100% |

Table 1.2 Fall Term 2007 (Census day)

Tables are a good way of organizing and displaying data. But graphs can be even more helpful in understanding the data. There are no strict rules concerning which graphs to use. Two graphs that are used to display qualitative(categorical) data are pie charts and bar graphs.

In a **pie chart**, categories of data are represented by wedges in a circle and are proportional in size to the percent of individuals in each category.

In a **bar graph**, the length of the bar for each category is proportional to the number or percent of individuals in each category. Bars may be vertical or horizontal.

A **Pareto chart** consists of bars that are sorted into order by category size (largest to smallest).

Look at **Figure 1.4** and **Figure 1.5** and determine which graph (pie or bar) you think displays the comparisons better.

It is a good idea to look at a variety of graphs to see which is the most helpful in displaying the data. We might make different choices of what we think is the "best" graph depending on the data and the context. Our choice also depends on what we are using the data for.

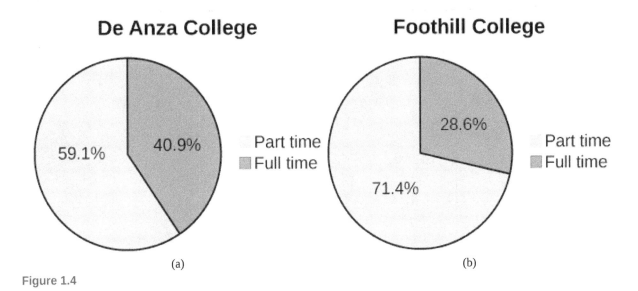

Figure 1.4

## Student Status

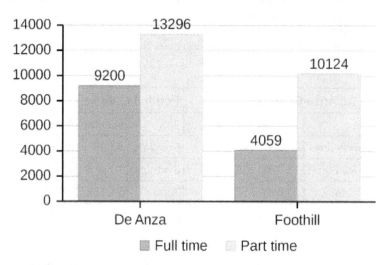

Figure 1.5

### Percentages That Add to More (or Less) Than 100%

Sometimes percentages add up to be more than 100% (or less than 100%). In the graph, the percentages add to more than 100% because students can be in more than one category. A bar graph is appropriate to compare the relative size of the categories. A pie chart cannot be used. It also could not be used if the percentages added to less than 100%.

| Characteristic/Category | Percent |
|---|---|
| Full-Time Students | 40.9% |
| Students who intend to transfer to a 4-year educational institution | 48.6% |
| Students under age 25 | 61.0% |
| TOTAL | 150.5% |

Table 1.3 De Anza College Spring 2010

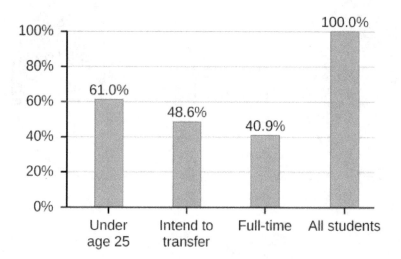

Figure 1.6

## Omitting Categories/Missing Data

The table displays Ethnicity of Students but is missing the "Other/Unknown" category. This category contains people who did not feel they fit into any of the ethnicity categories or declined to respond. Notice that the frequencies do not add up to the total number of students. In this situation, create a bar graph and not a pie chart.

|  | Frequency | Percent |
|---|---|---|
| Asian | 8,794 | 36.1% |
| Black | 1,412 | 5.8% |
| Filipino | 1,298 | 5.3% |
| Hispanic | 4,180 | 17.1% |
| Native American | 146 | 0.6% |
| Pacific Islander | 236 | 1.0% |
| White | 5,978 | 24.5% |
| TOTAL | 22,044 out of 24,382 | 90.4% out of 100% |

**Table 1.4 Ethnicity of Students at De Anza College Fall Term 2007 (Census Day)**

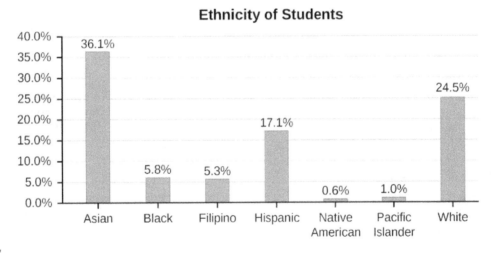

**Figure 1.7**

The following graph is the same as the previous graph but the "Other/Unknown" percent (9.6%) has been included. The "Other/Unknown" category is large compared to some of the other categories (Native American, 0.6%, Pacific Islander 1.0%). This is important to know when we think about what the data are telling us.

This particular bar graph in **Figure 1.8** can be difficult to understand visually. The graph in **Figure 1.9** is a Pareto chart. The Pareto chart has the bars sorted from largest to smallest and is easier to read and interpret.

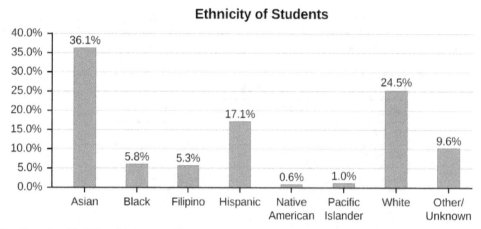

**Figure 1.8 Bar Graph with Other/Unknown Category**

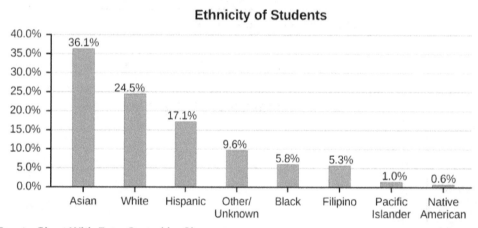

**Figure 1.9 Pareto Chart With Bars Sorted by Size**

## Pie Charts: No Missing Data

The following pie charts have the "Other/Unknown" category included (since the percentages must add to 100%). The chart in **Figure 1.10b** is organized by the size of each wedge, which makes it a more visually informative graph than the unsorted, alphabetical graph in **Figure 1.10a**.

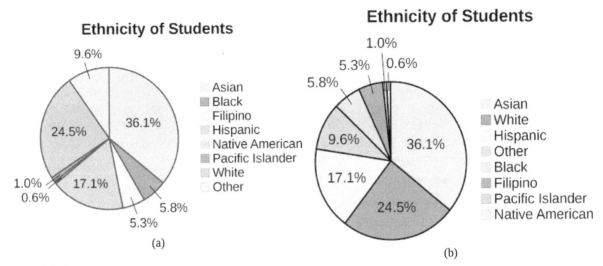

Figure 1.10

## Sampling

Gathering information about an entire population often costs too much or is virtually impossible. Instead, we use a sample of the population. **A sample should have the same characteristics as the population it is representing.** Most statisticians use various methods of random sampling in an attempt to achieve this goal. This section will describe a few of the most common methods. There are several different methods of **random sampling**. In each form of random sampling, each member of a population initially has an equal chance of being selected for the sample. Each method has pros and cons. The easiest method to describe is called a **simple random sample**. Any group of $n$ individuals is equally likely to be chosen as any other group of $n$ individuals if the simple random sampling technique is used. In other words, each sample of the same size has an equal chance of being selected.

Besides simple random sampling, there are other forms of sampling that involve a chance process for getting the sample. **Other well-known random sampling methods are the stratified sample, the cluster sample, and the systematic sample.**

To choose a **stratified sample**, divide the population into groups called strata and then take a **proportionate** number from each stratum. For example, you could stratify (group) your college population by department and then choose a proportionate simple random sample from each stratum (each department) to get a stratified random sample. To choose a simple random sample from each department, number each member of the first department, number each member of the second department, and do the same for the remaining departments. Then use simple random sampling to choose proportionate numbers from the first department and do the same for each of the remaining departments. Those numbers picked from the first department, picked from the second department, and so on represent the members who make up the stratified sample.

To choose a **cluster sample**, divide the population into clusters (groups) and then randomly select some of the clusters. All the members from these clusters are in the cluster sample. For example, if you randomly sample four departments from your college population, the four departments make up the cluster sample. Divide your college faculty by department. The departments are the clusters. Number each department, and then choose four different numbers using simple random sampling. All members of the four departments with those numbers are the cluster sample.

To choose a **systematic sample**, randomly select a starting point and take every $n^{th}$ piece of data from a listing of the population. For example, suppose you have to do a phone survey. Your phone book contains 20,000 residence listings. You must choose 400 names for the sample. Number the population 1–20,000 and then use a simple random sample to pick a number that represents the first name in the sample. Then choose every fiftieth name thereafter until you have a total of 400 names (you might have to go back to the beginning of your phone list). Systematic sampling is frequently chosen because it is a simple method.

A type of sampling that is non-random is convenience sampling. **Convenience sampling** involves using results that are readily available. For example, a computer software store conducts a marketing study by interviewing potential customers who happen to be in the store browsing through the available software. The results of convenience sampling may be very good in some cases and highly biased (favor certain outcomes) in others.

Sampling data should be done very carefully. Collecting data carelessly can have devastating results. Surveys mailed to households and then returned may be very biased (they may favor a certain group). It is better for the person conducting the survey to select the sample respondents.

True random sampling is done **with replacement**. That is, once a member is picked, that member goes back into the population and thus may be chosen more than once. However for practical reasons, in most populations, simple random sampling is done **without replacement**. Surveys are typically done without replacement. That is, a member of the population may be chosen only once. Most samples are taken from large populations and the sample tends to be small in comparison to the population. Since this is the case, sampling without replacement is approximately the same as sampling with replacement because the chance of picking the same individual more than once with replacement is very low.

In a college population of 10,000 people, suppose you want to pick a sample of 1,000 randomly for a survey. **For any particular sample of 1,000**, if you are sampling **with replacement**,

- the chance of picking the first person is 1,000 out of 10,000 (0.1000);
- the chance of picking a different second person for this sample is 999 out of 10,000 (0.0999);
- the chance of picking the same person again is 1 out of 10,000 (very low).

If you are sampling **without replacement**,

- the chance of picking the first person for any particular sample is 1000 out of 10,000 (0.1000);
- the chance of picking a different second person is 999 out of 9,999 (0.0999);
- you do not replace the first person before picking the next person.

Compare the fractions 999/10,000 and 999/9,999. For accuracy, carry the decimal answers to four decimal places. To four decimal places, these numbers are equivalent (0.0999).

Sampling without replacement instead of sampling with replacement becomes a mathematical issue only when the population is small. For example, if the population is 25 people, the sample is ten, and you are sampling **with replacement for any particular sample**, then the chance of picking the first person is ten out of 25, and the chance of picking a different second person is nine out of 25 (you replace the first person).

If you sample **without replacement**, then the chance of picking the first person is ten out of 25, and then the chance of picking the second person (who is different) is nine out of 24 (you do not replace the first person).

Compare the fractions 9/25 and 9/24. To four decimal places, 9/25 = 0.3600 and 9/24 = 0.3750. To four decimal places, these numbers are not equivalent.

When you analyze data, it is important to be aware of **sampling errors** and nonsampling errors. The actual process of sampling causes sampling errors. For example, the sample may not be large enough. Factors not related to the sampling process cause **nonsampling errors**. A defective counting device can cause a nonsampling error.

In reality, a sample will never be exactly representative of the population so there will always be some sampling error. As a rule, the larger the sample, the smaller the sampling error.

In statistics, **a sampling bias** is created when a sample is collected from a population and some members of the population are not as likely to be chosen as others (remember, each member of the population should have an equally likely chance of being chosen). When a sampling bias happens, there can be incorrect conclusions drawn about the population that is being studied.

## Critical Evaluation

We need to evaluate the statistical studies we read about critically and analyze them before accepting the results of the studies. Common problems to be aware of include

- Problems with samples: A sample must be representative of the population. A sample that is not representative of the population is biased. Biased samples that are not representative of the population give results that are inaccurate and not valid.
- Self-selected samples: Responses only by people who choose to respond, such as call-in surveys, are often unreliable.
- Sample size issues: Samples that are too small may be unreliable. Larger samples are better, if possible. In some situations, having small samples is unavoidable and can still be used to draw conclusions. Examples: crash testing cars or medical testing for rare conditions
- Undue influence: collecting data or asking questions in a way that influences the response
- Non-response or refusal of subject to participate: The collected responses may no longer be representative of the

population. Often, people with strong positive or negative opinions may answer surveys, which can affect the results.

- Causality: A relationship between two variables does not mean that one causes the other to occur. They may be related (correlated) because of their relationship through a different variable.

- Self-funded or self-interest studies: A study performed by a person or organization in order to support their claim. Is the study impartial? Read the study carefully to evaluate the work. Do not automatically assume that the study is good, but do not automatically assume the study is bad either. Evaluate it on its merits and the work done.

- Misleading use of data: improperly displayed graphs, incomplete data, or lack of context

- Confounding: When the effects of multiple factors on a response cannot be separated. Confounding makes it difficult or impossible to draw valid conclusions about the effect of each factor.

## Example 1.11

A study is done to determine the average tuition that San Jose State undergraduate students pay per semester. Each student in the following samples is asked how much tuition he or she paid for the Fall semester. What is the type of sampling in each case?

a. A sample of 100 undergraduate San Jose State students is taken by organizing the students' names by classification (freshman, sophomore, junior, or senior), and then selecting 25 students from each.

b. A random number generator is used to select a student from the alphabetical listing of all undergraduate students in the Fall semester. Starting with that student, every 50th student is chosen until 75 students are included in the sample.

c. A completely random method is used to select 75 students. Each undergraduate student in the fall semester has the same probability of being chosen at any stage of the sampling process.

d. The freshman, sophomore, junior, and senior years are numbered one, two, three, and four, respectively. A random number generator is used to pick two of those years. All students in those two years are in the sample.

e. An administrative assistant is asked to stand in front of the library one Wednesday and to ask the first 100 undergraduate students he encounters what they paid for tuition the Fall semester. Those 100 students are the sample.

Solution 1.11
a. stratified; b. systematic; c. simple random; d. cluster; e. convenience

## Example 1.12

Determine the type of sampling used (simple random, stratified, systematic, cluster, or convenience).

a. A soccer coach selects six players from a group of boys aged eight to ten, seven players from a group of boys aged 11 to 12, and three players from a group of boys aged 13 to 14 to form a recreational soccer team.

b. A pollster interviews all human resource personnel in five different high tech companies.

c. A high school educational researcher interviews 50 high school female teachers and 50 high school male teachers.

d. A medical researcher interviews every third cancer patient from a list of cancer patients at a local hospital.

e. A high school counselor uses a computer to generate 50 random numbers and then picks students whose names correspond to the numbers.

f. A student interviews classmates in his algebra class to determine how many pairs of jeans a student owns, on the average.

Solution 1.12
a. stratified; b. cluster; c. stratified; d. systematic; e. simple random; f.convenience

If we were to examine two samples representing the same population, even if we used random sampling methods for the samples, they would not be exactly the same. Just as there is variation in data, there is variation in samples. As you become accustomed to sampling, the variability will begin to seem natural.

## Example 1.13

Suppose ABC College has 10,000 part-time students (the population). We are interested in the average amount of money a part-time student spends on books in the fall term. Asking all 10,000 students is an almost impossible task.

Suppose we take two different samples.

First, we use convenience sampling and survey ten students from a first term organic chemistry class. Many of these students are taking first term calculus in addition to the organic chemistry class. The amount of money they spend on books is as follows:

$128; $87; $173; $116; $130; $204; $147; $189; $93; $153

The second sample is taken using a list of senior citizens who take P.E. classes and taking every fifth senior citizen on the list, for a total of ten senior citizens. They spend:

$50; $40; $36; $15; $50; $100; $40; $53; $22; $22

It is unlikely that any student is in both samples.

a. Do you think that either of these samples is representative of (or is characteristic of) the entire 10,000 part-time student population?

### Solution 1.13

a. No. The first sample probably consists of science-oriented students. Besides the chemistry course, some of them are also taking first-term calculus. Books for these classes tend to be expensive. Most of these students are, more than likely, paying more than the average part-time student for their books. The second sample is a group of senior citizens who are, more than likely, taking courses for health and interest. The amount of money they spend on books is probably much less than the average parttime student. Both samples are biased. Also, in both cases, not all students have a chance to be in either sample.

b. Since these samples are not representative of the entire population, is it wise to use the results to describe the entire population?

### Solution 1.13

b. No. For these samples, each member of the population did not have an equally likely chance of being chosen.

Now, suppose we take a third sample. We choose ten different part-time students from the disciplines of chemistry, math, English, psychology, sociology, history, nursing, physical education, art, and early childhood development. (We assume that these are the only disciplines in which part-time students at ABC College are enrolled and that an equal number of part-time students are enrolled in each of the disciplines.) Each student is chosen using simple random sampling. Using a calculator, random numbers are generated and a student from a particular discipline is selected if he or she has a corresponding number. The students spend the following amounts:

$180; $50; $150; $85; $260; $75; $180; $200; $200; $150

c. Is the sample biased?

### Solution 1.13

c. The sample is unbiased, but a larger sample would be recommended to increase the likelihood that the sample will be close to representative of the population. However, for a biased sampling technique, even a large sample runs the risk of not being representative of the population.

Students often ask if it is "good enough" to take a sample, instead of surveying the entire population. If the survey is done well, the answer is yes.

**1.13** A local radio station has a fan base of 20,000 listeners. The station wants to know if its audience would prefer more music or more talk shows. Asking all 20,000 listeners is an almost impossible task.

The station uses convenience sampling and surveys the first 200 people they meet at one of the station's music concert events. 24 people said they'd prefer more talk shows, and 176 people said they'd prefer more music.

Do you think that this sample is representative of (or is characteristic of) the entire 20,000 listener population?

## Variation in Data

**Variation** is present in any set of data. For example, 16-ounce cans of beverage may contain more or less than 16 ounces of liquid. In one study, eight 16 ounce cans were measured and produced the following amount (in ounces) of beverage:

15.8; 16.1; 15.2; 14.8; 15.8; 15.9; 16.0; 15.5

Measurements of the amount of beverage in a 16-ounce can may vary because different people make the measurements or because the exact amount, 16 ounces of liquid, was not put into the cans. Manufacturers regularly run tests to determine if the amount of beverage in a 16-ounce can falls within the desired range.

Be aware that as you take data, your data may vary somewhat from the data someone else is taking for the same purpose. This is completely natural. However, if two or more of you are taking the same data and get very different results, it is time for you and the others to reevaluate your data-taking methods and your accuracy.

## Variation in Samples

It was mentioned previously that two or more **samples** from the same **population**, taken randomly, and having close to the same characteristics of the population will likely be different from each other. Suppose Doreen and Jung both decide to study the average amount of time students at their college sleep each night. Doreen and Jung each take samples of 500 students. Doreen uses systematic sampling and Jung uses cluster sampling. Doreen's sample will be different from Jung's sample. Even if Doreen and Jung used the same sampling method, in all likelihood their samples would be different. Neither would be wrong, however.

Think about what contributes to making Doreen's and Jung's samples different.

If Doreen and Jung took larger samples (i.e. the number of data values is increased), their sample results (the average amount of time a student sleeps) might be closer to the actual population average. But still, their samples would be, in all likelihood, different from each other. This **variability in samples** cannot be stressed enough.

### Size of a Sample

The size of a sample (often called the number of observations, usually given the symbol n) is important. The examples you have seen in this book so far have been small. Samples of only a few hundred observations, or even smaller, are sufficient for many purposes. In polling, samples that are from 1,200 to 1,500 observations are considered large enough and good enough if the survey is random and is well done. Later we will find that even much smaller sample sizes will give very good results. You will learn why when you study confidence intervals.

Be aware that many large samples are biased. For example, call-in surveys are invariably biased, because people choose to respond or not.

# 1.3 | Levels of Measurement

Once you have a set of data, you will need to organize it so that you can analyze how frequently each datum occurs in the set. However, when calculating the frequency, you may need to round your answers so that they are as precise as possible.

## Levels of Measurement

The way a set of data is measured is called its **level of measurement**. Correct statistical procedures depend on a researcher being familiar with levels of measurement. Not every statistical operation can be used with every set of data. Data can be classified into four levels of measurement. They are (from lowest to highest level):

- **Nominal scale level**
- **Ordinal scale level**
- **Interval scale level**
- **Ratio scale level**

Data that is measured using a **nominal scale** is **qualitative (categorical)**. Categories, colors, names, labels and favorite foods along with yes or no responses are examples of nominal level data. Nominal scale data are not ordered. For example, trying to classify people according to their favorite food does not make any sense. Putting pizza first and sushi second is not meaningful.

Smartphone companies are another example of nominal scale data. The data are the names of the companies that make smartphones, but there is no agreed upon order of these brands, even though people may have personal preferences. Nominal scale data cannot be used in calculations.

Data that is measured using an **ordinal scale** is similar to nominal scale data but there is a big difference. The ordinal scale data can be ordered. An example of ordinal scale data is a list of the top five national parks in the United States. The top five national parks in the United States can be ranked from one to five but we cannot measure differences between the data.

Another example of using the ordinal scale is a cruise survey where the responses to questions about the cruise are "excellent," "good," "satisfactory," and "unsatisfactory." These responses are ordered from the most desired response to the least desired. But the differences between two pieces of data cannot be measured. Like the nominal scale data, ordinal scale data cannot be used in calculations.

Data that is measured using the **interval scale** is similar to ordinal level data because it has a definite ordering but there is a difference between data. The differences between interval scale data can be measured though the data does not have a starting point.

Temperature scales like Celsius (C) and Fahrenheit (F) are measured by using the interval scale. In both temperature measurements, 40° is equal to 100° minus 60°. Differences make sense. But 0 degrees does not because, in both scales, 0 is not the absolute lowest temperature. Temperatures like -10° F and -15° C exist and are colder than 0.

Interval level data can be used in calculations, but one type of comparison cannot be done. 80° C is not four times as hot as 20° C (nor is 80° F four times as hot as 20° F). There is no meaning to the ratio of 80 to 20 (or four to one).

Data that is measured using the **ratio scale** takes care of the ratio problem and gives you the most information. Ratio scale data is like interval scale data, but it has a 0 point and ratios can be calculated. For example, four multiple choice statistics final exam scores are 80, 68, 20 and 92 (out of a possible 100 points). The exams are machine-graded.

The data can be put in order from lowest to highest: 20, 68, 80, 92.

The differences between the data have meaning. The score 92 is more than the score 68 by 24 points. Ratios can be calculated. The smallest score is 0. So 80 is four times 20. The score of 80 is four times better than the score of 20.

## Frequency

Twenty students were asked how many hours they worked per day. Their responses, in hours, are as follows: 5; 6; 3; 3; 2; 4; 7; 5; 2; 3; 5; 6; 5; 4; 4; 3; 5; 2; 5; 3.

Table 1.5 lists the different data values in ascending order and their frequencies.

| DATA VALUE | FREQUENCY |
|---|---|
| 2 | 3 |
| 3 | 5 |
| 4 | 3 |
| 5 | 6 |
| 6 | 2 |
| 7 | 1 |

Table 1.5 Frequency Table of Student Work Hours

A **frequency** is the number of times a value of the data occurs. According to Table 1.5, there are three students who work two hours, five students who work three hours, and so on. The sum of the values in the frequency column, 20, represents the total number of students included in the sample.

A **relative frequency** is the ratio (fraction or proportion) of the number of times a value of the data occurs in the set of all outcomes to the total number of outcomes. To find the relative frequencies, divide each frequency by the total number of students in the sample—in this case, 20. Relative frequencies can be written as fractions, percents, or decimals.

| DATA VALUE | FREQUENCY | RELATIVE FREQUENCY |
|---|---|---|
| 2 | 3 | $\frac{3}{20}$ or 0.15 |
| 3 | 5 | $\frac{5}{20}$ or 0.25 |
| 4 | 3 | $\frac{3}{20}$ or 0.15 |
| 5 | 6 | $\frac{6}{20}$ or 0.30 |
| 6 | 2 | $\frac{2}{20}$ or 0.10 |
| 7 | 1 | $\frac{1}{20}$ or 0.05 |

Table 1.6 Frequency Table of Student Work Hours with Relative Frequencies

The sum of the values in the relative frequency column of **Table 1.6** is $\frac{20}{20}$ , or 1.

**Cumulative relative frequency** is the accumulation of the previous relative frequencies. To find the cumulative relative frequencies, add all the previous relative frequencies to the relative frequency for the current row, as shown in **Table 1.7**.

| DATA VALUE | FREQUENCY | RELATIVE FREQUENCY | CUMULATIVE RELATIVE FREQUENCY |
|---|---|---|---|
| 2 | 3 | $\frac{3}{20}$ or 0.15 | 0.15 |
| 3 | 5 | $\frac{5}{20}$ or 0.25 | 0.15 + 0.25 = 0.40 |
| 4 | 3 | $\frac{3}{20}$ or 0.15 | 0.40 + 0.15 = 0.55 |
| 5 | 6 | $\frac{6}{20}$ or 0.30 | 0.55 + 0.30 = 0.85 |
| 6 | 2 | $\frac{2}{20}$ or 0.10 | 0.85 + 0.10 = 0.95 |
| 7 | 1 | $\frac{1}{20}$ or 0.05 | 0.95 + 0.05 = 1.00 |

Table 1.7 Frequency Table of Student Work Hours with Relative and Cumulative Relative Frequencies

The last entry of the cumulative relative frequency column is one, indicating that one hundred percent of the data has been accumulated.

**NOTE**

Because of rounding, the relative frequency column may not always sum to one, and the last entry in the cumulative relative frequency column may not be one. However, they each should be close to one.

Table 1.8 represents the heights, in inches, of a sample of 100 male semiprofessional soccer players.

| HEIGHTS (INCHES) | FREQUENCY | RELATIVE FREQUENCY | CUMULATIVE RELATIVE FREQUENCY |
|---|---|---|---|
| 59.95–61.95 | 5 | $\frac{5}{100} = 0.05$ | 0.05 |
| 61.95–63.95 | 3 | $\frac{3}{100} = 0.03$ | 0.05 + 0.03 = 0.08 |
| 63.95–65.95 | 15 | $\frac{15}{100} = 0.15$ | 0.08 + 0.15 = 0.23 |
| 65.95–67.95 | 40 | $\frac{40}{100} = 0.40$ | 0.23 + 0.40 = 0.63 |
| 67.95–69.95 | 17 | $\frac{17}{100} = 0.17$ | 0.63 + 0.17 = 0.80 |
| 69.95–71.95 | 12 | $\frac{12}{100} = 0.12$ | 0.80 + 0.12 = 0.92 |
| 71.95–73.95 | 7 | $\frac{7}{100} = 0.07$ | 0.92 + 0.07 = 0.99 |
| 73.95–75.95 | 1 | $\frac{1}{100} = 0.01$ | 0.99 + 0.01 = 1.00 |
|  | Total = 100 | Total = 1.00 |  |

Table 1.8 Frequency Table of Soccer Player Height

The data in this table have been **grouped** into the following intervals:

- 59.95 to 61.95 inches
- 61.95 to 63.95 inches
- 63.95 to 65.95 inches
- 65.95 to 67.95 inches
- 67.95 to 69.95 inches
- 69.95 to 71.95 inches
- 71.95 to 73.95 inches
- 73.95 to 75.95 inches

In this sample, there are **five** players whose heights fall within the interval 59.95–61.95 inches, **three** players whose heights fall within the interval 61.95–63.95 inches, **15** players whose heights fall within the interval 63.95–65.95 inches, **40** players whose heights fall within the interval 65.95–67.95 inches, **17** players whose heights fall within the interval 67.95–69.95 inches, **12** players whose heights fall within the interval 69.95–71.95, **seven** players whose heights fall within the interval 71.95–73.95, and **one** player whose heights fall within the interval 73.95–75.95. All heights fall between the endpoints of an interval and not at the endpoints.

## Example 1.14

From Table 1.8, find the percentage of heights that are less than 65.95 inches.

### Solution 1.14
If you look at the first, second, and third rows, the heights are all less than 65.95 inches. There are 5 + 3 + 15 = 23

players whose heights are less than 65.95 inches. The percentage of heights less than 65.95 inches is then $\frac{23}{100}$ or 23%. This percentage is the cumulative relative frequency entry in the third row.

**1.14** Table 1.9 shows the amount, in inches, of annual rainfall in a sample of towns.

| Rainfall (Inches) | Frequency | Relative Frequency | Cumulative Relative Frequency |
|---|---|---|---|
| 2.95–4.97 | 6 | $\frac{6}{50}$ = 0.12 | 0.12 |
| 4.97–6.99 | 7 | $\frac{7}{50}$ = 0.14 | 0.12 + 0.14 = 0.26 |
| 6.99–9.01 | 15 | $\frac{15}{50}$ = 0.30 | 0.26 + 0.30 = 0.56 |
| 9.01–11.03 | 8 | $\frac{8}{50}$ = 0.16 | 0.56 + 0.16 = 0.72 |
| 11.03–13.05 | 9 | $\frac{9}{50}$ = 0.18 | 0.72 + 0.18 = 0.90 |
| 13.05–15.07 | 5 | $\frac{5}{50}$ = 0.10 | 0.90 + 0.10 = 1.00 |
|  | Total = 50 | Total = 1.00 |  |

Table 1.9

From Table 1.9, find the percentage of rainfall that is less than 9.01 inches.

## Example 1.15

From Table 1.8, find the percentage of heights that fall between 61.95 and 65.95 inches.

**Solution 1.15**
Add the relative frequencies in the second and third rows: 0.03 + 0.15 = 0.18 or 18%.

**1.15** From Table 1.9, find the percentage of rainfall that is between 6.99 and 13.05 inches.

## Example 1.16

Use the heights of the 100 male semiprofessional soccer players in Table 1.8. Fill in the blanks and check your answers.

a.  The percentage of heights that are from 67.95 to 71.95 inches is: ____.

b.  The percentage of heights that are from 67.95 to 73.95 inches is: ____.

c.  The percentage of heights that are more than 65.95 inches is: ____.

d.  The number of players in the sample who are between 61.95 and 71.95 inches tall is: ____.

e.  What kind of data are the heights?

f.  Describe how you could gather this data (the heights) so that the data are characteristic of all male semiprofessional soccer players.

Remember, you **count frequencies**. To find the relative frequency, divide the frequency by the total number of data values. To find the cumulative relative frequency, add all of the previous relative frequencies to the relative frequency for the current row.

Solution 1.16

a.  29%

b.  36%

c.  77%

d.  87

e.  quantitative continuous

f.  get rosters from each team and choose a simple random sample from each

## Example 1.17

Nineteen people were asked how many miles, to the nearest mile, they commute to work each day. The data are as follows: 2; 5; 7; 3; 2; 10; 18; 15; 20; 7; 10; 18; 5; 12; 13; 12; 4; 5; 10. **Table 1.10** was produced:

| DATA | FREQUENCY | RELATIVE FREQUENCY | CUMULATIVE RELATIVE FREQUENCY |
|------|-----------|--------------------|-------------------------------|
| 3 | 3 | $\frac{3}{19}$ | 0.1579 |
| 4 | 1 | $\frac{1}{19}$ | 0.2105 |
| 5 | 3 | $\frac{3}{19}$ | 0.1579 |
| 7 | 2 | $\frac{2}{19}$ | 0.2632 |
| 10 | 3 | $\frac{4}{19}$ | 0.4737 |
| 12 | 2 | $\frac{2}{19}$ | 0.7895 |
| 13 | 1 | $\frac{1}{19}$ | 0.8421 |
| 15 | 1 | $\frac{1}{19}$ | 0.8948 |
| 18 | 1 | $\frac{1}{19}$ | 0.9474 |
| 20 | 1 | $\frac{1}{19}$ | 1.0000 |

**Table 1.10 Frequency of Commuting Distances**

a. Is the table correct? If it is not correct, what is wrong?

b. True or False: Three percent of the people surveyed commute three miles. If the statement is not correct, what should it be? If the table is incorrect, make the corrections.

c. What fraction of the people surveyed commute five or seven miles?

d. What fraction of the people surveyed commute 12 miles or more? Less than 12 miles? Between five and 13 miles (not including five and 13 miles)?

### Solution 1.17

a. No. The frequency column sums to 18, not 19. Not all cumulative relative frequencies are correct.

b. False. The frequency for three miles should be one; for two miles (left out), two. The cumulative relative frequency column should read: 0.1052, 0.1579, 0.2105, 0.3684, 0.4737, 0.6316, 0.7368, 0.7895, 0.8421, 0.9474, 1.0000.

c. $\frac{5}{19}$

d. $\frac{7}{19}$, $\frac{12}{19}$, $\frac{7}{19}$

**1.17** Table 1.9 represents the amount, in inches, of annual rainfall in a sample of towns. What fraction of towns surveyed get between 11.03 and 13.05 inches of rainfall each year?

## Example 1.18

Table 1.11 contains the total number of deaths worldwide as a result of earthquakes for the period from 2000 to 2012.

| Year | Total Number of Deaths |
|------|------------------------|
| 2000 | 231 |
| 2001 | 21,357 |
| 2002 | 11,685 |
| 2003 | 33,819 |
| 2004 | 228,802 |
| 2005 | 88,003 |
| 2006 | 6,605 |
| 2007 | 712 |
| 2008 | 88,011 |
| 2009 | 1,790 |
| 2010 | 320,120 |
| 2011 | 21,953 |
| 2012 | 768 |
| Total | 823,856 |

Table 1.11

Answer the following questions.

   a.  What is the frequency of deaths measured from 2006 through 2009?

   b.  What percentage of deaths occurred after 2009?

   c.  What is the relative frequency of deaths that occurred in 2003 or earlier?

   d.  What is the percentage of deaths that occurred in 2004?

   e.  What kind of data are the numbers of deaths?

   f.  The Richter scale is used to quantify the energy produced by an earthquake. Examples of Richter scale numbers are 2.3, 4.0, 6.1, and 7.0. What kind of data are these numbers?

Solution 1.18
   a.  97,118 (11.8%)

   b.  41.6%

   c.  67,092/823,356 or 0.081 or 8.1 %

   d.  27.8%

    e.   Quantitative discrete

    f.   Quantitative continuous

**1.18** Table 1.12 contains the total number of fatal motor vehicle traffic crashes in the United States for the period from 1994 to 2011.

| Year | Total Number of Crashes | Year | Total Number of Crashes |
|------|-------------------------|------|-------------------------|
| 1994 | 36,254 | 2004 | 38,444 |
| 1995 | 37,241 | 2005 | 39,252 |
| 1996 | 37,494 | 2006 | 38,648 |
| 1997 | 37,324 | 2007 | 37,435 |
| 1998 | 37,107 | 2008 | 34,172 |
| 1999 | 37,140 | 2009 | 30,862 |
| 2000 | 37,526 | 2010 | 30,296 |
| 2001 | 37,862 | 2011 | 29,757 |
| 2002 | 38,491 | Total | 653,782 |
| 2003 | 38,477 |  |  |

Table 1.12

Answer the following questions.

a.   What is the frequency of deaths measured from 2000 through 2004?

b.   What percentage of deaths occurred after 2006?

c.   What is the relative frequency of deaths that occurred in 2000 or before?

d.   What is the percentage of deaths that occurred in 2011?

e.   What is the cumulative relative frequency for 2006? Explain what this number tells you about the data.

# 1.4 | Experimental Design and Ethics

Does aspirin reduce the risk of heart attacks? Is one brand of fertilizer more effective at growing roses than another? Is fatigue as dangerous to a driver as the influence of alcohol? Questions like these are answered using randomized experiments. In this module, you will learn important aspects of experimental design. Proper study design ensures the production of reliable, accurate data.

The purpose of an experiment is to investigate the relationship between two variables. When one variable causes change in another, we call the first variable the **independent variable** or **explanatory variable**. The affected variable is called the **dependent variable** or **response variable**: stimulus, response. In a randomized experiment, the researcher manipulates values of the explanatory variable and measures the resulting changes in the response variable. The different values of the explanatory variable are called **treatments**. An **experimental unit** is a single object or individual to be measured.

You want to investigate the effectiveness of vitamin E in preventing disease. You recruit a group of subjects and ask them if they regularly take vitamin E. You notice that the subjects who take vitamin E exhibit better health on average than those who do not. Does this prove that vitamin E is effective in disease prevention? It does not. There are many differences between the two groups compared in addition to vitamin E consumption. People who take vitamin E regularly often take other steps to improve their health: exercise, diet, other vitamin supplements, choosing not to smoke. Any one of these factors could be influencing health. As described, this study does not prove that vitamin E is the key to disease prevention.

Additional variables that can cloud a study are called **lurking variables**. In order to prove that the explanatory variable is causing a change in the response variable, it is necessary to isolate the explanatory variable. The researcher must design her experiment in such a way that there is only one difference between groups being compared: the planned treatments. This is accomplished by the **random assignment** of experimental units to treatment groups. When subjects are assigned treatments randomly, all of the potential lurking variables are spread equally among the groups. At this point the only difference between groups is the one imposed by the researcher. Different outcomes measured in the response variable, therefore, must be a direct result of the different treatments. In this way, an experiment can prove a cause-and-effect connection between the explanatory and response variables.

The power of suggestion can have an important influence on the outcome of an experiment. Studies have shown that the expectation of the study participant can be as important as the actual medication. In one study of performance-enhancing drugs, researchers noted:

*Results showed that believing one had taken the substance resulted in [performance] times almost as fast as those associated with consuming the drug itself. In contrast, taking the drug without knowledge yielded no significant performance increment.*[1]

When participation in a study prompts a physical response from a participant, it is difficult to isolate the effects of the explanatory variable. To counter the power of suggestion, researchers set aside one treatment group as a **control group**. This group is given a **placebo** treatment–a treatment that cannot influence the response variable. The control group helps researchers balance the effects of being in an experiment with the effects of the active treatments. Of course, if you are participating in a study and you know that you are receiving a pill which contains no actual medication, then the power of suggestion is no longer a factor. **Blinding** in a randomized experiment preserves the power of suggestion. When a person involved in a research study is blinded, he does not know who is receiving the active treatment(s) and who is receiving the placebo treatment. A **double-blind experiment** is one in which both the subjects and the researchers involved with the subjects are blinded.

## Example 1.19

The Smell & Taste Treatment and Research Foundation conducted a study to investigate whether smell can affect learning. Subjects completed mazes multiple times while wearing masks. They completed the pencil and paper mazes three times wearing floral-scented masks, and three times with unscented masks. Participants were assigned at random to wear the floral mask during the first three trials or during the last three trials. For each trial, researchers recorded the time it took to complete the maze and the subject's impression of the mask's scent: positive, negative, or neutral.

a. Describe the explanatory and response variables in this study.

b. What are the treatments?

c. Identify any lurking variables that could interfere with this study.

d. Is it possible to use blinding in this study?

### Solution 1.19

a. The explanatory variable is scent, and the response variable is the time it takes to complete the maze.

b. There are two treatments: a floral-scented mask and an unscented mask.

c. All subjects experienced both treatments. The order of treatments was randomly assigned so there were no differences between the treatment groups. Random assignment eliminates the problem of lurking variables.

d. Subjects will clearly know whether they can smell flowers or not, so subjects cannot be blinded in this study. Researchers timing the mazes can be blinded, though. The researcher who is observing a subject will not know which mask is being worn.

---

1. McClung, M. Collins, D. "Because I know it will!": placebo effects of an ergogenic aid on athletic performance. Journal of Sport & Exercise Psychology. 2007 Jun. 29(3):382-94. Web. April 30, 2013.

# KEY TERMS

**Average** also called mean or arithmetic mean; a number that describes the central tendency of the data

**Blinding** not telling participants which treatment a subject is receiving

**Categorical Variable** variables that take on values that are names or labels

**Cluster Sampling** a method for selecting a random sample and dividing the population into groups (clusters); use simple random sampling to select a set of clusters. Every individual in the chosen clusters is included in the sample.

**Continuous Random Variable** a random variable (RV) whose outcomes are measured; the height of trees in the forest is a continuous RV.

**Control Group** a group in a randomized experiment that receives an inactive treatment but is otherwise managed exactly as the other groups

**Convenience Sampling** a nonrandom method of selecting a sample; this method selects individuals that are easily accessible and may result in biased data.

**Cumulative Relative Frequency** The term applies to an ordered set of observations from smallest to largest. The cumulative relative frequency is the sum of the relative frequencies for all values that are less than or equal to the given value.

**Data** a set of observations (a set of possible outcomes); most data can be put into two groups: **qualitative** (an attribute whose value is indicated by a label) or **quantitative** (an attribute whose value is indicated by a number). Quantitative data can be separated into two subgroups: **discrete** and **continuous**. Data is discrete if it is the result of counting (such as the number of students of a given ethnic group in a class or the number of books on a shelf). Data is continuous if it is the result of measuring (such as distance traveled or weight of luggage)

**Discrete Random Variable** a random variable (RV) whose outcomes are counted

**Double-blinding** the act of blinding both the subjects of an experiment and the researchers who work with the subjects

**Experimental Unit** any individual or object to be measured

**Explanatory Variable** the **independent variable** in an experiment; the value controlled by researchers

**Frequency** the number of times a value of the data occurs

**Informed Consent** Any human subject in a research study must be cognizant of any risks or costs associated with the study. The subject has the right to know the nature of the treatments included in the study, their potential risks, and their potential benefits. Consent must be given freely by an informed, fit participant.

**Institutional Review Board** a committee tasked with oversight of research programs that involve human subjects

**Lurking Variable** a variable that has an effect on a study even though it is neither an explanatory variable nor a response variable

**Mathematical Models** a description of a phenomenon using mathematical concepts, such as equations, inequalities, distributions, etc.

**Nonsampling Error** an issue that affects the reliability of sampling data other than natural variation; it includes a variety of human errors including poor study design, biased sampling methods, inaccurate information provided by study participants, data entry errors, and poor analysis.

**Numerical Variable** variables that take on values that are indicated by numbers

**Observational Study** a study in which the independent variable is not manipulated by the researcher

**Parameter** a number that is used to represent a population characteristic and that generally cannot be determined easily

**Placebo** an inactive treatment that has no real effect on the explanatory variable

**Population** all individuals, objects, or measurements whose properties are being studied

**Probability** a number between zero and one, inclusive, that gives the likelihood that a specific event will occur

**Proportion** the number of successes divided by the total number in the sample

**Qualitative Data** See Data.

**Quantitative Data** See Data.

**Random Assignment** the act of organizing experimental units into treatment groups using random methods

**Random Sampling** a method of selecting a sample that gives every member of the population an equal chance of being selected.

**Relative Frequency** the ratio of the number of times a value of the data occurs in the set of all outcomes to the number of all outcomes to the total number of outcomes

**Representative Sample** a subset of the population that has the same characteristics as the population

**Response Variable** the **dependent variable** in an experiment; the value that is measured for change at the end of an experiment

**Sample** a subset of the population studied

**Sampling Bias** not all members of the population are equally likely to be selected

**Sampling Error** the natural variation that results from selecting a sample to represent a larger population; this variation decreases as the sample size increases, so selecting larger samples reduces sampling error.

**Sampling with Replacement** Once a member of the population is selected for inclusion in a sample, that member is returned to the population for the selection of the next individual.

**Sampling without Replacement** A member of the population may be chosen for inclusion in a sample only once. If chosen, the member is not returned to the population before the next selection.

**Simple Random Sampling** a straightforward method for selecting a random sample; give each member of the population a number. Use a random number generator to select a set of labels. These randomly selected labels identify the members of your sample.

**Statistic** a numerical characteristic of the sample; a statistic estimates the corresponding population parameter.

**Statistical Models** a description of a phenomenon using probability distributions that describe the expected behavior of the phenomenon and the variability in the expected observations.

**Stratified Sampling** a method for selecting a random sample used to ensure that subgroups of the population are represented adequately; divide the population into groups (strata). Use simple random sampling to identify a proportionate number of individuals from each stratum.

**Survey** a study in which data is collected as reported by individuals.

**Systematic Sampling** a method for selecting a random sample; list the members of the population. Use simple random sampling to select a starting point in the population. Let k = (number of individuals in the population)/(number of individuals needed in the sample). Choose every kth individual in the list starting with the one that was randomly selected. If necessary, return to the beginning of the population list to complete your sample.

**Treatments** different values or components of the explanatory variable applied in an experiment

**Variable** a characteristic of interest for each person or object in a population

# CHAPTER REVIEW

## 1.1 Definitions of Statistics, Probability, and Key Terms

The mathematical theory of statistics is easier to learn when you know the language. This module presents important terms that will be used throughout the text.

## 1.2 Data, Sampling, and Variation in Data and Sampling

Data are individual items of information that come from a population or sample. Data may be classified as qualitative (categorical), quantitative continuous, or quantitative discrete.

Because it is not practical to measure the entire population in a study, researchers use samples to represent the population. A random sample is a representative group from the population chosen by using a method that gives each individual in the population an equal chance of being included in the sample. Random sampling methods include simple random sampling, stratified sampling, cluster sampling, and systematic sampling. Convenience sampling is a nonrandom method of choosing a sample that often produces biased data.

Samples that contain different individuals result in different data. This is true even when the samples are well-chosen and representative of the population. When properly selected, larger samples model the population more closely than smaller samples. There are many different potential problems that can affect the reliability of a sample. Statistical data needs to be critically analyzed, not simply accepted.

## 1.3 Levels of Measurement

Some calculations generate numbers that are artificially precise. It is not necessary to report a value to eight decimal places when the measures that generated that value were only accurate to the nearest tenth. Round off your final answer to one more decimal place than was present in the original data. This means that if you have data measured to the nearest tenth of a unit, report the final statistic to the nearest hundredth.

In addition to rounding your answers, you can measure your data using the following four levels of measurement.

- **Nominal scale level:** data that cannot be ordered nor can it be used in calculations

- **Ordinal scale level:** data that can be ordered; the differences cannot be measured

- **Interval scale level:** data with a definite ordering but no starting point; the differences can be measured, but there is no such thing as a ratio.

- **Ratio scale level:** data with a starting point that can be ordered; the differences have meaning and ratios can be calculated.

When organizing data, it is important to know how many times a value appears. How many statistics students study five hours or more for an exam? What percent of families on our block own two pets? Frequency, relative frequency, and cumulative relative frequency are measures that answer questions like these.

## 1.4 Experimental Design and Ethics

A poorly designed study will not produce reliable data. There are certain key components that must be included in every experiment. To eliminate lurking variables, subjects must be assigned randomly to different treatment groups. One of the groups must act as a control group, demonstrating what happens when the active treatment is not applied. Participants in the control group receive a placebo treatment that looks exactly like the active treatments but cannot influence the response variable. To preserve the integrity of the placebo, both researchers and subjects may be blinded. When a study is designed properly, the only difference between treatment groups is the one imposed by the researcher. Therefore, when groups respond differently to different treatments, the difference must be due to the influence of the explanatory variable.

"An ethics problem arises when you are considering an action that benefits you or some cause you support, hurts or reduces benefits to others, and violates some rule."[2] Ethical violations in statistics are not always easy to spot. Professional associations and federal agencies post guidelines for proper conduct. It is important that you learn basic statistical procedures so that you can recognize proper data analysis.

---

2. Andrew Gelman, "Open Data and Open Methods," Ethics and Statistics, http://www.stat.columbia.edu/~gelman/research/published/ChanceEthics1.pdf (accessed May 1, 2013).

# HOMEWORK

## 1.1 Definitions of Statistics, Probability, and Key Terms

*For each of the following eight exercises, identify: a. the population, b. the sample, c. the parameter, d. the statistic, e. the variable, and f. the data. Give examples where appropriate.*

**1.** A fitness center is interested in the mean amount of time a client exercises in the center each week.

**2.** Ski resorts are interested in the mean age that children take their first ski and snowboard lessons. They need this information to plan their ski classes optimally.

**3.** A cardiologist is interested in the mean recovery period of her patients who have had heart attacks.

**4.** Insurance companies are interested in the mean health costs each year of their clients, so that they can determine the costs of health insurance.

**5.** A politician is interested in the proportion of voters in his district who think he is doing a good job.

**6.** A marriage counselor is interested in the proportion of clients she counsels who stay married.

**7.** Political pollsters may be interested in the proportion of people who will vote for a particular cause.

**8.** A marketing company is interested in the proportion of people who will buy a particular product.

*Use the following information to answer the next three exercises:* A Lake Tahoe Community College instructor is interested in the mean number of days Lake Tahoe Community College math students are absent from class during a quarter.

**9.** What is the population she is interested in?
    a.  all Lake Tahoe Community College students
    b.  all Lake Tahoe Community College English students
    c.  all Lake Tahoe Community College students in her classes
    d.  all Lake Tahoe Community College math students

**10.** Consider the following:

$X$ = number of days a Lake Tahoe Community College math student is absent

In this case, $X$ is an example of a:

    a.  variable.
    b.  population.
    c.  statistic.
    d.  data.

**11.** The instructor's sample produces a mean number of days absent of 3.5 days. This value is an example of a:
    a.  parameter.
    b.  data.
    c.  statistic.
    d.  variable.

## 1.2 Data, Sampling, and Variation in Data and Sampling

*For the following exercises, identify the type of data that would be used to describe a response (quantitative discrete, quantitative continuous, or qualitative), and give an example of the data.*

**12.** number of tickets sold to a concert

**13.** percent of body fat

**14.** favorite baseball team

**15.** time in line to buy groceries

**16.** number of students enrolled at Evergreen Valley College

**17.** most-watched television show

**18.** brand of toothpaste

**19.** distance to the closest movie theatre

**20.** age of executives in Fortune 500 companies

**21.** number of competing computer spreadsheet software packages

*Use the following information to answer the next two exercises:* A study was done to determine the age, number of times per week, and the duration (amount of time) of resident use of a local park in San Jose. The first house in the neighborhood around the park was selected randomly and then every 8th house in the neighborhood around the park was interviewed.

**22.** "Number of times per week" is what type of data?
   a. qualitative (categorical)
   b. quantitative discrete
   c. quantitative continuous

**23.** "Duration (amount of time)" is what type of data?
   a. qualitative (categorical)
   b. quantitative discrete
   c. quantitative continuous

**24.** Airline companies are interested in the consistency of the number of babies on each flight, so that they have adequate safety equipment. Suppose an airline conducts a survey. Over Thanksgiving weekend, it surveys six flights from Boston to Salt Lake City to determine the number of babies on the flights. It determines the amount of safety equipment needed by the result of that study.
   a. Using complete sentences, list three things wrong with the way the survey was conducted.
   b. Using complete sentences, list three ways that you would improve the survey if it were to be repeated.

**25.** Suppose you want to determine the mean number of students per statistics class in your state. Describe a possible sampling method in three to five complete sentences. Make the description detailed.

**26.** Suppose you want to determine the mean number of cans of soda drunk each month by students in their twenties at your school. Describe a possible sampling method in three to five complete sentences. Make the description detailed.

**27.** List some practical difficulties involved in getting accurate results from a telephone survey.

**28.** List some practical difficulties involved in getting accurate results from a mailed survey.

**29.** With your classmates, brainstorm some ways you could overcome these problems if you needed to conduct a phone or mail survey.

**30.** The instructor takes her sample by gathering data on five randomly selected students from each Lake Tahoe Community College math class. The type of sampling she used is
   a. cluster sampling
   b. stratified sampling
   c. simple random sampling
   d. convenience sampling

**31.** A study was done to determine the age, number of times per week, and the duration (amount of time) of residents using a local park in San Jose. The first house in the neighborhood around the park was selected randomly and then every eighth house in the neighborhood around the park was interviewed. The sampling method was:
   a. simple random
   b. systematic
   c. stratified
   d. cluster

**32.** Name the sampling method used in each of the following situations:

a. A woman in the airport is handing out questionnaires to travelers asking them to evaluate the airport's service. She does not ask travelers who are hurrying through the airport with their hands full of luggage, but instead asks all travelers who are sitting near gates and not taking naps while they wait.

b. A teacher wants to know if her students are doing homework, so she randomly selects rows two and five and then calls on all students in row two and all students in row five to present the solutions to homework problems to the class.

c. The marketing manager for an electronics chain store wants information about the ages of its customers. Over the next two weeks, at each store location, 100 randomly selected customers are given questionnaires to fill out asking for information about age, as well as about other variables of interest.

d. The librarian at a public library wants to determine what proportion of the library users are children. The librarian has a tally sheet on which she marks whether books are checked out by an adult or a child. She records this data for every fourth patron who checks out books.

e. A political party wants to know the reaction of voters to a debate between the candidates. The day after the debate, the party's polling staff calls 1,200 randomly selected phone numbers. If a registered voter answers the phone or is available to come to the phone, that registered voter is asked whom he or she intends to vote for and whether the debate changed his or her opinion of the candidates.

**33.** A "random survey" was conducted of 3,274 people of the "microprocessor generation" (people born since 1971, the year the microprocessor was invented). It was reported that 48% of those individuals surveyed stated that if they had $2,000 to spend, they would use it for computer equipment. Also, 66% of those surveyed considered themselves relatively savvy computer users.

a. Do you consider the sample size large enough for a study of this type? Why or why not?

b. Based on your "gut feeling," do you believe the percents accurately reflect the U.S. population for those individuals born since 1971? If not, do you think the percents of the population are actually higher or lower than the sample statistics? Why?
Additional information: The survey, reported by Intel Corporation, was filled out by individuals who visited the Los Angeles Convention Center to see the Smithsonian Institute's road show called "America's Smithsonian."

c. With this additional information, do you feel that all demographic and ethnic groups were equally represented at the event? Why or why not?

d. With the additional information, comment on how accurately you think the sample statistics reflect the population parameters.

**34.** The Well-Being Index is a survey that follows trends of U.S. residents on a regular basis. There are six areas of health and wellness covered in the survey: Life Evaluation, Emotional Health, Physical Health, Healthy Behavior, Work Environment, and Basic Access. Some of the questions used to measure the Index are listed below.

Identify the type of data obtained from each question used in this survey: qualitative(categorical), quantitative discrete, or quantitative continuous.

a. Do you have any health problems that prevent you from doing any of the things people your age can normally do?

b. During the past 30 days, for about how many days did poor health keep you from doing your usual activities?

c. In the last seven days, on how many days did you exercise for 30 minutes or more?

d. Do you have health insurance coverage?

**35.** In advance of the 1936 Presidential Election, a magazine titled Literary Digest released the results of an opinion poll predicting that the republican candidate Alf Landon would win by a large margin. The magazine sent post cards to approximately 10,000,000 prospective voters. These prospective voters were selected from the subscription list of the magazine, from automobile registration lists, from phone lists, and from club membership lists. Approximately 2,300,000 people returned the postcards.

a. Think about the state of the United States in 1936. Explain why a sample chosen from magazine subscription lists, automobile registration lists, phone books, and club membership lists was not representative of the population of the United States at that time.

b. What effect does the low response rate have on the reliability of the sample?

c. Are these problems examples of sampling error or nonsampling error?

d. During the same year, George Gallup conducted his own poll of 30,000 prospective voters. These researchers used a method they called "quota sampling" to obtain survey answers from specific subsets of the population. Quota sampling is an example of which sampling method described in this module?

**36.** Crime-related and demographic statistics for 47 US states in 1960 were collected from government agencies, including the FBI's *Uniform Crime Report*. One analysis of this data found a strong connection between education and crime indicating that higher levels of education in a community correspond to higher crime rates.

Which of the potential problems with samples discussed in Section 1.2 could explain this connection?

**37.** YouPolls is a website that allows anyone to create and respond to polls. One question posted April 15 asks:

"Do you feel happy paying your taxes when members of the Obama administration are allowed to ignore their tax liabilities?"[3]

As of April 25, 11 people responded to this question. Each participant answered "NO!"

Which of the potential problems with samples discussed in this module could explain this connection?

**38.** A scholarly article about response rates begins with the following quote:

"Declining contact and cooperation rates in random digit dial (RDD) national telephone surveys raise serious concerns about the validity of estimates drawn from such research."[4]

The Pew Research Center for People and the Press admits:

"The percentage of people we interview – out of all we try to interview – has been declining over the past decade or more."[5]

    a.   What are some reasons for the decline in response rate over the past decade?
    b.   Explain why researchers are concerned with the impact of the declining response rate on public opinion polls.

## 1.3 Levels of Measurement

**39.** Fifty part-time students were asked how many courses they were taking this term. The (incomplete) results are shown below:

| # of Courses | Frequency | Relative Frequency | Cumulative Relative Frequency |
|---|---|---|---|
| 1 | 30 | 0.6 | |
| 2 | 15 | | |
| 3 | | | |

Table 1.13 Part-time Student Course Loads

    a.   Fill in the blanks in Table 1.13.
    b.   What percent of students take exactly two courses?
    c.   What percent of students take one or two courses?

---

3.  lastbaldeagle. 2013. On Tax Day, House to Call for Firing Federal Workers Who Owe Back Taxes. Opinion poll posted online at: http://www.youpolls.com/details.aspx?id=12328 (accessed May 1, 2013).

4.  Scott Keeter et al., "Gauging the Impact of Growing Nonresponse on Estimates from a National RDD Telephone Survey," Public Opinion Quarterly 70 no. 5 (2006), http://poq.oxfordjournals.org/content/70/5/759.full (http://poq.oxfordjournals.org/content/70/5/759.full) (accessed May 1, 2013).

5.  Frequently Asked Questions, Pew Research Center for the People & the Press, http://www.people-press.org/methodology/frequently-asked-questions/#dont-you-have-trouble-getting-people-to-answer-your-polls (accessed May 1, 2013).

**40.** Sixty adults with gum disease were asked the number of times per week they used to floss before their diagnosis. The (incomplete) results are shown in Table 1.14.

| # Flossing per Week | Frequency | Relative Frequency | Cumulative Relative Freq. |
|---|---|---|---|
| 0 | 27 | 0.4500 | |
| 1 | 18 | | |
| 3 | | | 0.9333 |
| 6 | 3 | 0.0500 | |
| 7 | 1 | 0.0167 | |

Table 1.14 Flossing Frequency for Adults with Gum Disease

a. Fill in the blanks in Table 1.14.
b. What percent of adults flossed six times per week?
c. What percent flossed at most three times per week?

**41.** Nineteen immigrants to the U.S were asked how many years, to the nearest year, they have lived in the U.S. The data are as follows: 2; 5; 7; 2; 2; 10; 20; 15; 0; 7; 0; 20; 5; 12; 15; 12; 4; 5; 10.

Table 1.15 was produced.

| Data | Frequency | Relative Frequency | Cumulative Relative Frequency |
|------|-----------|--------------------|-------------------------------|
| 0 | 2 | $\frac{2}{19}$ | 0.1053 |
| 2 | 3 | $\frac{3}{19}$ | 0.2632 |
| 4 | 1 | $\frac{1}{19}$ | 0.3158 |
| 5 | 3 | $\frac{3}{19}$ | 0.4737 |
| 7 | 2 | $\frac{2}{19}$ | 0.5789 |
| 10 | 2 | $\frac{2}{19}$ | 0.6842 |
| 12 | 2 | $\frac{2}{19}$ | 0.7895 |
| 15 | 1 | $\frac{1}{19}$ | 0.8421 |
| 20 | 1 | $\frac{1}{19}$ | 1.0000 |

**Table 1.15 Frequency of Immigrant Survey Responses**

a. Fix the errors in Table 1.15. Also, explain how someone might have arrived at the incorrect number(s).
b. Explain what is wrong with this statement: "47 percent of the people surveyed have lived in the U.S. for 5 years."
c. Fix the statement in **b** to make it correct.
d. What fraction of the people surveyed have lived in the U.S. five or seven years?
e. What fraction of the people surveyed have lived in the U.S. at most 12 years?
f. What fraction of the people surveyed have lived in the U.S. fewer than 12 years?
g. What fraction of the people surveyed have lived in the U.S. from five to 20 years, inclusive?

**42.** How much time does it take to travel to work? Table 1.16 shows the mean commute time by state for workers at least 16 years old who are not working at home. Find the mean travel time, and round off the answer properly.

| | | | | | | | | | |
|------|------|------|------|------|------|------|------|------|------|
| 24.0 | 24.3 | 25.9 | 18.9 | 27.5 | 17.9 | 21.8 | 20.9 | 16.7 | 27.3 |
| 18.2 | 24.7 | 20.0 | 22.6 | 23.9 | 18.0 | 31.4 | 22.3 | 24.0 | 25.5 |
| 24.7 | 24.6 | 28.1 | 24.9 | 22.6 | 23.6 | 23.4 | 25.7 | 24.8 | 25.5 |
| 21.2 | 25.7 | 23.1 | 23.0 | 23.9 | 26.0 | 16.3 | 23.1 | 21.4 | 21.5 |
| 27.0 | 27.0 | 18.6 | 31.7 | 23.3 | 30.1 | 22.9 | 23.3 | 21.7 | 18.6 |

**Table 1.16**

**43.** *Forbes* magazine published data on the best small firms in 2012. These were firms which had been publicly traded for at least a year, have a stock price of at least $5 per share, and have reported annual revenue between $5 million and $1 billion. **Table 1.17** shows the ages of the chief executive officers for the first 60 ranked firms.

| Age | Frequency | Relative Frequency | Cumulative Relative Frequency |
|-----|-----------|--------------------|-------------------------------|
| 40–44 | 3 | | |
| 45–49 | 11 | | |
| 50–54 | 13 | | |
| 55–59 | 16 | | |
| 60–64 | 10 | | |
| 65–69 | 6 | | |
| 70–74 | 1 | | |

**Table 1.17**

a. What is the frequency for CEO ages between 54 and 65?
b. What percentage of CEOs are 65 years or older?
c. What is the relative frequency of ages under 50?
d. What is the cumulative relative frequency for CEOs younger than 55?
e. Which graph shows the relative frequency and which shows the cumulative relative frequency?

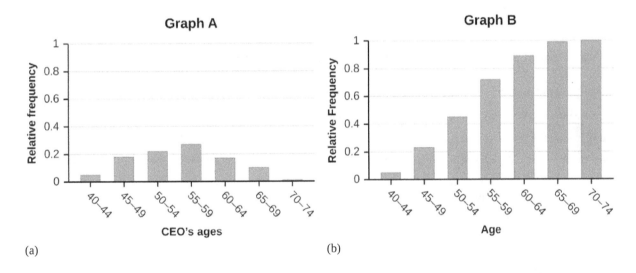

**Figure 1.11**

*Use the following information to answer the next two exercises:* **Table 1.18** contains data on hurricanes that have made direct hits on the U.S. Between 1851 and 2004. A hurricane is given a strength category rating based on the minimum wind speed generated by the storm.

| Category | Number of Direct Hits | Relative Frequency | Cumulative Frequency |
|----------|-----------------------|--------------------|----------------------|
| 1 | 109 | 0.3993 | 0.3993 |
| | Total = 273 | | |

| Category | Number of Direct Hits | Relative Frequency | Cumulative Frequency |
|----------|----------------------|--------------------|--------------------|
| 2 | 72 | 0.2637 | 0.6630 |
| 3 | 71 | 0.2601 | |
| 4 | 18 | | 0.9890 |
| 5 | 3 | 0.0110 | 1.0000 |
| | Total = 273 | | |

Table 1.18 Frequency of Hurricane Direct Hits

**44.** What is the relative frequency of direct hits that were category 4 hurricanes?
   a. 0.0768
   b. 0.0659
   c. 0.2601
   d. Not enough information to calculate

**45.** What is the relative frequency of direct hits that were AT MOST a category 3 storm?
   a. 0.3480
   b. 0.9231
   c. 0.2601
   d. 0.3370

# REFERENCES

## 1.1 Definitions of Statistics, Probability, and Key Terms

The Data and Story Library, http://lib.stat.cmu.edu/DASL/Stories/CrashTestDummies.html (accessed May 1, 2013).

## 1.2 Data, Sampling, and Variation in Data and Sampling

Gallup-Healthways Well-Being Index. http://www.well-beingindex.com/default.asp (accessed May 1, 2013).

Gallup-Healthways Well-Being Index. http://www.well-beingindex.com/methodology.asp (accessed May 1, 2013).

Gallup-Healthways Well-Being Index. http://www.gallup.com/poll/146822/gallup-healthways-index-questions.aspx (accessed May 1, 2013).

Data from http://www.bookofodds.com/Relationships-Society/Articles/A0374-How-George-Gallup-Picked-the-President

Dominic Lusinchi, "'President' Landon and the 1936 *Literary Digest* Poll: Were Automobile and Telephone Owners to Blame?" Social Science History 36, no. 1: 23-54 (2012), http://ssh.dukejournals.org/content/36/1/23.abstract (accessed May 1, 2013).

"The Literary Digest Poll," Virtual Laboratories in Probability and Statistics http://www.math.uah.edu/stat/data/LiteraryDigest.html (accessed May 1, 2013).

"Gallup Presidential Election Trial-Heat Trends, 1936–2008," Gallup Politics http://www.gallup.com/poll/110548/gallup-presidential-election-trialheat-trends-19362004.aspx#4 (accessed May 1, 2013).

The Data and Story Library, http://lib.stat.cmu.edu/DASL/Datafiles/USCrime.html (accessed May 1, 2013).

LBCC Distance Learning (DL) program data in 2010-2011, http://de.lbcc.edu/reports/2010-11/future/highlights.html#focus (accessed May 1, 2013).

Data from San Jose Mercury News

## 1.3 Levels of Measurement

"State & County QuickFacts," U.S. Census Bureau. http://quickfacts.census.gov/qfd/download_data.html (accessed May 1,

2013).

"State & County QuickFacts: Quick, easy access to facts about people, business, and geography," U.S. Census Bureau. http://quickfacts.census.gov/qfd/index.html (accessed May 1, 2013).

"Table 5: Direct hits by mainland United States Hurricanes (1851-2004)," National Hurricane Center, http://www.nhc.noaa.gov/gifs/table5.gif (accessed May 1, 2013).

"Levels of Measurement," http://infinity.cos.edu/faculty/woodbury/stats/tutorial/Data_Levels.htm (accessed May 1, 2013).

Courtney Taylor, "Levels of Measurement," about.com, http://statistics.about.com/od/HelpandTutorials/a/Levels-Of-Measurement.htm (accessed May 1, 2013).

David Lane. "Levels of Measurement," Connexions, http://cnx.org/content/m10809/latest/ (accessed May 1, 2013).

## 1.4 Experimental Design and Ethics

"Vitamin E and Health," Nutrition Source, Harvard School of Public Health, http://www.hsph.harvard.edu/nutritionsource/vitamin-e/ (accessed May 1, 2013).

Stan Reents. "Don't Underestimate the Power of Suggestion," athleteinme.com, http://www.athleteinme.com/ArticleView.aspx?id=1053 (accessed May 1, 2013).

Ankita Mehta. "Daily Dose of Aspiring Helps Reduce Heart Attacks: Study," International Business Times, July 21, 2011. Also available online at http://www.ibtimes.com/daily-dose-aspirin-helps-reduce-heart-attacks-study-300443 (accessed May 1, 2013).

The Data and Story Library, http://lib.stat.cmu.edu/DASL/Stories/ScentsandLearning.html (accessed May 1, 2013).

M.L. Jacskon et al., "Cognitive Components of Simulated Driving Performance: Sleep Loss effect and Predictors," Accident Analysis and Prevention Journal, Jan no. 50 (2013), http://www.ncbi.nlm.nih.gov/pubmed/22721550 (accessed May 1, 2013).

"Earthquake Information by Year," U.S. Geological Survey. http://earthquake.usgs.gov/earthquakes/eqarchives/year/ (accessed May 1, 2013).

"Fatality Analysis Report Systems (FARS) Encyclopedia," National Highway Traffic and Safety Administration. http://www-fars.nhtsa.dot.gov/Main/index.aspx (accessed May 1, 2013).

Data from www.businessweek.com (accessed May 1, 2013).

Data from www.forbes.com (accessed May 1, 2013).

"America's Best Small Companies," http://www.forbes.com/best-small-companies/list/ (accessed May 1, 2013).

U.S. Department of Health and Human Services, Code of Federal Regulations Title 45 Public Welfare Department of Health and Human Services Part 46 Protection of Human Subjects revised January 15, 2009. Section 46.111:Criteria for IRB Approval of Research.

"April 2013 Air Travel Consumer Report," U.S. Department of Transportation, April 11 (2013), http://www.dot.gov/airconsumer/april-2013-air-travel-consumer-report (accessed May 1, 2013).

Lori Alden, "Statistics can be Misleading," econoclass.com, http://www.econoclass.com/misleadingstats.html (accessed May 1, 2013).

Maria de los A. Medina, "Ethics in Statistics," Based on "Building an Ethics Module for Business, Science, and Engineering Students" by Jose A. Cruz-Cruz and William Frey, Connexions, http://cnx.org/content/m15555/latest/ (accessed May 1, 2013).

## SOLUTIONS

2

   a.  all children who take ski or snowboard lessons

   b.  a group of these children

   c.  the population mean age of children who take their first snowboard lesson

d. the sample mean age of children who take their first snowboard lesson

e. $X$ = the age of one child who takes his or her first ski or snowboard lesson

f. values for $X$, such as 3, 7, and so on

**4**

a. the clients of the insurance companies

b. a group of the clients

c. the mean health costs of the clients

d. the mean health costs of the sample

e. $X$ = the health costs of one client

f. values for $X$, such as 34, 9, 82, and so on

**6**

a. all the clients of this counselor

b. a group of clients of this marriage counselor

c. the proportion of all her clients who stay married

d. the proportion of the sample of the counselor's clients who stay married

e. $X$ = the number of couples who stay married

f. yes, no

**8**

a. all people (maybe in a certain geographic area, such as the United States)

b. a group of the people

c. the proportion of all people who will buy the product

d. the proportion of the sample who will buy the product

e. $X$ = the number of people who will buy it

f. buy, not buy

**10** a

**12** quantitative discrete, 150

**14** qualitative, Oakland A's

**16** quantitative discrete, 11,234 students

**18** qualitative, Crest

**20** quantitative continuous, 47.3 years

**22** b

**24**

a. The survey was conducted using six similar flights.
The survey would not be a true representation of the entire population of air travelers.
Conducting the survey on a holiday weekend will not produce representative results.

b. Conduct the survey during different times of the year.
Conduct the survey using flights to and from various locations.
Conduct the survey on different days of the week.

**26** Answers will vary. Sample Answer: You could use a systematic sampling method. Stop the tenth person as they leave one of the buildings on campus at 9:50 in the morning. Then stop the tenth person as they leave a different building on campus at 1:50 in the afternoon.

**28** Answers will vary. Sample Answer: Many people will not respond to mail surveys. If they do respond to the surveys, you can't be sure who is responding. In addition, mailing lists can be incomplete.

**30** b

**32** convenience; cluster; stratified ; systematic; simple random

**34**

a. qualitative(categorical)

b. quantitative discrete

c. quantitative discrete

d. qualitative(categorical)

**36** Causality: The fact that two variables are related does not guarantee that one variable is influencing the other. We cannot assume that crime rate impacts education level or that education level impacts crime rate. Confounding: There are many factors that define a community other than education level and crime rate. Communities with high crime rates and high education levels may have other lurking variables that distinguish them from communities with lower crime rates and lower education levels. Because we cannot isolate these variables of interest, we cannot draw valid conclusions about the connection between education and crime. Possible lurking variables include police expenditures, unemployment levels, region, average age, and size.

**38**

a. Possible reasons: increased use of caller id, decreased use of landlines, increased use of private numbers, voice mail, privacy managers, hectic nature of personal schedules, decreased willingness to be interviewed

b. When a large number of people refuse to participate, then the sample may not have the same characteristics of the population. Perhaps the majority of people willing to participate are doing so because they feel strongly about the subject of the survey.

**40**

a.

| # Flossing per Week | Frequency | Relative Frequency | Cumulative Relative Frequency |
|---|---|---|---|
| 0 | 27 | 0.4500 | 0.4500 |
| 1 | 18 | 0.3000 | 0.7500 |
| 3 | 11 | 0.1833 | 0.9333 |
| 6 | 3 | 0.0500 | 0.9833 |
| 7 | 1 | 0.0167 | 1 |

Table 1.19

b. 5.00%

c. 93.33%

**42** The sum of the travel times is 1,173.1. Divide the sum by 50 to calculate the mean value: 23.462. Because each state's travel time was measured to the nearest tenth, round this calculation to the nearest hundredth: 23.46.

**44** b

# 2 | DESCRIPTIVE STATISTICS

**Figure 2.1** When you have large amounts of data, you will need to organize it in a way that makes sense. These ballots from an election are rolled together with similar ballots to keep them organized. (credit: William Greeson)

## Introduction

Once you have collected data, what will you do with it? Data can be described and presented in many different formats. For example, suppose you are interested in buying a house in a particular area. You may have no clue about the house prices, so you might ask your real estate agent to give you a sample data set of prices. Looking at all the prices in the sample often is overwhelming. A better way might be to look at the median price and the variation of prices. The median and variation are just two ways that you will learn to describe data. Your agent might also provide you with a graph of the data.

In this chapter, you will study numerical and graphical ways to describe and display your data. This area of statistics is called **"Descriptive Statistics."** You will learn how to calculate, and even more importantly, how to interpret these measurements and graphs.

A statistical graph is a tool that helps you learn about the shape or distribution of a sample or a population. A graph can be a more effective way of presenting data than a mass of numbers because we can see where data clusters and where there are only a few data values. Newspapers and the Internet use graphs to show trends and to enable readers to compare facts and figures quickly. Statisticians often graph data first to get a picture of the data. Then, more formal tools may be applied.

Some of the types of graphs that are used to summarize and organize data are the dot plot, the bar graph, the histogram, the stem-and-leaf plot, the frequency polygon (a type of broken line graph), the pie chart, and the box plot. In this chapter, we will briefly look at stem-and-leaf plots, line graphs, and bar graphs, as well as frequency polygons, and time series graphs. Our emphasis will be on histograms and box plots.

# 2.1 | Display Data

## Stem-and-Leaf Graphs (Stemplots), Line Graphs, and Bar Graphs

One simple graph, the **stem-and-leaf graph** or **stemplot**, comes from the field of exploratory data analysis. It is a good choice when the data sets are small. To create the plot, divide each observation of data into a stem and a leaf. The leaf consists of a **final significant digit**. For example, 23 has stem two and leaf three. The number 432 has stem 43 and leaf two. Likewise, the number 5,432 has stem 543 and leaf two. The decimal 9.3 has stem nine and leaf three. Write the stems in a vertical line from smallest to largest. Draw a vertical line to the right of the stems. Then write the leaves in increasing order next to their corresponding stem.

---

### Example 2.1

For Susan Dean's spring pre-calculus class, scores for the first exam were as follows (smallest to largest):
33; 42; 49; 49; 53; 55; 55; 61; 63; 67; 68; 68; 69; 69; 72; 73; 74; 78; 80; 83; 88; 88; 88; 90; 92; 94; 94; 94; 94; 96; 100

| Stem | Leaf |
|------|------|
| 3 | 3 |
| 4 | 2 9 9 |
| 5 | 3 5 5 |
| 6 | 1 3 7 8 8 9 9 |
| 7 | 2 3 4 8 |
| 8 | 0 3 8 8 8 |
| 9 | 0 2 4 4 4 4 6 |
| 10 | 0 |

**Table 2.1 Stem-and-Leaf Graph**

The stemplot shows that most scores fell in the 60s, 70s, 80s, and 90s. Eight out of the 31 scores or approximately 26% $\left(\frac{8}{31}\right)$ were in the 90s or 100, a fairly high number of As.

---

## Try It $\Sigma$

**2.1** For the Park City basketball team, scores for the last 30 games were as follows (smallest to largest):
32; 32; 33; 34; 38; 40; 42; 42; 43; 44; 46; 47; 47; 48; 48; 48; 49; 50; 50; 51; 52; 52; 52; 53; 54; 56; 57; 57; 60; 61
Construct a stem plot for the data.

The stemplot is a quick way to graph data and gives an exact picture of the data. You want to look for an overall pattern and any outliers. An **outlier** is an observation of data that does not fit the rest of the data. It is sometimes called an **extreme value.** When you graph an outlier, it will appear not to fit the pattern of the graph. Some outliers are due to mistakes (for example, writing down 50 instead of 500) while others may indicate that something unusual is happening. It takes some

Download for free at https://openstax.org/details/books/introductory-business-statistics

background information to explain outliers, so we will cover them in more detail later.

The data are the distances (in kilometers) from a home to local supermarkets. Create a stemplot using the data:
1.1; 1.5; 2.3; 2.5; 2.7; 3.2; 3.3; 3.3; 3.5; 3.8; 4.0; 4.2; 4.5; 4.5; 4.7; 4.8; 5.5; 5.6; 6.5; 6.7; 12.3

Do the data seem to have any concentration of values?

The leaves are to the right of the decimal.

**Solution 2.2**

The value 12.3 may be an outlier. Values appear to concentrate at three and four kilometers.

| Stem | Leaf |
|------|------|
| 1 | 1 5 |
| 2 | 3 5 7 |
| 3 | 2 3 3 5 8 |
| 4 | 0 2 5 5 7 8 |
| 5 | 5 6 |
| 6 | 5 7 |
| 7 | |
| 8 | |
| 9 | |
| 10 | |
| 11 | |
| 12 | 3 |

Table 2.2

**2.2** The following data show the distances (in miles) from the homes of off-campus statistics students to the college. Create a stem plot using the data and identify any outliers:

0.5; 0.7; 1.1; 1.2; 1.2; 1.3; 1.3; 1.5; 1.5; 1.7; 1.7; 1.8; 1.9; 2.0; 2.2; 2.5; 2.6; 2.8; 2.8; 2.8; 3.5; 3.8; 4.4; 4.8; 4.9; 5.2; 5.5; 5.7; 5.8; 8.0

A **side-by-side stem-and-leaf plot** allows a comparison of the two data sets in two columns. In a side-by-side stem-and-leaf plot, two sets of leaves share the same stem. The leaves are to the left and the right of the stems.

Table 2.4 and Table 2.5 show the ages of presidents at their inauguration and at their death. Construct a side-by-side stem-and-leaf plot using this data.

Solution 2.3

| Ages at Inauguration | | Ages at Death |
|---|---|---|
| 9 9 8 7 7 7 6 3 2 | 4 | 6 9 |
| 8 7 7 7 7 6 6 6 5 5 5 5 4 4 4 4 4 2 1 1 1 1 1 1 0 | 5 | 3 6 6 7 7 8 |
| 9 5 4 4 2 1 1 1 0 | 6 | 0 0 3 3 4 4 5 6 7 7 7 8 |
| | 7 | 0 0 1 1 1 4 7 8 8 9 |
| | 8 | 0 1 3 5 8 |
| | 9 | 0 0 3 3 |

Table 2.3

| President | Age | President | Age | President | Age |
|---|---|---|---|---|---|
| Washington | 57 | Lincoln | 52 | Hoover | 54 |
| J. Adams | 61 | A. Johnson | 56 | F. Roosevelt | 51 |
| Jefferson | 57 | Grant | 46 | Truman | 60 |
| Madison | 57 | Hayes | 54 | Eisenhower | 62 |
| Monroe | 58 | Garfield | 49 | Kennedy | 43 |
| J. Q. Adams | 57 | Arthur | 51 | L. Johnson | 55 |
| Jackson | 61 | Cleveland | 47 | Nixon | 56 |
| Van Buren | 54 | B. Harrison | 55 | Ford | 61 |
| W. H. Harrison | 68 | Cleveland | 55 | Carter | 52 |
| Tyler | 51 | McKinley | 54 | Reagan | 69 |
| Polk | 49 | T. Roosevelt | 42 | G.H.W. Bush | 64 |
| Taylor | 64 | Taft | 51 | Clinton | 47 |
| Fillmore | 50 | Wilson | 56 | G. W. Bush | 54 |
| Pierce | 48 | Harding | 55 | Obama | 47 |
| Buchanan | 65 | Coolidge | 51 | | |

Table 2.4 Presidential Ages at Inauguration

| President | Age | President | Age | President | Age |
|---|---|---|---|---|---|
| Washington | 67 | Lincoln | 56 | Hoover | 90 |
| J. Adams | 90 | A. Johnson | 66 | F. Roosevelt | 63 |
| Jefferson | 83 | Grant | 63 | Truman | 88 |

Table 2.5 Presidential Age at Death

| President | Age | President | Age | President | Age |
|-----------|-----|-----------|-----|-----------|-----|
| Madison | 85 | Hayes | 70 | Eisenhower | 78 |
| Monroe | 73 | Garfield | 49 | Kennedy | 46 |
| J. Q. Adams | 80 | Arthur | 56 | L. Johnson | 64 |
| Jackson | 78 | Cleveland | 71 | Nixon | 81 |
| Van Buren | 79 | B. Harrison | 67 | Ford | 93 |
| W. H. Harrison | 68 | Cleveland | 71 | Reagan | 93 |
| Tyler | 71 | McKinley | 58 | | |
| Polk | 53 | T. Roosevelt | 60 | | |
| Taylor | 65 | Taft | 72 | | |
| Fillmore | 74 | Wilson | 67 | | |
| Pierce | 64 | Harding | 57 | | |
| Buchanan | 77 | Coolidge | 60 | | |

Table 2.5 Presidential Age at Death

Another type of graph that is useful for specific data values is a **line graph**. In the particular line graph shown in Example 2.4, the *x*-axis (horizontal axis) consists of **data values** and the *y*-axis (vertical axis) consists of **frequency points**. The frequency points are connected using line segments.

## Example 2.4

In a survey, 40 mothers were asked how many times per week a teenager must be reminded to do his or her chores. The results are shown in Table 2.6 and in Figure 2.2.

| Number of times teenager is reminded | Frequency |
|--------------------------------------|-----------|
| 0 | 2 |
| 1 | 5 |
| 2 | 8 |
| 3 | 14 |
| 4 | 7 |
| 5 | 4 |

Table 2.6

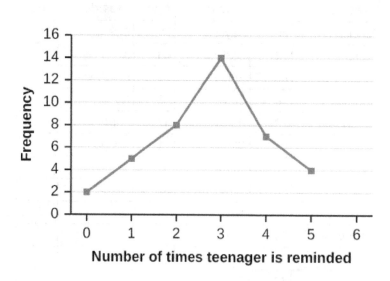

Figure 2.2

**2.4** In a survey, 40 people were asked how many times per year they had their car in the shop for repairs. The results are shown in **Table 2.7**. Construct a line graph.

| Number of times in shop | Frequency |
|---|---|
| 0 | 7 |
| 1 | 10 |
| 2 | 14 |
| 3 | 9 |

Table 2.7

**Bar graphs** consist of bars that are separated from each other. The bars can be rectangles or they can be rectangular boxes (used in three-dimensional plots), and they can be vertical or horizontal. The **bar graph** shown in **Example 2.5** has age groups represented on the *x*-axis and proportions on the *y*-axis.

## Example 2.5

By the end of 2011, Facebook had over 146 million users in the United States. Table 2.7 shows three age groups, the number of users in each age group, and the proportion (%) of users in each age group. Construct a bar graph using this data.

| Age groups | Number of Facebook users | Proportion (%) of Facebook users |
|---|---|---|
| 13–25 | 65,082,280 | 45% |
| 26–44 | 53,300,200 | 36% |
| 45–64 | 27,885,100 | 19% |

Table 2.8

**Solution 2.5**

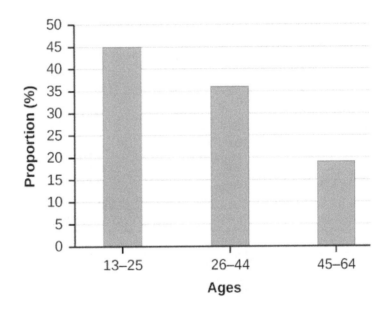

Figure 2.3

**2.5** The population in Park City is made up of children, working-age adults, and retirees. Table 2.9 shows the three age groups, the number of people in the town from each age group, and the proportion (%) of people in each age group. Construct a bar graph showing the proportions.

| Age groups | Number of people | Proportion of population |
|---|---|---|
| Children | 67,059 | 19% |
| Working-age adults | 152,198 | 43% |
| Retirees | 131,662 | 38% |

Table 2.9

## Example 2.6

The columns in Table 2.9 contain: the race or ethnicity of students in U.S. Public Schools for the class of 2011, percentages for the Advanced Placement examine population for that class, and percentages for the overall student population. Create a bar graph with the student race or ethnicity (qualitative data) on the x-axis, and the Advanced Placement examinee population percentages on the y-axis.

| Race/Ethnicity | AP Examinee Population | Overall Student Population |
|---|---|---|
| 1 = Asian, Asian American or Pacific Islander | 10.3% | 5.7% |
| 2 = Black or African American | 9.0% | 14.7% |
| 3 = Hispanic or Latino | 17.0% | 17.6% |
| 4 = American Indian or Alaska Native | 0.6% | 1.1% |
| 5 = White | 57.1% | 59.2% |
| 6 = Not reported/other | 6.0% | 1.7% |

Table 2.10

Solution 2.6

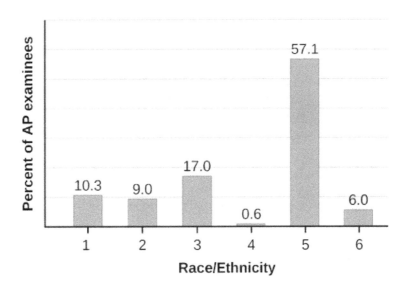

Figure 2.4

**2.6** Park city is broken down into six voting districts. The table shows the percent of the total registered voter population that lives in each district as well as the percent total of the entire population that lives in each district. Construct a bar graph that shows the registered voter population by district.

| District | Registered voter population | Overall city population |
|----------|------------------------------|--------------------------|
| 1 | 15.5% | 19.4% |
| 2 | 12.2% | 15.6% |
| 3 | 9.8% | 9.0% |
| 4 | 17.4% | 18.5% |
| 5 | 22.8% | 20.7% |
| 6 | 22.3% | 16.8% |

Table 2.11

## Example 2.7

Below is a two-way table showing the types of pets owned by men and women:

|       | Dogs | Cats | Fish | Total |
|-------|------|------|------|-------|
| Men   | 4    | 2    | 2    | 8     |
| Women | 4    | 6    | 2    | 12    |
| Total | 8    | 8    | 4    | 20    |

Table 2.12

Given these data, calculate the conditional distributions for the subpopulation of men who own each pet type.

**Solution 2.7**

Men who own dogs = 4/8 = 0.5

Men who own cats = 2/8 = 0.25

Men who own fish = 2/8 = 0.25

Note: The sum of all of the conditional distributions must equal one. In this case, 0.5 + 0.25 + 0.25 = 1; therefore, the solution "checks".

# Histograms, Frequency Polygons, and Time Series Graphs

For most of the work you do in this book, you will use a histogram to display the data. One advantage of a histogram is that it can readily display large data sets. A rule of thumb is to use a histogram when the data set consists of 100 values or more.

A **histogram** consists of contiguous (adjoining) boxes. It has both a horizontal axis and a vertical axis. The horizontal axis is labeled with what the data represents (for instance, distance from your home to school). The vertical axis is labeled either **frequency** or **relative frequency** (or percent frequency or probability). The graph will have the same shape with either label. The histogram (like the stemplot) can give you the shape of the data, the center, and the spread of the data.

The relative frequency is equal to the frequency for an observed value of the data divided by the total number of data values in the sample.(Remember, frequency is defined as the number of times an answer occurs.) If:

- $f$ = frequency
- $n$ = total number of data values (or the sum of the individual frequencies), and
- $RF$ = relative frequency,

then:

$$RF = \frac{f}{n}$$

For example, if three students in Mr. Ahab's English class of 40 students received from 90% to 100%, then, $f = 3$, $n = 40$, and $RF = \frac{f}{n} = \frac{3}{40} = 0.075$. 7.5% of the students received 90–100%. 90–100% are quantitative measures.

**To construct a histogram,** first decide how many **bars** or **intervals**, also called classes, represent the data. Many histograms consist of five to 15 bars or classes for clarity. The number of bars needs to be chosen. Choose a starting point for the first interval to be less than the smallest data value. A **convenient starting point** is a lower value carried out to one more decimal place than the value with the most decimal places. For example, if the value with the most decimal places is 6.1 and this is the smallest value, a convenient starting point is 6.05 (6.1 – 0.05 = 6.05). We say that 6.05 has more precision. If the value with the most decimal places is 2.23 and the lowest value is 1.5, a convenient starting point is 1.495 (1.5 – 0.005 = 1.495). If the value with the most decimal places is 3.234 and the lowest value is 1.0, a convenient starting point is 0.9995 (1.0 – 0.0005 = 0.9995). If all the data happen to be integers and the smallest value is two, then a convenient starting point is 1.5 (2 – 0.5 = 1.5). Also, when the starting point and other boundaries are carried to one additional decimal place, no data value will fall on a boundary. The next two examples go into detail about how to construct a histogram using continuous data and how to create a histogram using discrete data.

## Example 2.8

The following data are the heights (in inches to the nearest half inch) of 100 male semiprofessional soccer players. The heights are **continuous** data, since height is measured.

60; 60.5; 61; 61; 61.5

63.5; 63.5; 63.5

64; 64; 64; 64; 64; 64; 64; 64.5; 64.5; 64.5; 64.5; 64.5; 64.5; 64.5

66; 66; 66; 66; 66; 66; 66; 66; 66; 66; 66.5; 66.5; 66.5; 66.5; 66.5; 66.5; 66.5; 66.5; 66.5; 66.5; 66.5; 67; 67; 67; 67; 67; 67; 67; 67; 67; 67; 67; 67; 67.5; 67.5; 67.5; 67.5; 67.5; 67.5; 67.5

68; 68; 69; 69; 69; 69; 69; 69; 69; 69; 69; 69.5; 69.5; 69.5; 69.5; 69.5

70; 70; 70; 70; 70; 70; 70.5; 70.5; 70.5; 71; 71; 71

72; 72; 72; 72.5; 72.5; 73; 73.5

74

The smallest data value is 60. Since the data with the most decimal places has one decimal (for instance, 61.5), we want our starting point to have two decimal places. Since the numbers 0.5, 0.05, 0.005, etc. are convenient numbers, use 0.05 and subtract it from 60, the smallest value, for the convenient starting point.

$60 - 0.05 = 59.95$ which is more precise than, say, 61.5 by one decimal place. The starting point is, then, 59.95.

The largest value is 74, so $74 + 0.05 = 74.05$ is the ending value.

Next, calculate the width of each bar or class interval. To calculate this width, subtract the starting point from the ending value and divide by the number of bars (you must choose the number of bars you desire). Suppose you choose eight bars.

$$\frac{74.05 - 59.95}{8} = 1.76$$

### NOTE

We will round up to two and make each bar or class interval two units wide. Rounding up to two is one way to prevent a value from falling on a boundary. Rounding to the next number is often necessary even if it goes against the standard rules of rounding. For this example, using 1.76 as the width would also work. A guideline that is followed by some for the width of a bar or class interval is to take the square root of the number of data values and then round to the nearest whole number, if necessary. For example, if there are 150 values of data, take the square root of 150 and round to 12 bars or intervals.

The boundaries are:

- 59.95

- $59.95 + 2 = 61.95$

- $61.95 + 2 = 63.95$

- $63.95 + 2 = 65.95$

- $65.95 + 2 = 67.95$

- $67.95 + 2 = 69.95$

- $69.95 + 2 = 71.95$

- $71.95 + 2 = 73.95$

- $73.95 + 2 = 75.95$

The heights 60 through 61.5 inches are in the interval 59.95–61.95. The heights that are 63.5 are in the interval 61.95–63.95. The heights that are 64 through 64.5 are in the interval 63.95–65.95. The heights 66 through 67.5 are in the interval 65.95–67.95. The heights 68 through 69.5 are in the interval 67.95–69.95. The heights 70 through 71 are in the interval 69.95–71.95. The heights 72 through 73.5 are in the interval 71.95–73.95. The height 74 is in the interval 73.95–75.95.

The following histogram displays the heights on the *x*-axis and relative frequency on the *y*-axis.

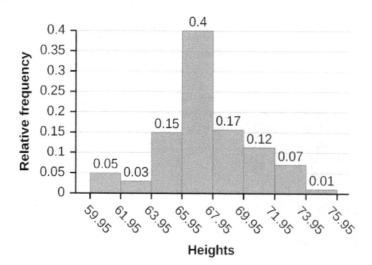

Figure 2.5

## Try It Σ

**2.8** The following data are the shoe sizes of 50 male students. The sizes are continuous data since shoe size is measured. Construct a histogram and calculate the width of each bar or class interval. Suppose you choose six bars.
9; 9; 9.5; 9.5; 10; 10; 10; 10; 10; 10; 10.5; 10.5; 10.5; 10.5; 10.5; 10.5; 10.5; 10.5
11; 11; 11; 11; 11; 11; 11; 11; 11; 11; 11; 11; 11; 11.5; 11.5; 11.5; 11.5; 11.5; 11.5; 11.5
12; 12; 12; 12; 12; 12; 12; 12.5; 12.5; 12.5; 12.5; 14

## Example 2.9

The following data are the number of books bought by 50 part-time college students at ABC College. The number of books is **discrete data**, since books are counted.
1; 1; 1; 1; 1; 1; 1; 1; 1; 1; 1
2; 2; 2; 2; 2; 2; 2; 2; 2; 2
3; 3; 3; 3; 3; 3; 3; 3; 3; 3; 3; 3; 3; 3; 3; 3
4; 4; 4; 4; 4; 4
5; 5; 5; 5; 5
6; 6

Eleven students buy one book. Ten students buy two books. Sixteen students buy three books. Six students buy four books. Five students buy five books. Two students buy six books.

Because the data are integers, subtract 0.5 from 1, the smallest data value and add 0.5 to 6, the largest data value. Then the starting point is 0.5 and the ending value is 6.5.

Next, calculate the width of each bar or class interval. If the data are discrete and there are not too many different values, a width that places the data values in the middle of the bar or class interval is the most convenient. Since the data consist of the numbers 1, 2, 3, 4, 5, 6, and the starting point is 0.5, a width of one places the 1 in the middle of the interval from 0.5 to 1.5, the 2 in the middle of the interval from 1.5 to 2.5, the 3 in the middle of the interval from 2.5 to 3.5, the 4 in the middle of the interval from _____ to _____, the 5 in the middle of the interval from _____ to _____, and the _____ in the middle of the interval from _____ to _____ .

Solution 2.9

- 3.5 to 4.5

- 4.5 to 5.5

- 6

- 5.5 to 6.5

Calculate the number of bars as follows:

$$\frac{6.5 - 0.5}{\text{number of bars}} = 1$$

where 1 is the width of a bar. Therefore, bars = 6.

The following histogram displays the number of books on the *x*-axis and the frequency on the *y*-axis.

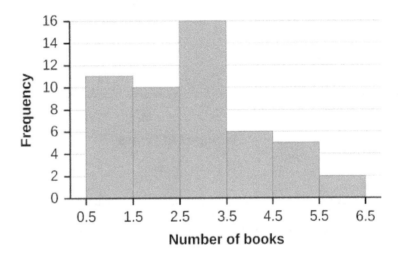

Figure 2.6

## Example 2.10

Using this data set, construct a histogram.

| Number of Hours My Classmates Spent Playing Video Games on Weekends | | | | |
|---|---|---|---|---|
| 9.95 | 10 | 2.25 | 16.75 | 0 |
| 19.5 | 22.5 | 7.5 | 15 | 12.75 |
| 5.5 | 11 | 10 | 20.75 | 17.5 |
| 23 | 21.9 | 24 | 23.75 | 18 |
| 20 | 15 | 22.9 | 18.8 | 20.5 |

Table 2.13

Solution 2.10

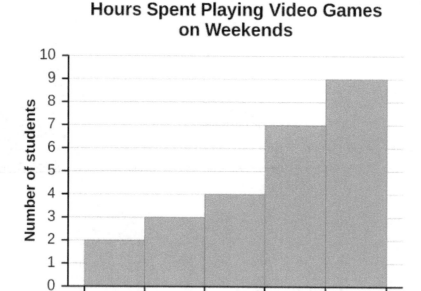

**Figure 2.7**

Some values in this data set fall on boundaries for the class intervals. A value is counted in a class interval if it falls on the left boundary, but not if it falls on the right boundary. Different researchers may set up histograms for the same data in different ways. There is more than one correct way to set up a histogram.

## Frequency Polygons

Frequency polygons are analogous to line graphs, and just as line graphs make continuous data visually easy to interpret, so too do frequency polygons.

To construct a frequency polygon, first examine the data and decide on the number of intervals, or class intervals, to use on the x-axis and y-axis. After choosing the appropriate ranges, begin plotting the data points. After all the points are plotted, draw line segments to connect them.

## Example 2.11

A frequency polygon was constructed from the frequency table below.

| Frequency Distribution for Calculus Final Test Scores | | | |
|---|---|---|---|
| **Lower Bound** | **Upper Bound** | **Frequency** | **Cumulative Frequency** |
| 49.5 | 59.5 | 5 | 5 |
| 59.5 | 69.5 | 10 | 15 |
| 69.5 | 79.5 | 30 | 45 |
| 79.5 | 89.5 | 40 | 85 |
| 89.5 | 99.5 | 15 | 100 |

Table 2.14

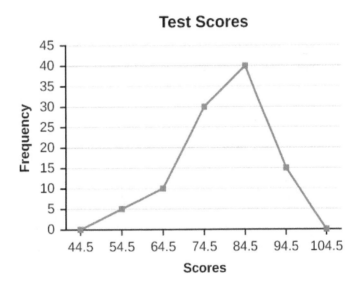

Figure 2.8

The first label on the *x*-axis is 44.5. This represents an interval extending from 39.5 to 49.5. Since the lowest test score is 54.5, this interval is used only to allow the graph to touch the *x*-axis. The point labeled 54.5 represents the next interval, or the first "real" interval from the table, and contains five scores. This reasoning is followed for each of the remaining intervals with the point 104.5 representing the interval from 99.5 to 109.5. Again, this interval contains no data and is only used so that the graph will touch the *x*-axis. Looking at the graph, we say that this distribution is skewed because one side of the graph does not mirror the other side.

**2.11** Construct a frequency polygon of U.S. Presidents' ages at inauguration shown in Table 2.15.

| Age at Inauguration | Frequency |
|:---:|:---:|
| 41.5–46.5 | 4 |
| 46.5–51.5 | 11 |
| 51.5–56.5 | 14 |
| 56.5–61.5 | 9 |
| 61.5–66.5 | 4 |
| 66.5–71.5 | 2 |

Table 2.15

Frequency polygons are useful for comparing distributions. This is achieved by overlaying the frequency polygons drawn for different data sets.

## Example 2.12

We will construct an overlay frequency polygon comparing the scores from **Example 2.11** with the students' final numeric grade.

| Frequency Distribution for Calculus Final Test Scores | | | |
|:---:|:---:|:---:|:---:|
| **Lower Bound** | **Upper Bound** | **Frequency** | **Cumulative Frequency** |
| 49.5 | 59.5 | 5 | 5 |
| 59.5 | 69.5 | 10 | 15 |
| 69.5 | 79.5 | 30 | 45 |
| 79.5 | 89.5 | 40 | 85 |
| 89.5 | 99.5 | 15 | 100 |

Table 2.16

| Frequency Distribution for Calculus Final Grades | | | |
|:---:|:---:|:---:|:---:|
| **Lower Bound** | **Upper Bound** | **Frequency** | **Cumulative Frequency** |
| 49.5 | 59.5 | 10 | 10 |
| 59.5 | 69.5 | 10 | 20 |
| 69.5 | 79.5 | 30 | 50 |
| 79.5 | 89.5 | 45 | 95 |
| 89.5 | 99.5 | 5 | 100 |

Table 2.17

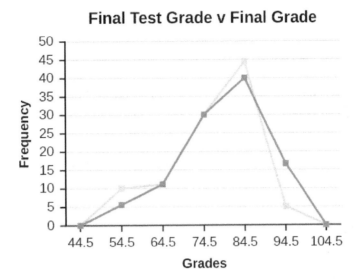

**Final Test Grade v Final Grade**

Figure 2.9

## Constructing a Time Series Graph

Suppose that we want to study the temperature range of a region for an entire month. Every day at noon we note the temperature and write this down in a log. A variety of statistical studies could be done with these data. We could find the mean or the median temperature for the month. We could construct a histogram displaying the number of days that temperatures reach a certain range of values. However, all of these methods ignore a portion of the data that we have collected.

One feature of the data that we may want to consider is that of time. Since each date is paired with the temperature reading for the day, we don't have to think of the data as being random. We can instead use the times given to impose a chronological order on the data. A graph that recognizes this ordering and displays the changing temperature as the month progresses is called a time series graph.

To construct a time series graph, we must look at both pieces of our **paired data set**. We start with a standard Cartesian coordinate system. The horizontal axis is used to plot the date or time increments, and the vertical axis is used to plot the values of the variable that we are measuring. By doing this, we make each point on the graph correspond to a date and a measured quantity. The points on the graph are typically connected by straight lines in the order in which they occur.

## Example 2.13

The following data shows the Annual Consumer Price Index, each month, for ten years. Construct a time series graph for the Annual Consumer Price Index data only.

| Year | Jan | Feb | Mar | Apr | May | Jun | Jul |
|------|------|------|------|------|------|------|------|
| 2003 | 181.7 | 183.1 | 184.2 | 183.8 | 183.5 | 183.7 | 183.9 |
| 2004 | 185.2 | 186.2 | 187.4 | 188.0 | 189.1 | 189.7 | 189.4 |
| 2005 | 190.7 | 191.8 | 193.3 | 194.6 | 194.4 | 194.5 | 195.4 |
| 2006 | 198.3 | 198.7 | 199.8 | 201.5 | 202.5 | 202.9 | 203.5 |
| 2007 | 202.416 | 203.499 | 205.352 | 206.686 | 207.949 | 208.352 | 208.299 |
| 2008 | 211.080 | 211.693 | 213.528 | 214.823 | 216.632 | 218.815 | 219.964 |
| 2009 | 211.143 | 212.193 | 212.709 | 213.240 | 213.856 | 215.693 | 215.351 |
| 2010 | 216.687 | 216.741 | 217.631 | 218.009 | 218.178 | 217.965 | 218.011 |
| 2011 | 220.223 | 221.309 | 223.467 | 224.906 | 225.964 | 225.722 | 225.922 |
| 2012 | 226.665 | 227.663 | 229.392 | 230.085 | 229.815 | 229.478 | 229.104 |

Table 2.18

| Year | Aug | Sep | Oct | Nov | Dec | Annual |
|------|------|------|------|------|------|--------|
| 2003 | 184.6 | 185.2 | 185.0 | 184.5 | 184.3 | 184.0 |
| 2004 | 189.5 | 189.9 | 190.9 | 191.0 | 190.3 | 188.9 |
| 2005 | 196.4 | 198.8 | 199.2 | 197.6 | 196.8 | 195.3 |
| 2006 | 203.9 | 202.9 | 201.8 | 201.5 | 201.8 | 201.6 |
| 2007 | 207.917 | 208.490 | 208.936 | 210.177 | 210.036 | 207.342 |
| 2008 | 219.086 | 218.783 | 216.573 | 212.425 | 210.228 | 215.303 |
| 2009 | 215.834 | 215.969 | 216.177 | 216.330 | 215.949 | 214.537 |
| 2010 | 218.312 | 218.439 | 218.711 | 218.803 | 219.179 | 218.056 |
| 2011 | 226.545 | 226.889 | 226.421 | 226.230 | 225.672 | 224.939 |
| 2012 | 230.379 | 231.407 | 231.317 | 230.221 | 229.601 | 229.594 |

Table 2.19

Solution 2.13

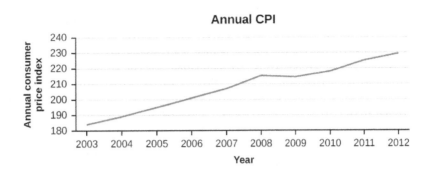

Figure 2.10

**2.13** The following table is a portion of a data set from www.worldbank.org. Use the table to construct a time series graph for $CO_2$ emissions for the United States.

| CO2 Emissions | | | |
|---|---|---|---|
| | **Ukraine** | **United Kingdom** | **United States** |
| 2003 | 352,259 | 540,640 | 5,681,664 |
| 2004 | 343,121 | 540,409 | 5,790,761 |
| 2005 | 339,029 | 541,990 | 5,826,394 |
| 2006 | 327,797 | 542,045 | 5,737,615 |
| 2007 | 328,357 | 528,631 | 5,828,697 |
| 2008 | 323,657 | 522,247 | 5,656,839 |
| 2009 | 272,176 | 474,579 | 5,299,563 |

Table 2.20

## Uses of a Time Series Graph

Time series graphs are important tools in various applications of statistics. When recording values of the same variable over an extended period of time, sometimes it is difficult to discern any trend or pattern. However, once the same data points are displayed graphically, some features jump out. Time series graphs make trends easy to spot.

## How NOT to Lie with Statistics

It is important to remember that the very reason we develop a variety of methods to present data is to develop insights into the subject of what the observations represent. We want to get a "sense" of the data. Are the observations all very much alike or are they spread across a wide range of values, are they bunched at one end of the spectrum or are they distributed evenly and so on. We are trying to get a visual picture of the numerical data. Shortly we will develop formal mathematical measures of the data, but our visual graphical presentation can say much. It can, unfortunately, also say much that is distracting, confusing and simply wrong in terms of the impression the visual leaves. Many years ago Darrell Huff wrote the book *How to Lie with Statistics*. It has been through 25 plus printings and sold more than one and one-half million copies. His perspective was a harsh one and used many actual examples that were designed to mislead. He wanted to make people aware of such deception, but perhaps more importantly to educate so that others do not make the same errors inadvertently.

Again, the goal is to enlighten with visuals that tell the story of the data. Pie charts have a number of common problems when used to convey the message of the data. Too many pieces of the pie overwhelm the reader. More than perhaps five or six categories ought to give an idea of the relative importance of each piece. This is after all the goal of a pie chart, what subset matters most relative to the others. If there are more components than this then perhaps an alternative approach would be better or perhaps some can be consolidated into an "other" category. Pie charts cannot show changes over time, although we see this attempted all too often. In federal, state, and city finance documents pie charts are often presented to show the components of revenue available to the governing body for appropriation: income tax, sales tax motor vehicle taxes and so on. In and of itself this is interesting information and can be nicely done with a pie chart. The error occurs when two years are set side-by-side. Because the total revenues change year to year, but the size of the pie is fixed, no real information is provided and the relative size of each piece of the pie cannot be meaningfully compared.

Histograms can be very helpful in understanding the data. Properly presented, they can be a quick visual way to present probabilities of different categories by the simple visual of comparing relative areas in each category. Here the error, purposeful or not, is to vary the width of the categories. This of course makes comparison to the other categories impossible. It does embellish the importance of the category with the expanded width because it has a greater area, inappropriately, and thus visually "says" that that category has a higher probability of occurrence.

Time series graphs perhaps are the most abused. A plot of some variable across time should never be presented on axes that change part way across the page either in the vertical or horizontal dimension. Perhaps the time frame is changed from years to months. Perhaps this is to save space or because monthly data was not available for early years. In either case this confounds the presentation and destroys any value of the graph. If this is not done to purposefully confuse the reader, then it certainly is either lazy or sloppy work.

Changing the units of measurement of the axis can smooth out a drop or accentuate one. If you want to show large changes, then measure the variable in small units, penny rather than thousands of dollars. And of course to continue the fraud, be sure that the axis does not begin at zero, zero. If it begins at zero, zero, then it becomes apparent that the axis has been manipulated.

Perhaps you have a client that is concerned with the volatility of the portfolio you manage. An easy way to present the data is to use long time periods on the time series graph. Use months or better, quarters rather than daily or weekly data. If that doesn't get the volatility down then spread the time axis relative to the rate of return or portfolio valuation axis. If you want to show "quick" dramatic growth, then shrink the time axis. Any positive growth will show visually "high" growth rates. Do note that if the growth is negative then this trick will show the portfolio is collapsing at a dramatic rate.

Again, the goal of descriptive statistics is to convey meaningful visuals that tell the story of the data. Purposeful manipulation is fraud and unethical at the worst, but even at its best, making these type of errors will lead to confusion on the part of the analysis.

## 2.2 | Measures of the Location of the Data

The common measures of location are **quartiles** and **percentiles**

Quartiles are special percentiles. The first quartile, $Q_1$, is the same as the $25^{th}$ percentile, and the third quartile, $Q_3$, is the same as the $75^{th}$ percentile. The median, $M$, is called both the second quartile and the $50^{th}$ percentile.

To calculate quartiles and percentiles, the data must be ordered from smallest to largest. Quartiles divide ordered data into quarters. Percentiles divide ordered data into hundredths. To score in the $90^{th}$ percentile of an exam does not mean, necessarily, that you received 90% on a test. It means that 90% of test scores are the same or less than your score and 10% of the test scores are the same or greater than your test score.

Percentiles are useful for comparing values. For this reason, universities and colleges use percentiles extensively. One instance in which colleges and universities use percentiles is when SAT results are used to determine a minimum testing score that will be used as an acceptance factor. For example, suppose Duke accepts SAT scores at or above the $75^{th}$ percentile. That translates into a score of at least 1220.

Percentiles are mostly used with very large populations. Therefore, if you were to say that 90% of the test scores are less (and not the same or less) than your score, it would be acceptable because removing one particular data value is not significant.

The **median** is a number that measures the "center" of the data. You can think of the median as the "middle value," but it does not actually have to be one of the observed values. It is a number that separates ordered data into halves. Half the values are the same number or smaller than the median, and half the values are the same number or larger. For example, consider the following data.
1; 11.5; 6; 7.2; 4; 8; 9; 10; 6.8; 8.3; 2; 2; 10; 1

Ordered from smallest to largest:
1; 1; 2; 2; 4; 6; 6.8; 7.2; 8; 8.3; 9; 10; 10; 11.5

Since there are 14 observations, the median is between the seventh value, 6.8, and the eighth value, 7.2. To find the median, add the two values together and divide by two.

$$\frac{6.8 + 7.2}{2} = 7$$

The median is seven. Half of the values are smaller than seven and half of the values are larger than seven.

**Quartiles** are numbers that separate the data into quarters. Quartiles may or may not be part of the data. To find the quartiles, first find the median or second quartile. The first quartile, $Q_1$, is the middle value of the lower half of the data, and the third quartile, $Q_3$, is the middle value, or median, of the upper half of the data. To get the idea, consider the same data set:
1; 1; 2; 2; 4; 6; 6.8; 7.2; 8; 8.3; 9; 10; 10; 11.5

The median or **second quartile** is seven. The lower half of the data are 1, 1, 2, 2, 4, 6, 6.8. The middle value of the lower half is two.
1; 1; 2; 2; 4; 6; 6.8

The number two, which is part of the data, is the **first quartile**. One-fourth of the entire sets of values are the same as or less than two and three-fourths of the values are more than two.

The upper half of the data is 7.2, 8, 8.3, 9, 10, 10, 11.5. The middle value of the upper half is nine.

The **third quartile**, $Q_3$, is nine. Three-fourths (75%) of the ordered data set are less than nine. One-fourth (25%) of the ordered data set are greater than nine. The third quartile is part of the data set in this example.

The **interquartile range** is a number that indicates the spread of the middle half or the middle 50% of the data. It is the difference between the third quartile ($Q_3$) and the first quartile ($Q_1$).

$IQR = Q_3 - Q_1$

The $IQR$ can help to determine potential **outliers**. **A value is suspected to be a potential outlier if it is less than (1.5)($IQR$) below the first quartile or more than (1.5)($IQR$) above the third quartile**. Potential outliers always require further investigation.

> **NOTE**
>
> A potential outlier is a data point that is significantly different from the other data points. These special data points may be errors or some kind of abnormality or they may be a key to understanding the data.

### Example 2.14

For the following 13 real estate prices, calculate the $IQR$ and determine if any prices are potential outliers. Prices are in dollars.
389,950; 230,500; 158,000; 479,000; 639,000; 114,950; 5,500,000; 387,000; 659,000; 529,000; 575,000; 488,800; 1,095,000

**Solution 2.14**

Order the data from smallest to largest.
114,950; 158,000; 230,500; 387,000; 389,950; 479,000; 488,800; 529,000; 575,000; 639,000; 659,000; 1,095,000; 5,500,000

$M = 488,800$

$$Q_1 = \frac{230,500 + 387,000}{2} = 308,750$$

$$Q_3 = \frac{639,000 + 659,000}{2} = 649,000$$

$IQR = 649,000 - 308,750 = 340,250$

$(1.5)(IQR) = (1.5)(340,250) = 510,375$

$Q_1 - (1.5)(IQR) = 308,750 - 510,375 = -201,625$

$Q_3 + (1.5)(IQR) = 649,000 + 510,375 = 1,159,375$

No house price is less than –201,625. However, 5,500,000 is more than 1,159,375. Therefore, 5,500,000 is a potential **outlier**.

## Example 2.15

For the two data sets in the **test scores example**, find the following:

a. The interquartile range. Compare the two interquartile ranges.

b. Any outliers in either set.

### Solution 2.15

The five number summary for the day and night classes is

| | Minimum | $Q_1$ | Median | $Q_3$ | Maximum |
|---|---|---|---|---|---|
| **Day** | 32 | 56 | 74.5 | 82.5 | 99 |
| **Night** | 25.5 | 78 | 81 | 89 | 98 |

**Table 2.21**

a. The IQR for the day group is $Q_3 - Q_1 = 82.5 - 56 = 26.5$
   The IQR for the night group is $Q_3 - Q_1 = 89 - 78 = 11$

   The interquartile range (the spread or variability) for the day class is larger than the night class $IQR$. This suggests more variation will be found in the day class's class test scores.

b. Day class outliers are found using the IQR times 1.5 rule. So,
   $Q_1 - IQR(1.5) = 56 - 26.5(1.5) = 16.25$
   $Q_3 + IQR(1.5) = 82.5 + 26.5(1.5) = 122.25$

   Since the minimum and maximum values for the day class are greater than 16.25 and less than 122.25, there are no outliers.

   Night class outliers are calculated as:

   $Q_1 - IQR(1.5) = 78 - 11(1.5) = 61.5$
   $Q_3 + IQR(1.5) = 89 + 11(1.5) = 105.5$

   For this class, any test score less than 61.5 is an outlier. Therefore, the scores of 45 and 25.5 are outliers. Since no test score is greater than 105.5, there is no upper end outlier.

## Example 2.16

Fifty statistics students were asked how much sleep they get per school night (rounded to the nearest hour). The results were:

| AMOUNT OF SLEEP PER SCHOOL NIGHT (HOURS) | FREQUENCY | RELATIVE FREQUENCY | CUMULATIVE RELATIVE FREQUENCY |
|---|---|---|---|
| 4 | 2 | 0.04 | 0.04 |
| 5 | 5 | 0.10 | 0.14 |
| 6 | 7 | 0.14 | 0.28 |
| 7 | 12 | 0.24 | 0.52 |
| 8 | 14 | 0.28 | 0.80 |
| 9 | 7 | 0.14 | 0.94 |
| 10 | 3 | 0.06 | 1.00 |

Table 2.22

**Find the 28$^{th}$ percentile**. Notice the 0.28 in the "cumulative relative frequency" column. Twenty-eight percent of 50 data values is 14 values. There are 14 values less than the 28$^{th}$ percentile. They include the two 4s, the five 5s, and the seven 6s. The 28$^{th}$ percentile is between the last six and the first seven. **The 28$^{th}$ percentile is 6.5.**

**Find the median**. Look again at the "cumulative relative frequency" column and find 0.52. The median is the 50$^{th}$ percentile or the second quartile. 50% of 50 is 25. There are 25 values less than the median. They include the two 4s, the five 5s, the seven 6s, and eleven of the 7s. The median or 50$^{th}$ percentile is between the 25$^{th}$, or seven, and 26$^{th}$, or seven, values. **The median is seven.**

**Find the third quartile**. The third quartile is the same as the 75$^{th}$ percentile. You can "eyeball" this answer. If you look at the "cumulative relative frequency" column, you find 0.52 and 0.80. When you have all the fours, fives, sixes and sevens, you have 52% of the data. When you include all the 8s, you have 80% of the data. **The 75$^{th}$ percentile, then, must be an eight**. Another way to look at the problem is to find 75% of 50, which is 37.5, and round up to 38. The third quartile, $Q_3$, is the 38$^{th}$ value, which is an eight. You can check this answer by counting the values. (There are 37 values below the third quartile and 12 values above.)

**2.16** Forty bus drivers were asked how many hours they spend each day running their routes (rounded to the nearest hour). Find the 65$^{th}$ percentile.

| Amount of time spent on route (hours) | Frequency | Relative Frequency | Cumulative Relative Frequency |
|---|---|---|---|
| 2 | 12 | 0.30 | 0.30 |
| 3 | 14 | 0.35 | 0.65 |
| 4 | 10 | 0.25 | 0.90 |
| 5 | 4 | 0.10 | 1.00 |

Table 2.23

## Example 2.17

Using **Table 2.22**:

a.  Find the $80^{th}$ percentile.

b.  Find the $90^{th}$ percentile.

c.  Find the first quartile. What is another name for the first quartile?

### Solution 2.17

Using the data from the frequency table, we have:

a.  The $80^{th}$ percentile is between the last eight and the first nine in the table (between the $40^{th}$ and $41^{st}$ values). Therefore, we need to take the mean of the $40^{th}$ an $41^{st}$ values. The $80^{th}$ percentile $= \frac{8+9}{2} = 8.5$

b.  The $90^{th}$ percentile will be the $45^{th}$ data value (location is 0.90(50) = 45) and the $45^{th}$ data value is nine.

c.  $Q_1$ is also the $25^{th}$ percentile. The $25^{th}$ percentile location calculation: $P_{25} = 0.25(50) = 12.5 \approx 13$ the $13^{th}$ data value. Thus, the 25th percentile is six.

## A Formula for Finding the *k*th Percentile

If you were to do a little research, you would find several formulas for calculating the $k^{th}$ percentile. Here is one of them.

$k$ = the $k^{th}$ percentile. It may or may not be part of the data.

$i$ = the index (ranking or position of a data value)

$n$ = the total number of data points, or observations

- Order the data from smallest to largest.

- Calculate $i = \frac{k}{100}(n + 1)$

- If $i$ is an integer, then the $k^{th}$ percentile is the data value in the $i^{th}$ position in the ordered set of data.

- If $i$ is not an integer, then round $i$ up and round $i$ down to the nearest integers. Average the two data values in these two positions in the ordered data set. This is easier to understand in an example.

## Example 2.18

Listed are 29 ages for Academy Award winning best actors *in order from smallest to largest.*
18; 21; 22; 25; 26; 27; 29; 30; 31; 33; 36; 37; 41; 42; 47; 52; 55; 57; 58; 62; 64; 67; 69; 71; 72; 73; 74; 76; 77

a.  Find the $70^{th}$ percentile.

b.  Find the $83^{rd}$ percentile.

### Solution 2.18

a.  $k = 70$
    $i$ = the index
    $n = 29$
    $i = \frac{k}{100}(n + 1) = (\frac{70}{100})(29 + 1) = 21$. Twenty-one is an integer, and the data value in the $21^{st}$ position in the ordered data set is 64. The $70^{th}$ percentile is 64 years.

b.  $k = 83^{rd}$ percentile

$i$ = the index

$n$ = 29

$i$ = $\frac{k}{100}$ ($n$ + 1) = ) $\frac{83}{100}$ )(29 + 1) = 24.9, which is NOT an integer. Round it down to 24 and up to 25. The age in the 24th position is 71 and the age in the 25th position is 72. Average 71 and 72. The 83rd percentile is 71.5 years.

## Try It $\Sigma$

**2.18** Listed are 29 ages for Academy Award winning best actors *in order from smallest to largest.*

18; 21; 22; 25; 26; 27; 29; 30; 31; 33; 36; 37; 41; 42; 47; 52; 55; 57; 58; 62; 64; 67; 69; 71; 72; 73; 74; 76; 77

Calculate the 20th percentile and the 55th percentile.

## A Formula for Finding the Percentile of a Value in a Data Set

- Order the data from smallest to largest.

- $x$ = the number of data values counting from the bottom of the data list up to but not including the data value for which you want to find the percentile.

- $y$ = the number of data values equal to the data value for which you want to find the percentile.

- $n$ = the total number of data.

- Calculate $\frac{x + 0.5y}{n}$ (100). Then round to the nearest integer.

### Example 2.19

Listed are 29 ages for Academy Award winning best actors *in order from smallest to largest.*
18; 21; 22; 25; 26; 27; 29; 30; 31; 33; 36; 37; 41; 42; 47; 52; 55; 57; 58; 62; 64; 67; 69; 71; 72; 73; 74; 76; 77

a. Find the percentile for 58.

b. Find the percentile for 25.

#### Solution 2.19

a. Counting from the bottom of the list, there are 18 data values less than 58. There is one value of 58.

$x$ = 18 and $y$ = 1. $\frac{x + 0.5y}{n}$ (100) = $\frac{18 + 0.5(1)}{29}$ (100) = 63.80. 58 is the 64th percentile.

b. Counting from the bottom of the list, there are three data values less than 25. There is one value of 25.

$x$ = 3 and $y$ = 1. $\frac{x + 0.5y}{n}$ (100) = $\frac{3 + 0.5(1)}{29}$ (100) = 12.07. Twenty-five is the 12th percentile.

## Interpreting Percentiles, Quartiles, and Median

A percentile indicates the relative standing of a data value when data are sorted into numerical order from smallest to largest. Percentages of data values are less than or equal to the pth percentile. For example, 15% of data values are less than or equal to the 15th percentile.

- Low percentiles always correspond to lower data values.

- High percentiles always correspond to higher data values.

A percentile may or may not correspond to a value judgment about whether it is "good" or "bad." The interpretation of whether a certain percentile is "good" or "bad" depends on the context of the situation to which the data applies. In some situations, a low percentile would be considered "good;" in other contexts a high percentile might be considered "good". In many situations, there is no value judgment that applies.

Understanding how to interpret percentiles properly is important not only when describing data, but also when calculating probabilities in later chapters of this text.

### GUIDELINE

When writing the interpretation of a percentile in the context of the given data, the sentence should contain the following information.

- information about the context of the situation being considered
- the data value (value of the variable) that represents the percentile
- the percent of individuals or items with data values below the percentile
- the percent of individuals or items with data values above the percentile.

### Example 2.20

On a timed math test, the first quartile for time it took to finish the exam was 35 minutes. Interpret the first quartile in the context of this situation.

#### Solution 2.20

- Twenty-five percent of students finished the exam in 35 minutes or less.
- Seventy-five percent of students finished the exam in 35 minutes or more.
- A low percentile could be considered good, as finishing more quickly on a timed exam is desirable. (If you take too long, you might not be able to finish.)

### Example 2.21

On a 20 question math test, the $70^{th}$ percentile for number of correct answers was 16. Interpret the $70^{th}$ percentile in the context of this situation.

#### Solution 2.21

- Seventy percent of students answered 16 or fewer questions correctly.
- Thirty percent of students answered 16 or more questions correctly.
- A higher percentile could be considered good, as answering more questions correctly is desirable.

## Try It Σ

**2.21** On a 60 point written assignment, the $80^{th}$ percentile for the number of points earned was 49. Interpret the $80^{th}$ percentile in the context of this situation.

### Example 2.22

At a community college, it was found that the $30^{th}$ percentile of credit units that students are enrolled for is seven units. Interpret the $30^{th}$ percentile in the context of this situation.

**Solution 2.22**

- Thirty percent of students are enrolled in seven or fewer credit units.

- Seventy percent of students are enrolled in seven or more credit units.

- In this example, there is no "good" or "bad" value judgment associated with a higher or lower percentile. Students attend community college for varied reasons and needs, and their course load varies according to their needs.

## Example 2.23

Sharpe Middle School is applying for a grant that will be used to add fitness equipment to the gym. The principal surveyed 15 anonymous students to determine how many minutes a day the students spend exercising. The results from the 15 anonymous students are shown.

0 minutes; 40 minutes; 60 minutes; 30 minutes; 60 minutes

10 minutes; 45 minutes; 30 minutes; 300 minutes; 90 minutes;

30 minutes; 120 minutes; 60 minutes; 0 minutes; 20 minutes

Determine the following five values.

Min = 0
$Q_1$ = 20
Med = 40
$Q_3$ = 60
Max = 300

If you were the principal, would you be justified in purchasing new fitness equipment? Since 75% of the students exercise for 60 minutes or less daily, and since the $IQR$ is 40 minutes (60 − 20 = 40), we know that half of the students surveyed exercise between 20 minutes and 60 minutes daily. This seems a reasonable amount of time spent exercising, so the principal would be justified in purchasing the new equipment.

However, the principal needs to be careful. The value 300 appears to be a potential outlier.

$Q_3 + 1.5(IQR) = 60 + (1.5)(40) = 120.$

The value 300 is greater than 120 so it is a potential outlier. If we delete it and calculate the five values, we get the following values:

Min = 0
$Q_1$ = 20
$Q_3$ = 60
Max = 120

We still have 75% of the students exercising for 60 minutes or less daily and half of the students exercising between 20 and 60 minutes a day. However, 15 students is a small sample and the principal should survey more students to be sure of his survey results.

# 2.3 | Measures of the Center of the Data

The "center" of a data set is also a way of describing location. The two most widely used measures of the "center" of the data are the **mean** (average) and the **median**. To calculate the **mean weight** of 50 people, add the 50 weights together and divide by 50. Technically this is the arithmetic mean. We will discuss the geometric mean later. To find the **median weight** of the 50 people, order the data and find the number that splits the data into two equal parts meaning an equal number of observations on each side. The weight of 25 people are below this weight and 25 people are heavier than this weight. The median is generally a better measure of the center when there are extreme values or outliers because it is not affected by the precise numerical values of the outliers. The mean is the most common measure of the center.

## NOTE

The words "mean" and "average" are often used interchangeably. The substitution of one word for the other is common practice. The technical term is "arithmetic mean" and "average" is technically a center location. Formally, the arithmetic mean is called the first moment of the distribution by mathematicians. However, in practice among non-statisticians, "average" is commonly accepted for "arithmetic mean."

When each value in the data set is not unique, the mean can be calculated by multiplying each distinct value by its frequency and then dividing the sum by the total number of data values. The letter used to represent the **sample mean** is an $x$ with a bar over it (pronounced "$x$ bar"): $\bar{x}$.

The Greek letter $\mu$ (pronounced "mew") represents the **population mean**. One of the requirements for the **sample mean** to be a good estimate of the **population mean** is for the sample taken to be truly random.

To see that both ways of calculating the mean are the same, consider the sample:
1; 1; 1; 2; 2; 3; 4; 4; 4; 4; 4

$$\bar{x} = \frac{1+1+1+2+2+3+4+4+4+4+4}{11} = 2.7$$

$$\bar{x} = \frac{3(1) + 2(2) + 1(3) + 5(4)}{11} = 2.7$$

In the second calculation, the frequencies are 3, 2, 1, and 5.

You can quickly find the location of the median by using the expression $\frac{n+1}{2}$.

The letter $n$ is the total number of data values in the sample. If $n$ is an odd number, the median is the middle value of the ordered data (ordered smallest to largest). If $n$ is an even number, the median is equal to the two middle values added together and divided by two after the data has been ordered. For example, if the total number of data values is 97, then $\frac{n+1}{2} = \frac{97+1}{2} = 49$. The median is the 49[th] value in the ordered data. If the total number of data values is 100, then $\frac{n+1}{2} = \frac{100+1}{2} = 50.5$. The median occurs midway between the 50th and 51st values. The location of the median and the value of the median are **not** the same. The upper case letter $M$ is often used to represent the median. The next example illustrates the location of the median and the value of the median.

## Example 2.24

AIDS data indicating the number of months a patient with AIDS lives after taking a new antibody drug are as follows (smallest to largest):
3; 4; 8; 8; 10; 11; 12; 13; 14; 15; 15; 16; 16; 17; 17; 18; 21; 22; 22; 24; 24; 25; 26; 26; 27; 27; 29; 29; 31; 32; 33; 33; 34; 34; 35; 37; 40; 44; 44; 47;
Calculate the mean and the median.

### Solution 2.24

The calculation for the mean is:

$$\bar{x} = \frac{[3 + 4 + (8)(2) + 10 + 11 + 12 + 13 + 14 + (15)(2) + (16)(2) + \ldots + 35 + 37 + 40 + (44)(2) + 47]}{40} = 23.6$$

To find the median, $M$, first use the formula for the location. The location is:
$$\frac{n+1}{2} = \frac{40+1}{2} = 20.5$$

Starting at the smallest value, the median is located between the 20th and 21st values (the two 24s):
3; 4; 8; 8; 10; 11; 12; 13; 14; 15; 15; 16; 16; 17; 17; 18; 21; 22; 22; 24; 24; 25; 26; 26; 27; 27; 29; 29; 31; 32; 33; 33; 34; 34; 35; 37; 40; 44; 44; 47;

$$M = \frac{24 + 24}{2} = 24$$

## Example 2.25

Suppose that in a small town of 50 people, one person earns $5,000,000 per year and the other 49 each earn $30,000. Which is the better measure of the "center": the mean or the median?

**Solution 2.25**

$$\bar{x} = \frac{5,000,000 + 49(30,000)}{50} = 129,400$$

$M = 30,000$

(There are 49 people who earn $30,000 and one person who earns $5,000,000.)

The median is a better measure of the "center" than the mean because 49 of the values are 30,000 and one is 5,000,000. The 5,000,000 is an outlier. The 30,000 gives us a better sense of the middle of the data.

Another measure of the center is the mode. The **mode** is the most frequent value. There can be more than one mode in a data set as long as those values have the same frequency and that frequency is the highest. A data set with two modes is called bimodal.

## Example 2.26

Statistics exam scores for 20 students are as follows:

50; 53; 59; 59; 63; 63; 72; 72; 72; 72; 72; 76; 78; 81; 83; 84; 84; 84; 90; 93

Find the mode.

**Solution 2.26**
The most frequent score is 72, which occurs five times. Mode = 72.

## Example 2.27

Five real estate exam scores are 430, 430, 480, 480, 495. The data set is bimodal because the scores 430 and 480 each occur twice.

When is the mode the best measure of the "center"? Consider a weight loss program that advertises a mean weight loss of six pounds the first week of the program. The mode might indicate that most people lose two pounds the first week, making the program less appealing.

### NOTE

The mode can be calculated for qualitative data as well as for quantitative data. For example, if the data set is: red, red, red, green, green, yellow, purple, black, blue, the mode is red.

## Calculating the Arithmetic Mean of Grouped Frequency Tables

When only grouped data is available, you do not know the individual data values (we only know intervals and interval frequencies); therefore, you cannot compute an exact mean for the data set. What we must do is estimate the actual mean by calculating the mean of a frequency table. A frequency table is a data representation in which grouped data is displayed along with the corresponding frequencies. To calculate the mean from a grouped frequency table we can apply the basic definition of mean: $mean = \dfrac{data\ sum}{number\ of\ data\ values}$ We simply need to modify the definition to fit within the restrictions of a frequency table.

Since we do not know the individual data values we can instead find the midpoint of each interval. The midpoint is $\dfrac{lower\ boundary + upper\ boundary}{2}$. We can now modify the mean definition to be

$$Mean\ of\ Frequency\ Table = \frac{\sum fm}{\sum f}$$ where $f$ = the frequency of the interval and $m$ = the midpoint of the interval.

## Example 2.28

A frequency table displaying professor Blount's last statistic test is shown. Find the best estimate of the class mean.

| Grade Interval | Number of Students |
|---|---|
| 50–56.5 | 1 |
| 56.5–62.5 | 0 |
| 62.5–68.5 | 4 |
| 68.5–74.5 | 4 |
| 74.5–80.5 | 2 |
| 80.5–86.5 | 3 |
| 86.5–92.5 | 4 |
| 92.5–98.5 | 1 |

Table 2.24

### Solution 2.28

- Find the midpoints for all intervals

| Grade Interval | Midpoint |
|---|---|
| 50–56.5 | 53.25 |
| 56.5–62.5 | 59.5 |
| 62.5–68.5 | 65.5 |
| 68.5–74.5 | 71.5 |
| 74.5–80.5 | 77.5 |
| 80.5–86.5 | 83.5 |
| 86.5–92.5 | 89.5 |
| 92.5–98.5 | 95.5 |

Table 2.25

- Calculate the sum of the product of each interval frequency and midpoint. $\sum fm$

$$53.25(1) + 59.5(0) + 65.5(4) + 71.5(4) + 77.5(2) + 83.5(3) + 89.5(4) + 95.5(1) = 1460.25$$

- $\mu = \dfrac{\sum fm}{\sum f} = \dfrac{1460.25}{19} = 76.86$

**2.28** Maris conducted a study on the effect that playing video games has on memory recall. As part of her study, she compiled the following data:

| Hours Teenagers Spend on Video Games | Number of Teenagers |
|---|---|
| 0–3.5 | 3 |
| 3.5–7.5 | 7 |
| 7.5–11.5 | 12 |
| 11.5–15.5 | 7 |
| 15.5–19.5 | 9 |

Table 2.26

What is the best estimate for the mean number of hours spent playing video games?

# 2.4 | Sigma Notation and Calculating the Arithmetic Mean

**Formula for Population Mean**

$$\mu = \frac{1}{N}\sum_{i=1}^{N} x_i$$

**Formula for Sample Mean**

$$\bar{x} = \frac{1}{n}\sum_{i=1}^{n} x_i$$

This unit is here to remind you of material that you once studied and said at the time "I am sure that I will never need this!"

Here are the formulas for a population mean and the sample mean. The Greek letter $\mu$ is the symbol for the population mean and $\bar{x}$ is the symbol for the sample mean. Both formulas have a mathematical symbol that tells us how to make the calculations. It is called Sigma notation because the symbol is the Greek capital letter sigma: $\Sigma$. Like all mathematical symbols it tells us what to do: just as the plus sign tells us to add and the x tells us to multiply. These are called mathematical operators. The $\Sigma$ symbol tells us to add a specific list of numbers.

Let's say we have a sample of animals from the local animal shelter and we are interested in their average age. If we list each value, or observation, in a column, you can give each one an index number. The first number will be number 1 and the second number 2 and so on.

| Animal | Age |
|--------|------|
| 1      | 9    |
| 2      | 1    |
| 3      | 8.5  |
| 4      | 10.5 |
| 5      | 10   |
| 6      | 8.5  |
| 7      | 12   |
| 8      | 8    |
| 9      | 1    |
| 10     | 9.5  |

Table 2.27

Each observation represents a particular animal in the sample. Purr is animal number one and is a 9 year old cat, Toto is animal number 2 and is a 1 year old puppy and so on.

To calculate the mean we are told by the formula to add up all these numbers, ages in this case, and then divide the sum by 10, the total number of animals in the sample.

Animal number one, the cat Purr, is designated as $X_1$, animal number 2, Toto, is designated as $X_2$ and so on through Dundee who is animal number 10 and is designated as $X_{10}$.

The i in the formula tells us which of the observations to add together. In this case it is $X_1$ through $X_{10}$ which is all of them. We know which ones to add by the indexing notation, the i = 1 and the n or capital N for the population. For this example the indexing notation would be i = 1 and because it is a sample we use a small n on the top of the $\Sigma$ which would be 10.

The standard deviation requires the same mathematical operator and so it would be helpful to recall this knowledge from your past.

The sum of the ages is found to be 78 and dividing by 10 gives us the sample mean age as 7.8 years.

# 2.5 | Geometric Mean

The mean (Arithmetic), median and mode are all measures of the "center" of the data, the "average". They are all in their own way trying to measure the "common" point within the data, that which is "normal". In the case of the arithmetic mean this is solved by finding the value from which all points are equal linear distances. We can imagine that all the data values are combined through addition and then distributed back to each data point in equal amounts. The sum of all the values is what is redistributed in equal amounts such that the total sum remains the same.

The geometric mean redistributes not the sum of the values but the product of multiplying all the individual values and then redistributing them in equal portions such that the total product remains the same. This can be seen from the formula for the geometric mean, $\tilde{x}$ : *(Pronounced x-tilde)*

$$\tilde{x} = \left( \prod_{i=1}^{n} x_i \right)^{\frac{1}{n}} = \sqrt[n]{x_1 * x_2 \cdots x_n} = \left( x_1 * x_2 \cdots x_n \right)^{\frac{1}{n}}$$

where $\pi$ is another mathematical operator, that tells us to multiply all the $x_i$ numbers in the same way capital Greek sigma tells us to add all the $x_i$ numbers. Remember that a fractional exponent is calling for the nth root of the number thus an exponent of 1/3 is the cube root of the number.

The geometric mean answers the question, "if all the quantities had the same value, what would that value have to be in order to achieve the same product?" The geometric mean gets its name from the fact that when redistributed in this way the sides form a geometric shape for which all sides have the same length. To see this, take the example of the numbers 10, 51.2 and 8. The geometric mean is the product of multiplying these three numbers together (4,096) and taking the cube root because there are three numbers among which this product is to be distributed. Thus the geometric mean of these three numbers is 16. This describes a cube 16x16x16 and has a volume of 4,096 units.

The geometric mean is relevant in Economics and Finance for dealing with growth: growth of markets, in investment, population and other variables the growth in which there is an interest. Imagine that our box of 4,096 units (perhaps dollars) is the value of an investment after three years and that the investment returns in percents were the three numbers in our example. The geometric mean will provide us with the answer to the question, what is the average rate of return: 16 percent. The arithmetic mean of these three numbers is 23.6 percent. The reason for this difference, 16 versus 23.6, is that the arithmetic mean is additive and thus does not account for the interest on the interest, compound interest, embedded in the investment growth process. The same issue arises when asking for the average rate of growth of a population or sales or market penetration, etc., knowing the annual rates of growth. The formula for the geometric mean rate of return, or any other growth rate, is:

$$r_s = (x_1 * x_2 \bullet\bullet\bullet x_n)^{\frac{1}{n}} - 1$$

Manipulating the formula for the geometric mean can also provide a calculation of the average rate of growth between two periods knowing only the initial value $a_0$ and the ending value $a_n$ and the number of periods, $n$. The following formula provides this information:

$$\left(\frac{a_n}{a_0}\right)^{\frac{1}{n}} = \tilde{x}$$

Finally, we note that the formula for the geometric mean requires that all numbers be positive, greater than zero. The reason of course is that the root of a negative number is undefined for use outside of mathematical theory. There are ways to avoid this problem however. In the case of rates of return and other simple growth problems we can convert the negative values to meaningful positive equivalent values. Imagine that the annual returns for the past three years are +12%, -8%, and +2%. Using the decimal multiplier equivalents of 1.12, 0.92, and 1.02, allows us to compute a geometric mean of 1.0167. Subtracting 1 from this value gives the geometric mean of +1.67% as a net rate of population growth (or financial return). From this example we can see that the geometric mean provides us with this formula for calculating the geometric (mean) rate of return for a series of annual rates of return:

$$r_s = \tilde{x} - 1$$

where $r_s$ is average rate of return and $\tilde{x}$ is the geometric mean of the returns during some number of time periods. Note that the length of each time period must be the same.

As a general rule one should convert the percent values to its decimal equivalent multiplier. It is important to recognize that when dealing with percents, the geometric mean of percent values does not equal the geometric mean of the decimal multiplier equivalents and it is the decimal multiplier equivalent geometric mean that is relevant.

## 2.6 | Skewness and the Mean, Median, and Mode

Consider the following data set.
4; 5; 6; 6; 6; 7; 7; 7; 7; 7; 7; 8; 8; 8; 9; 10

This data set can be represented by following histogram. Each interval has width one, and each value is located in the middle of an interval.

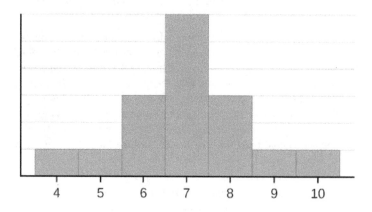

Figure 2.11

The histogram displays a **symmetrical** distribution of data. A distribution is symmetrical if a vertical line can be drawn at some point in the histogram such that the shape to the left and the right of the vertical line are mirror images of each other. The mean, the median, and the mode are each seven for these data. **In a perfectly symmetrical distribution, the mean and the median are the same.** This example has one mode (unimodal), and the mode is the same as the mean and median. In a symmetrical distribution that has two modes (bimodal), the two modes would be different from the mean and median.

The histogram for the data: 4; 5; 6; 6; 6; 7; 7; 7; 7; 8 is not symmetrical. The right-hand side seems "chopped off" compared to the left side. A distribution of this type is called **skewed to the left** because it is pulled out to the left. We can formally measure the skewness of a distribution just as we can mathematically measure the center weight of the data or its general "speadness". The mathematical formula for skewness is: $a_3 = \sum \dfrac{\left(x_i - \bar{x}\right)^3}{ns^3}$. The greater the deviation from zero indicates a greater degree of skewness. If the skewness is negative then the distribution is skewed left as in **Figure 2.12**. A positive measure of skewness indicates right skewness such as **Figure 2.13**.

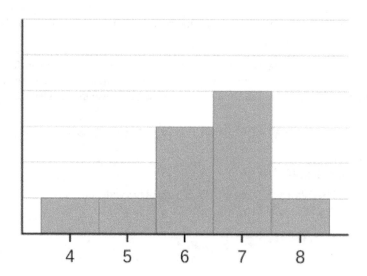

Figure 2.12

The mean is 6.3, the median is 6.5, and the mode is seven. **Notice that the mean is less than the median, and they are both less than the mode.** The mean and the median both reflect the skewing, but the mean reflects it more so.

The histogram for the data: 6; 7; 7; 7; 7; 8; 8; 8; 9; 10, is also not symmetrical. It is **skewed to the right**.

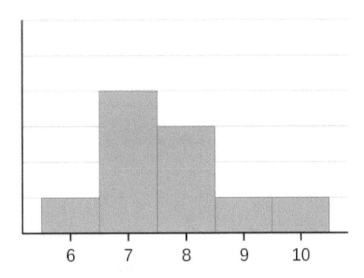

Figure 2.13

The mean is 7.7, the median is 7.5, and the mode is seven. Of the three statistics, **the mean is the largest, while the mode is the smallest**. Again, the mean reflects the skewing the most.

To summarize, generally if the distribution of data is skewed to the left, the mean is less than the median, which is often less than the mode. If the distribution of data is skewed to the right, the mode is often less than the median, which is less than the mean.

As with the mean, median and mode, and as we will see shortly, the variance, there are mathematical formulas that give us precise measures of these characteristics of the distribution of the data. Again looking at the formula for skewness we see that this is a relationship between the mean of the data and the individual observations cubed.

$$a_3 = \sum \frac{\left(x_i - \bar{x}\right)^3}{ns^3}$$

where $s$ is the sample standard deviation of the data, $X_i$ , and $\bar{x}$ is the arithmetic mean and $n$ is the sample size.

Formally the arithmetic mean is known as the first moment of the distribution. The second moment we will see is the variance, and skewness is the third moment. The variance measures the squared differences of the data from the mean and skewness measures the cubed differences of the data from the mean. While a variance can never be a negative number, the measure of skewness can and this is how we determine if the data are skewed right of left. The skewness for a normal distribution is zero, and any symmetric data should have skewness near zero. Negative values for the skewness indicate data that are skewed left and positive values for the skewness indicate data that are skewed right. By skewed left, we mean that the left tail is long relative to the right tail. Similarly, skewed right means that the right tail is long relative to the left tail. The skewness characterizes the degree of asymmetry of a distribution around its mean. While the mean and standard deviation are *dimensional* quantities (this is why we will take the square root of the variance ) that is, have the same units as the measured quantities $X_i$, the skewness is conventionally defined in such a way as to make it *nondimensional*. It is a

pure number that characterizes only the shape of the distribution. A positive value of skewness signifies a distribution with an asymmetric tail extending out towards more positive X and a negative value signifies a distribution whose tail extends out towards more negative X. A zero measure of skewness will indicate a symmetrical distribution.

Skewness and symmetry become important when we discuss probability distributions in later chapters.

## 2.7 | Measures of the Spread of the Data

An important characteristic of any set of data is the variation in the data. In some data sets, the data values are concentrated closely near the mean; in other data sets, the data values are more widely spread out from the mean. The most common measure of variation, or spread, is the standard deviation. The **standard deviation** is a number that measures how far data values are from their mean.

# The standard deviation

- provides a numerical measure of the overall amount of variation in a data set, and

- can be used to determine whether a particular data value is close to or far from the mean.

## The standard deviation provides a measure of the overall variation in a data set

The standard deviation is always positive or zero. The standard deviation is small when the data are all concentrated close to the mean, exhibiting little variation or spread. The standard deviation is larger when the data values are more spread out from the mean, exhibiting more variation.

Suppose that we are studying the amount of time customers wait in line at the checkout at supermarket $A$ and supermarket $B$. The average wait time at both supermarkets is five minutes. At supermarket $A$, the standard deviation for the wait time is two minutes; at supermarket $B$. The standard deviation for the wait time is four minutes.

Because supermarket $B$ has a higher standard deviation, we know that there is more variation in the wait times at supermarket $B$. Overall, wait times at supermarket $B$ are more spread out from the average; wait times at supermarket $A$ are more concentrated near the average.

## Calculating the Standard Deviation

If $x$ is a number, then the difference "$x$ minus the mean" is called its **deviation**. In a data set, there are as many deviations as there are items in the data set. The deviations are used to calculate the standard deviation. If the numbers belong to a population, in symbols a deviation is $x - \mu$. For sample data, in symbols a deviation is $x - \bar{x}$.

The procedure to calculate the standard deviation depends on whether the numbers are the entire population or are data from a sample. The calculations are similar, but not identical. Therefore the symbol used to represent the standard deviation depends on whether it is calculated from a population or a sample. The lower case letter s represents the sample standard deviation and the Greek letter $\sigma$ (sigma, lower case) represents the population standard deviation. If the sample has the same characteristics as the population, then s should be a good estimate of $\sigma$.

To calculate the standard deviation, we need to calculate the variance first. The **variance** is the **average of the squares of the deviations** (the $x - \bar{x}$ values for a sample, or the $x - \mu$ values for a population). The symbol $\sigma^2$ represents the population variance; the population standard deviation $\sigma$ is the square root of the population variance. The symbol $s^2$ represents the sample variance; the sample standard deviation $s$ is the square root of the sample variance. You can think of the standard deviation as a special average of the deviations. Formally, the variance is the second moment of the distribution or the first moment around the mean. Remember that the mean is the first moment of the distribution.

If the numbers come from a census of the entire **population** and not a sample, when we calculate the average of the squared deviations to find the variance, we divide by $N$, the number of items in the population. If the data are from a **sample** rather than a population, when we calculate the average of the squared deviations, we divide by $n - 1$, one less than the number of items in the sample.

## Formulas for the Sample Standard Deviation

- $s = \sqrt{\dfrac{\Sigma(x - \bar{x})^2}{n - 1}}$ or $s = \sqrt{\dfrac{\Sigma f(x - \bar{x})^2}{n - 1}}$ or $s = \sqrt{\dfrac{\left(\sum\limits_{i=1}^{n} x^2\right) - n\bar{x}^2}{n - 1}}$

- For the sample standard deviation, the denominator is $n - 1$, that is the sample size minus 1.

## Formulas for the Population Standard Deviation

- $\sigma = \sqrt{\dfrac{\Sigma(x - \mu)^2}{N}}$ or $\sigma = \sqrt{\dfrac{\Sigma f(x - \mu)^2}{N}}$ or $\sigma = \sqrt{\dfrac{\sum\limits_{i=1}^{N} x_i^2}{N} - \mu^2}$

- For the population standard deviation, the denominator is $N$, the number of items in the population.

In these formulas, $f$ represents the frequency with which a value appears. For example, if a value appears once, $f$ is one. If a value appears three times in the data set or population, $f$ is three. Two important observations concerning the variance and standard deviation: the deviations are measured from the mean and the deviations are squared. In principle, the deviations could be measured from any point, however, our interest is measurement from the center weight of the data, what is the "normal" or most usual value of the observation. Later we will be trying to measure the "unusualness" of an observation or a sample mean and thus we need a measure from the mean. The second observation is that the deviations are squared. This does two things, first it makes the deviations all positive and second it changes the units of measurement from that of the mean and the original observations. If the data are weights then the mean is measured in pounds, but the variance is measured in pounds-squared. One reason to use the standard deviation is to return to the original units of measurement by taking the square root of the variance. Further, when the deviations are squared it explodes their value. For example, a deviation of 10 from the mean when squared is 100, but a deviation of 100 from the mean is 10,000. What this does is place great weight on outliers when calculating the variance.

## Types of Variability in Samples

When trying to study a population, a sample is often used, either for convenience or because it is not possible to access the entire population. Variability is the term used to describe the differences that may occur in these outcomes. Common types of variability include the following:

- Observational or measurement variability

- Natural variability

- Induced variability

- Sample variability

Here are some examples to describe each type of variability.

### Example 1: Measurement variability

Measurement variability occurs when there are differences in the instruments used to measure or in the people using those instruments. If we are gathering data on how long it takes for a ball to drop from a height by having students measure the time of the drop with a stopwatch, we may experience measurement variability if the two stopwatches used were made by different manufacturers: For example, one stopwatch measures to the nearest second, whereas the other one measures to the nearest tenth of a second. We also may experience measurement variability because two different people are gathering the data. Their reaction times in pressing the button on the stopwatch may differ; thus, the outcomes will vary accordingly. The differences in outcomes may be affected by measurement variability.

### Example 2: Natural variability

Natural variability arises from the differences that naturally occur because members of a population differ from each other. For example, if we have two identical corn plants and we expose both plants to the same amount of water and sunlight, they may still grow at different rates simply because they are two different corn plants. The difference in outcomes may be explained by natural variability.

### Example 3: Induced variability

Induced variability is the counterpart to natural variability; this occurs because we have artificially induced an element of variation (that, by definition, was not present naturally): For example, we assign people to two different groups to study memory, and we induce a variable in one group by limiting the amount of sleep they get. The difference in outcomes may be affected by induced variability.

### Example 4: Sample variability

Sample variability occurs when multiple random samples are taken from the same population. For example, if I conduct four surveys of 50 people randomly selected from a given population, the differences in outcomes may be affected by sample variability.

## Example 2.29

In a fifth grade class, the teacher was interested in the average age and the sample standard deviation of the ages of her students. The following data are the ages for a SAMPLE of $n = 20$ fifth grade students. The ages are rounded to the nearest half year:

9; 9.5; 9.5; 10; 10; 10; 10; 10.5; 10.5; 10.5; 10.5; 11; 11; 11; 11; 11; 11; 11.5; 11.5; 11.5;

$$\bar{x} = \frac{9 + 9.5(2) + 10(4) + 10.5(4) + 11(6) + 11.5(3)}{20} = 10.525$$

The average age is 10.53 years, rounded to two places.

The variance may be calculated by using a table. Then the standard deviation is calculated by taking the square root of the variance. We will explain the parts of the table after calculating $s$.

| Data | Freq. | Deviations | Deviations$^2$ | (Freq.)(Deviations$^2$) |
|---|---|---|---|---|
| $x$ | $f$ | $(x - \bar{x})$ | $(x - \bar{x})^2$ | $(f)(x - \bar{x})^2$ |
| 9 | 1 | $9 - 10.525 = -1.525$ | $(-1.525)^2 = 2.325625$ | $1 \times 2.325625 = 2.325625$ |
| 9.5 | 2 | $9.5 - 10.525 = -1.025$ | $(-1.025)^2 = 1.050625$ | $2 \times 1.050625 = 2.101250$ |
| 10 | 4 | $10 - 10.525 = -0.525$ | $(-0.525)^2 = 0.275625$ | $4 \times 0.275625 = 1.1025$ |
| 10.5 | 4 | $10.5 - 10.525 = -0.025$ | $(-0.025)^2 = 0.000625$ | $4 \times 0.000625 = 0.0025$ |
| 11 | 6 | $11 - 10.525 = 0.475$ | $(0.475)^2 = 0.225625$ | $6 \times 0.225625 = 1.35375$ |
| 11.5 | 3 | $11.5 - 10.525 = 0.975$ | $(0.975)^2 = 0.950625$ | $3 \times 0.950625 = 2.851875$ |
| | | | | The total is 9.7375 |

Table 2.28

The sample variance, $s^2$, is equal to the sum of the last column (9.7375) divided by the total number of data values minus one (20 – 1):

$$s^2 = \frac{9.7375}{20 - 1} = 0.5125$$

The **sample standard deviation** $s$ is equal to the square root of the sample variance:

$$s = \sqrt{0.5125} = 0.715891, \quad \text{which is rounded to two decimal places, } s = 0.72.$$

## Explanation of the standard deviation calculation shown in the table

The deviations show how spread out the data are about the mean. The data value 11.5 is farther from the mean than is the data value 11 which is indicated by the deviations 0.97 and 0.47. A positive deviation occurs when the data value is greater than the mean, whereas a negative deviation occurs when the data value is less than the mean. The deviation is –1.525 for the data value nine. **If you add the deviations, the sum is always zero.** (For **Example 2.29**, there are $n = 20$ deviations.) So you cannot simply add the deviations to get the spread of the data. By squaring the deviations, you make them positive numbers, and the sum will also be positive. The variance, then, is the average squared deviation. By squaring the deviations we are placing an extreme penalty on observations that are far from the mean; these observations get greater weight in the calculations of the variance. We will see later on that the variance (standard deviation) plays the critical role in determining our conclusions in inferential statistics. We can begin now by using the standard deviation as a measure of "unusualness." "How did you do on the test?" "Terrific! Two standard deviations above the mean." This, we will see, is an unusually good exam grade.

The variance is a squared measure and does not have the same units as the data. Taking the square root solves the problem. The standard deviation measures the spread in the same units as the data.

Notice that instead of dividing by $n = 20$, the calculation divided by $n - 1 = 20 - 1 = 19$ because the data is a sample. For the **sample** variance, we divide by the sample size minus one ($n - 1$). Why not divide by $n$? The answer has to do with the population variance. **The sample variance is an estimate of the population variance.** This estimate requires us to use an estimate of the population mean rather than the actual population mean. Based on the theoretical mathematics that lies behind these calculations, dividing by $(n - 1)$ gives a better estimate of the population variance.

The standard deviation, $s$ or $\sigma$, is either zero or larger than zero. Describing the data with reference to the spread is called "variability". The variability in data depends upon the method by which the outcomes are obtained; for example, by measuring or by random sampling. When the standard deviation is zero, there is no spread; that is, the all the data values are equal to each other. The standard deviation is small when the data are all concentrated close to the mean, and is larger when the data values show more variation from the mean. When the standard deviation is a lot larger than zero, the data values are very spread out about the mean; outliers can make $s$ or $\sigma$ very large.

## Example 2.30

Use the following data (first exam scores) from Susan Dean's spring pre-calculus class:

33; 42; 49; 49; 53; 55; 55; 61; 63; 67; 68; 68; 69; 69; 72; 73; 74; 78; 80; 83; 88; 88; 88; 90; 92; 94; 94; 94; 96; 100

a. Create a chart containing the data, frequencies, relative frequencies, and cumulative relative frequencies to three decimal places.

b. Calculate the following to one decimal place:

    i. The sample mean

    ii. The sample standard deviation

    iii. The median

    iv. The first quartile

    v. The third quartile

    vi. *IQR*

### Solution 2.30

a. See **Table 2.29**

b.  i. The sample mean = 73.5

    ii. The sample standard deviation = 17.9

    iii. The median = 73

    iv. The first quartile = 61

    v. The third quartile = 90

    vi. *IQR* = 90 − 61 = 29

| Data | Frequency | Relative Frequency | Cumulative Relative Frequency |
|---|---|---|---|
| 33 | 1 | 0.032 | 0.032 |
| 42 | 1 | 0.032 | 0.064 |
| 49 | 2 | 0.065 | 0.129 |
| 53 | 1 | 0.032 | 0.161 |
| 55 | 2 | 0.065 | 0.226 |
| 61 | 1 | 0.032 | 0.258 |
| 63 | 1 | 0.032 | 0.29 |
| 67 | 1 | 0.032 | 0.322 |
| 68 | 2 | 0.065 | 0.387 |
| 69 | 2 | 0.065 | 0.452 |
| 72 | 1 | 0.032 | 0.484 |
| 73 | 1 | 0.032 | 0.516 |
| 74 | 1 | 0.032 | 0.548 |
| 78 | 1 | 0.032 | 0.580 |
| 80 | 1 | 0.032 | 0.612 |

**Table 2.29**

| Data | Frequency | Relative Frequency | Cumulative Relative Frequency |
|------|-----------|--------------------|-------------------------------|
| 83 | 1 | 0.032 | 0.644 |
| 88 | 3 | 0.097 | 0.741 |
| 90 | 1 | 0.032 | 0.773 |
| 92 | 1 | 0.032 | 0.805 |
| 94 | 4 | 0.129 | 0.934 |
| 96 | 1 | 0.032 | 0.966 |
| 100 | 1 | 0.032 | 0.998 (Why isn't this value 1? ANSWER: Rounding) |

Table 2.29

## Standard deviation of Grouped Frequency Tables

Recall that for grouped data we do not know individual data values, so we cannot describe the typical value of the data with precision. In other words, we cannot find the exact mean, median, or mode. We can, however, determine the best estimate of

the measures of center by finding the mean of the grouped data with the formula: $Mean\ of\ Frequency\ Table = \dfrac{\sum fm}{\sum f}$

where $f =$ interval frequencies and $m =$ interval midpoints.

Just as we could not find the exact mean, neither can we find the exact standard deviation. Remember that standard deviation describes numerically the expected deviation a data value has from the mean. In simple English, the standard deviation allows us to compare how "unusual" individual data is compared to the mean.

### Example 2.31

Find the standard deviation for the data in Table 2.30.

| Class | Frequency, $f$ | Midpoint, $m$ | $f * m$ | $f(m - \bar{x})^2$ |
|-------|----------------|---------------|---------|---------------------|
| 0–2 | 1 | 1 | $1 * 1 = 1$ | $1(1 - 7.58)^2 = 43.26$ |
| 3–5 | 6 | 4 | $6 * 4 = 24$ | $6(4 - 7.58)^2 = 76.77$ |
| 6-8 | 10 | 7 | $10 * 7 = 70$ | $10(7 - 7.58)^2 = 3.33$ |
| 9-11 | 7 | 10 | $7 * 10 = 70$ | $7(10 - 7.58)^2 = 41.10$ |
| 12-14 | 0 | 13 | $0 * 13 = 0$ | $0(13 - 7.58)^2 = 0$ |
|  | 26=n |  | $\bar{x} = \frac{197}{26} = 7.58$ | $s^2 = \frac{306.35}{26 - 1} = 12.25$ |

Table 2.30

For this data set, we have the mean, $\bar{x}$ = 7.58 and the standard deviation, $s_x$ = 3.5. This means that a randomly selected data value would be expected to be 3.5 units from the mean. If we look at the first class, we see that the class midpoint is equal to one. This is almost two full standard deviations from the mean since $7.58 - 3.5 - 3.5 =$

0.58. While the formula for calculating the standard deviation is not complicated, $s_x = \sqrt{\dfrac{\Sigma(m - \bar{x})^2 f}{n - 1}}$ where

$s_x$ = sample standard deviation, $\bar{x}$ = sample mean, the calculations are tedious. It is usually best to use technology when performing the calculations.

## Comparing Values from Different Data Sets

The standard deviation is useful when comparing data values that come from different data sets. If the data sets have different means and standard deviations, then comparing the data values directly can be misleading.

- For each data value x, calculate how many standard deviations away from its mean the value is.
- Use the formula: x = mean + (#ofSTDEVs)(standard deviation); solve for #ofSTDEVs.
- $\# \, ofSTDEVs = \dfrac{x - \text{mean}}{\text{standard deviation}}$
- Compare the results of this calculation.

#ofSTDEVs is often called a "z-score"; we can use the symbol $z$. In symbols, the formulas become:

| Sample | $x = \bar{x} + zs$ | $z = \dfrac{x - \bar{x}}{s}$ |
|---|---|---|
| Population | $x = \mu + z\sigma$ | $z = \dfrac{x - \mu}{\sigma}$ |

Table 2.31

## Example 2.32

Two students, John and Ali, from different high schools, wanted to find out who had the highest GPA when compared to his school. Which student had the highest GPA when compared to his school?

| Student | GPA | School Mean GPA | School Standard Deviation |
|---------|------|-----------------|---------------------------|
| John | 2.85 | 3.0 | 0.7 |
| Ali | 77 | 80 | 10 |

Table 2.32

### Solution 2.32

For each student, determine how many standard deviations (#ofSTDEVs) his GPA is away from the average, for his school. Pay careful attention to signs when comparing and interpreting the answer.

$$z = \# \text{ of STDEVs} = \frac{value \ - \ mean}{standard \ deviation} = \frac{x - \mu}{\sigma}$$

For John, $z = \# \, ofSTDEVs = \frac{2.85 - 3.0}{0.7} = -0.21$

For Ali, $z = \# \, ofSTDEVs = \frac{77 - 80}{10} = -0.3$

John has the better GPA when compared to his school because his GPA is 0.21 standard deviations **below** his school's mean while Ali's GPA is 0.3 standard deviations **below** his school's mean.

John's z-score of –0.21 is higher than Ali's z-score of –0.3. For GPA, higher values are better, so we conclude that John has the better GPA when compared to his school.

## Try It Σ

**2.32** Two swimmers, Angie and Beth, from different teams, wanted to find out who had the fastest time for the 50 meter freestyle when compared to her team. Which swimmer had the fastest time when compared to her team?

| Swimmer | Time (seconds) | Team Mean Time | Team Standard Deviation |
|---------|----------------|----------------|-------------------------|
| Angie | 26.2 | 27.2 | 0.8 |
| Beth | 27.3 | 30.1 | 1.4 |

Table 2.33

The following lists give a few facts that provide a little more insight into what the standard deviation tells us about the distribution of the data.

For ANY data set, no matter what the distribution of the data is:
- At least 75% of the data is within two standard deviations of the mean.
- At least 89% of the data is within three standard deviations of the mean.
- At least 95% of the data is within 4.5 standard deviations of the mean.
- This is known as Chebyshev's Rule.

For data having a Normal Distribution, which we will examine in great detail later:

- Approximately 68% of the data is within one standard deviation of the mean.

- Approximately 95% of the data is within two standard deviations of the mean.

- More than 99% of the data is within three standard deviations of the mean.

- This is known as the Empirical Rule.

- It is important to note that this rule only applies when the shape of the distribution of the data is bell-shaped and symmetric. We will learn more about this when studying the "Normal" or "Gaussian" probability distribution in later chapters.

## Coefficient of Variation

Another useful way to compare distributions besides simple comparisons of means or standard deviations is to adjust for differences in the scale of the data being measured. Quite simply, a large variation in data with a large mean is different than the same variation in data with a small mean. To adjust for the scale of the underlying data the Coefficient of Variation (CV) has been developed. Mathematically:

$$CV = \frac{s}{\bar{x}} * 100 \text{ conditioned upon } \bar{x} \neq 0, \text{ where } s \text{ is the standard deviation of the data and } \bar{x} \text{ is the mean.}$$

We can see that this measures the variability of the underlying data as a percentage of the mean value; the center weight of the data set. This measure is useful in comparing risk where an adjustment is warranted because of differences in scale of two data sets. In effect, the scale is changed to common scale, percentage differences, and allows direct comparison of the two or more magnitudes of variation of different data sets.

# KEY TERMS

**Frequency** the number of times a value of the data occurs

**Frequency Table** a data representation in which grouped data is displayed along with the corresponding frequencies

**Histogram** a graphical representation in $x$-$y$ form of the distribution of data in a data set; $x$ represents the data and $y$ represents the frequency, or relative frequency. The graph consists of contiguous rectangles.

**Interquartile Range** or $IQR$, is the range of the middle 50 percent of the data values; the $IQR$ is found by subtracting the first quartile from the third quartile.

**Mean (arithmetic)** a number that measures the central tendency of the data; a common name for mean is 'average.' The term 'mean' is a shortened form of 'arithmetic mean.' By definition, the mean for a sample (denoted by $\bar{x}$ ) is

$\bar{x} = \dfrac{\text{Sum of all values in the sample}}{\text{Number of values in the sample}}$, and the mean for a population (denoted by $\mu$) is

$\mu = \dfrac{\text{Sum of all values in the population}}{\text{Number of values in the population}}$.

**Mean (geometric)** a measure of central tendency that provides a measure of average geometric growth over multiple time periods.

**Median** a number that separates ordered data into halves; half the values are the same number or smaller than the median and half the values are the same number or larger than the median. The median may or may not be part of the data.

**Midpoint** the mean of an interval in a frequency table

**Mode** the value that appears most frequently in a set of data

**Outlier** an observation that does not fit the rest of the data

**Percentile** a number that divides ordered data into hundredths; percentiles may or may not be part of the data. The median of the data is the second quartile and the $50^{\text{th}}$ percentile. The first and third quartiles are the $25^{\text{th}}$ and the $75^{\text{th}}$ percentiles, respectively.

**Quartiles** the numbers that separate the data into quarters; quartiles may or may not be part of the data. The second quartile is the median of the data.

**Relative Frequency** the ratio of the number of times a value of the data occurs in the set of all outcomes to the number of all outcomes

**Standard Deviation** a number that is equal to the square root of the variance and measures how far data values are from their mean; notation: $s$ for sample standard deviation and $\sigma$ for population standard deviation.

**Variance** mean of the squared deviations from the mean, or the square of the standard deviation; for a set of data, a deviation can be represented as $x - \bar{x}$ where $x$ is a value of the data and $\bar{x}$ is the sample mean. The sample variance is equal to the sum of the squares of the deviations divided by the difference of the sample size and one.

# CHAPTER REVIEW

## 2.1 Display Data

A **stem-and-leaf plot** is a way to plot data and look at the distribution. In a stem-and-leaf plot, all data values within a class are visible. The advantage in a stem-and-leaf plot is that all values are listed, unlike a histogram, which gives classes of data values. A **line graph** is often used to represent a set of data values in which a quantity varies with time. These graphs are useful for finding trends. That is, finding a general pattern in data sets including temperature, sales, employment, company profit or cost over a period of time. A **bar graph** is a chart that uses either horizontal or vertical bars to show comparisons among categories. One axis of the chart shows the specific categories being compared, and the other axis represents a discrete value. Some bar graphs present bars clustered in groups of more than one (grouped bar graphs), and others show the bars divided into subparts to show cumulative effect (stacked bar graphs). Bar graphs are especially useful when categorical data is being used.

A **histogram** is a graphic version of a frequency distribution. The graph consists of bars of equal width drawn adjacent to each other. The horizontal scale represents classes of quantitative data values and the vertical scale represents frequencies. The heights of the bars correspond to frequency values. Histograms are typically used for large, continuous, quantitative data sets. A frequency polygon can also be used when graphing large data sets with data points that repeat. The data usually goes on $y$-axis with the frequency being graphed on the $x$-axis. Time series graphs can be helpful when looking at large amounts of data for one variable over a period of time.

### 2.2 Measures of the Location of the Data

The values that divide a rank-ordered set of data into 100 equal parts are called percentiles. Percentiles are used to compare and interpret data. For example, an observation at the $50^{th}$ percentile would be greater than 50 percent of the other obeservations in the set. Quartiles divide data into quarters. The first quartile ($Q_1$) is the $25^{th}$ percentile, the second quartile ($Q_2$ or median) is $50^{th}$ percentile, and the third quartile ($Q_3$) is the the $75^{th}$ percentile. The interquartile range, or $IQR$, is the range of the middle 50 percent of the data values. The $IQR$ is found by subtracting $Q_1$ from $Q_3$, and can help determine outliers by using the following two expressions.

- $Q_3 + IQR(1.5)$

- $Q_1 - IQR(1.5)$

### 2.3 Measures of the Center of the Data

The mean and the median can be calculated to help you find the "center" of a data set. The mean is the best estimate for the actual data set, but the median is the best measurement when a data set contains several outliers or extreme values. The mode will tell you the most frequently occuring datum (or data) in your data set. The mean, median, and mode are extremely helpful when you need to analyze your data, but if your data set consists of ranges which lack specific values, the mean may seem impossible to calculate. However, the mean can be approximated if you add the lower boundary with the upper boundary and divide by two to find the midpoint of each interval. Multiply each midpoint by the number of values found in the corresponding range. Divide the sum of these values by the total number of data values in the set.

### 2.6 Skewness and the Mean, Median, and Mode

Looking at the distribution of data can reveal a lot about the relationship between the mean, the median, and the mode. There are three types of distributions. A **right (or positive) skewed** distribution has a shape like **Figure 2.12**. A **left (or negative) skewed** distribution has a shape like **Figure 2.13**. A **symmetrical** distrubtion looks like **Figure 2.11**.

### 2.7 Measures of the Spread of the Data

The standard deviation can help you calculate the spread of data. There are different equations to use if are calculating the standard deviation of a sample or of a population.

- The Standard Deviation allows us to compare individual data or classes to the data set mean numerically.

- $s = \sqrt{\dfrac{\sum (x - \bar{x})^2}{n - 1}}$ or $s = \sqrt{\dfrac{\sum f(x - \bar{x})^2}{n - 1}}$ is the formula for calculating the standard deviation of a sample.

  To calculate the standard deviation of a population, we would use the population mean, $\mu$, and the formula $\sigma = \sqrt{\dfrac{\sum (x - \mu)^2}{N}}$ or $\sigma = \sqrt{\dfrac{\sum f(x - \mu)^2}{N}}$.

# FORMULA REVIEW

### 2.2 Measures of the Location of the Data

$$i = \left(\frac{k}{100}\right)(n + 1)$$

where $i$ = the ranking or position of a data value,

$k$ = the kth percentile,

$n$ = total number of data.

Expression for finding the percentile of a data value: $\left(\dfrac{x + 0.5y}{n}\right)(100)$

where $x$ = the number of values counting from the bottom of the data list up to but not including the data value for which you want to find the percentile,

$y$ = the number of data values equal to the data value for which you want to find the percentile,

$n$ = total number of data

## 2.3 Measures of the Center of the Data

$\mu = \dfrac{\sum fm}{\sum f}$ Where $f$ = interval frequencies and $m$ = interval midpoints.

The arithmetic mean for a sample (denoted by $\bar{x}$ ) is

$\bar{x} = \dfrac{\text{Sum of all values in the sample}}{\text{Number of values in the sample}}$

The arithmetic mean for a population (denoted by $\mu$) is

$\mu = \dfrac{\text{Sum of all values in the population}}{\text{Number of values in the population}}$

## 2.5 Geometric Mean

The Geometric Mean:

$\tilde{x} = \left(\prod_{i=1}^{n} x_i\right)^{\frac{1}{n}} = \sqrt[n]{x_1 * x_2 \cdots x_n} = (x_1 * x_2 \cdots x_n)^{\frac{1}{n}}$

## 2.6 Skewness and the Mean, Median, and Mode

Formula for skewness: $a_3 = \sum \dfrac{\left(x_i - \bar{x}\right)^3}{ns^3}$

Formula for Coefficient of Variation: $CV = \dfrac{s}{\bar{x}} * 100$ conditioned upon $\bar{x} \neq 0$

## 2.7 Measures of the Spread of the Data

$s_x = \sqrt{\dfrac{\sum fm^2}{n} - \bar{x}^2}$ where

$s_x$ = sample standard deviation

$\bar{x}$ = sample mean

Formulas for Sample Standard Deviation

$s = \sqrt{\dfrac{\Sigma(x - \bar{x})^2}{n-1}}$ or $s = \sqrt{\dfrac{\Sigma f(x - \bar{x})^2}{n-1}}$ or

$s = \sqrt{\dfrac{\left(\sum_{i=1}^{n} x^2\right) - n\bar{x}^2}{n-1}}$ For the sample standard deviation, the denominator is $n - 1$, that is the sample size - 1.

Formulas for Population Standard Deviation

$\sigma = \sqrt{\dfrac{\Sigma(x - \mu)^2}{N}}$ or $\sigma = \sqrt{\dfrac{\Sigma f(x - \mu)^2}{N}}$ or

$\sigma = \sqrt{\dfrac{\sum_{i=1}^{N} x_i^2}{N} - \mu^2}$ For the population standard deviation, the denominator is $N$, the number of items in the population.

# PRACTICE

## 2.1 Display Data

*For the next three exercises, use the data to construct a line graph.*

**1.** In a survey, 40 people were asked how many times they visited a store before making a major purchase. The results are shown in **Table 2.34**.

| Number of times in store | Frequency |
|---|---|
| 1 | 4 |
| 2 | 10 |
| 3 | 16 |
| 4 | 6 |
| 5 | 4 |

Table 2.34

**2.** In a survey, several people were asked how many years it has been since they purchased a mattress. The results are shown in **Table 2.35**.

| Years since last purchase | Frequency |
|---|---|
| 0 | 2 |
| 1 | 8 |
| 2 | 13 |
| 3 | 22 |
| 4 | 16 |
| 5 | 9 |

Table 2.35

**3.** Several children were asked how many TV shows they watch each day. The results of the survey are shown in **Table 2.36**.

| Number of TV Shows | Frequency |
|---|---|
| 0 | 12 |
| 1 | 18 |
| 2 | 36 |
| 3 | 7 |
| 4 | 2 |

Table 2.36

**4.** The students in Ms. Ramirez's math class have birthdays in each of the four seasons. **Table 2.37** shows the four seasons, the number of students who have birthdays in each season, and the percentage (%) of students in each group. Construct a bar graph showing the number of students.

| Seasons | Number of students | Proportion of population |
|---|---|---|
| Spring | 8 | 24% |
| Summer | 9 | 26% |
| Autumn | 11 | 32% |
| Winter | 6 | 18% |

Table 2.37

**5.** Using the data from Mrs. Ramirez's math class supplied in **Exercise 2.4**, construct a bar graph showing the percentages.

**6.** David County has six high schools. Each school sent students to participate in a county-wide science competition. **Table 2.38** shows the percentage breakdown of competitors from each school, and the percentage of the entire student population of the county that goes to each school. Construct a bar graph that shows the population percentage of competitors from each school.

| High School | Science competition population | Overall student population |
|---|---|---|
| Alabaster | 28.9% | 8.6% |
| Concordia | 7.6% | 23.2% |
| Genoa | 12.1% | 15.0% |
| Mocksville | 18.5% | 14.3% |
| Tynneson | 24.2% | 10.1% |
| West End | 8.7% | 28.8% |

Table 2.38

**7.** Use the data from the David County science competition supplied in **Exercise 2.6**. Construct a bar graph that shows the county-wide population percentage of students at each school.

**8.** Sixty-five randomly selected car salespersons were asked the number of cars they generally sell in one week. Fourteen people answered that they generally sell three cars; nineteen generally sell four cars; twelve generally sell five cars; nine generally sell six cars; eleven generally sell seven cars. Complete the table.

| Data Value (# cars) | Frequency | Relative Frequency | Cumulative Relative Frequency |
|---|---|---|---|
|  |  |  |  |
|  |  |  |  |
|  |  |  |  |
|  |  |  |  |
|  |  |  |  |

Table 2.39

**9.** What does the frequency column in **Table 2.39** sum to? Why?

**10.** What does the relative frequency column in **Table 2.39** sum to? Why?

**11.** What is the difference between relative frequency and frequency for each data value in **Table 2.39**?

**12.** What is the difference between cumulative relative frequency and relative frequency for each data value?

**13.** To construct the histogram for the data in **Table 2.39**, determine appropriate minimum and maximum $x$ and $y$ values and the scaling. Sketch the histogram. Label the horizontal and vertical axes with words. Include numerical scaling.

**Figure 2.14**

**14.** Construct a frequency polygon for the following:

a.

| Pulse Rates for Women | Frequency |
|:---:|:---:|
| 60–69 | 12 |
| 70–79 | 14 |
| 80–89 | 11 |
| 90–99 | 1 |
| 100–109 | 1 |
| 110–119 | 0 |
| 120–129 | 1 |

Table 2.40

b.

| Actual Speed in a 30 MPH Zone | Frequency |
|:---:|:---:|
| 42–45 | 25 |
| 46–49 | 14 |
| 50–53 | 7 |
| 54–57 | 3 |
| 58–61 | 1 |

Table 2.41

c.

| Tar (mg) in Nonfiltered Cigarettes | Frequency |
|:---:|:---:|
| 10–13 | 1 |
| 14–17 | 0 |
| 18–21 | 15 |
| 22–25 | 7 |
| 26–29 | 2 |

Table 2.42

**15.** Construct a frequency polygon from the frequency distribution for the 50 highest ranked countries for depth of hunger.

| Depth of Hunger | Frequency |
|---|---|
| 230–259 | 21 |
| 260–289 | 13 |
| 290–319 | 5 |
| 320–349 | 7 |
| 350–379 | 1 |
| 380–409 | 1 |
| 410–439 | 1 |

Table 2.43

**16.** Use the two frequency tables to compare the life expectancy of men and women from 20 randomly selected countries. Include an overlayed frequency polygon and discuss the shapes of the distributions, the center, the spread, and any outliers. What can we conclude about the life expectancy of women compared to men?

| Life Expectancy at Birth – Women | Frequency |
|---|---|
| 49–55 | 3 |
| 56–62 | 3 |
| 63–69 | 1 |
| 70–76 | 3 |
| 77–83 | 8 |
| 84–90 | 2 |

Table 2.44

| Life Expectancy at Birth – Men | Frequency |
|---|---|
| 49–55 | 3 |
| 56–62 | 3 |
| 63–69 | 1 |
| 70–76 | 1 |
| 77–83 | 7 |
| 84–90 | 5 |

Table 2.45

**17.** Construct a times series graph for (a) the number of male births, (b) the number of female births, and (c) the total number of births.

| Sex/Year | 1855 | 1856 | 1857 | 1858 | 1859 | 1860 | 1861 |
|---|---|---|---|---|---|---|---|
| Female | 45,545 | 49,582 | 50,257 | 50,324 | 51,915 | 51,220 | 52,403 |
| Male | 47,804 | 52,239 | 53,158 | 53,694 | 54,628 | 54,409 | 54,606 |
| Total | 93,349 | 101,821 | 103,415 | 104,018 | 106,543 | 105,629 | 107,009 |

Table 2.46

| Sex/Year | 1862 | 1863 | 1864 | 1865 | 1866 | 1867 | 1868 | 1869 |
|---|---|---|---|---|---|---|---|---|
| Female | 51,812 | 53,115 | 54,959 | 54,850 | 55,307 | 55,527 | 56,292 | 55,033 |
| Male | 55,257 | 56,226 | 57,374 | 58,220 | 58,360 | 58,517 | 59,222 | 58,321 |
| Total | 107,069 | 109,341 | 112,333 | 113,070 | 113,667 | 114,044 | 115,514 | 113,354 |

Table 2.47

| Sex/Year | 1871 | 1870 | 1872 | 1871 | 1872 | 1827 | 1874 | 1875 |
|---|---|---|---|---|---|---|---|---|
| Female | 56,099 | 56,431 | 57,472 | 56,099 | 57,472 | 58,233 | 60,109 | 60,146 |
| Male | 60,029 | 58,959 | 61,293 | 60,029 | 61,293 | 61,467 | 63,602 | 63,432 |
| Total | 116,128 | 115,390 | 118,765 | 116,128 | 118,765 | 119,700 | 123,711 | 123,578 |

Table 2.48

**18.** The following data sets list full time police per 100,000 citizens along with homicides per 100,000 citizens for the city of Detroit, Michigan during the period from 1961 to 1973.

| Year | 1961 | 1962 | 1963 | 1964 | 1965 | 1966 | 1967 |
|---|---|---|---|---|---|---|---|
| Police | 260.35 | 269.8 | 272.04 | 272.96 | 272.51 | 261.34 | 268.89 |
| Homicides | 8.6 | 8.9 | 8.52 | 8.89 | 13.07 | 14.57 | 21.36 |

Table 2.49

| Year | 1968 | 1969 | 1970 | 1971 | 1972 | 1973 |
|---|---|---|---|---|---|---|
| Police | 295.99 | 319.87 | 341.43 | 356.59 | 376.69 | 390.19 |
| Homicides | 28.03 | 31.49 | 37.39 | 46.26 | 47.24 | 52.33 |

Table 2.50

  a.  Construct a double time series graph using a common *x*-axis for both sets of data.
  b.  Which variable increased the fastest? Explain.
  c.  Did Detroit's increase in police officers have an impact on the murder rate? Explain.

## 2.2 Measures of the Location of the Data

**19.** Listed are 29 ages for Academy Award winning best actors *in order from smallest to largest.*

18; 21; 22; 25; 26; 27; 29; 30; 31; 33; 36; 37; 41; 42; 47; 52; 55; 57; 58; 62; 64; 67; 69; 71; 72; 73; 74; 76; 77

    a.  Find the $40^{th}$ percentile.

    b.  Find the $78^{th}$ percentile.

**20.** Listed are 32 ages for Academy Award winning best actors *in order from smallest to largest.*

18; 18; 21; 22; 25; 26; 27; 29; 30; 31; 31; 33; 36; 37; 37; 41; 42; 47; 52; 55; 57; 58; 62; 64; 67; 69; 71; 72; 73; 74; 76; 77

    a.  Find the percentile of 37.

    b.  Find the percentile of 72.

**21.** Jesse was ranked $37^{th}$ in his graduating class of 180 students. At what percentile is Jesse's ranking?

**22.**

    a.  For runners in a race, a low time means a faster run. The winners in a race have the shortest running times. Is it more desirable to have a finish time with a high or a low percentile when running a race?

    b.  The $20^{th}$ percentile of run times in a particular race is 5.2 minutes. Write a sentence interpreting the $20^{th}$ percentile in the context of the situation.

    c.  A bicyclist in the $90^{th}$ percentile of a bicycle race completed the race in 1 hour and 12 minutes. Is he among the fastest or slowest cyclists in the race? Write a sentence interpreting the $90^{th}$ percentile in the context of the situation.

**23.**

    a.  For runners in a race, a higher speed means a faster run. Is it more desirable to have a speed with a high or a low percentile when running a race?

    b.  The $40^{th}$ percentile of speeds in a particular race is 7.5 miles per hour. Write a sentence interpreting the $40^{th}$ percentile in the context of the situation.

**24.** On an exam, would it be more desirable to earn a grade with a high or low percentile? Explain.

**25.** Mina is waiting in line at the Department of Motor Vehicles (DMV). Her wait time of 32 minutes is the $85^{th}$ percentile of wait times. Is that good or bad? Write a sentence interpreting the $85^{th}$ percentile in the context of this situation.

**26.** In a survey collecting data about the salaries earned by recent college graduates, Li found that her salary was in the $78^{th}$ percentile. Should Li be pleased or upset by this result? Explain.

**27.** In a study collecting data about the repair costs of damage to automobiles in a certain type of crash tests, a certain model of car had \$1,700 in damage and was in the $90^{th}$ percentile. Should the manufacturer and the consumer be pleased or upset by this result? Explain and write a sentence that interprets the $90^{th}$ percentile in the context of this problem.

**28.** The University of California has two criteria used to set admission standards for freshman to be admitted to a college in the UC system:

    a.  Students' GPAs and scores on standardized tests (SATs and ACTs) are entered into a formula that calculates an "admissions index" score. The admissions index score is used to set eligibility standards intended to meet the goal of admitting the top 12% of high school students in the state. In this context, what percentile does the top 12% represent?

    b.  Students whose GPAs are at or above the $96^{th}$ percentile of all students at their high school are eligible (called eligible in the local context), even if they are not in the top 12% of all students in the state. What percentage of students from each high school are "eligible in the local context"?

**29.** Suppose that you are buying a house. You and your realtor have determined that the most expensive house you can afford is the $34^{th}$ percentile. The $34^{th}$ percentile of housing prices is \$240,000 in the town you want to move to. In this town, can you afford 34% of the houses or 66% of the houses?

Use **Exercise 2.21** to calculate the following values:

**30.** First quartile = _____

**31.** Second quartile = median = $50^{\text{th}}$ percentile = _____

**32.** Third quartile = _____

**33.** Interquartile range ($IQR$) = _____ – _____ = _____

**34.** $10^{\text{th}}$ percentile = _____

**35.** $70^{\text{th}}$ percentile = _____

## 2.3 Measures of the Center of the Data

**36.** Find the mean for the following frequency tables.

a.

| Grade | Frequency |
|-----------|-----------|
| 49.5–59.5 | 2 |
| 59.5–69.5 | 3 |
| 69.5–79.5 | 8 |
| 79.5–89.5 | 12 |
| 89.5–99.5 | 5 |

Table 2.51

b.

| Daily Low Temperature | Frequency |
|-----------------------|-----------|
| 49.5–59.5 | 53 |
| 59.5–69.5 | 32 |
| 69.5–79.5 | 15 |
| 79.5–89.5 | 1 |
| 89.5–99.5 | 0 |

Table 2.52

c.

| Points per Game | Frequency |
|-----------------|-----------|
| 49.5–59.5 | 14 |
| 59.5–69.5 | 32 |
| 69.5–79.5 | 15 |
| 79.5–89.5 | 23 |
| 89.5–99.5 | 2 |

Table 2.53

*Use the following information to answer the next three exercises:* The following data show the lengths of boats moored in a marina. The data are ordered from smallest to largest: 16; 17; 19; 20; 20; 21; 23; 24; 25; 25; 25; 26; 26; 27; 27; 27; 28; 29; 30; 32; 33; 33; 34; 35; 37; 39; 40

**37.** Calculate the mean.

**38.** Identify the median.

**39.** Identify the mode.

*Use the following information to answer the next three exercises:* Sixty-five randomly selected car salespersons were asked the number of cars they generally sell in one week. Fourteen people answered that they generally sell three cars; nineteen generally sell four cars; twelve generally sell five cars; nine generally sell six cars; eleven generally sell seven cars. Calculate the following:

**40.** sample mean = $\bar{x}$ = _____

**41.** median = _____

**42.** mode = _____

## 2.6 Skewness and the Mean, Median, and Mode

*Use the following information to answer the next three exercises:* State whether the data are symmetrical, skewed to the left, or skewed to the right.

**43.** 1; 1; 1; 2; 2; 2; 2; 3; 3; 3; 3; 3; 3; 3; 3; 4; 4; 4; 5; 5

**44.** 16; 17; 19; 22; 22; 22; 22; 22; 23

**45.** 87; 87; 87; 87; 87; 88; 89; 89; 90; 91

**46.** When the data are skewed left, what is the typical relationship between the mean and median?

**47.** When the data are symmetrical, what is the typical relationship between the mean and median?

**48.** What word describes a distribution that has two modes?

**49.** Describe the shape of this distribution.

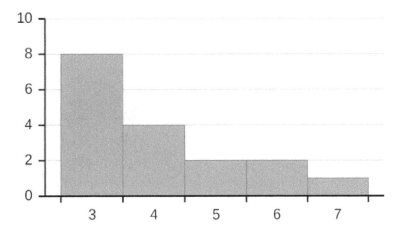

**Figure 2.15**

**50.** Describe the relationship between the mode and the median of this distribution.

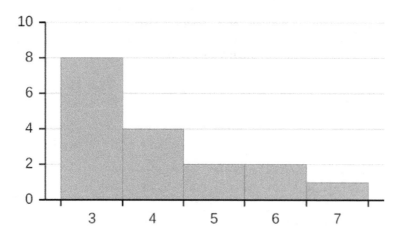

Figure 2.16

**51.** Describe the relationship between the mean and the median of this distribution.

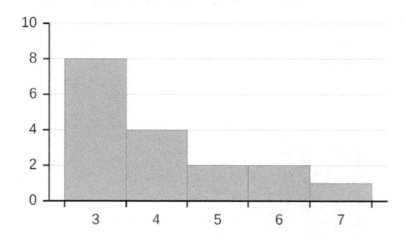

Figure 2.17

**52.** Describe the shape of this distribution.

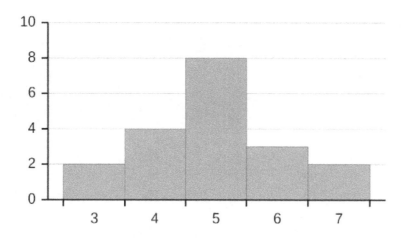

Figure 2.18

**53.** Describe the relationship between the mode and the median of this distribution.

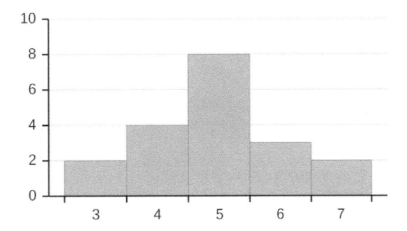

**54.** Are the mean and the median the exact same in this distribution? Why or why not?

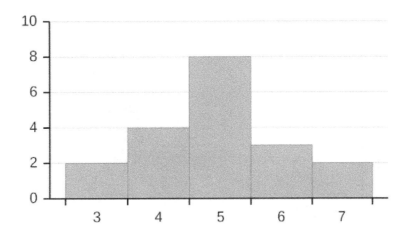

**55.** Describe the shape of this distribution.

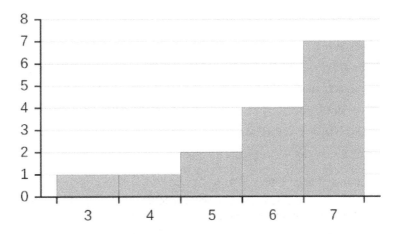

**56.** Describe the relationship between the mode and the median of this distribution.

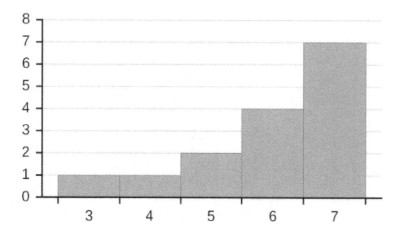

Figure 2.22

**57.** Describe the relationship between the mean and the median of this distribution.

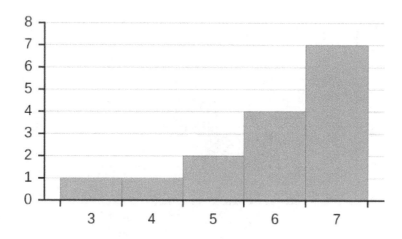

Figure 2.23

**58.** The mean and median for the data are the same.

3; 4; 5; 5; 6; 6; 6; 6; 7; 7; 7; 7; 7; 7; 7

Is the data perfectly symmetrical? Why or why not?

**59.** Which is the greatest, the mean, the mode, or the median of the data set?

11; 11; 12; 12; 12; 12; 13; 15; 17; 22; 22; 22

**60.** Which is the least, the mean, the mode, and the median of the data set?

56; 56; 56; 58; 59; 60; 62; 64; 64; 65; 67

**61.** Of the three measures, which tends to reflect skewing the most, the mean, the mode, or the median? Why?

**62.** In a perfectly symmetrical distribution, when would the mode be different from the mean and median?

## 2.7 Measures of the Spread of the Data

*Use the following information to answer the next two exercises*: The following data are the distances between 20 retail stores and a large distribution center. The distances are in miles.
29; 37; 38; 40; 58; 67; 68; 69; 76; 86; 87; 95; 96; 96; 99; 106; 112; 127; 145; 150

**63.** Use a graphing calculator or computer to find the standard deviation and round to the nearest tenth.

**64.** Find the value that is one standard deviation below the mean.

**65.** Two baseball players, Fredo and Karl, on different teams wanted to find out who had the higher batting average when compared to his team. Which baseball player had the higher batting average when compared to his team?

| Baseball Player | Batting Average | Team Batting Average | Team Standard Deviation |
|-----------------|-----------------|----------------------|-------------------------|
| Fredo | 0.158 | 0.166 | 0.012 |
| Karl | 0.177 | 0.189 | 0.015 |

Table 2.54

**66.** Use Table 2.54 to find the value that is three standard deviations:
**a.** above the mean
**b.** below the mean

*Find the standard deviation for the following frequency tables using the formula. Check the calculations with the TI 83/84.*

**67.** Find the standard deviation for the following frequency tables using the formula. Check the calculations with the TI 83/84.

a.

| Grade | Frequency |
|---|---|
| 49.5–59.5 | 2 |
| 59.5–69.5 | 3 |
| 69.5–79.5 | 8 |
| 79.5–89.5 | 12 |
| 89.5–99.5 | 5 |

Table 2.55

b.

| Daily Low Temperature | Frequency |
|---|---|
| 49.5–59.5 | 53 |
| 59.5–69.5 | 32 |
| 69.5–79.5 | 15 |
| 79.5–89.5 | 1 |
| 89.5–99.5 | 0 |

Table 2.56

c.

| Points per Game | Frequency |
|---|---|
| 49.5–59.5 | 14 |
| 59.5–69.5 | 32 |
| 69.5–79.5 | 15 |
| 79.5–89.5 | 23 |
| 89.5–99.5 | 2 |

Table 2.57

# HOMEWORK

## 2.1 Display Data

**68.** Table 2.58 contains the 2010 obesity rates in U.S. states and Washington, DC.

| State | Percent (%) | State | Percent (%) | State | Percent (%) |
|---|---|---|---|---|---|
| Alabama | 32.2 | Kentucky | 31.3 | North Dakota | 27.2 |
| Alaska | 24.5 | Louisiana | 31.0 | Ohio | 29.2 |
| Arizona | 24.3 | Maine | 26.8 | Oklahoma | 30.4 |
| Arkansas | 30.1 | Maryland | 27.1 | Oregon | 26.8 |
| California | 24.0 | Massachusetts | 23.0 | Pennsylvania | 28.6 |
| Colorado | 21.0 | Michigan | 30.9 | Rhode Island | 25.5 |
| Connecticut | 22.5 | Minnesota | 24.8 | South Carolina | 31.5 |
| Delaware | 28.0 | Mississippi | 34.0 | South Dakota | 27.3 |
| Washington, DC | 22.2 | Missouri | 30.5 | Tennessee | 30.8 |
| Florida | 26.6 | Montana | 23.0 | Texas | 31.0 |
| Georgia | 29.6 | Nebraska | 26.9 | Utah | 22.5 |
| Hawaii | 22.7 | Nevada | 22.4 | Vermont | 23.2 |
| Idaho | 26.5 | New Hampshire | 25.0 | Virginia | 26.0 |
| Illinois | 28.2 | New Jersey | 23.8 | Washington | 25.5 |
| Indiana | 29.6 | New Mexico | 25.1 | West Virginia | 32.5 |
| Iowa | 28.4 | New York | 23.9 | Wisconsin | 26.3 |
| Kansas | 29.4 | North Carolina | 27.8 | Wyoming | 25.1 |

Table 2.58

a. Use a random number generator to randomly pick eight states. Construct a bar graph of the obesity rates of those eight states.
b. Construct a bar graph for all the states beginning with the letter "A."
c. Construct a bar graph for all the states beginning with the letter "M."

**69.** Suppose that three book publishers were interested in the number of fiction paperbacks adult consumers purchase per month. Each publisher conducted a survey. In the survey, adult consumers were asked the number of fiction paperbacks they had purchased the previous month. The results are as follows:

| # of books | Freq. | Rel. Freq. |
|---|---|---|
| 0 | 10 | |
| 1 | 12 | |
| 2 | 16 | |
| 3 | 12 | |
| 4 | 8 | |
| 5 | 6 | |
| 6 | 2 | |
| 8 | 2 | |

Table 2.59 Publisher A

| # of books | Freq. | Rel. Freq. |
|---|---|---|
| 0 | 18 | |
| 1 | 24 | |
| 2 | 24 | |
| 3 | 22 | |
| 4 | 15 | |
| 5 | 10 | |
| 7 | 5 | |
| 9 | 1 | |

Table 2.60 Publisher B

| # of books | Freq. | Rel. Freq. |
|---|---|---|
| 0–1 | 20 | |
| 2–3 | 35 | |
| 4–5 | 12 | |
| 6–7 | 2 | |
| 8–9 | 1 | |

Table 2.61 Publisher C

a. Find the relative frequencies for each survey. Write them in the charts.
b. Use the frequency column to construct a histogram for each publisher's survey. For Publishers A and B, make bar widths of one. For Publisher C, make bar widths of two.
c. In complete sentences, give two reasons why the graphs for Publishers A and B are not identical.
d. Would you have expected the graph for Publisher C to look like the other two graphs? Why or why not?
e. Make new histograms for Publisher A and Publisher B. This time, make bar widths of two.
f. Now, compare the graph for Publisher C to the new graphs for Publishers A and B. Are the graphs more similar or more different? Explain your answer.

**70.** Often, cruise ships conduct all on-board transactions, with the exception of gambling, on a cashless basis. At the end of the cruise, guests pay one bill that covers all onboard transactions. Suppose that 60 single travelers and 70 couples were surveyed as to their on-board bills for a seven-day cruise from Los Angeles to the Mexican Riviera. Following is a summary of the bills for each group.

| Amount($) | Frequency | Rel. Frequency |
|-----------|-----------|----------------|
| 51–100    | 5         |                |
| 101–150   | 10        |                |
| 151–200   | 15        |                |
| 201–250   | 15        |                |
| 251–300   | 10        |                |
| 301–350   | 5         |                |

Table 2.62 Singles

| Amount($) | Frequency | Rel. Frequency |
|-----------|-----------|----------------|
| 100–150   | 5         |                |
| 201–250   | 5         |                |
| 251–300   | 5         |                |
| 301–350   | 5         |                |
| 351–400   | 10        |                |
| 401–450   | 10        |                |
| 451–500   | 10        |                |
| 501–550   | 10        |                |
| 551–600   | 5         |                |
| 601–650   | 5         |                |

Table 2.63 Couples

a. Fill in the relative frequency for each group.
b. Construct a histogram for the singles group. Scale the x-axis by $50 widths. Use relative frequency on the y-axis.
c. Construct a histogram for the couples group. Scale the x-axis by $50 widths. Use relative frequency on the y-axis.
d. Compare the two graphs:
    i. List two similarities between the graphs.
    ii. List two differences between the graphs.
    iii. Overall, are the graphs more similar or different?
e. Construct a new graph for the couples by hand. Since each couple is paying for two individuals, instead of scaling the x-axis by $50, scale it by $100. Use relative frequency on the y-axis.
f. Compare the graph for the singles with the new graph for the couples:
    i. List two similarities between the graphs.
    ii. Overall, are the graphs more similar or different?
g. How did scaling the couples graph differently change the way you compared it to the singles graph?
h. Based on the graphs, do you think that individuals spend the same amount, more or less, as singles as they do person by person as a couple? Explain why in one or two complete sentences.

**71.** Twenty-five randomly selected students were asked the number of movies they watched the previous week. The results are as follows.

| # of movies | Frequency | Relative Frequency | Cumulative Relative Frequency |
|---|---|---|---|
| 0 | 5 | | |
| 1 | 9 | | |
| 2 | 6 | | |
| 3 | 4 | | |
| 4 | 1 | | |

Table 2.64

a. Construct a histogram of the data.
b. Complete the columns of the chart.

*Use the following information to answer the next two exercises:* Suppose one hundred eleven people who shopped in a special t-shirt store were asked the number of t-shirts they own costing more than $19 each.

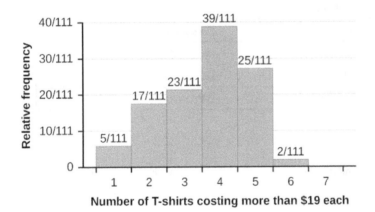

**72.** The percentage of people who own at most three t-shirts costing more than $19 each is approximately:
a. 21
b. 59
c. 41
d. Cannot be determined

**73.** If the data were collected by asking the first 111 people who entered the store, then the type of sampling is:
a. cluster
b. simple random
c. stratified
d. convenience

**74.** Following are the 2010 obesity rates by U.S. states and Washington, DC.

| State | Percent (%) | State | Percent (%) | State | Percent (%) |
|---|---|---|---|---|---|
| Alabama | 32.2 | Kentucky | 31.3 | North Dakota | 27.2 |
| Alaska | 24.5 | Louisiana | 31.0 | Ohio | 29.2 |
| Arizona | 24.3 | Maine | 26.8 | Oklahoma | 30.4 |
| Arkansas | 30.1 | Maryland | 27.1 | Oregon | 26.8 |
| California | 24.0 | Massachusetts | 23.0 | Pennsylvania | 28.6 |
| Colorado | 21.0 | Michigan | 30.9 | Rhode Island | 25.5 |
| Connecticut | 22.5 | Minnesota | 24.8 | South Carolina | 31.5 |
| Delaware | 28.0 | Mississippi | 34.0 | South Dakota | 27.3 |
| Washington, DC | 22.2 | Missouri | 30.5 | Tennessee | 30.8 |
| Florida | 26.6 | Montana | 23.0 | Texas | 31.0 |
| Georgia | 29.6 | Nebraska | 26.9 | Utah | 22.5 |
| Hawaii | 22.7 | Nevada | 22.4 | Vermont | 23.2 |
| Idaho | 26.5 | New Hampshire | 25.0 | Virginia | 26.0 |
| Illinois | 28.2 | New Jersey | 23.8 | Washington | 25.5 |
| Indiana | 29.6 | New Mexico | 25.1 | West Virginia | 32.5 |
| Iowa | 28.4 | New York | 23.9 | Wisconsin | 26.3 |
| Kansas | 29.4 | North Carolina | 27.8 | Wyoming | 25.1 |

Table 2.65

Construct a bar graph of obesity rates of your state and the four states closest to your state. Hint: Label the *x*-axis with the states.

## 2.2 Measures of the Location of the Data

**75.** The median age for U.S. blacks currently is 30.9 years; for U.S. whites it is 42.3 years.
   a. Based upon this information, give two reasons why the black median age could be lower than the white median age.
   b. Does the lower median age for blacks necessarily mean that blacks die younger than whites? Why or why not?
   c. How might it be possible for blacks and whites to die at approximately the same age, but for the median age for whites to be higher?

**76.** Six hundred adult Americans were asked by telephone poll, "What do you think constitutes a middle-class income?" The results are in Table 2.66. Also, include left endpoint, but not the right endpoint.

| Salary ($) | Relative Frequency |
|---|---|
| < 20,000 | 0.02 |
| 20,000–25,000 | 0.09 |
| 25,000–30,000 | 0.19 |
| 30,000–40,000 | 0.26 |
| 40,000–50,000 | 0.18 |
| 50,000–75,000 | 0.17 |
| 75,000–99,999 | 0.02 |
| 100,000+ | 0.01 |

Table 2.66

a. What percentage of the survey answered "not sure"?
b. What percentage think that middle-class is from $25,000 to $50,000?
c. Construct a histogram of the data.
    i. Should all bars have the same width, based on the data? Why or why not?
    ii. How should the <20,000 and the 100,000+ intervals be handled? Why?
d. Find the $40^{th}$ and $80^{th}$ percentiles
e. Construct a bar graph of the data

## 2.3 Measures of the Center of the Data

**77.** The most obese countries in the world have obesity rates that range from 11.4% to 74.6%. This data is summarized in the following table.

| Percent of Population Obese | Number of Countries |
|---|---|
| 11.4–20.45 | 29 |
| 20.45–29.45 | 13 |
| 29.45–38.45 | 4 |
| 38.45–47.45 | 0 |
| 47.45–56.45 | 2 |
| 56.45–65.45 | 1 |
| 65.45–74.45 | 0 |
| 74.45–83.45 | 1 |

Table 2.67

a. What is the best estimate of the average obesity percentage for these countries?
b. The United States has an average obesity rate of 33.9%. Is this rate above average or below?
c. How does the United States compare to other countries?

**78.** Table 2.68 gives the percent of children under five considered to be underweight. What is the best estimate for the mean percentage of underweight children?

| Percent of Underweight Children | Number of Countries |
|---|---|
| 16–21.45 | 23 |
| 21.45–26.9 | 4 |
| 26.9–32.35 | 9 |
| 32.35–37.8 | 7 |
| 37.8–43.25 | 6 |
| 43.25–48.7 | 1 |

Table 2.68

## 2.6 Skewness and the Mean, Median, and Mode

**79.** The median age of the U.S. population in 1980 was 30.0 years. In 1991, the median age was 33.1 years.
   a.  What does it mean for the median age to rise?
   b.  Give two reasons why the median age could rise.
   c.  For the median age to rise, is the actual number of children less in 1991 than it was in 1980? Why or why not?

## 2.7 Measures of the Spread of the Data

*Use the following information to answer the next nine exercises:* The population parameters below describe the full-time equivalent number of students (FTES) each year at Lake Tahoe Community College from 1976–1977 through 2004–2005.

- $\mu$ = 1000 FTES
- median = 1,014 FTES
- $\sigma$ = 474 FTES
- first quartile = 528.5 FTES
- third quartile = 1,447.5 FTES
- $n$ = 29 years

**80.** A sample of 11 years is taken. About how many are expected to have a FTES of 1014 or above? Explain how you determined your answer.

**81.** 75% of all years have an FTES:
   a.  at or below: _____
   b.  at or above: _____

**82.** The population standard deviation = _____

**83.** What percent of the FTES were from 528.5 to 1447.5? How do you know?

**84.** What is the *IQR*? What does the *IQR* represent?

**85.** How many standard deviations away from the mean is the median?

*Additional Information:* The population FTES for 2005–2006 through 2010–2011 was given in an updated report. The data are reported here.

| Year | 2005–06 | 2006–07 | 2007–08 | 2008–09 | 2009–10 | 2010–11 |
|------|---------|---------|---------|---------|---------|---------|
| Total FTES | 1,585 | 1,690 | 1,735 | 1,935 | 2,021 | 1,890 |

Table 2.69

**86.** Calculate the mean, median, standard deviation, the first quartile, the third quartile and the *IQR*. Round to one decimal place.

**87.** Compare the *IQR* for the FTES for 1976–77 through 2004–2005 with the *IQR* for the FTES for 2005-2006 through 2010–2011. Why do you suppose the *IQR*s are so different?

**88.** Three students were applying to the same graduate school. They came from schools with different grading systems. Which student had the best GPA when compared to other students at his school? Explain how you determined your answer.

| Student | GPA | School Average GPA | School Standard Deviation |
|---------|-----|--------------------|--------------------------|
| Thuy | 2.7 | 3.2 | 0.8 |
| Vichet | 87 | 75 | 20 |
| Kamala | 8.6 | 8 | 0.4 |

Table 2.70

**89.** A music school has budgeted to purchase three musical instruments. They plan to purchase a piano costing $3,000, a guitar costing $550, and a drum set costing $600. The mean cost for a piano is $4,000 with a standard deviation of $2,500. The mean cost for a guitar is $500 with a standard deviation of $200. The mean cost for drums is $700 with a standard deviation of $100. Which cost is the lowest, when compared to other instruments of the same type? Which cost is the highest when compared to other instruments of the same type. Justify your answer.

**90.** An elementary school class ran one mile with a mean of 11 minutes and a standard deviation of three minutes. Rachel, a student in the class, ran one mile in eight minutes. A junior high school class ran one mile with a mean of nine minutes and a standard deviation of two minutes. Kenji, a student in the class, ran 1 mile in 8.5 minutes. A high school class ran one mile with a mean of seven minutes and a standard deviation of four minutes. Nedda, a student in the class, ran one mile in eight minutes.
   a. Why is Kenji considered a better runner than Nedda, even though Nedda ran faster than he?
   b. Who is the fastest runner with respect to his or her class? Explain why.

**91.** The most obese countries in the world have obesity rates that range from 11.4% to 74.6%. This data is summarized in Table 14.

| Percent of Population Obese | Number of Countries |
|---|---|
| 11.4–20.45 | 29 |
| 20.45–29.45 | 13 |
| 29.45–38.45 | 4 |
| 38.45–47.45 | 0 |
| 47.45–56.45 | 2 |
| 56.45–65.45 | 1 |
| 65.45–74.45 | 0 |
| 74.45–83.45 | 1 |

Table 2.71

What is the best estimate of the average obesity percentage for these countries? What is the standard deviation for the listed obesity rates? The United States has an average obesity rate of 33.9%. Is this rate above average or below? How "unusual" is the United States' obesity rate compared to the average rate? Explain.

**92.** Table 2.72 gives the percent of children under five considered to be underweight.

| Percent of Underweight Children | Number of Countries |
|---|---|
| 16–21.45 | 23 |
| 21.45–26.9 | 4 |
| 26.9–32.35 | 9 |
| 32.35–37.8 | 7 |
| 37.8–43.25 | 6 |
| 43.25–48.7 | 1 |

Table 2.72

What is the best estimate for the mean percentage of underweight children? What is the standard deviation? Which interval(s) could be considered unusual? Explain.

# BRINGING IT TOGETHER: HOMEWORK

**93.** Javier and Ercilia are supervisors at a shopping mall. Each was given the task of estimating the mean distance that shoppers live from the mall. They each randomly surveyed 100 shoppers. The samples yielded the following information.

|  | Javier | Ercilia |
|---|---|---|
| $\overline{x}$ | 6.0 miles | 6.0 miles |
| $s$ | 4.0 miles | 7.0 miles |

Table 2.73

a. How can you determine which survey was correct ?
b. Explain what the difference in the results of the surveys implies about the data.
c. If the two histograms depict the distribution of values for each supervisor, which one depicts Ercilia's sample? How do you know?

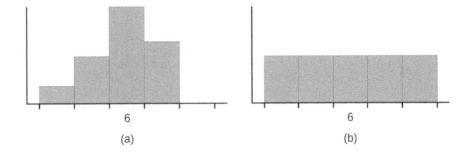

(a)                                    (b)

Figure 2.24

*Use the following information to answer the next three exercises*: We are interested in the number of years students in a particular elementary statistics class have lived in California. The information in the following table is from the entire section.

| Number of years | Frequency | Number of years | Frequency |
|---|---|---|---|
| 7 | 1 | 22 | 1 |
| 14 | 3 | 23 | 1 |
| 15 | 1 | 26 | 1 |
| 18 | 1 | 40 | 2 |
| 19 | 4 | 42 | 2 |
| 20 | 3 |  |  |
|  |  |  | Total = 20 |

Table 2.74

**94.** What is the *IQR*?
a. 8
b. 11
c. 15
d. 35

**95.** What is the mode?
  a. 19
  b. 19.5
  c. 14 and 20
  d. 22.65

**96.** Is this a sample or the entire population?
  a. sample
  b. entire population
  c. neither

**97.** Twenty-five randomly selected students were asked the number of movies they watched the previous week. The results are as follows:

| # of movies | Frequency |
|---|---|
| 0 | 5 |
| 1 | 9 |
| 2 | 6 |
| 3 | 4 |
| 4 | 1 |

Table 2.75

  a. Find the sample mean $\bar{x}$ .
  b. Find the approximate sample standard deviation, $s$.

**98.** Forty randomly selected students were asked the number of pairs of sneakers they owned. Let $X$ = the number of pairs of sneakers owned. The results are as follows:

| X | Frequency |
|---|---|
| 1 | 2 |
| 2 | 5 |
| 3 | 8 |
| 4 | 12 |
| 5 | 12 |
| 6 | 0 |
| 7 | 1 |

Table 2.76

a. Find the sample mean $\bar{x}$
b. Find the sample standard deviation, $s$
c. Construct a histogram of the data.
d. Complete the columns of the chart.
e. Find the first quartile.
f. Find the median.
g. Find the third quartile.
h. What percent of the students owned at least five pairs?
i. Find the 40$^{\text{th}}$ percentile.
j. Find the 90$^{\text{th}}$ percentile.
k. Construct a line graph of the data
l. Construct a stemplot of the data

**99.** Following are the published weights (in pounds) of all of the team members of the San Francisco 49ers from a previous year.

177; 205; 210; 210; 232; 205; 185; 185; 178; 210; 206; 212; 184; 174; 185; 242; 188; 212; 215; 247; 241; 223; 220; 260; 245; 259; 278; 270; 280; 295; 275; 285; 290; 272; 273; 280; 285; 286; 200; 215; 185; 230; 250; 241; 190; 260; 250; 302; 265; 290; 276; 228; 265

a. Organize the data from smallest to largest value.
b. Find the median.
c. Find the first quartile.
d. Find the third quartile.
e. The middle 50% of the weights are from _____ to _____.
f. If our population were all professional football players, would the above data be a sample of weights or the population of weights? Why?
g. If our population included every team member who ever played for the San Francisco 49ers, would the above data be a sample of weights or the population of weights? Why?
h. Assume the population was the San Francisco 49ers. Find:
    i. the population mean, $\mu$.
    ii. the population standard deviation, $\sigma$.
    iii. the weight that is two standard deviations below the mean.
    iv. When Steve Young, quarterback, played football, he weighed 205 pounds. How many standard deviations above or below the mean was he?
i. That same year, the mean weight for the Dallas Cowboys was 240.08 pounds with a standard deviation of 44.38 pounds. Emmit Smith weighed in at 209 pounds. With respect to his team, who was lighter, Smith or Young? How did you determine your answer?

**100.** One hundred teachers attended a seminar on mathematical problem solving. The attitudes of a representative sample of 12 of the teachers were measured before and after the seminar. A positive number for change in attitude indicates that a teacher's attitude toward math became more positive. The 12 change scores are as follows:

3; 8; –1; 2; 0; 5; –3; 1; –1; 6; 5; –2

a. What is the mean change score?
b. What is the standard deviation for this population?
c. What is the median change score?
d. Find the change score that is 2.2 standard deviations below the mean.

**101.** Refer to **Figure 2.25** determine which of the following are true and which are false. Explain your solution to each part in complete sentences.

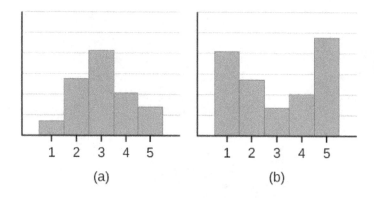

(a)                    (b)

**Figure 2.25**
a. The medians for both graphs are the same.
b. We cannot determine if any of the means for both graphs is different.
c. The standard deviation for graph b is larger than the standard deviation for graph a.
d. We cannot determine if any of the third quartiles for both graphs is different.

**102.** In a recent issue of the *IEEE Spectrum*, 84 engineering conferences were announced. Four conferences lasted two days. Thirty-six lasted three days. Eighteen lasted four days. Nineteen lasted five days. Four lasted six days. One lasted seven days. One lasted eight days. One lasted nine days. Let $X$ = the length (in days) of an engineering conference.

    a. Organize the data in a chart.
    b. Find the median, the first quartile, and the third quartile.
    c. Find the $65^{th}$ percentile.
    d. Find the $10^{th}$ percentile.
    e. The middle 50% of the conferences last from _____ days to _____ days.
    f. Calculate the sample mean of days of engineering conferences.
    g. Calculate the sample standard deviation of days of engineering conferences.
    h. Find the mode.
    i. If you were planning an engineering conference, which would you choose as the length of the conference: mean; median; or mode? Explain why you made that choice.
    j. Give two reasons why you think that three to five days seem to be popular lengths of engineering conferences.

**103.** A survey of enrollment at 35 community colleges across the United States yielded the following figures:

6414; 1550; 2109; 9350; 21828; 4300; 5944; 5722; 2825; 2044; 5481; 5200; 5853; 2750; 10012; 6357; 27000; 9414; 7681; 3200; 17500; 9200; 7380; 18314; 6557; 13713; 17768; 7493; 2771; 2861; 1263; 7285; 28165; 5080; 11622

    a. Organize the data into a chart with five intervals of equal width. Label the two columns "Enrollment" and "Frequency."
    b. Construct a histogram of the data.
    c. If you were to build a new community college, which piece of information would be more valuable: the mode or the mean?
    d. Calculate the sample mean.
    e. Calculate the sample standard deviation.
    f. A school with an enrollment of 8000 would be how many standard deviations away from the mean?

*Use the following information to answer the next two exercises.* $X$ = the number of days per week that 100 clients use a particular exercise facility.

| x | Frequency |
|---|---|
| 0 | 3 |
| 1 | 12 |
| 2 | 33 |
| 3 | 28 |
| 4 | 11 |
| 5 | 9 |
| 6 | 4 |

Table 2.77

**104.** The $80^{th}$ percentile is _____
    a. 5
    b. 80
    c. 3
    d. 4

**105.** The number that is 1.5 standard deviations BELOW the mean is approximately _____
   a.  0.7
   b.  4.8
   c.  −2.8
   d.  Cannot be determined

**106.** Suppose that a publisher conducted a survey asking adult consumers the number of fiction paperback books they had purchased in the previous month. The results are summarized in the Table 2.78.

| # of books | Freq. | Rel. Freq. |
|---|---|---|
| 0 | 18 | |
| 1 | 24 | |
| 2 | 24 | |
| 3 | 22 | |
| 4 | 15 | |
| 5 | 10 | |
| 7 | 5 | |
| 9 | 1 | |

Table 2.78

   a.  Are there any outliers in the data? Use an appropriate numerical test involving the *IQR* to identify outliers, if any, and clearly state your conclusion.
   b.  If a data value is identified as an outlier, what should be done about it?
   c.  Are any data values further than two standard deviations away from the mean? In some situations, statisticians may use this criteria to identify data values that are unusual, compared to the other data values. (Note that this criteria is most appropriate to use for data that is mound-shaped and symmetric, rather than for skewed data.)
   d.  Do parts a and c of this problem give the same answer?
   e.  Examine the shape of the data. Which part, a or c, of this question gives a more appropriate result for this data?
   f.  Based on the shape of the data which is the most appropriate measure of center for this data: mean, median or mode?

# REFERENCES

## 2.1 Display Data

Burbary, Ken. *Facebook Demographics Revisited – 2001 Statistics,* 2011. Available online at http://www.kenburbary.com/2011/03/facebook-demographics-revisited-2011-statistics-2/ (accessed August 21, 2013).

"9th Annual AP Report to the Nation." CollegeBoard, 2013. Available online at http://apreport.collegeboard.org/goals-and-findings/promoting-equity (accessed September 13, 2013).

"Overweight and Obesity: Adult Obesity Facts." Centers for Disease Control and Prevention. Available online at http://www.cdc.gov/obesity/data/adult.html (accessed September 13, 2013).

Data on annual homicides in Detroit, 1961–73, from Gunst & Mason's book 'Regression Analysis and its Application', Marcel Dekker

"Timeline: Guide to the U.S. Presidents: Information on every president's birthplace, political party, term of office, and more." Scholastic, 2013. Available online at http://www.scholastic.com/teachers/article/timeline-guide-us-presidents (accessed April 3, 2013).

"Presidents." Fact Monster. Pearson Education, 2007. Available online at http://www.factmonster.com/ipka/A0194030.html

(accessed April 3, 2013).

"Food Security Statistics." Food and Agriculture Organization of the United Nations. Available online at http://www.fao.org/economic/ess/ess-fs/en/ (accessed April 3, 2013).

"Consumer Price Index." United States Department of Labor: Bureau of Labor Statistics. Available online at http://data.bls.gov/pdq/SurveyOutputServlet (accessed April 3, 2013).

"CO2 emissions (kt)." The World Bank, 2013. Available online at http://databank.worldbank.org/data/home.aspx (accessed April 3, 2013).

"Births Time Series Data." General Register Office For Scotland, 2013. Available online at http://www.gro-scotland.gov.uk/statistics/theme/vital-events/births/time-series.html (accessed April 3, 2013).

"Demographics: Children under the age of 5 years underweight." Indexmundi. Available online at http://www.indexmundi.com/g/r.aspx?t=50&v=2224&aml=en (accessed April 3, 2013).

Gunst, Richard, Robert Mason. *Regression Analysis and Its Application: A Data-Oriented Approach*. CRC Press: 1980.

"Overweight and Obesity: Adult Obesity Facts." Centers for Disease Control and Prevention. Available online at http://www.cdc.gov/obesity/data/adult.html (accessed September 13, 2013).

**2.2 Measures of the Location of the Data**

Cauchon, Dennis, Paul Overberg. "Census data shows minorities now a majority of U.S. births." USA Today, 2012. Available online at http://usatoday30.usatoday.com/news/nation/story/2012-05-17/minority-birthscensus/55029100/1 (accessed April 3, 2013).

Data from the United States Department of Commerce: United States Census Bureau. Available online at http://www.census.gov/ (accessed April 3, 2013).

"1990 Census." United States Department of Commerce: United States Census Bureau. Available online at http://www.census.gov/main/www/cen1990.html (accessed April 3, 2013).

Data from *San Jose Mercury News*.

Data from *Time Magazine*; survey by Yankelovich Partners, Inc.

**2.3 Measures of the Center of the Data**

Data from The World Bank, available online at http://www.worldbank.org (accessed April 3, 2013).

"Demographics: Obesity – adult prevalence rate." Indexmundi. Available online at http://www.indexmundi.com/g/r.aspx?t=50&v=2228&l=en (accessed April 3, 2013).

**2.7 Measures of the Spread of the Data**

Data from Microsoft Bookshelf.

King, Bill."Graphically Speaking." Institutional Research, Lake Tahoe Community College. Available online at http://www.ltcc.edu/web/about/institutional-research (accessed April 3, 2013).

# SOLUTIONS

1

Figure 2.26

3

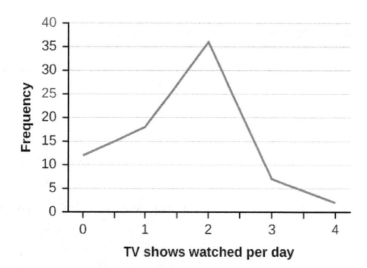

Figure 2.27

5

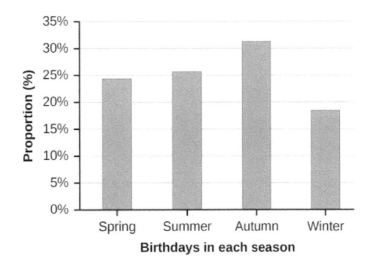

Figure 2.28

7

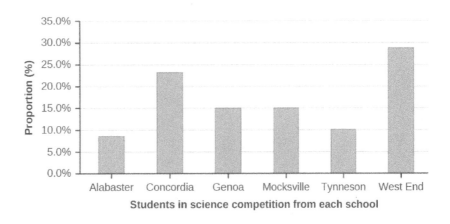

Figure 2.29

**9** 65

**11** The relative frequency shows the *proportion* of data points that have each value. The frequency tells the *number* of data points that have each value.

**13** Answers will vary. One possible histogram is shown:

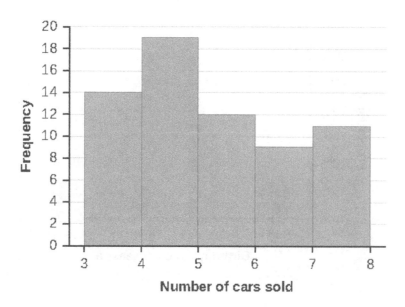

Figure 2.30

**15** Find the midpoint for each class. These will be graphed on the *x*-axis. The frequency values will be graphed on the *y*-axis values.

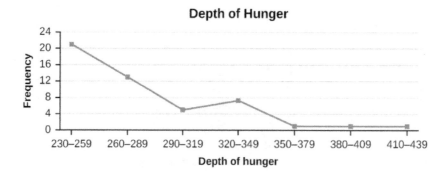

Figure 2.31

**17**

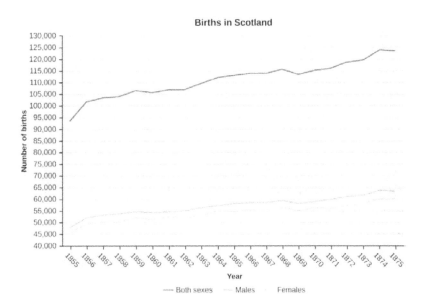

**Figure 2.32**

**19**

a.  The 40<sup>th</sup> percentile is 37 years.

b.  The 78<sup>th</sup> percentile is 70 years.

**21**  Jesse graduated 37<sup>th</sup> out of a class of 180 students. There are $180 - 37 = 143$ students ranked below Jesse. There is one rank of 37. $x = 143$ and $y = 1$. $\frac{x + 0.5y}{n}(100) = \frac{143 + 0.5(1)}{180}(100) = 79.72$. Jesse's rank of 37 puts him at the 80<sup>th</sup> percentile.

**23**

a.  For runners in a race it is more desirable to have a high percentile for speed. A high percentile means a higher speed which is faster.

b.  40% of runners ran at speeds of 7.5 miles per hour or less (slower). 60% of runners ran at speeds of 7.5 miles per hour or more (faster).

**25**  When waiting in line at the DMV, the 85<sup>th</sup> percentile would be a long wait time compared to the other people waiting. 85% of people had shorter wait times than Mina. In this context, Mina would prefer a wait time corresponding to a lower percentile. 85% of people at the DMV waited 32 minutes or less. 15% of people at the DMV waited 32 minutes or longer.

**27**  The manufacturer and the consumer would be upset. This is a large repair cost for the damages, compared to the other cars in the sample. INTERPRETATION: 90% of the crash tested cars had damage repair costs of $1700 or less; only 10% had damage repair costs of $1700 or more.

**29**  You can afford 34% of houses. 66% of the houses are too expensive for your budget. INTERPRETATION: 34% of houses cost $240,000 or less. 66% of houses cost $240,000 or more.

**31**  4

**33**  $6 - 4 = 2$

**35**  6

**37**  Mean: $16 + 17 + 19 + 20 + 20 + 21 + 23 + 24 + 25 + 25 + 25 + 26 + 26 + 27 + 27 + 27 + 28 + 29 + 30 + 32 + 33 + 33 + 34 + 35 + 37 + 39 + 40 = 738$; $\frac{738}{27} = 27.33$

**39**  The most frequent lengths are 25 and 27, which occur three times. Mode = 25, 27

**41** 4

**43** The data are symmetrical. The median is 3 and the mean is 2.85. They are close, and the mode lies close to the middle of the data, so the data are symmetrical.

**45** The data are skewed right. The median is 87.5 and the mean is 88.2. Even though they are close, the mode lies to the left of the middle of the data, and there are many more instances of 87 than any other number, so the data are skewed right.

**47** When the data are symmetrical, the mean and median are close or the same.

**49** The distribution is skewed right because it looks pulled out to the right.

**51** The mean is 4.1 and is slightly greater than the median, which is four.

**53** The mode and the median are the same. In this case, they are both five.

**55** The distribution is skewed left because it looks pulled out to the left.

**57** The mean and the median are both six.

**59** The mode is 12, the median is 13.5, and the mean is 15.1. The mean is the largest.

**61** The mean tends to reflect skewing the most because it is affected the most by outliers.

**63** $s = 34.5$

**65** For Fredo: $z = \dfrac{0.158 - 0.166}{0.012} = -0.67$ For Karl: $z = \dfrac{0.177 - 0.189}{0.015} = -0.8$ Fredo's $z$-score of $-0.67$ is higher than Karl's $z$-score of $-0.8$. For batting average, higher values are better, so Fredo has a better batting average compared to his team.

**67**

a. $s_x = \sqrt{\dfrac{\sum fm^2}{n} - \bar{x}^2} = \sqrt{\dfrac{193157.45}{30} - 79.5^2} = 10.88$

b. $s_x = \sqrt{\dfrac{\sum fm^2}{n} - \bar{x}^2} = \sqrt{\dfrac{380945.3}{101} - 60.94^2} = 7.62$

c. $s_x = \sqrt{\dfrac{\sum fm^2}{n} - \bar{x}^2} = \sqrt{\dfrac{440051.5}{86} - 70.66^2} = 11.14$

**68**

a. Example solution for using the random number generator for the TI-84+ to generate a simple random sample of 8 states. Instructions are as follows.

Number the entries in the table 1–51 (Includes Washington, DC; Numbered vertically)

Press MATH

Arrow over to PRB

Press 5:randInt(

Enter 51,1,8)

Eight numbers are generated (use the right arrow key to scroll through the numbers). The numbers correspond to the numbered states (for this example: {47 21 9 23 51 13 25 4}. If any numbers are repeated, generate a different number by using 5:randInt(51,1)). Here, the states (and Washington DC) are {Arkansas, Washington DC, Idaho, Maryland, Michigan, Mississippi, Virginia, Wyoming}.

Corresponding percents are {30.1, 22.2, 26.5, 27.1, 30.9, 34.0, 26.0, 25.1}.

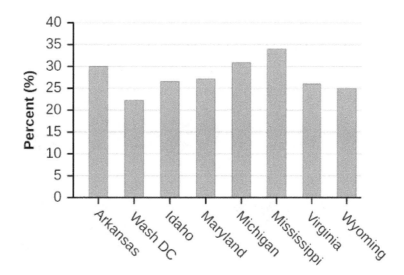

**Figure 2.33**

b.

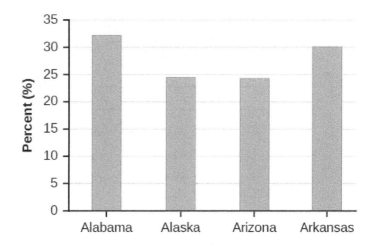

**Figure 2.34**

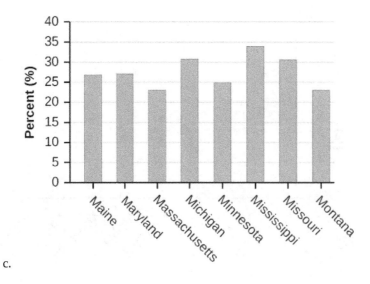

c.

**Figure 2.35**

70

| Amount($) | Frequency | Relative Frequency |
|-----------|-----------|--------------------|
| 51–100    | 5         | 0.08               |
| 101–150   | 10        | 0.17               |
| 151–200   | 15        | 0.25               |
| 201–250   | 15        | 0.25               |
| 251–300   | 10        | 0.17               |
| 301–350   | 5         | 0.08               |

Table 2.79 Singles

| Amount($) | Frequency | Relative Frequency |
|-----------|-----------|--------------------|
| 100–150   | 5         | 0.07               |
| 201–250   | 5         | 0.07               |
| 251–300   | 5         | 0.07               |
| 301–350   | 5         | 0.07               |
| 351–400   | 10        | 0.14               |
| 401–450   | 10        | 0.14               |
| 451–500   | 10        | 0.14               |
| 501–550   | 10        | 0.14               |
| 551–600   | 5         | 0.07               |
| 601–650   | 5         | 0.07               |

Table 2.80 Couples

a.  See Table 2.63 and Table 2.63.

b.  In the following histogram data values that fall on the right boundary are counted in the class interval, while values that fall on the left boundary are not counted (with the exception of the first interval where both boundary values are included).

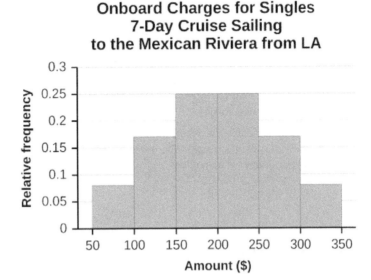

Figure 2.36

c.  In the following histogram, the data values that fall on the right boundary are counted in the class interval, while values that fall on the left boundary are not counted (with the exception of the first interval where values on both boundaries are included).

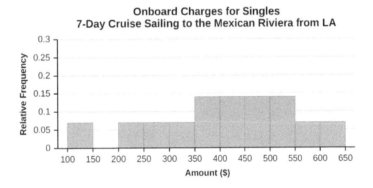

Figure 2.37

d.  Compare the two graphs:

i.  Answers may vary. Possible answers include:

- Both graphs have a single peak.
- Both graphs use class intervals with width equal to $50.

ii.  Answers may vary. Possible answers include:

- The couples graph has a class interval with no values.
- It takes almost twice as many class intervals to display the data for couples.

iii.  Answers may vary. Possible answers include: The graphs are more similar than different because the overall patterns for the graphs are the same.

e.  Check student's solution.

f.  Compare the graph for the Singles with the new graph for the Couples:

    i.    ▪ Both graphs have a single peak.

          ▪ Both graphs display 6 class intervals.

          ▪ Both graphs show the same general pattern.

    ii.  Answers may vary. Possible answers include: Although the width of the class intervals for couples is double that of the class intervals for singles, the graphs are more similar than they are different.

g.  Answers may vary. Possible answers include: You are able to compare the graphs interval by interval. It is easier to compare the overall patterns with the new scale on the Couples graph. Because a couple represents two individuals, the new scale leads to a more accurate comparison.

h.  Answers may vary. Possible answers include: Based on the histograms, it seems that spending does not vary much from singles to individuals who are part of a couple. The overall patterns are the same. The range of spending for couples is approximately double the range for individuals.

**72** c

**74** Answers will vary.

**76**

a.  $1 - (0.02+0.09+0.19+0.26+0.18+0.17+0.02+0.01) = 0.06$

b.  $0.19+0.26+0.18 = 0.63$

c.  Check student's solution.

d.  $40^{th}$ percentile will fall between 30,000 and 40,000

    $80^{th}$ percentile will fall between 50,000 and 75,000

e.  Check student's solution.

**78** The mean percentage, $\bar{x} = \dfrac{1328.65}{50} = 26.75$

**80** The median value is the middle value in the ordered list of data values. The median value of a set of 11 will be the 6th number in order. Six years will have totals at or below the median.

**82** 474 FTES

**84** 919

**86**

- mean = 1,809.3

- median = 1,812.5

- standard deviation = 151.2

- first quartile = 1,690

- third quartile = 1,935

- $IQR = 245$

**87** Hint: Think about the number of years covered by each time period and what happened to higher education during those periods.

**89** For pianos, the cost of the piano is 0.4 standard deviations BELOW the mean. For guitars, the cost of the guitar is 0.25 standard deviations ABOVE the mean. For drums, the cost of the drum set is 1.0 standard deviations BELOW the mean. Of the three, the drums cost the lowest in comparison to the cost of other instruments of the same type. The guitar costs the most in comparison to the cost of other instruments of the same type.

**91**

- $\overline{x} = 23.32$

- Using the TI 83/84, we obtain a standard deviation of: $s_x = 12.95$.

- The obesity rate of the United States is 10.58% higher than the average obesity rate.

- Since the standard deviation is 12.95, we see that $23.32 + 12.95 = 36.27$ is the obesity percentage that is one standard deviation from the mean. The United States obesity rate is slightly less than one standard deviation from the mean. Therefore, we can assume that the United States, while 34% obese, does not have an unusually high percentage of obese people.

**94** a

**96** b

**97**

a. 1.48

b. 1.12

**99**

a. 174; 177; 178; 184; 185; 185; 185; 185; 188; 190; 200; 205; 205; 206; 210; 210; 210; 212; 212; 215; 215; 220; 223; 228; 230; 232; 241; 241; 242; 245; 247; 250; 250; 259; 260; 260; 265; 265; 270; 272; 273; 275; 276; 278; 280; 280; 285; 285; 286; 290; 290; 295; 302

b. 241

c. 205.5

d. 272.5

e. 205.5, 272.5

f. sample

g. population

h.   i. 236.34

    ii. 37.50

    iii. 161.34

    iv. 0.84 std. dev. below the mean

i. Young

**101**

a. True

b. True

c. True

d. False

**103**

a.

| Enrollment | Frequency |
|------------|-----------|
| 1000-5000 | 10 |
| 5000-10000 | 16 |
| 10000-15000 | 3 |
| 15000-20000 | 3 |

Table 2.81

| Enrollment | Frequency |
|------------|-----------|
| 20000-25000 | 1 |
| 25000-30000 | 2 |

Table 2.81

b. Check student's solution.

c. mode

d. 8628.74

e. 6943.88

f. −0.09

**105** a

# 3 | PROBABILITY TOPICS

**Figure 3.1** Meteor showers are rare, but the probability of them occurring can be calculated. (credit: Navicore/flickr)

## Introduction

It is often necessary to "guess" about the outcome of an event in order to make a decision. Politicians study polls to guess their likelihood of winning an election. Teachers choose a particular course of study based on what they think students can comprehend. Doctors choose the treatments needed for various diseases based on their assessment of likely results. You may have visited a casino where people play games chosen because of the belief that the likelihood of winning is good. You may have chosen your course of study based on the probable availability of jobs.

You have, more than likely, used probability. In fact, you probably have an intuitive sense of probability. Probability deals with the chance of an event occurring. Whenever you weigh the odds of whether or not to do your homework or to study for an exam, you are using probability. In this chapter, you will learn how to solve probability problems using a systematic approach.

## 3.1 | Terminology

Probability is a measure that is associated with how certain we are of outcomes of a particular experiment or activity. An **experiment** is a planned operation carried out under controlled conditions. If the result is not predetermined, then the experiment is said to be a **chance** experiment. Flipping one fair coin twice is an example of an experiment.

A result of an experiment is called an **outcome**. The **sample space** of an experiment is the set of all possible outcomes. Three ways to represent a sample space are: to list the possible outcomes, to create a tree diagram, or to create a Venn diagram. The uppercase letter $S$ is used to denote the sample space. For example, if you flip one fair coin, $S = \{H, T\}$ where $H$ = heads and $T$ = tails are the outcomes.

An **event** is any combination of outcomes. Upper case letters like $A$ and $B$ represent events. For example, if the experiment is to flip one fair coin, event $A$ might be getting at most one head. The probability of an event $A$ is written $P(A)$.

The **probability** of any outcome is the **long-term relative frequency** of that outcome. **Probabilities are between zero and one, inclusive** (that is, zero and one and all numbers between these values). $P(A) = 0$ means the event $A$ can never happen. $P(A) = 1$ means the event $A$ always happens. $P(A) = 0.5$ means the event $A$ is equally likely to occur or not to occur. For example, if you flip one fair coin repeatedly (from 20 to 2,000 to 20,000 times) the relative frequency of heads approaches

0.5 (the probability of heads).

**Equally likely** means that each outcome of an experiment occurs with equal probability. For example, if you toss a **fair**, six-sided die, each face (1, 2, 3, 4, 5, or 6) is as likely to occur as any other face. If you toss a fair coin, a Head (*H*) and a Tail (*T*) are equally likely to occur. If you randomly guess the answer to a true/false question on an exam, you are equally likely to select a correct answer or an incorrect answer.

**To calculate the probability of an event *A* when all outcomes in the sample space are equally likely**, count the number of outcomes for event *A* and divide by the total number of outcomes in the sample space. For example, if you toss a fair dime and a fair nickel, the sample space is {*HH, TH, HT, TT*} where *T* = tails and *H* = heads. The sample space has four outcomes. *A* = getting one head. There are two outcomes that meet this condition {*HT, TH*}, so $P(A) = \frac{2}{4} = 0.5$.

Suppose you roll one fair six-sided die, with the numbers {1, 2, 3, 4, 5, 6} on its faces. Let event *E* = rolling a number that is at least five. There are two outcomes {5, 6}. $P(E) = \frac{2}{6}$. If you were to roll the die only a few times, you would not be surprised if your observed results did not match the probability. If you were to roll the die a very large number of times, you would expect that, overall, $\frac{2}{6}$ of the rolls would result in an outcome of "at least five". You would not expect exactly $\frac{2}{6}$.

The long-term relative frequency of obtaining this result would approach the theoretical probability of $\frac{2}{6}$ as the number of repetitions grows larger and larger.

This important characteristic of probability experiments is known as the **law of large numbers** which states that as the number of repetitions of an experiment is increased, the relative frequency obtained in the experiment tends to become closer and closer to the theoretical probability. Even though the outcomes do not happen according to any set pattern or order, overall, the long-term observed relative frequency will approach the theoretical probability. (The word **empirical** is often used instead of the word observed.)

It is important to realize that in many situations, the outcomes are not equally likely. A coin or die may be **unfair**, or **biased**. Two math professors in Europe had their statistics students test the Belgian one Euro coin and discovered that in 250 trials, a head was obtained 56% of the time and a tail was obtained 44% of the time. The data seem to show that the coin is not a fair coin; more repetitions would be helpful to draw a more accurate conclusion about such bias. Some dice may be biased. Look at the dice in a game you have at home; the spots on each face are usually small holes carved out and then painted to make the spots visible. Your dice may or may not be biased; it is possible that the outcomes may be affected by the slight weight differences due to the different numbers of holes in the faces. Gambling casinos make a lot of money depending on outcomes from rolling dice, so casino dice are made differently to eliminate bias. Casino dice have flat faces; the holes are completely filled with paint having the same density as the material that the dice are made out of so that each face is equally likely to occur. Later we will learn techniques to use to work with probabilities for events that are not equally likely.

### " ∪ " Event: The Union

An outcome is in the event *A* ∪ *B* if the outcome is in *A* or is in *B* or is in both *A* and *B*. For example, let *A* = {1, 2, 3, 4, 5} and *B* = {4, 5, 6, 7, 8}. *A* ∪ *B* = {1, 2, 3, 4, 5, 6, 7, 8}. Notice that 4 and 5 are NOT listed twice.

### " ∩ " Event: The Intersection

An outcome is in the event *A* ∩ *B* if the outcome is in both *A* and *B* at the same time. For example, let *A* and *B* be {1, 2, 3, 4, 5} and {4, 5, 6, 7, 8}, respectively. Then *A* ∩ *B* = {4, 5}.

The **complement** of event *A* is denoted *A′* (read "*A* prime"). *A′* consists of all outcomes that are **NOT** in *A*. Notice that *P*(*A*) + *P*(*A′*) = 1. For example, let *S* = {1, 2, 3, 4, 5, 6} and let *A* = {1, 2, 3, 4}. Then, *A′* = {5, 6}. $P(A) = \frac{4}{6}$, $P(A') = \frac{2}{6}$, and

$$P(A) + P(A') = \frac{4}{6} + \frac{2}{6} = 1$$

The **conditional probability** of *A* given *B* is written *P*(*A* | *B*). *P*(*A* | *B*) is the probability that event *A* will occur given that the event *B* has already occurred. **A conditional reduces the sample space**. We calculate the probability of *A* from the reduced sample space *B*. The formula to calculate *P*(*A* | *B*) is $P(A \mid B) = \frac{P(A \cap B)}{P(B)}$ where *P*(*B*) is greater than zero.

For example, suppose we toss one fair, six-sided die. The sample space *S* = {1, 2, 3, 4, 5, 6}. Let *A* = face is 2 or 3 and *B* =

face is even (2, 4, 6). To calculate $P(A \mid B)$, we count the number of outcomes 2 or 3 in the sample space $B = \{2, 4, 6\}$. Then we divide that by the number of outcomes $B$ (rather than $S$).

We get the same result by using the formula. Remember that $S$ has six outcomes.

$$P(A \mid B) = \frac{P(A \cap B)}{P(B)} = \frac{\frac{\text{(the number of outcomes that are 2 or 3 and even in } S)}{6}}{\frac{\text{(the number of outcomes that are even in } S)}{6}} = \frac{\frac{1}{6}}{\frac{3}{6}} = \frac{1}{3}$$

## Odds

The odds of an event presents the probability as a ratio of success to failure. This is common in various gambling formats. Mathematically, the odds of an event can be defined as:

$$\frac{P(A)}{1 - P(A)}$$

where $P(A)$ is the probability of success and of course $1 - P(A)$ is the probability of failure. Odds are always quoted as "numerator to denominator," e.g. 2 to 1. Here the probability of winning is twice that of losing; thus, the probability of winning is 0.66. A probability of winning of 0.60 would generate odds in favor of winning of 3 to 2. While the calculation of odds can be useful in gambling venues in determining payoff amounts, it is not helpful for understanding probability or statistical theory.

## Understanding Terminology and Symbols

It is important to read each problem carefully to think about and understand what the events are. Understanding the wording is the first very important step in solving probability problems. Reread the problem several times if necessary. Clearly identify the event of interest. Determine whether there is a condition stated in the wording that would indicate that the probability is conditional; carefully identify the condition, if any.

### Example 3.1

The sample space $S$ is the whole numbers starting at one and less than 20.

a. $S = $ _____
   Let event $A$ = the even numbers and event $B$ = numbers greater than 13.

b. $A = $ _____, $B = $ _____

c. $P(A) = $ _____, $P(B) = $ _____

d. $A \cap B = $ _____, $A$ OR $B = $ _____

e. $P(A \cap B) = $ _____, $P(A \cup B) = $ _____

f. $A' = $ _____, $P(A') = $ _____

g. $P(A) + P(A') = $ _____

h. $P(A \mid B) = $ _____, $P(B \mid A) = $ _____; are the probabilities equal?

### Solution 3.1

a. $S = \{1, 2, 3, 4, 5, 6, 7, 8, 9, 10, 11, 12, 13, 14, 15, 16, 17, 18, 19\}$

b. $A = \{2, 4, 6, 8, 10, 12, 14, 16, 18\}$, $B = \{14, 15, 16, 17, 18, 19\}$

c. $P(A) = \frac{9}{19}$, $P(B) = \frac{6}{19}$

d. $A \cap B = \{14, 16, 18\}$, $A$ OR $B = \{2, 4, 6, 8, 10, 12, 14, 15, 16, 17, 18, 19\}$

e. $P(A \cap B) = \frac{3}{19}$, $P(A \cup B) = \frac{12}{19}$

f. $A' = 1, 3, 5, 7, 9, 11, 13, 15, 17, 19$; $P(A') = \frac{10}{19}$

g. $P(A) + P(A') = 1$ ( $\frac{9}{19} + \frac{10}{19} = 1$ )

h. $P(A \mid B) = \frac{P(A \cap B)}{P(B)} = \frac{3}{6}$, $P(B \mid A) = \frac{P(A \cap B)}{P(A)} = \frac{3}{9}$, No

## Try It Σ

**3.1** The sample space $S$ is all the ordered pairs of two whole numbers, the first from one to three and the second from one to four (Example: (1, 4)).

a. $S =$ _____

Let event $A$ = the sum is even and event $B$ = the first number is prime.

b. $A =$ _____, $B =$ _____

c. $P(A) =$ _____, $P(B) =$ _____

d. $A \cap B =$ _____, $A \cup B =$ _____

e. $P(A \cap B) =$ _____, $P(A \cup B) =$ _____

f. $B' =$ _____, $P(B') =$ _____

g. $P(A) + P(A') =$ _____

h. $P(A \mid B) =$ _____, $P(B \mid A) =$ _____; are the probabilities equal?

## Example 3.2

A fair, six-sided die is rolled. Describe the sample space $S$, identify each of the following events with a subset of $S$ and compute its probability (an outcome is the number of dots that show up).

a. Event $T$ = the outcome is two.

b. Event $A$ = the outcome is an even number.

c. Event $B$ = the outcome is less than four.

d. The complement of $A$.

e. $A \mid B$

f. $B \mid A$

g. $A \cap B$

h. $A \cup B$

i. $A \cup B'$

j. Event $N$ = the outcome is a prime number.

k. Event $I$ = the outcome is seven.

### Solution 3.2

a. $T = \{2\}$, $P(T) = \frac{1}{6}$

b. $A = \{2, 4, 6\}$, $P(A) = \frac{1}{2}$

c. $B = \{1, 2, 3\}$, $P(B) = \frac{1}{2}$

d. $A' = \{1, 3, 5\}$, $P(A') = \frac{1}{2}$

e. $A \mid B = \{2\}$, $P(A \mid B) = \frac{1}{3}$

f. $B \mid A = \{2\}$, $P(B \mid A) = \frac{1}{3}$

g. $A \cap B = \{2\}$, $P(A \cap B) = \frac{1}{6}$

h. $A \cup B = \{1, 2, 3, 4, 6\}$, $P(A \cup B) = \frac{5}{6}$

i. $A \cup B' = \{2, 4, 5, 6\}$, $P(A \cup B') = \frac{2}{3}$

j. $N = \{2, 3, 5\}$, $P(N) = \frac{1}{2}$

k. A six-sided die does not have seven dots. $P(7) = 0$.

## Example 3.3

Table 3.1 describes the distribution of a random sample $S$ of 100 individuals, organized by gender and whether they are right- or left-handed.

|  | Right-handed | Left-handed |
|---|---|---|
| Males | 43 | 9 |
| Females | 44 | 4 |

Table 3.1

Let's denote the events $M$ = the subject is male, $F$ = the subject is female, $R$ = the subject is right-handed, $L$ = the subject is left-handed. Compute the following probabilities:

a. $P(M)$

b. $P(F)$

c. $P(R)$

d. $P(L)$

e. $P(M \cap R)$

f. $P(F \cap L)$

g. $P(M \cup F)$

h. $P(M \cup R)$

i. $P(F \cup L)$

j. $P(M')$

   k.  $P(R\,|\,M)$

   l.  $P(F\,|\,L)$

   m.  $P(L\,|\,F)$

**Solution 3.3**
   a.  $P(M) = 0.52$

   b.  $P(F) = 0.48$

   c.  $P(R) = 0.87$

   d.  $P(L) = 0.13$

   e.  $P(M \cap R) = 0.43$

   f.  $P(F \cap L) = 0.04$

   g.  $P(M \cup F) = 1$

   h.  $P(M \cup R) = 0.96$

   i.  $P(F \cup L) = 0.57$

   j.  $P(M') = 0.48$

   k.  $P(R\,|\,M) = 0.8269$ (rounded to four decimal places)

   l.  $P(F\,|\,L) = 0.3077$ (rounded to four decimal places)

   m.  $P(L\,|\,F) = 0.0833$

# 3.2 | Independent and Mutually Exclusive Events

Independent and mutually exclusive do **not** mean the same thing.

## Independent Events

Two events are independent if one of the following are true:

- $P(A|B) = P(A)$

- $P(B|A) = P(B)$

- $P(A \cap B) = P(A)P(B)$

Two events $A$ and $B$ are **independent** if the knowledge that one occurred does not affect the chance the other occurs. For example, the outcomes of two roles of a fair die are independent events. The outcome of the first roll does not change the probability for the outcome of the second roll. To show two events are independent, you must show **only one** of the above conditions. If two events are NOT independent, then we say that they are **dependent**.

Sampling may be done **with replacement** or **without replacement**.

- **With replacement**: If each member of a population is replaced after it is picked, then that member has the possibility of being chosen more than once. When sampling is done with replacement, then events are considered to be independent, meaning the result of the first pick will not change the probabilities for the second pick.

- **Without replacement**: When sampling is done without replacement, each member of a population may be chosen only once. In this case, the probabilities for the second pick are affected by the result of the first pick. The events are considered to be dependent or not independent.

If it is not known whether $A$ and $B$ are independent or dependent, **assume they are dependent until you can show otherwise**.

## Example 3.4

You have a fair, well-shuffled deck of 52 cards. It consists of four suits. The suits are clubs, diamonds, hearts and spades. There are 13 cards in each suit consisting of 1, 2, 3, 4, 5, 6, 7, 8, 9, 10, J (jack), Q (queen), K (king) of that suit.

a. Sampling with replacement:
Suppose you pick three cards with replacement. The first card you pick out of the 52 cards is the Q of spades. You put this card back, reshuffle the cards and pick a second card from the 52-card deck. It is the ten of clubs. You put this card back, reshuffle the cards and pick a third card from the 52-card deck. This time, the card is the Q of spades again. Your picks are {Q of spades, ten of clubs, Q of spades}. You have picked the Q of spades twice. You pick each card from the 52-card deck.

b. Sampling without replacement:
Suppose you pick three cards without replacement. The first card you pick out of the 52 cards is the K of hearts. You put this card aside and pick the second card from the 51 cards remaining in the deck. It is the three of diamonds. You put this card aside and pick the third card from the remaining 50 cards in the deck. The third card is the J of spades. Your picks are {K of hearts, three of diamonds, J of spades}. Because you have picked the cards without replacement, you cannot pick the same card twice. The probability of picking the three of diamonds is called a conditional probability because it is conditioned on what was picked first. This is true also of the probability of picking the J of spades. The probability of picking the J of spades is actually conditioned on *both* the previous picks.

## Try It Σ

**3.4** You have a fair, well-shuffled deck of 52 cards. It consists of four suits. The suits are clubs, diamonds, hearts and spades. There are 13 cards in each suit consisting of 1, 2, 3, 4, 5, 6, 7, 8, 9, 10, J (jack), Q (queen), K (king) of that suit. Three cards are picked at random.

a. Suppose you know that the picked cards are Q of spades, K of hearts and Q of spades. Can you decide if the sampling was with or without replacement?

b. Suppose you know that the picked cards are Q of spades, K of hearts, and J of spades. Can you decide if the sampling was with or without replacement?

## Example 3.5

You have a fair, well-shuffled deck of 52 cards. It consists of four suits. The suits are clubs, diamonds, hearts, and spades. There are 13 cards in each suit consisting of 1, 2, 3, 4, 5, 6, 7, 8, 9, 10, J (jack), Q (queen), and K (king) of that suit. S = spades, H = Hearts, D = Diamonds, C = Clubs.

a. Suppose you pick four cards, but do not put any cards back into the deck. Your cards are QS, 1D, 1C, QD.

b. Suppose you pick four cards and put each card back before you pick the next card. Your cards are KH, 7D, 6D, KH.

Which of a. or b. did you sample with replacement and which did you sample without replacement?

### Solution 3.5

a. Without replacement; b. With replacement

**3.5** You have a fair, well-shuffled deck of 52 cards. It consists of four suits. The suits are clubs, diamonds, hearts, and spades. There are 13 cards in each suit consisting of 1, 2, 3, 4, 5, 6, 7, 8, 9, 10, $J$ (jack), $Q$ (queen), and $K$ (king) of that suit. $S$ = spades, $H$ = Hearts, $D$ = Diamonds, $C$ = Clubs. Suppose that you sample four cards without replacement. Which of the following outcomes are possible? Answer the same question for sampling with replacement.

a. $QS, 1D, 1C, QD$

b. $KH, 7D, 6D, KH$

c. $QS, 7D, 6D, KS$

## Mutually Exclusive Events

$A$ and $B$ are **mutually exclusive** events if they cannot occur at the same time. Said another way, If $A$ occurred then $B$ cannot occur and vise-a-versa. This means that $A$ and $B$ do not share any outcomes and $P(A \cap B) = 0$.

For example, suppose the sample space $S$ = {1, 2, 3, 4, 5, 6, 7, 8, 9, 10}. Let $A$ = {1, 2, 3, 4, 5}, $B$ = {4, 5, 6, 7, 8}, and $C$ = {7, 9}. $A \cap B$ = {4, 5}. $P(A \cap B) = \frac{2}{10}$ and is not equal to zero. Therefore, $A$ and $B$ are not mutually exclusive. $A$ and $C$ do not have any numbers in common so $P(A \cap C) = 0$. Therefore, $A$ and $C$ are mutually exclusive.

If it is not known whether $A$ and $B$ are mutually exclusive, **assume they are not until you can show otherwise**. The following examples illustrate these definitions and terms.

## Example 3.6

Flip two fair coins. (This is an experiment.)

The sample space is {*HH, HT, TH, TT*} where *T* = tails and *H* = heads. The outcomes are *HH, HT, TH,* and *TT*. The outcomes HT and TH are different. The *HT* means that the first coin showed heads and the second coin showed tails. The *TH* means that the first coin showed tails and the second coin showed heads.

- Let *A* = the event of getting **at most one tail**. (At most one tail means zero or one tail.) Then *A* can be written as {*HH, HT, TH*}. The outcome *HH* shows zero tails. *HT* and *TH* each show one tail.

- Let *B* = the event of getting all tails. *B* can be written as {*TT*}. *B* is the **complement** of *A*, so *B* = *A'*. Also, *P*(*A*) + *P*(*B*) = *P*(*A*) + *P*(*A'*) = 1.

- The probabilities for *A* and for *B* are $P(A) = \frac{3}{4}$ and $P(B) = \frac{1}{4}$.

- Let *C* = the event of getting all heads. *C* = {*HH*}. Since *B* = {*TT*}, $P(B \cap C) = 0$. *B* and *C* are mutually exclusive. (*B* and *C* have no members in common because you cannot have all tails and all heads at the same time.)

- Let *D* = event of getting **more than one** tail. *D* = {*TT*}. $P(D) = \frac{1}{4}$

- Let *E* = event of getting a head on the first roll. (This implies you can get either a head or tail on the second roll.) *E* = {*HT, HH*}. $P(E) = \frac{2}{4}$

- Find the probability of getting **at least one** (one or two) tail in two flips. Let *F* = event of getting at least one tail in two flips. *F* = {*HT, TH, TT*}. $P(F) = \frac{3}{4}$

## Try It Σ

**3.6** Draw two cards from a standard 52-card deck with replacement. Find the probability of getting at least one black card.

## Example 3.7

Flip two fair coins. Find the probabilities of the events.

a. Let *F* = the event of getting at most one tail (zero or one tail).

b. Let *G* = the event of getting two faces that are the same.

c. Let *H* = the event of getting a head on the first flip followed by a head or tail on the second flip.

d. Are *F* and *G* mutually exclusive?

e. Let *J* = the event of getting all tails. Are *J* and *H* mutually exclusive?

**Solution 3.7**

Look at the sample space in Example 3.6.

a. Zero (0) or one (1) tails occur when the outcomes *HH, TH, HT* show up. $P(F) = \frac{3}{4}$

b. Two faces are the same if *HH* or *TT* show up. $P(G) = \frac{2}{4}$

c. A head on the first flip followed by a head or tail on the second flip occurs when *HH* or *HT* show up. *P*(*H*)

$= \frac{2}{4}$

   d.  *F* and *G* share *HH* so $P(F \cap G)$ is not equal to zero (0). *F* and *G* are not mutually exclusive.

   e.  Getting all tails occurs when tails shows up on both coins (*TT*). *H*'s outcomes are *HH* and *HT*.

*J* and *H* have nothing in common so $P(J \cap H) = 0$. *J* and *H* are mutually exclusive.

## Try It Σ

**3.7** A box has two balls, one white and one red. We select one ball, put it back in the box, and select a second ball (sampling with replacement). Find the probability of the following events:

   a.  Let *F* = the event of getting the white ball twice.

   b.  Let *G* = the event of getting two balls of different colors.

   c.  Let *H* = the event of getting white on the first pick.

   d.  Are *F* and *G* mutually exclusive?

   e.  Are *G* and *H* mutually exclusive?

## Example 3.8

Roll one fair, six-sided die. The sample space is {1, 2, 3, 4, 5, 6}. Let event *A* = a face is odd. Then *A* = {1, 3, 5}. Let event *B* = a face is even. Then *B* = {2, 4, 6}.

- Find the complement of *A*, *A'*. The complement of *A*, *A'*, is *B* because *A* and *B* together make up the sample space. $P(A) + P(B) = P(A) + P(A') = 1$. Also, $P(A) = \frac{3}{6}$ and $P(B) = \frac{3}{6}$.

- Let event *C* = odd faces larger than two. Then *C* = {3, 5}. Let event *D* = all even faces smaller than five. Then *D* = {2, 4}. $P(C \cap D) = 0$ because you cannot have an odd and even face at the same time. Therefore, *C* and *D* are mutually exclusive events.

- Let event *E* = all faces less than five. *E* = {1, 2, 3, 4}.

Are *C* and *E* mutually exclusive events? (Answer yes or no.) Why or why not?

**Solution 3.8**

No. *C* = {3, 5} and *E* = {1, 2, 3, 4}. $P\left(C \cap E\right) = \frac{1}{6}$. To be mutually exclusive, $P(C \cap E)$ must be zero.

- Find $P(C|A)$. This is a conditional probability. Recall that the event *C* is {3, 5} and event *A* is {1, 3, 5}. To find $P(C|A)$, find the probability of *C* using the sample space *A*. You have reduced the sample space from the original sample space {1, 2, 3, 4, 5, 6} to {1, 3, 5}. So, $P\left(C|A\right) = \frac{2}{3}$.

## Try It Σ

**3.8** Let event *A* = learning Spanish. Let event *B* = learning German. Then $A \cap B =$ learning Spanish and German. Suppose $P(A) = 0.4$ and $P(B) = 0.2$. $P(A \cap B) = 0.08$. Are events *A* and *B* independent? Hint: You must show

ONE of the following:

- $P(A|B) = P(A)$

- $P(B|A) = P(B)$

- $P(A \cap B) = P(A)P(B)$

## Example 3.9

Let event $G$ = taking a math class. Let event $H$ = taking a science class. Then, G $\cap$ H = taking a math class and a science class. Suppose $P(G) = 0.6$, $P(H) = 0.5$, and $P(G \cap H) = 0.3$. Are $G$ and $H$ independent?

If $G$ and $H$ are independent, then you must show **ONE** of the following:

- $P(G|H) = P(G)$

- $P(H|G) = P(H)$

- $P(G \cap H) = P(G)P(H)$

### NOTE

**The choice you make depends on the information you have.** You could choose any of the methods here because you have the necessary information.

a. Show that $P(G|H) = P(G)$.

**Solution 3.9**

$$P\left(G\middle|H\right) = \frac{P(G \cap H)}{P(H)} = \frac{0.3}{0.5} = 0.6 = P\left(G\right)$$

b. Show $P(G \cap H) = P(G)P(H)$.

**Solution 3.9**

$$P(G)P(H) = (0.6)(0.5) = 0.3 = P(G \cap H)$$

Since $G$ and $H$ are independent, knowing that a person is taking a science class does not change the chance that he or she is taking a math class. If the two events had not been independent (that is, they are dependent) then knowing that a person is taking a science class would change the chance he or she is taking math. For practice, show that $P(H|G) = P(H)$ to show that $G$ and $H$ are independent events.

## Try It Σ

**3.9** In a bag, there are six red marbles and four green marbles. The red marbles are marked with the numbers 1, 2, 3, 4, 5, and 6. The green marbles are marked with the numbers 1, 2, 3, and 4.

- $R$ = a red marble
- $G$ = a green marble
- $O$ = an odd-numbered marble
- The sample space is $S$ = {R1, R2, R3, R4, R5, R6, G1, G2, G3, G4}.

$S$ has ten outcomes. What is $P(G \cap O)$?

## Example 3.10

Let event $C$ = taking an English class. Let event $D$ = taking a speech class.

Suppose $P(C) = 0.75$, $P(D) = 0.3$, $P(C|D) = 0.75$ and $P(C \cap D) = 0.225$.

Justify your answers to the following questions numerically.

a.  Are $C$ and $D$ independent?

b.  Are $C$ and $D$ mutually exclusive?

c.  What is $P(D|C)$?

### Solution 3.10

a.  Yes, because $P(C|D) = P(C)$.

b.  No, because $P(C \cap D)$ is not equal to zero.

c.  $P\left(D\middle|C\right) = \frac{P(C \cap D)}{P(C)} = \frac{0.225}{0.75} = 0.3$

## Try It Σ

**3.10** A student goes to the library. Let events $B$ = the student checks out a book and $D$ = the student checks out a DVD. Suppose that $P(B) = 0.40$, $P(D) = 0.30$ and $P(B \cap D) = 0.20$.

a.  Find $P(B|D)$.

b.  Find $P(D|B)$.

c.  Are $B$ and $D$ independent?

d.  Are $B$ and $D$ mutually exclusive?

## Example 3.11

In a box there are three red cards and five blue cards. The red cards are marked with the numbers 1, 2, and 3, and the blue cards are marked with the numbers 1, 2, 3, 4, and 5. The cards are well-shuffled. You reach into the box (you cannot see into it) and draw one card.

Let $R$ = red card is drawn, $B$ = blue card is drawn, $E$ = even-numbered card is drawn.

The sample space $S$ = R1, R2, R3, B1, B2, B3, B4, B5. $S$ has eight outcomes.

- $P\left(R\right) = \frac{3}{8}.P\left(B\right) = \frac{5}{8}.P\left(R \cap B\right) = 0$. (You cannot draw one card that is both red and blue.)

- $P(E) = \frac{3}{8}$. (There are three even-numbered cards, R2, B2, and B4.)

- $P(E|B) = \frac{2}{5}$. (There are five blue cards: B1, B2, B3, B4, and B5. Out of the blue cards, there are two even cards; B2 and B4.)

- $P(B|E) = \frac{2}{3}$. (There are three even-numbered cards: R2, B2, and B4. Out of the even-numbered cards, to are blue; B2 and B4.)

- The events R and B are mutually exclusive because $P(R \cap B) = 0$.

- Let G = card with a number greater than 3. G = {B4, B5}. $P(G) = \frac{2}{8}$. Let H = blue card numbered between one and four, inclusive. H = {B1, B2, B3, B4}. $P(G|H) = \frac{1}{4}$. (The only card in H that has a number greater than three is B4.) Since $\frac{2}{8} = \frac{1}{4}$, $P(G) = P(G|H)$, which means that G and H are independent.

**3.11** In a basketball arena,

- 70% of the fans are rooting for the home team.

- 25% of the fans are wearing blue.

- 20% of the fans are wearing blue and are rooting for the away team.

- Of the fans rooting for the away team, 67% are wearing blue.

Let A be the event that a fan is rooting for the away team.
Let B be the event that a fan is wearing blue.
Are the events of rooting for the away team and wearing blue independent? Are they mutually exclusive?

## Example 3.12

In a particular college class, 60% of the students are female. Fifty percent of all students in the class have long hair. Forty-five percent of the students are female and have long hair. Of the female students, 75% have long hair. Let F be the event that a student is female. Let L be the event that a student has long hair. One student is picked randomly. Are the events of being female and having long hair independent?

- The following probabilities are given in this example:

- $P(F)=0.60$; $P(L)=0.50$

- $P(F \cap L) = 0.45$

- $P(L|F) = 0.75$

NOTE

**The choice you make depends on the information you have.** You could use the first or last condition on the list for this example. You do not know $P(F|L)$ yet, so you cannot use the second condition.

**Solution 1**

Check whether $P(F \cap L) = P(F)P(L)$. We are given that $P(F \cap L) = 0.45$, but $P(F)P(L) = (0.60)(0.50) = 0.30$. The events of being female and having long hair are not independent because $P(F \cap L)$ does not equal $P(F)P(L)$.

**Solution 2**

Check whether $P(L|F)$ equals $P(L)$. We are given that $P(L|F) = 0.75$, but $P(L) = 0.50$; they are not equal. The events of being female and having long hair are not independent.

**Interpretation of Results**

The events of being female and having long hair are not independent; knowing that a student is female changes the probability that a student has long hair.

# Try It Σ

**3.12** Mark is deciding which route to take to work. His choices are $I$ = the Interstate and $F$ = Fifth Street.

- $P(I) = 0.44$ and $P(F) = 0.56$

- $P(I \cap F) = 0$ because Mark will take only one route to work.

What is the probability of $P(I \cup F)$?

## Example 3.13

a. Toss one fair coin (the coin has two sides, $H$ and $T$). The outcomes are _____. Count the outcomes. There are ____ outcomes.

b. Toss one fair, six-sided die (the die has 1, 2, 3, 4, 5 or 6 dots on a side). The outcomes are _____. Count the outcomes. There are ____ outcomes.

c. Multiply the two numbers of outcomes. The answer is _____.

d. If you flip one fair coin and follow it with the toss of one fair, six-sided die, the answer to c is the number of outcomes (size of the sample space). What are the outcomes? (Hint: Two of the outcomes are $H1$ and $T6$.)

e. Event $A$ = heads ($H$) on the coin followed by an even number (2, 4, 6) on the die.
$A$ = {_____}. Find $P(A)$.

f. Event $B$ = heads on the coin followed by a three on the die. $B$ = {_____}. Find $P(B)$.

g. Are $A$ and $B$ mutually exclusive? (Hint: What is $P(A \cap B)$? If $P(A \cap B) = 0$, then $A$ and $B$ are mutually exclusive.)

h. Are $A$ and $B$ independent? (Hint: Is $P(A \cap B) = P(A)P(B)$? If $P(A \cap B) = P(A)P(B)$, then $A$ and $B$ are independent. If not, then they are dependent).

**Solution 3.13**

a. $H$ and $T$; 2

b. 1, 2, 3, 4, 5, 6; 6

c. 2(6) = 12

d. $T1, T2, T3, T4, T5, T6, H1, H2, H3, H4, H5, H6$

e. $A$ = {$H2, H4, H6$}; $P(A) = \frac{3}{12}$

f.   $B = \{H3\}$; $P(B) = \frac{1}{12}$

g.   Yes, because $P(A \cap B) = 0$

h.   $P(A \cap B) = 0$. $P(A)P(B) = (\frac{3}{12})$. $P(A \cap B)$ does not equal $P(A)P(B)$, so $A$ and $B$ are dependent.

## Try It Σ

**3.13** A box has two balls, one white and one red. We select one ball, put it back in the box, and select a second ball (sampling with replacement). Let $T$ be the event of getting the white ball twice, $F$ the event of picking the white ball first, $S$ the event of picking the white ball in the second drawing.

a.   Compute $P(T)$.

b.   Compute $P(T|F)$.

c.   Are $T$ and $F$ independent?.

d.   Are $F$ and $S$ mutually exclusive?

e.   Are $F$ and $S$ independent?

# 3.3 | Two Basic Rules of Probability

When calculating probability, there are two rules to consider when determining if two events are independent or dependent and if they are mutually exclusive or not.

## The Multiplication Rule

If $A$ and $B$ are two events defined on a **sample space**, then: $P(A \cap B) = P(B)P(A|B)$. We can think of the intersection symbol as substituting for the word "and".

This rule may also be written as: $P(A|B) = \frac{P(A \cap B)}{P(B)}$

This equation is read as the probability of $A$ given $B$ equals the probability of $A$ and $B$ divided by the probability of $B$.

If $A$ and $B$ are **independent**, then $P(A|B) = P(A)$. Then $P(A \cap B) = P(A|B)P(B)$ becomes $P(A \cap B) = P(A)(B)$ because the $P(A|B) = P(A)$ if $A$ and $B$ are independent.

One easy way to remember the multiplication rule is that the word "and" means that the event has to satisfy two conditions. For example the name drawn from the class roster is to be both a female and a sophomore. It is harder to satisfy two conditions than only one and of course when we multiply fractions the result is always smaller. This reflects the increasing difficulty of satisfying two conditions.

## The Addition Rule

If $A$ and $B$ are defined on a sample space, then: $P(A \cup B) = P(A) + P(B) - P(A \cap B)$. We can think of the union symbol substituting for the word "or". The reason we subtract the intersection of $A$ and $B$ is to keep from double counting elements that are in both $A$ and $B$.

If $A$ and $B$ are **mutually exclusive**, then $P(A \cap B) = 0$. Then $P(A \cup B) = P(A) + P(B) - P(A \cap B)$ becomes $P(A \cup B) = P(A) + P(B)$.

## Example 3.14

Klaus is trying to choose where to go on vacation. His two choices are: $A$ = New Zealand and $B$ = Alaska

- Klaus can only afford one vacation. The probability that he chooses $A$ is $P(A) = 0.6$ and the probability that he chooses $B$ is $P(B) = 0.35$.

- $P(A \cap B) = 0$ because Klaus can only afford to take one vacation

- Therefore, the probability that he chooses either New Zealand or Alaska is $P(A \cup B) = P(A) + P(B) = 0.6 + 0.35 = 0.95$. Note that the probability that he does not choose to go anywhere on vacation must be 0.05.

## Example 3.15

Carlos plays college soccer. He makes a goal 65% of the time he shoots. Carlos is going to attempt two goals in a row in the next game. $A$ = the event Carlos is successful on his first attempt. $P(A) = 0.65$. $B$ = the event Carlos is successful on his second attempt. $P(B) = 0.65$. Carlos tends to shoot in streaks. The probability that he makes the second goal | that he made the first goal is 0.90.

a. What is the probability that he makes both goals?

**Solution 3.15**

a. The problem is asking you to find $P(A \cap B) = P(B \cap A)$. Since $P(B|A) = 0.90$: $P(B \cap A) = P(B|A)$
$P(A) = (0.90)(0.65) = 0.585$

Carlos makes the first and second goals with probability 0.585.

b. What is the probability that Carlos makes either the first goal or the second goal?

**Solution 3.15**

b. The problem is asking you to find $P(A \cup B)$.

$P(A \cup B) = P(A) + P(B) - P(A \cap B) = 0.65 + 0.65 - 0.585 = 0.715$

Carlos makes either the first goal or the second goal with probability 0.715.

c. Are $A$ and $B$ independent?

**Solution 3.15**

c. No, they are not, because $P(B \cap A) = 0.585$.

$P(B)P(A) = (0.65)(0.65) = 0.423$

$0.423 \neq 0.585 = P(B \cap A)$

So, $P(B \cap A)$ is **not** equal to $P(B)P(A)$.

d. Are $A$ and $B$ mutually exclusive?

**Solution 3.15**

d. No, they are not because $P(A \cap B) = 0.585$.

To be mutually exclusive, $P(A \cap B)$ must equal zero.

**3.15** Helen plays basketball. For free throws, she makes the shot 75% of the time. Helen must now attempt two free throws. $C$ = the event that Helen makes the first shot. $P(C) = 0.75$. $D$ = the event Helen makes the second shot. $P(D) = 0.75$. The probability that Helen makes the second free throw given that she made the first is 0.85. What is the probability that Helen makes both free throws?

## Example 3.16

A community swim team has **150** members. **Seventy-five** of the members are advanced swimmers. **Forty-seven** of the members are intermediate swimmers. The remainder are novice swimmers. **Forty** of the advanced swimmers practice four times a week. **Thirty** of the intermediate swimmers practice four times a week. **Ten** of the novice swimmers practice four times a week. Suppose one member of the swim team is chosen randomly.

a. What is the probability that the member is a novice swimmer?

**Solution 3.16**

a. $\frac{28}{150}$

b. What is the probability that the member practices four times a week?

**Solution 3.16**

b. $\frac{80}{150}$

c. What is the probability that the member is an advanced swimmer and practices four times a week?

**Solution 3.16**

c. $\frac{40}{150}$

d. What is the probability that a member is an advanced swimmer and an intermediate swimmer? Are being an advanced swimmer and an intermediate swimmer mutually exclusive? Why or why not?

**Solution 3.16**

d. $P(\text{advanced} \cap \text{intermediate}) = 0$, so these are mutually exclusive events. A swimmer cannot be an advanced swimmer and an intermediate swimmer at the same time.

e. Are being a novice swimmer and practicing four times a week independent events? Why or why not?

**Solution 3.16**

e. No, these are not independent events.
$P(\text{novice} \cap \text{practices four times per week}) = 0.0667$
$P(\text{novice})P(\text{practices four times per week}) = 0.0996$
$0.0667 \neq 0.0996$

## Try It ∑

**3.16** A school has 200 seniors of whom 140 will be going to college next year. Forty will be going directly to work. The remainder are taking a gap year. Fifty of the seniors going to college play sports. Thirty of the seniors going directly to work play sports. Five of the seniors taking a gap year play sports. What is the probability that a senior is taking a gap year?

## Example 3.17

Felicity attends Modesto JC in Modesto, CA. The probability that Felicity enrolls in a math class is 0.2 and the probability that she enrolls in a speech class is 0.65. The probability that she enrolls in a math class | that she enrolls in speech class is 0.25.

Let: $M$ = math class, $S$ = speech class, $M \mid S$ = math given speech

a. What is the probability that Felicity enrolls in math and speech?
Find $P(M \cap S) = P(M \mid S)P(S)$.

b. What is the probability that Felicity enrolls in math or speech classes?
Find $P(M \cup S) = P(M) + P(S) - P(M \cap S)$.

c. Are $M$ and $S$ independent? Is $P(M \mid S) = P(M)$?

d. Are $M$ and $S$ mutually exclusive? Is $P(M \cap S) = 0$?

**Solution 3.17**
a. 0.1625, b. 0.6875, c. No, d. No

**3.17** A student goes to the library. Let events $B$ = the student checks out a book and $D$ = the student check out a DVD. Suppose that $P(B) = 0.40$, $P(D) = 0.30$ and $P(D \mid B) = 0.5$.

a. Find $P(B \cap D)$.

b. Find $P(B \cup D)$.

## Example 3.18

Studies show that about one woman in seven (approximately 14.3%) who live to be 90 will develop breast cancer. Suppose that of those women who develop breast cancer, a test is negative 2% of the time. Also suppose that in the general population of women, the test for breast cancer is negative about 85% of the time. Let $B$ = woman develops breast cancer and let $N$ = tests negative. Suppose one woman is selected at random.

a. What is the probability that the woman develops breast cancer? What is the probability that woman tests negative?

**Solution 3.18**
a. $P(B) = 0.143$; $P(N) = 0.85$

b. Given that the woman has breast cancer, what is the probability that she tests negative?

**Solution 3.18**
b. $P(N \mid B) = 0.02$

c. What is the probability that the woman has breast cancer AND tests negative?

**Solution 3.18**
c. $P(B \cap N) = P(B)P(N \mid B) = (0.143)(0.02) = 0.0029$

d. What is the probability that the woman has breast cancer or tests negative?

**Solution 3.18**

d. $P(B \cup N) = P(B) + P(N) - P(B \cap N) = 0.143 + 0.85 - 0.0029 = 0.9901$

e. Are having breast cancer and testing negative independent events?

**Solution 3.18**

e. No. $P(N) = 0.85$; $P(N|B) = 0.02$. So, $P(N|B)$ does not equal $P(N)$.

f. Are having breast cancer and testing negative mutually exclusive?

**Solution 3.18**

f. No. $P(B \cap N) = 0.0029$. For $B$ and $N$ to be mutually exclusive, $P(B \cap N)$ must be zero.

## Try It Σ

**3.18** A school has 200 seniors of whom 140 will be going to college next year. Forty will be going directly to work. The remainder are taking a gap year. Fifty of the seniors going to college play sports. Thirty of the seniors going directly to work play sports. Five of the seniors taking a gap year play sports. What is the probability that a senior is going to college and plays sports?

## Example 3.19

Refer to the information in **Example 3.18**. $P$ = tests positive.

a. Given that a woman develops breast cancer, what is the probability that she tests positive. Find $P(P|B) = 1 - P(N|B)$.

b. What is the probability that a woman develops breast cancer and tests positive. Find $P(B \cap P) = P(P|B)P(B)$.

c. What is the probability that a woman does not develop breast cancer. Find $P(B') = 1 - P(B)$.

d. What is the probability that a woman tests positive for breast cancer. Find $P(P) = 1 - P(N)$.

**Solution 3.19**

a. 0.98; b. 0.1401; c. 0.857; d. 0.15

## Try It Σ

**3.19** A student goes to the library. Let events $B$ = the student checks out a book and $D$ = the student checks out a DVD. Suppose that $P(B) = 0.40$, $P(D) = 0.30$ and $P(D|B) = 0.5$.

a. Find $P(B')$.

b. Find $P(D \cap B)$.

c. Find $P(B|D)$.

d. Find $P(D \cap B')$.

e.   Find $P(D \mid B')$.

# 3.4 | Contingency Tables and Probability Trees
## Contingency Tables

A **contingency table** provides a way of portraying data that can facilitate calculating probabilities. The table helps in determining conditional probabilities quite easily. The table displays sample values in relation to two different variables that may be dependent or contingent on one another. Later on, we will use contingency tables again, but in another manner.

Suppose a study of speeding violations and drivers who use cell phones produced the following fictional data:

|  | Speeding violation in the last year | No speeding violation in the last year | Total |
|---|---|---|---|
| Cell phone user | 25 | 280 | 305 |
| Not a cell phone user | 45 | 405 | 450 |
| Total | 70 | 685 | 755 |

Table 3.2

The total number of people in the sample is 755. The row totals are 305 and 450. The column totals are 70 and 685. Notice that 305 + 450 = 755 and 70 + 685 = 755.

Calculate the following probabilities using the table.

a. Find $P$(Person is a car phone user).

Solution 3.20

a.   $\dfrac{\text{number of car phone users}}{\text{total number in study}} = \dfrac{305}{755}$

b. Find $P$(person had no violation in the last year).

Solution 3.20

b.   $\dfrac{\text{number that had no violation}}{\text{total number in study}} = \dfrac{685}{755}$

c. Find $P$(Person had no violation in the last year $\cap$ was a car phone user).

Solution 3.20

c.   $\dfrac{280}{755}$

d. Find $P$(Person is a car phone user $\cup$ person had no violation in the last year).

**Solution 3.20**

d. $\left(\frac{305}{755} + \frac{685}{755}\right) - \frac{280}{755} = \frac{710}{755}$

e. Find $P$(Person is a car phone user | person had a violation in the last year).

**Solution 3.20**

e. $\frac{25}{70}$ (The sample space is reduced to the number of persons who had a violation.)

f. Find $P$(Person had no violation last year | person was not a car phone user)

**Solution 3.20**

f. $\frac{405}{450}$ (The sample space is reduced to the number of persons who were not car phone users.)

**3.20** Table 3.3 shows the number of athletes who stretch before exercising and how many had injuries within the past year.

|                   | Injury in last year | No injury in last year | Total |
|-------------------|---------------------|------------------------|-------|
| Stretches         | 55                  | 295                    | 350   |
| Does not stretch  | 231                 | 219                    | 450   |
| Total             | 286                 | 514                    | 800   |

Table 3.3

a.   What is $P$(athlete stretches before exercising)?
b.   What is $P$(athlete stretches before exercising | no injury in the last year)?

## Example 3.21

Table 3.4 shows a random sample of 100 hikers and the areas of hiking they prefer.

| Sex    | The Coastline | Near Lakes and Streams | On Mountain Peaks | Total |
|--------|---------------|------------------------|-------------------|-------|
| Female | 18            | 16                     | ___               | 45    |
| Male   | ___           | ___                    | 14                | 55    |
| Total  | ___           | 41                     | ___               | ___   |

Table 3.4 Hiking Area Preference

a. Complete the table.

**Solution 3.21**

a.

| Sex | The Coastline | Near Lakes and Streams | On Mountain Peaks | Total |
|---|---|---|---|---|
| Female | 18 | 16 | **11** | 45 |
| Male | **16** | **25** | 14 | 55 |
| Total | **34** | 41 | **25** | **100** |

**Table 3.5 Hiking Area Preference**

b. Are the events "being female" and "preferring the coastline" independent events?

Let $F$ = being female and let $C$ = preferring the coastline.

1. Find $P(F \cap C)$.

2. Find $P(F)P(C)$

Are these two numbers the same? If they are, then $F$ and $C$ are independent. If they are not, then $F$ and $C$ are not independent.

**Solution 3.21**

b.

1. $P\left(F \cap C\right) = \frac{18}{100} = 0.18$

2. $P(F)P(C) = \left(\frac{45}{100}\right)\left(\frac{34}{100}\right) = (0.45)(0.34) = 0.153$

$P(F \cap C) \neq P(F)P(C)$, so the events $F$ and $C$ are not independent.

c. Find the probability that a person is male given that the person prefers hiking near lakes and streams. Let $M$ = being male, and let $L$ = prefers hiking near lakes and streams.

1. What word tells you this is a conditional?

2. Fill in the blanks and calculate the probability: $P(\_\_\_ | \_\_\_) = \_\_\_$.

3. Is the sample space for this problem all 100 hikers? If not, what is it?

**Solution 3.21**

c.

1. The word 'given' tells you that this is a conditional.

2. $P(M | L) = \frac{25}{41}$

3. No, the sample space for this problem is the 41 hikers who prefer lakes and streams.

d. Find the probability that a person is female or prefers hiking on mountain peaks. Let $F$ = being female, and let $P$ = prefers mountain peaks.

1. Find $P(F)$.

2. Find $P(P)$.

3. Find $P(F \cap P)$.

4.  Find $P(F \cup P)$.

**Solution 3.21**

d.

1.  $P(F) = \dfrac{45}{100}$

2.  $P(P) = \dfrac{25}{100}$

3.  $P(F \cap P) = \dfrac{11}{100}$

4.  $P(F \cup P) = \dfrac{45}{100} + \dfrac{25}{100} - \dfrac{11}{100} = \dfrac{59}{100}$

# Try It Σ

**3.21** **Table 3.6** shows a random sample of 200 cyclists and the routes they prefer. Let $M$ = males and $H$ = hilly path.

| Gender | Lake Path | Hilly Path | Wooded Path | Total |
|--------|-----------|------------|-------------|-------|
| Female | 45 | 38 | 27 | 110 |
| Male | 26 | 52 | 12 | 90 |
| Total | 71 | 90 | 39 | 200 |

**Table 3.6**

a.  Out of the males, what is the probability that the cyclist prefers a hilly path?

b.  Are the events "being male" and "preferring the hilly path" independent events?

## Example 3.22

Muddy Mouse lives in a cage with three doors. If Muddy goes out the first door, the probability that he gets caught by Alissa the cat is $\dfrac{1}{5}$ and the probability he is not caught is $\dfrac{4}{5}$. If he goes out the second door, the probability he gets caught by Alissa is $\dfrac{1}{4}$ and the probability he is not caught is $\dfrac{3}{4}$. The probability that Alissa catches Muddy coming out of the third door is $\dfrac{1}{2}$ and the probability she does not catch Muddy is $\dfrac{1}{2}$. It is equally likely that Muddy will choose any of the three doors so the probability of choosing each door is $\dfrac{1}{3}$.

| Caught or Not | Door One | Door Two | Door Three | Total |
|---------------|----------|----------|------------|-------|
| Caught | $\dfrac{1}{15}$ | $\dfrac{1}{12}$ | $\dfrac{1}{6}$ | ____ |

**Table 3.7 Door Choice**

| Caught or Not | Door One | Door Two | Door Three | Total |
|---|---|---|---|---|
| Not Caught | $\frac{4}{15}$ | $\frac{3}{12}$ | $\frac{1}{6}$ | —— |
| Total | —— | —— | —— | 1 |

Table 3.7 Door Choice

- The first entry $\frac{1}{15} = \left(\frac{1}{5}\right)\left(\frac{1}{3}\right)$ is $P$(Door One $\cap$ Caught)

- The entry $\frac{4}{15} = \left(\frac{4}{5}\right)\left(\frac{1}{3}\right)$ is $P$(Door One $\cap$ Not Caught)

Verify the remaining entries.

a. Complete the probability contingency table. Calculate the entries for the totals. Verify that the lower-right corner entry is 1.

**Solution 3.22**
a.

| Caught or Not | Door One | Door Two | Door Three | Total |
|---|---|---|---|---|
| Caught | $\frac{1}{15}$ | $\frac{1}{12}$ | $\frac{1}{6}$ | $\frac{19}{60}$ |
| Not Caught | $\frac{4}{15}$ | $\frac{3}{12}$ | $\frac{1}{6}$ | $\frac{41}{60}$ |
| Total | $\frac{5}{15}$ | $\frac{4}{12}$ | $\frac{2}{6}$ | 1 |

Table 3.8 Door Choice

b. What is the probability that Alissa does not catch Muddy?

**Solution 3.22**
b. $\frac{41}{60}$

c. What is the probability that Muddy chooses Door One $\cup$ Door Two given that Muddy is caught by Alissa?

**Solution 3.22**
c. $\frac{9}{19}$

## Example 3.23

Table 3.9 contains the number of crimes per 100,000 inhabitants from 2008 to 2011 in the U.S.

| Year | Robbery | Burglary | Rape | Vehicle | Total |
|------|---------|----------|------|---------|-------|
| 2008 | 145.7 | 732.1 | 29.7 | 314.7 | |
| 2009 | 133.1 | 717.7 | 29.1 | 259.2 | |
| 2010 | 119.3 | 701 | 27.7 | 239.1 | |
| 2011 | 113.7 | 702.2 | 26.8 | 229.6 | |
| Total | | | | | |

**Table 3.9 United States Crime Index Rates Per 100,000 Inhabitants 2008–2011**

TOTAL each column and each row. Total data = 4,520.7

a. Find $P(2009 \cap \text{Robbery})$.

b. Find $P(2010 \cap \text{Burglary})$.

c. Find $P(2010 \cup \text{Burglary})$.

d. Find $P(2011 \mid \text{Rape})$.

e. Find $P(\text{Vehicle} \mid 2008)$.

**Solution 3.23**
a. 0.0294, b. 0.1551, c. 0.7165, d. 0.2365, e. 0.2575

## Try It Σ

**3.23** Table 3.10 relates the weights and heights of a group of individuals participating in an observational study.

| Weight/Height | Tall | Medium | Short | Totals |
|---------------|------|--------|-------|--------|
| Obese | 18 | 28 | 14 | |
| Normal | 20 | 51 | 28 | |
| Underweight | 12 | 25 | 9 | |
| Totals | | | | |

Table 3.10

a. Find the total for each row and column

b. Find the probability that a randomly chosen individual from this group is Tall.

c. Find the probability that a randomly chosen individual from this group is Obese and Tall.

d. Find the probability that a randomly chosen individual from this group is Tall given that the idividual is Obese.

e. Find the probability that a randomly chosen individual from this group is Obese given that the individual is Tall.

f. Find the probability a randomly chosen individual from this group is Tall and Underweight.

g. Are the events Obese and Tall independent?

# Tree Diagrams

Sometimes, when the probability problems are complex, it can be helpful to graph the situation. Tree diagrams can be used to visualize and solve conditional probabilities.

### Tree Diagrams

A **tree diagram** is a special type of graph used to determine the outcomes of an experiment. It consists of "branches" that are labeled with either frequencies or probabilities. Tree diagrams can make some probability problems easier to visualize and solve. The following example illustrates how to use a tree diagram.

## Example 3.24

In an urn, there are 11 balls. Three balls are red ($R$) and eight balls are blue ($B$). Draw two balls, one at a time, **with replacement**. "With replacement" means that you put the first ball back in the urn before you select the second ball. The tree diagram using frequencies that show all the possible outcomes follows.

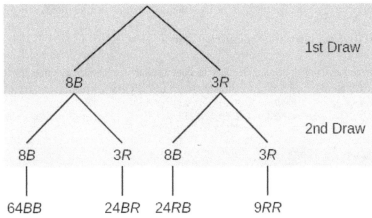

**Figure 3.2**  Total = 64 + 24 + 24 + 9 = 121

The first set of branches represents the first draw. The second set of branches represents the second draw. Each of the outcomes is distinct. In fact, we can list each red ball as $R1$, $R2$, and $R3$ and each blue ball as $B1$, $B2$, $B3$, $B4$, $B5$, $B6$, $B7$, and $B8$. Then the nine $RR$ outcomes can be written as:

$R1R1$; $R1R2$; $R1R3$; $R2R1$; $R2R2$; $R2R3$; $R3R1$; $R3R2$; $R3R3$

The other outcomes are similar.

There are a total of 11 balls in the urn. Draw two balls, one at a time, with replacement. There are 11(11) = 121 outcomes, the size of the **sample space**.

a. List the 24 $BR$ outcomes: $B1R1$, $B1R2$, $B1R3$, ...

**Solution 3.24**
a. $B1R1$; $B1R2$; $B1R3$; $B2R1$; $B2R2$; $B2R3$; $B3R1$; $B3R2$; $B3R3$; $B4R1$; $B4R2$; $B4R3$; $B5R1$; $B5R2$; $B5R3$; $B6R1$; $B6R2$; $B6R3$; $B7R1$; $B7R2$; $B7R3$; $B8R1$; $B8R2$; $B8R3$

b. Using the tree diagram, calculate $P(RR)$.

**Solution 3.24**
b. $P(RR) = \left(\frac{3}{11}\right)\left(\frac{3}{11}\right) = \frac{9}{121}$

c. Using the tree diagram, calculate $P(RB \cup BR)$.

**Solution 3.24**

c. $P(RB \cup BR) = \left(\frac{3}{11}\right)\left(\frac{8}{11}\right) + \left(\frac{8}{11}\right)\left(\frac{3}{11}\right) = \frac{48}{121}$

d. Using the tree diagram, calculate $P(R \text{ on 1st draw} \cap B \text{ on 2nd draw})$.

**Solution 3.24**

d. $P(R \text{ on 1st draw} \cap B \text{ on 2nd draw}) = \left(\frac{3}{11}\right)\left(\frac{8}{11}\right) = \frac{24}{121}$

e. Using the tree diagram, calculate $P(R \text{ on 2nd draw} \mid B \text{ on 1st draw})$.

**Solution 3.24**

e. $P(R \text{ on 2nd draw} \mid B \text{ on 1st draw}) = P(R \text{ on 2nd} \mid B \text{ on 1st}) = \frac{24}{88} = \frac{3}{11}$

This problem is a conditional one. The sample space has been reduced to those outcomes that already have a blue on the first draw. There are $24 + 64 = 88$ possible outcomes (24 *BR* and 64 *BB*). Twenty-four of the 88 possible outcomes are *BR*. $\frac{24}{88} = \frac{3}{11}$.

f. Using the tree diagram, calculate $P(BB)$.

**Solution 3.24**

f. $P(BB) = \frac{64}{121}$

g. Using the tree diagram, calculate $P(B \text{ on the 2nd draw} \mid R \text{ on the first draw})$.

**Solution 3.24**

g. $P(B \text{ on 2nd draw} \mid R \text{ on 1st draw}) = \frac{8}{11}$

There are $9 + 24$ outcomes that have *R* on the first draw (9 *RR* and 24 *RB*). The sample space is then $9 + 24 = 33$. 24 of the 33 outcomes have *B* on the second draw. The probability is then $\frac{24}{33}$.

## Try It Σ

**3.24** In a standard deck, there are 52 cards. 12 cards are face cards (event *F*) and 40 cards are not face cards (event *N*). Draw two cards, one at a time, with replacement. All possible outcomes are shown in the tree diagram as frequencies. Using the tree diagram, calculate $P(FF)$.

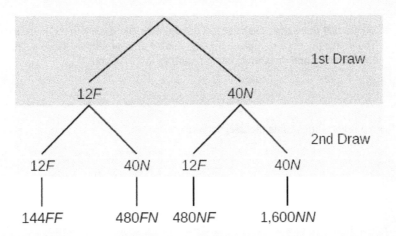

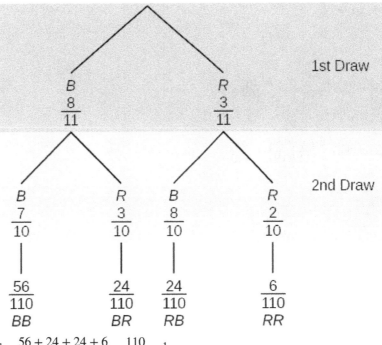

**Figure 3.3**

---

## Example 3.25

An urn has three red marbles and eight blue marbles in it. Draw two marbles, one at a time, this time without replacement, from the urn. **"Without replacement"** means that you do not put the first ball back before you select the second marble. Following is a tree diagram for this situation. The branches are labeled with probabilities instead of frequencies. The numbers at the ends of the branches are calculated by multiplying the numbers on the two corresponding branches, for example, $\left(\frac{3}{11}\right)\left(\frac{2}{10}\right) = \frac{6}{110}$.

**Figure 3.4**  Total = $\frac{56 + 24 + 24 + 6}{110} = \frac{110}{110} = 1$

**NOTE**

If you draw a red on the first draw from the three red possibilities, there are two red marbles left to draw on the second draw. You do not put back or replace the first marble after you have drawn it. You draw **without replacement**, so that on the second draw there are ten marbles left in the urn.

Calculate the following probabilities using the tree diagram.

a. $P(RR) = $ _____

**Solution 3.25**

a. $P(RR) = \left(\frac{3}{11}\right)\left(\frac{2}{10}\right) = \frac{6}{110}$

b. Fill in the blanks:

$P(RB \cup BR) = \left(\frac{3}{11}\right)\left(\frac{8}{10}\right) + (\underline{\quad})(\underline{\quad}) = \frac{48}{110}$

**Solution 3.25**

b. $P(RB \cup BR) = \left(\frac{3}{11}\right)\left(\frac{8}{10}\right) + \left(\frac{8}{11}\right)\left(\frac{3}{10}\right) = \frac{48}{110}$

c. $P(R \text{ on 2nd} \mid B \text{ on 1st}) = $

**Solution 3.25**

c. $P(R \text{ on 2nd} \mid B \text{ on 1st}) = \frac{3}{10}$

d. Fill in the blanks.

$P(R \text{ on 1st} \cap B \text{ on 2nd}) = (\underline{\quad})(\underline{\quad}) = \frac{24}{100}$

**Solution 3.25**

d. $P(R \text{ on 1st} \cap B \text{ on 2nd}) = \left(\frac{3}{11}\right)\left(\frac{8}{10}\right) = \frac{24}{100}$

e. Find $P(BB)$.

**Solution 3.25**

e. $P(BB) = \left(\frac{8}{11}\right)\left(\frac{7}{10}\right)$

f. Find $P(B \text{ on 2nd} \mid R \text{ on 1st})$.

**Solution 3.25**

f. Using the tree diagram, $P(B \text{ on 2nd} \mid R \text{ on 1st}) = P(R \mid B) = \frac{8}{10}$.

If we are using probabilities, we can label the tree in the following general way.

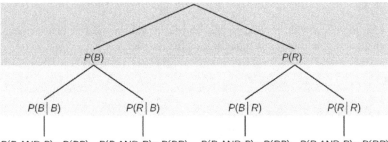

- $P(R \mid R)$ here means $P(R$ on 2nd $\mid R$ on 1st)

- $P(B \mid R)$ here means $P(B$ on 2nd $\mid R$ on 1st)

- $P(R \mid B)$ here means $P(R$ on 2nd $\mid B$ on 1st)

- $P(B \mid B)$ here means $P(B$ on 2nd $\mid B$ on 1st)

**3.25** In a standard deck, there are 52 cards. Twelve cards are face cards ($F$) and 40 cards are not face cards ($N$). Draw two cards, one at a time, without replacement. The tree diagram is labeled with all possible probabilities.

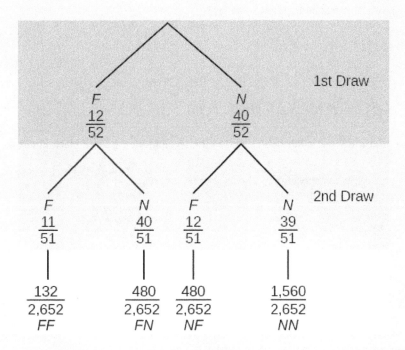

Figure 3.5

a. Find $P(FN \cup NF)$.

b. Find $P(N \mid F)$.

c. Find $P$(at most one face card).
   Hint: "At most one face card" means zero or one face card.

d. Find $P$(at least on face card).
   Hint: "At least one face card" means one or two face cards.

## Example 3.26

A litter of kittens available for adoption at the Humane Society has four tabby kittens and five black kittens. A family comes in and randomly selects two kittens (without replacement) for adoption.

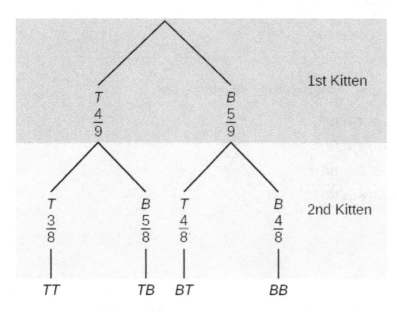

a.   What is the probability that both kittens are tabby?

   a. $\left(\frac{1}{2}\right)\left(\frac{1}{2}\right)$  b. $\left(\frac{4}{9}\right)\left(\frac{4}{9}\right)$  c. $\left(\frac{4}{9}\right)\left(\frac{3}{8}\right)$  d. $\left(\frac{4}{9}\right)\left(\frac{5}{9}\right)$

b.   What is the probability that one kitten of each coloring is selected?

   a. $\left(\frac{4}{9}\right)\left(\frac{5}{9}\right)$  b. $\left(\frac{4}{9}\right)\left(\frac{5}{8}\right)$  c. $\left(\frac{4}{9}\right)\left(\frac{5}{9}\right)+\left(\frac{5}{9}\right)\left(\frac{4}{9}\right)$  d. $\left(\frac{4}{9}\right)\left(\frac{5}{8}\right)+\left(\frac{5}{9}\right)\left(\frac{4}{8}\right)$

c.   What is the probability that a tabby is chosen as the second kitten when a black kitten was chosen as the first?

d.   What is the probability of choosing two kittens of the same color?

**Solution 3.26**

a. c, b. d, c. $\frac{4}{8}$, d. $\frac{32}{72}$

**3.26** Suppose there are four red balls and three yellow balls in a box. Two balls are drawn from the box without replacement. What is the probability that one ball of each coloring is selected?

# 3.5 | Venn Diagrams

## Venn Diagrams

A **Venn diagram** is a picture that represents the outcomes of an experiment. It generally consists of a box that represents the sample space S together with circles or ovals. The circles or ovals represent events. Venn diagrams also help us to convert common English words into mathematical terms that help add precision.

Venn diagrams are named for their inventor, John Venn, a mathematics professor at Cambridge and an Anglican minister. His main work was conducted during the late 1870's and gave rise to a whole branch of mathematics and a new way to approach issues of logic. We will develop the probability rules just covered using this powerful way to demonstrate the probability postulates including the Addition Rule, Multiplication Rule, Complement Rule, Independence, and Conditional Probability.

## Example 3.27

Suppose an experiment has the outcomes 1, 2, 3, ... , 12 where each outcome has an equal chance of occurring. Let event $A$ = {1, 2, 3, 4, 5, 6} and event $B$ = {6, 7, 8, 9}. Then $A$ intersect $B$ = $A \cap B$ = {6} and $A$ union $B$ = $A \cup B$ = {1, 2, 3, 4, 5, 6, 7, 8, 9}.. The Venn diagram is as follows:

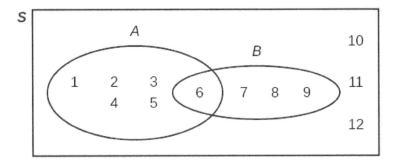

**Figure 3.6**

**Figure 3.6** shows the most basic relationship among these numbers. First, the numbers are in groups called sets; set A and set B. Some number are in both sets; we say in set A ∩ in set B. The English word "and" means inclusive, meaning having the characteristics of both A and B, or in this case, being a part of both A and B. This condition is called the INTERSECTION of the two sets. All members that are part of both sets constitute the intersection of the two sets. The intersection is written as $A \cap B$ where ∩ is the mathematical symbol for intersection. The statement $A \cap B$ is read as "A intersect B." You can remember this by thinking of the intersection of two streets.

There are also those numbers that form a group that, for membership, the number must be in either one or the other group. The number does not have to be in BOTH groups, but instead only in either one of the two. These numbers are called the UNION of the two sets and in this case they are the numbers 1-5 (from A exclusively), 7-9 (from set B exclusively) and also 6, which is in both sets A and B. The symbol for the UNION is ∪ , thus $A \cup B$ = numbers 1-9, but excludes number 10, 11, and 12. The values 10, 11, and 12 are part of the universe, but are not in either of the two sets.

Translating the English word "AND" into the mathematical logic symbol ∩ , intersection, and the word "OR" into the mathematical symbol ∪ , union, provides a very precise way to discuss the issues of probability and logic. The general terminology for the three areas of the Venn diagram in **Figure 3.6** is shown in **Figure 3.7**.

 **Try It**

**3.27** Suppose an experiment has outcomes black, white, red, orange, yellow, green, blue, and purple, where each outcome has an equal chance of occurring. Let event $C$ = {green, blue, purple} and event $P$ = {red, yellow, blue}. Then $C \cap P$ = {blue} and $C \cup P$ = {green, blue, purple, red, yellow} . Draw a Venn diagram representing this situation.

### Example 3.28

Flip two fair coins. Let $A$ = tails on the first coin. Let $B$ = tails on the second coin. Then $A$ = {$TT$, $TH$} and $B$ = {$TT$, $HT$}. Therefore, $A \cap B$ = {TT} . $A \cup B$ = {TH, TT, HT} .

The sample space when you flip two fair coins is $X$ = {$HH$, $HT$, $TH$, $TT$}. The outcome $HH$ is in NEITHER $A$ NOR $B$. The Venn diagram is as follows:

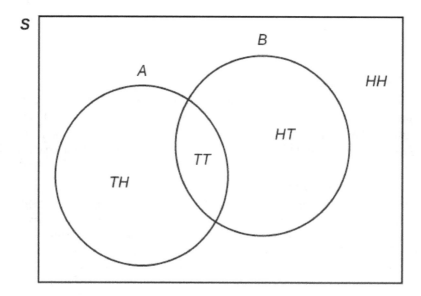

Figure 3.7

**Try It**

**3.28** Roll a fair, six-sided die. Let $A$ = a prime number of dots is rolled. Let $B$ = an odd number of dots is rolled. Then $A$ = {2, 3, 5} and $B$ = {1, 3, 5}. Therefore, $A \cap B$ = {3, 5} . $A \cup B$ = {1, 2, 3, 5} . The sample space for rolling a fair die is $S$ = {1, 2, 3, 4, 5, 6}. Draw a Venn diagram representing this situation.

## Example 3.29

A person with type O blood and a negative Rh factor (Rh-) can donate blood to any person with any blood type. Four percent of African Americans have type O blood and a negative RH factor, 5–10% of African Americans have the Rh- factor, and 51% have type O blood.

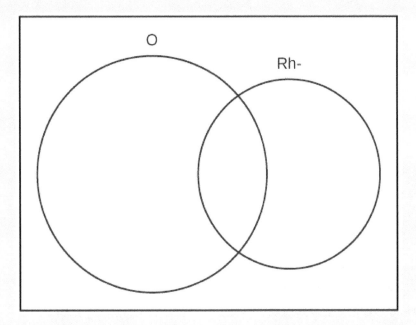

**Figure 3.8**

The "O" circle represents the African Americans with type O blood. The "Rh-" oval represents the African Americans with the Rh- factor.

We will take the average of 5% and 10% and use 7.5% as the percent of African Americans who have the Rh- factor. Let $O$ = African American with Type O blood and $R$ = African American with Rh- factor.

a.  $P(O) = $ _____

b.  $P(R) = $ _____

c.  $P(O \cap R) = $ _____

d.  $P(O \cup R) = $ _____

e.  In the Venn Diagram, describe the overlapping area using a complete sentence.

f.  In the Venn Diagram, describe the area in the rectangle but outside both the circle and the oval using a complete sentence.

## Example 3.30

**Forty percent** of the students at a local college belong to a club and **50%** work part time. **Five percent** of the students work part time and belong to a club. Draw a Venn diagram showing the relationships. Let $C$ = student belongs to a club and $PT$ = student works part time.

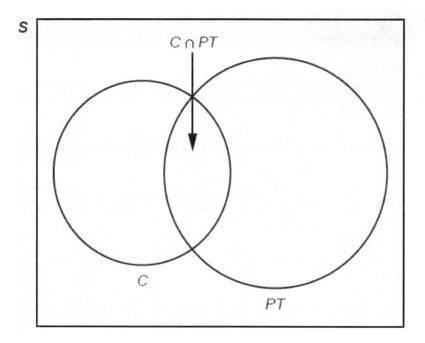

Figure 3.9

If a student is selected at random, find

- the probability that the student belongs to a club. $P(C) = 0.40$

- the probability that the student works part time. $P(PT) = 0.50$

- the probability that the student belongs to a club AND works part time. $P(C \cap PT) = 0.05$

- the probability that the student belongs to a club **given** that the student works part time.
  $P(C|PT) = \dfrac{P(C \cap PT)}{P(PT)} = \dfrac{0.05}{0.50} = 0.1$

- the probability that the student belongs to a club **OR** works part time.
  $P(C \cup PT) = P(C) + P(PT) - P(C \cap PT) = 0.40 + 0.50 - 0.05 = 0.85$

In order to solve **Example 3.30** we had to draw upon the concept of conditional probability from the previous section. There we used tree diagrams to track the changes in the probabilities, because the sample space changed as we drew without replacement. In short, conditional probability is the chance that something will happen given that some other event has already happened. Put another way, the probability that something will happen conditioned upon the situation that something else is also true. In **Example 3.30** the probability $P(C \mid PT)$ is the conditional probability that the randomly drawn student is a member of the club, conditioned upon the fact that the student also is working part time. This allows us to see the relationship between Venn diagrams and the probability postulates.

**3.30** Fifty percent of the workers at a factory work a second job, 25% have a spouse who also works, 5% work a second job and have a spouse who also works. Draw a Venn diagram showing the relationships. Let $W$ = works a second job and $S$ = spouse also works.

**3.30** In a bookstore, the probability that the customer buys a novel is 0.6, and the probability that the customer buys a non-fiction book is 0.4. Suppose that the probability that the customer buys both is 0.2.

a. Draw a Venn diagram representing the situation.

b. Find the probability that the customer buys either a novel or a non-fiction book.

c. In the Venn diagram, describe the overlapping area using a complete sentence.

d. Suppose that some customers buy only compact disks. Draw an oval in your Venn diagram representing this event.

## Example 3.31

A set of 20 German Shepherd dogs is observed. 12 are male, 8 are female, 10 have some brown coloring, and 5 have some white sections of fur. Answer the following using Venn Diagrams.

Draw a Venn diagram simply showing the sets of male and female dogs.

### Solution 3.31

The Venn diagram below demonstrates the situation of mutually exclusive events where the outcomes are independent events. If a dog cannot be both male and female, then there is no intersection. Being male precludes being female and being female precludes being male: in this case, the characteristic gender is therefore mutually exclusive. A Venn diagram shows this as two sets with no intersection. The intersection is said to be the null set using the mathematical symbol $\varnothing$.

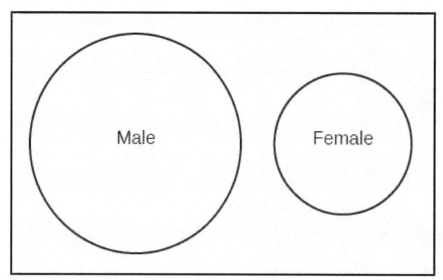

Figure 3.10

Draw a second Venn diagram illustrating that 10 of the male dogs have brown coloring.

### Solution 3.31

The Venn diagram below shows the overlap between male and brown where the number 10 is placed in it. This represents Male ∩ Brown : both male and brown. This is the intersection of these two characteristics. To get the union of Male and Brown, then it is simply the two circled areas minus the overlap. In proper terms, Male ∪ Brown = Male + Brown − Male ∩ Brown will give us the number of dogs in the union of these two sets. If we did not subtract the intersection, we would have double counted some of the dogs.

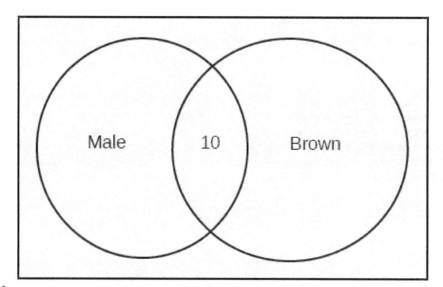

Figure 3.11

Now draw a situation depicting a scenario in which the non-shaded region represents "No white fur and female," or *White fur'* ∩ *Female.* the prime above "fur" indicates "not white fur." The prime above a set means not in that set, e.g. $A'$ means not $A$. Sometimes, the notation used is a line above the letter. For example, $\bar{A} = A'$.

Solution 3.31

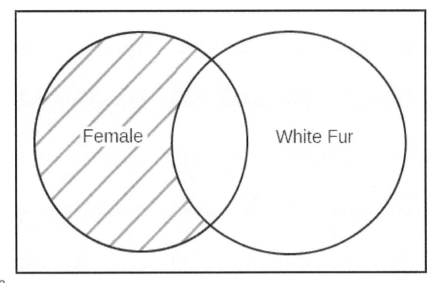

Figure 3.12

### The Addition Rule of Probability

We met the addition rule earlier but without the help of Venn diagrams. Venn diagrams help visualize the counting process that is inherent in the calculation of probability. To restate the Addition Rule of Probability:

$$P(A \cup B) = P(A) + P(B) - P(A \cap B)$$

Remember that probability is simply the proportion of the objects we are interested in relative to the total number of objects. This is why we can see the usefulness of the Venn diagrams. **Example 3.31** shows how we can use Venn diagrams to count the number of dogs in the union of brown and male by reminding us to subtract the intersection of brown and male. We can see the effect of this directly on probabilities in the addition rule.

### Example 3.32

Let's sample 50 students who are in a statistics class. 20 are freshmen and 30 are sophomores. 15 students get a "B" in the course, and 5 students both get a "B" and are freshmen.

Find the probability of selecting a student who either earns a "B" OR is a freshmen. We are translating the word OR to the mathematical symbol for the addition rule, which is the union of the two sets.

Solution 3.32

We know that there are 50 students in our sample, so we know the denominator of our fraction to give us probability. We need only to find the number of students that meet the characteristics we are interested in, i.e. any freshman and any student who earned a grade of "B." With the Addition Rule of probability, we can skip directly to probabilities.

Let "A" = the number of freshmen, and let "B" = the grade of "B." Below we can see the process for using Venn diagrams to solve this.

The $P\!\left(A\right) = \frac{20}{50} = 0.40$, $P\!\left(B\right) = \frac{15}{50} = 0.30$, and $P\!\left(A \cap B\right) = \frac{5}{50} = 0.10$.

Therefore, $P(A \cap B) = 0.40 + 0.30 - 0.10 = 0.60$.

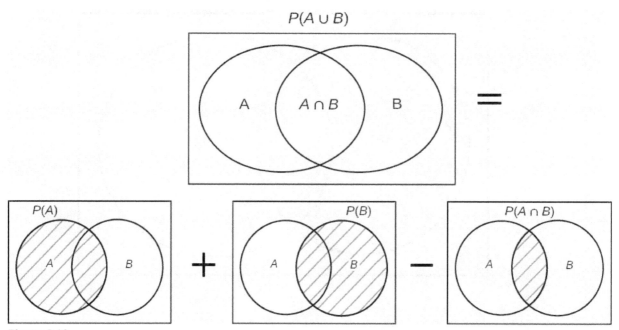

**Figure 3.13**

If two events are mutually exclusive, then, like the example where we diagram the male and female dogs, the addition rule is simplified to just $P(A \cup B) = P(A) + P(B) - 0$. This is true because, as we saw earlier, the union of mutually exclusive events is the null set, $\emptyset$. The diagrams below demonstrate this.

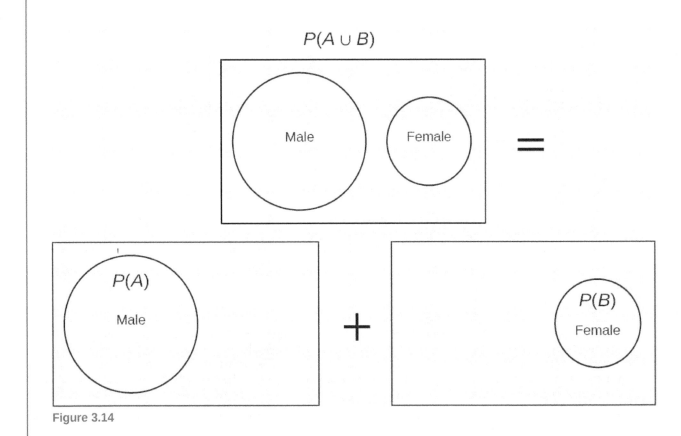

**Figure 3.14**

### The Multiplication Rule of Probability

Restating the Multiplication Rule of Probability using the notation of Venn diagrams, we have:

$$P(A \cap B) = P(A|B) \cdot P(B)$$

The multiplication rule can be modified with a bit of algebra into the following conditional rule. Then Venn diagrams can then be used to demonstrate the process.

The conditional rule:  $P(A|B) = \dfrac{P(A \cap B)}{P(B)}$

Using the same facts from **Example 3.32** above, find the probability that someone will earn a "B" if they are a "freshman."

$$P(A|B) = \frac{0.10}{0.30} = \frac{1}{3}$$

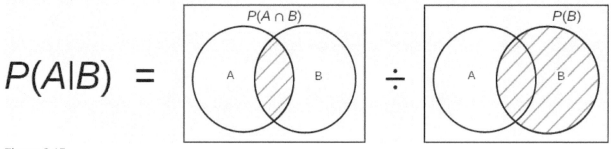

Figure 3.15

The multiplication rule must also be altered if the two events are independent. Independent events are defined as a situation where the conditional probability is simply the probability of the event of interest. Formally, independence of events is defined as $P(A|B) = P(A)$ or $P(B|A) = P(B)$. When flipping coins, the outcome of the second flip is independent of the outcome of the first flip; coins do not have memory. The Multiplication Rule of Probability for independent events thus becomes:

$$P(A \cap B) = P(A) \cdot P(B)$$

One easy way to remember this is to consider what we mean by the word "and." We see that the Multiplication Rule has translated the word "and" to the Venn notation for intersection. Therefore, the outcome must meet the two conditions of freshmen and grade of "B" in the above example. It is harder, less probable, to meet two conditions than just one or some other one. We can attempt to see the logic of the Multiplication Rule of probability due to the fact that fractions multiplied times each other become smaller.

The development of the Rules of Probability with the use of Venn diagrams can be shown to help as we wish to calculate probabilities from data arranged in a contingency table.

## Example 3.33

Table 3.11 is from a sample of 200 people who were asked how much education they completed. The columns represent the highest education they completed, and the rows separate the individuals by male and female.

|         | Less than High School Grad | High School Grad | Some College | College Grad | **Total** |
|---------|-----------|-----------|-----------|-----------|-----------|
| Male    | 5         | 15        | 40        | 60        | 120       |
| Female  | 8         | 12        | 30        | 30        | 80        |
| **Total** | 13      | 27        | 70        | 90        | **200**   |

Table 3.11

Now, we can use this table to answer probability questions. The following examples are designed to help understand the format above while connecting the knowledge to both Venn diagrams and the probability rules.

What is the probability that a selected person both finished college and is female?

### Solution 3.33

This is a simple task of finding the value where the two characteristics intersect on the table, and then applying the postulate of probability, which states that the probability of an event is the proportion of outcomes that match the event in which we are interested as a proportion of all total possible outcomes.

$P(College\ Grad\ \cap\ Female) = \dfrac{30}{200} = 0.15$

What is the probability of selecting either a female or someone who finished college?

### Solution 3.33

This task involves the use of the addition rule to solve for this probability.

$P(College\ Grad\ \cup\ Female) = P(F) + P(CG) - P(F\ \cap\ CG)$

$P(College\ Grad\ \cup\ Female) = \dfrac{80}{200} + \dfrac{90}{200} - \dfrac{30}{200} = \dfrac{140}{200} = 0.70$

What is the probability of selecting a high school graduate if we only select from the group of males?

### Solution 3.33

Here we must use the conditional probability rule (the modified multiplication rule) to solve for this probability.

$P(HS\ Grad\ |\ Male = \dfrac{P(HS\ Grad\ \cap\ Male)}{P(Male)} = \dfrac{\left(\frac{15}{200}\right)}{\left(\frac{120}{200}\right)} = \dfrac{15}{120} = 0.125$

Can we conclude that the level of education attained by these 200 people is independent of the gender of the person?

### Solution 3.33

There are two ways to approach this test. The first method seeks to test if the intersection of two events equals the product of the events separately remembering that if two events are independent than $P(A)*P(B) = P(A\ \cap\ B)$. For simplicity's sake, we can use calculated values from above.

*Does $P(College\ Grad\ \cap\ Female) = P(CG) \cdot P(F)$?*

$\dfrac{30}{200} \neq \dfrac{90}{200} \cdot \dfrac{80}{200}$ *because* $0.15 \neq 0.18$.

Therefore, gender and education here are **not** independent.

The second method is to test if the conditional probability of *A given B* is equal to the probability of *A*. Again for simplicity, we can use an already calculated value from above.

*Does $P(HS\ Grad\ |\ Male) = P(HS\ Grad)$?*

$\dfrac{15}{120} \neq \dfrac{27}{200}$ *because* $0.125 \neq 0.135$.

Therefore, again gender and education here are **not** independent.

# KEY TERMS

**Conditional Probability** the likelihood that an event will occur given that another event has already occurred

**Contingency Table** the method of displaying a frequency distribution as a table with rows and columns to show how two variables may be dependent (contingent) upon each other; the table provides an easy way to calculate conditional probabilities.

**Dependent Events** If two events are NOT independent, then we say that they are dependent.

**Equally Likely** Each outcome of an experiment has the same probability.

**Event** a subset of the set of all outcomes of an experiment; the set of all outcomes of an experiment is called a **sample space** and is usually denoted by *S*. An event is an arbitrary subset in *S*. It can contain one outcome, two outcomes, no outcomes (empty subset), the entire sample space, and the like. Standard notations for events are capital letters such as *A*, *B*, *C*, and so on.

**Experiment** a planned activity carried out under controlled conditions

**Independent Events** The occurrence of one event has no effect on the probability of the occurrence of another event. Events *A* and *B* are independent if one of the following is true:

1. $P(A|B) = P(A)$
2. $P(B|A) = P(B)$
3. $P(A \cap B) = P(A)P(B)$

**Mutually Exclusive** Two events are mutually exclusive if the probability that they both happen at the same time is zero. If events *A* and *B* are mutually exclusive, then $P(A \cap B) = 0$.

**Outcome** a particular result of an experiment

**Probability** a number between zero and one, inclusive, that gives the likelihood that a specific event will occur; the foundation of statistics is given by the following 3 axioms (by A.N. Kolmogorov, 1930's): Let *S* denote the sample space and *A* and *B* are two events in *S*. Then:

- $0 \le P(A) \le 1$
- If *A* and *B* are any two mutually exclusive events, then $P(A \cup B) = P(A) + P(B)$.
- $P(S) = 1$

**Sample Space** the set of all possible outcomes of an experiment

**Sampling with Replacement** If each member of a population is replaced after it is picked, then that member has the possibility of being chosen more than once.

**Sampling without Replacement** When sampling is done without replacement, each member of a population may be chosen only once.

**The Complement Event** The complement of event *A* consists of all outcomes that are NOT in *A*.

**The Conditional Probability of *A* | *B*** $P(A \mid B)$ is the probability that event *A* will occur given that the event *B* has already occurred.

**The Intersection: the ∩ Event** An outcome is in the event $A \cap B$ if the outcome is in both $A \cap B$ at the same time.

**The Union: the ∪ Event** An outcome is in the event $A \cup B$ if the outcome is in *A* or is in *B* or is in both *A* and *B*.

**Tree Diagram** the useful visual representation of a sample space and events in the form of a "tree" with branches marked by possible outcomes together with associated probabilities (frequencies, relative frequencies)

**Venn Diagram** the visual representation of a sample space and events in the form of circles or ovals showing their intersections

# CHAPTER REVIEW

### 3.1 Terminology

In this module we learned the basic terminology of probability. The set of all possible outcomes of an experiment is called the sample space. Events are subsets of the sample space, and they are assigned a probability that is a number between zero and one, inclusive.

### 3.2 Independent and Mutually Exclusive Events

Two events $A$ and $B$ are independent if the knowledge that one occurred does not affect the chance the other occurs. If two events are not independent, then we say that they are dependent.

In sampling with replacement, each member of a population is replaced after it is picked, so that member has the possibility of being chosen more than once, and the events are considered to be independent. In sampling without replacement, each member of a population may be chosen only once, and the events are considered not to be independent. When events do not share outcomes, they are mutually exclusive of each other.

### 3.3 Two Basic Rules of Probability

The multiplication rule and the addition rule are used for computing the probability of $A$ and $B$, as well as the probability of $A$ or $B$ for two given events $A$, $B$ defined on the sample space. In sampling with replacement each member of a population is replaced after it is picked, so that member has the possibility of being chosen more than once, and the events are considered to be independent. In sampling without replacement, each member of a population may be chosen only once, and the events are considered to be not independent. The events $A$ and $B$ are mutually exclusive events when they do not have any outcomes in common.

### 3.4 Contingency Tables and Probability Trees

There are several tools you can use to help organize and sort data when calculating probabilities. Contingency tables help display data and are particularly useful when calculating probabilites that have multiple dependent variables.

A tree diagram use branches to show the different outcomes of experiments and makes complex probability questions easy to visualize.

### 3.5 Venn Diagrams

A Venn diagram is a picture that represents the outcomes of an experiment. It generally consists of a box that represents the sample space S or universe of the objects of interest together with circles or ovals. The circles or ovals represent groups of events called sets. A Venn diagram is especially helpful for visualizing the $\cup$ event, the $\cap$ event, and the complement of an event and for understanding conditional probabilities. A Venn diagram is especially helpful for visualizing an Intersection of two events, a Union of two events, or a Complement of one event. A system of Venn diagrams can also help to understand Conditional probabilities. Venn diagrams connect the brain and eyes by matching the literal arithmetic to a picture. It is important to note that more than one Venn diagram is needed to solve the probability rule formulas introduced in **Section 3.3**.

# FORMULA REVIEW

### 3.1 Terminology

$A$ and $B$ are events

$P(S) = 1$ where $S$ is the sample space

$0 \leq P(A) \leq 1$

$P(A \mid B) = \dfrac{P(A \cap B)}{P(B)}$

### 3.2 Independent and Mutually Exclusive Events

If $A$ and $B$ are independent, $P(A \cap B) = P(A)P(B)$, $P(A|B) = P(A)$ and $P(B|A) = P(B)$.

If $A$ and $B$ are mutually exclusive, $P(A \cup B) = P(A) + P(B)$ and $P(A \cap B) = 0$.

### 3.3 Two Basic Rules of Probability

**The multiplication rule:** $P(A \cap B) = P(A \mid B)P(B)$

**The addition rule:** $P(A \cup B) = P(A) + P(B) - P(A \cap B)$

# PRACTICE

## 3.1 Terminology

**1.** In a particular college class, there are male and female students. Some students have long hair and some students have short hair. Write the **symbols** for the probabilities of the events for parts a through j. (Note that you cannot find numerical answers here. You were not given enough information to find any probability values yet; concentrate on understanding the symbols.)

- Let $F$ be the event that a student is female.
- Let $M$ be the event that a student is male.
- Let $S$ be the event that a student has short hair.
- Let $L$ be the event that a student has long hair.

    a. The probability that a student does not have long hair.
    b. The probability that a student is male or has short hair.
    c. The probability that a student is a female and has long hair.
    d. The probability that a student is male, given that the student has long hair.
    e. The probability that a student has long hair, given that the student is male.
    f. Of all the female students, the probability that a student has short hair.
    g. Of all students with long hair, the probability that a student is female.
    h. The probability that a student is female or has long hair.
    i. The probability that a randomly selected student is a male student with short hair.
    j. The probability that a student is female.

*Use the following information to answer the next four exercises.* A box is filled with several party favors. It contains 12 hats, 15 noisemakers, ten finger traps, and five bags of confetti.

Let $H$ = the event of getting a hat.
Let $N$ = the event of getting a noisemaker.
Let $F$ = the event of getting a finger trap.
Let $C$ = the event of getting a bag of confetti.

**2.** Find $P(H)$.

**3.** Find $P(N)$.

**4.** Find $P(F)$.

**5.** Find $P(C)$.

*Use the following information to answer the next six exercises.* A jar of 150 jelly beans contains 22 red jelly beans, 38 yellow, 20 green, 28 purple, 26 blue, and the rest are orange.

Let $B$ = the event of getting a blue jelly bean
Let $G$ = the event of getting a green jelly bean.
Let $O$ = the event of getting an orange jelly bean.
Let $P$ = the event of getting a purple jelly bean.
Let $R$ = the event of getting a red jelly bean.
Let $Y$ = the event of getting a yellow jelly bean.

**6.** Find $P(B)$.

**7.** Find $P(G)$.

**8.** Find $P(P)$.

**9.** Find $P(R)$.

**10.** Find $P(Y)$.

**11.** Find $P(O)$.

*Use the following information to answer the next six exercises.* There are 23 countries in North America, 12 countries in South America, 47 countries in Europe, 44 countries in Asia, 54 countries in Africa, and 14 in Oceania (Pacific Ocean region).
Let $A$ = the event that a country is in Asia.
Let $E$ = the event that a country is in Europe.
Let $F$ = the event that a country is in Africa.
Let $N$ = the event that a country is in North America.
Let $O$ = the event that a country is in Oceania.
Let $S$ = the event that a country is in South America.

**12.** Find $P(A)$.

**13.** Find $P(E)$.

**14.** Find $P(F)$.

**15.** Find $P(N)$.

**16.** Find $P(O)$.

**17.** Find $P(S)$.

**18.** What is the probability of drawing a red card in a standard deck of 52 cards?

**19.** What is the probability of drawing a club in a standard deck of 52 cards?

**20.** What is the probability of rolling an even number of dots with a fair, six-sided die numbered one through six?

**21.** What is the probability of rolling a prime number of dots with a fair, six-sided die numbered one through six?

*Use the following information to answer the next two exercises.* You see a game at a local fair. You have to throw a dart at a color wheel. Each section on the color wheel is equal in area.

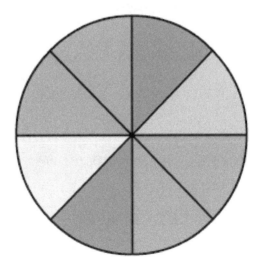

Figure 3.16

Let $B$ = the event of landing on blue.
Let $R$ = the event of landing on red.
Let $G$ = the event of landing on green.
Let $Y$ = the event of landing on yellow.

**22.** If you land on $Y$, you get the biggest prize. Find $P(Y)$.

**23.** If you land on red, you don't get a prize. What is $P(R)$?

*Use the following information to answer the next ten exercises.* On a baseball team, there are infielders and outfielders. Some players are great hitters, and some players are not great hitters.

Let $I$ = the event that a player in an infielder.

Let $O$ = the event that a player is an outfielder.

Let $H$ = the event that a player is a great hitter.

Let $N$ = the event that a player is not a great hitter.

**24.** Write the symbols for the probability that a player is not an outfielder.

**25.** Write the symbols for the probability that a player is an outfielder or is a great hitter.

**26.** Write the symbols for the probability that a player is an infielder and is not a great hitter.

**27.** Write the symbols for the probability that a player is a great hitter, given that the player is an infielder.

**28.** Write the symbols for the probability that a player is an infielder, given that the player is a great hitter.

**29.** Write the symbols for the probability that of all the outfielders, a player is not a great hitter.

**30.** Write the symbols for the probability that of all the great hitters, a player is an outfielder.

**31.** Write the symbols for the probability that a player is an infielder or is not a great hitter.

**32.** Write the symbols for the probability that a player is an outfielder and is a great hitter.

**33.** Write the symbols for the probability that a player is an infielder.

**34.** What is the word for the set of all possible outcomes?

**35.** What is conditional probability?

**36.** A shelf holds 12 books. Eight are fiction and the rest are nonfiction. Each is a different book with a unique title. The fiction books are numbered one to eight. The nonfiction books are numbered one to four. Randomly select one book
Let $F$ = event that book is fiction
Let $N$ = event that book is nonfiction
What is the sample space?

**37.** What is the sum of the probabilities of an event and its complement?

*Use the following information to answer the next two exercises.* You are rolling a fair, six-sided number cube. Let $E$ = the event that it lands on an even number. Let $M$ = the event that it lands on a multiple of three.

**38.** What does $P(E \mid M)$ mean in words?

**39.** What does $P(E \cup M)$ mean in words?

## 3.2 Independent and Mutually Exclusive Events

**40.** $E$ and $F$ are mutually exclusive events. $P(E) = 0.4$; $P(F) = 0.5$. Find $P(E \mid F)$.

**41.** $J$ and $K$ are independent events. $P(J|K) = 0.3$. Find $P(J)$.

**42.** $U$ and $V$ are mutually exclusive events. $P(U) = 0.26$; $P(V) = 0.37$. Find:
   a. $P(U \cap V) =$
   b. $P(U|V) =$
   c. $P(U \cup V) =$

**43.** $Q$ and $R$ are independent events. $P(Q) = 0.4$ and $P(Q \cap R) = 0.1$. Find $P(R)$.

## 3.3 Two Basic Rules of Probability

*Use the following information to answer the next ten exercises.* Forty-eight percent of all Californians registered voters prefer life in prison without parole over the death penalty for a person convicted of first degree murder. Among Latino California registered voters, 55% prefer life in prison without parole over the death penalty for a person convicted of first degree murder. 37.6% of all Californians are Latino.

In this problem, let:

- *C* = Californians (registered voters) preferring life in prison without parole over the death penalty for a person convicted of first degree murder.

- *L* = Latino Californians

Suppose that one Californian is randomly selected.

**44.** Find *P*(*C*).

**45.** Find *P*(*L*).

**46.** Find *P*(*C* | *L*).

**47.** In words, what is *C* | *L*?

**48.** Find *P*(*L* ∩ *C*).

**49.** In words, what is *L* ∩ *C*?

**50.** Are *L* and *C* independent events? Show why or why not.

**51.** Find *P*(*L* ∪ *C*).

**52.** In words, what is *L* ∪ *C*?

**53.** Are *L* and *C* mutually exclusive events? Show why or why not.

### 3.5 Venn Diagrams

*Use the following information to answer the next four exercises.* Table 3.12 shows a random sample of musicians and how they learned to play their instruments.

| Gender | Self-taught | Studied in School | Private Instruction | Total |
|--------|-------------|-------------------|---------------------|-------|
| Female | 12 | 38 | 22 | 72 |
| Male | 19 | 24 | 15 | 58 |
| Total | 31 | 62 | 37 | 130 |

Table 3.12

**54.** Find *P*(musician is a female).

**55.** Find *P*(musician is a male ∩ had private instruction).

**56.** Find *P*(musician is a female ∪ is self taught).

**57.** Are the events "being a female musician" and "learning music in school" mutually exclusive events?

**58.** The probability that a man develops some form of cancer in his lifetime is 0.4567. The probability that a man has at least one false positive test result (meaning the test comes back for cancer when the man does not have it) is 0.51. Let: *C* = a man develops cancer in his lifetime; *P* = man has at least one false positive. Construct a tree diagram of the situation.

## BRINGING IT TOGETHER: PRACTICE

Use the following information to answer the next seven exercises. An article in the *New England Journal of Medicine*, reported about a study of smokers in California and Hawaii. In one part of the report, the self-reported ethnicity and smoking levels per day were given. Of the people smoking at most ten cigarettes per day, there were 9,886 African Americans, 2,745 Native Hawaiians, 12,831 Latinos, 8,378 Japanese Americans, and 7,650 Whites. Of the people smoking 11 to 20 cigarettes per day, there were 6,514 African Americans, 3,062 Native Hawaiians, 4,932 Latinos, 10,680 Japanese Americans, and 9,877 Whites. Of the people smoking 21 to 30 cigarettes per day, there were 1,671 African Americans, 1,419 Native Hawaiians, 1,406 Latinos, 4,715 Japanese Americans, and 6,062 Whites. Of the people smoking at least 31 cigarettes per day, there were 759 African Americans, 788 Native Hawaiians, 800 Latinos, 2,305 Japanese Americans, and 3,970 Whites.

**59.** Complete the table using the data provided. Suppose that one person from the study is randomly selected. Find the probability that person smoked 11 to 20 cigarettes per day.

| Smoking Level | African American | Native Hawaiian | Latino | Japanese Americans | White | TOTALS |
|---|---|---|---|---|---|---|
| 1–10 | | | | | | |
| 11–20 | | | | | | |
| 21–30 | | | | | | |
| 31+ | | | | | | |
| TOTALS | | | | | | |

Table 3.13 Smoking Levels by Ethnicity

**60.** Suppose that one person from the study is randomly selected. Find the probability that person smoked 11 to 20 cigarettes per day.

**61.** Find the probability that the person was Latino.

**62.** In words, explain what it means to pick one person from the study who is "Japanese American **AND** smokes 21 to 30 cigarettes per day." Also, find the probability.

**63.** In words, explain what it means to pick one person from the study who is "Japanese American ∪ smokes 21 to 30 cigarettes per day." Also, find the probability.

**64.** In words, explain what it means to pick one person from the study who is "Japanese American | that person smokes 21 to 30 cigarettes per day." Also, find the probability.

**65.** Prove that smoking level/day and ethnicity are dependent events.

*Use the following information to answer the next two exercises.* Suppose that you have eight cards. Five are green and three are yellow. The cards are well shuffled.

**66.** Suppose that you randomly draw two cards, one at a time, **with replacement**.
Let $G_1$ = first card is green
Let $G_2$ = second card is green
    a. Draw a tree diagram of the situation.
    b. Find $P(G_1 \cap G_2)$.
    c. Find $P$(at least one green).
    d. Find $P(G_2 | G_1)$.
    e. Are $G_2$ and $G_1$ independent events? Explain why or why not.

**67.** Suppose that you randomly draw two cards, one at a time, **without replacement**.
$G_1$ = first card is green
$G_2$ = second card is green
    a. Draw a tree diagram of the situation.
    b. Find $P(G_1 \cap G_2)$.
    c. Find $P$(at least one green).
    d. Find $P(G_2 | G_1)$.
    e. Are $G_2$ and $G_1$ independent events? Explain why or why not.

*Use the following information to answer the next two exercises.* The percent of licensed U.S. drivers (from a recent year) that are female is 48.60. Of the females, 5.03% are age 19 and under; 81.36% are age 20–64; 13.61% are age 65 or over. Of the licensed U.S. male drivers, 5.04% are age 19 and under; 81.43% are age 20–64; 13.53% are age 65 or over.

**68.** Complete the following.
   a.  Construct a table or a tree diagram of the situation.
   b.  Find $P$(driver is female).
   c.  Find $P$(driver is age 65 or over | driver is female).
   d.  Find $P$(driver is age 65 or over ∩ female).
   e.  In words, explain the difference between the probabilities in part c and part d.
   f.  Find $P$(driver is age 65 or over).
   g.  Are being age 65 or over and being female mutually exclusive events? How do you know?

**69.** Suppose that 10,000 U.S. licensed drivers are randomly selected.
   a.  How many would you expect to be male?
   b.  Using the table or tree diagram, construct a contingency table of gender versus age group.
   c.  Using the contingency table, find the probability that out of the age 20–64 group, a randomly selected driver is female.

**70.** Approximately 86.5% of Americans commute to work by car, truck, or van. Out of that group, 84.6% drive alone and 15.4% drive in a carpool. Approximately 3.9% walk to work and approximately 5.3% take public transportation.
   a.  Construct a table or a tree diagram of the situation. Include a branch for all other modes of transportation to work.
   b.  Assuming that the walkers walk alone, what percent of all commuters travel alone to work?
   c.  Suppose that 1,000 workers are randomly selected. How many would you expect to travel alone to work?
   d.  Suppose that 1,000 workers are randomly selected. How many would you expect to drive in a carpool?

**71.** When the Euro coin was introduced in 2002, two math professors had their statistics students test whether the Belgian one Euro coin was a fair coin. They spun the coin rather than tossing it and found that out of 250 spins, 140 showed a head (event $H$) while 110 showed a tail (event $T$). On that basis, they claimed that it is not a fair coin.
   a.  Based on the given data, find $P(H)$ and $P(T)$.
   b.  Use a tree to find the probabilities of each possible outcome for the experiment of tossing the coin twice.
   c.  Use the tree to find the probability of obtaining exactly one head in two tosses of the coin.
   d.  Use the tree to find the probability of obtaining at least one head.

# HOMEWORK

## 3.1 Terminology

**72.**

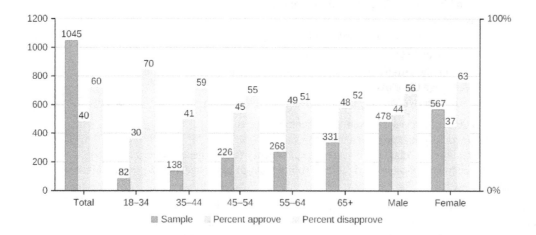

**Figure 3.17** The graph in **Figure 3.17** displays the sample sizes and percentages of people in different age and gender groups who were polled concerning their approval of Mayor Ford's actions in office. The total number in the sample of all the age groups is 1,045.

    a. Define three events in the graph.
    b. Describe in words what the entry 40 means.
    c. Describe in words the complement of the entry in question 2.
    d. Describe in words what the entry 30 means.
    e. Out of the males and females, what percent are males?
    f. Out of the females, what percent disapprove of Mayor Ford?
    g. Out of all the age groups, what percent approve of Mayor Ford?
    h. Find $P$(Approve | Male).
    i. Out of the age groups, what percent are more than 44 years old?
    j. Find $P$(Approve | Age < 35).

**73.** Explain what is wrong with the following statements. Use complete sentences.
    a. If there is a 60% chance of rain on Saturday and a 70% chance of rain on Sunday, then there is a 130% chance of rain over the weekend.
    b. The probability that a baseball player hits a home run is greater than the probability that he gets a successful hit.

## 3.2 Independent and Mutually Exclusive Events

*Use the following information to answer the next 12 exercises.* The graph shown is based on more than 170,000 interviews done by Gallup that took place from January through December 2012. The sample consists of employed Americans 18 years of age or older. The Emotional Health Index Scores are the sample space. We randomly sample one Emotional Health Index Score.

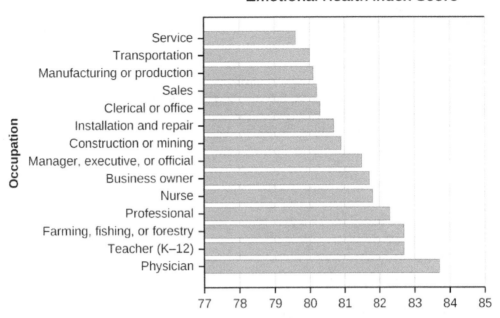

**Figure 3.18**

**74.** Find the probability that an Emotional Health Index Score is 82.7.

**75.** Find the probability that an Emotional Health Index Score is 81.0.

**76.** Find the probability that an Emotional Health Index Score is more than 81?

**77.** Find the probability that an Emotional Health Index Score is between 80.5 and 82?

**78.** If we know an Emotional Health Index Score is 81.5 or more, what is the probability that it is 82.7?

**79.** What is the probability that an Emotional Health Index Score is 80.7 or 82.7?

**80.** What is the probability that an Emotional Health Index Score is less than 80.2 given that it is already less than 81.

**81.** What occupation has the highest emotional index score?

**82.** What occupation has the lowest emotional index score?

**83.** What is the range of the data?

**84.** Compute the average EHIS.

**85.** If all occupations are equally likely for a certain individual, what is the probability that he or she will have an occupation with lower than average EHIS?

## 3.3 Two Basic Rules of Probability

**86.** On February 28, 2013, a Field Poll Survey reported that 61% of California registered voters approved of allowing two people of the same gender to marry and have regular marriage laws apply to them. Among 18 to 39 year olds (California registered voters), the approval rating was 78%. Six in ten California registered voters said that the upcoming Supreme Court's ruling about the constitutionality of California's Proposition 8 was either very or somewhat important to them. Out of those CA registered voters who support same-sex marriage, 75% say the ruling is important to them.

In this problem, let:

- $C$ = California registered voters who support same-sex marriage.
- $B$ = California registered voters who say the Supreme Court's ruling about the constitutionality of California's Proposition 8 is very or somewhat important to them
- $A$ = California registered voters who are 18 to 39 years old.

    a. Find $P(C)$.
    b. Find $P(B)$.
    c. Find $P(C \mid A)$.
    d. Find $P(B|C)$.
    e. In words, what is $C \mid A$?
    f. In words, what is $B \mid C$?
    g. Find $P(C \cap B)$.
    h. In words, what is $C \cap B$?
    i. Find $P(C \cup B)$.
    j. Are $C$ and $B$ mutually exclusive events? Show why or why not.

**87.** After Rob Ford, the mayor of Toronto, announced his plans to cut budget costs in late 2011, the Forum Research polled 1,046 people to measure the mayor's popularity. Everyone polled expressed either approval or disapproval. These are the results their poll produced:

- In early 2011, 60 percent of the population approved of Mayor Ford's actions in office.
- In mid-2011, 57 percent of the population approved of his actions.
- In late 2011, the percentage of popular approval was measured at 42 percent.

    a. What is the sample size for this study?
    b. What proportion in the poll disapproved of Mayor Ford, according to the results from late 2011?
    c. How many people polled responded that they approved of Mayor Ford in late 2011?
    d. What is the probability that a person supported Mayor Ford, based on the data collected in mid-2011?
    e. What is the probability that a person supported Mayor Ford, based on the data collected in early 2011?

*Use the following information to answer the next three exercises.* The casino game, roulette, allows the gambler to bet on the probability of a ball, which spins in the roulette wheel, landing on a particular color, number, or range of numbers. The table used to place bets contains of 38 numbers, and each number is assigned to a color and a range.

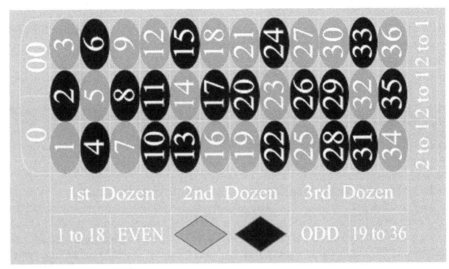

**Figure 3.19** (credit: film8ker/wikibooks)

**88.**
    a. List the sample space of the 38 possible outcomes in roulette.
    b. You bet on red. Find $P$(red).
    c. You bet on -1st 12- (1st Dozen). Find $P$(-1st 12-).
    d. You bet on an even number. Find $P$(even number).
    e. Is getting an odd number the complement of getting an even number? Why?
    f. Find two mutually exclusive events.
    g. Are the events Even and 1st Dozen independent?

**89.** Compute the probability of winning the following types of bets:
    a. Betting on two lines that touch each other on the table as in 1-2-3-4-5-6
    b. Betting on three numbers in a line, as in 1-2-3
    c. Betting on one number
    d. Betting on four numbers that touch each other to form a square, as in 10-11-13-14
    e. Betting on two numbers that touch each other on the table, as in 10-11 or 10-13
    f. Betting on 0-00-1-2-3
    g. Betting on 0-1-2; or 0-00-2; or 00-2-3

**90.** Compute the probability of winning the following types of bets:
    a. Betting on a color
    b. Betting on one of the dozen groups
    c. Betting on the range of numbers from 1 to 18
    d. Betting on the range of numbers 19–36
    e. Betting on one of the columns
    f. Betting on an even or odd number (excluding zero)

**91.** Suppose that you have eight cards. Five are green and three are yellow. The five green cards are numbered 1, 2, 3, 4, and 5. The three yellow cards are numbered 1, 2, and 3. The cards are well shuffled. You randomly draw one card.
- $G$ = card drawn is green
- $E$ = card drawn is even-numbered
    a. List the sample space.
    b. $P(G) = $ \_\_\_\_\_
    c. $P(G \mid E) = $ \_\_\_\_\_
    d. $P(G \cap E) = $ \_\_\_\_\_
    e. $P(G \cup E) = $ \_\_\_\_\_
    f. Are $G$ and $E$ mutually exclusive? Justify your answer numerically.

**92.** Roll two fair dice separately. Each die has six faces.
  a.  List the sample space.
  b.  Let *A* be the event that either a three or four is rolled first, followed by an even number. Find *P*(*A*).
  c.  Let *B* be the event that the sum of the two rolls is at most seven. Find *P*(*B*).
  d.  In words, explain what "*P*(*A* | *B*)" represents. Find *P*(*A* | *B*).
  e.  Are *A* and *B* mutually exclusive events? Explain your answer in one to three complete sentences, including numerical justification.
  f.  Are *A* and *B* independent events? Explain your answer in one to three complete sentences, including numerical justification.

**93.** A special deck of cards has ten cards. Four are green, three are blue, and three are red. When a card is picked, its color of it is recorded. An experiment consists of first picking a card and then tossing a coin.
  a.  List the sample space.
  b.  Let *A* be the event that a blue card is picked first, followed by landing a head on the coin toss. Find *P*(*A*).
  c.  Let *B* be the event that a red or green is picked, followed by landing a head on the coin toss. Are the events *A* and *B* mutually exclusive? Explain your answer in one to three complete sentences, including numerical justification.
  d.  Let *C* be the event that a red or blue is picked, followed by landing a head on the coin toss. Are the events *A* and *C* mutually exclusive? Explain your answer in one to three complete sentences, including numerical justification.

**94.** An experiment consists of first rolling a die and then tossing a coin.
  a.  List the sample space.
  b.  Let *A* be the event that either a three or a four is rolled first, followed by landing a head on the coin toss. Find *P*(*A*).
  c.  Let *B* be the event that the first and second tosses land on heads. Are the events *A* and *B* mutually exclusive? Explain your answer in one to three complete sentences, including numerical justification.

**95.** An experiment consists of tossing a nickel, a dime, and a quarter. Of interest is the side the coin lands on.
  a.  List the sample space.
  b.  Let *A* be the event that there are at least two tails. Find *P*(*A*).
  c.  Let *B* be the event that the first and second tosses land on heads. Are the events *A* and *B* mutually exclusive? Explain your answer in one to three complete sentences, including justification.

**96.** Consider the following scenario:
Let *P*(*C*) = 0.4.
Let *P*(*D*) = 0.5.
Let *P*(*C* | *D*) = 0.6.
  a.  Find *P*(*C* ∩ *D*).
  b.  Are *C* and *D* mutually exclusive? Why or why not?
  c.  Are *C* and *D* independent events? Why or why not?
  d.  Find *P*(*C* ∪ *D*).
  e.  Find *P*(*D* | *C*).

**97.** *Y* and *Z* are independent events.
  a.  Rewrite the basic Addition Rule *P*(*Y* ∪ *Z*) = *P*(*Y*) + *P*(*Z*) - *P*(*Y* ∩ *Z*) using the information that *Y* and *Z* are independent events.
  b.  Use the rewritten rule to find *P*(*Z*) if *P*(*Y* ∪ *Z*) = 0.71 and *P*(*Y*) = 0.42.

**98.** *G* and *H* are mutually exclusive events. *P*(*G*) = 0.5 *P*(*H*) = 0.3
  a.  Explain why the following statement MUST be false: *P*(*H* | *G*) = 0.4.
  b.  Find *P*(*H* ∪ *G*).
  c.  Are *G* and *H* independent or dependent events? Explain in a complete sentence.

**99.** Approximately 281,000,000 people over age five live in the United States. Of these people, 55,000,000 speak a language other than English at home. Of those who speak another language at home, 62.3% speak Spanish.

Let: $E$ = speaks English at home; $E'$ = speaks another language at home; $S$ = speaks Spanish;

Finish each probability statement by matching the correct answer.

| Probability Statements | Answers |
|---|---|
| a. $P(E') =$ | i. 0.8043 |
| b. $P(E) =$ | ii. 0.623 |
| c. $P(S \cap E') =$ | iii. 0.1957 |
| d. $P(S \mid E') =$ | iv. 0.1219 |

Table 3.14

**100.** 1994, the U.S. government held a lottery to issue 55,000 Green Cards (permits for non-citizens to work legally in the U.S.). Renate Deutsch, from Germany, was one of approximately 6.5 million people who entered this lottery. Let $G$ = won green card.
   a. What was Renate's chance of winning a Green Card? Write your answer as a probability statement.
   b. In the summer of 1994, Renate received a letter stating she was one of 110,000 finalists chosen. Once the finalists were chosen, assuming that each finalist had an equal chance to win, what was Renate's chance of winning a Green Card? Write your answer as a conditional probability statement. Let $F$ = was a finalist.
   c. Are $G$ and $F$ independent or dependent events? Justify your answer numerically and also explain why.
   d. Are $G$ and $F$ mutually exclusive events? Justify your answer numerically and explain why.

**101.** Three professors at George Washington University did an experiment to determine if economists are more selfish than other people. They dropped 64 stamped, addressed envelopes with $10 cash in different classrooms on the George Washington campus. 44% were returned overall. From the economics classes 56% of the envelopes were returned. From the business, psychology, and history classes 31% were returned.

Let: $R$ = money returned; $E$ = economics classes; $O$ = other classes

   a. Write a probability statement for the overall percent of money returned.
   b. Write a probability statement for the percent of money returned out of the economics classes.
   c. Write a probability statement for the percent of money returned out of the other classes.
   d. Is money being returned independent of the class? Justify your answer numerically and explain it.
   e. Based upon this study, do you think that economists are more selfish than other people? Explain why or why not. Include numbers to justify your answer.

**102.** The following table of data obtained from www.baseball-almanac.com shows hit information for four players. Suppose that one hit from the table is randomly selected.

| Name | Single | Double | Triple | Home Run | Total Hits |
|------|--------|--------|--------|----------|------------|
| Babe Ruth | 1,517 | 506 | 136 | 714 | 2,873 |
| Jackie Robinson | 1,054 | 273 | 54 | 137 | 1,518 |
| Ty Cobb | 3,603 | 174 | 295 | 114 | 4,189 |
| Hank Aaron | 2,294 | 624 | 98 | 755 | 3,771 |
| Total | 8,471 | 1,577 | 583 | 1,720 | 12,351 |

Table 3.15

Are "the hit being made by Hank Aaron" and "the hit being a double" independent events?

    a. Yes, because $P$(hit by Hank Aaron | hit is a double) = $P$(hit by Hank Aaron)
    b. No, because $P$(hit by Hank Aaron | hit is a double) ≠ $P$(hit is a double)
    c. No, because $P$(hit is by Hank Aaron | hit is a double) ≠ $P$(hit by Hank Aaron)
    d. Yes, because $P$(hit is by Hank Aaron | hit is a double) = $P$(hit is a double)

**103.** United Blood Services is a blood bank that serves more than 500 hospitals in 18 states. According to their website, a person with type O blood and a negative Rh factor (Rh-) can donate blood to any person with any bloodtype. Their data show that 43% of people have type O blood and 15% of people have Rh- factor; 52% of people have type O or Rh- factor.

    a. Find the probability that a person has both type O blood and the Rh- factor.
    b. Find the probability that a person does NOT have both type O blood and the Rh- factor.

**104.** At a college, 72% of courses have final exams and 46% of courses require research papers. Suppose that 32% of courses have a research paper and a final exam. Let $F$ be the event that a course has a final exam. Let $R$ be the event that a course requires a research paper.
    a. Find the probability that a course has a final exam or a research project.
    b. Find the probability that a course has NEITHER of these two requirements.

**105.** In a box of assorted cookies, 36% contain chocolate and 12% contain nuts. Of those, 8% contain both chocolate and nuts. Sean is allergic to both chocolate and nuts.
    a. Find the probability that a cookie contains chocolate or nuts (he can't eat it).
    b. Find the probability that a cookie does not contain chocolate or nuts (he can eat it).

**106.** A college finds that 10% of students have taken a distance learning class and that 40% of students are part time students. Of the part time students, 20% have taken a distance learning class. Let $D$ = event that a student takes a distance learning class and $E$ = event that a student is a part time student
    a. Find $P(D \cap E)$.
    b. Find $P(E | D)$.
    c. Find $P(D \cup E)$.
    d. Using an appropriate test, show whether $D$ and $E$ are independent.
    e. Using an appropriate test, show whether $D$ and $E$ are mutually exclusive.

## 3.5 Venn Diagrams

*Use the information in the Table 3.16 to answer the next eight exercises.* The table shows the political party affiliation of each of 67 members of the US Senate in June 2012, and when they are up for reelection.

| Up for reelection: | Democratic Party | Republican Party | Other | Total |
|---|---|---|---|---|
| November 2014 | 20 | 13 | 0 | |
| November 2016 | 10 | 24 | 0 | |
| Total | | | | |

Table 3.16

**107.** What is the probability that a randomly selected senator has an "Other" affiliation?

**108.** What is the probability that a randomly selected senator is up for reelection in November 2016?

**109.** What is the probability that a randomly selected senator is a Democrat and up for reelection in November 2016?

**110.** What is the probability that a randomly selected senator is a Republican or is up for reelection in November 2014?

**111.** Suppose that a member of the US Senate is randomly selected. Given that the randomly selected senator is up for reelection in November 2016, what is the probability that this senator is a Democrat?

**112.** Suppose that a member of the US Senate is randomly selected. What is the probability that the senator is up for reelection in November 2014, knowing that this senator is a Republican?

**113.** The events "Republican" and "Up for reelection in 2016" are _____
   a. mutually exclusive.
   b. independent.
   c. both mutually exclusive and independent.
   d. neither mutually exclusive nor independent.

**114.** The events "Other" and "Up for reelection in November 2016" are _____
   a. mutually exclusive.
   b. independent.
   c. both mutually exclusive and independent.
   d. neither mutually exclusive nor independent.

**115.** Table 3.17 gives the number of suicides estimated in the U.S. for a recent year by age, race (black or white), and sex. We are interested in possible relationships between age, race, and sex. We will let suicide victims be our population.

| Race and Sex | 1–14 | 15–24 | 25–64 | over 64 | TOTALS |
|---|---|---|---|---|---|
| white, male | 210 | 3,360 | 13,610 | | 22,050 |
| white, female | 80 | 580 | 3,380 | | 4,930 |
| black, male | 10 | 460 | 1,060 | | 1,670 |
| black, female | 0 | 40 | 270 | | 330 |
| all others | | | | | |
| TOTALS | 310 | 4,650 | 18,780 | | 29,760 |

Table 3.17

Do not include "all others" for parts f and g.

a. Fill in the column for the suicides for individuals over age 64.
b. Fill in the row for all other races.
c. Find the probability that a randomly selected individual was a white male.
d. Find the probability that a randomly selected individual was a black female.
e. Find the probability that a randomly selected individual was black
f. Find the probability that a randomly selected individual was male.
g. Out of the individuals over age 64, find the probability that a randomly selected individual was a black or white male.

*Use the following information to answer the next two exercises.* The table of data obtained from *www.baseball-almanac.com* shows hit information for four well known baseball players. Suppose that one hit from the table is randomly selected.

| NAME | Single | Double | Triple | Home Run | TOTAL HITS |
|---|---|---|---|---|---|
| Babe Ruth | 1,517 | 506 | 136 | 714 | 2,873 |
| Jackie Robinson | 1,054 | 273 | 54 | 137 | 1,518 |
| Ty Cobb | 3,603 | 174 | 295 | 114 | 4,189 |
| Hank Aaron | 2,294 | 624 | 98 | 755 | 3,771 |
| TOTAL | 8,471 | 1,577 | 583 | 1,720 | 12,351 |

Table 3.18

**116.** Find $P$(hit was made by Babe Ruth).
   a. $\frac{1518}{2873}$
   b. $\frac{2873}{12351}$
   c. $\frac{583}{12351}$
   d. $\frac{4189}{12351}$

**117.** Find $P$(hit was made by Ty Cobb|The hit was a Home Run).

    a. $\dfrac{4189}{12351}$

    b. $\dfrac{114}{1720}$

    c. $\dfrac{1720}{4189}$

    d. $\dfrac{114}{12351}$

**118.** Table 3.19 identifies a group of children by one of four hair colors, and by type of hair.

| Hair Type | Brown | Blond | Black | Red | Totals |
|---|---|---|---|---|---|
| Wavy | 20 | | 15 | 3 | 43 |
| Straight | 80 | 15 | | 12 | |
| Totals | | 20 | | | 215 |

Table 3.19

    a. Complete the table.
    b. What is the probability that a randomly selected child will have wavy hair?
    c. What is the probability that a randomly selected child will have either brown or blond hair?
    d. What is the probability that a randomly selected child will have wavy brown hair?
    e. What is the probability that a randomly selected child will have red hair, given that he or she has straight hair?
    f. If $B$ is the event of a child having brown hair, find the probability of the complement of $B$.
    g. In words, what does the complement of $B$ represent?

**119.** In a previous year, the weights of the members of the **San Francisco 49ers** and the **Dallas Cowboys** were published in the *San Jose Mercury News*. The factual data were compiled into the following table.

| Shirt# | ≤ 210 | 211–250 | 251–290 | > 290 |
|---|---|---|---|---|
| 1–33 | 21 | 5 | 0 | 0 |
| 34–66 | 6 | 18 | 7 | 4 |
| 66–99 | 6 | 12 | 22 | 5 |

Table 3.20

For the following, suppose that you randomly select one player from the 49ers or Cowboys.

    a. Find the probability that his shirt number is from 1 to 33.
    b. Find the probability that he weighs at most 210 pounds.
    c. Find the probability that his shirt number is from 1 to 33 AND he weighs at most 210 pounds.
    d. Find the probability that his shirt number is from 1 to 33 OR he weighs at most 210 pounds.
    e. Find the probability that his shirt number is from 1 to 33 GIVEN that he weighs at most 210 pounds.

*Use the following information to answer the next two exercises.* This tree diagram shows the tossing of an unfair coin followed by drawing one bead from a cup containing three red ($R$), four yellow ($Y$) and five blue ($B$) beads. For the coin, $P(H) = \frac{2}{3}$ and $P(T) = \frac{1}{3}$ where $H$ is heads and $T$ is tails.

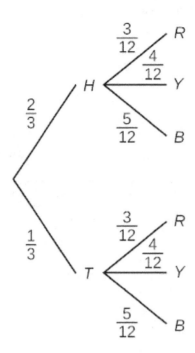

**Figure 3.20**

**120.** Find $P$(tossing a Head on the coin AND a Red bead)

    a.  $\frac{2}{3}$

    b.  $\frac{5}{15}$

    c.  $\frac{6}{36}$

    d.  $\frac{5}{36}$

**121.** Find $P$(Blue bead).

    a.  $\frac{15}{36}$

    b.  $\frac{10}{36}$

    c.  $\frac{10}{12}$

    d.  $\frac{6}{36}$

**122.** A box of cookies contains three chocolate and seven butter cookies. Miguel randomly selects a cookie and eats it. Then he randomly selects another cookie and eats it. (How many cookies did he take?)

    a.  Draw the tree that represents the possibilities for the cookie selections. Write the probabilities along each branch of the tree.

    b.  Are the probabilities for the flavor of the SECOND cookie that Miguel selects independent of his first selection? Explain.

    c.  For each complete path through the tree, write the event it represents and find the probabilities.

    d.  Let S be the event that both cookies selected were the same flavor. Find $P(S)$.

    e.  Let $T$ be the event that the cookies selected were different flavors. Find $P(T)$ by two different methods: by using the complement rule and by using the branches of the tree. Your answers should be the same with both methods.

    f.  Let $U$ be the event that the second cookie selected is a butter cookie. Find $P(U)$.

## BRINGING IT TOGETHER: HOMEWORK

**123.** A previous year, the weights of the members of the **San Francisco 49ers** and the **Dallas Cowboys** were published in the *San Jose Mercury News*. The factual data are compiled into Table 3.21.

| Shirt# | ≤ 210 | 211–250 | 251–290 | 290≤ |
|--------|-------|---------|---------|------|
| 1–33 | 21 | 5 | 0 | 0 |
| 34–66 | 6 | 18 | 7 | 4 |
| 66–99 | 6 | 12 | 22 | 5 |

Table 3.21

For the following, suppose that you randomly select one player from the 49ers or Cowboys.

If having a shirt number from one to 33 and weighing at most 210 pounds were independent events, then what should be true about $P$(Shirt# 1–33|≤ 210 pounds)?

**124.** The probability that a male develops some form of cancer in his lifetime is 0.4567. The probability that a male has at least one false positive test result (meaning the test comes back for cancer when the man does not have it) is 0.51. Some of the following questions do not have enough information for you to answer them. Write "not enough information" for those answers. Let $C$ = a man develops cancer in his lifetime and $P$ = man has at least one false positive.
   a.   $P(C) = $ _____
   b.   $P(P|C) = $ _____
   c.   $P(P|C') = $ _____
   d.   If a test comes up positive, based upon numerical values, can you assume that man has cancer? Justify numerically and explain why or why not.

**125.** Given events $G$ and $H$: $P(G) = 0.43$; $P(H) = 0.26$; $P(H \cap G) = 0.14$
   a.   Find $P(H \cup G)$.
   b.   Find the probability of the complement of event $(H \cap G)$.
   c.   Find the probability of the complement of event $(H \cup G)$.

**126.** Given events $J$ and $K$ : $P(J) = 0.18$; $P(K) = 0.37$; $P(J \cup K) = 0.45$
   a.   Find $P(J \cap K)$.
   b.   Find the probability of the complement of event $(J \cap K)$.
   c.   Find the probability of the complement of event $(J \cap K)$.

## REFERENCES

### 3.1 Terminology

"Countries List by Continent." Worldatlas, 2013. Available online at http://www.worldatlas.com/cntycont.htm (accessed May 2, 2013).

### 3.2 Independent and Mutually Exclusive Events

Lopez, Shane, Preety Sidhu. "U.S. Teachers Love Their Lives, but Struggle in the Workplace." Gallup Wellbeing, 2013. http://www.gallup.com/poll/161516/teachers-love-lives-struggle-workplace.aspx (accessed May 2, 2013).

Data from Gallup. Available online at www.gallup.com/ (accessed May 2, 2013).

### 3.3 Two Basic Rules of Probability

DiCamillo, Mark, Mervin Field. "The File Poll." Field Research Corporation. Available online at http://www.field.com/fieldpollonline/subscribers/Rls2443.pdf (accessed May 2, 2013).

Rider, David, "Ford support plummeting, poll suggests," The Star, September 14, 2011. Available online at http://www.thestar.com/news/gta/2011/09/14/ford_support_plummeting_poll_suggests.html (accessed May 2, 2013).

"Mayor's Approval Down." News Release by Forum Research Inc. Available online at http://www.forumresearch.com/forms/News                                    Archives/News                                    Releases/74209_TO_Issues_-_Mayoral_Approval_%28Forum_Research%29%2820130320%29.pdf (accessed May 2, 2013).

"Roulette." Wikipedia. Available online at http://en.wikipedia.org/wiki/Roulette (accessed May 2, 2013).

Shin, Hyon B., Robert A. Kominski. "Language Use in the United States: 2007." United States Census Bureau. Available online at http://www.census.gov/hhes/socdemo/language/data/acs/ACS-12.pdf (accessed May 2, 2013).

Data from the Baseball-Almanac, 2013. Available online at www.baseball-almanac.com (accessed May 2, 2013).

Data from U.S. Census Bureau.

Data from the Wall Street Journal.

Data from The Roper Center: Public Opinion Archives at the University of Connecticut. Available online at http://www.ropercenter.uconn.edu/ (accessed May 2, 2013).

Data from Field Research Corporation. Available online at www.field.com/fieldpollonline (accessed May 2,2 013).

## 3.4 Contingency Tables and Probability Trees

"Blood Types." American Red Cross, 2013. Available online at http://www.redcrossblood.org/learn-about-blood/blood-types (accessed May 3, 2013).

Data from the National Center for Health Statistics, part of the United States Department of Health and Human Services.

Data from United States Senate. Available online at www.senate.gov (accessed May 2, 2013).

"Human Blood Types." Unite Blood Services, 2011. Available online at http://www.unitedbloodservices.org/learnMore.aspx (accessed May 2, 2013).

Haiman, Christopher A., Daniel O. Stram, Lynn R. Wilkens, Malcom C. Pike, Laurence N. Kolonel, Brien E. Henderson, and Loïc Le Marchand. "Ethnic and Racial Differences in the Smoking-Related Risk of Lung Cancer." The New England Journal of Medicine, 2013. Available online at http://www.nejm.org/doi/full/10.1056/NEJMoa033250 (accessed May 2, 2013).

Samuel, T. M. "Strange Facts about RH Negative Blood." eHow Health, 2013. Available online at http://www.ehow.com/facts_5552003_strange-rh-negative-blood.html (accessed May 2, 2013).

"United States: Uniform Crime Report – State Statistics from 1960–2011." The Disaster Center. Available online at http://www.disastercenter.com/crime/ (accessed May 2, 2013).

Data from Clara County Public H.D.

Data from the American Cancer Society.

Data from The Data and Story Library, 1996. Available online at http://lib.stat.cmu.edu/DASL/ (accessed May 2, 2013).

Data from the Federal Highway Administration, part of the United States Department of Transportation.

Data from the United States Census Bureau, part of the United States Department of Commerce.

Data from USA Today.

"Environment." The World Bank, 2013. Available online at http://data.worldbank.org/topic/environment (accessed May 2, 2013).

"Search for Datasets." Roper Center: Public Opinion Archives, University of Connecticut., 2013. Available online at http://www.ropercenter.uconn.edu/data_access/data/search_for_datasets.html (accessed May 2, 2013).

## SOLUTIONS

1

  a.  $P(L') = P(S)$

  b.  $P(M \cup S)$

  c.  $P(F \cap L)$

  d.  $P(M \mid L)$

  e.  $P(L \mid M)$

  f.  $P(S \mid F)$

  g.  $P(F \mid L)$

  h.  $P(F \cup L)$

  i.  $P(M \cap S)$

  j.  $P(F)$

3  $P(N) = \dfrac{15}{42} = \dfrac{5}{14} = 0.36$

5  $P(C) = \dfrac{5}{42} = 0.12$

7  $P(G) = \dfrac{20}{150} = \dfrac{2}{15} = 0.13$

9  $P(R) = \dfrac{22}{150} = \dfrac{11}{75} = 0.15$

11  $P(O) = \dfrac{150 - 22 - 38 - 20 - 28 - 26}{150} = \dfrac{16}{150} = \dfrac{8}{75} = 0.11$

13  $P(E) = \dfrac{47}{194} = 0.24$

15  $P(N) = \dfrac{23}{194} = 0.12$

17  $P(S) = \dfrac{12}{194} = \dfrac{6}{97} = 0.06$

19  $\dfrac{13}{52} = \dfrac{1}{4} = 0.25$

21  $\dfrac{3}{6} = \dfrac{1}{2} = 0.5$

23  $P(R) = \dfrac{4}{8} = 0.5$

25  $P(O \cup H)$

27  $P(H \mid I)$

29  $P(N \mid O)$

31  $P(I \cup N)$

33  $P(I)$

35  The likelihood that an event will occur given that another event has already occurred.

37  1

**39** the probability of landing on an even number or a multiple of three

**41** $P(J) = 0.3$

**43** $P(Q \cap R) = P(Q)P(R)$  $0.1 = (0.4)P(R)$  $P(R) = 0.25$

**45** 0.376

**47** $C | L$ means, given the person chosen is a Latino Californian, the person is a registered voter who prefers life in prison without parole for a person convicted of first degree murder.

**49** $L \cap C$ is the event that the person chosen is a Latino California registered voter who prefers life without parole over the death penalty for a person convicted of first degree murder.

**51** 0.6492

**53** No, because $P(L \cap C)$ does not equal 0.

**55** $P(\text{musician is a male} \cap \text{had private instruction}) = \frac{15}{130} = \frac{3}{26} = 0.12$

**57** $P(\text{being a female musician} \cap \text{learning music in school}) = \frac{38}{130} = \frac{19}{65} = 0.29$ $P(\text{being a female musician})P(\text{learning music in school}) = \left(\frac{72}{130}\right)\left(\frac{62}{130}\right) = \frac{4,464}{16,900} = \frac{1,116}{4,225} = 0.26$ No, they are not independent because $P(\text{being a female musician} \cap \text{learning music in school})$ is not equal to $P(\text{being a female musician})P(\text{learning music in school})$.

**58**

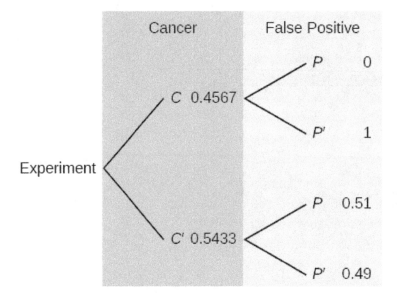

**Figure 3.21**

**60** $\frac{35,065}{100,450}$

**62** To pick one person from the study who is Japanese American AND smokes 21 to 30 cigarettes per day means that the person has to meet both criteria: both Japanese American and smokes 21 to 30 cigarettes. The sample space should include everyone in the study. The probability is $\frac{4,715}{100,450}$.

**64** To pick one person from the study who is Japanese American given that person smokes 21-30 cigarettes per day, means that the person must fulfill both criteria and the sample space is reduced to those who smoke 21-30 cigarettes per day. The probability is $\frac{4715}{15,273}$.

66

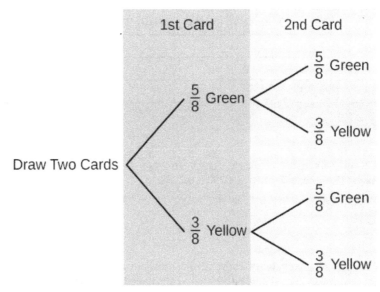

a.

**Figure 3.22**

b. $P(GG) = \left(\frac{5}{8}\right)\left(\frac{5}{8}\right) = \frac{25}{64}$

c. $P(\text{at least one green}) = P(GG) + P(GY) + P(YG) = \frac{25}{64} + \frac{15}{64} + \frac{15}{64} = \frac{55}{64}$

d. $P(G \mid G) = \frac{5}{8}$

e. Yes, they are independent because the first card is placed back in the bag before the second card is drawn; the composition of cards in the bag remains the same from draw one to draw two.

68

a.

|  | <20 | 20–64 | >64 | Totals |
|---|---|---|---|---|
| **Female** | 0.0244 | 0.3954 | 0.0661 | 0.486 |
| **Male** | 0.0259 | 0.4186 | 0.0695 | 0.514 |
| **Totals** | 0.0503 | 0.8140 | 0.1356 | 1 |

**Table 3.22**

b. $P(F) = 0.486$

c. $P(>64 \mid F) = 0.1361$

d. $P(>64 \text{ and } F) = P(F) \, P(>64|F) = (0.486)(0.1361) = 0.0661$

e. $P(>64 \mid F)$ is the percentage of female drivers who are 65 or older and $P(>64 \cap F)$ is the percentage of drivers who are female and 65 or older.

f. $P(>64) = P(>64 \cap F) + P(>64 \cap M) = 0.1356$

g. No, being female and 65 or older are not mutually exclusive because they can occur at the same time $P(>64 \cap F) = 0.0661$.

**70**

a.

|            | Car, Truck or Van | Walk   | Public Transportation | Other  | Totals |
|------------|-------------------|--------|-----------------------|--------|--------|
| **Alone**     | 0.7318            |        |                       |        |        |
| **Not Alone** | 0.1332            |        |                       |        |        |
| **Totals**    | 0.8650            | 0.0390 | 0.0530                | 0.0430 | 1      |

Table 3.23

b. If we assume that all walkers are alone and that none from the other two groups travel alone (which is a big assumption) we have: $P(\text{Alone}) = 0.7318 + 0.0390 = 0.7708$.

c. Make the same assumptions as in (b) we have: $(0.7708)(1,000) = 771$

d. $(0.1332)(1,000) = 133$

**73**

a. You can't calculate the joint probability knowing the probability of both events occurring, which is not in the information given; the probabilities should be multiplied, not added; and probability is never greater than 100%

b. A home run by definition is a successful hit, so he has to have at least as many successful hits as home runs.

**75** 0

**77** 0.3571

**79** 0.2142

**81** Physician (83.7)

**83** $83.7 - 79.6 = 4.1$

**85** $P(\text{Occupation} < 81.3) = 0.5$

**87**

a. The Forum Research surveyed 1,046 Torontonians.

b. 58%

c. 42% of 1,046 = 439 (rounding to the nearest integer)

d. 0.57

e. 0.60.

**89**

a. $P(\text{Betting on two line that touch each other on the table}) = \frac{6}{38}$

b. $P(\text{Betting on three numbers in a line}) = \frac{3}{38}$

c. $P(\text{Bettting on one number}) = \frac{1}{38}$

d. $P(\text{Betting on four number that touch each other to form a square}) = \frac{4}{38}$

e. $P(\text{Betting on two number that touch each other on the table }) = \frac{2}{38}$

f. $P(\text{Betting on 0-00-1-2-3}) = \frac{5}{38}$

g. $P$(Betting on 0-1-2; or 0-00-2; or 00-2-3) $= \frac{3}{38}$

**91**

a. $\{G1, G2, G3, G4, G5, Y1, Y2, Y3\}$

b. $\frac{5}{8}$

c. $\frac{2}{3}$

d. $\frac{2}{8}$

e. $\frac{6}{8}$

f. No, because $P(G \cap E)$ does not equal 0.

**93**

> **NOTE**
>
> The coin toss is independent of the card picked first.

a. $\{(G,H) (G,T) (B,H) (B,T) (R,H) (R,T)\}$

b. $P(A) = P(\text{blue})P(\text{head}) = \left(\frac{3}{10}\right)\left(\frac{1}{2}\right) = \frac{3}{20}$

c. Yes, $A$ and $B$ are mutually exclusive because they cannot happen at the same time; you cannot pick a card that is both blue and also (red or green). $P(A \cap B) = 0$

d. No, $A$ and $C$ are not mutually exclusive because they can occur at the same time. In fact, $C$ includes all of the outcomes of $A$; if the card chosen is blue it is also (red or blue). $P(A \cap C) = P(A) = \frac{3}{20}$

**95**

a. $S = \{(HHH), (HHT), (HTH), (HTT), (THH), (THT), (TTH), (TTT)\}$

b. $\frac{4}{8}$

c. Yes, because if $A$ has occurred, it is impossible to obtain two tails. In other words, $P(A \cap B) = 0$.

**97**

a. If $Y$ and $Z$ are independent, then $P(Y \cap Z) = P(Y)P(Z)$, so $P(Y \cup Z) = P(Y) + P(Z) - P(Y)P(Z)$.

b. 0.5

**99** iii; i; iv; ii

**101**

a. $P(R) = 0.44$

b. $P(R \mid E) = 0.56$

c. $P(R \mid O) = 0.31$

d. No, whether the money is returned is not independent of which class the money was placed in. There are several ways to justify this mathematically, but one is that the money placed in economics classes is not returned at the same overall rate; $P(R \mid E) \neq P(R)$.

e. No, this study definitely does not support that notion; *in fact*, it suggests the opposite. The money placed in the economics classrooms was returned at a higher rate than the money place in all classes collectively; $P(R \mid E) > P(R)$.

**103**

a.  $P(\text{type O} \cup \text{Rh-}) = P(\text{type O}) + P(\text{Rh-}) - P(\text{type O} \cap \text{Rh-})$

    $0.52 = 0.43 + 0.15 - P(\text{type O} \cap \text{Rh-})$; solve to find $P(\text{type O} \cap \text{Rh-}) = 0.06$

    6% of people have type O, Rh- blood

b.  $P(\text{NOT}(\text{type O} \cap \text{Rh-})) = 1 - P(\text{type O} \cap \text{Rh-}) = 1 - 0.06 = 0.94$

    94% of people do not have type O, Rh- blood

**105**

a.  Let $C$ = be the event that the cookie contains chocolate. Let $N$ = the event that the cookie contains nuts.

b.  $P(C \cup N) = P(C) + P(N) - P(C \cap N) = 0.36 + 0.12 - 0.08 = 0.40$

c.  $P(\text{NEITHER chocolate NOR nuts}) = 1 - P(C \cup N) = 1 - 0.40 = 0.60$

**107** 0

**109** $\frac{10}{67}$

**111** $\frac{10}{34}$

**113** d

**115**

a.

| Race and Sex | 1–14 | 15–24 | 25–64 | over 64 | TOTALS |
|---|---|---|---|---|---|
| white, male | 210 | 3,360 | 13,610 | 4,870 | 22,050 |
| white, female | 80 | 580 | 3,380 | 890 | 4,930 |
| black, male | 10 | 460 | 1,060 | 140 | 1,670 |
| black, female | 0 | 40 | 270 | 20 | 330 |
| all others | | | | 100 | |
| TOTALS | 310 | 4,650 | 18,780 | 6,020 | 29,760 |

Table 3.24

b.

| Race and Sex | 1–14 | 15–24 | 25–64 | over 64 | TOTALS |
|---|---|---|---|---|---|
| white, male | 210 | 3,360 | 13,610 | 4,870 | 22,050 |
| white, female | 80 | 580 | 3,380 | 890 | 4,930 |
| black, male | 10 | 460 | 1,060 | 140 | 1,670 |
| black, female | 0 | 40 | 270 | 20 | 330 |
| all others | 10 | 210 | 460 | 100 | 780 |
| TOTALS | 310 | 4,650 | 18,780 | 6,020 | 29,760 |

Table 3.25

c.  $\dfrac{22{,}050}{29{,}760}$

d.  $\dfrac{330}{29{,}760}$

e.  $\dfrac{2{,}000}{29{,}760}$

f.  $\dfrac{23{,}720}{29{,}760}$

g.  $\dfrac{5{,}010}{6{,}020}$

**117** b

**119**

a.  $\dfrac{26}{106}$

b.  $\dfrac{33}{106}$

c.  $\dfrac{21}{106}$

d.  $\left(\dfrac{26}{106}\right) + \left(\dfrac{33}{106}\right) - \left(\dfrac{21}{106}\right) = \left(\dfrac{38}{106}\right)$

e.  $\dfrac{21}{33}$

**121** a

**124**

a.  $P(C) = 0.4567$

b.  not enough information

c.  not enough information

d.  No, because over half (0.51) of men have at least one false positive text

**126**

a.  $(J \cup K) = P(\,J\,) + P(K) - P(J \cap K)$; $0.45 = 0.18 + 0.37 - P(J \cap K)$; solve to fin  $P(J \cap K) = 0.10$

b.  $P(\text{NOT}(J \cap K)) = 1 - P(J \cap K) = 1 - 0.10 = 0.90$

c.  $P(\text{NOT}(J \cup K)) = 1 - P(J \cup K) = 1 - 0.45 = 0.55$

# 4 | DISCRETE RANDOM VARIABLES

**Figure 4.1** You can use probability and discrete random variables to calculate the likelihood of lightning striking the ground five times during a half-hour thunderstorm. (Credit: Leszek Leszczynski)

## Introduction

A student takes a ten-question, true-false quiz. Because the student had such a busy schedule, he or she could not study and guesses randomly at each answer. What is the probability of the student passing the test with at least a 70%?

Small companies might be interested in the number of long-distance phone calls their employees make during the peak time of the day. Suppose the historical average is 20 calls. What is the probability that the employees make more than 20 long-distance phone calls during the peak time?

These two examples illustrate two different types of probability problems involving discrete random variables. Recall that discrete data are data that you can count, that is, the random variable can only take on whole number values. A **random variable** describes the outcomes of a statistical experiment in words. The values of a random variable can vary with each repetition of an experiment, often called a trial.

### Random Variable Notation

The upper case letter $X$ denotes a random variable. Lower case letters like $x$ or $y$ denote the value of a random variable. If $X$ **is a random variable, then $X$ is written in words, and $x$ is given as a number.**

For example, let $X$ = the number of heads you get when you toss three fair coins. The sample space for the toss of three fair coins is *TTT*; *THH*; *HTH*; *HHT*; *HTT*; *THT*; *TTH*; *HHH*. Then, $x$ = 0, 1, 2, 3. $X$ is in words and $x$ is a number. Notice that for this example, the $x$ values are countable outcomes. Because you can count the possible values as whole numbers that $X$ can take on and the outcomes are random (the $x$ values 0, 1, 2, 3), $X$ is a discrete random variable.

## Probability Density Functions (PDF) for a Random Variable

A **probability density function** or **probability distribution function** has two characteristics:

1.  Each probability is between zero and one, inclusive.

2.  The sum of the probabilities is one.

A probability density function is a mathematical formula that calculates probabilities for specific types of events, what we have been calling experiments. There is a sort of magic to a probability density function (Pdf) partially because the same formula often describes very different types of events. For example, the binomial Pdf will calculate probabilities for flipping coins, yes/no questions on an exam, opinions of voters in an up or down opinion poll, indeed any binary event. Other probability density functions will provide probabilities for the time until a part will fail, when a customer will arrive at the turnpike booth, the number of telephone calls arriving at a central switchboard, the growth rate of a bacterium, and on and on. There are whole families of probability density functions that are used in a wide variety of applications, including medicine, business and finance, physics and engineering, among others.

For our needs here we will concentrate on only a few probability density functions as we develop the tools of inferential statistics.

## Counting Formulas and the Combinational Formula

To repeat, the probability of event A , P(A), is simply the number of ways the experiment will result in A, relative to the total number of possible outcomes of the experiment.

As an equation this is:

$$P(A) = \frac{\text{number of ways to get A}}{\text{Total number of possible outcomes}}$$

When we looked at the sample space for flipping 3 coins we could easily write the full sample space and thus could easily count the number of events that met our desired result, e.g. x = 1 , where X is the random variable defined as the number of heads.

As we have larger numbers of items in the sample space, such as a full deck of 52 cards, the ability to write out the sample space becomes impossible.

We see that probabilities are nothing more than counting the events in each group we are interested in and dividing by the number of elements in the universe, or sample space. This is easy enough if we are counting sophomores in a Stat class, but in more complicated cases listing all the possible outcomes may take a life time. There are, for example, 36 possible outcomes from throwing just two six-sided dice where the random variable is the sum of the number of spots on the up-facing sides. If there were four dice then the total number of possible outcomes would become 1,296. There are more than 2.5 MILLION possible 5 card poker hands in a standard deck of 52 cards. Obviously keeping track of all these possibilities and counting them to get at a single probability would be tedious at best.

An alternative to listing the complete sample space and counting the number of elements we are interested in, is to skip the step of listing the sample space, and simply figuring out the number of elements in it and doing the appropriate division. If we are after a probability we really do not need to see each and every element in the sample space, we only need to know how many elements are there. Counting formulas were invented to do just this. They tell us the number of unordered subsets of a certain size that can be created from a set of unique elements. By unordered it is meant that, for example, when dealing cards, it does not matter if you got {ace, ace, ace, ace, king} or {king, ace, ace, ace, ace} or {ace, king, ace, ace, ace} and so on. Each of these subsets are the same because they each have 4 aces and one king.

### Combinational Formula

$$\binom{n}{x} = {}_nC_x = \frac{n!}{x!(n-x)!}$$

This is the formula that tells the number of unique unordered subsets of size x that can be created from n unique elements. The formula is read "n combinatorial x". Sometimes it is read as "n choose x." The exclamation point "!" is called a factorial and tells us to take all the numbers from 1 through the number before the ! and multiply them together thus 4! is 1*2*3*4=24. By definition 0! = 1. The formula is called the Combinatorial Formula. It is also called the Binomial Coefficient, for reasons that will be clear shortly. While this mathematical concept was understood long before 1653, Blaise

Pascal is given major credit for his proof that he published in that year. Further, he developed a generalized method of calculating the values for combinatorials known to us as the Pascal Triangle. Pascal was one of the geniuses of an era of extraordinary intellectual advancement which included the work of Galileo, Rene Descartes, Isaac Newton, William Shakespeare and the refinement of the scientific method, the very rationale for the topic of this text.

Let's find the hard way the total number of combinations of the four aces in a deck of cards if we were going to take them two at a time. The sample space would be:

S={Spade,Heart),(Spade, Diamond),(Spade,Club), (Diamond,Club),(Heart,Diamond),(Heart,Club)}

There are 6 combinations; formally, six unique unordered subsets of size 2 that can be created from 4 unique elements. To use the combinatorial formula we would solve the formula as follows:

$$\binom{4}{2} = \frac{4!}{(4-2)!2!} = \frac{4 \cdot 3 \cdot 2 \cdot 1}{2 \cdot 1 \cdot 2 \cdot 1} = 6$$

If we wanted to know the number of unique 5 card poker hands that could be created from a 52 card deck we simply compute:

$$\binom{52}{5}$$

where 52 is the total number of unique elements from which we are drawing and 5 is the size group we are putting them into.

With the combinatorial formula we can count the number of elements in a sample space without having to write each one of them down, truly a lifetime's work for just the number of 5 card hands from a deck of 52 cards. We can now apply this tool to a very important probability density function, the hypergeometric distribution.

Remember, a probability density function computes probabilities for us. We simply put the appropriate numbers in the formula and we get the probability of specific events. However, for these formulas to work they must be applied only to cases for which they were designed.

# 4.1 | Hypergeometric Distribution

The simplest probability density function is the hypergeometric. This is the most basic one because it is created by combining our knowledge of probabilities from Venn diagrams, the addition and multiplication rules, and the combinatorial counting formula.

To find the number of ways to get 2 aces from the four in the deck we computed:

$$\binom{4}{2} = \frac{4!}{2!(4-2)!} = 6$$

And if we did not care what else we had in our hand for the other three cards we would compute:

$$\binom{48}{3} = \frac{48!}{3!45!} = 17,296$$

Putting this together, we can compute the probability of getting exactly two aces in a 5 card poker hand as:

$$\frac{\binom{4}{2}\binom{48}{3}}{\binom{52}{5}} = .0399$$

This solution is really just the probability distribution known as the Hypergeometric. The generalized formula is:

$$h(x) = \frac{\binom{A}{x}\binom{N-A}{n-x}}{\binom{N}{n}}$$

where $x$ = the number we are interested in coming from the group with A objects.

h(x) is the probability of x successes, in n attempts, when A successes (aces in this case) are in a population that contains N elements. The hypergeometric distribution is an example of a discrete probability distribution because there is no possibility of partial success, that is, there can be no poker hands with 2 1/2 aces. Said another way, a discrete random variable has to be a whole, or counting, number only. This probability distribution works in cases where the probability of a success changes with each draw. Another way of saying this is that the events are NOT independent. In using a deck of cards, we are sampling WITHOUT replacement. If we put each card back after it was drawn then the hypergeometric distribution be an inappropriate Pdf.

For the hypergeometric to work,

1. the population must be dividable into two and only two independent subsets (aces and non-aces in our example). The random variable X = the number of items from the group of interest.

2. the experiment must have changing probabilities of success with each experiment (the fact that cards are not replaced after the draw in our example makes this true in this case). Another way to say this is that you sample without replacement and therefore each pick is not independent.

3. the random variable must be discrete, rather than continuous.

## Example 4.1

A candy dish contains 30 jelly beans and 20 gumdrops. Ten candies are picked at random. What is the probability that 5 of the 10 are gumdrops? The two groups are jelly beans and gumdrops. Since the probability question asks for the probability of picking gumdrops, the group of interest (first group A in the formula) is gumdrops. The size of the group of interest (first group) is 30. The size of the second group is 20. The size of the sample is 10 (jelly beans or gumdrops). Let $X$ = the number of gumdrops in the sample of 10. $X$ takes on the values $x$ = 0, 1, 2, ..., 10. a. What is the probability statement written mathematically? b. What is the hypergeometric probability density function written out to solve this problem? c. What is the answer to the question "What is the probability of drawing 5 gumdrops in 10 picks from the dish?"

**Solution 4.1**

a. $P(x = 5)$

b. $P(x = 5) = \dfrac{\binom{30}{5}\binom{20}{5}}{\binom{50}{10}}$

c. $P(x = 5) = 0.215$

## Try It $\Sigma$

**4.1** A bag contains letter tiles. Forty-four of the tiles are vowels, and 56 are consonants. Seven tiles are picked at random. You want to know the probability that four of the seven tiles are vowels. What is the group of interest, the size of the group of interest, and the size of the sample?

# 4.2 | Binomial Distribution

A more valuable probability density function with many applications is the binomial distribution. This distribution will compute probabilities for any binomial process. A binomial process, often called a Bernoulli process after the first person to fully develop its properties, is any case where there are only two possible outcomes in any one trial, called successes and failures. It gets its name from the binary number system where all numbers are reduced to either 1's or 0's, which is the basis for computer technology and CD music recordings.

## Binomial Formula

$$b(x) = \binom{n}{x} p^x q^{n-x}$$

where b(x) is the probability of X successes in n trials when the probability of a success in ANY ONE TRIAL is p. And of course q=(1-p) and is the probability of a failure in any one trial.

We can see now why the combinatorial formula is also called the binomial coefficient because it reappears here again in the binomial probability function. For the binomial formula to work, the probability of a success in any one trial must be the same from trial to trial, or in other words, the outcomes of each trial must be independent. Flipping a coin is a binomial process because the probability of getting a head in one flip does not depend upon what has happened in PREVIOUS flips. (At this time it should be noted that using p for the parameter of the binomial distribution is a violation of the rule that population parameters are designated with Greek letters. In many textbooks $\theta$ (pronounced theta) is used instead of p and this is how it should be.

Just like a set of data, a probability density function has a mean and a standard deviation that describes the data set. For the binomial distribution these are given by the formulas:

$$\mu = np$$

$$\sigma = \sqrt{npq}$$

Notice that p is the only parameter in these equations. The binomial distribution is thus seen as coming from the one-parameter family of probability distributions. In short, we know all there is to know about the binomial once we know p, the probability of a success in any one trial.

In probability theory, under certain circumstances, one probability distribution can be used to approximate another. We say that one is the limiting distribution of the other. If a small number is to be drawn from a large population, even if there is no replacement, we can still use the binomial even thought this is not a binomial process. If there is no replacement it violates the independence rule of the binomial. Nevertheless, we can use the binomial to approximate a probability that is really a hypergeometric distribution if we are drawing fewer than 10 percent of the population, i.e. n is less than 10 percent of N in the formula for the hypergeometric function. The rationale for this argument is that when drawing a small percentage of the population we do not alter the probability of a success from draw to draw in any meaningful way. Imagine drawing from not one deck of 52 cards but from 6 decks of cards. The probability of say drawing an ace does not change the conditional probability of what happens on a second draw in the same way it would if there were only 4 aces rather than the 24 aces now to draw from. This ability to use one probability distribution to estimate others will become very valuable to us later.

There are three characteristics of a binomial experiment.

1.  There are a fixed number of trials. Think of trials as repetitions of an experiment. The letter $n$ denotes the number of trials.

2.  The random variable, $x$, number of successes, is discrete.

3.  There are only two possible outcomes, called "success" and "failure," for each trial. The letter $p$ denotes the probability of a success on any one trial, and $q$ denotes the probability of a failure on any one trial. $p + q = 1$.

4.  The $n$ trials are independent and are repeated using identical conditions. Think of this as drawing WITH replacement. Because the $n$ trials are independent, the outcome of one trial does not help in predicting the outcome of another trial. Another way of saying this is that for each individual trial, the probability, $p$, of a success and probability, $q$, of a failure remain the same. For example, randomly guessing at a true-false statistics question has only two outcomes. If a success is guessing correctly, then a failure is guessing incorrectly. Suppose Joe always guesses correctly on any statistics true-false question with a probability $p = 0.6$. Then, $q = 0.4$. This means that for every true-false statistics question Joe answers, his probability of success ($p = 0.6$) and his probability of failure ($q = 0.4$) remain the same.

The outcomes of a binomial experiment fit a **binomial probability distribution**. The random variable $X$ = the number of successes obtained in the $n$ independent trials.

The mean, $\mu$, and variance, $\sigma^2$, for the binomial probability distribution are $\mu = np$ and $\sigma^2 = npq$. The standard deviation, $\sigma$, is then $\sigma = \sqrt{npq}$.

Any experiment that has characteristics three and four and where $n = 1$ is called a **Bernoulli Trial** (named after Jacob Bernoulli who, in the late 1600s, studied them extensively). A binomial experiment takes place when the number of successes is counted in one or more Bernoulli Trials.

## Example 4.2

Suppose you play a game that you can only either win or lose. The probability that you win any game is 55%, and the probability that you lose is 45%. Each game you play is independent. If you play the game 20 times, write the function that describes the probability that you win 15 of the 20 times. Here, if you define $X$ as the number of wins, then $X$ takes on the values 0, 1, 2, 3, ..., 20. The probability of a success is $p = 0.55$. The probability of a failure is $q = 0.45$. The number of trials is $n = 20$. The probability question can be stated mathematically as $P(x = 15)$.

**4.2** A trainer is teaching a dolphin to do tricks. The probability that the dolphin successfully performs the trick is 35%, and the probability that the dolphin does not successfully perform the trick is 65%. Out of 20 attempts, you want to find the probability that the dolphin succeeds 12 times. Find the $P(X=12)$ using the binomial Pdf.

## Example 4.3

A fair coin is flipped 15 times. Each flip is independent. What is the probability of getting more than ten heads? Let $X$ = the number of heads in 15 flips of the fair coin. $X$ takes on the values 0, 1, 2, 3, ..., 15. Since the coin is fair, $p = 0.5$ and $q = 0.5$. The number of trials is $n = 15$. State the probability question mathematically.

**Solution 4.3**
$P(x > 10)$

## Example 4.4

Approximately 70% of statistics students do their homework in time for it to be collected and graded. Each student does homework independently. In a statistics class of 50 students, what is the probability that at least 40 will do their homework on time? Students are selected randomly.

a. This is a binomial problem because there is only a success or a _____, there are a fixed number of trials, and the probability of a success is 0.70 for each trial.

**Solution 4.4**
a. failure

b. If we are interested in the number of students who do their homework on time, then how do we define $X$?

**Solution 4.4**
b. $X$ = the number of statistics students who do their homework on time

c. What values does $x$ take on?

**Solution 4.4**
c. 0, 1, 2, ..., 50

d. What is a "failure," in words?

**Solution 4.4**

d. Failure is defined as a student who does not complete his or her homework on time.

The probability of a success is $p = 0.70$. The number of trials is $n = 50$.

e. If $p + q = 1$, then what is $q$?

**Solution 4.4**
e. $q = 0.30$

f. The words "at least" translate as what kind of inequality for the probability question $P(x \_\_\_\_ 40)$.

**Solution 4.4**
f. greater than or equal to ($\geq$)
The probability question is $P(x \geq 40)$.

**Try It** $\Sigma$

**4.4** Sixty-five percent of people pass the state driver's exam on the first try. A group of 50 individuals who have taken the driver's exam is randomly selected. Give two reasons why this is a binomial problem.

**Try It** $\Sigma$

**4.4** During the 2013 regular NBA season, DeAndre Jordan of the Los Angeles Clippers had the highest field goal completion rate in the league. DeAndre scored with 61.3% of his shots. Suppose you choose a random sample of 80 shots made by DeAndre during the 2013 season. Let $X$ = the number of shots that scored points.

a. What is the probability distribution for $X$?

b. Using the formulas, calculate the (i) mean and (ii) standard deviation of $X$.

c. Find the probability that DeAndre scored with 60 of these shots.

d. Find the probability that DeAndre scored with more than 50 of these shots.

# 4.3 | Geometric Distribution

The geometric probability density function builds upon what we have learned from the binomial distribution. In this case the experiment continues until either a success or a failure occurs rather than for a set number of trials. There are three main characteristics of a geometric experiment.

1.  There are one or more Bernoulli trials with all failures except the last one, which is a success. In other words, you keep repeating what you are doing until the first success. Then you stop. For example, you throw a dart at a bullseye until you hit the bullseye. The first time you hit the bullseye is a "success" so you stop throwing the dart. It might take six tries until you hit the bullseye. You can think of the trials as failure, failure, failure, failure, failure, success, STOP.

2.  In theory, the number of trials could go on forever.

3.  The probability, $p$, of a success and the probability, $q$, of a failure is the same for each trial. $p + q = 1$ and $q = 1 - p$. For example, the probability of rolling a three when you throw one fair die is $\frac{1}{6}$. This is true no matter how many times you roll the die. Suppose you want to know the probability of getting the first three on the fifth roll. On rolls one through four, you do not get a face with a three. The probability for each of the rolls is $q = \frac{5}{6}$, the probability of a failure. The probability of getting a three on the fifth roll is $\left(\frac{5}{6}\right)\left(\frac{5}{6}\right)\left(\frac{5}{6}\right)\left(\frac{5}{6}\right)\left(\frac{1}{6}\right) = 0.0804$

4.  $X$ = the number of independent trials until the first success.

### Example 4.5

You play a game of chance that you can either win or lose (there are no other possibilities) **until** you lose. Your probability of losing is $p = 0.57$. What is the probability that it takes five games until you lose? Let $X$ = the number of games you play until you lose (includes the losing game). Then $X$ takes on the values 1, 2, 3, ... (could go on indefinitely). The probability question is $P(x = 5)$.

**4.5** You throw darts at a board until you hit the center area. Your probability of hitting the center area is $p = 0.17$. You want to find the probability that it takes eight throws until you hit the center. What values does $X$ take on?

### Example 4.6

A safety engineer feels that 35% of all industrial accidents in her plant are caused by failure of employees to follow instructions. She decides to look at the accident reports (selected randomly and replaced in the pile after reading) **until** she finds one that shows an accident caused by failure of employees to follow instructions. On average, how many reports would the safety engineer **expect** to look at until she finds a report showing an accident caused by employee failure to follow instructions? What is the probability that the safety engineer will have to examine at least three reports until she finds a report showing an accident caused by employee failure to follow instructions?

Let $X$ = the number of accidents the safety engineer must examine **until** she finds a report showing an accident caused by employee failure to follow instructions. $X$ takes on the values 1, 2, 3, .... The first question asks you to find the **expected value** or the mean. The second question asks you to find $P(x \geq 3)$. ("At least" translates to a "greater than or equal to" symbol).

**4.6** An instructor feels that 15% of students get below a C on their final exam. She decides to look at final exams (selected randomly and replaced in the pile after reading) until she finds one that shows a grade below a C. We want to know the probability that the instructor will have to examine at least ten exams until she finds one with a grade below a C. What is the probability question stated mathematically?

### Example 4.7

Suppose that you are looking for a student at your college who lives within five miles of you. You know that 55% of the 25,000 students do live within five miles of you. You randomly contact students from the college **until** one says he or she lives within five miles of you. What is the probability that you need to contact four people?

This is a geometric problem because you may have a number of failures before you have the one success you desire. Also, the probability of a success stays approximately the same each time you ask a student if he or she lives within five miles of you. There is no definite number of trials (number of times you ask a student).

a. Let $X$ = the number of _____ you must ask _____ one says yes.

**Solution 4.7**

a. Let $X$ = the number of **students** you must ask **until** one says yes.

b. What values does $X$ take on?

**Solution 4.7**
b. 1, 2, 3, …, (total number of students)

c. What are $p$ and $q$?

**Solution 4.7**
c. $p = 0.55$; $q = 0.45$

d. The probability question is $P(\underline{\hspace{1.5cm}})$.

**Solution 4.7**
d. $P(x = 4)$

## Notation for the Geometric: G = Geometric Probability Distribution Function

$X \sim G(p)$

Read this as "$X$ is a random variable with a **geometric distribution**." The parameter is $p$; $p$ = the probability of a success for each trial.

The Geometric Pdf tells us the probability that the first occurrence of success requires x number of independent trials, each with success probability p. If the probability of success on each trial is $p$, then the probability that the $x$th trial (out of x trials) is the first success is:

$$P(X = x) = (1 - p)^{x-1}p$$

for $x$ = 1, 2, 3, ....

The expected value of X, the mean of this distribution, is 1/p. This tells us how many trials we have to expect until we get the first success including in the count the trial that results in success. The above form of the Geometric distribution is used for modeling the number of trials until the first success. The number of trials includes the one that is a success: x = all trials including the one that is a success. This can be seen in the form of the formula. If X = number of trials including the success, then we must multiply the probability of failure, (1-p), times the number of failures, that is X-1.

By contrast, the following form of the geometric distribution is used for modeling number of failures until the first success:

$$P(X = x) = (1 - p)^{x}p$$

for $x$ = 0, 1, 2, 3, ....

In this case the trial that is a success is not counted as a trial in the formula: x = number of failures. The expected value, mean, of this distribution is $\mu = \dfrac{(1 - p)}{p}$. This tells us how many failures to expect before we have a success. In either case, the sequence of probabilities is a geometric sequence.

### Example 4.8

Assume that the probability of a defective computer component is 0.02. Components are randomly selected. Find the probability that the first defect is caused by the seventh component tested. How many components do you expect to test until one is found to be defective?

Let $X$ = the number of computer components tested until the first defect is found.

$X$ takes on the values 1, 2, 3, ... where $p = 0.02$. $X \sim G(0.02)$

Find $P(x = 7)$. Answer: $P(x = 7) = (1 - 0.02)^{7-1} \times 0.02 = 0.0177$.

The probability that the seventh component is the first defect is 0.0177.

The graph of $X \sim G(0.02)$ is:

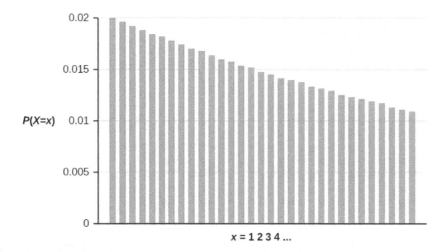

**Figure 4.2**

The $y$-axis contains the probability of $x$, where $X$ = the number of computer components tested. Notice that the probabilities decline by a common increment. This increment is the same ratio between each number and is called a geometric progression and thus the name for this probability density function.

The number of components that you would expect to test until you find the first defective component is the mean, $\mu = 50$.

The formula for the mean for the random variable defined as number of failures until first success is $\mu = \frac{1}{p} = \frac{1}{0.02} = 50$

See **Example 4.9** for an example where the geometric random variable is defined as number of trials until first success. The expected value of this formula for the geometric will be different from this version of the distribution.

The formula for the variance is $\sigma^2 = \left(\frac{1}{p}\right)\left(\frac{1}{p} - 1\right) = \left(\frac{1}{0.02}\right)\left(\frac{1}{0.02} - 1\right) = 2{,}450$

The standard deviation is $\sigma = \sqrt{\left(\frac{1}{p}\right)\left(\frac{1}{p} - 1\right)} = \sqrt{\left(\frac{1}{0.02}\right)\left(\frac{1}{0.02} - 1\right)} = 49.5$

## Example 4.9

The lifetime risk of developing pancreatic cancer is about one in 78 (1.28%). Let $X$ = the number of people you ask before one says he or she has pancreatic cancer. The random variable $X$ in this case includes only the number of trials that were failures and does not count the trial that was a success in finding a person who had the disease. The appropriate formula for this random variable is the second one presented above. Then $X$ is a discrete random variable with a geometric distribution: $X \sim G\left(\frac{1}{78}\right)$ or $X \sim G(0.0128)$.

   a.  What is the probability of that you ask 9 people before one says he or she has pancreatic cancer? This is asking, what is the probability that you ask 9 people unsuccessfully and the tenth person is a success?

   b.  What is the probability that you must ask 20 people?

c. Find the (i) mean and (ii) standard deviation of $X$.

**Solution 4.9**

a. $P(x = 9) = (1 - 0.0128)^9 * 0.0128 = 0.0114$

b. $P(x = 20) = (1 - 0.0128)^{19} * 0.0128 = 0.01$

c.    i.   Mean $= \mu = \dfrac{(1 - p)}{p} = \dfrac{(1 - 0.0128)}{0.0128} = 77.12$

      ii.   Standard Deviation $= \sigma = \sqrt{\dfrac{1 - p}{p^2}} = \sqrt{\dfrac{1 - 0.0128}{0.0128^2}} \approx 77.62$

## Try It $\Sigma$

**4.9** The literacy rate for a nation measures the proportion of people age 15 and over who can read and write. The literacy rate for women in The United Colonies of Independence is 12%. Let $X$ = the number of women you ask until one says that she is literate.

a. What is the probability distribution of $X$?

b. What is the probability that you ask five women before one says she is literate?

c. What is the probability that you must ask ten women?

## Example 4.10

A baseball player has a batting average of 0.320. This is the general probability that he gets a hit each time he is at bat.

What is the probability that he gets his first hit in the third trip to bat?

**Solution 4.10**

$P(x=3) = (1-0.32)^{3-1} \times .32 = 0.1480$

In this case the sequence is failure, failure success.

How many trips to bat do you expect the hitter to need before getting a hit?

**Solution 4.10**

$\mu = \dfrac{1}{p} = \dfrac{1}{0.320} = 3.125 \approx 3$

This is simply the expected value of successes and therefore the mean of the distribution.

## Example 4.11

There is an 80% chance that a Dalmatian dog has 13 black spots. You go to a dog show and count the spots on Dalmatians. What is the probability that you will review the spots on 3 dogs before you find one that has 13 black spots?

**Solution 4.11**

$P(x=3) = (1 - 0.80)^3 \times 0.80 = 0.0064$

# 4.4 | Poisson Distribution

Another useful probability distribution is the Poisson distribution, or waiting time distribution. This distribution is used to determine how many checkout clerks are needed to keep the waiting time in line to specified levels, how may telephone lines are needed to keep the system from overloading, and many other practical applications. A modification of the Poisson, the Pascal, invented nearly four centuries ago, is used today by telecommunications companies worldwide for load factors, satellite hookup levels and Internet capacity problems. The distribution gets its name from Simeon Poisson who presented it in 1837 as an extension of the binomial distribution which we will see can be estimated with the Poisson.

There are two main characteristics of a Poisson experiment.

1. The **Poisson probability distribution** gives the probability of a number of events occurring in a **fixed interval** of time or space if these events happen with a known average rate.

2. The events are independently of the time since the last event. For example, a book editor might be interested in the number of words spelled incorrectly in a particular book. It might be that, on the average, there are five words spelled incorrectly in 100 pages. The interval is the 100 pages and it is assumed that there is no relationship between when misspellings occur.

3. The random variable $X$ = the number of occurrences in the interval of interest.

---

### Example 4.12

A bank expects to receive six bad checks per day, on average. What is the probability of the bank getting fewer than five bad checks on any given day? Of interest is the number of checks the bank receives in one day, so the time interval of interest is one day. Let $X$ = the number of bad checks the bank receives in one day. If the bank expects to receive six bad checks per day then the average is six checks per day. Write a mathematical statement for the probability question.

**Solution 4.12**

$P(x < 5)$

---

### Example 4.13

You notice that a news reporter says "uh," on average, two times per broadcast. What is the probability that the news reporter says "uh" more than two times per broadcast.

This is a Poisson problem because you are interested in knowing the number of times the news reporter says "uh" during a broadcast.

a. What is the interval of interest?

**Solution 4.13**

a. one broadcast measured in minutes

b. What is the average number of times the news reporter says "uh" during one broadcast?

**Solution 4.13**

b. 2

c. Let $X$ = _____. What values does $X$ take on?

**Solution 4.13**

c. Let $X$ = the number of times the news reporter says "uh" during one broadcast.

$x = 0, 1, 2, 3, ...$

d. The probability question is $P(\underline{\hspace{1cm}})$.

**Solution 4.13**

d. $P(x > 2)$

## Notation for the Poisson: P = Poisson Probability Distribution Function

$X \sim P(\mu)$

Read this as "$X$ is a random variable with a Poisson distribution." The parameter is $\mu$ (or $\lambda$); $\mu$ (or $\lambda$) = the mean for the interval of interest. The mean is the number of occurrences that occur on average during the interval period.

The formula for computing probabilities that are from a Poisson process is:

$$P(x) = \frac{\mu^x e^{-\mu}}{x!}$$

where $P(X)$ is the probability of $X$ successes, $\mu$ is the expected number of successes based upon historical data, $e$ is the natural logarithm approximately equal to 2.718, and $X$ is the number of successes per unit, usually per unit of time.

In order to use the Poisson distribution, certain assumptions must hold. These are: the probability of a success, $\mu$, is unchanged within the interval, there cannot be simultaneous successes within the interval, and finally, that the probability of a success among intervals is independent, the same assumption of the binomial distribution.

In a way, the Poisson distribution can be thought of as a clever way to convert a continuous random variable, usually time, into a discrete random variable by breaking up time into discrete independent intervals. This way of thinking about the Poisson helps us understand why it can be used to estimate the probability for the discrete random variable from the binomial distribution. The Poisson is asking for the probability of a number of successes during a period of time while the binomial is asking for the probability of a certain number of successes for a given number of trials.

## Example 4.14

Leah's answering machine receives about six telephone calls between 8 a.m. and 10 a.m. What is the probability that Leah receives more than one call **in the next 15 minutes?**

Let $X$ = the number of calls Leah receives in 15 minutes. (The **interval of interest** is 15 minutes or $\frac{1}{4}$ hour.)

$x = 0, 1, 2, 3, \ldots$

If Leah receives, on the average, six telephone calls in two hours, and there are eight 15 minute intervals in two hours, then Leah receives

$\left(\frac{1}{8}\right)(6) = 0.75$ calls in 15 minutes, on average. So, $\mu = 0.75$ for this problem.

$X \sim P(0.75)$

Find $P(x > 1)$. $P(x > 1) = 0.1734$

Probability that Leah receives more than one telephone call in the next 15 minutes is about 0.1734.

The graph of $X \sim P(0.75)$ is:

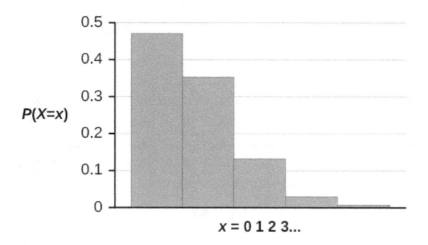

Figure 4.3

The *y*-axis contains the probability of *x* where *X* = the number of calls in 15 minutes.

## Example 4.15

According to a survey a university professor gets, on average, 7 emails per day. Let *X* = the number of emails a professor receives per day. The discrete random variable *X* takes on the values *x* = 0, 1, 2 …. The random variable *X* has a Poisson distribution: $X \sim P(7)$. The mean is 7 emails.

a.  What is the probability that an email user receives exactly 2 emails per day?

b.  What is the probability that an email user receives at most 2 emails per day?

c.  What is the standard deviation?

**Solution 4.15**

a.  $P\left(x = 2\right) = \frac{\mu^x e^{-\mu}}{x!} = \frac{7^2 e^{-7}}{2!} = 0.022$

b.  $P\left(x \le 2\right) = \frac{7^0 e^{-7}}{0!} + \frac{7^1 e^{-7}}{1!} + \frac{7^2 e^{-7}}{2!} = 0.029$

c.  Standard Deviation = $\sigma = \sqrt{\mu} = \sqrt{7} \approx 2.65$

## Example 4.16

Text message users receive or send an average of 41.5 text messages per day.

a.  How many text messages does a text message user receive or send per hour?

b.  What is the probability that a text message user receives or sends two messages per hour?

c.  What is the probability that a text message user receives or sends more than two messages per hour?

**Solution 4.16**

a.  Let *X* = the number of texts that a user sends or receives in one hour. The average number of texts received per hour is $\frac{41.5}{24} \approx 1.7292$.

b. $P\left(x=2\right)=\frac{\mu^{x}e^{-\mu}}{x!}=\frac{1.729^{2}e^{-1.729}}{2!}=0.265$

c. $P\left(x>2\right)=1-P\left(x\leq2\right)=1-\left[\frac{7^{0}e^{-7}}{0!}+\frac{7^{1}e^{-7}}{1!}+\frac{7^{2}e^{-7}}{2!}\right]=0.250$

## Example 4.17

On May 13, 2013, starting at 4:30 PM, the probability of low seismic activity for the next 48 hours in Alaska was reported as about 1.02%. Use this information for the next 200 days to find the probability that there will be low seismic activity in ten of the next 200 days. Use both the binomial and Poisson distributions to calculate the probabilities. Are they close?

### Solution 4.17

Let $X$ = the number of days with low seismic activity.

Using the binomial distribution:

- $P\left(x=10\right)=\frac{200!}{10!(200-10)!}\times.0102^{10}=0.000039$

Using the Poisson distribution:

- Calculate $\mu=np=200(0.0102)\approx2.04$
- $P\left(x=10\right)=\frac{\mu^{x}e^{-\mu}}{x!}=\frac{2.04^{10}e^{-2.04}}{10!}=0.000045$

We expect the approximation to be good because $n$ is large (greater than 20) and $p$ is small (less than 0.05). The results are close—both probabilities reported are almost 0.

## Estimating the Binomial Distribution with the Poisson Distribution

We found before that the binomial distribution provided an approximation for the hypergeometric distribution. Now we find that the Poisson distribution can provide an approximation for the binomial. We say that the binomial distribution approaches the Poisson. The binomial distribution approaches the Poisson distribution is as $n$ gets larger and $p$ is small such that $np$ becomes a constant value. There are several rules of thumb for when one can say they will use a Poisson to estimate a binomial. One suggests that $np$, the mean of the binomial, should be less than 25. Another author suggests that it should be less than 7. And another, noting that the mean and variance of the Poisson are both the same, suggests that $np$ and $npq$, the mean and variance of the binomial, should be greater than 5. There is no one broadly accepted rule of thumb for when one can use the Poisson to estimate the binomial.

As we move through these probability distributions we are getting to more sophisticated distributions that, in a sense, contain the less sophisticated distributions within them. This proposition has been proven by mathematicians. This gets us to the highest level of sophistication in the next probability distribution which can be used as an approximation to all of those that we have discussed so far. This is the normal distribution.

## Example 4.18

A survey of 500 seniors in the Price Business School yields the following information. 75% go straight to work after graduation. 15% go on to work on their MBA. 9% stay to get a minor in another program. 1% go on to get a Master's in Finance.

What is the probability that more than 2 seniors go to graduate school for their Master's in finance?

### Solution 4.18

This is clearly a binomial probability distribution problem. The choices are binary when we define the results as "Graduate School in Finance" versus "all other options." The random variable is discrete, and the events are, we could assume, independent. Solving as a binomial problem, we have:

**Binomial Solution**

$$n * p = 500 * 0.01 = 5 = \mu$$

$$P(0) = \frac{500!}{0!(500-0)!} 0.01^0 (1-0.01)^{500-0} = 0.00657$$

$$P(1) = \frac{500!}{1!(500-1)!} 0.01^1 (1-0.01)^{500-1} = 0.03318$$

$$P(2) = \frac{500!}{2!(500-2)!} 0.01^2 (1-0.01)^{500-2} = 0.08363$$

*Adding all 3 together* = 0.12339

$$1 - 0.12339 = 0.87661$$

**Poisson approximation**

$$n * p = 500 * 0.01 = 5 = \mu$$

$$n * p * (1-p) = 500 * 0.01 * (0.99) \approx 5 = \sigma^2 = \mu$$

$$P(X) = \frac{e^{-np}(np)^x}{x!} = \left\{ P(0) = \frac{e^{-5} * 5^0}{0!} \right\} + \left\{ P(1) = \frac{e^{-5} * 5^1}{1!} \right\} + \left\{ P(2) = \frac{e^{-5} * 5^2}{2!} \right\}$$

$$0.0067 + 0.0337 + 0.0842 = 0.1247$$

$$1 - 0.1247 = 0.8753$$

An approximation that is off by 1 one thousandth is certainly an acceptable approximation.

# KEY TERMS

**Bernoulli Trials** an experiment with the following characteristics:

1. There are only two possible outcomes called "success" and "failure" for each trial.

2. The probability $p$ of a success is the same for any trial (so the probability $q = 1 - p$ of a failure is the same for any trial).

**Binomial Experiment** a statistical experiment that satisfies the following three conditions:

1. There are a fixed number of trials, $n$.

2. There are only two possible outcomes, called "success" and, "failure," for each trial. The letter $p$ denotes the probability of a success on one trial, and $q$ denotes the probability of a failure on one trial.

3. The $n$ trials are independent and are repeated using identical conditions.

**Binomial Probability Distribution** a discrete random variable (RV) that arises from Bernoulli trials; there are a fixed number, $n$, of independent trials. "Independent" means that the result of any trial (for example, trial one) does not affect the results of the following trials, and all trials are conducted under the same conditions. Under these circumstances the binomial RV $X$ is defined as the number of successes in $n$ trials. The mean is $\mu = np$ and the standard deviation is $\sigma = \sqrt{npq}$. The probability of exactly $x$ successes in $n$ trials is

$$P(X = x) = \binom{n}{x} p^x q^{n-x}.$$

**Geometric Distribution** a discrete random variable (RV) that arises from the Bernoulli trials; the trials are repeated until the first success. The geometric variable $X$ is defined as the number of trials until the first success. The mean is $\mu = \frac{1}{p}$ and the standard deviation is $\sigma = \sqrt{\frac{1}{p}\left(\frac{1}{p} - 1\right)}$. The probability of exactly $x$ failures before the first success is given by the formula: $P(X = x) = p(1-p)^{x-1}$ where one wants to know probability for the number of trials until the first success: the xth trail is the first success.

An alternative formulation of the geometric distribution asks the question: what is the probability of $x$ failures until the first success? In this formulation the trial that resulted in the first success is not counted. The formula for this presentation of the geometric is: $P(X = x) = p(1-p)^x$

The expected value in this form of the geometric distribution is $\mu = \frac{1-p}{p}$

The easiest way to keep these two forms of the geometric distribution straight is to remember that $p$ is the probability of success and $(1-p)$ is the probability of failure. In the formula the exponents simply count the number of successes and number of failures of the desired outcome of the experiment. Of course the sum of these two numbers must add to the number of trials in the experiment.

**Geometric Experiment** a statistical experiment with the following properties:

1. There are one or more Bernoulli trials with all failures except the last one, which is a success.

2. In theory, the number of trials could go on forever. There must be at least one trial.

3. The probability, $p$, of a success and the probability, $q$, of a failure do not change from trial to trial.

**Hypergeometric Experiment** a statistical experiment with the following properties:

1. You take samples from two groups.

2. You are concerned with a group of interest, called the first group.

3. You sample without replacement from the combined groups.

4. Each pick is not independent, since sampling is without replacement.

**Hypergeometric Probability** a discrete random variable (RV) that is characterized by:

1. A fixed number of trials.

2. The probability of success is not the same from trial to trial.

We sample from two groups of items when we are interested in only one group. $X$ is defined as the number of successes out of the total number of items chosen.

**Poisson Probability Distribution** a discrete random variable (RV) that counts the number of times a certain event will occur in a specific interval; characteristics of the variable:

- The probability that the event occurs in a given interval is the same for all intervals.

- The events occur with a known mean and independently of the time since the last event.

The distribution is defined by the mean $\mu$ of the event in the interval. The mean is $\mu = np$. The standard deviation is $\sigma = \sqrt{\mu}$. The probability of having exactly $x$ successes in $r$ trials is $P(x) = \dfrac{\mu^x e^{-\mu}}{x!}$. The Poisson distribution is often used to approximate the binomial distribution, when $n$ is "large" and $p$ is "small" (a general rule is that $np$ should be greater than or equal to 25 and $p$ should be less than or equal to 0.01).

**Probability Distribution Function (PDF)** a mathematical description of a discrete random variable (RV), given either in the form of an equation (formula) or in the form of a table listing all the possible outcomes of an experiment and the probability associated with each outcome.

**Random Variable (RV)** a characteristic of interest in a population being studied; common notation for variables are upper case Latin letters $X$, $Y$, $Z$,...; common notation for a specific value from the domain (set of all possible values of a variable) are lower case Latin letters $x$, $y$, and $z$. For example, if $X$ is the number of children in a family, then $x$ represents a specific integer 0, 1, 2, 3,.... Variables in statistics differ from variables in intermediate algebra in the two following ways.

- The domain of the random variable (RV) is not necessarily a numerical set; the domain may be expressed in words; for example, if $X$ = hair color then the domain is {black, blond, gray, green, orange}.

- We can tell what specific value $x$ the random variable $X$ takes only after performing the experiment.

# CHAPTER REVIEW

## 4.0 Introduction

The characteristics of a probability distribution or density function (PDF) are as follows:

1. Each probability is between zero and one, inclusive (*inclusive* means to include zero and one).

2. The sum of the probabilities is one.

## 4.1 Hypergeometric Distribution

The combinatorial formula can provide the number of unique subsets of size x that can be created from n unique objects to help us calculate probabilities. The combinatorial formula is $\binom{n}{x} = {}_nC_x = \dfrac{n!}{x!(n-x)!}$

A **hypergeometric experiment** is a statistical experiment with the following properties:

1. You take samples from two groups.

2. You are concerned with a group of interest, called the first group.

3. You sample without replacement from the combined groups.

4. Each pick is not independent, since sampling is without replacement.

The outcomes of a hypergeometric experiment fit a hypergeometric probability distribution. The random variable $X$ = the number of items from the group of interest. $h(x) = \dfrac{\binom{A}{x}\binom{N-A}{n-x}}{\binom{N}{n}}$.

## 4.2 Binomial Distribution

A statistical experiment can be classified as a binomial experiment if the following conditions are met:

1. There are a fixed number of trials, $n$.

2. There are only two possible outcomes, called "success" and, "failure" for each trial. The letter $p$ denotes the probability

of a success on one trial and $q$ denotes the probability of a failure on one trial.

3.  The $n$ trials are independent and are repeated using identical conditions.

The outcomes of a binomial experiment fit a binomial probability distribution. The random variable $X$ = the number of successes obtained in the $n$ independent trials. The mean of $X$ can be calculated using the formula $\mu = np$, and the standard deviation is given by the formula $\sigma = \sqrt{npq}$.

The formula for the Binomial probability density function is

$$P(x) = \frac{n!}{x!(n-x)!} \cdot p^x q^{(n-x)}$$

## 4.3 Geometric Distribution

There are three characteristics of a geometric experiment:

1.  There are one or more Bernoulli trials with all failures except the last one, which is a success.

2.  In theory, the number of trials could go on forever. There must be at least one trial.

3.  The probability, $p$, of a success and the probability, $q$, of a failure are the same for each trial.

In a geometric experiment, define the discrete random variable $X$ as the number of independent trials until the first success. We say that X has a geometric distribution and write $X \sim G(p)$ where $p$ is the probability of success in a single trial.

The mean of the geometric distribution $X \sim G(p)$ is $\mu = 1 / p$ where x = number of trials until first success for the formula $P(X = x) = (1-p)^{x-1} p$ where the number of trials is up and including the first success.

An alternative formulation of the geometric distribution asks the question: what is the probability of $x$ failures until the first success? In this formulation the trial that resulted in the first success is not counted. The formula for this presentation of the geometric is:

$$P(X = x) = p(1-p)^x$$

The expected value in this form of the geometric distribution is

$$\mu = \frac{1-p}{p}$$

The easiest way to keep these two forms of the geometric distribution straight is to remember that $p$ is the probability of success and (1−p) is the probability of failure. In the formula the exponents simply count the number of successes and number of failures of the desired outcome of the experiment. Of course the sum of these two numbers must add to the number of trials in the experiment.

## 4.4 Poisson Distribution

A **Poisson probability distribution** of a discrete random variable gives the probability of a number of events occurring in a fixed interval of time or space, if these events happen at a known average rate and independently of the time since the last event. The Poisson distribution may be used to approximate the binomial, if the probability of success is "small" (less than or equal to 0.01) and the number of trials is "large" (greater than or equal to 25). Other rules of thumb are also suggested by different authors, but all recognize that the Poisson distribution is the limiting distribution of the binomial as $n$ increases and $p$ approaches zero.

The formula for computing probabilities that are from a Poisson process is:

$$P(x) = \frac{\mu^x e^{-\mu}}{x!}$$

where P(X) is the probability of successes, μ (pronounced mu) is the expected number of successes, e is the natural logarithm approximately equal to 2.718, and X is the number of successes per unit, usually per unit of time.

# FORMULA REVIEW

## 4.1 Hypergeometric Distribution

$$h(x) = \frac{\binom{A}{x}\binom{N-A}{n-x}}{\binom{N}{n}}$$

## 4.2 Binomial Distribution

$X \sim B(n, p)$ means that the discrete random variable $X$ has a binomial probability distribution with $n$ trials and probability of success $p$.

$X$ = the number of successes in $n$ independent trials

$n$ = the number of independent trials

$X$ takes on the values $x = 0, 1, 2, 3, ..., n$

$p$ = the probability of a success for any trial

$q$ = the probability of a failure for any trial

$p + q = 1$

$q = 1 - p$

The mean of $X$ is $\mu = np$. The standard deviation of $X$ is $\sigma = \sqrt{npq}$.

$$P(x) = \frac{n!}{x!(n-x)!} \cdot p^x q^{(n-x)}$$

where P(X) is the probability of X successes in n trials when the probability of a success in ANY ONE TRIAL is p.

## 4.3 Geometric Distribution

$$P(X = x) = p(1-p)^{x-1}$$

$X \sim G(p)$ means that the discrete random variable $X$ has a geometric probability distribution with probability of success in a single trial $p$.

$X$ = the number of independent trials until the first success

$X$ takes on the values $x = 1, 2, 3, ...$

$p$ = the probability of a success for any trial

$q$ = the probability of a failure for any trial $p + q = 1$
$q = 1 - p$

The mean is $\mu = \frac{1}{p}$.

The standard deviation is $\sigma = \sqrt{\frac{1-p}{p^2}} = \sqrt{\frac{1}{p}\left(\frac{1}{p} - 1\right)}$.

## 4.4 Poisson Distribution

$X \sim P(\mu)$ means that $X$ has a Poisson probability distribution where $X$ = the number of occurrences in the interval of interest.

$X$ takes on the values $x = 0, 1, 2, 3, ...$

The mean $\mu$ or $\lambda$ is typically given.

The variance is $\sigma^2 = \mu$, and the standard deviation is $\sigma = \sqrt{\mu}$.

When $P(\mu)$ is used to approximate a binomial distribution, $\mu = np$ where $n$ represents the number of independent trials and $p$ represents the probability of success in a single trial.

$$P(x) = \frac{\mu^x e^{-\mu}}{x!}$$

# PRACTICE

## 4.0 Introduction

*Use the following information to answer the next five exercises:* A company wants to evaluate its attrition rate, in other words, how long new hires stay with the company. Over the years, they have established the following probability distribution.

Let $X$ = the number of years a new hire will stay with the company.

Let $P(x)$ = the probability that a new hire will stay with the company $x$ years.

**1.** Complete Table 4.1 using the data provided.

| x | P(x) |
|---|------|
| 0 | 0.12 |
| 1 | 0.18 |
| 2 | 0.30 |
| 3 | 0.15 |
| 4 |      |
| 5 | 0.10 |
| 6 | 0.05 |

Table 4.1

**2.** $P(x = 4) = $ _____

**3.** $P(x \geq 5) = $ _____

**4.** On average, how long would you expect a new hire to stay with the company?

**5.** What does the column "$P(x)$" sum to?

*Use the following information to answer the next six exercises:* A baker is deciding how many batches of muffins to make to sell in his bakery. He wants to make enough to sell every one and no fewer. Through observation, the baker has established a probability distribution.

| x | P(x) |
|---|------|
| 1 | 0.15 |
| 2 | 0.35 |
| 3 | 0.40 |
| 4 | 0.10 |

Table 4.2

**6.** Define the random variable $X$.

**7.** What is the probability the baker will sell more than one batch? $P(x > 1) = $ _____

**8.** What is the probability the baker will sell exactly one batch? $P(x = 1) = $ _____

**9.** On average, how many batches should the baker make?

*Use the following information to answer the next four exercises:* Ellen has music practice three days a week. She practices for all of the three days 85% of the time, two days 8% of the time, one day 4% of the time, and no days 3% of the time. One week is selected at random.

**10.** Define the random variable $X$.

**11.** Construct a probability distribution table for the data.

**12.** We know that for a probability distribution function to be discrete, it must have two characteristics. One is that the sum of the probabilities is one. What is the other characteristic?

*Use the following information to answer the next five exercises:* Javier volunteers in community events each month. He does not do more than five events in a month. He attends exactly five events 35% of the time, four events 25% of the time, three events 20% of the time, two events 10% of the time, one event 5% of the time, and no events 5% of the time.

**13.** Define the random variable $X$.

**14.** What values does $x$ take on?

**15.** Construct a PDF table.

**16.** Find the probability that Javier volunteers for less than three events each month. $P(x < 3) =$ _____

**17.** Find the probability that Javier volunteers for at least one event each month. $P(x > 0) =$ _____

## 4.1 Hypergeometric Distribution

*Use the following information to answer the next five exercises:* Suppose that a group of statistics students is divided into two groups: business majors and non-business majors. There are 16 business majors in the group and seven non-business majors in the group. A random sample of nine students is taken. We are interested in the number of business majors in the sample.

**18.** In words, define the random variable $X$.

**19.** What values does $X$ take on?

## 4.2 Binomial Distribution

*Use the following information to answer the next eight exercises:* The Higher Education Research Institute at UCLA collected data from 203,967 incoming first-time, full-time freshmen from 270 four-year colleges and universities in the U.S. 71.3% of those students replied that, yes, they believe that same-sex couples should have the right to legal marital status. Suppose that you randomly pick eight first-time, full-time freshmen from the survey. You are interested in the number that believes that same sex-couples should have the right to legal marital status.

**20.** In words, define the random variable $X$.

**21.** $X \sim$ _____(_____,_____)

**22.** What values does the random variable $X$ take on?

**23.** Construct the probability distribution function (PDF).

| x | P(x) |
|---|------|
|   |      |
|   |      |
|   |      |
|   |      |
|   |      |
|   |      |
|   |      |
|   |      |
|   |      |

Table 4.3

**24.** On average ($\mu$), how many would you expect to answer yes?

**25.** What is the standard deviation ($\sigma$)?

**26.** What is the probability that at most five of the freshmen reply "yes"?

**27.** What is the probability that at least two of the freshmen reply "yes"?

## 4.3 Geometric Distribution

*Use the following information to answer the next six exercises:* The Higher Education Research Institute at UCLA collected data from 203,967 incoming first-time, full-time freshmen from 270 four-year colleges and universities in the U.S. 71.3% of those students replied that, yes, they believe that same-sex couples should have the right to legal marital status. Suppose that you randomly select freshman from the study until you find one who replies "yes." You are interested in the number of freshmen you must ask.

**28.** In words, define the random variable $X$.

**29.** $X \sim$ _____(_____,_____)

**30.** What values does the random variable $X$ take on?

**31.** Construct the probability distribution function (PDF). Stop at $x = 6$.

| x | P(x) |
|---|------|
| 1 | |
| 2 | |
| 3 | |
| 4 | |
| 5 | |
| 6 | |

Table 4.4

**32.** On average ($\mu$), how many freshmen would you expect to have to ask until you found one who replies "yes?"

**33.** What is the probability that you will need to ask fewer than three freshmen?

## 4.4 Poisson Distribution

*Use the following information to answer the next six exercises:* On average, a clothing store gets 120 customers per day.

**34.** Assume the event occurs independently in any given day. Define the random variable $X$.

**35.** What values does $X$ take on?

**36.** What is the probability of getting 150 customers in one day?

**37.** What is the probability of getting 35 customers in the first four hours? Assume the store is open 12 hours each day.

**38.** What is the probability that the store will have more than 12 customers in the first hour?

**39.** What is the probability that the store will have fewer than 12 customers in the first two hours?

**40.** Which type of distribution can the Poisson model be used to approximate? When would you do this?

*Use the following information to answer the next six exercises:* On average, eight teens in the U.S. die from motor vehicle injuries per day. As a result, states across the country are debating raising the driving age.

**41.** Assume the event occurs independently in any given day. In words, define the random variable $X$.

**42.** $X \sim$ _____(_____,_____)

**43.** What values does $X$ take on?

**44.** For the given values of the random variable $X$, fill in the corresponding probabilities.

**45.** Is it likely that there will be no teens killed from motor vehicle injuries on any given day in the U.S? Justify your answer numerically.

**46.** Is it likely that there will be more than 20 teens killed from motor vehicle injuries on any given day in the U.S.? Justify your answer numerically.

# HOMEWORK

## 4.1 Hypergeometric Distribution

**47.** A group of Martial Arts students is planning on participating in an upcoming demonstration. Six are students of Tae Kwon Do; seven are students of Shotokan Karate. Suppose that eight students are randomly picked to be in the first demonstration. We are interested in the number of Shotokan Karate students in that first demonstration.
- a. In words, define the random variable $X$.
- b. List the values that $X$ may take on.
- c. How many Shotokan Karate students do we expect to be in that first demonstration?

**48.** In one of its Spring catalogs, L.L. Bean® advertised footwear on 29 of its 192 catalog pages. Suppose we randomly survey 20 pages. We are interested in the number of pages that advertise footwear. Each page may be picked at most once.

- a. In words, define the random variable $X$.
- b. List the values that $X$ may take on.
- c. How many pages do you expect to advertise footwear on them?
- d. Calculate the standard deviation.

**49.** Suppose that a technology task force is being formed to study technology awareness among instructors. Assume that ten people will be randomly chosen to be on the committee from a group of 28 volunteers, 20 who are technically proficient and eight who are not. We are interested in the number on the committee who are **not** technically proficient.
- a. In words, define the random variable $X$.
- b. List the values that $X$ may take on.
- c. How many instructors do you expect on the committee who are **not** technically proficient?
- d. Find the probability that at least five on the committee are not technically proficient.
- e. Find the probability that at most three on the committee are not technically proficient.

**50.** Suppose that nine Massachusetts athletes are scheduled to appear at a charity benefit. The nine are randomly chosen from eight volunteers from the Boston Celtics and four volunteers from the New England Patriots. We are interested in the number of Patriots picked.
- a. In words, define the random variable $X$.
- b. List the values that $X$ may take on.
- c. Are you choosing the nine athletes with or without replacement?

**51.** A bridge hand is defined as 13 cards selected at random and without replacement from a deck of 52 cards. In a standard deck of cards, there are 13 cards from each suit: hearts, spades, clubs, and diamonds. What is the probability of being dealt a hand that does not contain a heart?
- a. What is the group of interest?
- b. How many are in the group of interest?
- c. How many are in the other group?
- d. Let $X$ = _____. What values does $X$ take on?
- e. The probability question is $P($_____$)$.
- f. Find the probability in question.
- g. Find the (i) mean and (ii) standard deviation of $X$.

## 4.2 Binomial Distribution

**52.** According to a recent article the average number of babies born with significant hearing loss (deafness) is approximately two per 1,000 babies in a healthy baby nursery. The number climbs to an average of 30 per 1,000 babies in an intensive care nursery.

Suppose that 1,000 babies from healthy baby nurseries were randomly surveyed. Find the probability that exactly two babies were born deaf.

Use the following information to answer the next four exercises. Recently, a nurse commented that when a patient calls the medical advice line claiming to have the flu, the chance that he or she truly has the flu (and not just a nasty cold) is only about 4%. Of the next 25 patients calling in claiming to have the flu, we are interested in how many actually have the flu.

**53.** Define the random variable and list its possible values.

**54.** State the distribution of $X$.

**55.** Find the probability that at least four of the 25 patients actually have the flu.

**56.** On average, for every 25 patients calling in, how many do you expect to have the flu?

**57.** People visiting video rental stores often rent more than one DVD at a time. The probability distribution for DVD rentals per customer at Video To Go is given Table 4.5. There is five-video limit per customer at this store, so nobody ever rents more than five DVDs.

| x | P(x) |
|---|------|
| 0 | 0.03 |
| 1 | 0.50 |
| 2 | 0.24 |
| 3 |      |
| 4 | 0.07 |
| 5 | 0.04 |

Table 4.5

a. Describe the random variable $X$ in words.
b. Find the probability that a customer rents three DVDs.
c. Find the probability that a customer rents at least four DVDs.
d. Find the probability that a customer rents at most two DVDs.

**58.** A school newspaper reporter decides to randomly survey 12 students to see if they will attend Tet (Vietnamese New Year) festivities this year. Based on past years, she knows that 18% of students attend Tet festivities. We are interested in the number of students who will attend the festivities.
a. In words, define the random variable $X$.
b. List the values that $X$ may take on.
c. Give the distribution of $X$. $X \sim$ _____(_____,_____)
d. How many of the 12 students do we expect to attend the festivities?
e. Find the probability that at most four students will attend.
f. Find the probability that more than two students will attend.

*Use the following information to answer the next two exercises:* The probability that the San Jose Sharks will win any given game is 0.3694 based on a 13-year win history of 382 wins out of 1,034 games played (as of a certain date). An upcoming monthly schedule contains 12 games.

**59.** The expected number of wins for that upcoming month is:
a. 1.67
b. 12
c. $\frac{382}{1043}$
d. 4.43

Let $X$ = the number of games won in that upcoming month.

**60.** What is the probability that the San Jose Sharks win six games in that upcoming month?
a. 0.1476
b. 0.2336
c. 0.7664
d. 0.8903

**61.** What is the probability that the San Jose Sharks win at least five games in that upcoming month
a. 0.3694
b. 0.5266
c. 0.4734
d. 0.2305

**62.** A student takes a ten-question true-false quiz, but did not study and randomly guesses each answer. Find the probability that the student passes the quiz with a grade of at least 70% of the questions correct.

**63.** A student takes a 32-question multiple-choice exam, but did not study and randomly guesses each answer. Each question has three possible choices for the answer. Find the probability that the student guesses **more than** 75% of the questions correctly.

**64.** Six different colored dice are rolled. Of interest is the number of dice that show a one.
   a. In words, define the random variable $X$.
   b. List the values that $X$ may take on.
   c. On average, how many dice would you expect to show a one?
   d. Find the probability that all six dice show a one.
   e. Is it more likely that three or that four dice will show a one? Use numbers to justify your answer numerically.

**65.** More than 96 percent of the very largest colleges and universities (more than 15,000 total enrollments) have some online offerings. Suppose you randomly pick 13 such institutions. We are interested in the number that offer distance learning courses.
   a. In words, define the random variable $X$.
   b. List the values that $X$ may take on.
   c. Give the distribution of $X$. $X \sim$ _____(_____,_____)
   d. On average, how many schools would you expect to offer such courses?
   e. Find the probability that at most ten offer such courses.
   f. Is it more likely that 12 or that 13 will offer such courses? Use numbers to justify your answer numerically and answer in a complete sentence.

**66.** Suppose that about 85% of graduating students attend their graduation. A group of 22 graduating students is randomly chosen.
   a. In words, define the random variable $X$.
   b. List the values that $X$ may take on.
   c. Give the distribution of $X$. $X \sim$ _____(_____,_____)
   d. How many are expected to attend their graduation?
   e. Find the probability that 17 or 18 attend.
   f. Based on numerical values, would you be surprised if all 22 attended graduation? Justify your answer numerically.

**67.** At The Fencing Center, 60% of the fencers use the foil as their main weapon. We randomly survey 25 fencers at The Fencing Center. We are interested in the number of fencers who do **not** use the foil as their main weapon.
   a. In words, define the random variable $X$.
   b. List the values that $X$ may take on.
   c. Give the distribution of $X$. $X \sim$ _____(_____,_____)
   d. How many are expected to **not** to use the foil as their main weapon?
   e. Find the probability that six do **not** use the foil as their main weapon.
   f. Based on numerical values, would you be surprised if all 25 did **not** use foil as their main weapon? Justify your answer numerically.

**68.** Approximately 8% of students at a local high school participate in after-school sports all four years of high school. A group of 60 seniors is randomly chosen. Of interest is the number who participated in after-school sports all four years of high school.
   a. In words, define the random variable $X$.
   b. List the values that $X$ may take on.
   c. Give the distribution of $X$. $X \sim$ _____(_____,_____)
   d. How many seniors are expected to have participated in after-school sports all four years of high school?
   e. Based on numerical values, would you be surprised if none of the seniors participated in after-school sports all four years of high school? Justify your answer numerically.
   f. Based upon numerical values, is it more likely that four or that five of the seniors participated in after-school sports all four years of high school? Justify your answer numerically.

**69.** The chance of an IRS audit for a tax return with over $25,000 in income is about 2% per year. We are interested in the expected number of audits a person with that income has in a 20-year period. Assume each year is independent.

    a. In words, define the random variable $X$.
    b. List the values that $X$ may take on.
    c. Give the distribution of $X$. $X \sim$ \_\_\_\_\_(\_\_\_\_\_,\_\_\_\_\_)
    d. How many audits are expected in a 20-year period?
    e. Find the probability that a person is not audited at all.
    f. Find the probability that a person is audited more than twice.

**70.** It has been estimated that only about 30% of California residents have adequate earthquake supplies. Suppose you randomly survey 11 California residents. We are interested in the number who have adequate earthquake supplies.

    a. In words, define the random variable $X$.
    b. List the values that $X$ may take on.
    c. Give the distribution of $X$. $X \sim$ \_\_\_\_\_(\_\_\_\_\_,\_\_\_\_\_)
    d. What is the probability that at least eight have adequate earthquake supplies?
    e. Is it more likely that none or that all of the residents surveyed will have adequate earthquake supplies? Why?
    f. How many residents do you expect will have adequate earthquake supplies?

**71.** There are two similar games played for Chinese New Year and Vietnamese New Year. In the Chinese version, fair dice with numbers 1, 2, 3, 4, 5, and 6 are used, along with a board with those numbers. In the Vietnamese version, fair dice with pictures of a gourd, fish, rooster, crab, crayfish, and deer are used. The board has those six objects on it, also. We will play with bets being $1. The player places a bet on a number or object. The "house" rolls three dice. If none of the dice show the number or object that was bet, the house keeps the $1 bet. If one of the dice shows the number or object bet (and the other two do not show it), the player gets back his or her $1 bet, plus $1 profit. If two of the dice show the number or object bet (and the third die does not show it), the player gets back his or her $1 bet, plus $2 profit. If all three dice show the number or object bet, the player gets back his or her $1 bet, plus $3 profit. Let $X$ = number of matches and $Y$ = profit per game.

    a. In words, define the random variable $X$.
    b. List the values that $X$ may take on.
    c. List the values that $Y$ may take on. Then, construct one PDF table that includes both $X$ and $Y$ and their probabilities.
    d. Calculate the average expected matches over the long run of playing this game for the player.
    e. Calculate the average expected earnings over the long run of playing this game for the player.
    f. Determine who has the advantage, the player or the house.

**72.** According to The World Bank, only 9% of the population of Uganda had access to electricity as of 2009. Suppose we randomly sample 150 people in Uganda. Let $X$ = the number of people who have access to electricity.

    a. What is the probability distribution for $X$?
    b. Using the formulas, calculate the mean and standard deviation of $X$.
    c. Find the probability that 15 people in the sample have access to electricity.
    d. Find the probability that at most ten people in the sample have access to electricity.
    e. Find the probability that more than 25 people in the sample have access to electricity.

**73.** The literacy rate for a nation measures the proportion of people age 15 and over that can read and write. The literacy rate in Afghanistan is 28.1%. Suppose you choose 15 people in Afghanistan at random. Let $X$ = the number of people who are literate.

    a. Sketch a graph of the probability distribution of $X$.
    b. Using the formulas, calculate the (i) mean and (ii) standard deviation of $X$.
    c. Find the probability that more than five people in the sample are literate. Is it is more likely that three people or four people are literate.

## 4.3 Geometric Distribution

**74.** A consumer looking to buy a used red Miata car will call dealerships until she finds a dealership that carries the car. She estimates the probability that any independent dealership will have the car will be 28%. We are interested in the number of dealerships she must call.
  a. In words, define the random variable $X$.
  b. List the values that $X$ may take on.
  c. Give the distribution of $X$. $X \sim$ _____(_____,_____)
  d. On average, how many dealerships would we expect her to have to call until she finds one that has the car?
  e. Find the probability that she must call at most four dealerships.
  f. Find the probability that she must call three or four dealerships.

**75.** Suppose that the probability that an adult in America will watch the Super Bowl is 40%. Each person is considered independent. We are interested in the number of adults in America we must survey until we find one who will watch the Super Bowl.
  a. In words, define the random variable $X$.
  b. List the values that $X$ may take on.
  c. Give the distribution of $X$. $X \sim$ _____(_____,_____)
  d. How many adults in America do you expect to survey until you find one who will watch the Super Bowl?
  e. Find the probability that you must ask seven people.
  f. Find the probability that you must ask three or four people.

**76.** It has been estimated that only about 30% of California residents have adequate earthquake supplies. Suppose we are interested in the number of California residents we must survey until we find a resident who does **not** have adequate earthquake supplies.
  a. In words, define the random variable $X$.
  b. List the values that $X$ may take on.
  c. Give the distribution of $X$. $X \sim$ _____(_____,_____)
  d. What is the probability that we must survey just one or two residents until we find a California resident who does not have adequate earthquake supplies?
  e. What is the probability that we must survey at least three California residents until we find a California resident who does not have adequate earthquake supplies?
  f. How many California residents do you expect to need to survey until you find a California resident who **does not** have adequate earthquake supplies?
  g. How many California residents do you expect to need to survey until you find a California resident who **does** have adequate earthquake supplies?

**77.** In one of its Spring catalogs, L.L. Bean® advertised footwear on 29 of its 192 catalog pages. Suppose we randomly survey 20 pages. We are interested in the number of pages that advertise footwear. Each page may be picked more than once.
  a. In words, define the random variable $X$.
  b. List the values that $X$ may take on.
  c. Give the distribution of $X$. $X \sim$ _____(_____,_____)
  d. How many pages do you expect to advertise footwear on them?
  e. Is it probable that all twenty will advertise footwear on them? Why or why not?
  f. What is the probability that fewer than ten will advertise footwear on them?
  g. Reminder: A page may be picked more than once. We are interested in the number of pages that we must randomly survey until we find one that has footwear advertised on it. Define the random variable $X$ and give its distribution.
  h. What is the probability that you only need to survey at most three pages in order to find one that advertises footwear on it?
  i. How many pages do you expect to need to survey in order to find one that advertises footwear?

**78.** Suppose that you are performing the probability experiment of rolling one fair six-sided die. Let $F$ be the event of rolling a four or a five. You are interested in how many times you need to roll the die in order to obtain the first four or five as the outcome.
- $p$ = probability of success (event $F$ occurs)
- $q$ = probability of failure (event $F$ does not occur)

    a. Write the description of the random variable $X$.
    b. What are the values that $X$ can take on?
    c. Find the values of $p$ and $q$.
    d. Find the probability that the first occurrence of event $F$ (rolling a four or five) is on the second trial.

**79.** Ellen has music practice three days a week. She practices for all of the three days 85% of the time, two days 8% of the time, one day 4% of the time, and no days 3% of the time. One week is selected at random. What values does $X$ take on?

**80.** The World Bank records the prevalence of HIV in countries around the world. According to their data, "Prevalence of HIV refers to the percentage of people ages 15 to 49 who are infected with HIV."[1] In South Africa, the prevalence of HIV is 17.3%. Let $X$ = the number of people you test until you find a person infected with HIV.
    a. Sketch a graph of the distribution of the discrete random variable $X$.
    b. What is the probability that you must test 30 people to find one with HIV?
    c. What is the probability that you must ask ten people?
    d. Find the (i) mean and (ii) standard deviation of the distribution of $X$.

**81.** According to a recent Pew Research poll, 75% of millenials (people born between 1981 and 1995) have a profile on a social networking site. Let $X$ = the number of millenials you ask until you find a person without a profile on a social networking site.
    a. Describe the distribution of $X$.
    b. Find the (i) mean and (ii) standard deviation of $X$.
    c. What is the probability that you must ask ten people to find one person without a social networking site?
    d. What is the probability that you must ask 20 people to find one person without a social networking site?
    e. What is the probability that you must ask *at most* five people?

## 4.4 Poisson Distribution

**82.** The switchboard in a Minneapolis law office gets an average of 5.5 incoming phone calls during the noon hour on Mondays. Experience shows that the existing staff can handle up to six calls in an hour. Let $X$ = the number of calls received at noon.
    a. Find the mean and standard deviation of $X$.
    b. What is the probability that the office receives at most six calls at noon on Monday?
    c. Find the probability that the law office receives six calls at noon. What does this mean to the law office staff who get, on average, 5.5 incoming phone calls at noon?
    d. What is the probability that the office receives more than eight calls at noon?

**83.** The maternity ward at Dr. Jose Fabella Memorial Hospital in Manila in the Philippines is one of the busiest in the world with an average of 60 births per day. Let $X$ = the number of births in an hour.
    a. Find the mean and standard deviation of $X$.
    b. Sketch a graph of the probability distribution of $X$.
    c. What is the probability that the maternity ward will deliver three babies in one hour?
    d. What is the probability that the maternity ward will deliver at most three babies in one hour?
    e. What is the probability that the maternity ward will deliver more than five babies in one hour?

**84.** A manufacturer of Christmas tree light bulbs knows that 3% of its bulbs are defective. Find the probability that a string of 100 lights contains at most four defective bulbs using both the binomial and Poisson distributions.

---

1. "Prevalence of HIV, total (% of populations ages 15-49)," The World Bank, 2013. Available online at http://data.worldbank.org/indicator/
SH.DYN.AIDS.ZS?order=wbapi_data_value_2011+wbapi_data_value+wbapi_data_value-last&sort=desc (accessed May 15, 2013).

**85.** The average number of children a Japanese woman has in her lifetime is 1.37. Suppose that one Japanese woman is randomly chosen.
  a.  In words, define the random variable $X$.
  b.  List the values that $X$ may take on.
  c.  Find the probability that she has no children.
  d.  Find the probability that she has fewer children than the Japanese average.
  e.  Find the probability that she has more children than the Japanese average.

**86.** The average number of children a Spanish woman has in her lifetime is 1.47. Suppose that one Spanish woman is randomly chosen.
  a.  In words, define the Random Variable $X$.
  b.  List the values that $X$ may take on.
  c.  Find the probability that she has no children.
  d.  Find the probability that she has fewer children than the Spanish average.
  e.  Find the probability that she has more children than the Spanish average .

**87.** Fertile, female cats produce an average of three litters per year. Suppose that one fertile, female cat is randomly chosen. In one year, find the probability she produces:
  a.  In words, define the random variable $X$.
  b.  List the values that $X$ may take on.
  c.  Give the distribution of $X$. $X \sim$ _____
  d.  Find the probability that she has no litters in one year.
  e.  Find the probability that she has at least two litters in one year.
  f.  Find the probability that she has exactly three litters in one year.

**88.** The chance of having an extra fortune in a fortune cookie is about 3%. Given a bag of 144 fortune cookies, we are interested in the number of cookies with an extra fortune. Two distributions may be used to solve this problem, but only use one distribution to solve the problem.
  a.  In words, define the random variable $X$.
  b.  List the values that $X$ may take on.
  c.  How many cookies do we expect to have an extra fortune?
  d.  Find the probability that none of the cookies have an extra fortune.
  e.  Find the probability that more than three have an extra fortune.
  f.  As $n$ increases, what happens involving the probabilities using the two distributions? Explain in complete sentences.

**89.** According to the South Carolina Department of Mental Health web site, for every 200 U.S. women, the average number who suffer from anorexia is one. Out of a randomly chosen group of 600 U.S. women determine the following.
  a.  In words, define the random variable $X$.
  b.  List the values that $X$ may take on.
  c.  Give the distribution of $X$. $X \sim$ _____(_____,_____)
  d.  How many are expected to suffer from anorexia?
  e.  Find the probability that no one suffers from anorexia.
  f.  Find the probability that more than four suffer from anorexia.

**90.** The chance of an IRS audit for a tax return with over $25,000 in income is about 2% per year. Suppose that 100 people with tax returns over $25,000 are randomly picked. We are interested in the number of people audited in one year. Use a Poisson distribution to anwer the following questions.
  a.  In words, define the random variable $X$.
  b.  List the values that $X$ may take on.
  c.  How many are expected to be audited?
  d.  Find the probability that no one was audited.
  e.  Find the probability that at least three were audited.

**91.** Approximately 8% of students at a local high school participate in after-school sports all four years of high school. A group of 60 seniors is randomly chosen. Of interest is the number that participated in after-school sports all four years of high school.

    a. In words, define the random variable $X$.

    b. List the values that $X$ may take on.

    c. How many seniors are expected to have participated in after-school sports all four years of high school?

    d. Based on numerical values, would you be surprised if none of the seniors participated in after-school sports all four years of high school? Justify your answer numerically.

    e. Based on numerical values, is it more likely that four or that five of the seniors participated in after-school sports all four years of high school? Justify your answer numerically.

**92.** On average, Pierre, an amateur chef, drops three pieces of egg shell into every two cake batters he makes. Suppose that you buy one of his cakes.

    a. In words, define the random variable $X$.

    b. List the values that $X$ may take on.

    c. On average, how many pieces of egg shell do you expect to be in the cake?

    d. What is the probability that there will not be any pieces of egg shell in the cake?

    e. Let's say that you buy one of Pierre's cakes each week for six weeks. What is the probability that there will not be any egg shell in any of the cakes?

    f. Based upon the average given for Pierre, is it possible for there to be seven pieces of shell in the cake? Why?

*Use the following information to answer the next two exercises:* The average number of times per week that Mrs. Plum's cats wake her up at night because they want to play is ten. We are interested in the number of times her cats wake her up each week.

**93.** In words, the random variable $X$ = _____

    a. the number of times Mrs. Plum's cats wake her up each week.

    b. the number of times Mrs. Plum's cats wake her up each hour.

    c. the number of times Mrs. Plum's cats wake her up each night.

    d. the number of times Mrs. Plum's cats wake her up.

**94.** Find the probability that her cats will wake her up no more than five times next week.

    a. 0.5000

    b. 0.9329

    c. 0.0378

    d. 0.0671

# REFERENCES

### 4.2 Binomial Distribution

"Access to electricity (% of population)," The World Bank, 2013. Available online at http://data.worldbank.org/indicator/ EG.ELC.ACCS.ZS?order=wbapi_data_value_2009%20wbapi_data_value%20wbapi_data_value-first&sort=asc (accessed May 15, 2015).

"Distance Education." Wikipedia. Available online at http://en.wikipedia.org/wiki/Distance_education (accessed May 15, 2013).

"NBA Statistics – 2013," ESPN NBA, 2013. Available online at http://espn.go.com/nba/statistics/_/seasontype/2 (accessed May 15, 2013).

Newport, Frank. "Americans Still Enjoy Saving Rather than Spending: Few demographic differences seen in these views other than by income," GALLUP® Economy, 2013. Available online at http://www.gallup.com/poll/162368/americans-enjoy-saving-rather-spending.aspx (accessed May 15, 2013).

Pryor, John H., Linda DeAngelo, Laura Palucki Blake, Sylvia Hurtado, Serge Tran. *The American Freshman: National Norms Fall 2011*. Los Angeles: Cooperative Institutional Research Program at the Higher Education Research Institute at UCLA, 2011. Also available online at http://heri.ucla.edu/PDFs/pubs/TFS/Norms/Monographs/ TheAmericanFreshman2011.pdf (accessed May 15, 2013).

"The World FactBook," Central Intelligence Agency. Available online at https://www.cia.gov/library/publications/the-world-factbook/geos/af.html (accessed May 15, 2013).

"What are the key statistics about pancreatic cancer?" American Cancer Society, 2013. Available online at http://www.cancer.org/cancer/pancreaticcancer/detailedguide/pancreatic-cancer-key-statistics (accessed May 15, 2013).

## 4.3 Geometric Distribution

"Millennials: A Portrait of Generation Next," PewResearchCenter. Available online at http://www.pewsocialtrends.org/files/2010/10/millennials-confident-connected-open-to-change.pdf (accessed May 15, 2013).

"Millennials: Confident. Connected. Open to Change." Executive Summary by PewResearch Social & Demographic Trends, 2013. Available online at http://www.pewsocialtrends.org/2010/02/24/millennials-confident-connected-open-to-change/ (accessed May 15, 2013).

"Prevalence of HIV, total (% of populations ages 15-49)," The World Bank, 2013. Available online at http://data.worldbank.org/indicator/SH.DYN.AIDS.ZS?order=wbapi_data_value_2011+wbapi_data_value+wbapi_data_value-last&sort=desc (accessed May 15, 2013).

Pryor, John H., Linda DeAngelo, Laura Palucki Blake, Sylvia Hurtado, Serge Tran. *The American Freshman: National Norms Fall 2011*. Los Angeles: Cooperative Institutional Research Program at the Higher Education Research Institute at UCLA, 2011. Also available online at http://heri.ucla.edu/PDFs/pubs/TFS/Norms/Monographs/TheAmericanFreshman2011.pdf (accessed May 15, 2013).

"Summary of the National Risk and Vulnerability Assessment 2007/8: A profile of Afghanistan," The European Union and ICON-Institute. Available online at http://ec.europa.eu/europeaid/where/asia/documents/afgh_brochure_summary_en.pdf (accessed May 15, 2013).

"The World FactBook," Central Intelligence Agency. Available online at https://www.cia.gov/library/publications/the-world-factbook/geos/af.html (accessed May 15, 2013).

"UNICEF reports on Female Literacy Centers in Afghanistan established to teach women and girls basic resading [sic] and writing skills," UNICEF Television. Video available online at http://www.unicefusa.org/assets/video/afghan-female-literacy-centers.html (accessed May 15, 2013).

## 4.4 Poisson Distribution

"ATL Fact Sheet," Department of Aviation at the Hartsfield-Jackson Atlanta International Airport, 2013. Available online at http://www.atlanta-airport.com/Airport/ATL/ATL_FactSheet.aspx (accessed May 15, 2013).

Center for Disease Control and Prevention. "Teen Drivers: Fact Sheet," Injury Prevention & Control: Motor Vehicle Safety, October 2, 2012. Available online at http://www.cdc.gov/Motorvehiclesafety/Teen_Drivers/teendrivers_factsheet.html (accessed May 15, 2013).

"Children and Childrearing," Ministry of Health, Labour, and Welfare. Available online at http://www.mhlw.go.jp/english/policy/children/children-childrearing/index.html (accessed May 15, 2013).

"Eating Disorder Statistics," South Carolina Department of Mental Health, 2006. Available online at http://www.state.sc.us/dmh/anorexia/statistics.htm (accessed May 15, 2013).

"Giving Birth in Manila: The maternity ward at the Dr Jose Fabella Memorial Hospital in Manila, the busiest in the Philippines, where there is an average of 60 births a day," theguardian, 2013. Available online at http://www.theguardian.com/world/gallery/2011/jun/08/philippines-health#/?picture=375471900&index=2 (accessed May 15, 2013).

"How Americans Use Text Messaging," Pew Internet, 2013. Available online at http://pewinternet.org/Reports/2011/Cell-Phone-Texting-2011/Main-Report.aspx (accessed May 15, 2013).

Lenhart, Amanda. "Teens, Smartphones & Testing: Texting volum is up while the frequency of voice calling is down. About one in four teens say they own smartphones," Pew Internet, 2012. Available online at http://www.pewinternet.org/~/media/Files/Reports/2012/PIP_Teens_Smartphones_and_Texting.pdf (accessed May 15, 2013).

"One born every minute: the maternity unit where mothers are THREE to a bed," MailOnline. Available online at http://www.dailymail.co.uk/news/article-2001422/Busiest-maternity-ward-planet-averages-60-babies-day-mothers-bed.html (accessed May 15, 2013).

Vanderkam, Laura. "Stop Checking Your Email, Now." CNNMoney, 2013. Available online at http://management.fortune.cnn.com/2012/10/08/stop-checking-your-email-now/ (accessed May 15, 2013).

"World Earthquakes: Live Earthquake News and Highlights," World Earthquakes, 2012. http://www.world-earthquakes.com/index.php?option=ethq_prediction (accessed May 15, 2013).

## SOLUTIONS

1

| x | P(x) |
|---|------|
| 0 | 0.12 |
| 1 | 0.18 |
| 2 | 0.30 |
| 3 | 0.15 |
| 4 | 0.10 |
| 5 | 0.10 |
| 6 | 0.05 |

Table 4.6

3  $0.10 + 0.05 = 0.15$

5  1

7  $0.35 + 0.40 + 0.10 = 0.85$

9  $1(0.15) + 2(0.35) + 3(0.40) + 4(0.10) = 0.15 + 0.70 + 1.20 + 0.40 = 2.45$

11

| x | P(x) |
|---|------|
| 0 | 0.03 |
| 1 | 0.04 |
| 2 | 0.08 |
| 3 | 0.85 |

Table 4.7

13  Let $X$ = the number of events Javier volunteers for each month.

**15**

| x | P(x) |
|---|------|
| 0 | 0.05 |
| 1 | 0.05 |
| 2 | 0.10 |
| 3 | 0.20 |
| 4 | 0.25 |
| 5 | 0.35 |

Table 4.8

**17** $1 - 0.05 = 0.95$

**18** $X$ = the number of business majors in the sample.

**19** 2, 3, 4, 5, 6, 7, 8, 9

**20** $X$ = the number that reply "yes"

**22** 0, 1, 2, 3, 4, 5, 6, 7, 8

**24** 5.7

**26** 0.4151

**28** $X$ = the number of freshmen selected from the study until one replied "yes" that same-sex couples should have the right to legal marital status.

**30** 1,2,…

**32** 1.4

**35** 0, 1, 2, 3, 4, …

**37** 0.0485

**39** 0.0214

**41** $X$ = the number of U.S. teens who die from motor vehicle injuries per day.

**43** 0, 1, 2, 3, 4, ...

**45** No

**48**

a. $X$ = the number of pages that advertise footwear

b. 0, 1, 2, 3, ..., 20

c. 3.03

d. 1.5197

**50**

a. $X$ = the number of Patriots picked

b. 0, 1, 2, 3, 4

c. Without replacement

**53** $X$ = the number of patients calling in claiming to have the flu, who actually have the flu. $X$ = 0, 1, 2, ...25

**55** 0.0165

**57**

  a.  $X$ = the number of DVDs a Video to Go customer rents

  b.  0.12

  c.  0.11

  d.  0.77

**59** d. 4.43

**61** c

**63**

  •  $X$ = number of questions answered correctly

  •  $X \sim B\left(32, \frac{1}{3}\right)$

  •  We are interested in MORE THAN 75% of 32 questions correct. 75% of 32 is 24. We want to find $P(x > 24)$. The event "more than 24" is the complement of "less than or equal to 24."

  •  $P(x > 24) = 0$

  •  The probability of getting more than 75% of the 32 questions correct when randomly guessing is very small and practically zero.

**65**

  a.  $X$ = the number of college and universities that offer online offerings.

  b.  0, 1, 2, ..., 13

  c.  $X \sim B(13, 0.96)$

  d.  12.48

  e.  0.0135

  f.  $P(x = 12) = 0.3186$ $P(x = 13) = 0.5882$ More likely to get 13.

**67**

  a.  $X$ = the number of fencers who do **not** use the foil as their main weapon

  b.  0, 1, 2, 3,... 25

  c.  $X \sim B(25, 0.40)$

  d.  10

  e.  0.0442

  f.  The probability that all 25 not use the foil is almost zero. Therefore, it would be very surprising.

**69**

  a.  $X$ = the number of audits in a 20-year period

  b.  0, 1, 2, ..., 20

  c.  $X \sim B(20, 0.02)$

  d.  0.4

  e.  0.6676

  f.  0.0071

**71**

  1.  $X$ = the number of matches

  2.  0, 1, 2, 3

  3.  In dollars: −1, 1, 2, 3

4. $\frac{1}{2}$

5. The answer is −0.0787. You lose about eight cents, on average, per game.

6. The house has the advantage.

**73**

a. $X \sim B(15, 0.281)$

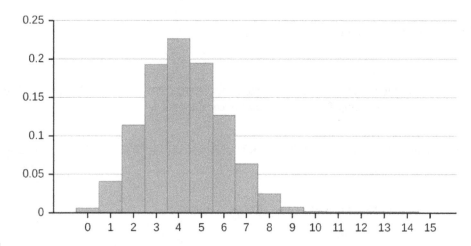

Figure 4.4

b.   i.   Mean = $\mu = np = 15(0.281) = 4.215$

   ii.   Standard Deviation = $\sigma = \sqrt{npq} = \sqrt{15(0.281)(0.719)} = 1.7409$

c. $P(x > 5)=1 - 0.7754 = 0.2246$
$P(x = 3) = 0.1927$
$P(x = 4) = 0.2259$
It is more likely that four people are literate that three people are.

**75**

a. $X$ = the number of adults in America who are surveyed until one says he or she will watch the Super Bowl.

b. $X \sim G(0.40)$

c. 2.5

d. 0.0187

e. 0.2304

**77**

a. $X$ = the number of pages that advertise footwear

b. $X$ takes on the values 0, 1, 2, ..., 20

c. $X \sim B(20, \frac{29}{192})$

d. 3.02

e. No

f. 0.9997

g. $X$ = the number of pages we must survey until we find one that advertises footwear. $X \sim G(\frac{29}{192})$

h. 0.3881

i. 6.6207 pages

**79** 0, 1, 2, and 3

**81**

a. $X \sim G(0.25)$

b.    i.   Mean = $\mu = \dfrac{1}{p} = \dfrac{1}{0.25} = 4$

     ii.   Standard Deviation = $\sigma = \sqrt{\dfrac{1-p}{p^2}} = \sqrt{\dfrac{1-0.25}{0.25^2}} \approx 3.4641$

c. $P(x = 10) = 0.0188$

d. $P(x = 20) = 0.0011$

e. $P(x \le 5) = 0.7627$

**82**

a. $X \sim P(5.5)$; $\mu = 5.5$; $\sigma = \sqrt{5.5} \approx 2.3452$

b. $P(x \le 6) \approx 0.6860$

c. There is a 15.7% probability that the law staff will receive more calls than they can handle.

d. $P(x > 8) = 1 - P(x \le 8) \approx 1 - 0.8944 = 0.1056$

**84** Let $X$ = the number of defective bulbs in a string. Using the Poisson distribution:
- $\mu = np = 100(0.03) = 3$

- $X \sim P(3)$

- $P(x \le 4) \approx 0.8153$

Using the binomial distribution:
- $X \sim B(100, 0.03)$

- $P(x \le 4) = 0.8179$

The Poisson approximation is very good—the difference between the probabilities is only 0.0026.

**86**

a. $X$ = the number of children for a Spanish woman

b. 0, 1, 2, 3,...

c. 0.2299

d. 0.5679

e. 0.4321

**88**

a. $X$ = the number of fortune cookies that have an extra fortune

b. 0, 1, 2, 3,... 144

c. 4.32

d. 0.0124 or 0.0133

e. 0.6300 or 0.6264

f. As $n$ gets larger, the probabilities get closer together.

**90**

a. $X$ = the number of people audited in one year

b. 0, 1, 2, ..., 100

   c.  2

   d.  0.1353

   e.  0.3233

**92**

   a.  $X$ = the number of shell pieces in one cake

   b.  0, 1, 2, 3,...

   c.  1.5

   d.  0.2231

   e.  0.0001

   f.  Yes

**94** d

# 5 | CONTINUOUS RANDOM VARIABLES

**Figure 5.1** The heights of these radish plants are continuous random variables. (Credit: Rev Stan)

## Introduction

Continuous random variables have many applications. Baseball batting averages, IQ scores, the length of time a long distance telephone call lasts, the amount of money a person carries, the length of time a computer chip lasts, rates of return from an investment, and SAT scores are just a few. The field of reliability depends on a variety of continuous random variables, as do all areas of risk analysis.

> **NOTE**
>
> The values of discrete and continuous random variables can be ambiguous. For example, if $X$ is equal to the number of miles (to the nearest mile) you drive to work, then $X$ is a discrete random variable. You count the miles. If $X$ is the distance you drive to work, then you measure values of $X$ and $X$ is a continuous random variable. For a second

example, if $X$ is equal to the number of books in a backpack, then $X$ is a discrete random variable. If $X$ is the weight of a book, then $X$ is a continuous random variable because weights are measured. How the random variable is defined is very important.

# 5.1 | Properties of Continuous Probability Density Functions

The graph of a continuous probability distribution is a curve. Probability is represented by area under the curve. We have already met this concept when we developed relative frequencies with histograms in Chapter 2. The relative area for a range of values was the probability of drawing at random an observation in that group. Again with the Poisson distribution in Chapter 4, the graph in Example 4.14 used boxes to represent the probability of specific values of the random variable. In this case, we were being a bit casual because the random variables of a Poisson distribution are discrete, whole numbers, and a box has width. Notice that the horizontal axis, the random variable x, purposefully did not mark the points along the axis. The probability of a specific value of a continuous random variable will be zero because the area under a point is zero. Probability is area.

The curve is called the **probability density function** (abbreviated as **pdf**). We use the symbol $f(x)$ to represent the curve. $f(x)$ is the function that corresponds to the graph; we use the density function $f(x)$ to draw the graph of the probability distribution.

**Area under the curve** is given by a different function called the **cumulative distribution function** (abbreviated as **cdf**). The cumulative distribution function is used to evaluate probability as area. Mathematically, the cumulative probability density function is the integral of the pdf, and the probability between two values of a continuous random variable will be the integral of the pdf between these two values: the area under the curve between these values. Remember that the area under the pdf for all possible values of the random variable is one, certainty. Probability thus can be seen as the relative percent of certainty between the two values of interest.

- The outcomes are measured, not counted.
- The entire area under the curve and above the x-axis is equal to one.
- Probability is found for intervals of $x$ values rather than for individual $x$ values.
- $P(c < x < d)$ is the probability that the random variable $X$ is in the interval between the values $c$ and $d$. $P(c < x < d)$ is the area under the curve, above the $x$-axis, to the right of $c$ and the left of $d$.
- $P(x = c) = 0$ The probability that $x$ takes on any single individual value is zero. The area below the curve, above the $x$-axis, and between $x = c$ and $x = c$ has no width, and therefore no area (area = 0). Since the probability is equal to the area, the probability is also zero.
- $P(c < x < d)$ is the same as $P(c \leq x \leq d)$ because probability is equal to area.

We will find the area that represents probability by using geometry, formulas, technology, or probability tables. In general, integral calculus is needed to find the area under the curve for many probability density functions. When we use formulas to find the area in this textbook, the formulas were found by using the techniques of integral calculus.

There are many continuous probability distributions. When using a continuous probability distribution to model probability, the distribution used is selected to model and fit the particular situation in the best way.

In this chapter and the next, we will study the uniform distribution, the exponential distribution, and the normal distribution. The following graphs illustrate these distributions.

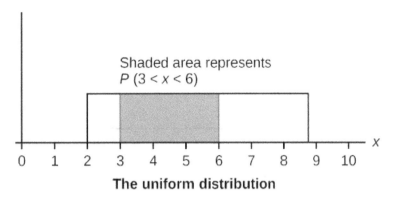

The uniform distribution

**Figure 5.2** The graph shows a Uniform Distribution with the area between $x = 3$ and $x = 6$ shaded to represent the probability that the value of the random variable $X$ is in the interval between three and six.

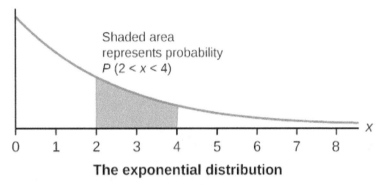

The exponential distribution

**Figure 5.3** The graph shows an Exponential Distribution with the area between $x = 2$ and $x = 4$ shaded to represent the probability that the value of the random variable $X$ is in the interval between two and four.

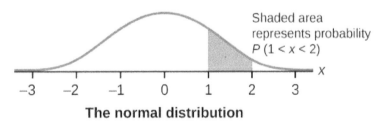

The normal distribution

**Figure 5.4** The graph shows the Standard Normal Distribution with the area between $x = 1$ and $x = 2$ shaded to represent the probability that the value of the random variable $X$ is in the interval between one and two.

**For continuous probability distributions, PROBABILITY = AREA.**

## Example 5.1

Consider the function $f(x) = \frac{1}{20}$ for $0 \le x \le 20$. $x$ = a real number. The graph of $f(x) = \frac{1}{20}$ is a horizontal line.

However, since $0 \le x \le 20$, $f(x)$ is restricted to the portion between $x = 0$ and $x = 20$, inclusive.

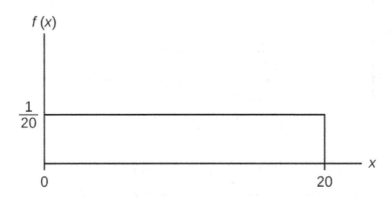

**Figure 5.5**

$f(x) = \frac{1}{20}$ **for** $0 \le x \le 20$.

The graph of $f(x) = \frac{1}{20}$ is a horizontal line segment when $0 \le x \le 20$.

The area between $f(x) = \frac{1}{20}$ where $0 \le x \le 20$ and the $x$-axis is the area of a rectangle with base = 20 and height

= $\frac{1}{20}$.

$$\text{AREA} = 20\left(\frac{1}{20}\right) = 1$$

**Suppose we want to find the area between $f(x) = \frac{1}{20}$ and the $x$-axis where $0 < x < 2$.**

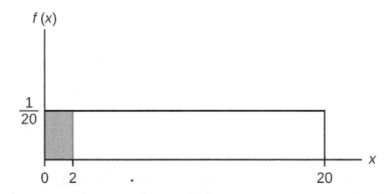

**Figure 5.6**

$$\text{AREA} = (2 - 0)\left(\frac{1}{20}\right) = 0.1$$

$(2 - 0) = 2 = $ base of a rectangle

**REMINDER**

area of a rectangle = (base)(height).

The area corresponds to a probability. The probability that $x$ is between zero and two is 0.1, which can be written mathematically as $P(0 < x < 2) = P(x < 2) = 0.1$.

**Suppose we want to find the area between $f(x) = \frac{1}{20}$ and the $x$-axis where $4 < x < 15$.**

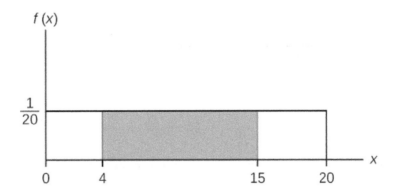

**Figure 5.7**

$$\text{AREA} = (15 - 4)\left(\frac{1}{20}\right) = 0.55$$

$(15 - 4) = 11 = $ the base of a rectangle

The area corresponds to the probability $P(4 < x < 15) = 0.55$.

Suppose we want to find $P(x = 15)$. On an x-y graph, $x = 15$ is a vertical line. A vertical line has no width (or zero width). Therefore, $P(x = 15) = $ (base)(height) $= (0)\left(\frac{1}{20}\right) = 0$

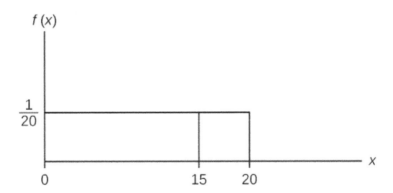

**Figure 5.8**

$P(X \leq x)$, which can also be written as $P(X < x)$ for continuous distributions, is called the cumulative distribution function or CDF. Notice the "less than or equal to" symbol. We can also use the CDF to calculate $P(X > x)$. The CDF gives "area to the left" and $P(X > x)$ gives "area to the right." We calculate $P(X > x)$ for continuous distributions as follows: $P(X > x) = 1 - P(X < x)$.

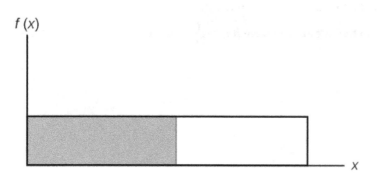

**Figure 5.9**

Label the graph with $f(x)$ and $x$. Scale the $x$ and $y$ axes with the maximum $x$ and $y$ values. $f(x) = \frac{1}{20}$, $0 \le x \le 20$.

To calculate the probability that $x$ is between two values, look at the following graph. Shade the region between $x = 2.3$ and $x = 12.7$. Then calculate the shaded area of a rectangle.

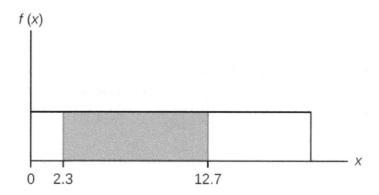

**Figure 5.10**

$$P(2.3 < x < 12.7) = (\text{base})(\text{height}) = (12.7 - 2.3)\left(\frac{1}{20}\right) = 0.52$$

## Try It Σ

**5.1** Consider the function $f(x) = \frac{1}{8}$ for $0 \le x \le 8$. Draw the graph of $f(x)$ and find $P(2.5 < x < 7.5)$.

## 5.2 | The Uniform Distribution

The uniform distribution is a continuous probability distribution and is concerned with events that are equally likely to occur. When working out problems that have a uniform distribution, be careful to note if the data is inclusive or exclusive of endpoints.

The mathematical statement of the uniform distribution is

$$f(x) = \frac{1}{b - a} \text{ for } a \le x \le b$$

where $a$ = the lowest value of $x$ and $b$ = the highest value of $x$.

Formulas for the theoretical mean and standard deviation are

$$\mu = \frac{a + b}{2} \text{ and } \sigma = \sqrt{\frac{(b - a)^2}{12}}$$

## Try It Σ

**5.1** The data that follow are the number of passengers on 35 different charter fishing boats. The sample mean = 7.9 and the sample standard deviation = 4.33. The data follow a uniform distribution where all values between and including zero and 14 are equally likely. State the values of $a$ and $b$. Write the distribution in proper notation, and calculate the theoretical mean and standard deviation.

| 1 | 12 | 4 | 10 | 4 | 14 | 11 |
|---|----|---|----|---|----|----|
| 7 | 11 | 4 | 13 | 2 | 4 | 6 |
| 3 | 10 | 0 | 12 | 6 | 9 | 10 |
| 5 | 13 | 4 | 10 | 14 | 12 | 11 |
| 6 | 10 | 11 | 0 | 11 | 13 | 2 |

**Table 5.1**

## Example 5.2

The amount of time, in minutes, that a person must wait for a bus is uniformly distributed between zero and 15 minutes, inclusive.

a. What is the probability that a person waits fewer than 12.5 minutes?

### Solution 5.2

a. Let $X$ = the number of minutes a person must wait for a bus. $a = 0$ and $b = 15$. $X \sim U(0, 15)$. Write the probability density function. $f(x) = \frac{1}{15 - 0} = \frac{1}{15}$ for $0 \le x \le 15$.

Find $P(x < 12.5)$. Draw a graph.

$$P(x < k) = (\text{base})(\text{height}) = (12.5 - 0)\left(\frac{1}{15}\right) = 0.8333$$

The probability a person waits less than 12.5 minutes is 0.8333.

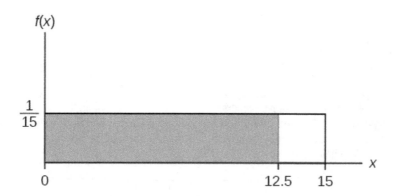

**Figure 5.11**

b. On the average, how long must a person wait? Find the mean, $\mu$, and the standard deviation, $\sigma$.

**Solution 5.2**

b. $\mu = \dfrac{a + b}{2} = \dfrac{15 + 0}{2} = 7.5$. On the average, a person must wait 7.5 minutes.

$\sigma = \sqrt{\dfrac{(b-a)^2}{12}} = \sqrt{\dfrac{(15-0)^2}{12}} = 4.3$. The Standard deviation is 4.3 minutes.

c. Ninety percent of the time, the time a person must wait falls below what value?

This asks for the 90th percentile.

**Solution 5.2**

c. Find the 90th percentile. Draw a graph. Let $k$ = the 90th percentile.

$P(x < k) = (\text{base})(\text{height}) = (k - 0)(\frac{1}{15})$

$0.90 = (k)\left(\dfrac{1}{15}\right)$

$k = (0.90)(15) = 13.5$

The 90th percentile is 13.5 minutes. Ninety percent of the time, a person must wait at most 13.5 minutes.

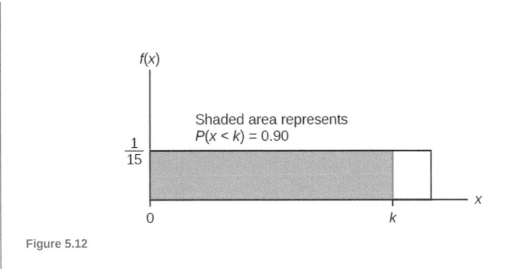

**Figure 5.12**

**5.2** The total duration of baseball games in the major league in the 2011 season is uniformly distributed between 447 hours and 521 hours inclusive.

   a.  Find $a$ and $b$ and describe what they represent.

   b.  Write the distribution.

   c.  Find the mean and the standard deviation.

   d.  What is the probability that the duration of games for a team for the 2011 season is between 480 and 500 hours?

# 5.3 | The Exponential Distribution

The **exponential distribution** is often concerned with the amount of time until some specific event occurs. For example, the amount of time (beginning now) until an earthquake occurs has an exponential distribution. Other examples include the length of time, in minutes, of long distance business telephone calls, and the amount of time, in months, a car battery lasts. It can be shown, too, that the value of the change that you have in your pocket or purse approximately follows an exponential distribution.

Values for an exponential random variable occur in the following way. There are fewer large values and more small values. For example, marketing studies have shown that the amount of money customers spend in one trip to the supermarket follows an exponential distribution. There are more people who spend small amounts of money and fewer people who spend large amounts of money.

Exponential distributions are commonly used in calculations of product reliability, or the length of time a product lasts.

The random variable for the exponential distribution is continuous and often measures a passage of time, although it can be used in other applications. Typical questions may be, "what is the probability that some event will occur within the next $x$ hours or days, or what is the probability that some event will occur between $x_1$ hours and $x_2$ hours, or what is the probability that the event will take more than $x_1$ hours to perform?" In short, the random variable $X$ equals ($a$) the time between events or ($b$) the passage of time to complete an action, e.g. wait on a customer. The probability density function is given by:

$$f(x) = \frac{1}{\mu}e^{-\frac{1}{\mu}x}$$

where μ is the historical average waiting time.

and has a mean and standard deviation of 1/μ.

An alternative form of the exponential distribution formula recognizes what is often called the decay factor. The decay factor simply measures how rapidly the probability of an event declines as the random variable $X$ increases. When the notation using the decay parameter $m$ is used, the probability density function is presented as:

$$f(x) \;=\; me^{-mx}$$

where $m = \frac{1}{\mu}$

In order to calculate probabilities for specific probability density functions, the cumulative density function is used. The cumulative density function (cdf) is simply the integral of the pdf and is:

$$F\left(x\right) = \int_0^\infty \left[\frac{1}{\mu}e^{-\frac{x}{\mu}}\right] = 1 - e^{-\frac{x}{\mu}}$$

## Example 5.3

Let $X$ = amount of time (in minutes) a postal clerk spends with a customer. The time is known from historical data to have an average amount of time equal to four minutes.

It is given that $\mu$ = 4 minutes, that is, the average time the clerk spends with a customer is 4 minutes. Remember that we are still doing probability and thus we have to be told the population parameters such as the mean. To do any calculations, we need to know the mean of the distribution: the historical time to provide a service, for example. Knowing the historical mean allows the calculation of the decay parameter, $m$.

$m = \frac{1}{\mu}$. Therefore, $m = \frac{1}{4} = 0.25$.

When the notation used the decay parameter, $m$, the probability density function is presented as

$f(x) \;=\; me^{-mx}$, which is simply the original formula with $m$ substituted for $\frac{1}{\mu}$, or $f(x) = \frac{1}{\mu}e^{-\frac{1}{\mu}x}$.

To calculate probabilities for an exponential probability density function, we need to use the cumulative density function. As shown below, the curve for the cumulative density function is:

$f(x) = 0.25e^{-0.25x}$ where $x$ is at least zero and $m = 0.25$.

For example, $f(5) = 0.25e^{(-0.25)(5)} = 0.072$. In other words, the function has a value of .072 when $x = 5$.

The graph is as follows:

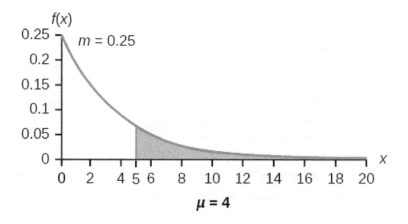

Figure 5.13

Notice the graph is a declining curve. When $x = 0$,

$f(x) = 0.25e^{(-0.25)(0)} = (0.25)(1) = 0.25 = m$. The maximum value on the $y$-axis is always $m$, one divided by the mean.

**5.3** The amount of time spouses shop for anniversary cards can be modeled by an exponential distribution with the average amount of time equal to eight minutes. Write the distribution, state the probability density function, and graph the distribution.

## Example 5.4

a. Using the information in **Example 5.3**, find the probability that a clerk spends four to five minutes with a randomly selected customer.

### Solution 5.4

a. Find $P(4 < x < 5)$.
The **cumulative distribution function (CDF)** gives the area to the left.
$P(x < x) = 1 - e^{-mx}$
$P(x < 5) = 1 - e^{(-0.25)(5)} = 0.7135$ and $P(x < 4) = 1 - e^{(-0.25)(4)} = 0.6321$
$P(4 < x < 5) = 0.7135 - 0.6321 = 0.0814$

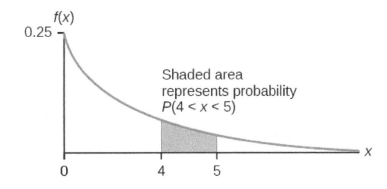

Figure 5.14

**5.4** The number of days ahead travelers purchase their airline tickets can be modeled by an exponential distribution with the average amount of time equal to 15 days. Find the probability that a traveler will purchase a ticket fewer than ten days in advance. How many days do half of all travelers wait?

## Example 5.5

On the average, a certain computer part lasts ten years. The length of time the computer part lasts is exponentially distributed.

a. What is the probability that a computer part lasts more than 7 years?

**Solution 5.5**

a. Let $x$ = the amount of time (in years) a computer part lasts.

$\mu = 10$ so $m = \frac{1}{\mu} = \frac{1}{10} = 0.1$

Find $P(x > 7)$. Draw the graph.

$P(x > 7) = 1 - P(x < 7)$.

Since $P(X < x) = 1 - e^{-mx}$ then $P(X > x) = 1 - (1 - e^{-mx}) = e^{-mx}$

$P(x > 7) = e^{(-0.1)(7)} = 0.4966$. The probability that a computer part lasts more than seven years is 0.4966.

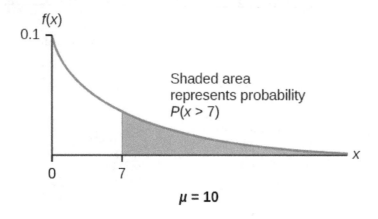

**Figure 5.15**

b. On the average, how long would five computer parts last if they are used one after another?

**Solution 5.5**

b. On the average, one computer part lasts ten years. Therefore, five computer parts, if they are used one right after the other would last, on the average, $(5)(10) = 50$ years.

d. What is the probability that a computer part lasts between nine and 11 years?

**Solution 5.5**

d. Find $P(9 < x < 11)$. Draw the graph.

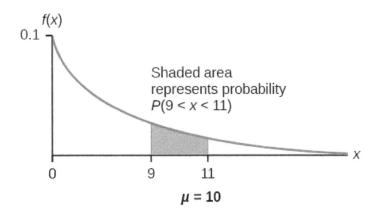

**Figure 5.16**

$P(9 < x < 11) = P(x < 11) - P(x < 9) = (1 - e^{(-0.1)(11)}) - (1 - e^{(-0.1)(9)}) = 0.6671 - 0.5934 = 0.0737$. The probability that a computer part lasts between nine and 11 years is 0.0737.

## Try It Σ

**5.5** On average, a pair of running shoes can last 18 months if used every day. The length of time running shoes last is exponentially distributed. What is the probability that a pair of running shoes last more than 15 months? On average, how long would six pairs of running shoes last if they are used one after the other? Eighty percent of running shoes last at most how long if used every day?

## Example 5.6

Suppose that the length of a phone call, in minutes, is an exponential random variable with decay parameter $\frac{1}{12}$. The decay p[parameter is another way to view $1/\lambda$. If another person arrives at a public telephone just before you, find the probability that you will have to wait more than five minutes. Let $X$ = the length of a phone call, in minutes.

What is $m$, $\mu$, and $\sigma$? The probability that you must wait more than five minutes is _____ .

**Solution 5.6**
- $m = \frac{1}{12}$

- $\mu = 12$

- $\sigma = 12$

$P(x > 5) = 0.6592$

## Example 5.7

The time spent waiting between events is often modeled using the exponential distribution. For example, suppose that an average of 30 customers per hour arrive at a store and the time between arrivals is exponentially distributed.

a. On average, how many minutes elapse between two successive arrivals?

b. When the store first opens, how long on average does it take for three customers to arrive?

c. After a customer arrives, find the probability that it takes less than one minute for the next customer to arrive.

d. After a customer arrives, find the probability that it takes more than five minutes for the next customer to arrive.

e. Is an exponential distribution reasonable for this situation?

### Solution 5.7

a. Since we expect 30 customers to arrive per hour (60 minutes), we expect on average one customer to arrive every two minutes on average.

b. Since one customer arrives every two minutes on average, it will take six minutes on average for three customers to arrive.

c. Let $X$ = the time between arrivals, in minutes. By part a, $\mu = 2$, so $m = \frac{1}{2} = 0.5$.

The cumulative distribution function is $P(X < x) = 1 - e^{(-0.5)(x)}$

**Therefore** $P(X < 1) = 1 - e^{(-0.5)(1)} = 0.3935$.

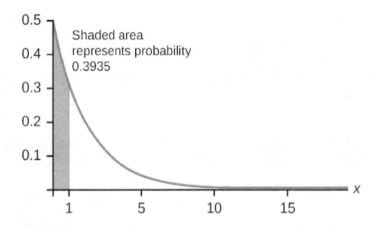

**Figure 5.17**

d. $P(X > 5) = 1 - P(X < 5) = 1 - (1 - e^{(-0.5)(5)}) = e^{-2.5} \approx 0.0821$.

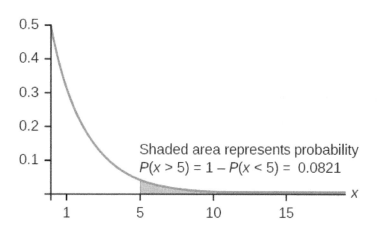

Figure 5.18

e. This model assumes that a single customer arrives at a time, which may not be reasonable since people might shop in groups, leading to several customers arriving at the same time. It also assumes that the flow of customers does not change throughout the day, which is not valid if some times of the day are busier than others.

## Memorylessness of the Exponential Distribution

Recall that the amount of time between customers for the postal clerk discussed earlier is exponentially distributed with a mean of two minutes. Suppose that five minutes have elapsed since the last customer arrived. Since an unusually long amount of time has now elapsed, it would seem to be more likely for a customer to arrive within the next minute. With the exponential distribution, this is not the case–the additional time spent waiting for the next customer does not depend on how much time has already elapsed since the last customer. This is referred to as the **memoryless property**. The exponential and geometric probability density functions are the only probability functions that have the memoryless property. Specifically, the **memoryless property** says that

$P(X > r + t \mid X > r) = P(X > t)$ for all $r \geq 0$ and $t \geq 0$

For example, if five minutes have elapsed since the last customer arrived, then the probability that more than one minute will elapse before the next customer arrives is computed by using $r = 5$ and $t = 1$ in the foregoing equation.

$P(X > 5 + 1 \mid X > 5) = P(X > 1) = e^{(-0.5)(1)} = 0.6065.$

*This is the same* probability as that of waiting more than one minute for a customer to arrive after the previous arrival.

The exponential distribution is often used to model the longevity of an electrical or mechanical device. In Example 5.5, the lifetime of a certain computer part has the exponential distribution with a mean of ten years. The **memoryless property** says that knowledge of what has occurred in the past has no effect on future probabilities. In this case it means that an old part is not any more likely to break down at any particular time than a brand new part. In other words, the part stays as good as new until it suddenly breaks. For example, if the part has already lasted ten years, then the probability that it lasts another seven years is $P(X > 17 \mid X > 10) = P(X > 7) = 0.4966$, where the vertical line is read as "given".

## Example 5.8

Refer back tb the postal clerk again where the time a postal clerk spends with his or her customer has an exponential distribution with a mean of four minutes. Suppose a customer has spent four minutes with a postal clerk. What is the probability that he or she will spend at least an additional three minutes with the postal clerk?

The decay parameter of X is $m = \frac{1}{4} = 0.25$, so $X \sim Exp(0.25)$.

The cumulative distribution function is $P(X < x) = 1 - e^{-0.25x}$.

We want to find $P(X > 7|X > 4)$. The **memoryless property** says that $P(X > 7|X > 4) = P(X > 3)$, so we just need to find the probability that a customer spends more than three minutes with a postal clerk.

This is $P(X > 3) = 1 - P(X < 3) = 1 - (1 - e^{-0.25 \cdot 3}) = e^{-0.75} \approx 0.4724$.

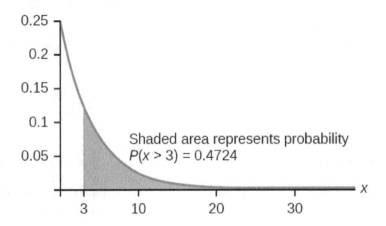

**Figure 5.19**

## Relationship between the Poisson and the Exponential Distribution

There is an interesting relationship between the exponential distribution and the Poisson distribution. Suppose that the time that elapses between two successive events follows the exponential distribution with a mean of $\mu$ units of time. Also assume that these times are independent, meaning that the time between events is not affected by the times between previous events. If these assumptions hold, then the number of events per unit time follows a Poisson distribution with mean $\mu$. Recall that if

X has the Poisson distribution with mean $\mu$, then $P(X = x) = \dfrac{\mu^x e^{-\mu}}{x!}$.

The formula for the exponential distribution: $P(X = x) = me^{-mx} = \dfrac{1}{\mu}e^{-\frac{1}{\mu}x}$ Where m = the rate parameter, or $\mu$ = average time between occurrences.

We see that the exponential is the cousin of the Poisson distribution and they are linked through this formula. There are important differences that make each distribution relevant for different types of probability problems.

First, the Poisson has a discrete random variable, x, where time; a continuous variable is artificially broken into discrete pieces. We saw that the number of occurrences of an event in a given time interval, x, follows the Poisson distribution.

For example, the **number** of times the telephone rings per hour. By contrast, the time **between** occurrences follows the exponential distribution. For example. The telephone just rang, how long will it be until it rings again? We are measuring length of time of the interval, a continuous random variable, exponential, not events during an interval, Poisson.

### The Exponential Distribution v. the Poisson Distribution

A visual way to show both the similarities and differences between these two distributions is with a time line.

**Exponential Distribution**
X = passage of time: $t_1$ to next event

**Poisson Distribution**
X = number of events $t_1$ to $t_2$

Figure 5.20

The random variable for the Poisson distribution is discrete and thus counts events during a given time period, $t_1$ to $t_2$ on **Figure 5.20**, and calculates the probability of that number occurring. The number of events, four in the graph, is measured in counting numbers; therefore, the random variable of the Poisson is a discrete random variable.

The exponential probability distribution calculates probabilities of the passage of time, a continuous random variable. In **Figure 5.20** this is shown as the bracket from $t_1$ to the next occurrence of the event marked with a triangle.

Classic Poisson distribution questions are "how many people will arrive at my checkout window in the next hour?".

Classic exponential distribution questions are "how long it will be until the next person arrives," or a variant, "how long will the person remain here once they have arrived?".

Again, the formula for the exponential distribution is:

$$f(x) = me^{-mx} \text{ or } f(x) = \frac{1}{\mu}e^{-\frac{1}{\mu}x}$$

We see immediately the similarity between the exponential formula and the Poisson formula.

$$P(x) = \frac{\mu^x e^{-\mu}}{x!}$$

Both probability density functions are based upon the relationship between time and exponential growth or decay. The "e" in the formula is a constant with the approximate value of 2.71828 and is the base of the natural logarithmic exponential growth formula. When people say that something has grown exponentially this is what they are talking about.

An example of the exponential and the Poisson will make clear the differences been the two. It will also show the interesting applications they have.

**Poisson Distribution**

Suppose that historically 10 customers arrive at the checkout lines each hour. Remember that this is still probability so we have to be told these historical values. We see this is a Poisson probability problem.

We can put this information into the Poisson probability density function and get a general formula that will calculate the probability of **any** specific number of customers arriving in the next hour.

The formula is for any value of the random variable we chose, and so the x is put into the formula. This is the formula:

$$f(x) = \frac{10^x e^{-10}}{x!}$$

As an example, the probability of 15 people arriving at the checkout counter in the next hour would be

$$P(x = 15) = \frac{10^{15} e^{-10}}{15!} = 0.0611$$

Here we have inserted x = 15 and calculated the probability that in the next hour 15 people will arrive is .061.

**Exponential Distribution**

If we keep the same historical facts that 10 customers arrive each hour, but we now are interested in the service time a person spends at the counter, then we would use the exponential distribution. The exponential probability function for any value of x, the random variable, for this particular checkout counter historical data is:

$$f(x) = \frac{1}{.1}e^{\frac{-x}{.1}} = 10e^{-10x}$$

To calculate $\mu$, the historical average service time, we simply divide the number of people that arrive per hour, 10 , into the time period, one hour, and have $\mu = 0.1$. Historically, people spend 0.1 of an hour at the checkout counter, or 6 minutes. This explains the .1 in the formula.

There is a natural confusion with $\mu$ in both the Poisson and exponential formulas. They have different meanings, although they have the same symbol. The mean of the exponential is one divided by the mean of the Poisson. If you are given the historical number of arrivals you have the mean of the Poisson. If you are given an historical length of time between events you have the mean of an exponential.

Continuing with our example at the checkout clerk; if we wanted to know the probability that a person would spend 9 minutes or less checking out, then we use this formula. First, we convert to the same time units which are parts of one hour. Nine minutes is 0.15 of one hour. Next we note that we are asking for a range of values. This is always the case for a continuous random variable. We write the probability question as:

$$p\left(x \le 9\right) = 1 - 10e^{-10x}$$

We can now put the numbers into the formula and we have our result.

$$p(x = .15) = 1 - 10e^{-10(.15)} = 0.7769$$

The probability that a customer will spend 9 minutes or less checking out is 0.7769.

We see that we have a high probability of getting out in less than nine minutes and a tiny probability of having 15 customers arriving in the next hour.

# KEY TERMS

**Conditional Probability** the likelihood that an event will occur given that another event has already occurred.

**decay parameter** The decay parameter describes the rate at which probabilities decay to zero for increasing values of $x$. It is the value $m$ in the probability density function $f(x) = me^{(-mx)}$ of an exponential random variable. It is also equal to $m = \frac{1}{\mu}$ , where $\mu$ is the mean of the random variable.

**Exponential Distribution** a continuous random variable (RV) that appears when we are interested in the intervals of time between some random events, for example, the length of time between emergency arrivals at a hospital. The mean is $\mu = \frac{1}{m}$ and the standard deviation is $\sigma = \frac{1}{m}$. The probability density function is $f(x) = me^{-mx}$ or $f(x) = \frac{1}{\mu}e^{-\frac{1}{\mu}x}$ , $x \geq 0$ and the cumulative distribution function is $P(X \leq x) = 1 - e^{-mx}$ or $P(X \leq x) = 1 - e^{-\frac{1}{\mu}x}$.

.

**memoryless property** For an exponential random variable $X$, the memoryless property is the statement that knowledge of what has occurred in the past has no effect on future probabilities. This means that the probability that $X$ exceeds $x + t$, given that it has exceeded $x$, is the same as the probability that $X$ would exceed $t$ if we had no knowledge about it. In symbols we say that $P(X > x + t | X > x) = P(X > t)$.

**Poisson distribution** If there is a known average of $\mu$ events occurring per unit time, and these events are independent of each other, then the number of events $X$ occurring in one unit of time has the Poisson distribution. The probability of $x$ events occurring in one unit time is equal to $P(X = x) = \frac{\mu^x e^{-\mu}}{x!}$.

**Uniform Distribution** a continuous random variable (RV) that has equally likely outcomes over the domain, $a < x < b$; it is often referred as the **rectangular distribution** because the graph of the pdf has the form of a rectangle. The mean is $\mu = \frac{a+b}{2}$ and the standard deviation is $\sigma = \sqrt{\frac{(b-a)^2}{12}}$. The probability density function is $f(x) = \frac{1}{b-a}$ for $a < x < b$ or $a \leq x \leq b$. The cumulative distribution is $P(X \leq x) = \frac{x-a}{b-a}$.

# CHAPTER REVIEW

## 5.1 Properties of Continuous Probability Density Functions

The probability density function (pdf) is used to describe probabilities for continuous random variables. The area under the density curve between two points corresponds to the probability that the variable falls between those two values. In other words, the area under the density curve between points $a$ and $b$ is equal to $P(a < x < b)$. The cumulative distribution function (cdf) gives the probability as an area. If $X$ is a continuous random variable, the probability density function (pdf), $f(x)$, is used to draw the graph of the probability distribution. The total area under the graph of $f(x)$ is one. The area under the graph of $f(x)$ and between values $a$ and $b$ gives the probability $P(a < x < b)$.

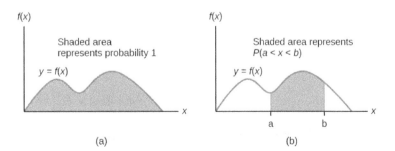

**Figure 5.21**

The cumulative distribution function (cdf) of $X$ is defined by $P(X \le x)$. It is a function of $x$ that gives the probability that the random variable is less than or equal to $x$.

## 5.2 The Uniform Distribution

If $X$ has a uniform distribution where $a < x < b$ or $a \le x \le b$, then $X$ takes on values between $a$ and $b$ (may include $a$ and $b$). All values $x$ are equally likely. We write $X \sim U(a, b)$. The mean of $X$ is $\mu = \frac{a+b}{2}$. The standard deviation of $X$ is $\sigma = \sqrt{\frac{(b-a)^2}{12}}$. The probability density function of $X$ is $f(x) = \frac{1}{b-a}$ for $a \le x \le b$. The cumulative distribution function of $X$ is $P(X \le x) = \frac{x-a}{b-a}$. $X$ is continuous.

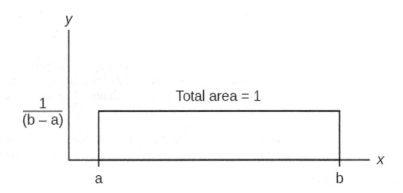

**Figure 5.22**

The probability $P(c < X < d)$ may be found by computing the area under $f(x)$, between $c$ and $d$. Since the corresponding area is a rectangle, the area may be found simply by multiplying the width and the height.

## 5.3 The Exponential Distribution

If $X$ has an **exponential distribution** with mean $\mu$, then the **decay parameter** is $m = \frac{1}{\mu}$. The probability density function of $X$ is $f(x) = me^{-mx}$ (or equivalently $f(x) = \frac{1}{\mu}e^{-x/\mu}$. The cumulative distribution function of $X$ is $P(X \le x) = 1 - e^{-mx}$.

# FORMULA REVIEW

### 5.1 Properties of Continuous Probability Density Functions

Probability density function (pdf) $f(x)$:

- $f(x) \ge 0$
- The total area under the curve $f(x)$ is one.

Cumulative distribution function (cdf): $P(X \le x)$

### 5.2 The Uniform Distribution

$X$ = a real number between $a$ and $b$ (in some instances, $X$ can take on the values $a$ and $b$). $a$ = smallest $X$; $b$ = largest $X$

$X \sim U(a, b)$

The mean is $\mu = \frac{a+b}{2}$

The standard deviation is $\sigma = \sqrt{\frac{(b-a)^2}{12}}$

**Probability density function:** $f(x) = \frac{1}{b-a}$ for $a \le X \le b$

**Area to the Left of $x$:** $P(X < x) = (x-a)\left(\frac{1}{b-a}\right)$

**Area to the Right of $x$:** $P(X > x) = (b-x)\left(\frac{1}{b-a}\right)$

**Area Between $c$ and $d$:** $P(c < x < d) = $ (base)(height) = $(d$

$- c)\left(\frac{1}{b-a}\right)$

- pdf: $f(x) = \frac{1}{b-a}$ for $a \le x \le b$

- cdf: $P(X \le x) = \frac{x-a}{b-a}$

- mean $\mu = \frac{a+b}{2}$

- standard deviation $\sigma = \sqrt{\frac{(b-a)^2}{12}}$

- $P(c < X < d) = (d-c)\left(\frac{1}{b-a}\right)$

- pdf: $f(x) = me^{(-mx)}$ where $x \ge 0$ and $m > 0$

- cdf: $P(X \le x) = 1 - e^{(-mx)}$

- mean $\mu = \frac{1}{m}$

- standard deviation $\sigma = \mu$

- Additionally
  - $P(X > x) = e^{(-mx)}$
  - $P(a < X < b) = e^{(-ma)} - e^{(-mb)}$

- Poisson probability: $P(X = x) = \frac{\mu^x e^{-\mu}}{x!}$ with mean and variance of $\mu$

## 5.3 The Exponential Distribution

# PRACTICE

### 5.1 Properties of Continuous Probability Density Functions

**1.** Which type of distribution does the graph illustrate?

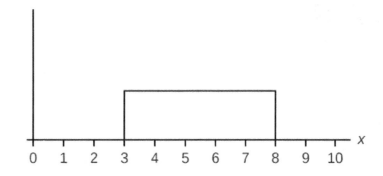

Figure 5.23

**2.** Which type of distribution does the graph illustrate?

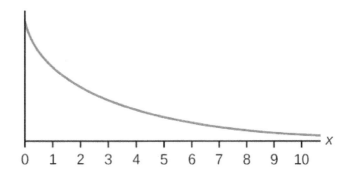

Figure 5.24

**3.** Which type of distribution does the graph illustrate?

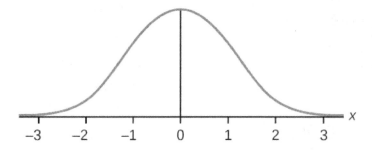

Figure 5.25

**4.** What does the shaded area represent? $P(\_\_ < x < \_\_)$

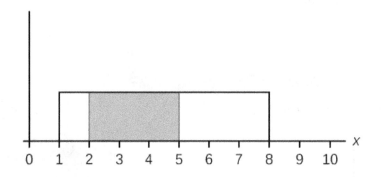

Figure 5.26

**5.** What does the shaded area represent? $P(\_\_ < x < \_\_)$

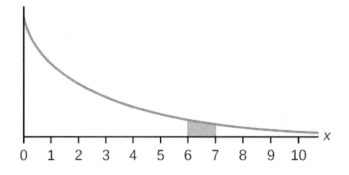

Figure 5.27

**6.** For a continuous probablity distribution, $0 \le x \le 15$. What is $P(x > 15)$?

**7.** What is the area under $f(x)$ if the function is a continuous probability density function?

**8.** For a continuous probability distribution, $0 \le x \le 10$. What is $P(x = 7)$?

**9.** A **continuous** probability function is restricted to the portion between $x = 0$ and 7. What is $P(x = 10)$?

**10.** $f(x)$ for a continuous probability function is $\frac{1}{5}$, and the function is restricted to $0 \le x \le 5$. What is $P(x < 0)$?

**11.** $f(x)$, a continuous probability function, is equal to $\frac{1}{12}$, and the function is restricted to $0 \le x \le 12$. What is $P(0 < x < 12)$?

**12.** Find the probability that *x* falls in the shaded area.

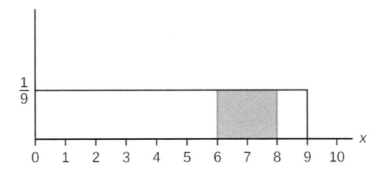

Figure 5.28

**13.** Find the probability that *x* falls in the shaded area.

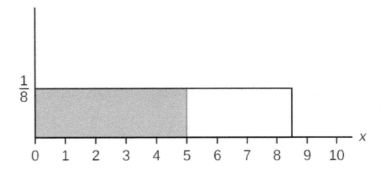

Figure 5.29

**14.** Find the probability that *x* falls in the shaded area.

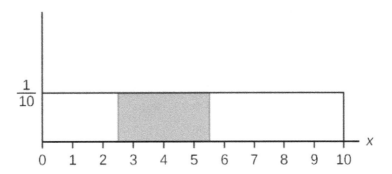

Figure 5.30

**15.** *f*(*x*), a continuous probability function, is equal to $\frac{1}{3}$ and the function is restricted to $1 \leq x \leq 4$. Describe $P\left(x > \frac{3}{2}\right)$.

## 5.2 The Uniform Distribution

*Use the following information to answer the next ten questions.* The data that follow are the square footage (in 1,000 feet squared) of 28 homes.

| 1.5 | 2.4 | 3.6 | 2.6 | 1.6 | 2.4 | 2.0 |
|-----|-----|-----|-----|-----|-----|-----|
| 3.5 | 2.5 | 1.8 | 2.4 | 2.5 | 3.5 | 4.0 |
| 2.6 | 1.6 | 2.2 | 1.8 | 3.8 | 2.5 | 1.5 |
| 2.8 | 1.8 | 4.5 | 1.9 | 1.9 | 3.1 | 1.6 |

Table 5.2

The sample mean = 2.50 and the sample standard deviation = 0.8302.

The distribution can be written as $X \sim U(1.5, 4.5)$.

**16.** What type of distribution is this?

**17.** In this distribution, outcomes are equally likely. What does this mean?

**18.** What is the height of $f(x)$ for the continuous probability distribution?

**19.** What are the constraints for the values of $x$?

**20.** Graph $P(2 < x < 3)$.

**21.** What is $P(2 < x < 3)$?

**22.** What is $P(x < 3.5 \mid x < 4)$?

**23.** What is $P(x = 1.5)$?

**24.** Find the probability that a randomly selected home has more than 3,000 square feet given that you already know the house has more than 2,000 square feet.

*Use the following information to answer the next eight exercises.* A distribution is given as $X \sim U(0, 12)$.

**25.** What is $a$? What does it represent?

**26.** What is $b$? What does it represent?

**27.** What is the probability density function?

**28.** What is the theoretical mean?

**29.** What is the theoretical standard deviation?

**30.** Draw the graph of the distribution for $P(x > 9)$.

**31.** Find $P(x > 9)$.

*Use the following information to answer the next eleven exercises.* The age of cars in the staff parking lot of a suburban college is uniformly distributed from six months (0.5 years) to 9.5 years.

**32.** What is being measured here?

**33.** In words, define the random variable $X$.

**34.** Are the data discrete or continuous?

**35.** The interval of values for $x$ is _____.

**36.** The distribution for $X$ is _____.

**37.** Write the probability density function.

**38.** Graph the probability distribution.

    a.  Sketch the graph of the probability distribution.

    **Figure 5.31**

    b.  Identify the following values:

        i.   Lowest value for $\bar{x}$ : _____

        ii.  Highest value for $\bar{x}$ : _____

        iii.  Height of the rectangle: _____

        iv.  Label for $x$-axis (words): _____

        v.   Label for $y$-axis (words): _____

**39.** Find the average age of the cars in the lot.

**40.** Find the probability that a randomly chosen car in the lot was less than four years old.

    a.  Sketch the graph, and shade the area of interest.

    **Figure 5.32**

    b.  Find the probability. $P(x < 4)$ = _____

**41.** Considering only the cars less than 7.5 years old, find the probability that a randomly chosen car in the lot was less than four years old.

  a.   Sketch the graph, shade the area of interest.

  Figure 5.33

  b.   Find the probability. $P(x < 4 \mid x < 7.5)$ = _____

**42.** What has changed in the previous two problems that made the solutions different?

**43.** Find the third quartile of ages of cars in the lot. This means you will have to find the value such that $\frac{3}{4}$, or 75%, of the cars are at most (less than or equal to) that age.

  a.   Sketch the graph, and shade the area of interest.

  Figure 5.34

  b.   Find the value $k$ such that $P(x < k) = 0.75$.

  c.   The third quartile is _____

## 5.3 The Exponential Distribution

*Use the following information to answer the next ten exercises.* A customer service representative must spend different amounts of time with each customer to resolve various concerns. The amount of time spent with each customer can be modeled by the following distribution: $X \sim Exp(0.2)$

**44.** What type of distribution is this?

**45.** Are outcomes equally likely in this distribution? Why or why not?

**46.** What is $m$? What does it represent?

**47.** What is the mean?

**48.** What is the standard deviation?

**49.** State the probability density function.

**50.** Graph the distribution.

**51.** Find $P(2 < x < 10)$.

**52.** Find $P(x > 6)$.

**53.** Find the 70th percentile.

*Use the following information to answer the next seven exercises.* A distribution is given as $X \sim Exp(0.75)$.

**54.** What is $m$?

**55.** What is the probability density function?

**56.** What is the cumulative distribution function?

**57.** Draw the distribution.

**58.** Find $P(x < 4)$.

**59.** Find the 30th percentile.

**60.** Find the median.

**61.** Which is larger, the mean or the median?

*Use the following information to answer the next 16 exercises.* Carbon-14 is a radioactive element with a half-life of about 5,730 years. Carbon-14 is said to decay exponentially. The decay rate is 0.000121. We start with one gram of carbon-14. We are interested in the time (years) it takes to decay carbon-14.

**62.** What is being measured here?

**63.** Are the data discrete or continuous?

**64.** In words, define the random variable $X$.

**65.** What is the decay rate ($m$)?

**66.** The distribution for $X$ is _____.

**67.** Find the amount (percent of one gram) of carbon-14 lasting less than 5,730 years. This means, find $P(x < 5,730)$.

    a.  Sketch the graph, and shade the area of interest.

**Figure 5.35**

    b.  Find the probability. $P(x < 5,730) =$ _____

**68.** Find the percentage of carbon-14 lasting longer than 10,000 years.

   a.   Sketch the graph, and shade the area of interest.

   **Figure 5.36**

   b.   Find the probability. $P(x > 10{,}000) =$ _____

**69.** Thirty percent (30%) of carbon-14 will decay within how many years?

   a.   Sketch the graph, and shade the area of interest.

   **Figure 5.37**

   b.   Find the value $k$ such that $P(x < k) = 0.30$.

# HOMEWORK

## 5.1 Properties of Continuous Probability Density Functions

*For each probability and percentile problem, draw the picture.*

**70.** Consider the following experiment. You are one of 100 people enlisted to take part in a study to determine the percent of nurses in America with an R.N. (registered nurse) degree. You ask nurses if they have an R.N. degree. The nurses answer "yes" or "no." You then calculate the percentage of nurses with an R.N. degree. You give that percentage to your supervisor.

   a.   What part of the experiment will yield discrete data?

   b.   What part of the experiment will yield continuous data?

**71.** When age is rounded to the nearest year, do the data stay continuous, or do they become discrete? Why?

## 5.2 The Uniform Distribution

*For each probability and percentile problem, draw the picture.*

**72.** Births are approximately uniformly distributed between the 52 weeks of the year. They can be said to follow a uniform distribution from one to 53 (spread of 52 weeks).
   a. Graph the probability distribution.
   b. $f(x) =$ _____
   c. $\mu =$ _____
   d. $\sigma =$ _____
   e. Find the probability that a person is born at the exact moment week 19 starts. That is, find $P(x = 19) =$ _____
   f. $P(2 < x < 31) =$ _____
   g. Find the probability that a person is born after week 40.
   h. $P(12 < x \mid x < 28) =$ _____

**73.** A random number generator picks a number from one to nine in a uniform manner.
   a. Graph the probability distribution.
   b. $f(x) =$ _____
   c. $\mu =$ _____
   d. $\sigma =$ _____
   e. $P(3.5 < x < 7.25) =$ _____
   f. $P(x > 5.67)$
   g. $P(x > 5 \mid x > 3) =$ _____

**74.** According to a study by Dr. John McDougall of his live-in weight loss program at St. Helena Hospital, the people who follow his program lose between six and 15 pounds a month until they approach trim body weight. Let's suppose that the weight loss is uniformly distributed. We are interested in the weight loss of a randomly selected individual following the program for one month.
   a. Define the random variable. $X =$ _____
   b. Graph the probability distribution.
   c. $f(x) =$ _____
   d. $\mu =$ _____
   e. $\sigma =$ _____
   f. Find the probability that the individual lost more than ten pounds in a month.
   g. Suppose it is known that the individual lost more than ten pounds in a month. Find the probability that he lost less than 12 pounds in the month.
   h. $P(7 < x < 13 \mid x > 9) =$ _____. State this in a probability question, similarly to parts g and h, draw the picture, and find the probability.

**75.** A subway train on the Red Line arrives every eight minutes during rush hour. We are interested in the length of time a commuter must wait for a train to arrive. The time follows a uniform distribution.
   a. Define the random variable. $X =$ _____
   b. Graph the probability distribution.
   c. $f(x) =$ _____
   d. $\mu =$ _____
   e. $\sigma =$ _____
   f. Find the probability that the commuter waits less than one minute.
   g. Find the probability that the commuter waits between three and four minutes.

**76.** The age of a first grader on September 1 at Garden Elementary School is uniformly distributed from 5.8 to 6.8 years. We randomly select one first grader from the class.
   a. Define the random variable. $X =$ _____
   b. Graph the probability distribution.
   c. $f(x) =$ _____
   d. $\mu =$ _____
   e. $\sigma =$ _____
   f. Find the probability that she is over 6.5 years old.
   g. Find the probability that she is between four and six years old.

*Use the following information to answer the next three exercises.* The Sky Train from the terminal to the rental–car and long–term parking center is supposed to arrive every eight minutes. The waiting times for the train are known to follow a uniform distribution.

**77.** What is the average waiting time (in minutes)?
    a.  zero
    b.  two
    c.  three
    d.  four

**78.** The probability of waiting more than seven minutes given a person has waited more than four minutes is?
    a.  0.125
    b.  0.25
    c.  0.5
    d.  0.75

**79.** The time (in minutes) until the next bus departs a major bus depot follows a distribution with $f(x) = \frac{1}{20}$ where $x$ goes from 25 to 45 minutes.
    a.  Define the random variable. $X =$ _____
    b.  Graph the probability distribution.
    c.  The distribution is _____ (name of distribution). It is _____ (discrete or continuous).
    d.  $\mu =$ _____
    e.  $\sigma =$ _____
    f.  Find the probability that the time is at most 30 minutes. Sketch and label a graph of the distribution. Shade the area of interest. Write the answer in a probability statement.
    g.  Find the probability that the time is between 30 and 40 minutes. Sketch and label a graph of the distribution. Shade the area of interest. Write the answer in a probability statement.
    h.  $P(25 < x < 55) =$ _____. State this in a probability statement, similarly to parts g and h, draw the picture, and find the probability.

**80.** Suppose that the value of a stock varies each day from $16 to $25 with a uniform distribution.
    a.  Find the probability that the value of the stock is more than $19.
    b.  Find the probability that the value of the stock is between $19 and $22.
    c.  Given that the stock is greater than $18, find the probability that the stock is more than $21.

**81.** A fireworks show is designed so that the time between fireworks is between one and five seconds, and follows a uniform distribution.
    a.  Find the average time between fireworks.
    b.  Find probability that the time between fireworks is greater than four seconds.

**82.** The number of miles driven by a truck driver falls between 300 and 700, and follows a uniform distribution.
    a.  Find the probability that the truck driver goes more than 650 miles in a day.
    b.  Find the probability that the truck drivers goes between 400 and 650 miles in a day.

## 5.3 The Exponential Distribution

**83.** Suppose that the length of long distance phone calls, measured in minutes, is known to have an exponential distribution with the average length of a call equal to eight minutes.
    a.  Define the random variable. $X =$ _____.
    b.  Is $X$ continuous or discrete?
    c.  $\mu =$ _____
    d.  $\sigma =$ _____
    e.  Draw a graph of the probability distribution. Label the axes.
    f.  Find the probability that a phone call lasts less than nine minutes.
    g.  Find the probability that a phone call lasts more than nine minutes.
    h.  Find the probability that a phone call lasts between seven and nine minutes.
    i.  If 25 phone calls are made one after another, on average, what would you expect the total to be? Why?

**84.** Suppose that the useful life of a particular car battery, measured in months, decays with parameter 0.025. We are interested in the life of the battery.

    a. Define the random variable. $X =$ _____.

    b. Is $X$ continuous or discrete?

    c. On average, how long would you expect one car battery to last?

    d. On average, how long would you expect nine car batteries to last, if they are used one after another?

    e. Find the probability that a car battery lasts more than 36 months.

    f. Seventy percent of the batteries last at least how long?

**85.** The percent of persons (ages five and older) in each state who speak a language at home other than English is approximately exponentially distributed with a mean of 9.848. Suppose we randomly pick a state.

    a. Define the random variable. $X =$ _____.

    b. Is $X$ continuous or discrete?

    c. $\mu =$ _____

    d. $\sigma =$ _____

    e. Draw a graph of the probability distribution. Label the axes.

    f. Find the probability that the percent is less than 12.

    g. Find the probability that the percent is between eight and 14.

    h. The percent of all individuals living in the United States who speak a language at home other than English is 13.8.

        i. Why is this number different from 9.848%?

        ii. What would make this number higher than 9.848%?

**86.** The time (in years) **after** reaching age 60 that it takes an individual to retire is approximately exponentially distributed with a mean of about five years. Suppose we randomly pick one retired individual. We are interested in the time after age 60 to retirement.

    a. Define the random variable. $X =$ _____.

    b. Is $X$ continuous or discrete?

    c. $\mu =$ _____

    d. $\sigma =$ _____

    e. Draw a graph of the probability distribution. Label the axes.

    f. Find the probability that the person retired after age 70.

    g. Do more people retire before age 65 or after age 65?

    h. In a room of 1,000 people over age 80, how many do you expect will NOT have retired yet?

**87.** The cost of all maintenance for a car during its first year is approximately exponentially distributed with a mean of $150.

    a. Define the random variable. $X =$ _____.

    b. $\mu =$ _____

    c. $\sigma =$ _____

    d. Draw a graph of the probability distribution. Label the axes.

    e. Find the probability that a car required over $300 for maintenance during its first year.

*Use the following information to answer the next three exercises.* The average lifetime of a certain new cell phone is three years. The manufacturer will replace any cell phone failing within two years of the date of purchase. The lifetime of these cell phones is known to follow an exponential distribution.

**88.** The decay rate is:

    a. 0.3333

    b. 0.5000

    c. 2

    d. 3

**89.** What is the probability that a phone will fail within two years of the date of purchase?

    a. 0.8647

    b. 0.4866

    c. 0.2212

    d. 0.9997

**90.** What is the median lifetime of these phones (in years)?
   a. 0.1941
   b. 1.3863
   c. 2.0794
   d. 5.5452

**91.** At a 911 call center, calls come in at an average rate of one call every two minutes. Assume that the time that elapses from one call to the next has the exponential distribution.
   a. On average, how much time occurs between five consecutive calls?
   b. Find the probability that after a call is received, it takes more than three minutes for the next call to occur.
   c. Ninety-percent of all calls occur within how many minutes of the previous call?
   d. Suppose that two minutes have elapsed since the last call. Find the probability that the next call will occur within the next minute.
   e. Find the probability that less than 20 calls occur within an hour.

**92.** In major league baseball, a no-hitter is a game in which a pitcher, or pitchers, doesn't give up any hits throughout the game. No-hitters occur at a rate of about three per season. Assume that the duration of time between no-hitters is exponential.
   a. What is the probability that an entire season elapses with a single no-hitter?
   b. If an entire season elapses without any no-hitters, what is the probability that there are no no-hitters in the following season?
   c. What is the probability that there are more than 3 no-hitters in a single season?

**93.** During the years 1998–2012, a total of 29 earthquakes of magnitude greater than 6.5 have occurred in Papua New Guinea. Assume that the time spent waiting between earthquakes is exponential.
   a. What is the probability that the next earthquake occurs within the next three months?
   b. Given that six months has passed without an earthquake in Papua New Guinea, what is the probability that the next three months will be free of earthquakes?
   c. What is the probability of zero earthquakes occurring in 2014?
   d. What is the probability that at least two earthquakes will occur in 2014?

**94.** According to the American Red Cross, about one out of nine people in the U.S. have Type B blood. Suppose the blood types of people arriving at a blood drive are independent. In this case, the number of Type B blood types that arrive roughly follows the Poisson distribution.
   a. If 100 people arrive, how many on average would be expected to have Type B blood?
   b. What is the probability that over 10 people out of these 100 have type B blood?
   c. What is the probability that more than 20 people arrive before a person with type B blood is found?

**95.** A web site experiences traffic during normal working hours at a rate of 12 visits per hour. Assume that the duration between visits has the exponential distribution.
   a. Find the probability that the duration between two successive visits to the web site is more than ten minutes.
   b. The top 25% of durations between visits are at least how long?
   c. Suppose that 20 minutes have passed since the last visit to the web site. What is the probability that the next visit will occur within the next 5 minutes?
   d. Find the probability that less than 7 visits occur within a one-hour period.

**96.** At an urgent care facility, patients arrive at an average rate of one patient every seven minutes. Assume that the duration between arrivals is exponentially distributed.
   a. Find the probability that the time between two successive visits to the urgent care facility is less than 2 minutes.
   b. Find the probability that the time between two successive visits to the urgent care facility is more than 15 minutes.
   c. If 10 minutes have passed since the last arrival, what is the probability that the next person will arrive within the next five minutes?
   d. Find the probability that more than eight patients arrive during a half-hour period.

# REFERENCES

## 5.2 The Uniform Distribution

McDougall, John A. The McDougall Program for Maximum Weight Loss. Plume, 1995.

## 5.3 The Exponential Distribution

Data from the United States Census Bureau.

Data from World Earthquakes, 2013. Available online at http://www.world-earthquakes.com/ (accessed June 11, 2013).

"No-hitter." Baseball-Reference.com, 2013. Available online at http://www.baseball-reference.com/bullpen/No-hitter (accessed June 11, 2013).

Zhou, Rick. "Exponential Distribution lecture slides." Available online at www.public.iastate.edu/~riczw/stat330s11/lecture/lec13.pdf (accessed June 11, 2013).

## SOLUTIONS

**1** Uniform Distribution

**3** Normal Distribution

**5** $P(6 < x < 7)$

**7** one

**9** zero

**11** one

**13** 0.625

**15** The probability is equal to the area from $x = \frac{3}{2}$ to $x = 4$ above the x-axis and up to $f(x) = \frac{1}{3}$.

**17** It means that the value of $x$ is just as likely to be any number between 1.5 and 4.5.

**19** $1.5 \le x \le 4.5$

**21** 0.3333

**23** zero

**24** 0.6

**26** $b$ is 12, and it represents the highest value of $x$.

**28** six

**30**

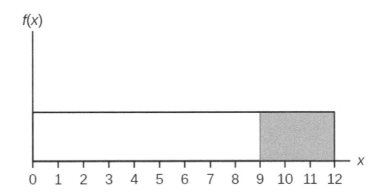

**Figure 5.38**

**33** $X$ = The age (in years) of cars in the staff parking lot

**35** 0.5 to 9.5

**37** $f(x) = \frac{1}{9}$ where $x$ is between 0.5 and 9.5, inclusive.

**39** $\mu = 5$

**41**

  a. Check student's solution.

  b. $\frac{3.5}{7}$

**43**

  a. Check student's solution.

  b. $k = 7.25$

  c. 7.25

**45** No, outcomes are not equally likely. In this distribution, more people require a little bit of time, and fewer people require a lot of time, so it is more likely that someone will require less time.

**47** five

**49** $f(x) = 0.2e^{-0.2x}$

**51** 0.5350

**53** 6.02

**55** $f(x) = 0.75e^{-0.75x}$

**57**

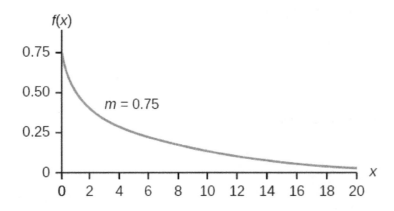

Figure 5.39

**59** 0.4756

**61** The mean is larger. The mean is $\frac{1}{m} = \frac{1}{0.75} \approx 1.33$, which is greater than 0.9242.

**63** continuous

**65** $m = 0.000121$

**67**

  a. Check student's solution

  b. $P(x < 5{,}730) = 0.5001$

**69**

  a. Check student's solution.

  b. $k = 2947.73$

**71** Age is a measurement, regardless of the accuracy used.

**73**

a. Check student's solution.

b. $f(x) = \frac{1}{8}$ where $1 \le x \le 9$

c. five

d. 2.3

e. $\frac{15}{32}$

f. $\frac{333}{800}$

g. $\frac{2}{3}$

**75**

a. $X$ represents the length of time a commuter must wait for a train to arrive on the Red Line.

b. Graph the probability distribution.

c. $f(x) = \frac{1}{8}$ where $0 \le x \le 8$

d. four

e. 2.31

f. $\frac{1}{8}$

g. $\frac{1}{8}$

**77** d

**78** b

**80**

a. The probability density function of $X$ is $\frac{1}{25 - 16} = \frac{1}{9}$.

$P(X > 19) = (25 - 19)\left(\frac{1}{9}\right) = \frac{6}{9} = \frac{2}{3}$.

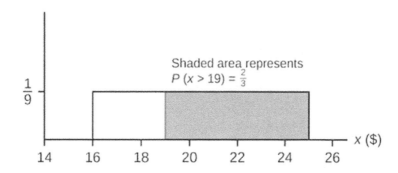

**Figure 5.40**

b. $P(19 < X < 22) = (22 - 19)\left(\frac{1}{9}\right) = \frac{3}{9} = \frac{1}{3}$.

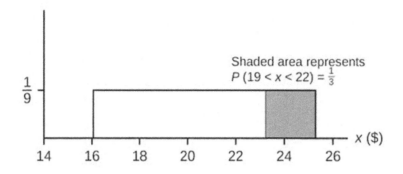

**Figure 5.41**

c.   This is a conditional probability question. P(x > 21  |  x > 18). You can do this two ways:

- Draw the graph where a is now 18 and b is still 25. The height is $\dfrac{1}{(25 - 18)} = \dfrac{1}{7}$

  So, $P(x > 21 \mid x > 18) = (25 - 21)\left(\dfrac{1}{7}\right) = 4/7.$

- Use the formula: $P(x > 21 \mid x > 18) = \dfrac{P(x > 21 \cap x > 18)}{P(x > 18)}$

  $= \dfrac{P(x > 21)}{P(x > 18)} = \dfrac{(25 - 21)}{(25 - 18)} = \dfrac{4}{7}.$

**82**

a.   $P(X > 650) = \dfrac{700 - 650}{700 - 300} = \dfrac{50}{400} = \dfrac{1}{8} = 0.125.$

b.   $P(400 < X < 650) = \dfrac{650 - 400}{700 - 300} = \dfrac{250}{400} = 0.625$

**84**

a.   $X$ = the useful life of a particular car battery, measured in months.

b.   $X$ is continuous.

c.   40 months

d.   360 months

e.   0.4066

f.   14.27

**86**

a.   $X$ = the time (in years) after reaching age 60 that it takes an individual to retire

b.   $X$ is continuous.

c.   five

d.   five

e.   Check student's solution.

f.   0.1353

g.   before

h.   18.3

**88** a

**90** c

**92** Let $X$ = the number of no-hitters throughout a season. Since the duration of time between no-hitters is exponential, the number of no-hitters per season is Poisson with mean $\lambda = 3$.

Therefore, $(X = 0) = \dfrac{3^0 e^{-3}}{0!} = e^{-3} \approx 0.0498$

---

You could let $T$ = duration of time between no-hitters. Since the time is exponential and there are 3 no-hitters per season, then the time between no-hitters is $\dfrac{1}{3}$ season. For the exponential, $\mu = \dfrac{1}{3}$.

Therefore, $m = \dfrac{1}{\mu} = 3$ and $T \sim Exp(3)$.

---

a.  The desired probability is $P(T > 1) = 1 - P(T < 1) = 1 - (1 - e^{-3}) = e^{-3} \approx 0.0498$.

b.  Let $T$ = duration of time between no-hitters. We find $P(T > 2 | T > 1)$, and by the **memoryless property** this is simply $P(T > 1)$, which we found to be 0.0498 in part a.

c.  Let $X$ = the number of no-hitters is a season. Assume that $X$ is Poisson with mean $\lambda = 3$. Then $P(X > 3) = 1 - P(X \le 3)$ = 0.3528.

**94**

a.  $\dfrac{100}{9} = 11.11$

b.  $P(X > 10) = 1 - P(X \le 10) = 1 - \text{Poissoncdf}(11.11, 10) \approx 0.5532$.

c.  The number of people with Type B blood encountered roughly follows the Poisson distribution, so the number of people $X$ who arrive between successive Type B arrivals is roughly exponential with mean $\mu = 9$ and $m = \dfrac{1}{9}$. The cumulative distribution function of $X$ is $P(X < x) = 1 - e^{-\frac{x}{9}}$. Thus hus, $P(X > 20) = 1 - P(X \le 20) = 1 - \left(1 - e^{-\frac{20}{9}}\right) \approx 0.1084$.

### NOTE

We could also deduce that each person arriving has a 8/9 chance of not having Type B blood. So the probability that none of the first 20 people arrive have Type B blood is $\left(\dfrac{8}{9}\right)^{20} \approx 0.0948$. (The geometric distribution is more appropriate than the exponential because the number of people between Type B people is discrete instead of continuous.)

**96** Let $T$ = duration (in minutes) between successive visits. Since patients arrive at a rate of one patient every seven minutes, $\mu = 7$ and the decay constant is $m = \dfrac{1}{7}$. The cdf is $P(T < t) = 1 - e^{\frac{t}{7}}$

a.  $P(T < 2) = 1 - 1 - e^{-\frac{2}{7}} \approx 0.2485$.

b.  $P(T > 15) = 1 - P(T < 15) = 1 - \left(1 - e^{-\frac{15}{7}}\right) \approx e^{-\frac{15}{7}} \approx 0.1173$.

c.  $P(T > 15 | T > 10) = P(T > 5) = 1 - \left(1 - e^{-\frac{5}{7}}\right) = e^{-\frac{5}{7}} \approx 0.4895$.

d.  Let $X$ = # of patients arriving during a half-hour period. Then $X$ has the Poisson distribution with a mean of $\frac{30}{7}$, $X \sim$ Poisson $\left(\frac{30}{7}\right)$. Find $P(X > 8) = 1 - P(X \le 8) \approx 0.0311$.

# 6 | THE NORMAL DISTRIBUTION

**Figure 6.1** If you ask enough people about their shoe size, you will find that your graphed data is shaped like a bell curve and can be described as normally distributed. (credit: Ömer Ünlü)

## Introduction

The normal probability density function, a continuous distribution, is the most important of all the distributions. It is widely used and even more widely abused. Its graph is bell-shaped. You see the bell curve in almost all disciplines. Some of these include psychology, business, economics, the sciences, nursing, and, of course, mathematics. Some of your instructors may use the normal distribution to help determine your grade. Most IQ scores are normally distributed. Often real-estate prices fit a normal distribution.

The normal distribution is extremely important, but it cannot be applied to everything in the real world. Remember here that we are still talking about the distribution of population data. This is a discussion of probability and thus it is the population data that may be normally distributed, and if it is, then this is how we can find probabilities of specific events just as we did for population data that may be binomially distributed or Poisson distributed. This caution is here because in the next chapter we will see that the normal distribution describes something very different from raw data and forms the foundation of inferential statistics.

The normal distribution has two parameters (two numerical descriptive measures): the mean ($\mu$) and the standard deviation

($\sigma$). If $X$ is a quantity to be measured that has a normal distribution with mean ($\mu$) and standard deviation ($\sigma$), we designate this by writing the following formula of the normal probability density function:

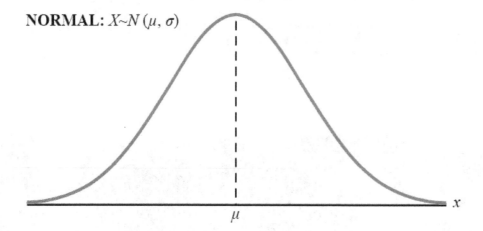

**NORMAL:** $X \sim N(\mu, \sigma)$

**Figure 6.2**

The probability density function is a rather complicated function. **Do not memorize it**. It is not necessary.

$$f(x) = \frac{1}{\sigma \cdot \sqrt{2 \cdot \pi}} \cdot e^{-\frac{1}{2} \cdot \left(\frac{x-\mu}{\sigma}\right)^2}$$

The curve is symmetric about a vertical line drawn through the mean, $\mu$. The mean is the same as the median, which is the same as the mode, because the graph is symmetric about $\mu$. As the notation indicates, the normal distribution depends only on the mean and the standard deviation. Note that this is unlike several probability density functions we have already studied, such as the Poisson, where the mean is equal to $\mu$ and the standard deviation simply the square root of the mean, or the binomial, where $p$ is used to determine both the mean and standard deviation. Since the area under the curve must equal one, a change in the standard deviation, $\sigma$, causes a change in the shape of the normal curve; the curve becomes fatter and wider or skinnier and taller depending on $\sigma$. A change in $\mu$ causes the graph to shift to the left or right. This means there are an infinite number of normal probability distributions. One of special interest is called the **standard normal distribution**.

# 6.1 | The Standard Normal Distribution

The **standard normal distribution** is a normal distribution of **standardized values called z-scores**. **A z-score is measured in units of the standard deviation.**

The mean for the standard normal distribution is zero, and the standard deviation is one. What this does is dramatically simplify the mathematical calculation of probabilities. Take a moment and substitute zero and one in the appropriate places in the above formula and you can see that the equation collapses into one that can be much more easily solved using integral calculus. The transformation $z = \frac{x - \mu}{\sigma}$ produces the distribution $Z \sim N(0, 1)$. The value $x$ in the given equation comes from a known normal distribution with known mean $\mu$ and known standard deviation $\sigma$. The z-score tells how many standard deviations a particular x is away from the mean.

## Z-Scores

If $X$ is a normally distributed random variable and $X \sim N(\mu, \sigma)$, then the z-score for a particular $x$ is:

$$z = \frac{x - \mu}{\sigma}$$

**The z-score tells you how many standard deviations the value $x$ is above (to the right of) or below (to the left of) the mean, $\mu$.** Values of $x$ that are larger than the mean have positive z-scores, and values of $x$ that are smaller than the mean have negative z-scores. If $x$ equals the mean, then $x$ has a z-score of zero.

## Example 6.1

Suppose $X \sim N(5, 6)$. This says that $X$ is a normally distributed random variable with mean $\mu = 5$ and standard deviation $\sigma = 6$. Suppose $x = 17$. Then:

$$z = \frac{x - \mu}{\sigma} = \frac{17 - 5}{6} = 2$$

This means that $x = 17$ is **two standard deviations** ($2\sigma$) above or to the right of the mean $\mu = 5$.

Now suppose $x = 1$. Then: $z = \frac{x - \mu}{\sigma} = \frac{1 - 5}{6} = -0.67$ (rounded to two decimal places)

This means that $x = 1$ is **0.67 standard deviations ($-0.67\sigma$) below or to the left of the mean $\mu = 5$.**

### The Empirical Rule

If $X$ is a random variable and has a normal distribution with mean $\mu$ and standard deviation $\sigma$, then the **Empirical Rule** states the following:

- About 68% of the $x$ values lie between $-1\sigma$ and $+1\sigma$ of the mean $\mu$ (within one standard deviation of the mean).

- About 95% of the $x$ values lie between $-2\sigma$ and $+2\sigma$ of the mean $\mu$ (within two standard deviations of the mean).

- About 99.7% of the $x$ values lie between $-3\sigma$ and $+3\sigma$ of the mean $\mu$ (within three standard deviations of the mean). Notice that almost all the $x$ values lie within three standard deviations of the mean.

- The $z$-scores for $+1\sigma$ and $-1\sigma$ are $+1$ and $-1$, respectively.

- The $z$-scores for $+2\sigma$ and $-2\sigma$ are $+2$ and $-2$, respectively.

- The $z$-scores for $+3\sigma$ and $-3\sigma$ are $+3$ and $-3$ respectively.

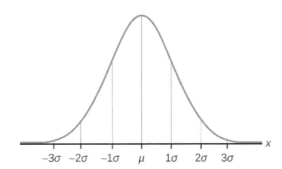

Figure 6.3

## Example 6.2

Suppose $x$ has a normal distribution with mean 50 and standard deviation 6.

- About 68% of the $x$ values lie within one standard deviation of the mean. Therefore, about 68% of the x values lie between $-1\sigma = (-1)(6) = -6$ and $1\sigma = (1)(6) = 6$ of the mean 50. The values $50 - 6 = 44$ and $50 + 6 = 56$ are within one standard deviation from the mean 50. The $z$-scores are $-1$ and $+1$ for 44 and 56, respectively.

- About 95% of the $x$ values lie within two standard deviations of the mean. Therefore, about 95% of the x values lie between $-2\sigma = (-2)(6) = -12$ and $2\sigma = (2)(6) = 12$. The values $50 - 12 = 38$ and $50 + 12 = 62$ are within two standard deviations from the mean 50. The $z$-scores are $-2$ and $+2$ for 38 and 62, respectively.

- About 99.7% of the $x$ values lie within three standard deviations of the mean. Therefore, about 95% of the x values lie between $-3\sigma = (-3)(6) = -18$ and $3\sigma = (3)(6) = 18$ of the mean 50. The values $50 - 18 = 32$ and $50$

+ 18 = 68 are within three standard deviations from the mean 50. The z-scores are –3 and +3 for 32 and 68, respectively.

# 6.2 | Using the Normal Distribution

The shaded area in the following graph indicates the area to the right of $x$. This area is represented by the probability $P(X > x)$. Normal tables provide the probability between the mean, zero for the standard normal distribution, and a specific value such as $x_1$. This is the unshaded part of the graph from the mean to $x_1$.

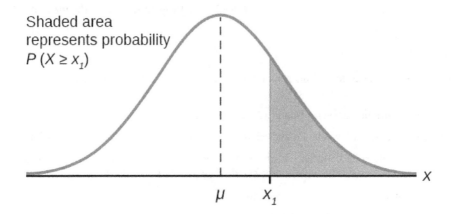

**Figure 6.4**

Because the normal distribution is symmetrical , if $x_1$ were the same distance to the left of the mean the area, probability, in the left tail, would be the same as the shaded area in the right tail. Also, bear in mind that because of the symmetry of this distribution, one-half of the probability is to the right of the mean and one-half is to the left of the mean.

## Calculations of Probabilities

To find the probability for probability density functions with a continuous random variable we need to calculate the area under the function across the values of X we are interested in. For the normal distribution this seems a difficult task given the complexity of the formula. There is, however, a simply way to get what we want. Here again is the formula for the normal distribution:

$$f(x) = \frac{1}{\sigma \cdot \sqrt{2 \cdot \pi}} \cdot e^{-\frac{1}{2} \cdot \left(\frac{x-\mu}{\sigma}\right)^2}$$

Looking at the formula for the normal distribution it is not clear just how we are going to solve for the probability doing it the same way we did it with the previous probability functions. There we put the data into the formula and did the math.

To solve this puzzle we start knowing that the area under a probability density function is the probability.

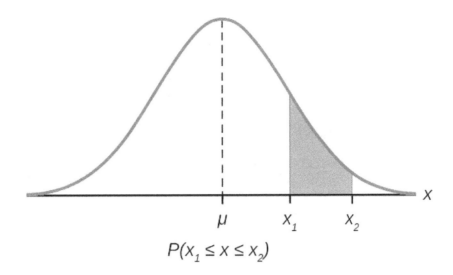

$$P(X_1 \leq X \leq X_2)$$

**Figure 6.5**

This shows that the area between $X_1$ and $X_2$ is the probability as stated in the formula: $P(X_1 \leq x \leq X_2)$

The mathematical tool needed to find the area under a curve is integral calculus. The integral of the normal probability density function between the two points $x_1$ and $x_2$ is the area under the curve between these two points and is the probability between these two points.

Doing these integrals is no fun and can be very time consuming. But now, remembering that there are an infinite number of normal distributions out there, we can consider the one with a mean of zero and a standard deviation of 1. This particular normal distribution is given the name Standard Normal Distribution. Putting these values into the formula it reduces to a very simple equation. We can now quite easily calculate all probabilities for any value of x, for this particular normal distribution, that has a mean of zero and a standard deviation of 1. These have been produced and are available here in the appendix to the text or everywhere on the web. They are presented in various ways. The table in this text is the most common presentation and is set up with probabilities for one-half the distribution beginning with zero, the mean, and moving outward. The shaded area in the graph at the top of the table in Statistical Tables represents the probability from zero to the specific Z value noted on the horizontal axis, Z.

The only problem is that even with this table, it would be a ridiculous coincidence that our data had a mean of zero and a standard deviation of one. The solution is to convert the distribution we have with its mean and standard deviation to this new Standard Normal Distribution. The Standard Normal has a random variable called Z.

Using the standard normal table, typically called the normal table, to find the probability of one standard deviation, go to the Z column, reading down to 1.0 and then read at column 0. That number, 0.3413 is the probability from zero to 1 standard deviation. At the top of the table is the shaded area in the distribution which is the probability for one standard deviation. The table has solved our integral calculus problem. But only if our data has a mean of zero and a standard deviation of 1.

However, the essential point here is, the probability for one standard deviation on one normal distribution is the same on every normal distribution. If the population data set has a mean of 10 and a standard deviation of 5 then the probability from 10 to 15, one standard deviation, is the same as from zero to 1, one standard deviation on the standard normal distribution. To compute probabilities, areas, for any normal distribution, we need only to convert the particular normal distribution to the standard normal distribution and look up the answer in the tables. As review, here again is the **standardizing formula**:

$$Z = \frac{x - \mu}{\sigma}$$

where Z is the value on the standard normal distribution, X is the value from a normal distribution one wishes to convert to the standard normal, $\mu$ and $\sigma$ are, respectively, the mean and standard deviation of that population. Note that the equation uses $\mu$ and $\sigma$ which denotes population parameters. This is still dealing with probability so we always are dealing with the population, with **known** parameter values and a **known** distribution. It is also important to note that because the normal distribution is symmetrical it does not matter if the z-score is positive or negative when calculating a probability. One standard deviation to the left (negative Z-score) covers the same area as one standard deviation to the right (positive Z-score). This fact is why the Standard Normal tables do not provide areas for the left side of the distribution. Because of this symmetry, the Z-score formula is sometimes written as:

$$Z = \frac{|x - \mu|}{\sigma}$$

Where the vertical lines in the equation means the absolute value of the number.

What the standardizing formula is really doing is computing the number of standard deviations X is from the mean of its own distribution. The standardizing formula and the concept of counting standard deviations from the mean is the secret of all that we will do in this statistics class. The reason this is true is that **all** of statistics boils down to variation, and the counting of standard deviations is a measure of variation.

This formula, in many disguises, will reappear over and over throughout this course.

## Example 6.3

The final exam scores in a statistics class were normally distributed with a mean of 63 and a standard deviation of five.

a. Find the probability that a randomly selected student scored more than 65 on the exam.
b. Find the probability that a randomly selected student scored less than 85.

### Solution 6.3

a. Let $X$ = a score on the final exam. $X \sim N(63, 5)$, where $\mu = 63$ and $\sigma = 5$.

Draw a graph.

Then, find $P(x > 65)$.

$P(x > 65) = 0.3446$

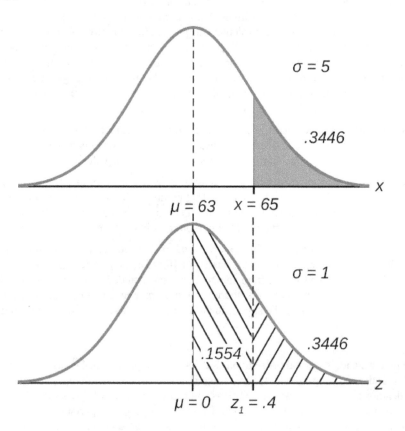

**Figure 6.6**

$$Z_1 = \frac{x_1 - \mu}{\sigma} = \frac{65 - 63}{5} = 0.4$$

$P(x \geq x_1) = P(Z \geq Z_1) = 0.3446$

The probability that any student selected at random scores more than 65 is 0.3446. Here is how we found this answer.

The normal table provides probabilities from zero to the value $Z_1$. For this problem the question can be written as: $P(X \geq 65) = P(Z \geq Z_1)$, which is the area in the tail. To find this area the formula would be $0.5 - P(X \leq 65)$. One half of the probability is above the mean value because this is a symmetrical distribution. The graph shows how to find the area in the tail by subtracting that portion from the mean, zero, to the $Z_1$ value. The final answer is: $P(X \geq 63) = P(Z \geq 0.4) = 0.3446$

$$z = \frac{65 - 63}{5} = 0.4$$

Area to the left of $Z_1$ to the mean of zero is 0.1554

$P(x > 65) = P(z > 0.4) = 0.5 - 0.1554 = 0.3446$

**Solution 6.3**

b.

$$Z = \frac{x - \mu}{\sigma} = \frac{85 - 63}{5} = 4.4$$ which is larger than the maximum value on the Standard Normal Table. Therefore, the probability that one student scores less than 85 is approximately one or 100%.

A score of 85 is 4.4 standard deviations from the mean of 63 which is beyond the range of the standard normal table. Therefore, the probability that one student scores less than 85 is approximately one (or 100%).

**6.3** The golf scores for a school team were normally distributed with a mean of 68 and a standard deviation of three. Find the probability that a randomly selected golfer scored less than 65.

## Example 6.4

A personal computer is used for office work at home, research, communication, personal finances, education, entertainment, social networking, and a myriad of other things. Suppose that the average number of hours a household personal computer is used for entertainment is two hours per day. Assume the times for entertainment are normally distributed and the standard deviation for the times is half an hour.

a. Find the probability that a household personal computer is used for entertainment between 1.8 and 2.75 hours per day.

**Solution 6.4**

a. Let $X$ = the amount of time (in hours) a household personal computer is used for entertainment. $X \sim N(2, 0.5)$ where $\mu = 2$ and $\sigma = 0.5$.

Find $P(1.8 < x < 2.75)$.

The probability for which you are looking is the area **between** $x = 1.8$ and $x = 2.75$. $P(1.8 < x < 2.75) = 0.5886$

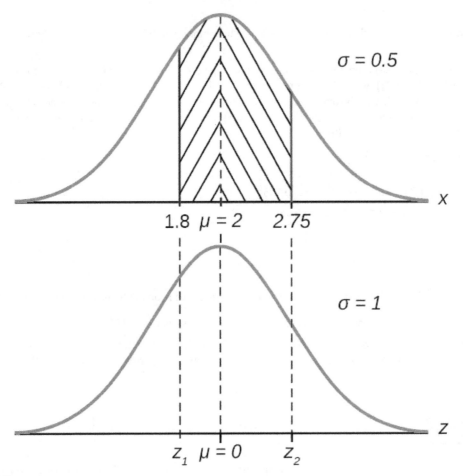

**Figure 6.7**

$P(1.8 \leq x \leq 2.75) = P(Z_i \leq Z \leq Z_2)$

The probability that a household personal computer is used between 1.8 and 2.75 hours per day for entertainment is 0.5886.

b. Find the maximum number of hours per day that the bottom quartile of households uses a personal computer for entertainment.

### Solution 6.4

b. To find the maximum number of hours per day that the bottom quartile of households uses a personal computer for entertainment, **find the 25th percentile**, $k$, where $P(x < k) = 0.25$.

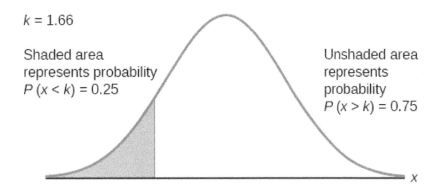

$k = 1.66$

Shaded area represents probability $P(x < k) = 0.25$

Unshaded area represents probability $P(x > k) = 0.75$

$x$

**Figure 6.8**

$f(Z) = 0.5 - 0.25 = 0.25$, *therefore* $Z \approx -0.675$ (*or just 0.67 using the table*) $Z = \frac{x - \mu}{\sigma} = \frac{x - 2}{0.5} = -0.675$, *therefore* $x = -0.675 * 0.5 + 2 = 1.66$ *hours.*

The maximum number of hours per day that the bottom quartile of households uses a personal computer for entertainment is 1.66 hours.

**6.4** The golf scores for a school team were normally distributed with a mean of 68 and a standard deviation of three. Find the probability that a golfer scored between 66 and 70.

## Example 6.5

In the United States the ages 13 to 55+ of smartphone users approximately follow a normal distribution with approximate mean and standard deviation of 36.9 years and 13.9 years, respectively.

a. Determine the probability that a random smartphone user in the age range 13 to 55+ is between 23 and 64.7 years old.

**Solution 6.5**
a. 0.8186

b. Determine the probability that a randomly selected smartphone user in the age range 13 to 55+ is at most 50.8 years old.

**Solution 6.5**
b. 0.8413

## Example 6.6

A citrus farmer who grows mandarin oranges finds that the diameters of mandarin oranges harvested on his farm follow a normal distribution with a mean diameter of 5.85 cm and a standard deviation of 0.24 cm.

a. Find the probability that a randomly selected mandarin orange from this farm has a diameter larger than 6.0 cm. Sketch the graph.

**Solution 6.6**

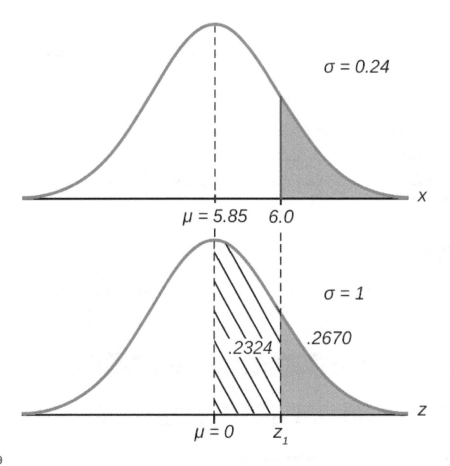

Figure 6.9

$$Z_1 = \frac{6 - 5.85}{.24} = .625$$

$P(x \geq 6) = P(z \geq 0.625) = 0.2670$

b. The middle 20% of mandarin oranges from this farm have diameters between _____ and _____.

**Solution 6.6**

$f(Z) = \frac{0.20}{2} = 0.10$ , *therefore* $Z \approx \pm 0.25$

$Z = \frac{x - \mu}{\sigma} = \frac{x - 5.85}{0.24} = \pm 0.25 \rightarrow \pm 0.25 * 0.24 + 5.85 = \left(5.79, 5.91\right)$

# 6.3 | Estimating the Binomial with the Normal Distribution

We found earlier that various probability density functions are the limiting distributions of others; thus, we can estimate one with another under certain circumstances. We will find here that the normal distribution can be used to estimate a binomial process. The Poisson was used to estimate the binomial previously, and the binomial was used to estimate the hypergeometric distribution.

In the case of the relationship between the hypergeometric distribution and the binomial, we had to recognize that a binomial process assumes that the probability of a success remains constant from trial to trial: a head on the last flip cannot have an effect on the probability of a head on the next flip. In the hypergeometric distribution this is the essence of the question because the experiment assumes that any "draw" is without replacement. If one draws without replacement, then all subsequent "draws" are conditional probabilities. We found that if the hypergeometric experiment draws only a small percentage of the total objects, then we can ignore the impact on the probability from draw to draw.

Imagine that there are 312 cards in a deck comprised of 6 normal decks. If the experiment called for drawing only 10 cards, less than 5% of the total, than we will accept the binomial estimate of the probability, even though this is actually a hypergeometric distribution because the cards are presumably drawn without replacement.

The Poisson likewise was considered an appropriate estimate of the binomial under certain circumstances. In **Chapter 4** we found that if the number of trials of interest is large and the probability of success is small, such that $\mu = np < 7$, the

Poisson can be used to estimate the binomial with good results. Again, these rules of thumb do not in any way claim that the actual probability is what the estimate determines, only that the difference is in the third or fourth decimal and is thus *de minimus*.

Here, again, we find that the normal distribution makes particularly accurate estimates of a binomial process under certain circumstances. **Figure 6.10** is a frequency distribution of a binomial process for the experiment of flipping three coins where the random variable is the number of heads. The sample space is listed below the distribution. The experiment assumed that the probability of a success is 0.5; the probability of a failure, a tail, is thus also 0.5. In observing **Figure 6.10** we are struck by the fact that the distribution is symmetrical. The root of this result is that the probabilities of success and failure are the same, 0.5. If the probability of success were smaller than 0.5, the distribution becomes skewed right. Indeed, as the probability of success diminishes, the degree of skewness increases. If the probability of success increases from 0.5, then the skewness increases in the lower tail, resulting in a left-skewed distribution.

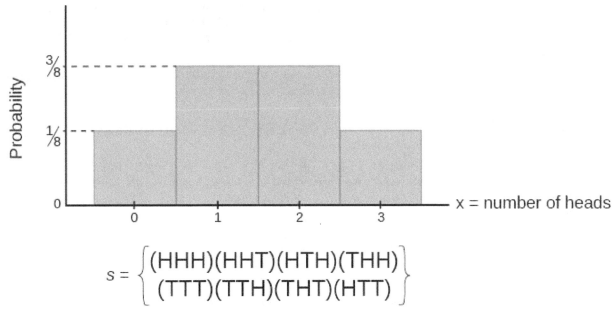

Figure 6.10

The reason the skewness of the binomial distribution is important is because if it is to be estimated with a normal distribution, then we need to recognize that the normal distribution is symmetrical. The closer the underlying binomial distribution is to being symmetrical, the better the estimate that is produced by the normal distribution. **Figure 6.11** shows a symmetrical normal distribution transposed on a graph of a binomial distribution where $p = 0.2$ and $n = 5$. The discrepancy between the estimated probability using a normal distribution and the probability of the original binomial distribution is apparent. The criteria for using a normal distribution to estimate a binomial thus addresses this problem by requiring BOTH $np$ AND $n(1 - p)$ are greater than five. Again, this is a rule of thumb, but is effective and results in acceptable estimates of the binomial probability.

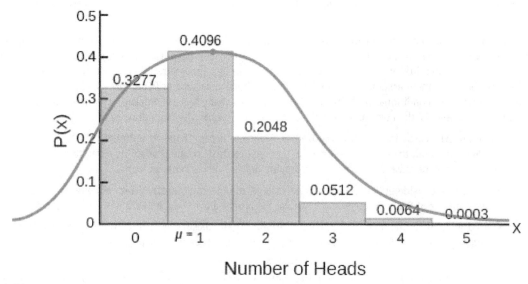

**Figure 6.11**

## Example 6.7

Imagine that it is known that only 10% of Australian Shepherd puppies are born with what is called "perfect symmetry" in their three colors, black, white, and copper. Perfect symmetry is defined as equal coverage on all parts of the dog when looked at in the face and measuring left and right down the centerline. A kennel would have a good reputation for breeding Australian Shepherds if they had a high percentage of dogs that met this criterion. During the past 5 years and out of the 100 dogs born to Dundee Kennels, 16 were born with this coloring characteristic.

What is the probability that, in 100 births, more than 16 would have this characteristic?

### Solution 6.7

If we assume that one dog's coloring is independent of other dogs' coloring, a bit of a brave assumption, this becomes a classic binomial probability problem.

The statement of the probability requested is $1 - [p(X = 0) + p(X = 1) + p(X = 2) + \ldots + p(X = 16)]$. This requires us to calculate 17 binomial formulas and add them together and then subtract from one to get the right hand part of the distribution. Alternatively, we can use the normal distribution to get an acceptable answer and in much less time.

First, we need to check if the binomial distribution is symmetrical enough to use the normal distribution. We know that the binomial for this problem is skewed because the probability of success, 0.1, is not the same as the probability of failure, 0.9. Nevertheless, both $np = 10$ and $n(1 - p) = 90$ are larger than 5, the cutoff for using the normal distribution to estimate the binomial.

Figure 6.11 below shows the binomial distribution and marks the area we wish to know. The mean of the binomial, 10, is also marked, and the standard deviation is written on the side of the graph: $\sigma = \sqrt{npq} = 3$.

The area under the distribution from zero to 16 is the probability requested, and has been shaded in. Below the binomial distribution is a normal distribution to be used to estimate this probability. That probability has also been shaded.

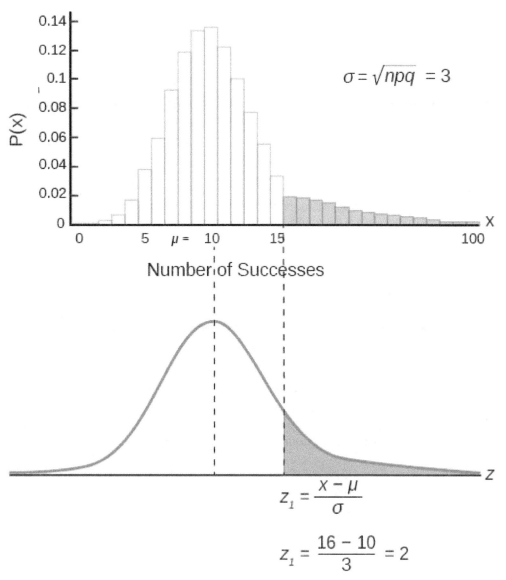

Figure 6.12

Standardizing from the binomial to the normal distribution as done in the past shows where we are asking for the probability from 16 to positive infinity, or 100 in this case. We need to calculate the number of standard deviations 16 is away from the mean: 10.

$$Z = \frac{x - \mu}{\sigma} = \frac{16 - 10}{3} = 2$$

We are asking for the probability beyond two standard deviations, a very unlikely event. We look up two standard deviations in the standard normal table and find the area from zero to two standard deviations is 0.4772. We are interested in the tail, however, so we subtract 0.4772 from 0.5 and thus find the area in the tail. Our conclusion is the probability of a kennel having 16 dogs with "perfect symmetry" is 0.0228. Dundee Kennels has an extraordinary record in this regard.

Mathematically, we write this as:

$$1 - [p(X = 0) + p(X = 1) + p(X = 2) + \ ... \ + p(X = 16)] = p(X > 16) = p(Z > 2) = 0.0228$$

# KEY TERMS

**Normal Distribution**

a continuous random variable (RV) with pdf $f(x) = \frac{1}{\sigma\sqrt{2\pi}} e^{\frac{-(x-\mu)^2}{2\sigma^2}}$, where $\mu$ is the mean of the distribution and $\sigma$ is the standard deviation; notation: $X \sim N(\mu, \sigma)$. If $\mu = 0$ and $\sigma = 1$, the RV, Z, is called the **standard normal distribution**.

**Standard Normal Distribution**  a continuous random variable (RV) $X \sim N(0, 1)$; when $X$ follows the standard normal distribution, it is often noted as $Z \sim N(0, 1)$.

**z-score**  the linear transformation of the form $z = \frac{x - \mu}{\sigma}$ or written as $z = \frac{|x - \mu|}{\sigma}$; if this transformation is applied to any normal distribution $X \sim N(\mu, \sigma)$ the result is the standard normal distribution $Z \sim N(0,1)$. If this transformation is applied to any specific value $x$ of the RV with mean $\mu$ and standard deviation $\sigma$, the result is called the z-score of $x$. The z-score allows us to compare data that are normally distributed but scaled differently. A z-score is the number of standard deviations a particular $x$ is away from its mean value.

# CHAPTER REVIEW

## 6.1 The Standard Normal Distribution

A z-score is a standardized value. Its distribution is the standard normal, $Z \sim N(0, 1)$. The mean of the z-scores is zero and the standard deviation is one. If $z$ is the z-score for a value $x$ from the normal distribution $N(\mu, \sigma)$ then $z$ tells you how many standard deviations $x$ is above (greater than) or below (less than) $\mu$.

## 6.3 Estimating the Binomial with the Normal Distribution

The normal distribution, which is continuous, is the most important of all the probability distributions. Its graph is bell-shaped. This bell-shaped curve is used in almost all disciplines. Since it is a continuous distribution, the total area under the curve is one. The parameters of the normal are the mean $\mu$ and the standard deviation $\sigma$. A special normal distribution, called the standard normal distribution is the distribution of z-scores. Its mean is zero, and its standard deviation is one.

# FORMULA REVIEW

## 6.0 Introduction

$X \sim N(\mu, \sigma)$

$\mu$ = the mean; $\sigma$ = the standard deviation

## 6.1 The Standard Normal Distribution

$Z \sim N(0, 1)$

$z$ = a standardized value (z-score)

mean = 0; standard deviation = 1

To find the $k^{th}$ percentile of $X$ when the z-scores is known:
$k = \mu + (z)\sigma$

z-score: $z = \frac{x - \mu}{\sigma}$ or $z = \frac{|x - \mu|}{\sigma}$

$Z$ = the random variable for z-scores

$Z \sim N(0, 1)$

## 6.3 Estimating the Binomial with the Normal Distribution

Normal Distribution: $X \sim N(\mu, \sigma)$ where $\mu$ is the mean and $\sigma$ is the standard deviation.

Standard Normal Distribution: $Z \sim N(0, 1)$.

# PRACTICE

## 6.1 The Standard Normal Distribution

**1.** A bottle of water contains 12.05 fluid ounces with a standard deviation of 0.01 ounces. Define the random variable $X$ in words. $X = $ _____.

**2.** A normal distribution has a mean of 61 and a standard deviation of 15. What is the median?

**3.** $X \sim N(1, 2)$

$\sigma = $ _____

**4.** A company manufactures rubber balls. The mean diameter of a ball is 12 cm with a standard deviation of 0.2 cm. Define the random variable $X$ in words. $X = $ _____.

**5.** $X \sim N(-4, 1)$

What is the median?

**6.** $X \sim N(3, 5)$

$\sigma = $ _____

**7.** $X \sim N(-2, 1)$

$\mu = $ _____

**8.** What does a $z$-score measure?

**9.** What does standardizing a normal distribution do to the mean?

**10.** Is $X \sim N(0, 1)$ a standardized normal distribution? Why or why not?

**11.** What is the $z$-score of $x = 12$, if it is two standard deviations to the right of the mean?

**12.** What is the $z$-score of $x = 9$, if it is 1.5 standard deviations to the left of the mean?

**13.** What is the $z$-score of $x = -2$, if it is 2.78 standard deviations to the right of the mean?

**14.** What is the $z$-score of $x = 7$, if it is 0.133 standard deviations to the left of the mean?

**15.** Suppose $X \sim N(2, 6)$. What value of $x$ has a $z$-score of three?

**16.** Suppose $X \sim N(8, 1)$. What value of $x$ has a $z$-score of $-2.25$?

**17.** Suppose $X \sim N(9, 5)$. What value of $x$ has a $z$-score of $-0.5$?

**18.** Suppose $X \sim N(2, 3)$. What value of $x$ has a $z$-score of $-0.67$?

**19.** Suppose $X \sim N(4, 2)$. What value of $x$ is 1.5 standard deviations to the left of the mean?

**20.** Suppose $X \sim N(4, 2)$. What value of $x$ is two standard deviations to the right of the mean?

**21.** Suppose $X \sim N(8, 9)$. What value of $x$ is 0.67 standard deviations to the left of the mean?

**22.** Suppose $X \sim N(-1, 2)$. What is the $z$-score of $x = 2$?

**23.** Suppose $X \sim N(12, 6)$. What is the $z$-score of $x = 2$?

**24.** Suppose $X \sim N(9, 3)$. What is the $z$-score of $x = 9$?

**25.** Suppose a normal distribution has a mean of six and a standard deviation of 1.5. What is the $z$-score of $x = 5.5$?

**26.** In a normal distribution, $x = 5$ and $z = -1.25$. This tells you that $x = 5$ is _____ standard deviations to the _____ (right or left) of the mean.

**27.** In a normal distribution, $x = 3$ and $z = 0.67$. This tells you that $x = 3$ is _____ standard deviations to the _____ (right or left) of the mean.

**28.** In a normal distribution, $x = -2$ and $z = 6$. This tells you that $x = -2$ is _____ standard deviations to the _____ (right or left) of the mean.

**29.** In a normal distribution, $x = -5$ and $z = -3.14$. This tells you that $x = -5$ is _____ standard deviations to the _____ (right or left) of the mean.

**30.** In a normal distribution, $x = 6$ and $z = -1.7$. This tells you that $x = 6$ is _____ standard deviations to the _____ (right or left) of the mean.

**31.** About what percent of $x$ values from a normal distribution lie within one standard deviation (left and right) of the mean of that distribution?

**32.** About what percent of the *x* values from a normal distribution lie within two standard deviations (left and right) of the mean of that distribution?

**33.** About what percent of *x* values lie between the second and third standard deviations (both sides)?

**34.** Suppose $X \sim N(15, 3)$. Between what *x* values does 68.27% of the data lie? The range of *x* values is centered at the mean of the distribution (i.e., 15).

**35.** Suppose $X \sim N(-3, 1)$. Between what *x* values does 95.45% of the data lie? The range of *x* values is centered at the mean of the distribution(i.e., –3).

**36.** Suppose $X \sim N(-3, 1)$. Between what *x* values does 34.14% of the data lie?

**37.** About what percent of *x* values lie between the mean and three standard deviations?

**38.** About what percent of *x* values lie between the mean and one standard deviation?

**39.** About what percent of *x* values lie between the first and second standard deviations from the mean (both sides)?

**40.** About what percent of *x* values lie betwween the first and third standard deviations(both sides)?

*Use the following information to answer the next two exercises:* The life of Sunshine CD players is normally distributed with mean of 4.1 years and a standard deviation of 1.3 years. A CD player is guaranteed for three years. We are interested in the length of time a CD player lasts.

**41.** Define the random variable *X* in words. *X* = _____.

**42.** $X \sim$ _____(_____,_____)

## 6.3 Estimating the Binomial with the Normal Distribution

**43.** How would you represent the area to the left of one in a probability statement?

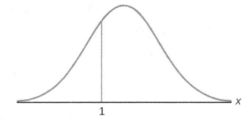

**Figure 6.13**

**44.** What is the area to the right of one?

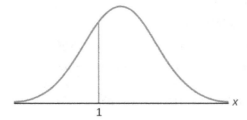

**Figure 6.14**

**45.** Is $P(x < 1)$ equal to $P(x \le 1)$? Why?

**46.** How would you represent the area to the left of three in a probability statement?

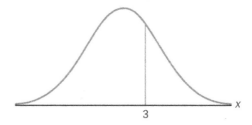

Figure 6.15

**47.** What is the area to the right of three?

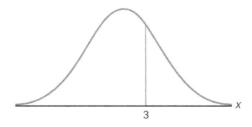

Figure 6.16

**48.** If the area to the left of $x$ in a normal distribution is 0.123, what is the area to the right of $x$?

**49.** If the area to the right of $x$ in a normal distribution is 0.543, what is the area to the left of $x$?

*Use the following information to answer the next four exercises:*

$X \sim N(54, 8)$

**50.** Find the probability that $x > 56$.

**51.** Find the probability that $x < 30$.

**52.** $X \sim N(6, 2)$

Find the probability that $x$ is between three and nine.

**53.** $X \sim N(-3, 4)$

Find the probability that $x$ is between one and four.

**54.** $X \sim N(4, 5)$

Find the maximum of $x$ in the bottom quartile.

**55.** *Use the following information to answer the next three exercise:* The life of Sunshine CD players is normally distributed with a mean of 4.1 years and a standard deviation of 1.3 years. A CD player is guaranteed for three years. We are interested in the length of time a CD player lasts. Find the probability that a CD player will break down during the guarantee period.

    a.  Sketch the situation. Label and scale the axes. Shade the region corresponding to the probability.

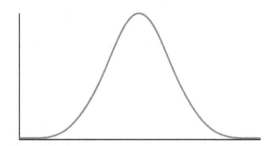

**Figure 6.17**

    b.  $P(0 < x < \underline{\hspace{2cm}}) = \underline{\hspace{2cm}}$ (Use zero for the minimum value of $x$.)

**56.** Find the probability that a CD player will last between 2.8 and six years.
    a.  Sketch the situation. Label and scale the axes. Shade the region corresponding to the probability.

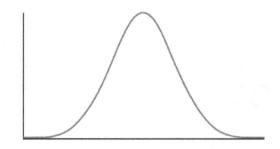

**Figure 6.18**

    b.  $P(\underline{\hspace{2cm}} < x < \underline{\hspace{2cm}}) = \underline{\hspace{2cm}}$

# HOMEWORK

## 6.1 The Standard Normal Distribution

*Use the following information to answer the next two exercises:* The patient recovery time from a particular surgical procedure is normally distributed with a mean of 5.3 days and a standard deviation of 2.1 days.

**57.** What is the median recovery time?
    a.  2.7
    b.  5.3
    c.  7.4
    d.  2.1

**58.** What is the $z$-score for a patient who takes ten days to recover?
    a.  1.5
    b.  0.2
    c.  2.2
    d.  7.3

**59.** The length of time to find it takes to find a parking space at 9 A.M. follows a normal distribution with a mean of five minutes and a standard deviation of two minutes. If the mean is significantly greater than the standard deviation, which of the following statements is true?
>   I.   The data cannot follow the uniform distribution.
>   II.  The data cannot follow the exponential distribution..
>   III. The data cannot follow the normal distribution.

>   a.  I only
>   b.  II only
>   c.  III only
>   d.  I, II, and III

**60.** The heights of the 430 National Basketball Association players were listed on team rosters at the start of the 2005–2006 season. The heights of basketball players have an approximate normal distribution with mean, $\mu = 79$ inches and a standard deviation, $\sigma = 3.89$ inches. For each of the following heights, calculate the $z$-score and interpret it using complete sentences.

>   a.  77 inches
>   b.  85 inches
>   c.  If an NBA player reported his height had a $z$-score of 3.5, would you believe him? Explain your answer.

**61.** The systolic blood pressure (given in millimeters) of males has an approximately normal distribution with mean $\mu = 125$ and standard deviation $\sigma = 14$. Systolic blood pressure for males follows a normal distribution.
>   a.  Calculate the $z$-scores for the male systolic blood pressures 100 and 150 millimeters.
>   b.  If a male friend of yours said he thought his systolic blood pressure was 2.5 standard deviations below the mean, but that he believed his blood pressure was between 100 and 150 millimeters, what would you say to him?

**62.** Kyle's doctor told him that the $z$-score for his systolic blood pressure is 1.75. Which of the following is the best interpretation of this standardized score? The systolic blood pressure (given in millimeters) of males has an approximately normal distribution with mean $\mu = 125$ and standard deviation $\sigma = 14$. If $X$ = a systolic blood pressure score then $X \sim N (125, 14)$.
>   a.  Which answer(s) **is/are** correct?
>>       i.   Kyle's systolic blood pressure is 175.
>>       ii.  Kyle's systolic blood pressure is 1.75 times the average blood pressure of men his age.
>>       iii. Kyle's systolic blood pressure is 1.75 above the average systolic blood pressure of men his age.
>>       iv.  Kyles's systolic blood pressure is 1.75 standard deviations above the average systolic blood pressure for men.
>   b.  Calculate Kyle's blood pressure.

**63.** Height and weight are two measurements used to track a child's development. The World Health Organization measures child development by comparing the weights of children who are the same height and the same gender. In 2009, weights for all 80 cm girls in the reference population had a mean $\mu = 10.2$ kg and standard deviation $\sigma = 0.8$ kg. Weights are normally distributed. $X \sim N(10.2, 0.8)$. Calculate the $z$-scores that correspond to the following weights and interpret them.
>   a.  11 kg
>   b.  7.9 kg
>   c.  12.2 kg

**64.** In 2005, 1,475,623 students heading to college took the SAT. The distribution of scores in the math section of the SAT follows a normal distribution with mean $\mu = 520$ and standard deviation $\sigma = 115$.
>   a.  Calculate the $z$-score for an SAT score of 720. Interpret it using a complete sentence.
>   b.  What math SAT score is 1.5 standard deviations above the mean? What can you say about this SAT score?
>   c.  For 2012, the SAT math test had a mean of 514 and standard deviation 117. The ACT math test is an alternate to the SAT and is approximately normally distributed with mean 21 and standard deviation 5.3. If one person took the SAT math test and scored 700 and a second person took the ACT math test and scored 30, who did better with respect to the test they took?

## 6.3 Estimating the Binomial with the Normal Distribution

*Use the following information to answer the next two exercises:* The patient recovery time from a particular surgical procedure is normally distributed with a mean of 5.3 days and a standard deviation of 2.1 days.

**65.** What is the probability of spending more than two days in recovery?
   a.  0.0580
   b.  0.8447
   c.  0.0553
   d.  0.9420

*Use the following information to answer the next three exercises:* The length of time it takes to find a parking space at 9 A.M. follows a normal distribution with a mean of five minutes and a standard deviation of two minutes.

**66.** Based upon the given information and numerically justified, would you be surprised if it took less than one minute to find a parking space?
   a.  Yes
   b.  No
   c.  Unable to determine

**67.** Find the probability that it takes at least eight minutes to find a parking space.
   a.  0.0001
   b.  0.9270
   c.  0.1862
   d.  0.0668

**68.** Seventy percent of the time, it takes more than how many minutes to find a parking space?
   a.  1.24
   b.  2.41
   c.  3.95
   d.  6.05

**69.** According to a study done by De Anza students, the height for Asian adult males is normally distributed with an average of 66 inches and a standard deviation of 2.5 inches. Suppose one Asian adult male is randomly chosen. Let $X$ = height of the individual.
   a.  $X \sim$ _____(_____,_____)
   b.  Find the probability that the person is between 65 and 69 inches. Include a sketch of the graph, and write a probability statement.
   c.  Would you expect to meet many Asian adult males over 72 inches? Explain why or why not, and justify your answer numerically.
   d.  The middle 40% of heights fall between what two values? Sketch the graph, and write the probability statement.

**70.** IQ is normally distributed with a mean of 100 and a standard deviation of 15. Suppose one individual is randomly chosen. Let $X$ = IQ of an individual.
   a.  $X \sim$ _____(_____,_____)
   b.  Find the probability that the person has an IQ greater than 120. Include a sketch of the graph, and write a probability statement.
   c.  MENSA is an organization whose members have the top 2% of all IQs. Find the minimum IQ needed to qualify for the MENSA organization. Sketch the graph, and write the probability statement.
   d.  The middle 50% of IQs fall between what two values? Sketch the graph and write the probability statement.

**71.** The percent of fat calories that a person in America consumes each day is normally distributed with a mean of about 36 and a standard deviation of 10. Suppose that one individual is randomly chosen. Let $X$ = percent of fat calories.
   a.  $X \sim$ _____(_____,_____)
   b.  Find the probability that the percent of fat calories a person consumes is more than 40. Graph the situation. Shade in the area to be determined.
   c.  Find the maximum number for the lower quarter of percent of fat calories. Sketch the graph and write the probability statement.

**72.** Suppose that the distance of fly balls hit to the outfield (in baseball) is normally distributed with a mean of 250 feet and a standard deviation of 50 feet.
   a.  If $X$ = distance in feet for a fly ball, then $X \sim$ _____(_____,_____)
   b.  If one fly ball is randomly chosen from this distribution, what is the probability that this ball traveled fewer than 220 feet? Sketch the graph. Scale the horizontal axis $X$. Shade the region corresponding to the probability. Find the probability.

**73.** In China, four-year-olds average three hours a day unsupervised. Most of the unsupervised children live in rural areas, considered safe. Suppose that the standard deviation is 1.5 hours and the amount of time spent alone is normally distributed. We randomly select one Chinese four-year-old living in a rural area. We are interested in the amount of time the child spends alone per day.

    a. In words, define the random variable $X$.

    b. $X \sim$ _____(_____,_____)

    c. Find the probability that the child spends less than one hour per day unsupervised. Sketch the graph, and write the probability statement.

    d. What percent of the children spend over ten hours per day unsupervised?

    e. Seventy percent of the children spend at least how long per day unsupervised?

**74.** In the 1992 presidential election, Alaska's 40 election districts averaged 1,956.8 votes per district for President Clinton. The standard deviation was 572.3. (There are only 40 election districts in Alaska.) The distribution of the votes per district for President Clinton was bell-shaped. Let $X$ = number of votes for President Clinton for an election district.

    a. State the approximate distribution of $X$.

    b. Is 1,956.8 a population mean or a sample mean? How do you know?

    c. Find the probability that a randomly selected district had fewer than 1,600 votes for President Clinton. Sketch the graph and write the probability statement.

    d. Find the probability that a randomly selected district had between 1,800 and 2,000 votes for President Clinton.

    e. Find the third quartile for votes for President Clinton.

**75.** Suppose that the duration of a particular type of criminal trial is known to be normally distributed with a mean of 21 days and a standard deviation of seven days.

    a. In words, define the random variable $X$.

    b. $X \sim$ _____(_____,_____)

    c. If one of the trials is randomly chosen, find the probability that it lasted at least 24 days. Sketch the graph and write the probability statement.

    d. Sixty percent of all trials of this type are completed within how many days?

**76.** Terri Vogel, an amateur motorcycle racer, averages 129.71 seconds per 2.5 mile lap (in a seven-lap race) with a standard deviation of 2.28 seconds. The distribution of her race times is normally distributed. We are interested in one of her randomly selected laps.

    a. In words, define the random variable $X$.

    b. $X \sim$ _____(_____,_____)

    c. Find the percent of her laps that are completed in less than 130 seconds.

    d. The fastest 3% of her laps are under _____.

    e. The middle 80% of her laps are from _____ seconds to _____ seconds.

**77.** Thuy Dau, Ngoc Bui, Sam Su, and Lan Voung conducted a survey as to how long customers at Lucky claimed to wait in the checkout line until their turn. Let $X$ = time in line. **Table 6.1** displays the ordered real data (in minutes):

| 0.50 | 4.25 | 5    | 6    | 7.25  |
|------|------|------|------|-------|
| 1.75 | 4.25 | 5.25 | 6    | 7.25  |
| 2    | 4.25 | 5.25 | 6.25 | 7.25  |
| 2.25 | 4.25 | 5.5  | 6.25 | 7.75  |
| 2.25 | 4.5  | 5.5  | 6.5  | 8     |
| 2.5  | 4.75 | 5.5  | 6.5  | 8.25  |
| 2.75 | 4.75 | 5.75 | 6.5  | 9.5   |
| 3.25 | 4.75 | 5.75 | 6.75 | 9.5   |
| 3.75 | 5    | 6    | 6.75 | 9.75  |
| 3.75 | 5    | 6    | 6.75 | 10.75 |

Table 6.1

a.  Calculate the sample mean and the sample standard deviation.
b.  Construct a histogram.
c.  Draw a smooth curve through the midpoints of the tops of the bars.
d.  In words, describe the shape of your histogram and smooth curve.
e.  Let the sample mean approximate $\mu$ and the sample standard deviation approximate $\sigma$. The distribution of $X$ can then be approximated by $X \sim$ _____(_____,_____)
f.  Use the distribution in part e to calculate the probability that a person will wait fewer than 6.1 minutes.
g.  Determine the cumulative relative frequency for waiting less than 6.1 minutes.
h.  Why aren't the answers to part f and part g exactly the same?
i.  Why are the answers to part f and part g as close as they are?
j.  If only ten customers has been surveyed rather than 50, do you think the answers to part f and part g would have been closer together or farther apart? Explain your conclusion.

**78.** Suppose that Ricardo and Anita attend different colleges. Ricardo's GPA is the same as the average GPA at his school. Anita's GPA is 0.70 standard deviations above her school average. In complete sentences, explain why each of the following statements may be false.
a.  Ricardo's actual GPA is lower than Anita's actual GPA.
b.  Ricardo is not passing because his $z$-score is zero.
c.  Anita is in the 70th percentile of students at her college.

**79.** An expert witness for a paternity lawsuit testifies that the length of a pregnancy is normally distributed with a mean of 280 days and a standard deviation of 13 days. An alleged father was out of the country from 240 to 306 days before the birth of the child, so the pregnancy would have been less than 240 days or more than 306 days long if he was the father. The birth was uncomplicated, and the child needed no medical intervention. What is the probability that he was NOT the father? What is the probability that he could be the father? Calculate the $z$-scores first, and then use those to calculate the probability.

**80.** A NUMMI assembly line, which has been operating since 1984, has built an average of 6,000 cars and trucks a week. Generally, 10% of the cars were defective coming off the assembly line. Suppose we draw a random sample of $n = 100$ cars. Let $X$ represent the number of defective cars in the sample. What can we say about $X$ in regard to the 68-95-99.7 empirical rule (one standard deviation, two standard deviations and three standard deviations from the mean are being referred to)? Assume a normal distribution for the defective cars in the sample.

**81.** We flip a coin 100 times ($n = 100$) and note that it only comes up heads 20% ($p = 0.20$) of the time. The mean and standard deviation for the number of times the coin lands on heads is $\mu = 20$ and $\sigma = 4$ (verify the mean and standard deviation). Solve the following:

    a.  There is about a 68% chance that the number of heads will be somewhere between ___ and ___.

    b.  There is about a ____chance that the number of heads will be somewhere between 12 and 28.

    c.  There is about a ____ chance that the number of heads will be somewhere between eight and 32.

**82.** A $1 scratch off lotto ticket will be a winner one out of five times. Out of a shipment of $n = 190$ lotto tickets, find the probability for the lotto tickets that there are

    a.  somewhere between 34 and 54 prizes.

    b.  somewhere between 54 and 64 prizes.

    c.  more than 64 prizes.

**83.** Facebook provides a variety of statistics on its Web site that detail the growth and popularity of the site.

On average, 28 percent of 18 to 34 year olds check their Facebook profiles before getting out of bed in the morning. Suppose this percentage follows a normal distribution with a standard deviation of five percent.

# REFERENCES

### 6.1 The Standard Normal Distribution

"Blood Pressure of Males and Females." StatCruch, 2013. Available online at http://www.statcrunch.com/5.0/viewreport.php?reportid=11960 (accessed May 14, 2013).

"The Use of Epidemiological Tools in Conflict-affected populations: Open-access educational resources for policy-makers: Calculation of z-scores." London School of Hygiene and Tropical Medicine, 2009. Available online at http://conflict.lshtm.ac.uk/page_125.htm (accessed May 14, 2013).

"2012 College-Bound Seniors Total Group Profile Report." CollegeBoard, 2012. Available online at http://media.collegeboard.com/digitalServices/pdf/research/TotalGroup-2012.pdf (accessed May 14, 2013).

"Digest of Education Statistics: ACT score average and standard deviations by sex and race/ethnicity and percentage of ACT test takers, by selected composite score ranges and planned fields of study: Selected years, 1995 through 2009." National Center for Education Statistics. Available online at http://nces.ed.gov/programs/digest/d09/tables/dt09_147.asp (accessed May 14, 2013).

Data from the *San Jose Mercury News*.

Data from *The World Almanac and Book of Facts*.

"List of stadiums by capacity." Wikipedia. Available online at https://en.wikipedia.org/wiki/List_of_stadiums_by_capacity (accessed May 14, 2013).

Data from the National Basketball Association. Available online at www.nba.com (accessed May 14, 2013).

### 6.2 Using the Normal Distribution

"Naegele's rule." Wikipedia. Available online at http://en.wikipedia.org/wiki/Naegele's_rule (accessed May 14, 2013).

"403: NUMMI." Chicago Public Media & Ira Glass, 2013. Available online at http://www.thisamericanlife.org/radio-archives/episode/403/nummi (accessed May 14, 2013).

"Scratch-Off Lottery Ticket Playing Tips." WinAtTheLottery.com, 2013. Available online at http://www.winatthelottery.com/public/department40.cfm (accessed May 14, 2013).

"Smart Phone Users, By The Numbers." Visual.ly, 2013. Available online at http://visual.ly/smart-phone-users-numbers (accessed May 14, 2013).

"Facebook Statistics." Statistics Brain. Available online at http://www.statisticbrain.com/facebook-statistics/(accessed May 14, 2013).

# SOLUTIONS

1 ounces of water in a bottle

3 2

5 –4

7 –2

9 The mean becomes zero.

11 $z = 2$

13 $z = 2.78$

15 $x = 20$

17 $x = 6.5$

19 $x = 1$

21 $x = 1.97$

23 $z = -1.67$

25 $z \approx -0.33$

27 0.67, right

29 3.14, left

31 about 68%

33 about 4%

35 between –5 and –1

37 about 50%

39 about 27%

41 The lifetime of a Sunshine CD player measured in years.

43 $P(x < 1)$

45 Yes, because they are the same in a continuous distribution: $P(x = 1) = 0$

47 $1 - P(x < 3)$ or $P(x > 3)$

49 $1 - 0.543 = 0.457$

51 0.0013

53 0.1186

55
  a. Check student's solution.

  b. 3, 0.1979

58 c

60
  a. Use the z-score formula. $z = -0.5141$. The height of 77 inches is 0.5141 standard deviations below the mean. An NBA player whose height is 77 inches is shorter than average.

  b. Use the z-score formula. $z = 1.5424$. The height 85 inches is 1.5424 standard deviations above the mean. An NBA player whose height is 85 inches is taller than average.

  c. Height = 79 + 3.5(3.89) = 90.67 inches, which is over 7.7 feet tall. There are very few NBA players this tall so the answer is no, not likely.

62
  a. iv

b. Kyle's blood pressure is equal to $125 + (1.75)(14) = 149.5$.

64 Let $X$ = an SAT math score and $Y$ = an ACT math score.

a. $X = 720$ $\frac{720 - 520}{15} = 1.74$ The exam score of 720 is 1.74 standard deviations above the mean of 520.

b. $z = 1.5$

The math SAT score is $520 + 1.5(115) \approx 692.5$. The exam score of 692.5 is 1.5 standard deviations above the mean of 520.

c. $\frac{X - \mu}{\sigma} = \frac{700 - 514}{117} \approx 1.59$, the z-score for the SAT. $\frac{Y - \mu}{\sigma} = \frac{30 - 21}{5.3} \approx 1.70$, the z-scores for the ACT. With respect to the test they took, the person who took the ACT did better (has the higher z-score).

67 d

69

a. $X \sim N(66, 2.5)$

b. 0.5404

c. No, the probability that an Asian male is over 72 inches tall is 0.0082

71

a. $X \sim N(36, 10)$

b. The probability that a person consumes more than 40% of their calories as fat is 0.3446.

c. Approximately 25% of people consume less than 29.26% of their calories as fat.

73

a. $X$ = number of hours that a Chinese four-year-old in a rural area is unsupervised during the day.

b. $X \sim N(3, 1.5)$

c. The probability that the child spends less than one hour a day unsupervised is 0.0918.

d. The probability that a child spends over ten hours a day unsupervised is less than 0.0001.

e. 2.21 hours

75

a. $X$ = the distribution of the number of days a particular type of criminal trial will take

b. $X \sim N(21, 7)$

c. The probability that a randomly selected trial will last more than 24 days is 0.3336.

d. 22.77

77

a. mean = 5.51, $s$ = 2.15

b. Check student's solution.

c. Check student's solution.

d. Check student's solution.

e. $X \sim N(5.51, 2.15)$

f. 0.6029

g. The cumulative frequency for less than 6.1 minutes is 0.64.

h. The answers to part f and part g are not exactly the same, because the normal distribution is only an approximation to the real one.

i. The answers to part f and part g are close, because a normal distribution is an excellent approximation when the sample size is greater than 30.

  j. The approximation would have been less accurate, because the smaller sample size means that the data does not fit normal curve as well.

**80**

$n = 100; p = 0.1; q = 0.9$

$\mu = np = (100)(0.10) = 10$

$\sigma = \sqrt{npq} = \sqrt{(100)(0.1)(0.9)} = 3$

  i.   $z = \pm 1 : x_1 = \mu + z\sigma = 10 + 1(3) = 13$ and $x2 = \mu - z\sigma = 10 - 1(3) = 7.68\%$ of the defective cars will fall between seven and 13.

  ii.   $z = \pm 2 : x_1 = \mu + z\sigma = 10 + 2(3) = 16$ and $x2 = \mu - z\sigma = 10 - 2(3) = 4.95\%$ of the defective cars will fall between four and 16

  iii.   $z = \pm 3 : x_1 = \mu + z\sigma = 10 + 3(3) = 19$ and $x2 = \mu - z\sigma = 10 - 3(3) = 1.99.7\%$ of the defective cars will fall between one and 19.

**82**

$n = 190; p = \dfrac{1}{5} = 0.2; q = 0.8$

$\mu = np = (190)(0.2) = 38$

$\sigma = \sqrt{npq} = \sqrt{(190)(0.2)(0.8)} = 5.5136$

  a.   For this problem: $P(34 < x < 54) = 0.7641$

  b.   For this problem: $P(54 < x < 64) = 0.0018$

  c.   For this problem: $P(x > 64) = 0.0000012$ (approximately 0)

# 7 | THE CENTRAL LIMIT THEOREM

**Figure 7.1** If you want to figure out the distribution of the change people carry in their pockets, using the Central Limit Theorem and assuming your sample is large enough, you will find that the distribution is the normal probability density function. (credit: John Lodder)

## Introduction

Why are we so concerned with means? Two reasons are: they give us a middle ground for comparison, and they are easy to calculate. In this chapter, you will study means and the **Central Limit Theorem**.

The **Central Limit Theorem** is one of the most powerful and useful ideas in all of statistics. The Central Limit Theorem is a theorem which means that it is NOT a theory or just somebody's idea of the way things work. As a theorem it ranks with the Pythagorean Theorem, or the theorem that tells us that the sum of the angles of a triangle must add to 180. These are facts of the ways of the world rigorously demonstrated with mathematical precision and logic. As we will see this powerful theorem will determine just what we can, and cannot say, in inferential statistics. The Central Limit Theorem is concerned with drawing finite samples of size $n$ from a population with a known mean, $\mu$, and a known standard deviation, $\sigma$. The conclusion is that if we collect samples of size $n$ with a "large enough $n$," calculate each sample's mean, and create a histogram (distribution) of those means, then the resulting distribution will tend to have an approximate normal distribution.

**The astounding result is that it does not matter what the distribution of the original population is, or whether**

**you even need to know it. The important fact is that the distribution of sample means tend to follow the normal distribution.**

The size of the sample, *n*, that is required in order to be "large enough" depends on the original population from which the samples are drawn (the sample size should be at least 30 or the data should come from a normal distribution). If the original population is far from normal, then more observations are needed for the sample means. **Sampling is done randomly and with replacement in the theoretical model.**

# 7.1 | The Central Limit Theorem for Sample Means

The sampling distribution is a theoretical distribution. It is created by taking many many samples of size n from a population. Each sample mean is then treated like a single observation of this new distribution, the sampling distribution. The genius of thinking this way is that it recognizes that when we sample we are creating an observation and that observation must come from some particular distribution. The Central Limit Theorem answers the question: from what distribution did a sample mean come? If this is discovered, then we can treat a sample mean just like any other observation and calculate probabilities about what values it might take on. We have effectively moved from the world of statistics where we know only what we have from the sample, to the world of probability where we know the distribution from which the sample mean came and the parameters of that distribution.

The reasons that one samples a population are obvious. The time and expense of checking every invoice to determine its validity or every shipment to see if it contains all the items may well exceed the cost of errors in billing or shipping. For some products, sampling would require destroying them, called destructive sampling. One such example is measuring the ability of a metal to withstand saltwater corrosion for parts on ocean going vessels.

Sampling thus raises an important question; just which sample was drawn. Even if the sample were randomly drawn, there are theoretically an almost infinite number of samples. With just 100 items, there are more than 75 million unique samples of size five that can be drawn. If six are in the sample, the number of possible samples increases to just more than one billion. Of the 75 million possible samples, then, which one did you get? If there is variation in the items to be sampled, there will be variation in the samples. One could draw an "unlucky" sample and make very wrong conclusions concerning the population. This recognition that any sample we draw is really only one from a distribution of samples provides us with what is probably the single most important theorem is statistics: **the Central Limit Theorem**. Without the Central Limit Theorem it would be impossible to proceed to inferential statistics from simple probability theory. In its most basic form, the Central Limit Theorem states that **regardless** of the underlying probability density function of the population data, the theoretical distribution of the means of samples from the population will be normally distributed. In essence, this says that the mean of a sample should be treated like an observation drawn from a normal distribution. The Central Limit Theorem only holds if the sample size is "large enough" which has been shown to be only 30 observations or more.

**Figure 7.2** graphically displays this very important proposition.

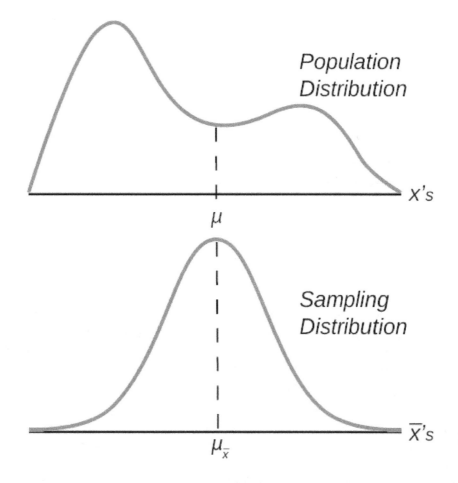

**Figure 7.2**

Notice that the horizontal axis in the top panel is labeled X. These are the individual observations of the population. This is the **unknown** distribution of the population values. The graph is purposefully drawn all squiggly to show that it does not matter just how odd ball it really is. Remember, we will never know what this distribution looks like, or its mean or standard deviation for that matter.

The horizontal axis in the bottom panel is labeled $\bar{X}$ 's. This is the theoretical distribution called the sampling distribution of the means. Each observation on this distribution is a sample mean. All these sample means were calculated from individual samples with the same sample size. The theoretical sampling distribution contains all of the sample mean values from all the possible samples that could have been taken from the population. Of course, no one would ever actually take all of these samples, but if they did this is how they would look. And the Central Limit Theorem says that they will be normally distributed.

The Central Limit Theorem goes even further and tells us the mean and standard deviation of this theoretical distribution.

| Parameter | Population Distribution | Sample | Sampling Distribution of $\bar{X}$ 's |
|---|---|---|---|
| Mean | μ | $\bar{X}$ | $\mu_{\bar{x}}$    and $E(\mu_{\bar{x}}) = \mu$ |
| Standard Deviation | σ | s | $\sigma_{\bar{x}} = \dfrac{\sigma}{\sqrt{n}}$ |

**Table 7.1**

The practical significance of The Central Limit Theorem is that now we can compute probabilities for drawing a sample mean, $\bar{X}$, in just the same way as we did for drawing specific observations, X's, when we knew the population mean and standard deviation and that the population data were normally distributed.. The standardizing formula has to be amended to recognize that the mean and standard deviation of the sampling distribution, sometimes, called the standard error of the mean, are different from those of the population distribution, but otherwise nothing has changed. The new standardizing formula is

$$Z = \frac{\bar{X} - \mu_{\bar{X}}}{\sigma_{\bar{X}}} = \frac{\bar{X} - \mu}{\frac{\sigma}{\sqrt{n}}}$$

Notice that $\mu_{\bar{X}}$ in the first formula has been changed to simply $\mu$ in the second version. The reason is that mathematically it can be shown that the expected value of $\mu_{\bar{X}}$ is equal to $\mu$. This was stated in **Table 7.1** above. Mathematically, the E(x) symbol read the "expected value of x". This formula will be used in the next unit to provide estimates of the **unknown** population parameter $\mu$.

# 7.2 | Using the Central Limit Theorem
## Examples of the Central Limit Theorem
### Law of Large Numbers

The **law of large numbers** says that if you take samples of larger and larger size from any population, then the mean of the sampling distribution, $\mu_{\bar{x}}$ tends to get closer and closer to the true population mean, $\mu$. From the Central Limit Theorem, we know that as $n$ gets larger and larger, the sample means follow a normal distribution. The larger $n$ gets, the smaller the standard deviation of the sampling distribution gets. (Remember that the standard deviation for the sampling distribution of $\bar{X}$ is $\frac{\sigma}{\sqrt{n}}$.) This means that the sample mean $\bar{x}$ must be closer to the population mean $\mu$ as $n$ increases. We can say that $\mu$ is the value that the sample means approach as $n$ gets larger. The Central Limit Theorem illustrates the law of large numbers.

This concept is so important and plays such a critical role in what follows it deserves to be developed further. Indeed, there are two critical issues that flow from the Central Limit Theorem and the application of the Law of Large numbers to it. These are

1. The probability density function of the sampling distribution of means is normally distributed **regardless** of the underlying distribution of the population observations and

2. standard deviation of the sampling distribution decreases as the size of the samples that were used to calculate the means for the sampling distribution increases.

Taking these in order. It would seem counterintuitive that the population may have **any** distribution and the distribution of means coming from it would be normally distributed. With the use of computers, experiments can be simulated that show the process by which the sampling distribution changes as the sample size is increased. These simulations show visually the results of the mathematical proof of the Central Limit Theorem.

Here are three examples of very different population distributions and the evolution of the sampling distribution to a normal distribution as the sample size increases. The top panel in these cases represents the histogram for the original data. The three panels show the histograms for 1,000 randomly drawn samples for different sample sizes: n=10, n= 25 and n=50. As the sample size increases, and the number of samples taken remains constant, the distribution of the 1,000 sample means becomes closer to the smooth line that represents the normal distribution.

**Figure 7.3** is for a normal distribution of individual observations and we would expect the sampling distribution to converge on the normal quickly. The results show this and show that even at a very small sample size the distribution is close to the normal distribution.

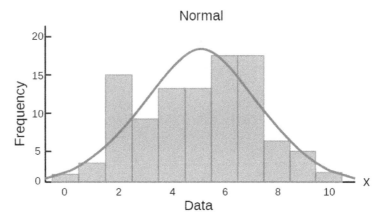

Data

Sample Size $n = 10$

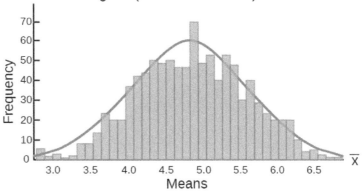

Means

Sample Size $n = 25$

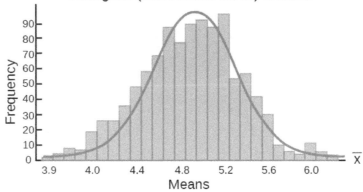

Means

Sample Size $n = 50$

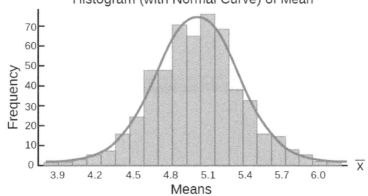

Means

**Figure 7.3**

**Figure 7.4** is a uniform distribution which, a bit amazingly, quickly approached the normal distribution even with only a sample of 10.

Distribution of Random Variable

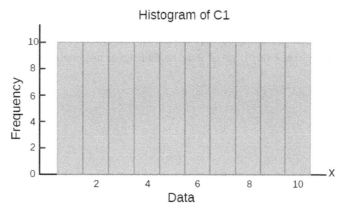

Sample Size *n* = 10

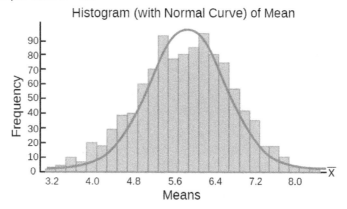

Sample Size *n* = 25

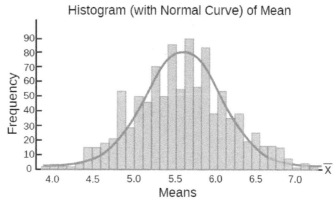

Sample Size *n* = 50

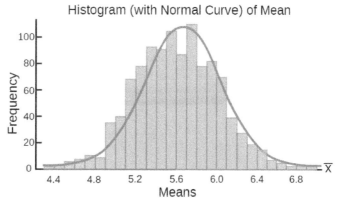

**Figure 7.4**

**Figure 7.5** is a skewed distribution. This last one could be an exponential, geometric, or binomial with a small probability of success creating the skew in the distribution. For skewed distributions our intuition would say that this will take larger sample sizes to move to a normal distribution and indeed that is what we observe from the simulation. Nevertheless, at a sample size of 50, not considered a very large sample, the distribution of sample means has very decidedly gained the shape of the normal distribution.

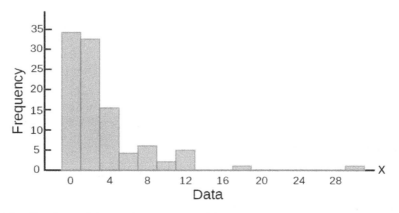

Distribution of Sample means with *n* = 10

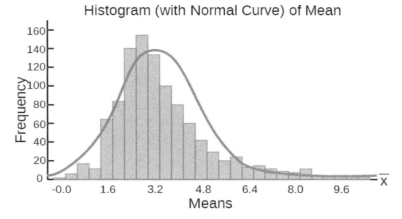

Distribution of Sample means with *n* = 25

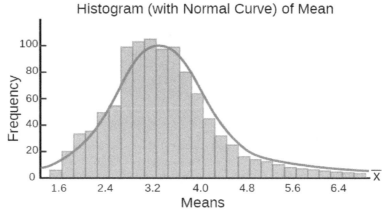

Distribution of Sample means with *n* = 50

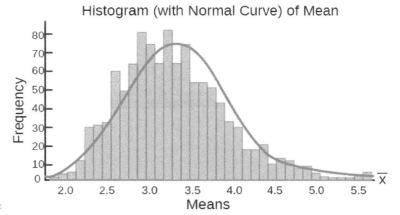

Figure 7.5

The Central Limit Theorem provides more than the proof that the sampling distribution of means is normally distributed. It also provides us with the mean and standard deviation of this distribution. Further, as discussed above, the expected value of the mean, $\mu_{\bar{x}}$, is equal to the mean of the population of the original data which is what we are interested in estimating from the sample we took. We have already inserted this conclusion of the Central Limit Theorem into the formula we use for standardizing from the sampling distribution to the standard normal distribution. And finally, the Central Limit Theorem has also provided the standard deviation of the sampling distribution, $\sigma_{\bar{x}} = \frac{\sigma}{\sqrt{n}}$, and this is critical to have to calculate probabilities of values of the new random variable, $\bar{x}$.

Figure 7.6 shows a sampling distribution. The mean has been marked on the horizontal axis of the $\bar{x}$ 's and the standard deviation has been written to the right above the distribution. Notice that the standard deviation of the sampling distribution is the original standard deviation of the population, divided by the sample size. We have already seen that as the sample size increases the sampling distribution becomes closer and closer to the normal distribution. As this happens, the standard deviation of the sampling distribution changes in another way; the standard deviation decreases as n increases. At very very large n, the standard deviation of the sampling distribution becomes very small and at infinity it collapses on top of the population mean. This is what it means that the expected value of $\mu_{\bar{x}}$ is the population mean, μ.

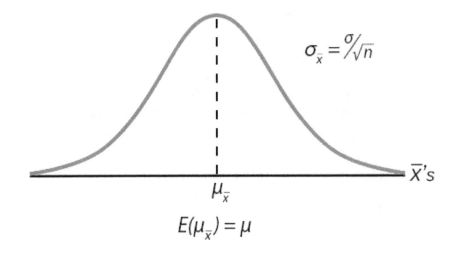

Figure 7.6

At non-extreme values of n, this relationship between the standard deviation of the sampling distribution and the sample size plays a very important part in our ability to estimate the parameters we are interested in.

Figure 7.7 shows three sampling distributions. The only change that was made is the sample size that was used to get the sample means for each distribution. As the sample size increases, n goes from 10 to 30 to 50, the standard deviations of the respective sampling distributions decrease because the sample size is in the denominator of the standard deviations of the sampling distributions.

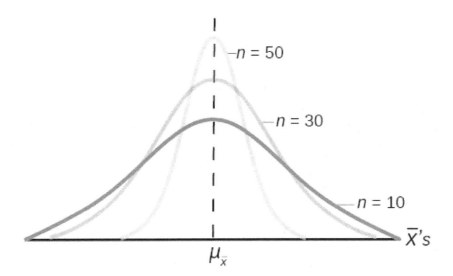

Figure 7.7

The implications for this are very important. **Figure 7.8** shows the effect of the sample size on the confidence we will have in our estimates. These are two sampling distributions from the same population. One sampling distribution was created with samples of size 10 and the other with samples of size 50. All other things constant, the sampling distribution with sample size 50 has a smaller standard deviation that causes the graph to be higher and narrower. The important effect of this is that for the same probability of one standard deviation from the mean, this distribution covers much less of a range of possible values than the other distribution. One standard deviation is marked on the $\overline{X}$ axis for each distribution. This is shown by the two arrows that are plus or minus one standard deviation for each distribution. If the probability that the true mean is one standard deviation away from the mean, then for the sampling distribution with the smaller sample size, the possible range of values is much greater. A simple question is, would you rather have a sample mean from the narrow, tight distribution, or the flat, wide distribution as the estimate of the population mean? Your answer tells us why people intuitively will always choose data from a large sample rather than a small sample. The sample mean they are getting is coming from a more compact distribution. This concept will be the foundation for what will be called level of confidence in the next unit.

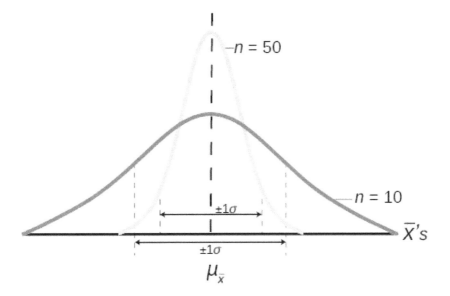

Figure 7.8

# 7.3 | The Central Limit Theorem for Proportions

The Central Limit Theorem tells us that the point estimate for the sample mean, $\bar{x}$, comes from a normal distribution of $\bar{x}$ 's. This theoretical distribution is called the sampling distribution of $\bar{x}$ 's. We now investigate the sampling distribution for another important parameter we wish to estimate; p from the binomial probability density function.

If the random variable is discrete, such as for categorical data, then the parameter we wish to estimate is the population proportion. This is, of course, the probability of drawing a success in any one random draw. Unlike the case just discussed for a continuous random variable where we did not know the population distribution of X's, here we actually know the underlying probability density function for these data; it is the binomial. The random variable is X = the number of successes and the parameter we wish to know is p, the probability of drawing a success which is of course the proportion of successes in the population. The question at issue is: from what distribution was the sample proportion, $p' = \frac{x}{n}$ drawn? The sample size is n and X is the number of successes found in that sample. This is a parallel question that was just answered by the Central Limit Theorem: from what distribution was the sample mean, $\bar{x}$, drawn? We saw that once we knew that the distribution was the Normal distribution then we were able to create confidence intervals for the population parameter, μ. We will also use this same information to test hypotheses about the population mean later. We wish now to be able to develop confidence intervals for the population parameter "p" from the binomial probability density function.

In order to find the distribution from which sample proportions come we need to develop the sampling distribution of sample proportions just as we did for sample means. So again imagine that we randomly sample say 50 people and ask them if they support the new school bond issue. From this we find a sample proportion, p', and graph it on the axis of p's. We do this again and again etc., etc. until we have the theoretical distribution of p's. Some sample proportions will show high favorability toward the bond issue and others will show low favorability because random sampling will reflect the variation of views within the population. What we have done can be seen in **Figure 7.9**. The top panel is the population distributions of probabilities for each possible value of the random variable X. While we do not know what the specific distribution looks like because we do not know p, the population parameter, we do know that it must look something like this. In reality, we do not know either the mean or the standard deviation of this population distribution, the same difficulty we faced when analyzing the X's previously.

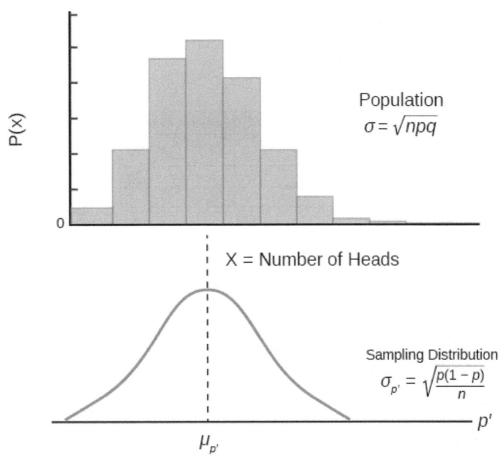

**Figure 7.9**

**Figure 7.9** places the mean on the distribution of population probabilities as $\mu = np$ but of course we do not actually know the population mean because we do not know the population probability of success, $p$. Below the distribution of the population values is the sampling distribution of $p$'s. Again the Central Limit Theorem tells us that this distribution is normally distributed just like the case of the sampling distribution for $\bar{x}$'s. This sampling distribution also has a mean, the mean of the $p$'s, and a standard deviation, $\sigma_{p'}$.

Importantly, in the case of the analysis of the distribution of sample means, the Central Limit Theorem told us the expected value of the mean of the sample means in the sampling distribution, and the standard deviation of the sampling distribution. Again the Central Limit Theorem provides this information for the sampling distribution for proportions. The answers are:

1.  The expected value of the mean of sampling distribution of sample proportions, $\mu_{p'}$, is the population proportion, p.

2.  The standard deviation of the sampling distribution of sample proportions, $\sigma_{p'}$, is the population standard deviation divided by the square root of the sample size, n.

Both these conclusions are the same as we found for the sampling distribution for sample means. However in this case, because the mean and standard deviation of the binomial distribution both rely upon $p$, the formula for the standard deviation of the sampling distribution requires algebraic manipulation to be useful. We will take that up in the next chapter. The proof of these important conclusions from the Central Limit Theorem is provided below.

$$E(p') = E\left(\frac{x}{n}\right) = \left(\frac{1}{n}\right)E(x) = \left(\frac{1}{n}\right)np = p$$

(The expected value of X, E(x), is simply the mean of the binomial distribution which we know to be np.)

$$\sigma_{p'}^2 = \text{Var}(p') = \text{Var}\left(\frac{x}{n}\right) = \frac{1}{n^2}(\text{Var}(x)) = \frac{1}{n^2}(np(1-p)) = \frac{p(1-p)}{n}$$

The standard deviation of the sampling distribution for proportions is thus:

$$\sigma_{p'} = \sqrt{\frac{p(1-P)}{n}}$$

| Parameter | Population Distribution | Sample | Sampling Distribution of $p's$ |
|---|---|---|---|
| Mean | $\mu = np$ | $p' = \frac{x}{n}$ | $p'$ and $E(p') = p$ |
| Standard Deviation | $\sigma = \sqrt{npq}$ | | $\sigma_{p'} = \sqrt{\frac{p(1-p)}{n}}$ |

**Table 7.2**

Table 7.2 summarizes these results and shows the relationship between the population, sample and sampling distribution. Notice the parallel between this Table and Table 7.1 for the case where the random variable is continuous and we were developing the sampling distribution for means.

Reviewing the formula for the standard deviation of the sampling distribution for proportions we see that as n increases the standard deviation decreases. This is the same observation we made for the standard deviation for the sampling distribution for means. Again, as the sample size increases, the point estimate for either $\mu$ or $p$ is found to come from a distribution with a narrower and narrower distribution. We concluded that with a given level of probability, the range from which the point estimate comes is smaller as the sample size, n, increases. Figure 7.8 shows this result for the case of sample means. Simply substitute $p'$ for $\bar{x}$ and we can see the impact of the sample size on the estimate of the sample proportion.

# 7.4 | Finite Population Correction Factor

We saw that the sample size has an important effect on the variance and thus the standard deviation of the sampling distribution. Also of interest is the proportion of the total population that has been sampled. We have assumed that the population is extremely large and that we have sampled a small part of the population. As the population becomes smaller and we sample a larger number of observations the sample observations are not independent of each other. To correct for the impact of this, the Finite Correction Factor can be used to adjust the variance of the sampling distribution. It is appropriate when more than 5% of the population is being sampled and the population has a known population size. There are cases when the population is known, and therefore the correction factor must be applied. The issue arises for both the sampling distribution of the means and the sampling distribution of proportions. The Finite Population Correction Factor for the variance of the means shown in the standardizing formula is:

$$Z = \frac{\bar{x} - \mu}{\frac{\sigma}{\sqrt{n}} * \sqrt{\frac{N-n}{N-1}}}$$

and for the variance of proportions is:

$$\sigma_{p'} = \sqrt{\frac{p(1-p)}{n}} \times \sqrt{\frac{N-n}{N-1}}$$

The following examples show how to apply the factor. Sampling variances get adjusted using the above formula.

## Example 7.1

It is learned that the population of White German Shepherds in the USA is 4,000 dogs, and the mean weight for German Shepherds is 75.45 pounds. It is also learned that the population standard deviation is 10.37 pounds.

If the sample size is 100 dogs, then find the probability that a sample will have a mean that differs from the true probability mean by less than 2 pounds.

**Solution 7.1**

$N = 4000, \quad n = 100, \quad \sigma = 10.37, \quad \mu = 75.45, \quad \left(\bar{x} - \mu\right) = \pm 2$

$$Z = \frac{\bar{x} - \mu}{\frac{\sigma}{\sqrt{n}} * \sqrt{\frac{N-n}{N-1}}} = \frac{\pm 2}{\frac{10.37}{\sqrt{100}} * \sqrt{\frac{4000-100}{4000-1}}} = \pm 1.95$$

$$f(Z) = 0.4744 * 2 = 0.9488$$

Note that "differs by less" references the area on both sides of the mean within 2 pounds right or left.

## Example 7.2

When a customer places an order with Rudy's On-Line Office Supplies, a computerized accounting information system (AIS) automatically checks to see if the customer has exceeded his or her credit limit. Past records indicate that the probability of customers exceeding their credit limit is .06.

Suppose that on a given day, 3,000 orders are placed in total. If we randomly select 360 orders, what is the probability that between 10 and 20 customers will exceed their credit limit?

**Solution 7.2**

$N = 3000, \quad n = 360, \quad p = 0.06$

$$\sigma_{p'} = \sqrt{\frac{p(1-p)}{n}} \times \sqrt{\frac{N-n}{N-1}} = \sqrt{\frac{0.06(1-0.06)}{360}} \times \sqrt{\frac{3000-360}{3000-1}} = 0.0117$$

$$p_1 = \frac{10}{360} = 0.0278, \quad p_2 = \frac{20}{360} = 0.0556$$

$$Z = \frac{p' - p}{\sqrt{\frac{p(1-p)}{n}} * \sqrt{\frac{N-n}{N-1}}} = \frac{0.0278 - 0.06}{0.011744} = -2.74$$

$$Z = \frac{p' - p}{\sqrt{\frac{p(1-p)}{n}} * \sqrt{\frac{N-n}{N-1}}} = \frac{0.0556 - 0.06}{0.011744} = -0.38$$

$$p\left(\frac{0.0278 - 0.06}{0.011744} \angle z \angle \frac{0.0556 - 0.06}{0.011744}\right) = p\left(-2.74 \angle z \angle -0.38\right) = 0.4969 - 0.1480 = 0.3489$$

# KEY TERMS

**Average** a number that describes the central tendency of the data; there are a number of specialized averages, including the arithmetic mean, weighted mean, median, mode, and geometric mean.

**Central Limit Theorem** Given a random variable with known mean $\mu$ and known standard deviation, $\sigma$, we are sampling with size $n$, and we are interested in two new RVs: the sample mean, $\overline{X}$ . If the size ($n$) of the sample is sufficiently large, then $\overline{X} \sim N(\mu, \frac{\sigma}{\sqrt{n}})$. If the size ($n$) of the sample is sufficiently large, then the distribution of the sample means will approximate a normal distributions regardless of the shape of the population. The mean of the sample means will equal the population mean. The standard deviation of the distribution of the sample means, $\frac{\sigma}{\sqrt{n}}$, is called the standard error of the mean.

**Finite Population Correction Factor** adjusts the variance of the sampling distribution if the population is known and more than 5% of the population is being sampled.

**Mean** a number that measures the central tendency; a common name for mean is "average." The term "mean" is a shortened form of "arithmetic mean." By definition, the mean for a sample (denoted by $\overline{x}$ ) is

$$\overline{x} = \frac{\text{Sum of all values in the sample}}{\text{Number of values in the sample}},$$ and the mean for a population (denoted by $\mu$) is

$$\mu = \frac{\text{Sum of all values in the population}}{\text{Number of values in the population}}.$$

**Normal Distribution**

a continuous random variable with pdf $f(x) = \frac{1}{\sigma\sqrt{2\pi}} \, e^{\frac{-(x-\mu)^2}{2\sigma^2}}$ , where $\mu$ is the mean of the distribution and $\sigma$ is the standard deviation.; notation: $X \sim N(\mu, \sigma)$. If $\mu = 0$ and $\sigma = 1$, the random variable, Z, is called the **standard normal distribution**.

**Sampling Distribution** Given simple random samples of size $n$ from a given population with a measured characteristic such as mean, proportion, or standard deviation for each sample, the probability distribution of all the measured characteristics is called a sampling distribution.

**Standard Error of the Mean** the standard deviation of the distribution of the sample means, or $\frac{\sigma}{\sqrt{n}}$ .

**Standard Error of the Proportion** the standard deviation of the sampling distribution of proportions

# CHAPTER REVIEW

## 7.1 The Central Limit Theorem for Sample Means

In a population whose distribution may be known or unknown, if the size ($n$) of samples is sufficiently large, the distribution of the sample means will be approximately normal. The mean of the sample means will equal the population mean. The standard deviation of the distribution of the sample means, called the standard error of the mean, is equal to the population standard deviation divided by the square root of the sample size ($n$).

## 7.2 Using the Central Limit Theorem

The Central Limit Theorem can be used to illustrate the law of large numbers. The law of large numbers states that the larger the sample size you take from a population, the closer the sample mean $\overline{x}$ gets to $\mu$.

## 7.3 The Central Limit Theorem for Proportions

The Central Limit Theorem can also be used to illustrate that the sampling distribution of sample proportions is normally distributed with the expected value of p and a standard deviation of $\sigma_{p'} = \sqrt{\frac{p(1-p)}{n}}$

# FORMULA REVIEW

## 7.1 The Central Limit Theorem for Sample Means

The Central Limit Theorem for Sample Means:

$$\bar{X} \sim N\left(\mu_{\bar{x}}, \frac{\sigma}{\sqrt{n}}\right)$$

$$Z = \frac{\bar{X} - \mu_{\bar{X}}}{\sigma_{\bar{X}}} = \frac{\bar{X} - \mu}{\sigma/\sqrt{n}}$$

The Mean $\bar{X}$ : $\mu_{\bar{x}}$

Central Limit Theorem for Sample Means z-score

$$z = \frac{\bar{x} - \mu_{\bar{x}}}{\left(\frac{\sigma}{\sqrt{n}}\right)}$$

Standard Error of the Mean (Standard Deviation ($\bar{X}$)):

$$\frac{\sigma}{\sqrt{n}}$$

Finite Population Correction Factor for the sampling distribution of means: $Z = \dfrac{x - \mu}{\frac{\sigma}{\sqrt{n}} * \sqrt{\frac{N-n}{N-1}}}$

Finite Population Correction Factor for the sampling distribution of proportions: $\sigma_{p'} = \sqrt{\frac{p(1-p)}{n}} \times \sqrt{\frac{N-n}{N-1}}$

# PRACTICE

## 7.2 Using the Central Limit Theorem

*Use the following information to answer the next ten exercises:* A manufacturer produces 25-pound lifting weights. The lowest actual weight is 24 pounds, and the highest is 26 pounds. Each weight is equally likely so the distribution of weights is uniform. A sample of 100 weights is taken.

**1.**
   a. What is the distribution for the weights of one 25-pound lifting weight? What is the mean and standard deivation?
   b. What is the distribution for the mean weight of 100 25-pound lifting weights?
   c. Find the probability that the mean actual weight for the 100 weights is less than 24.9.

**2.** Draw the graph from **Exercise 7.1**

**3.** Find the probability that the mean actual weight for the 100 weights is greater than 25.2.

**4.** Draw the graph from **Exercise 7.3**

**5.** Find the 90$^{th}$ percentile for the mean weight for the 100 weights.

**6.** Draw the graph from **Exercise 7.5**

**7.**
   a. What is the distribution for the sum of the weights of 100 25-pound lifting weights?
   b. Find $P(\Sigma x < 2{,}450)$.

**8.** Draw the graph from **Exercise 7.7**

**9.** Find the 90$^{th}$ percentile for the total weight of the 100 weights.

**10.** Draw the graph from **Exercise 7.9**

*Use the following information to answer the next five exercises:* The length of time a particular smartphone's battery lasts follows an exponential distribution with a mean of ten months. A sample of 64 of these smartphones is taken.

**11.**
   a. What is the standard deviation?
   b. What is the parameter $m$?

**12.** What is the distribution for the length of time one battery lasts?

**13.** What is the distribution for the mean length of time 64 batteries last?

**14.** What is the distribution for the total length of time 64 batteries last?

**15.** Find the probability that the sample mean is between seven and 11.

**16.** Find the $80^{th}$ percentile for the total length of time 64 batteries last.

**17.** Find the *IQR* for the mean amount of time 64 batteries last.

**18.** Find the middle 80% for the total amount of time 64 batteries last.

*Use the following information to answer the next eight exercises:* A uniform distribution has a minimum of six and a maximum of ten. A sample of 50 is taken.

**19.** Find $P(\Sigma x > 420)$.

**20.** Find the $90^{th}$ percentile for the sums.

**21.** Find the $15^{th}$ percentile for the sums.

**22.** Find the first quartile for the sums.

**23.** Find the third quartile for the sums.

**24.** Find the $80^{th}$ percentile for the sums.

# HOMEWORK

## 7.1 The Central Limit Theorem for Sample Means

**25.** Previously, De Anza statistics students estimated that the amount of change daytime statistics students carry is exponentially distributed with a mean of $0.88. Suppose that we randomly pick 25 daytime statistics students.
  a.  In words, $X =$ _____
  b.  $X \sim$ _____(_____,_____)
  c.  In words, $\bar{X} =$ _____
  d.  $\bar{X} \sim$ _____ (_____, _____)
  e.  Find the probability that an individual had between $0.80 and $1.00. Graph the situation, and shade in the area to be determined.
  f.  Find the probability that the average of the 25 students was between $0.80 and $1.00. Graph the situation, and shade in the area to be determined.
  g.  Explain why there is a difference in part e and part f.

**26.** Suppose that the distance of fly balls hit to the outfield (in baseball) is normally distributed with a mean of 250 feet and a standard deviation of 50 feet. We randomly sample 49 fly balls.
  a.  If $\bar{X}$ = average distance in feet for 49 fly balls, then $\bar{X} \sim$ _____(_____,_____)
  b.  What is the probability that the 49 balls traveled an average of less than 240 feet? Sketch the graph. Scale the horizontal axis for $\bar{X}$. Shade the region corresponding to the probability. Find the probability.
  c.  Find the $80^{th}$ percentile of the distribution of the average of 49 fly balls.

**27.** According to the Internal Revenue Service, the average length of time for an individual to complete (keep records for, learn, prepare, copy, assemble, and send) IRS Form 1040 is 10.53 hours (without any attached schedules). The distribution is unknown. Let us assume that the standard deviation is two hours. Suppose we randomly sample 36 taxpayers.

    a.  In words, $X$ = _____

    b.  In words, $\overline{X}$ = _____

    c.  $\overline{X}$ ~ _____(_____,_____)

    d.  Would you be surprised if the 36 taxpayers finished their Form 1040s in an average of more than 12 hours? Explain why or why not in complete sentences.

    e.  Would you be surprised if one taxpayer finished his or her Form 1040 in more than 12 hours? In a complete sentence, explain why.

**28.** Suppose that a category of world-class runners are known to run a marathon (26 miles) in an average of 145 minutes with a standard deviation of 14 minutes. Consider 49 of the races. Let $\overline{X}$ the average of the 49 races.

    a.  $\overline{X}$ ~ _____(_____,_____)

    b.  Find the probability that the runner will average between 142 and 146 minutes in these 49 marathons.

    c.  Find the $80^{th}$ percentile for the average of these 49 marathons.

    d.  Find the median of the average running times.

**29.** The length of songs in a collector's iTunes album collection is uniformly distributed from two to 3.5 minutes. Suppose we randomly pick five albums from the collection. There are a total of 43 songs on the five albums.

    a.  In words, $X$ = _____

    b.  $X$ ~ _____

    c.  In words, $\overline{X}$ = _____

    d.  $\overline{X}$ ~ _____(_____,_____)

    e.  Find the first quartile for the average song length.

    f.  The IQR(interquartile range) for the average song length is from _____–_____.

**30.** In 1940 the average size of a U.S. farm was 174 acres. Let's say that the standard deviation was 55 acres. Suppose we randomly survey 38 farmers from 1940.

    a.  In words, $X$ = _____

    b.  In words, $\overline{X}$ = _____

    c.  $\overline{X}$ ~ _____(_____,_____)

    d.  The IQR for $\overline{X}$ is from _____ acres to _____ acres.

**31.** Determine which of the following are true and which are false. Then, in complete sentences, justify your answers.

    a.  When the sample size is large, the mean of $\overline{X}$ is approximately equal to the mean of $X$.

    b.  When the sample size is large, $\overline{X}$ is approximately normally distributed.

    c.  When the sample size is large, the standard deviation of $\overline{X}$ is approximately the same as the standard deviation of $X$.

**32.** The percent of fat calories that a person in America consumes each day is normally distributed with a mean of about 36 and a standard deviation of about ten. Suppose that 16 individuals are randomly chosen. Let $\overline{X}$ = average percent of fat calories.

    a.  $\overline{X}$ ~ _____(_____, _____)

    b.  For the group of 16, find the probability that the average percent of fat calories consumed is more than five. Graph the situation and shade in the area to be determined.

    c.  Find the first quartile for the average percent of fat calories.

**33.** The distribution of income in some Third World countries is considered wedge shaped (many very poor people, very few middle income people, and even fewer wealthy people). Suppose we pick a country with a wedge shaped distribution. Let the average salary be $2,000 per year with a standard deviation of $8,000. We randomly survey 1,000 residents of that country.

    a. In words, $X =$ _____

    b. In words, $\bar{X} =$ _____

    c. $\bar{X} \sim$ _____(_____,_____)

    d. How is it possible for the standard deviation to be greater than the average?

    e. Why is it more likely that the average of the 1,000 residents will be from $2,000 to $2,100 than from $2,100 to $2,200?

**34.** Which of the following is NOT TRUE about the distribution for averages?

    a. The mean, median, and mode are equal.

    b. The area under the curve is one.

    c. The curve never touches the $x$-axis.

    d. The curve is skewed to the right.

**35.** The cost of unleaded gasoline in the Bay Area once followed an unknown distribution with a mean of $4.59 and a standard deviation of $0.10. Sixteen gas stations from the Bay Area are randomly chosen. We are interested in the average cost of gasoline for the 16 gas stations. The distribution to use for the average cost of gasoline for the 16 gas stations is:

    a. $\bar{X} \sim N(4.59, 0.10)$

    b. $\bar{X} \sim N\left(4.59, \dfrac{0.10}{\sqrt{16}}\right)$

    c. $\bar{X} \sim N\left(4.59, \dfrac{16}{0.10}\right)$

    d. $\bar{X} \sim N\left(4.59, \dfrac{\sqrt{16}}{0.10}\right)$

# REFERENCES

## 7.1 The Central Limit Theorem for Sample Means

Baran, Daya. "20 Percent of Americans Have Never Used Email."WebGuild, 2010. Available online at http://www.webguild.org/20080519/20-percent-of-americans-have-never-used-email (accessed May 17, 2013).

Data from The Flurry Blog, 2013. Available online at http://blog.flurry.com (accessed May 17, 2013).

Data from the United States Department of Agriculture.

# SOLUTIONS

**1**

    a. $U(24, 26)$, 25, 0.5774

    b. $N(25, 0.0577)$

    c. 0.0416

**3** 0.0003

**5** 25.07

**7**

    a. $N(2,500, 5.7735)$

    b. 0

**9** 2,507.40

**11**
  a.  10

  b.  $\frac{1}{10}$

**13** $N\left(10, \frac{10}{8}\right)$

**15** 0.7799

**17** 1.69

**19** 0.0072

**21** 391.54

**23** 405.51

**25**
  a.  $X$ = amount of change students carry

  b.  $X \sim E(0.88, 0.88)$

  c.  $\bar{X}$ = average amount of change carried by a sample of 25 students.

  d.  $\bar{X} \sim N(0.88, 0.176)$

  e.  0.0819

  f.  0.1882

  g.  The distributions are different. Part a is exponential and part b is normal.

**27**
  a.  length of time for an individual to complete IRS form 1040, in hours.

  b.  mean length of time for a sample of 36 taxpayers to complete IRS form 1040, in hours.

  c.  $N\left(10.53, \frac{1}{3}\right)$

  d.  Yes. I would be surprised, because the probability is almost 0.

  e.  No. I would not be totally surprised because the probability is 0.2312

**29**
  a.  the length of a song, in minutes, in the collection

  b.  $U(2, 3.5)$

  c.  the average length, in minutes, of the songs from a sample of five albums from the collection

  d.  $N(2.75, 0.066)$

  e.  2.74 minutes

  f.  0.03 minutes

**31**
  a.  True. The mean of a sampling distribution of the means is approximately the mean of the data distribution.

  b.  True. According to the Central Limit Theorem, the larger the sample, the closer the sampling distribution of the means becomes normal.

  c.  The standard deviation of the sampling distribution of the means will decrease making it approximately the same as the standard deviation of X as the sample size increases.

**33**

a.  $X$ = the yearly income of someone in a third world country

b.  the average salary from samples of 1,000 residents of a third world country

c.  $\bar{X} \sim N\left(2000, \frac{8000}{\sqrt{1000}}\right)$

d.  Very wide differences in data values can have averages smaller than standard deviations.

e.  The distribution of the sample mean will have higher probabilities closer to the population mean.
   $P(2000 < \bar{X} < 2100) = 0.1537$
   $P(2100 < \bar{X} < 2200) = 0.1317$

**35** b

# 8 | CONFIDENCE INTERVALS

**Figure 8.1** Have you ever wondered what the average number of M&Ms in a bag at the grocery store is? You can use confidence intervals to answer this question. (credit: comedy_nose/flickr)

## Introduction

Suppose you were trying to determine the mean rent of a two-bedroom apartment in your town. You might look in the classified section of the newspaper, write down several rents listed, and average them together. You would have obtained a point estimate of the true mean. If you are trying to determine the percentage of times you make a basket when shooting a basketball, you might count the number of shots you make and divide that by the number of shots you attempted. In this case, you would have obtained a point estimate for the true proportion the parameter p in the binomial probability density function.

We use sample data to make generalizations about an unknown population. This part of statistics is called **inferential statistics**. **The sample data help us to make an estimate of a population parameter**. We realize that the point estimate is most likely not the exact value of the population parameter, but close to it. After calculating point estimates, we construct interval estimates, called confidence intervals. What statistics provides us beyond a simple average, or point estimate, is an estimate to which we can attach a probability of accuracy, what we will call a confidence level. We make inferences with a known level of probability.

In this chapter, you will learn to construct and interpret confidence intervals. You will also learn a new distribution, the Student's-t, and how it is used with these intervals. Throughout the chapter, it is important to keep in mind that the confidence interval is a random variable. It is the population parameter that is fixed.

If you worked in the marketing department of an entertainment company, you might be interested in the mean number of songs a consumer downloads a month from iTunes. If so, you could conduct a survey and calculate the sample mean, $\bar{x}$ , and the sample standard deviation, $s$. You would use $\bar{x}$ to estimate the population mean and $s$ to estimate the population standard deviation. The sample mean, $\bar{x}$ , is the **point estimate** for the population mean, $\mu$. The sample standard deviation, $s$, is the point estimate for the population standard deviation, $\sigma$.

$\bar{x}$ and $s$ are each called a statistic.

A **confidence interval** is another type of estimate but, instead of being just one number, it is an interval of numbers. The interval of numbers is a range of values calculated from a given set of sample data. The confidence interval is likely to include the unknown population parameter.

Suppose, for the iTunes example, we do not know the population mean $\mu$, but we do know that the population standard deviation is $\sigma = 1$ and our sample size is 100. Then, by the central limit theorem, the standard deviation of the sampling distribution of the sample means is

$$\frac{\sigma}{\sqrt{n}} = \frac{1}{\sqrt{100}} = 0.1 \, .$$

The **empirical rule**, which applies to the normal distribution, says that in approximately 95% of the samples, the sample mean, $\bar{x}$ , will be within two standard deviations of the population mean $\mu$. For our iTunes example, two standard deviations is $(2)(0.1) = 0.2$. The sample mean $\bar{x}$ is likely to be within 0.2 units of $\mu$.

Because $\bar{x}$ is within 0.2 units of $\mu$, which is unknown, then $\mu$ is likely to be within 0.2 units of $\bar{x}$ with 95% probability. The population mean $\mu$ is contained in an interval whose lower number is calculated by taking the sample mean and subtracting two standard deviations $(2)(0.1)$ and whose upper number is calculated by taking the sample mean and adding two standard deviations. In other words, $\mu$ is between $\bar{x} - 0.2$ and $\bar{x} + 0.2$ in 95% of all the samples.

For the iTunes example, suppose that a sample produced a sample mean $\bar{x} = 2$ . Then with 95% probability the unknown population mean $\mu$ is between

$$\bar{x} - 0.2 = 2 - 0.2 = 1.8 \text{ and } \bar{x} + 0.2 = 2 + 0.2 = 2.2$$

We say that we are **95% confident** that the unknown population mean number of songs downloaded from iTunes per month is between 1.8 and 2.2. **The 95% confidence interval is (1.8, 2.2).** Please note that we talked in terms of 95% confidence using the empirical rule. The empirical rule for two standard deviations is only approximately 95% of the probability under the normal distribution. To be precise, two standard deviations under a normal distribution is actually 95.44% of the probability. To calculate the exact 95% confidence level we would use 1.96 standard deviations.

The 95% confidence interval implies two possibilities. Either the interval (1.8, 2.2) contains the true mean $\mu$, or our sample produced an $\bar{x}$ that is not within 0.2 units of the true mean $\mu$. The second possibility happens for only 5% of all the samples (95% minus 100% = 5%).

Remember that a confidence interval is created for an unknown population parameter like the population mean, $\mu$.

For the confidence interval for a mean the formula would be:

$$\mu = \bar{X} \pm Z_\alpha \frac{\sigma}{\sqrt{n}}$$

Or written another way as:

$$\bar{X} - Z_\alpha \frac{\sigma}{\sqrt{n}} \leq \mu \leq \bar{X} + Z_\alpha \frac{\sigma}{\sqrt{n}}$$

Where $\bar{X}$ is the sample mean. $Z_\alpha$ is determined by the level of confidence desired by the analyst, and $\frac{\sigma}{\sqrt{n}}$ is the standard deviation of the sampling distribution for means given to us by the Central Limit Theorem.

# 8.1 | A Confidence Interval for a Population Standard Deviation, Known or Large Sample Size

A confidence interval for a population mean with a known population standard deviation is based on the conclusion of the Central Limit Theorem that the sampling distribution of the sample means follow an approximately normal distribution.

## Calculating the Confidence Interval

Consider the standardizing formula for the sampling distribution developed in the discussion of the Central Limit Theorem:

$$Z_1 = \frac{\bar{X} - \mu_{\bar{X}}}{\sigma_{\bar{X}}} = \frac{\bar{X} - \mu}{\frac{\sigma}{\sqrt{n}}}$$

Notice that $\mu$ is substituted for $\mu_{\bar{x}}$ because we know that the expected value of $\mu_{\bar{x}}$ is $\mu$ from the Central Limit theorem and $\sigma_{\bar{x}}$ is replaced with $\frac{\sigma}{\sqrt{n}}$, also from the Central Limit Theorem.

In this formula we know $\bar{X}$, $\sigma_{\bar{x}}$ and n, the sample size. (In actuality we do not know the population standard deviation, but we do have a point estimate for it, s, from the sample we took. More on this later.) What we do not know is $\mu$ or $Z_1$. We can solve for either one of these in terms of the other. Solving for $\mu$ in terms of $Z_1$ gives:

$$\mu = \bar{X} \pm Z_1 \frac{\sigma}{\sqrt{n}}$$

Remembering that the Central Limit Theorem tells us that the distribution of the $\bar{X}$'s, the sampling distribution for means, is normal, and that the normal distribution is symmetrical, we can rearrange terms thus:

$$\bar{X} - Z_\alpha \left(\frac{\sigma}{\sqrt{n}}\right) \leq \mu \leq \bar{X} + Z_\alpha \left(\frac{\sigma}{\sqrt{n}}\right)$$

This is the formula for a confidence interval for the mean of a population.

Notice that $Z_\alpha$ has been substituted for $Z_1$ in this equation. This is where a choice must be made by the statistician. The analyst must decide the level of confidence they wish to impose on the confidence interval. $\alpha$ is the probability that the interval will not contain the true population mean. The confidence level is defined as $(1-\alpha)$. $Z_\alpha$ is the number of standard deviations $\bar{X}$ lies from the mean with a certain probability. If we chose $Z_\alpha = 1.96$ we are asking for the 95% confidence interval because we are setting the probability that the true mean lies within the range at 0.95. If we set $Z_\alpha$ at 1.64 we are asking for the 90% confidence interval because we have set the probability at 0.90. These numbers can be verified by consulting the Standard Normal table. Divide either 0.95 or 0.90 in half and find that probability inside the body of the table. Then read on the top and left margins the number of standard deviations it takes to get this level of probability.

In reality, we can set whatever level of confidence we desire simply by changing the $Z_\alpha$ value in the formula. It is the analyst's choice. Common convention in Economics and most social sciences sets confidence intervals at either 90, 95, or 99 percent levels. Levels less than 90% are considered of little value. The level of confidence of a particular interval estimate is called by $(1-\alpha)$.

A good way to see the development of a confidence interval is to graphically depict the solution to a problem requesting a confidence interval. This is presented in **Figure 8.2** for the example in the introduction concerning the number of downloads from iTunes. That case was for a 95% confidence interval, but other levels of confidence could have just as easily been chosen depending on the need of the analyst. However, the level of confidence MUST be pre-set and not subject to revision as a result of the calculations.

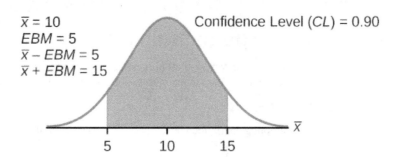

Figure 8.2

For this example, let's say we know that the actual population mean number of iTunes downloads is 2.1. The true population mean falls within the range of the 95% confidence interval. There is absolutely nothing to guarantee that this will happen. **Further, if the true mean falls outside of the interval we will never know it. We must always remember that we will never ever know the true mean.** Statistics simply allows us, with a given level of probability (confidence), to say that the true mean is within the range calculated. This is what was called in the introduction, the "level of ignorance admitted".

## Changing the Confidence Level or Sample Size

Here again is the formula for a confidence interval for an unknown population mean assuming we know the population standard deviation:

$$\dot{X} - Z_\alpha\left(\frac{\sigma}{\sqrt{n}}\right) \leq \mu \leq \dot{X} + Z_\alpha\left(\frac{\sigma}{\sqrt{n}}\right)$$

It is clear that the confidence interval is driven by two things, the chosen level of confidence, $Z_\alpha$, and the standard deviation of the sampling distribution. The Standard deviation of the sampling distribution is further affected by two things, the standard deviation of the population and the sample size we chose for our data. Here we wish to examine the effects of each of the choices we have made on the calculated confidence interval, the confidence level and the sample size.

For a moment we should ask just what we desire in a confidence interval. Our goal was to estimate the population mean from a sample. We have forsaken the hope that we will ever find the true population mean, and population standard deviation for that matter, for any case except where we have an extremely small population and the cost of gathering the data of interest is very small. In all other cases we must rely on samples. With the Central Limit Theorem we have the tools to provide a meaningful confidence interval with a given level of confidence, meaning a known probability of being wrong. By meaningful confidence interval we mean one that is useful. Imagine that you are asked for a confidence interval for the ages of your classmates. You have taken a sample and find a mean of 19.8 years. You wish to be very confident so you report an interval between 9.8 years and 29.8 years. This interval would certainly contain the true population mean and have a very high confidence level. However, it hardly qualifies as meaningful. The very best confidence interval is narrow while having high confidence. There is a natural tension between these two goals. The higher the level of confidence the wider the confidence interval as the case of the students' ages above. We can see this tension in the equation for the confidence interval.

$$\mu = \bar{x} \pm Z_\alpha\left(\frac{\sigma}{\sqrt{n}}\right)$$

The confidence interval will increase in width as $Z\alpha$ increases, $Z\alpha$ increases as the level of confidence increases. There is a tradeoff between the level of confidence and the width of the interval. Now let's look at the formula again and we see that the sample size also plays an important role in the width of the confidence interval. The sample sized, $n$, shows up in the denominator of the standard deviation of the sampling distribution. As the sample size increases, the standard deviation of the sampling distribution decreases and thus the width of the confidence interval, while holding constant the level of confidence. This relationship was demonstrated in Figure 7.80. Again we see the importance of having large samples for our analysis although we then face a second constraint, the cost of gathering data.

## Calculating the Confidence Interval: An Alternative Approach

Another way to approach confidence intervals is through the use of something called the Error Bound. The Error Bound gets its name from the recognition that it provides the boundary of the interval derived from the standard error of the sampling distribution. In the equations above it is seen that the interval is simply the estimated mean, sample mean, plus or minus something. That something is the Error Bound and is driven by the probability we desire to maintain in our estimate, $Z_\alpha$, times the standard deviation of the sampling distribution. The Error Bound for a mean is given the name, **Error Bound Mean**, or *EBM*.

To construct a confidence interval for a single unknown population mean $\mu$, **where the population standard deviation is known**, we need $\bar{x}$ as an estimate for $\mu$ and we need the margin of error. Here, the margin of error (*EBM*) is called the error bound for a population mean (abbreviated **EBM**). The sample mean $\bar{x}$ is the **point estimate** of the unknown population mean $\mu$.

**The confidence interval estimate will have the form:**

(point estimate - error bound, point estimate + error bound) or, in symbols,( $\bar{x} - EBM,\ \bar{x} + EBM$ )

The mathematical formula for this confidence interval is:

$$\bar{X} - Z_\alpha\left(\frac{\sigma}{\sqrt{n}}\right) \le \mu \le \bar{X} + Z_\alpha\left(\frac{\sigma}{\sqrt{n}}\right)$$

The margin of error (*EBM*) depends on the **confidence level** (abbreviated **CL**). The confidence level is often considered the probability that the calculated confidence interval estimate will contain the true population parameter. However, it is more accurate to state that the confidence level is the percent of confidence intervals that contain the true population parameter when repeated samples are taken. Most often, it is the choice of the person constructing the confidence interval to choose a confidence level of 90% or higher because that person wants to be reasonably certain of his or her conclusions.

There is another probability called alpha ($\alpha$). $\alpha$ is related to the confidence level, *CL*. $\alpha$ is the probability that the interval does not contain the unknown population parameter.
Mathematically, $1 - \alpha = CL$.

A confidence interval for a population mean with a **known** standard deviation is based on the fact that the sampling distribution of the sample means follow an approximately normal distribution. Suppose that our sample has a mean of $\bar{x}$ = 10, and we have constructed the 90% confidence interval (5, 15) where *EBM* = 5.

To get a 90% confidence interval, we must include the central 90% of the probability of the normal distribution. If we include the central 90%, we leave out a total of $\alpha$ = 10% in both tails, or 5% in each tail, of the normal distribution.

This is a normal distribution curve. The peak of the curve coincides with the point 10 on the horizontal axis. The points 5 and 15 are labeled on the axis. Vertical lines are drawn from these points to the curve, and the region between the lines is shaded. The shaded region has area equal to 0.90.

Figure 8.3

To capture the central 90%, we must go out 1.645 standard deviations on either side of the calculated sample mean. The value 1.645 is the *z*-score from a standard normal probability distribution that puts an area of 0.90 in the center, an area of 0.05 in the far left tail, and an area of 0.05 in the far right tail.

It is important that the standard deviation used must be appropriate for the parameter we are estimating, so in this section we need to use the standard deviation that applies to the sampling distribution for means which we studied with the Central Limit Theorem and is, $\frac{\sigma}{\sqrt{n}}$.

## Calculating the Confidence Interval Using EMB

To construct a confidence interval estimate for an unknown population mean, we need data from a random sample. The steps to construct and interpret the confidence interval are:

- Calculate the sample mean $\bar{x}$ from the sample data. Remember, in this section we know the population standard deviation $\sigma$.
- Find the *z*-score from the standard normal table that corresponds to the confidence level desired.
- Calculate the error bound *EBM*.
- Construct the confidence interval.
- Write a sentence that interprets the estimate in the context of the situation in the problem.

We will first examine each step in more detail, and then illustrate the process with some examples.

### Finding the *z*-score for the Stated Confidence Level

When we know the population standard deviation $\sigma$, we use a standard normal distribution to calculate the error bound EBM and construct the confidence interval. We need to find the value of $z$ that puts an area equal to the confidence level (in decimal form) in the middle of the standard normal distribution $Z \sim N(0, 1)$.

The confidence level, *CL*, is the area in the middle of the standard normal distribution. $CL = 1 - \alpha$, so $\alpha$ is the area that is split equally between the two tails. Each of the tails contains an area equal to $\frac{\alpha}{2}$.

The z-score that has an area to the right of $\frac{\alpha}{2}$ is denoted by $Z_{\frac{\alpha}{2}}$.

For example, when $CL = 0.95$, $\alpha = 0.05$ and $\frac{\alpha}{2} = 0.025$; we write $Z_{\frac{\alpha}{2}} = Z_{0.025}$.

The area to the right of $Z_{0.025}$ is 0.025 and the area to the left of $Z_{0.025}$ is $1 - 0.025 = 0.975$.

$Z_{\frac{\alpha}{2}} = Z_{0.025} = 1.96$, using a standard normal probability table. We will see later that we can use a different probability table, the Student's t-distribution, for finding the number of standard deviations of commonly used levels of confidence.

### Calculating the Error Bound (*EBM*)

The error bound formula for an unknown population mean $\mu$ when the population standard deviation $\sigma$ is known is

- $EBM = \left(Z_{\frac{\alpha}{2}}\right)\left(\frac{\sigma}{\sqrt{n}}\right)$

### Constructing the Confidence Interval

- The confidence interval estimate has the format $(\bar{x} - EBM, \bar{x} + EBM)$ or the formula:

$$\bar{X} - Z_{\alpha}\left(\frac{\sigma}{\sqrt{n}}\right) \leq \mu \leq \bar{X} + Z_{\alpha}\left(\frac{\sigma}{\sqrt{n}}\right)$$

The graph gives a picture of the entire situation.

$CL + \frac{\alpha}{2} + \frac{\alpha}{2} = CL + \alpha = 1$.

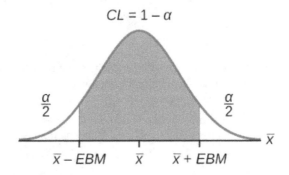

**Figure 8.4**

---

### Example 8.1

Suppose we are interested in the mean scores on an exam. A random sample of 36 scores is taken and gives a sample mean (sample mean score) of 68 ($\bar{X} = 68$). In this example we have the unusual knowledge that the population standard deviation is 3 points. Do not count on knowing the population parameters outside of textbook examples. Find a confidence interval estimate for the population mean exam score (the mean score on all exams).

Find a 90% confidence interval for the true (population) mean of statistics exam scores.

**Solution 8.1**
- The solution is shown step-by-step.

To find the confidence interval, you need the sample mean, $\bar{x}$, and the *EBM*.

$\bar{x} = 68$

$$EBM = \left(Z_{\frac{\alpha}{2}}\right)\left(\frac{\sigma}{\sqrt{n}}\right)$$

$\sigma = 3$; $n = 36$; The confidence level is 90% ($CL = 0.90$)

$CL = 0.90$ so $\alpha = 1 - CL = 1 - 0.90 = 0.10$

$\frac{\alpha}{2} = 0.05$   $Z_{\frac{\alpha}{2}} = z_{0.05}$

The area to the right of $Z_{0.05}$ is 0.05 and the area to the left of $Z_{0.05}$ is $1 - 0.05 = 0.95$.

$Z_{\frac{\alpha}{2}} = Z_{0.05} = 1.645$

This can be found using a computer, or using a probability table for the standard normal distribution. Because the common levels of confidence in the social sciences are 90%, 95% and 99% it will not be long until you become familiar with the numbers , 1.645, 1.96, and 2.56

$$EBM = (1.645)\left(\frac{3}{\sqrt{36}}\right) = 0.8225$$

$\bar{x} - EBM = 68 - 0.8225 = 67.1775$

$\bar{x} + EBM = 68 + 0.8225 = 68.8225$

The 90% confidence interval is **(67.1775, 68.8225).**

**Interpretation**

We estimate with 90% confidence that the true population mean exam score for all statistics students is between 67.18 and 68.82.

## Example 8.2

Suppose we change the original problem in **Example 8.1** by using a 95% confidence level. Find a 95% confidence interval for the true (population) mean statistics exam score.

**Solution 8.2**

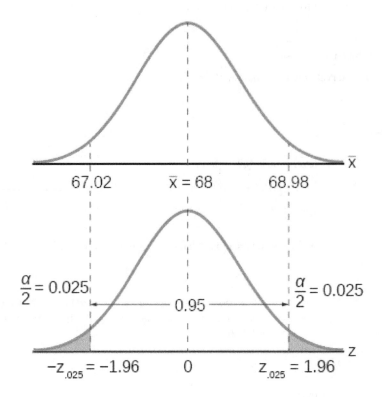

**Figure 8.5**

$$\mu = \bar{x} \pm Z_\alpha\left(\frac{\sigma}{\sqrt{n}}\right)$$

$$\mu = 68 \pm 1.96\left(\frac{3}{\sqrt{36}}\right)$$

$$67.02 \le \mu \le 68.98$$

$\sigma = 3$; $n = 36$; The confidence level is 95% ($CL = 0.95$).

$CL = 0.95$ so $\alpha = 1 - CL = 1 - 0.95 = 0.05$

$Z_{\frac{\alpha}{2}} = Z_{0.025} = 1.96$

Notice that the *EBM* is larger for a 95% confidence level in the original problem.

**Comparing the results**

The 90% confidence interval is (67.18, 68.82). The 95% confidence interval is (67.02, 68.98). The 95% confidence interval is wider. If you look at the graphs, because the area 0.95 is larger than the area 0.90, it makes sense that the 95% confidence interval is wider. To be more confident that the confidence interval actually does contain the true value of the population mean for all statistics exam scores, the confidence interval necessarily needs to be wider. This demonstrates a very important principle of confidence intervals. There is a trade off between the level of confidence and the width of the interval. Our desire is to have a narrow confidence interval, huge wide intervals provide little information that is useful. But we would also like to have a high level of confidence in our interval. This demonstrates that we cannot have both.

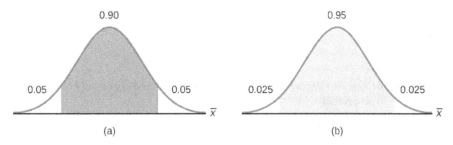

Figure 8.6

**Summary: Effect of Changing the Confidence Level**
- Increasing the confidence level makes the confidence interval wider.
- Decreasing the confidence level makes the confidence interval narrower.

And again here is the formula for a confidence interval for an unknown mean assuming we have the population standard deviation:

$$\bar{X} - Z_\alpha\left(\frac{\sigma}{\sqrt{n}}\right) \leq \mu \leq \bar{X} + Z_\alpha\left(\frac{\sigma}{\sqrt{n}}\right)$$

The standard deviation of the sampling distribution was provided by the Central Limit Theorem as $\frac{\sigma}{\sqrt{n}}$. While we infrequently get to choose the sample size it plays an important role in the confidence interval. Because the sample size is in the denominator of the equation, as $n$ increases it causes the standard deviation of the sampling distribution to idecrease and thus the width of the confidence interval to decrease. We have met this before as we reviewed the effects of sample size on the Central Limit Theorem. There we saw that as $n$ increases the sampling distribution narrows until in the limit it collapses on the true population mean.

## Example 8.3

Suppose we change the original problem in **Example 8.1** to see what happens to the confidence interval if the sample size is changed.

Leave everything the same except the sample size. Use the original 90% confidence level. What happens to the confidence interval if we increase the sample size and use $n$ = 100 instead of $n$ = 36? What happens if we decrease the sample size to $n$ = 25 instead of $n$ = 36?

Solution 8.3

**Solution A**

$$\mu = \bar{x} \pm Z_\alpha\left(\frac{\sigma}{\sqrt{n}}\right)$$

$$\mu = 68 \pm 1.645\left(\frac{3}{\sqrt{100}}\right)$$

$$67.5065 \leq \mu \leq 68.4935$$

If we **increase** the sample size $n$ to 100, we **decrease** the width of the confidence interval relative to the original sample size of 36 observations.

Solution 8.3

**Solution B**

$$\mu = \bar{x} \pm Z_\alpha\left(\frac{\sigma}{\sqrt{n}}\right)$$

$$\mu = 68 \pm 1.645\left(\frac{3}{\sqrt{25}}\right)$$

$$67.013 \le \mu \le 68.987$$

If we **decrease** the sample size $n$ to 25, we **increase** the width of the confidence interval by comparison to the original sample size of 36 observations.

Summary: Effect of Changing the Sample Size

- Increasing the sample size makes the confidence interval narrower.

- Decreasing the sample size makes the confidence interval wider.

We have already seen this effect when we reviewed the effects of changing the size of the sample, $n$, on the Central Limit Theorem. See **Figure 7.7** to see this effect. Before we saw that as the sample size increased the standard deviation of the sampling distribution decreases. This was why we choose the sample mean from a large sample as compared to a small sample, all other things held constant.

Thus far we assumed that we knew the population standard deviation. This will virtually never be the case. We will have the sample standard deviation, $s$, however. This is a point estimate for the population standard deviation and can be substituted into the formula for confidence intervals for a mean under certain circumstances. We just saw the effect the sample size has on the width of confidence interval and the impact on the sampling distribution for our discussion of the Central Limit Theorem. We can invoke this to substitute the point estimate for the standard deviation if the sample size is large "enough". Simulation studies indicate that 30 observations or more will be sufficient to eliminate any meaningful bias in the estimated confidence interval.

## Example 8.4

Spring break can be a very expensive holiday. A sample of 80 students is surveyed, and the average amount spent by students on travel and beverages is $593.84. The sample standard deviation is approximately $369.34.

Construct a 92% confidence interval for the population mean amount of money spent by spring breakers.

### Solution 8.4

We begin with the confidence interval for a mean. We use the formula for a mean because the random variable is dollars spent and this is a continuous random variable. The point estimate for the population standard deviation, $s$, has been substituted for the true population standard deviation because with 80 observations there is no concern for bias in the estimate of the confidence interval.

$$\mu = \bar{x} \pm \left[Z_{(\alpha/2)}\frac{s}{\sqrt{n}}\right]$$

Substituting the values into the formula, we have:

$$\mu = 593.84 \pm \left[1.75\frac{369.34}{\sqrt{80}}\right]$$

$Z_{(\alpha/2)}$ is found on the standard normal table by looking up 0.46 in the body of the table and finding the number of standard deviations on the side and top of the table; 1.75. The solution for the interval is thus:

$$\mu = 593.84 \pm 72.2636 = (521.57,\ 666.10)$$

$$\$\ 521.58 \le \mu \le \$\ 666.10$$

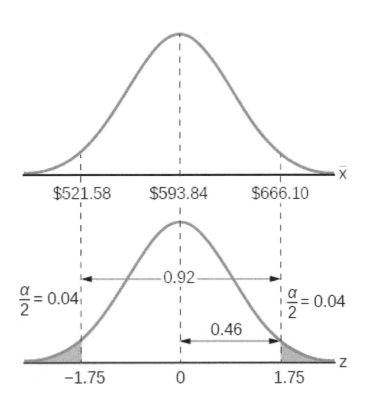

Figure 8.7

## Formula Review

The general form for a confidence interval for a single population mean, known standard deviation, normal distribution is given by $\bar{X} - Z_\alpha\left(\frac{\sigma}{\sqrt{n}}\right) \leq \mu \leq \bar{X} + Z_\alpha\left(\frac{\sigma}{\sqrt{n}}\right)$ This formula is used when the population standard deviation is known.

$CL$ = confidence level, or the proportion of confidence intervals created that are expected to contain the true population parameter

$\alpha = 1 - CL$ = the proportion of confidence intervals that will not contain the population parameter

$z_{\frac{\alpha}{2}}$ = the z-score with the property that the area to the right of the z-score is $\frac{\alpha}{2}$ this is the z-score used in the calculation of "EBM where $\alpha = 1 - CL$.

# 8.2 | A Confidence Interval for a Population Standard Deviation Unknown, Small Sample Case

In practice, we rarely know the population **standard deviation**. In the past, when the sample size was large, this did not present a problem to statisticians. They used the sample standard deviation $s$ as an estimate for $\sigma$ and proceeded as before to calculate a **confidence interval** with close enough results. This is what we did in **Example 8.4** above. The point estimate for the standard deviation, s, was substituted in the formula for the confidence interval for the population standard deviation. In this case there 80 observation well above the suggested 30 observations to eliminate any bias from a small sample. However, statisticians ran into problems when the sample size was small. A small sample size caused inaccuracies in the confidence interval.

William S. Goset (1876–1937) of the Guinness brewery in Dublin, Ireland ran into this problem. His experiments with hops and barley produced very few samples. Just replacing $\sigma$ with $s$ did not produce accurate results when he tried to calculate a confidence interval. He realized that he could not use a normal distribution for the calculation; he found that the actual distribution depends on the sample size. This problem led him to "discover" what is called the **Student's t-distribution**.

The name comes from the fact that Gosset wrote under the pen name "A Student."

Up until the mid-1970s, some statisticians used the **normal distribution** approximation for large sample sizes and used the Student's t-distribution only for sample sizes of at most 30 observations.

If you draw a simple random sample of size $n$ from a population with mean $\mu$ and unknown population standard deviation $\sigma$ and calculate the $t$-score $t = \dfrac{\bar{x} - \mu}{\left(\frac{s}{\sqrt{n}}\right)}$, then the $t$-scores follow a **Student's t-distribution with $n - 1$ degrees of freedom**.

The $t$-score has the same interpretation as the **$z$-score**. It measures how far in standard deviation units $\bar{x}$ is from its mean $\mu$. For each sample size $n$, there is a different Student's t-distribution.

The **degrees of freedom, $n - 1$**, come from the calculation of the sample standard deviation $s$. Remember when we first calculated a sample standard deviation we divided the sum of the squared deviations by $n - 1$, but we used $n$ deviations ($x - \bar{x}$ values) to calculate $s$. Because the sum of the deviations is zero, we can find the last deviation once we know the other $n - 1$ deviations. The other $n - 1$ deviations can change or vary freely. **We call the number $n - 1$ the degrees of freedom (df)** in recognition that one is lost in the calculations. The effect of losing a degree of freedom is that the t-value increases and the confidence interval increases in width.

## Properties of the Student's t-Distribution

- The graph for the Student's t-distribution is similar to the standard normal curve and at infinite degrees of freedom it is the normal distribution. You can confirm this by reading the bottom line at infinite degrees of freedom for a familiar level of confidence, e.g. at column 0.05, 95% level of confidence, we find the t-value of 1.96 at infinite degrees of freedom.

- The mean for the Student's t-distribution is zero and the distribution is symmetric about zero, again like the standard normal distribution.

- The Student's t-distribution has more probability in its tails than the standard normal distribution because the spread of the t-distribution is greater than the spread of the standard normal. So the graph of the Student's t-distribution will be thicker in the tails and shorter in the center than the graph of the standard normal distribution.

- The exact shape of the Student's t-distribution depends on the degrees of freedom. As the degrees of freedom increases, the graph of Student's t-distribution becomes more like the graph of the standard normal distribution.

- The underlying population of individual observations is assumed to be normally distributed with unknown population mean $\mu$ and unknown population standard deviation $\sigma$. This assumption comes from the Central Limit theorem because the individual observations in this case are the $\bar{x}$ s of the sampling distribution. The size of the underlying population is generally not relevant unless it is very small. If it is normal then the assumption is met and doesn't need discussion.

A probability table for the Student's t-distribution is used to calculate t-values at various commonly-used levels of confidence. The table gives t-scores that correspond to the confidence level (column) and degrees of freedom (row). When using a $t$-table, note that some tables are formatted to show the confidence level in the column headings, while the column headings in some tables may show only corresponding area in one or both tails. Notice that at the bottom the table will show the t-value for infinite degrees of freedom. Mathematically, as the degrees of freedom increase, the t distribution approaches the standard normal distribution. You can find familiar Z-values by looking in the relevant alpha column and reading value in the last row.

A Student's t table (See Appendix A) gives $t$-scores given the degrees of freedom and the right-tailed probability.

The Student's t distribution has one of the most desirable properties of the normal: it is symmetrical. What the Student's t distribution does is spread out the horizontal axis so it takes a larger number of standard deviations to capture the same amount of probability. In reality there are an infinite number of Student's t distributions, one for each adjustment to the sample size. As the sample size increases, the Student's t distribution become more and more like the normal distribution. When the sample size reaches 30 the normal distribution is usually substituted for the Student's t because they are so much alike. This relationship between the Student's t distribution and the normal distribution is shown in Figure 8.8.

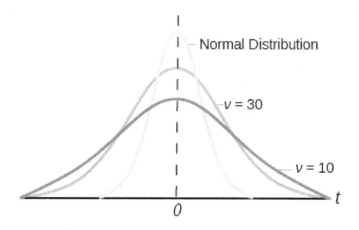

**Figure 8.8**

This is another example of one distribution limiting another one, in this case the normal distribution is the limiting distribution of the Student's t when the degrees of freedom in the Student's t approaches infinity. This conclusion comes directly from the [1]derivation of the Student's t distribution by Mr. Gosset. He recognized the problem as having few observations and no estimate of the population standard deviation. He was substituting the sample standard deviation and getting volatile results. He therefore created the Student's t distribution as a ratio of the normal distribution and Chi squared distribution. The Chi squared distribution is itself a ratio of two variances, in this case the sample variance and the unknown population variance. The Student's t distribution thus is tied to the normal distribution, but has degrees of freedom that come from those of the Chi squared distribution. The algebraic solution demonstrates this result.

Development of Student's t-distribution:

1. $t = \dfrac{z}{\sqrt{\dfrac{\chi^2}{v}}}$

    Where $Z$ is the standard normal distribution and $\chi^2$ is the chi-squared distribution with $v$ degrees of freedom.

2. $t = \dfrac{\dfrac{\left(\bar{x} - \mu\right)}{\sigma}}{\sqrt{\dfrac{\dfrac{s^2}{(n-1)}}{\dfrac{\sigma^2}{(n-1)}}}}$

    by substitution, and thus Student's t with $v = n - 1$ degrees of freedom is:

3. $t = \dfrac{\bar{x} - \mu}{\dfrac{s}{\sqrt{n}}}$

Restating the formula for a confidence interval for the mean for cases when the sample size is smaller than 30 and we do not know the population standard deviation, σ:

$$\bar{x} - t_{v,\alpha}\left(\dfrac{s}{\sqrt{n}}\right) \le \mu \le \bar{x} + t_{v,\alpha}\left(\dfrac{s}{\sqrt{n}}\right)$$

Here the point estimate of the population standard deviation, s has been substituted for the population standard deviation, σ, and $t_{v,\alpha}$ has been substituted for $Z_{\alpha}$. The Greek letter ν (pronounced nu) is placed in the general formula in recognition that there are many Student $t_v$ distributions, one for each sample size. ν is the symbol for the degrees of freedom of the distribution and depends on the size of the sample. Often df is used to abbreviate degrees of freedom. **For this type of problem,** the degrees of freedom is ν = n-1, where n is the sample size. To look up a probability in the Student's t table we have to know the degrees of freedom in the problem.

## Example 8.5

The average earnings per share (EPS) for 10 industrial stocks randomly selected from those listed on the Dow-Jones Industrial Average was found to be $\bar{X} = 1.85$ with a standard deviation of s=0.395. Calculate a 99% confidence interval for the average EPS of all the industrials listed on the DJIA.

$$\bar{x} - t_{v,\alpha}\left(\frac{s}{\sqrt{n}}\right) \leq \mu \leq \bar{x} + t_{v,\alpha}\left(\frac{s}{\sqrt{n}}\right)$$

### Solution 8.5

To help visualize the process of calculating a confident interval we draw the appropriate distribution for the problem. In this case this is the Student's t because we do not know the population standard deviation and the sample is small, less than 30.

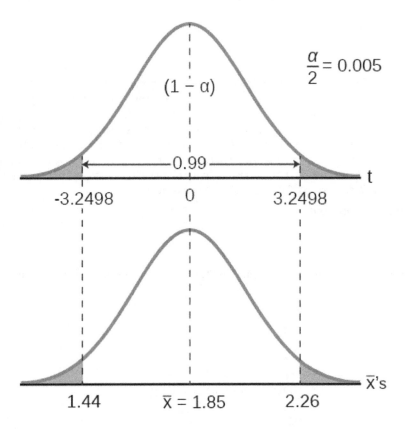

**Figure 8.9**

To find the appropriate t-value requires two pieces of information, the level of confidence desired and the degrees of freedom. The question asked for a 99% confidence level. On the graph this is shown where (1-α) , the level of confidence , is in the unshaded area. The tails, thus, have .005 probability each, α/2. The degrees of freedom for this type of problem is n-1= 9. From the Student's t table, at the row marked 9 and column marked .005, is the number of standard deviations to capture 99% of the probability, 3.2498. These are then placed on the graph remembering that the Student's t is symmetrical and so the t-value is both plus or minus on each side of the mean.

Inserting these values into the formula gives the result. These values can be placed on the graph to see the relationship between the distribution of the sample means, $\bar{X}$ 's and the Student's t distribution.

$$\mu = \bar{X} \pm t_{\alpha/2, df=n-1}\frac{s}{\sqrt{n}} = 1.851 \pm 3.2498\frac{0.395}{\sqrt{10}} = 1.8551 \pm 0.406$$

$$1.445 \leq \mu \leq 2.257$$

We state the formal conclusion as :

With 99% confidence level, the average EPS of all the industries listed at DJIA is from $1.44 to $2.26.

**8.5** You do a study of hypnotherapy to determine how effective it is in increasing the number of hours of sleep subjects get each night. You measure hours of sleep for 12 subjects with the following results. Construct a 95% confidence interval for the mean number of hours slept for the population (assumed normal) from which you took the data.

8.2; 9.1; 7.7; 8.6; 6.9; 11.2; 10.1; 9.9; 8.9; 9.2; 7.5; 10.5

# 8.3 | A Confidence Interval for A Population Proportion

During an election year, we see articles in the newspaper that state **confidence intervals** in terms of proportions or percentages. For example, a poll for a particular candidate running for president might show that the candidate has 40% of the vote within three percentage points (if the sample is large enough). Often, election polls are calculated with 95% confidence, so, the pollsters would be 95% confident that the true proportion of voters who favored the candidate would be between 0.37 and 0.43.

Investors in the stock market are interested in the true proportion of stocks that go up and down each week. Businesses that sell personal computers are interested in the proportion of households in the United States that own personal computers. Confidence intervals can be calculated for the true proportion of stocks that go up or down each week and for the true proportion of households in the United States that own personal computers.

The procedure to find the confidence interval for a population proportion is similar to that for the population mean, but the formulas are a bit different although conceptually identical. While the formulas are different, they are based upon the same mathematical foundation given to us by the Central Limit Theorem. Because of this we will see the same basic format using the same three pieces of information: the sample value of the parameter in question, the standard deviation of the relevant sampling distribution, and the number of standard deviations we need to have the confidence in our estimate that we desire.

**How do you know you are dealing with a proportion problem?** First, the underlying **distribution has a binary random variable and therefore is a binomial distribution**. (There is no mention of a mean or average.) If $X$ is a binomial random variable, then $X \sim B(n, p)$ where $n$ is the number of trials and $p$ is the probability of a success. To form a sample proportion, take $X$, the random variable for the number of successes and divide it by $n$, the number of trials (or the sample size). The random variable $P'$ (read "P prime") is the sample proportion,

$$P' = \frac{X}{n}$$

(Sometimes the random variable is denoted as $\overset{\wedge}{P}$, read "P hat".)

$p'$ = the **estimated proportion** of successes or sample proportion of successes ($p'$ is a **point estimate** for $p$, the true population proportion, and thus $q$ is the probability of a failure in any one trial.)

$x$ = the **number** of successes in the sample

$n$ = the size of the sample

The formula for the confidence interval for a population proportion follows the same format as that for an estimate of a population mean. Remembering the sampling distribution for the proportion from **Chapter 7**, the standard deviation was found to be:

$$\sigma_{p'} = \sqrt{\frac{p(1 - p)}{n}}$$

The confidence interval for a population proportion, therefore, becomes:

$$p = p' \pm \left[ Z_{\left(\frac{a}{2}\right)} \sqrt{\frac{p'(1 - p')}{n}} \right]$$

$Z_{\left(\frac{a}{2}\right)}$ is set according to our desired degree of confidence and $\sqrt{\dfrac{p'(1 - p')}{n}}$ is the standard deviation of the sampling distribution.

The **sample proportions $p'$ and $q'$ are estimates of the unknown population proportions $p$ and $q$**. The estimated proportions $p'$ and $q'$ are used because $p$ and $q$ are not known.

Remember that as $p$ moves further from 0.5 the binomial distribution becomes less symmetrical. Because we are estimating the binomial with the symmetrical normal distribution the further away from symmetrical the binomial becomes the less confidence we have in the estimate.

This conclusion can be demonstrated through the following analysis. Proportions are based upon the binomial probability distribution. The possible outcomes are binary, either "success" or "failure". This gives rise to a proportion, meaning the percentage of the outcomes that are "successes". It was shown that the binomial distribution could be fully understood if we knew only the probability of a success in any one trial, called p. The mean and the standard deviation of the binomial were found to be:

$$\mu = np$$

$$\sigma = \sqrt{npq}$$

It was also shown that the binomial could be estimated by the normal distribution if BOTH np AND nq were greater than 5. From the discussion above, it was found that the standardizing formula for the binomial distribution is:

$$Z = \frac{p' - p}{\sqrt{\left(\frac{pq}{n}\right)}}$$

which is nothing more than a restatement of the general standardizing formula with appropriate substitutions for $\mu$ and $\sigma$ from the binomial. We can use the standard normal distribution, the reason Z is in the equation, because the normal distribution is the limiting distribution of the binomial. This is another example of the Central Limit Theorem. We have already seen that the sampling distribution of means is normally distributed. Recall the extended discussion in Chapter 7 concerning the sampling distribution of proportions and the conclusions of the Central Limit Theorem.

We can now manipulate this formula in just the same way we did for finding the confidence intervals for a mean, but to find the confidence interval for the binomial population parameter, p.

$$p' - Z_\alpha \sqrt{\frac{p'q'}{n}} \leq p \leq p' + Z_\alpha \sqrt{\frac{p'q'}{n}}$$

Where $p' = x/n$, the point estimate of p taken from the sample. Notice that $p'$ has replaced p in the formula. This is because we do not know p, indeed, this is just what we are trying to estimate.

Unfortunately, there is no correction factor for cases where the sample size is small so $np'$ and $nq'$ must always be greater than 5 to develop an interval estimate for p.

## Example 8.6

Suppose that a market research firm is hired to estimate the percent of adults living in a large city who have cell phones. Five hundred randomly selected adult residents in this city are surveyed to determine whether they have cell phones. Of the 500 people sampled, 421 responded yes - they own cell phones. Using a 95% confidence level, compute a confidence interval estimate for the true proportion of adult residents of this city who have cell phones.

### Solution 8.6
- The solution step-by-step.

Let $X$ = the number of people in the sample who have cell phones. $X$ is binomial: the random variable is binary, people either have a cell phone or they do not.

To calculate the confidence interval, we must find $p', q'$.

$n = 500$

$x$ = the number of successes in the sample = 421

$$p' = \frac{x}{n} = \frac{421}{500} = 0.842$$

$p' = 0.842$ is the sample proportion; this is the point estimate of the population proportion.

$q' = 1 - p' = 1 - 0.842 = 0.158$

Since the requested confidence level is $CL = 0.95$, then $\alpha = 1 - CL = 1 - 0.95 = 0.05 \left(\frac{\alpha}{2}\right) = 0.025$.

Then $z_{\frac{\alpha}{2}} = z_{0.025} = 1.96$

This can be found using the Standard Normal probability table in **Appendix A**. This can also be found in the students t table at the 0.025 column and infinity degrees of freedom because at infinite degrees of freedom the students t distribution becomes the standard normal distribution, Z.

The confidence interval for the true binomial population proportion is

$$\text{p'} - Z_\alpha \sqrt{\frac{\text{p'q'}}{n}} \le p \le \text{p'} + Z_\alpha \sqrt{\frac{\text{p'q'}}{n}}$$

Substituting in the values from above we find he confidence inte val is : $0.810 \le p \le 0.874$

**Interpretation**

We estimate with 95% confidence that between 81% and 87.4% of all adult residents of this city have cell phones.

**Explanation of 95% Confidence Level**

Ninety-five percent of the confidence intervals constructed in this way would contain the true value for the population proportion of all adult residents of this city who have cell phones.

**Try It** Σ

**8.6** Suppose 250 randomly selected people are surveyed to determine if they own a tablet. Of the 250 surveyed, 98 reported owning a tablet. Using a 95% confidence level, compute a confidence interval estimate for the true proportion of people who own tablets.

## Example 8.7

The Dundee Dog Training School has a larger than average proportion of clients who compete in competitive professional events. A confidence interval for the population proportion of dogs that compete in professional events from 150 different training schools is constructed. The lower limit is determined to be 0.08 and the upper limit is determined to be 0.16. Determine the level of confidence used to construct the interval of the population proportion of dogs that compete in professional events.

### Solution 8.7

We begin with the formula for a confidence interval for a proportion because the random variable is binary; either the client competes in professional competitive dog events or they don't.

$$p = p' \pm \left[ Z_{\left(\frac{a}{2}\right)} \sqrt{\frac{p'(1 - p')}{n}} \right]$$

Next we find the sample proportion:

$$p' = \frac{0.08 + 0.16}{2} = 0.12$$

The ± that makes up the confidence interval is thus 0.04; 0.12 + 0.04 = 0.16 and 0.12 − 0.04 = 0.08, the boundaries of the confidence interval. Finally, we solve for $Z$.

$$\left[ Z \cdot \sqrt{\frac{0.12(1 - 0.12)}{150}} \right] = 0.04 \text{, } \textbf{\textit{therefore Z = 1.51}}$$

And then look up the probability for 1.51 standard deviations on the standard normal table.

$$p(Z = 1.51) = 0.4345 \text{, } p(Z) \cdot 2 = 0.8690 \textbf{ \textit{or}} \ 86.90 \ \% \ .$$

## Example 8.8

A financial officer for a company wants to estimate the percent of accounts receivable that are more than 30 days overdue. He surveys 500 accounts and finds that 300 are more than 30 days overdue. Compute a 90% confidence interval for the true percent of accounts receivable that are more than 30 days overdue, and interpret the confidence interval.

### Solution 8.8

- The solution is step-by-step:

$x = 300$ and $n = 500$

$$p' = \frac{x}{n} = \frac{300}{500} = 0.600$$

$$q' = 1 - p' = 1 - 0.600 = 0.400$$

Since confidence level = 0.90, then $\alpha = 1 - $ confidence level $= (1 - 0.90) = 0.10 \left(\frac{\alpha}{2}\right) = 0.05$

$$Z_{\frac{\alpha}{2}} = Z_{0.05} = 1.645$$

This Z-value can be found using a standard normal probability table. The student's t-table can also be used by entering the table at the 0.05 column and reading at the line for infinite degrees of freedom. The t-distribution is the normal distribution at infinite degrees of freedom. This is a handy trick to remember in finding Z-values for commonly used levels of confidence. We use this formula for a confidence interval for a proportion:

$$p' - Z_\alpha \sqrt{\frac{p'q'}{n}} \le p \le p' + Z_\alpha \sqrt{\frac{p'q'}{n}}$$

Substituting in the values from above we find the confidence interval for the true binomial population proportion is $0.564 \le p \le 0.636$

### Interpretation

- We estimate with 90% confidence that the true percent of all accounts receivable overdue 30 days is between 56.4% and 63.6%.

- Alternate Wording: We estimate with 90% confidence that between 56.4% and 63.6% of ALL accounts are overdue 30 days.

### Explanation of 90% Confidence Level

Ninety percent of all confidence intervals constructed in this way contain the true value for the population percent of accounts receivable that are overdue 30 days.

**8.8** A student polls his school to see if students in the school district are for or against the new legislation regarding school uniforms. She surveys 600 students and finds that 480 are against the new legislation.

a. Compute a 90% confidence interval for the true percent of students who are against the new legislation, and interpret the confidence interval.

b. In a sample of 300 students, 68% said they own an iPod and a smart phone. Compute a 97% confidence interval for the true percent of students who own an iPod and a smartphone.

# 8.4 | Calculating the Sample Size n: Continuous and

# Binary Random Variables

## Continuous Random Variables

Usually we have no control over the sample size of a data set. However, if we are able to set the sample size, as in cases where we are taking a survey, it is very helpful to know just how large it should be to provide the most information. Sampling can be very costly in both time and product. Simple telephone surveys will cost approximately $30.00 each, for example, and some sampling requires the destruction of the product.

If we go back to our standardizing formula for the sampling distribution for means, we can see that it is possible to solve it for n. If we do this we have $\left(\bar{X} - \mu\right)$ in the denominator.

$$n = \frac{Z_\alpha^2 \sigma^2}{\left(\bar{X} - \mu\right)^2} = \frac{Z_\alpha^2 \sigma^2}{e^2}$$

Because we have not taken a sample yet we do not know any of the variables in the formula except that we can set $Z_\alpha$ to the level of confidence we desire just as we did when determining confidence intervals. If we set a predetermined acceptable error, or tolerance, for the difference between $\bar{X}$ and μ, called e in the formula, we are much further in solving for the sample size n. We still do not know the population standard deviation, σ. In practice, a pre-survey is usually done which allows for fine tuning the questionnaire and will give a sample standard deviation that can be used. In other cases, previous information from other surveys may be used for σ in the formula. While crude, this method of determining the sample size may help in reducing cost significantly. It will be the actual data gathered that determines the inferences about the population, so caution in the sample size is appropriate calling for high levels of confidence and small sampling errors.

## Binary Random Variables

What was done in cases when looking for the mean of a distribution can also be done when sampling to determine the population parameter p for proportions. Manipulation of the standardizing formula for proportions gives:

$$n = \frac{Z_\alpha^2 pq}{e^2}$$

where e = (p'-p), and is the acceptable sampling error, or tolerance, for this application. This will be measured in percentage points.

In this case the very object of our search is in the formula, p, and of course q because q =1-p. This result occurs because the binomial distribution is a one parameter distribution. If we know p then we know the mean and the standard deviation. Therefore, p shows up in the standard deviation of the sampling distribution which is where we got this formula. If, in an abundance of caution, we substitute 0.5 for p we will draw the largest required sample size that will provide the level of confidence specified by $Z_\alpha$ and the tolerance we have selected. This is true because of all combinations of two fractions that add to one, the largest multiple is when each is 0.5. Without any other information concerning the population parameter p, this is the common practice. This may result in oversampling, but certainly not under sampling, thus, this is a cautious approach.

There is an interesting trade-off between the level of confidence and the sample size that shows up here when considering the cost of sampling. Table 8.1 shows the appropriate sample size at different levels of confidence and different level of the acceptable error, or tolerance.

| Required Sample Size (90%) | Required Sample Size (95%) | Tolerance Level |
|---|---|---|
| 1691 | 2401 | 2% |
| 752 | 1067 | 3% |
| 271 | 384 | 5% |
| 68 | 96 | 10% |

Table 8.1

This table is designed to show the maximum sample size required at different levels of confidence given an assumed p= 0.5

and q=0.5 as discussed above.

The acceptable error, called tolerance in the table, is measured in plus or minus values from the actual proportion. For example, an acceptable error of 5% means that if the sample proportion was found to be 26 percent, the conclusion would be that the actual population proportion is between 21 and 31 percent with a 90 percent level of confidence if a sample of 271 had been taken. Likewise, if the acceptable error was set at 2%, then the population proportion would be between 24 and 28 percent with a 90 percent level of confidence, but would require that the sample size be increased from 271 to 1,691. If we wished a higher level of confidence, we would require a larger sample size. Moving from a 90 percent level of confidence to a 95 percent level at a plus or minus 5% tolerance requires changing the sample size from 271 to 384. A very common sample size often seen reported in political surveys is 384. With the survey results it is frequently stated that the results are good to a plus or minus 5% level of "accuracy".

### Example 8.9

Suppose a mobile phone company wants to determine the current percentage of customers aged 50+ who use text messaging on their cell phones. How many customers aged 50+ should the company survey in order to be 90% confident that the estimated (sample) proportion is within three percentage points of the true population proportion of customers aged 50+ who use text messaging on their cell phones.

#### Solution 8.9

From the problem, we know that the acceptable error, $e$, is **0.03** (3%=0.03) and $z_{\frac{\alpha}{2}}$ $z_{0.05}$ = 1.645 because the confidence level is 90%. The acceptable error, $e$, is the difference between the actual population proportion $p$, and the sample proportion we expect to get from the sample.

However, in order to find $n$, we need to know the estimated (sample) proportion $p'$. Remember that $q' = 1 - p'$. But, we do not know $p'$ yet. Since we multiply $p'$ and $q'$ together, we make them both equal to 0.5 because $p'q' = (0.5)(0.5) = 0.25$ results in the largest possible product. (Try other products: $(0.6)(0.4) = 0.24$; $(0.3)(0.7) = 0.21$; $(0.2)(0.8) = 0.16$ and so on). The largest possible product gives us the largest $n$. This gives us a large enough sample so that we can be 90% confident that we are within three percentage points of the true population proportion. To calculate the sample size $n$, use the formula and make the substitutions.

$$n = \frac{z^2 p' q'}{e^2} \text{ gives } n = \frac{1.645^2(0.5)(0.5)}{0.03^2} = 751.7$$

Round the answer to the next higher value. The sample size should be 752 cell phone customers aged 50+ in order to be 90% confident that the estimated (sample) proportion is within three percentage points of the true population proportion of all customers aged 50+ who use text messaging on their cell phones.

**8.9** Suppose an internet marketing company wants to determine the current percentage of customers who click on ads on their smartphones. How many customers should the company survey in order to be 90% confident that the estimated proportion is within five percentage points of the true population proportion of customers who click on ads on their smartphones?

# KEY TERMS

**Binomial Distribution** a discrete random variable (RV) which arises from Bernoulli trials; there are a fixed number, $n$, of independent trials. "Independent" means that the result of any trial (for example, trial 1) does not affect the results of the following trials, and all trials are conducted under the same conditions. Under these circumstances the binomial RV $X$ is defined as the number of successes in $n$ trials. The notation is: $X \sim B(\mathbf{n}, \mathbf{p})$. The mean is $\mu = np$ and the standard deviation is $\sigma = \sqrt{npq}$. The probability of exactly $x$ successes in $n$ trials is $P(X = x) = \binom{n}{x} p^x q^{n-x}$.

.

**Confidence Interval (CI)** an interval estimate for an unknown population parameter. This depends on:

- the desired confidence level,
- information that is known about the distribution (for example, known standard deviation),
- the sample and its size.

**Confidence Level (CL)** the percent expression for the probability that the confidence interval contains the true population parameter; for example, if the CL = 90%, then in 90 out of 100 samples the interval estimate will enclose the true population parameter.

**Degrees of Freedom (*df*)** the number of objects in a sample that are free to vary

**Error Bound for a Population Mean (*EBM*)** the margin of error; depends on the confidence level, sample size, and known or estimated population standard deviation.

**Error Bound for a Population Proportion (EBP)** the margin of error; depends on the confidence level, the sample size, and the estimated (from the sample) proportion of successes.

**Inferential Statistics** also called statistical inference or inductive statistics; this facet of statistics deals with estimating a population parameter based on a sample statistic. For example, if four out of the 100 calculators sampled are defective we might infer that four percent of the production is defective.

**Normal Distribution**
a continuous random variable (RV) with pdf $f(x) = \frac{1}{\sigma\sqrt{2\pi}} e^{-(x-\mu)^2 / 2\sigma^2}$, where $\mu$ is the mean of the distribution and $\sigma$ is the standard deviation, notation: $X \sim N(\mu, \sigma)$. If $\mu = 0$ and $\sigma = 1$, the RV is called **the standard normal distribution**.

**Parameter** a numerical characteristic of a population

**Point Estimate** a single number computed from a sample and used to estimate a population parameter

**Standard Deviation** a number that is equal to the square root of the variance and measures how far data values are from their mean; notation: $s$ for sample standard deviation and $\sigma$ for population standard deviation

**Student's t-Distribution** investigated and reported by William S. Gossett in 1908 and published under the pseudonym Student; the major characteristics of this random variable (RV) are:

- It is continuous and assumes any real values.
- The pdf is symmetrical about its mean of zero.
- It approaches the standard normal distribution as $n$ get larger.
- There is a "family of t–distributions: each representative of the family is completely defined by the number of degrees of freedom, which depends upon the application for which the t is being used.

# CHAPTER REVIEW

## 8.2 A Confidence Interval for a Population Standard Deviation Unknown, Small Sample Case

In many cases, the researcher does not know the population standard deviation, $\sigma$, of the measure being studied. In these cases, it is common to use the sample standard deviation, *s*, as an estimate of σ. The normal distribution creates accurate confidence intervals when σ is known, but it is not as accurate when *s* is used as an estimate. In this case, the Student's t-distribution is much better. Define a t-score using the following formula:

$$t = \frac{\bar{x} - \mu}{\frac{s}{\sqrt{n}}}$$

The *t*-score follows the Student's t-distribution with $n - 1$ degrees of freedom. The confidence interval under this distribution is calculated with $\bar{x} \pm \left(t_{\frac{\alpha}{2}}\right)\frac{s}{\sqrt{n}}$ where $t_{\frac{\alpha}{2}}$ is the *t*-score with area to the right equal to $\frac{\alpha}{2}$, *s* is the sample standard deviation, and *n* is the sample size. Use a table, calculator, or computer to find $t_{\frac{\alpha}{2}}$ for a given α.

### 8.3 A Confidence Interval for A Population Proportion

Some statistical measures, like many survey questions, measure qualitative rather than quantitative data. In this case, the population parameter being estimated is a proportion. It is possible to create a confidence interval for the true population proportion following procedures similar to those used in creating confidence intervals for population means. The formulas are slightly different, but they follow the same reasoning.

Let $p'$ represent the sample proportion, $x/n$, where *x* represents the number of successes and *n* represents the sample size. Let $q' = 1 - p'$. Then the confidence interval for a population proportion is given by the following formula:

$$p' - Z_\alpha \sqrt{\frac{p'q'}{n}} \leq p \leq p' + Z_\alpha \sqrt{\frac{p'q'}{n}}$$

### 8.4 Calculating the Sample Size n: Continuous and Binary Random Variables

Sometimes researchers know in advance that they want to estimate a population mean within a specific margin of error for a given level of confidence. In that case, solve the relevant confidence interval formula for *n* to discover the size of the sample that is needed to achieve this goal:

$$n = \frac{Z_\alpha^2 \sigma^2}{(\bar{x} - \mu)^2}$$

If the random variable is binary then the formula for the appropriate sample size to maintain a particular level of confidence with a specific tolerance level is given by

$$n = \frac{Z_\alpha^2 pq}{e^2}$$

# FORMULA REVIEW

### 8.2 A Confidence Interval for a Population Standard Deviation Unknown, Small Sample Case

*s* = the standard deviation of sample values.

$t = \frac{\bar{x} - \mu}{\frac{s}{\sqrt{n}}}$ is the formula for the *t*-score which measures how far away a measure is from the population mean in the Student's t-distribution

$df = n - 1$; the degrees of freedom for a Student's t-distribution where n represents the size of the sample

$T \sim t_{df}$ the random variable, *T*, has a Student's t-distribution with *df* degrees of freedom

The general form for a confidence interval for a single mean, population standard deviation unknown, and sample size less than 30 Student's t is given by:

$$\bar{x} - t_{v,\alpha}\left(\frac{s}{\sqrt{n}}\right) \leq \mu \leq \bar{x} + t_{v,\alpha}\left(\frac{s}{\sqrt{n}}\right)$$

### 8.3 A Confidence Interval for A Population Proportion

$p' = \frac{x}{n}$ where *x* represents the number of successes in a sample and *n* represents the sample size. The variable $p'$ is the sample proportion and serves as the point estimate for the true population proportion.

$q' = 1 - p'$

The variable $p'$ has a binomial distribution that can be approximated with the normal distribution shown here. The confidence interval for the true population proportion is given by the formula:

$$p' - Z_\alpha \sqrt{\frac{p'q'}{n}} \le p \le p' + Z_\alpha \sqrt{\frac{p'q'}{n}}$$

$$n = \frac{Z_{\frac{\alpha}{2}}^2 p'q'}{e^2}$$ provides the number of observations

needed to sample to estimate the population proportion, $p$, with confidence $1 - \alpha$ and margin of error $e$. Where $e$ = the acceptable difference between the actual population proportion and the sample proportion.

## 8.4 Calculating the Sample Size n: Continuous and Binary Random Variables

$$n = \frac{Z^2\sigma^2}{(\bar{x} - \mu)^2}$$ = the formula used to determine the sample

size ($n$) needed to achieve a desired margin of error at a given level of confidence for a continuous random variable

$$n = \frac{Z_\alpha^2 pq}{e^2}$$ = the formula used to determine the sample

size if the random variable is binary

# PRACTICE

## 8.2 A Confidence Interval for a Population Standard Deviation Unknown, Small Sample Case

*Use the following information to answer the next five exercises.* A hospital is trying to cut down on emergency room wait times. It is interested in the amount of time patients must wait before being called back to be examined. An investigation committee randomly surveyed 70 patients. The sample mean was 1.5 hours with a sample standard deviation of 0.5 hours.

**1.** Identify the following:
   a.   $\bar{x} =$_____
   b.   $s_x =$_____
   c.   $n =$_____
   d.   $n-1 =$_____

**2.** Define the random variables $X$ and $\bar{X}$ in words.

**3.** Which distribution should you use for this problem?

**4.** Construct a 95% confidence interval for the population mean time spent waiting. State the confidence interval, sketch the graph, and calculate the error bound.

**5.** Explain in complete sentences what the confidence interval means.

*Use the following information to answer the next six exercises:* One hundred eight Americans were surveyed to determine the number of hours they spend watching television each month. It was revealed that they watched an average of 151 hours each month with a standard deviation of 32 hours. Assume that the underlying population distribution is normal.

**6.** Identify the following:
   a.   $\bar{x} =$_____
   b.   $s_x =$_____
   c.   $n =$_____
   d.   $n-1 =$_____

**7.** Define the random variable $X$ in words.

**8.** Define the random variable $\bar{X}$ in words.

**9.** Which distribution should you use for this problem?

**10.** Construct a 99% confidence interval for the population mean hours spent watching television per month. (a) State the confidence interval, (b) sketch the graph, and (c) calculate the error bound.

**11.** Why would the error bound change if the confidence level were lowered to 95%?

*Use the following information to answer the next 13 exercises:* The data in **Table 8.2** are the result of a random survey of 39 national flags (with replacement between picks) from various countries. We are interested in finding a confidence interval for the true mean number of colors on a national flag. Let $X$ = the number of colors on a national flag.

| X | Freq. |
|---|---|
| 1 | 1 |
| 2 | 7 |
| 3 | 18 |
| 4 | 7 |
| 5 | 6 |

Table 8.2

**12.** Calculate the following:
    a.  $\bar{x}$ =_____
    b.  $s_x$ =_____
    c.  $n$ =_____

**13.** Define the random variable $\bar{X}$ in words.

**14.** What is $\bar{x}$ estimating?

**15.** Is $\sigma_x$ known?

**16.** As a result of your answer to **Exercise 8.15**, state the exact distribution to use when calculating the confidence interval.

*Construct a 95% confidence interval for the true mean number of colors on national flags.*

**17.** How much area is in both tails (combined)?

**18.** How much area is in each tail?

**19.** Calculate the following:
    a.  lower limit
    b.  upper limit
    c.  error bound

**20.** The 95% confidence interval is_____.

**21.** Fill in the blanks on the graph with the areas, the upper and lower limits of the Confidence Interval and the sample mean.

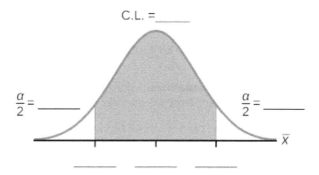

Figure 8.10

**22.** In one complete sentence, explain what the interval means.

**23.** Using the same $\bar{x}$, $s_x$, and level of confidence, suppose that $n$ were 69 instead of 39. Would the error bound become larger or smaller? How do you know?

**24.** Using the same $\bar{x}$, $s_x$, and $n = 39$, how would the error bound change if the confidence level were reduced to 90%? Why?

## 8.3 A Confidence Interval for A Population Proportion

*Use the following information to answer the next two exercises:* Marketing companies are interested in knowing the population percent of women who make the majority of household purchasing decisions.

**25.** When designing a study to determine this population proportion, what is the minimum number you would need to survey to be 90% confident that the population proportion is estimated to within 0.05?

**26.** If it were later determined that it was important to be more than 90% confident and a new survey were commissioned, how would it affect the minimum number you need to survey? Why?

*Use the following information to answer the next five exercises:* Suppose the marketing company did do a survey. They randomly surveyed 200 households and found that in 120 of them, the woman made the majority of the purchasing decisions. We are interested in the population proportion of households where women make the majority of the purchasing decisions.

**27.** Identify the following:
   a.  $x =$ _____
   b.  $n =$ _____
   c.  $p' =$ _____

**28.** Define the random variables $X$ and $P'$ in words.

**29.** Which distribution should you use for this problem?

**30.** Construct a 95% confidence interval for the population proportion of households where the women make the majority of the purchasing decisions. State the confidence interval, sketch the graph, and calculate the error bound.

**31.** List two difficulties the company might have in obtaining random results, if this survey were done by email.

*Use the following information to answer the next five exercises:* Of 1,050 randomly selected adults, 360 identified themselves as manual laborers, 280 identified themselves as non-manual wage earners, 250 identified themselves as mid-level managers, and 160 identified themselves as executives. In the survey, 82% of manual laborers preferred trucks, 62% of non-manual wage earners preferred trucks, 54% of mid-level managers preferred trucks, and 26% of executives preferred trucks.

**32.** We are interested in finding the 95% confidence interval for the percent of executives who prefer trucks. Define random variables $X$ and $P'$ in words.

**33.** Which distribution should you use for this problem?

**34.** Construct a 95% confidence interval. State the confidence interval, sketch the graph, and calculate the error bound.

**35.** Suppose we want to lower the sampling error. What is one way to accomplish that?

**36.** The sampling error given in the survey is ±2%. Explain what the ±2% means.

*Use the following information to answer the next five exercises:* A poll of 1,200 voters asked what the most significant issue was in the upcoming election. Sixty-five percent answered the economy. We are interested in the population proportion of voters who feel the economy is the most important.

**37.** Define the random variable $X$ in words.

**38.** Define the random variable $P'$ in words.

**39.** Which distribution should you use for this problem?

**40.** Construct a 90% confidence interval, and state the confidence interval and the error bound.

**41.** What would happen to the confidence interval if the level of confidence were 95%?

*Use the following information to answer the next 16 exercises:* The Ice Chalet offers dozens of different beginning ice-skating classes. All of the class names are put into a bucket. The 5 P.M., Monday night, ages 8 to 12, beginning ice-skating class was picked. In that class were 64 girls and 16 boys. Suppose that we are interested in the true proportion of girls, ages 8 to 12, in all beginning ice-skating classes at the Ice Chalet. Assume that the children in the selected class are a random sample of the population.

**42.** What is being counted?

**43.** In words, define the random variable $X$.

**44.** Calculate the following:
    a.  $x =$ _____
    b.  $n =$ _____
    c.  $p' =$ _____

**45.** State the estimated distribution of $X$. $X \sim$ _____

**46.** Define a new random variable $P'$. What is $p'$ estimating?

**47.** In words, define the random variable $P'$.

**48.** State the estimated distribution of $P'$. Construct a 92% Confidence Interval for the true proportion of girls in the ages 8 to 12 beginning ice-skating classes at the Ice Chalet.

**49.** How much area is in both tails (combined)?

**50.** How much area is in each tail?

**51.** Calculate the following:
    a.  lower limit
    b.  upper limit
    c.  error bound

**52.** The 92% confidence interval is _____.

**53.** Fill in the blanks on the graph with the areas, upper and lower limits of the confidence interval, and the sample proportion.

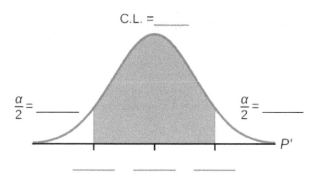

Figure 8.11

**54.** In one complete sentence, explain what the interval means.

**55.** Using the same $p'$ and level of confidence, suppose that $n$ were increased to 100. Would the error bound become larger or smaller? How do you know?

**56.** Using the same $p'$ and $n = 80$, how would the error bound change if the confidence level were increased to 98%? Why?

**57.** If you decreased the allowable error bound, why would the minimum sample size increase (keeping the same level of confidence)?

## 8.4 Calculating the Sample Size n: Continuous and Binary Random Variables

*Use the following information to answer the next five exercises:* The standard deviation of the weights of elephants is known to be approximately 15 pounds. We wish to construct a 95% confidence interval for the mean weight of newborn elephant calves. Fifty newborn elephants are weighed. The sample mean is 244 pounds. The sample standard deviation is 11 pounds.

**58.** Identify the following:
   a.   $\bar{x}$ = _____
   b.   $\sigma$ = _____
   c.   $n$ = _____

**59.** In words, define the random variables $X$ and $\bar{X}$ .

**60.** Which distribution should you use for this problem?

**61.** Construct a 95% confidence interval for the population mean weight of newborn elephants. State the confidence interval, sketch the graph, and calculate the error bound.

**62.** What will happen to the confidence interval obtained, if 500 newborn elephants are weighed instead of 50? Why?

*Use the following information to answer the next seven exercises:* The U.S. Census Bureau conducts a study to determine the time needed to complete the short form. The Bureau surveys 200 people. The sample mean is 8.2 minutes. There is a known standard deviation of 2.2 minutes. The population distribution is assumed to be normal.

**63.** Identify the following:
   a.   $\bar{x}$ = _____
   b.   $\sigma$ = _____
   c.   $n$ = _____

**64.** In words, define the random variables $X$ and $\bar{X}$ .

**65.** Which distribution should you use for this problem?

**66.** Construct a 90% confidence interval for the population mean time to complete the forms. State the confidence interval, sketch the graph, and calculate the error bound.

**67.** If the Census wants to increase its level of confidence and keep the error bound the same by taking another survey, what changes should it make?

**68.** If the Census did another survey, kept the error bound the same, and surveyed only 50 people instead of 200, what would happen to the level of confidence? Why?

**69.** Suppose the Census needed to be 98% confident of the population mean length of time. Would the Census have to survey more people? Why or why not?

*Use the following information to answer the next ten exercises:* A sample of 20 heads of lettuce was selected. Assume that the population distribution of head weight is normal. The weight of each head of lettuce was then recorded. The mean weight was 2.2 pounds with a standard deviation of 0.1 pounds. The population standard deviation is known to be 0.2 pounds.

**70.** Identify the following:
   a.   $\bar{x}$ = _____
   b.   $\sigma$ = _____
   c.   $n$ = _____

**71.** In words, define the random variable $X$.

**72.** In words, define the random variable $\bar{X}$ .

**73.** Which distribution should you use for this problem?

**74.** Construct a 90% confidence interval for the population mean weight of the heads of lettuce. State the confidence interval, sketch the graph, and calculate the error bound.

**75.** Construct a 95% confidence interval for the population mean weight of the heads of lettuce. State the confidence interval, sketch the graph, and calculate the error bound.

**76.** In complete sentences, explain why the confidence interval in Exercise 8.74 is larger than in Exercise 8.75.

**77.** In complete sentences, give an interpretation of what the interval in Exercise 8.75 means.

**78.** What would happen if 40 heads of lettuce were sampled instead of 20, and the error bound remained the same?

**79.** What would happen if 40 heads of lettuce were sampled instead of 20, and the confidence level remained the same?

*Use the following information to answer the next 14 exercises:* The mean age for all Foothill College students for a recent Fall term was 33.2. The population standard deviation has been pretty consistent at 15. Suppose that twenty-five Winter students were randomly selected. The mean age for the sample was 30.4. We are interested in the true mean age for Winter Foothill College students. Let $X$ = the age of a Winter Foothill College student.

**80.** $\bar{x}$ = _____

**81.** $n$ = _____

**82.** _____ = 15

**83.** In words, define the random variable $\bar{X}$.

**84.** What is $\bar{x}$ estimating?

**85.** Is $\sigma_x$ known?

**86.** As a result of your answer to **Exercise 8.83**, state the exact distribution to use when calculating the confidence interval.

*Construct a 95% Confidence Interval for the true mean age of Winter Foothill College students by working out then answering the next seven exercises.*

**87.** How much area is in both tails (combined)? $\alpha$ = _____

**88.** How much area is in each tail? $\frac{\alpha}{2}$ = _____

**89.** Identify the following specifications:
   a. lower limit
   b. upper limit
   c. error bound

**90.** The 95% confidence interval is: _____.

**91.** Fill in the blanks on the graph with the areas, upper and lower limits of the confidence interval, and the sample mean.

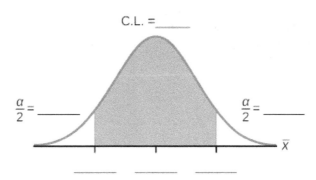

Figure 8.12

**92.** In one complete sentence, explain what the interval means.

**93.** Using the same mean, standard deviation, and level of confidence, suppose that $n$ were 69 instead of 25. Would the error bound become larger or smaller? How do you know?

**94.** Using the same mean, standard deviation, and sample size, how would the error bound change if the confidence level were reduced to 90%? Why?

# HOMEWORK

## 8.2 A Confidence Interval for a Population Standard Deviation Unknown, Small Sample Case

**95.** In six packages of "The Flintstones® Real Fruit Snacks" there were five Bam-Bam snack pieces. The total number of snack pieces in the six bags was 68. We wish to calculate a 96% confidence interval for the population proportion of Bam-Bam snack pieces.

    a.  Define the random variables $X$ and $P'$ in words.

    b.  Which distribution should you use for this problem? Explain your choice

    c.  Calculate $p'$.

    d.  Construct a 96% confidence interval for the population proportion of Bam-Bam snack pieces per bag.

        i.  State the confidence interval.

        ii.  Sketch the graph.

        iii.  Calculate the error bound.

    e.  Do you think that six packages of fruit snacks yield enough data to give accurate results? Why or why not?

**96.** A random survey of enrollment at 35 community colleges across the United States yielded the following figures: 6,414; 1,550; 2,109; 9,350; 21,828; 4,300; 5,944; 5,722; 2,825; 2,044; 5,481; 5,200; 5,853; 2,750; 10,012; 6,357; 27,000; 9,414; 7,681; 3,200; 17,500; 9,200; 7,380; 18,314; 6,557; 13,713; 17,768; 7,493; 2,771; 2,861; 1,263; 7,285; 28,165; 5,080; 11,622. Assume the underlying population is normal.

    a.

        i.  $\bar{x} = $ _____

        ii.  $s_x = $ _____

        iii.  $n = $ _____

        iv.  $n - 1 = $ _____

    b.  Define the random variables $X$ and $\bar{X}$ in words.

    c.  Which distribution should you use for this problem? Explain your choice.

    d.  Construct a 95% confidence interval for the population mean enrollment at community colleges in the United States.

        i.  State the confidence interval.

        ii.  Sketch the graph.

    e.  What will happen to the error bound and confidence interval if 500 community colleges were surveyed? Why?

**97.** Suppose that a committee is studying whether or not there is waste of time in our judicial system. It is interested in the mean amount of time individuals waste at the courthouse waiting to be called for jury duty. The committee randomly surveyed 81 people who recently served as jurors. The sample mean wait time was eight hours with a sample standard deviation of four hours.

    a.

        i.  $\bar{x} = $ _____

        ii.  $s_x = $ _____

        iii.  $n = $ _____

        iv.  $n - 1 = $ _____

    b.  Define the random variables $X$ and $\bar{X}$ in words.

    c.  Which distribution should you use for this problem? Explain your choice.

    d.  Construct a 95% confidence interval for the population mean time wasted.

        i.  State the confidence interval.

        ii.  Sketch the graph.

    e.  Explain in a complete sentence what the confidence interval means.

**98.** A pharmaceutical company makes tranquilizers. It is assumed that the distribution for the length of time they last is approximately normal. Researchers in a hospital used the drug on a random sample of nine patients. The effective period of the tranquilizer for each patient (in hours) was as follows: 2.7; 2.8; 3.0; 2.3; 2.3; 2.2; 2.8; 2.1; and 2.4.

    a.
        i.   $\bar{x}$ = _____
        ii.   $s_x$ = _____
        iii.   $n$ = _____
        iv.   $n - 1$ = _____

    b.  Define the random variable $X$ in words.

    c.  Define the random variable $\bar{X}$ in words.

    d.  Which distribution should you use for this problem? Explain your choice.

    e.  Construct a 95% confidence interval for the population mean length of time.

        i.  State the confidence interval.
        ii.  Sketch the graph.

    f.  What does it mean to be "95% confident" in this problem?

**99.** Suppose that 14 children, who were learning to ride two-wheel bikes, were surveyed to determine how long they had to use training wheels. It was revealed that they used them an average of six months with a sample standard deviation of three months. Assume that the underlying population distribution is normal.

    a.
        i.   $\bar{x}$ = _____
        ii.   $s_x$ = _____
        iii.   $n$ = _____
        iv.   $n - 1$ = _____

    b.  Define the random variable $X$ in words.

    c.  Define the random variable $\bar{X}$ in words.

    d.  Which distribution should you use for this problem? Explain your choice.

    e.  Construct a 99% confidence interval for the population mean length of time using training wheels.

        i.  State the confidence interval.
        ii.  Sketch the graph.

    f.  Why would the error bound change if the confidence level were lowered to 90%?

**100.** The Federal Election Commission (FEC) collects information about campaign contributions and disbursements for candidates and political committees each election cycle. A political action committee (PAC) is a committee formed to raise money for candidates and campaigns. A Leadership PAC is a PAC formed by a federal politician (senator or representative) to raise money to help other candidates' campaigns.

The FEC has reported financial information for 556 Leadership PACs that operating during the 2011–2012 election cycle. The following table shows the total receipts during this cycle for a random selection of 30 Leadership PACs.

| $46,500.00 | $0 | $40,966.50 | $105,887.20 | $5,175.00 |
|---|---|---|---|---|
| $29,050.00 | $19,500.00 | $181,557.20 | $31,500.00 | $149,970.80 |
| $2,555,363.20 | $12,025.00 | $409,000.00 | $60,521.70 | $18,000.00 |
| $61,810.20 | $76,530.80 | $119,459.20 | $0 | $63,520.00 |
| $6,500.00 | $502,578.00 | $705,061.10 | $708,258.90 | $135,810.00 |
| $2,000.00 | $2,000.00 | $0 | $1,287,933.80 | $219,148.30 |

Table 8.3

$\bar{x} = \$251,854.23$

$s = \$521,130.41$

Use this sample data to construct a 95% confidence interval for the mean amount of money raised by all Leadership PACs during the 2011–2012 election cycle. Use the Student's t-distribution.

**101.** *Forbes* magazine published data on the best small firms in 2012. These were firms that had been publicly traded for at least a year, have a stock price of at least $5 per share, and have reported annual revenue between $5 million and $1 billion. The Table 8.4 shows the ages of the corporate CEOs for a random sample of these firms.

| 48 | 58 | 51 | 61 | 56 |
|---|---|---|---|---|
| 59 | 74 | 63 | 53 | 50 |
| 59 | 60 | 60 | 57 | 46 |
| 55 | 63 | 57 | 47 | 55 |
| 57 | 43 | 61 | 62 | 49 |
| 67 | 67 | 55 | 55 | 49 |

Table 8.4

Use this sample data to construct a 90% confidence interval for the mean age of CEO's for these top small firms. Use the Student's t-distribution.

**102.** Unoccupied seats on flights cause airlines to lose revenue. Suppose a large airline wants to estimate its mean number of unoccupied seats per flight over the past year. To accomplish this, the records of 225 flights are randomly selected and the number of unoccupied seats is noted for each of the sampled flights. The sample mean is 11.6 seats and the sample standard deviation is 4.1 seats.

    a.

        i.   $\bar{x}$ = _____

        ii.   $s_X$ = _____

        iii.   $n$ = _____

        iv.   $n$-1 = _____

    b.   Define the random variables $X$ and $\bar{X}$ in words.

    c.   Which distribution should you use for this problem? Explain your choice.

    d.   Construct a 92% confidence interval for the population mean number of unoccupied seats per flight.

        i.   State the confidence interval.

        ii.   Sketch the graph.

**103.** In a recent sample of 84 used car sales costs, the sample mean was $6,425 with a standard deviation of $3,156. Assume the underlying distribution is approximately normal.

    a.   Which distribution should you use for this problem? Explain your choice.

    b.   Define the random variable $\bar{X}$ in words.

    c.   Construct a 95% confidence interval for the population mean cost of a used car.

        i.   State the confidence interval.

        ii.   Sketch the graph.

    d.   Explain what a "95% confidence interval" means for this study.

**104.** Six different national brands of chocolate chip cookies were randomly selected at the supermarket. The grams of fat per serving are as follows: 8; 8; 10; 7; 9; 9. Assume the underlying distribution is approximately normal.

    a.   Construct a 90% confidence interval for the population mean grams of fat per serving of chocolate chip cookies sold in supermarkets.

        i.   State the confidence interval.

        ii.   Sketch the graph.

    b.   If you wanted a smaller error bound while keeping the same level of confidence, what should have been changed in the study before it was done?

    c.   Go to the store and record the grams of fat per serving of six brands of chocolate chip cookies.

    d.   Calculate the mean.

    e.   Is the mean within the interval you calculated in part a? Did you expect it to be? Why or why not?

**105.** A survey of the mean number of cents off that coupons give was conducted by randomly surveying one coupon per page from the coupon sections of a recent San Jose Mercury News. The following data were collected: 20¢; 75¢; 50¢; 65¢; 30¢; 55¢; 40¢; 40¢; 30¢; 55¢; $1.50; 40¢; 65¢; 40¢. Assume the underlying distribution is approximately normal.

    a.

        i.   $\bar{x}$ = _____

        ii.   $s_X$ = _____

        iii.   $n$ = _____

        iv.   $n$-1 = _____

    b.   Define the random variables $X$ and $\bar{X}$ in words.

    c.   Which distribution should you use for this problem? Explain your choice.

    d.   Construct a 95% confidence interval for the population mean worth of coupons.

        i.   State the confidence interval.

        ii.   Sketch the graph.

    e.   If many random samples were taken of size 14, what percent of the confidence intervals constructed should contain the population mean worth of coupons? Explain why.

*Use the following information to answer the next two exercises:* A quality control specialist for a restaurant chain takes a random sample of size 12 to check the amount of soda served in the 16 oz. serving size. The sample mean is 13.30 with a sample standard deviation of 1.55. Assume the underlying population is normally distributed.

**106.** Find the 95% Confidence Interval for the true population mean for the amount of soda served.
  a. (12.42, 14.18)
  b. (12.32, 14.29)
  c. (12.50, 14.10)
  d. Impossible to determine

## 8.3 A Confidence Interval for A Population Proportion

**107.** Insurance companies are interested in knowing the population percent of drivers who always buckle up before riding in a car.
  a. When designing a study to determine this population proportion, what is the minimum number you would need to survey to be 95% confident that the population proportion is estimated to within 0.03?
  b. If it were later determined that it was important to be more than 95% confident and a new survey was commissioned, how would that affect the minimum number you would need to survey? Why?

**108.** Suppose that the insurance companies did do a survey. They randomly surveyed 400 drivers and found that 320 claimed they always buckle up. We are interested in the population proportion of drivers who claim they always buckle up.

  a.
      i.  $x =$ _____
      ii. $n =$ _____
      iii. $p' =$ _____
  b. Define the random variables $X$ and $P'$, in words.
  c. Which distribution should you use for this problem? Explain your choice.
  d. Construct a 95% confidence interval for the population proportion who claim they always buckle up.
      i.  State the confidence interval.
      ii. Sketch the graph.
  e. If this survey were done by telephone, list three difficulties the companies might have in obtaining random results.

**109.** According to a recent survey of 1,200 people, 61% feel that the president is doing an acceptable job. We are interested in the population proportion of people who feel the president is doing an acceptable job.
  a. Define the random variables $X$ and $P'$ in words.
  b. Which distribution should you use for this problem? Explain your choice.
  c. Construct a 90% confidence interval for the population proportion of people who feel the president is doing an acceptable job.
      i.  State the confidence interval.
      ii. Sketch the graph.

**110.** An article regarding interracial dating and marriage recently appeared in the *Washington Post*. Of the 1,709 randomly selected adults, 315 identified themselves as Latinos, 323 identified themselves as blacks, 254 identified themselves as Asians, and 779 identified themselves as whites. In this survey, 86% of blacks said that they would welcome a white person into their families. Among Asians, 77% would welcome a white person into their families, 71% would welcome a Latino, and 66% would welcome a black person.
  a. We are interested in finding the 95% confidence interval for the percent of all black adults who would welcome a white person into their families. Define the random variables $X$ and $P'$, in words.
  b. Which distribution should you use for this problem? Explain your choice.
  c. Construct a 95% confidence interval.
      i.  State the confidence interval.
      ii. Sketch the graph.

**111.** Refer to the information in **Exercise 8.110**.
  a. Construct three 95% confidence intervals.
      i.   percent of all Asians who would welcome a white person into their families.
      ii.  percent of all Asians who would welcome a Latino into their families.
      iii. percent of all Asians who would welcome a black person into their families.

  b. Even though the three point estimates are different, do any of the confidence intervals overlap? Which?
  c. For any intervals that do overlap, in words, what does this imply about the significance of the differences in the true proportions?
  d. For any intervals that do not overlap, in words, what does this imply about the significance of the differences in the true proportions?

**112.** Stanford University conducted a study of whether running is healthy for men and women over age 50. During the first eight years of the study, 1.5% of the 451 members of the 50-Plus Fitness Association died. We are interested in the proportion of people over 50 who ran and died in the same eight-year period.

    a. Define the random variables $X$ and $P'$ in words.

    b. Which distribution should you use for this problem? Explain your choice.

    c. Construct a 97% confidence interval for the population proportion of people over 50 who ran and died in the same eight–year period.

        i. State the confidence interval.

        ii. Sketch the graph.

    d. Explain what a "97% confidence interval" means for this study.

**113.** A telephone poll of 1,000 adult Americans was reported in an issue of *Time Magazine*. One of the questions asked was "What is the main problem facing the country?" Twenty percent answered "crime." We are interested in the population proportion of adult Americans who feel that crime is the main problem.

    a. Define the random variables $X$ and $P'$ in words.

    b. Which distribution should you use for this problem? Explain your choice.

    c. Construct a 95% confidence interval for the population proportion of adult Americans who feel that crime is the main problem.

        i. State the confidence interval.

        ii. Sketch the graph.

    d. Suppose we want to lower the sampling error. What is one way to accomplish that?

    e. The sampling error given by Yankelovich Partners, Inc. (which conducted the poll) is ±3%. In one to three complete sentences, explain what the ±3% represents.

**114.** Refer to Exercise 8.113. Another question in the poll was "[How much are] you worried about the quality of education in our schools?" Sixty-three percent responded "a lot". We are interested in the population proportion of adult Americans who are worried a lot about the quality of education in our schools.

    a. Define the random variables $X$ and $P'$ in words.

    b. Which distribution should you use for this problem? Explain your choice.

    c. Construct a 95% confidence interval for the population proportion of adult Americans who are worried a lot about the quality of education in our schools.

        i. State the confidence interval.

        ii. Sketch the graph.

    d. The sampling error given by Yankelovich Partners, Inc. (which conducted the poll) is ±3%. In one to three complete sentences, explain what the ±3% represents.

*Use the following information to answer the next three exercises:* According to a Field Poll, 79% of California adults (actual results are 400 out of 506 surveyed) feel that "education and our schools" is one of the top issues facing California. We wish to construct a 90% confidence interval for the true proportion of California adults who feel that education and the schools is one of the top issues facing California.

**115.** A point estimate for the true population proportion is:

    a. 0.90

    b. 1.27

    c. 0.79

    d. 400

**116.** A 90% confidence interval for the population proportion is _____.

    a. (0.761, 0.820)

    b. (0.125, 0.188)

    c. (0.755, 0.826)

    d. (0.130, 0.183)

*Use the following information to answer the next two exercises:* Five hundred and eleven (511) homes in a certain southern California community are randomly surveyed to determine if they meet minimal earthquake preparedness recommendations. One hundred seventy-three (173) of the homes surveyed met the minimum recommendations for earthquake preparedness, and 338 did not.

**117.** Find the confidence interval at the 90% Confidence Level for the true population proportion of southern California community homes meeting at least the minimum recommendations for earthquake preparedness.
   a. (0.2975, 0.3796)
   b. (0.6270, 0.6959)
   c. (0.3041, 0.3730)
   d. (0.6204, 0.7025)

**118.** The point estimate for the population proportion of homes that do not meet the minimum recommendations for earthquake preparedness is _____.
   a. 0.6614
   b. 0.3386
   c. 173
   d. 338

**119.** On May 23, 2013, Gallup reported that of the 1,005 people surveyed, 76% of U.S. workers believe that they will continue working past retirement age. The confidence level for this study was reported at 95% with a ±3% margin of error.

   a. Determine the estimated proportion from the sample.
   b. Determine the sample size.
   c. Identify *CL* and $\alpha$.
   d. Calculate the error bound based on the information provided.
   e. Compare the error bound in part d to the margin of error reported by Gallup. Explain any differences between the values.
   f. Create a confidence interval for the results of this study.
   g. A reporter is covering the release of this study for a local news station. How should she explain the confidence interval to her audience?

**120.** A national survey of 1,000 adults was conducted on May 13, 2013 by Rasmussen Reports. It concluded with 95% confidence that 49% to 55% of Americans believe that big-time college sports programs corrupt the process of higher education.
   a. Find the point estimate and the error bound for this confidence interval.
   b. Can we (with 95% confidence) conclude that more than half of all American adults believe this?
   c. Use the point estimate from part a and *n* = 1,000 to calculate a 75% confidence interval for the proportion of American adults that believe that major college sports programs corrupt higher education.
   d. Can we (with 75% confidence) conclude that at least half of all American adults believe this?

**121.** Public Policy Polling recently conducted a survey asking adults across the U.S. about music preferences. When asked, 80 of the 571 participants admitted that they have illegally downloaded music.
   a. Create a 99% confidence interval for the true proportion of American adults who have illegally downloaded music.
   b. This survey was conducted through automated telephone interviews on May 6 and 7, 2013. The error bound of the survey compensates for sampling error, or natural variability among samples. List some factors that could affect the survey's outcome that are not covered by the margin of error.
   c. Without performing any calculations, describe how the confidence interval would change if the confidence level changed from 99% to 90%.

**122.** You plan to conduct a survey on your college campus to learn about the political awareness of students. You want to estimate the true proportion of college students on your campus who voted in the 2012 presidential election with 95% confidence and a margin of error no greater than five percent. How many students must you interview?

## 8.4 Calculating the Sample Size n: Continuous and Binary Random Variables

**123.** Among various ethnic groups, the standard deviation of heights is known to be approximately three inches. We wish to construct a 95% confidence interval for the mean height of male Swedes. Forty-eight male Swedes are surveyed. The sample mean is 71 inches. The sample standard deviation is 2.8 inches.

    a.

        i.  $\bar{x} =$_____

        ii.  $\sigma =$_____

        iii.  $n =$_____

    b.  In words, define the random variables $X$ and $\bar{X}$.

    c.  Which distribution should you use for this problem? Explain your choice.

    d.  Construct a 95% confidence interval for the population mean height of male Swedes.

        i.  State the confidence interval.

        ii.  Sketch the graph.

    e.  What will happen to the level of confidence obtained if 1,000 male Swedes are surveyed instead of 48? Why?

**124.** Announcements for 84 upcoming engineering conferences were randomly picked from a stack of IEEE Spectrum magazines. The mean length of the conferences was 3.94 days, with a standard deviation of 1.28 days. Assume the underlying population is normal.

    a.  In words, define the random variables $X$ and $\bar{X}$.

    b.  Which distribution should you use for this problem? Explain your choice.

    c.  Construct a 95% confidence interval for the population mean length of engineering conferences.

        i.  State the confidence interval.

        ii.  Sketch the graph.

**125.** Suppose that an accounting firm does a study to determine the time needed to complete one person's tax forms. It randomly surveys 100 people. The sample mean is 23.6 hours. There is a known standard deviation of 7.0 hours. The population distribution is assumed to be normal.

    a.

        i.  $\bar{x} =$_____

        ii.  $\sigma =$_____

        iii.  $n =$_____

    b.  In words, define the random variables $X$ and $\bar{X}$.

    c.  Which distribution should you use for this problem? Explain your choice.

    d.  Construct a 90% confidence interval for the population mean time to complete the tax forms.

        i.  State the confidence interval.

        ii.  Sketch the graph.

    e.  If the firm wished to increase its level of confidence and keep the error bound the same by taking another survey, what changes should it make?

    f.  If the firm did another survey, kept the error bound the same, and only surveyed 49 people, what would happen to the level of confidence? Why?

    g.  Suppose that the firm decided that it needed to be at least 96% confident of the population mean length of time to within one hour. How would the number of people the firm surveys change? Why?

**126.** A sample of 16 small bags of the same brand of candies was selected. Assume that the population distribution of bag weights is normal. The weight of each bag was then recorded. The mean weight was two ounces with a standard deviation of 0.12 ounces. The population standard deviation is known to be 0.1 ounce.

    a.
        i.  $\bar{x}$ =_____
        ii.  $\sigma$ =_____
        iii.  $s_x$ =_____

    b.  In words, define the random variable $X$.
    c.  In words, define the random variable $\bar{X}$.
    d.  Which distribution should you use for this problem? Explain your choice.
    e.  Construct a 90% confidence interval for the population mean weight of the candies.
        i.  State the confidence interval.
        ii.  Sketch the graph.
    f.  Construct a 98% confidence interval for the population mean weight of the candies.
        i.  State the confidence interval.
        ii.  Sketch the graph.
        iii.  Calculate the error bound.
    g.  In complete sentences, explain why the confidence interval in part f is larger than the confidence interval in part e.
    h.  In complete sentences, give an interpretation of what the interval in part f means.

**127.** A camp director is interested in the mean number of letters each child sends during his or her camp session. The population standard deviation is known to be 2.5. A survey of 20 campers is taken. The mean from the sample is 7.9 with a sample standard deviation of 2.8.

    a.
        i.  $\bar{x}$ =_____
        ii.  $\sigma$ =_____
        iii.  $n$ =_____

    b.  Define the random variables $X$ and $\bar{X}$ in words.
    c.  Which distribution should you use for this problem? Explain your choice.
    d.  Construct a 90% confidence interval for the population mean number of letters campers send home.
        i.  State the confidence interval.
        ii.  Sketch the graph.
    e.  What will happen to the error bound and confidence interval if 500 campers are surveyed? Why?

**128.** What is meant by the term "90% confident" when constructing a confidence interval for a mean?
    a.  If we took repeated samples, approximately 90% of the samples would produce the same confidence interval.
    b.  If we took repeated samples, approximately 90% of the confidence intervals calculated from those samples would contain the sample mean.
    c.  If we took repeated samples, approximately 90% of the confidence intervals calculated from those samples would contain the true value of the population mean.
    d.  If we took repeated samples, the sample mean would equal the population mean in approximately 90% of the samples.

**129.** The Federal Election Commission collects information about campaign contributions and disbursements for candidates and political committees each election cycle. During the 2012 campaign season, there were 1,619 candidates for the House of Representatives across the United States who received contributions from individuals. **Table 8.5** shows the total receipts from individuals for a random selection of 40 House candidates rounded to the nearest $100. The standard deviation for this data to the nearest hundred is $\sigma$ = $909,200.

| | | | | |
|---|---|---|---|---|
| $3,600 | $1,243,900 | $10,900 | $385,200 | $581,500 |
| $7,400 | $2,900 | $400 | $3,714,500 | $632,500 |
| $391,000 | $467,400 | $56,800 | $5,800 | $405,200 |
| $733,200 | $8,000 | $468,700 | $75,200 | $41,000 |
| $13,300 | $9,500 | $953,800 | $1,113,500 | $1,109,300 |
| $353,900 | $986,100 | $88,600 | $378,200 | $13,200 |
| $3,800 | $745,100 | $5,800 | $3,072,100 | $1,626,700 |
| $512,900 | $2,309,200 | $6,600 | $202,400 | $15,800 |

**Table 8.5**

a. Find the point estimate for the population mean.
b. Using 95% confidence, calculate the error bound.
c. Create a 95% confidence interval for the mean total individual contributions.
d. Interpret the confidence interval in the context of the problem.

**130.** The American Community Survey (ACS), part of the United States Census Bureau, conducts a yearly census similar to the one taken every ten years, but with a smaller percentage of participants. The most recent survey estimates with 90% confidence that the mean household income in the U.S. falls between $69,720 and $69,922. Find the point estimate for mean U.S. household income and the error bound for mean U.S. household income.

**131.** The average height of young adult males has a normal distribution with standard deviation of 2.5 inches. You want to estimate the mean height of students at your college or university to within one inch with 93% confidence. How many male students must you measure?

# REFERENCES

**8.1 A Confidence Interval for a Population Standard Deviation, Known or Large Sample Size**

"American Fact Finder." U.S. Census Bureau. Available online at http://factfinder2.census.gov/faces/nav/jsf/pages/searchresults.xhtml?refresh=t (accessed July 2, 2013).

"Disclosure Data Catalog: Candidate Summary Report 2012." U.S. Federal Election Commission. Available online at http://www.fec.gov/data/index.jsp (accessed July 2, 2013).

"Headcount Enrollment Trends by Student Demographics Ten-Year Fall Trends to Most Recently Completed Fall." Foothill De Anza Community College District. Available online at http://research.fhda.edu/factbook/FH_Demo_Trends/FoothillDemographicTrends.htm (accessed September 30,2013).

Kuczmarski, Robert J., Cynthia L. Ogden, Shumei S. Guo, Laurence M. Grummer-Strawn, Katherine M. Flegal, Zuguo Mei, Rong Wei, Lester R. Curtin, Alex F. Roche, Clifford L. Johnson. "2000 CDC Growth Charts for the United States: Methods and Development." Centers for Disease Control and Prevention. Available online at http://www.cdc.gov/growthcharts/2000growthchart-us.pdf (accessed July 2, 2013).

La, Lynn, Kent German. "Cell Phone Radiation Levels." c|net part of CBX Interactive Inc. Available online at http://reviews.cnet.com/cell-phone-radiation-levels/ (accessed July 2, 2013).

"Mean Income in the Past 12 Months (in 2011 Inflaction-Adjusted Dollars): 2011 American Community Survey 1-Year

Estimates." American Fact Finder, U.S. Census Bureau. Available online at http://factfinder2.census.gov/faces/tableservices/jsf/pages/productview.xhtml?pid=ACS_11_1YR_S1902&prodType=table (accessed July 2, 2013).

"Metadata Description of Candidate Summary File." U.S. Federal Election Commission. Available online at http://www.fec.gov/finance/disclosure/metadata/metadataforcandidatesummary.shtml (accessed July 2, 2013).

"National Health and Nutrition Examination Survey." Centers for Disease Control and Prevention. Available online at http://www.cdc.gov/nchs/nhanes.htm (accessed July 2, 2013).

## 8.2 A Confidence Interval for a Population Standard Deviation Unknown, Small Sample Case

"America's Best Small Companies." Forbes, 2013. Available online at http://www.forbes.com/best-small-companies/list/ (accessed July 2, 2013).

Data from *Microsoft Bookshelf.*

Data from http://www.businessweek.com/.

Data from http://www.forbes.com/.

"Disclosure Data Catalog: Leadership PAC and Sponsors Report, 2012." Federal Election Commission. Available online at http://www.fec.gov/data/index.jsp (accessed July 2,2013).

"Human Toxome Project: Mapping the Pollution in People." Environmental Working Group. Available online at http://www.ewg.org/sites/humantoxome/participants/participant-group.php?group=in+utero%2Fnewborn (accessed July 2, 2013).

"Metadata Description of Leadership PAC List." Federal Election Commission. Available online at http://www.fec.gov/finance/disclosure/metadata/metadataLeadershipPacList.shtml (accessed July 2, 2013).

## 8.3 A Confidence Interval for A Population Proportion

Jensen, Tom. "Democrats, Republicans Divided on Opinion of Music Icons." Public Policy Polling. Available online at http://www.publicpolicypolling.com/Day2MusicPoll.pdf (accessed July 2, 2013).

Madden, Mary, Amanda Lenhart, Sandra Coresi, Urs Gasser, Maeve Duggan, Aaron Smith, and Meredith Beaton. "Teens, Social Media, and Privacy." PewInternet, 2013. Available online at http://www.pewinternet.org/Reports/2013/Teens-Social-Media-And-Privacy.aspx (accessed July 2, 2013).

Prince Survey Research Associates International. "2013 Teen and Privacy Management Survey." Pew Research Center: Internet and American Life Project. Available online at http://www.pewinternet.org/~/media//Files/Questionnaire/2013/Methods%20and%20Questions_Teens%20and%20Social%20Media.pdf (accessed July 2, 2013).

Saad, Lydia. "Three in Four U.S. Workers Plan to Work Pas Retirement Age: Slightly more say they will do this by choice rather than necessity." Gallup® Economy, 2013. Available online at http://www.gallup.com/poll/162758/three-four-workers-plan-work-past-retirement-age.aspx (accessed July 2, 2013).

The Field Poll. Available online at http://field.com/fieldpollonline/subscribers/ (accessed July 2, 2013).

Zogby. "New SUNYIT/Zogby Analytics Poll: Few Americans Worry about Emergency Situations Occurring in Their Community; Only one in three have an Emergency Plan; 70% Support Infrastructure 'Investment' for National Security." Zogby Analytics, 2013. Available online at http://www.zogbyanalytics.com/news/299-americans-neither-worried-nor-prepared-in-case-of-a-disaster-sunyit-zogby-analytics-poll (accessed July 2, 2013).

"52% Say Big-Time College Athletics Corrupt Education Process." Rasmussen Reports, 2013. Available online at http://www.rasmussenreports.com/public_content/lifestyle/sports/may_2013/52_say_big_time_college_athletics_corrupt_education_process (accessed July 2, 2013).

## SOLUTIONS

2 $X$ is the number of hours a patient waits in the emergency room before being called back to be examined. $\bar{X}$ is the mean wait time of 70 patients in the emergency room.

4 CI: (1.3808, 1.6192)

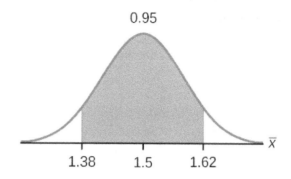

**Figure 8.13**

*EBM* = 0.12

6
   a.   $\bar{x}$ = 151
   b.   $s_x$ = 32
   c.   $n$ = 108
   d.   $n - 1$ = 107

8  $\bar{X}$ is the mean number of hours spent watching television per month from a sample of 108 Americans.

10  CI: (142.92, 159.08)

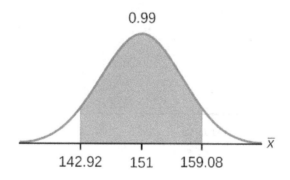

**Figure 8.14**

*EBM* = 8.08

12
   a.   3.26
   b.   1.02
   c.   39

14  $\mu$

16  $t_{38}$

18  0.025

20  (2.93, 3.59)

22  We are 95% confident that the true mean number of colors for national flags is between 2.93 colors and 3.59 colors.

23  The error bound would become EBM = 0.245. This error bound decreases because as sample sizes increase, variability

decreases and we need less interval length to capture the true mean.

**26** It would decrease, because the z-score would decrease, which reducing the numerator and lowering the number.

**28** $X$ is the number of "successes" where the woman makes the majority of the purchasing decisions for the household. $P'$ is the percentage of households sampled where the woman makes the majority of the purchasing decisions for the household.

**30** CI: (0.5321, 0.6679)

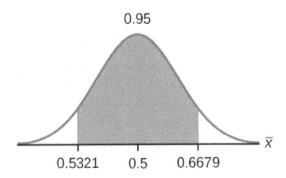

**Figure 8.15**

*EBM*: 0.0679

**32** $X$ is the number of "successes" where an executive prefers a truck. $P'$ is the percentage of executives sampled who prefer a truck.

**34** CI: (0.19432, 0.33068)

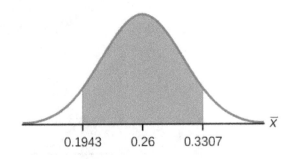

**Figure 8.16**

**36** The sampling error means that the true mean can be 2% above or below the sample mean.

**38** $P'$ is the proportion of voters sampled who said the economy is the most important issue in the upcoming election.

**40** CI: (0.62735, 0.67265) *EBM*: 0.02265

**42** The number of girls, ages 8 to 12, in the 5 P.M. Monday night beginning ice-skating class.

**44**
   a. $x = 64$
   b. $n = 80$
   c. $p' = 0.8$

**46** $p$

**48** $P' \sim N\left(0.8, \sqrt{\frac{(0.8)(0.2)}{80}}\right)$. (0.72171, 0.87829).

**50** 0.04

**52** (0.72; 0.88)

**54** With 92% confidence, we estimate the proportion of girls, ages 8 to 12, in a beginning ice-skating class at the Ice Chalet to be between 72% and 88%.

**56** The error bound would increase. Assuming all other variables are kept constant, as the confidence level increases, the area under the curve corresponding to the confidence level becomes larger, which creates a wider interval and thus a larger error.

**58**
  a.  244
  b.  15
  c.  50

**60** $N\left(244, \frac{15}{\sqrt{50}}\right)$

**62** As the sample size increases, there will be less variability in the mean, so the interval size decreases.

**64** $X$ is the time in minutes it takes to complete the U.S. Census short form. $\bar{X}$ is the mean time it took a sample of 200 people to complete the U.S. Census short form.

**66** CI: (7.9441, 8.4559)

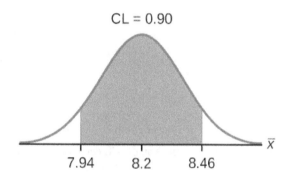

CL = 0.90

7.94   8.2   8.46

$\bar{X}$

Figure 8.17

**68** The level of confidence would decrease because decreasing $n$ makes the confidence interval wider, so at the same error bound, the confidence level decreases.

**70**
  a.  $\bar{x} = 2.2$
  b.  $\sigma = 0.2$
  c.  $n = 20$

**72** $\bar{X}$ is the mean weight of a sample of 20 heads of lettuce.

**74** $EBM = 0.07$
CI: (2.1264, 2.2736)

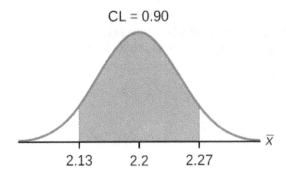

**Figure 8.18**

**76** The interval is greater because the level of confidence increased. If the only change made in the analysis is a change in confidence level, then all we are doing is changing how much area is being calculated for the normal distribution. Therefore, a larger confidence level results in larger areas and larger intervals.

**78** The confidence level would increase.

**80** 30.4

**82** $\sigma$

**84** $\mu$

**86** normal

**88** 0.025

**90** (24.52,36.28)

**92** We are 95% confident that the true mean age for Winger Foothill College students is between 24.52 and 36.28.

**94** The error bound for the mean would decrease because as the CL decreases, you need less area under the normal curve (which translates into a smaller interval) to capture the true population mean.

**96**

   a.   i.  8629

         ii.  6944

         iii.  35

         iv.  34

   b.  $t_{34}$

   c.   i.  CI: (6244, 11,014)

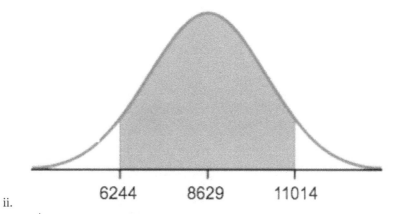

ii.

**Figure 8.19**

d. It will become smaller

**98**

a.  i.  $\bar{x} = 2.51$

ii.  $s_x = 0.318$

iii.  $n = 9$

iv.  $n - 1 = 8$

b. the effective length of time for a tranquilizer

c. the mean effective length of time of tranquilizers from a sample of nine patients

d. We need to use a Student's-t distribution, because we do not know the population standard deviation.

e.  i.  CI: (2.27, 2.76)

ii.  Check student's solution.

f. If we were to sample many groups of nine patients, 95% of the samples would contain the true population mean length of time.

**100**  $\bar{x} = \$251, 854.23$  $s = \$521, 130.41$ Note that we are not given the population standard deviation, only the standard deviation of the sample. There are 30 measures in the sample, so $n = 30$, and $df = 30 - 1 = 29$ $CL = 0.96$, so $\alpha = 1 - CL = 1 - 0.96 = 0.04$ $\frac{\alpha}{2} = 0.02 t_{\frac{\alpha}{2}} = t_{0.02} = 2.150$ $EBM = t_{\frac{\alpha}{2}}\left(\frac{s}{\sqrt{n}}\right) = 2.150\left(\frac{521, 130.41}{\sqrt{30}}\right)$ ~ $\$204, 561.66$ $\bar{x} - EBM = \$251,854.23 - \$204,561.66 = \$47,292.57$ $\bar{x} + EBM = \$251,854.23 + \$204,561.66 = \$456,415.89$ We estimate with 96% confidence that the mean amount of money raised by all Leadership PACs during the 2011–2012 election cycle lies between \$47,292.57 and \$456,415.89.

**102**

a.  i.  $\bar{x} = 11.6$

ii.  $s_x = 4.1$

iii.  $n = 225$

iv.  $n - 1 = 224$

b. $X$ is the number of unoccupied seats on a single flight. $\bar{X}$ is the mean number of unoccupied seats from a sample of 225 flights.

d. We will use a Student's-t distribution, because we do not know the population standard deviation.

     i.   CI: (11.12 , 12.08)

    ii.   Check student's solution.

**104**

a.   i.   CI: (7.64 , 9.36)

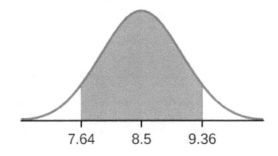

    ii.

**Figure 8.20**

b.   The sample should have been increased.

c.   Answers will vary.

d.   Answers will vary.

e.   Answers will vary.

**106** b

**107**

a.   1,068

b.   The sample size would need to be increased since the critical value increases as the confidence level increases.

**109**

a.   $X$ = the number of people who feel that the president is doing an acceptable job;

    $P'$ = the proportion of people in a sample who feel that the president is doing an acceptable job.

b.   $N\left(0.61, \sqrt{\dfrac{(0.61)(0.39)}{1200}}\right)$

c.   i.   CI: (0.59, 0.63)

    ii.   Check student's solution

**111**

a.   i.    (0.72, 0.82)

    ii.    (0.65, 0.76)

    iii.   (0.60, 0.72)

b.   Yes, the intervals (0.72, 0.82) and (0.65, 0.76) overlap, and the intervals (0.65, 0.76) and (0.60, 0.72) overlap.

c.   We can say that there does not appear to be a significant difference between the proportion of Asian adults who say that their families would welcome a white person into their families and the proportion of Asian adults who say that their families would welcome a Latino person into their families.

d.   We can say that there is a significant difference between the proportion of Asian adults who say that their families would welcome a white person into their families and the proportion of Asian adults who say that their families would welcome a black person into their families.

**113**

a. $X$ = the number of adult Americans who feel that crime is the main problem; $P'$ = the proportion of adult Americans who feel that crime is the main problem

b. Since we are estimating a proportion, given $P' = 0.2$ and $n = 1000$, the distribution we should use is $N\left(0.2, \sqrt{\frac{(0.2)(0.8)}{1000}}\right)$.

c.   i. CI: (0.18, 0.22)

    ii. Check student's solution.

d. One way to lower the sampling error is to increase the sample size.

e. The stated "± 3%" represents the maximum error bound. This means that those doing the study are reporting a maximum error of 3%. Thus, they estimate the percentage of adult Americans who feel that crime is the main problem to be between 18% and 22%.

**115** c

**118** a

**120**

a. $p' = \frac{(0.55 + 0.49)}{2} = 0.52$; $EBP = 0.55 - 0.52 = 0.03$

b. No, the confidence interval includes values less than or equal to 0.50. It is possible that less than half of the population believe this.

c. $CL = 0.75$, so $\alpha = 1 - 0.75 = 0.25$ and $\frac{\alpha}{2} = 0.125$   $z_{\frac{\alpha}{2}} = 1.150$. (The area to the right of this $z$ is 0.125, so the area to the left is $1 - 0.125 = 0.875$.)

$EBP = (1.150)\sqrt{\frac{0.52(0.48)}{1,000}} \approx 0.018$

$(p' - EBP, p' + EBP) = (0.52 - 0.018, 0.52 + 0.018) = (0.502, 0.538)$

d. Yes – this interval does not fall less than 0.50 so we can conclude that at least half of all American adults believe that major sports programs corrupt education – but we do so with only 75% confidence.

**123**

a.   i. 71

    ii. 2.8

    iii. 48

b. X is the height of a male Swede, and $\bar{x}$ is the mean height from a sample of 48 male Swedes.

c. Normal. We know the standard deviation for the population, and the sample size is greater than 30.

d.   i. CI: (70.151, 71.85)

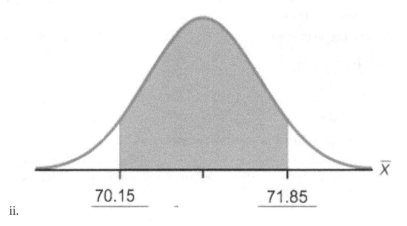

ii.

**Figure 8.21**

e. The confidence interval will decrease in size, because the sample size increased. Recall, when all factors remain unchanged, an increase in sample size decreases variability. Thus, we do not need as large an interval to capture the true population mean.

**125**

a.  i.  $\bar{x} = 23.6$

ii.  $\sigma = 7$

iii.  n = 100

b. $X$ is the time needed to complete an individual tax form. $\bar{X}$ is the mean time to complete tax forms from a sample of 100 customers.

c. $N\left(23.6, \dfrac{7}{\sqrt{100}}\right)$ because we know sigma.

d.  i.  (22.228, 24.972)

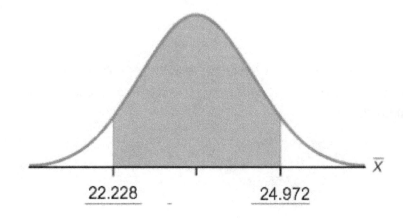

ii.

**Figure 8.22**

e. It will need to change the sample size. The firm needs to determine what the confidence level should be, then apply the error bound formula to determine the necessary sample size.

f. The confidence level would increase as a result of a larger interval. Smaller sample sizes result in more variability. To capture the true population mean, we need to have a larger interval.

g. According to the error bound formula, the firm needs to survey 206 people. Since we increase the confidence level, we need to increase either our error bound or the sample size.

**127**

a.  i.  7.9

ii.  2.5

iii.  20

b. X is the number of letters a single camper will send home. $\bar{X}$ is the mean number of letters sent home from a sample of 20 campers.

c. $N\ 7.9\left(\dfrac{2.5}{\sqrt{20}}\right)$

d.  i.  CI: (6.98, 8.82)

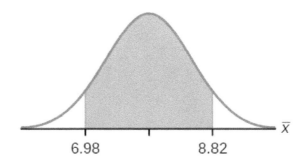

ii.

**Figure 8.23**

e. The error bound and confidence interval will decrease.

**129**

a. $\bar{x} = \$568{,}873$

b. $CL = 0.95\ \alpha = 1 - 0.95 = 0.05\ z_{\frac{\alpha}{2}} = 1.96$

$$EBM = z_{0.025}\frac{\sigma}{\sqrt{n}} = 1.96\ \frac{909200}{\sqrt{40}} = \$281{,}764$$

c. $\bar{x} - EBM = 568{,}873 - 281{,}764 = 287{,}109$

$\bar{x} + EBM = 568{,}873 + 281{,}764 = 850{,}637$

d. We estimate with 95% confidence that the mean amount of contributions received from all individuals by House candidates is between $287,109 and $850,637.

# 9 | HYPOTHESIS TESTING WITH ONE SAMPLE

**Figure 9.1** You can use a hypothesis test to decide if a dog breeder's claim that every Dalmatian has 35 spots is statistically sound. (Credit: Robert Neff)

## Introduction

Now we are down to the bread and butter work of the statistician: developing and testing hypotheses. It is important to put this material in a broader context so that the method by which a hypothesis is formed is understood completely. Using textbook examples often clouds the real source of statistical hypotheses.

Statistical testing is part of a much larger process known as the scientific method. This method was developed more than two centuries ago as the accepted way that new knowledge could be created. Until then, and unfortunately even today, among some, "knowledge" could be created simply by some authority saying something was so, *ipso dicta*. Superstition and conspiracy theories were (are?) accepted uncritically.

The scientific method, briefly, states that only by following a careful and specific process can some assertion be included in the accepted body of knowledge. This process begins with a set of assumptions upon which a theory, sometimes called a model, is built. This theory, if it has any validity, will lead to predictions; what we call hypotheses.

As an example, in Microeconomics the theory of consumer choice begins with certain assumption concerning human behavior. From these assumptions a theory of how consumers make choices using indifference curves and the budget line. This theory gave rise to a very important prediction, namely, that there was an inverse relationship between price and quantity demanded. This relationship was known as the demand curve. The negative slope of the demand curve is really just a prediction, or a hypothesis, that can be tested with statistical tools.

Unless hundreds and hundreds of statistical tests of this hypothesis had not confirmed this relationship, the so-called Law of Demand would have been discarded years ago. This is the role of statistics, to test the hypotheses of various theories to determine if they should be admitted into the accepted body of knowledge; how we understand our world. Once admitted, however, they may be later discarded if new theories come along that make better predictions.

Not long ago two scientists claimed that they could get more energy out of a process than was put in. This caused a tremendous stir for obvious reasons. They were on the cover of *Time* and were offered extravagant sums to bring their research work to private industry and any number of universities. It was not long until their work was subjected to the rigorous tests of the scientific method and found to be a failure. No other lab could replicate their findings. Consequently they have sunk into obscurity and their theory discarded. It may surface again when someone can pass the tests of the hypotheses required by the scientific method, but until then it is just a curiosity. Many pure frauds have been attempted over time, but most have been found out by applying the process of the scientific method.

This discussion is meant to show just where in this process statistics falls. Statistics and statisticians are not necessarily in the business of developing theories, but in the business of testing others' theories. Hypotheses come from these theories based upon an explicit set of assumptions and sound logic. The hypothesis comes first, before any data are gathered. Data do not create hypotheses; they are used to test them. If we bear this in mind as we study this section the process of forming and testing hypotheses will make more sense.

One job of a statistician is to make statistical inferences about populations based on samples taken from the population. **Confidence intervals** are one way to estimate a population parameter. Another way to make a statistical inference is to make a decision about the value of a specific parameter. For instance, a car dealer advertises that its new small truck gets 35 miles per gallon, on average. A tutoring service claims that its method of tutoring helps 90% of its students get an A or a B. A company says that women managers in their company earn an average of $60,000 per year.

A statistician will make a decision about these claims. This process is called " **hypothesis testing**." A hypothesis test involves collecting data from a sample and evaluating the data. Then, the statistician makes a decision as to whether or not there is sufficient evidence, based upon analyses of the data, to reject the null hypothesis.

In this chapter, you will conduct hypothesis tests on single means and single proportions. You will also learn about the errors associated with these tests.

# 9.1 | Null and Alternative Hypotheses

The actual test begins by considering two **hypotheses**. They are called the **null hypothesis** and the **alternative hypothesis**. These hypotheses contain opposing viewpoints.

$H_0$: **The null hypothesis:** It is a statement of no difference between a sample mean or proportion and a population mean or proportion. In other words, the difference equals 0. This can often be considered the status quo and as a result if you cannot accept the null it requires some action.

$H_a$: **The alternative hypothesis:** It is a claim about the population that is contradictory to $H_0$ and what we conclude when we cannot accept $H_0$. The alternative hypothesis is the contender and must win with significant evidence to overthrow the status quo. This concept is sometimes referred to the tyranny of the status quo because as we will see later, to overthrow the null hypothesis takes usually 90 or greater confidence that this is the proper decision.

Since the null and alternative hypotheses are contradictory, you must examine evidence to decide if you have enough evidence to reject the null hypothesis or not. The evidence is in the form of sample data.

After you have determined which hypothesis the sample supports, you make a **decision.** There are two options for a decision. They are "cannot accept $H_0$" if the sample information favors the alternative hypothesis or "do not reject $H_0$" or "decline to reject $H_0$" if the sample information is insufficient to reject the null hypothesis. These conclusions are all based upon a level of probability, a significance level, that is set my the analyst.

Table 9.1 presents the various hypotheses in the relevant pairs. For example, if the null hypothesis is equal to some value, the alternative has to be not equal to that value.

| $H_0$ | $H_a$ |
|---|---|
| equal (=) | not equal (≠) |
| greater than or equal to (≥) | less than (<) |
| less than or equal to (≤) | more than (>) |

Table 9.1

**NOTE**

As a mathematical convention $H_0$ always has a symbol with an equal in it. $H_a$ never has a symbol with an equal in it. The choice of symbol depends on the wording of the hypothesis test.

## Example 9.1

$H_0$: No more than 30% of the registered voters in Santa Clara County voted in the primary election. $p \leq 30$
$H_a$: More than 30% of the registered voters in Santa Clara County voted in the primary election. $p > 30$

## Example 9.2

We want to test whether the mean GPA of students in American colleges is different from 2.0 (out of 4.0). The null and alternative hypotheses are:
$H_0$: $\mu = 2.0$
$H_a$: $\mu \neq 2.0$

## Example 9.3

We want to test if college students take less than five years to graduate from college, on the average. The null and alternative hypotheses are:
$H_0$: $\mu \geq 5$
$H_a$: $\mu < 5$

# 9.2 | Outcomes and the Type I and Type II Errors

When you perform a hypothesis test, there are four possible outcomes depending on the actual truth (or falseness) of the null hypothesis $H_0$ and the decision to reject or not. The outcomes are summarized in the following table:

| STATISTICAL DECISION | $H_0$ IS ACTUALLY... | |
|---|---|---|
| | True | False |
| **Cannot reject $H_0$** | Correct Outcome | Type II error |
| **Cannot accept $H_0$** | Type I Error | Correct Outcome |

Table 9.2

The four possible outcomes in the table are:

1.  The decision is **cannot reject $H_0$** when **$H_0$ is true (correct decision).**

2.  The decision is **cannot accept $H_0$** when **$H_0$ is true** (incorrect decision known as a **Type I error**). This case is described as "rejecting a good null". As we will see later, it is this type of error that we will guard against by setting the probability of making such an error. The goal is to NOT take an action that is an error.

3.  The decision is **cannot reject $H_0$** when, in fact, **$H_0$ is false** (incorrect decision known as a **Type II error**). This is called "accepting a false null". In this situation you have allowed the status quo to remain in force when it should be overturned. As we will see, the null hypothesis has the advantage in competition with the alternative.

4.  The decision is **cannot accept $H_0$** when **$H_0$ is false (correct decision).**

Each of the errors occurs with a particular probability. The Greek letters $\alpha$ and $\beta$ represent the probabilities.

$\alpha$ = probability of a Type I error = **P(Type I error)** = probability of rejecting the null hypothesis when the null hypothesis is true: rejecting a good null.

$\beta$ = probability of a Type II error = **P(Type II error)** = probability of not rejecting the null hypothesis when the null hypothesis is false. $(1 - \beta)$ is called the **Power of the Test**.

$\alpha$ and $\beta$ should be as small as possible because they are probabilities of errors.

Statistics allows us to set the probability that we are making a Type I error. The probability of making a Type I error is $\alpha$. Recall that the confidence intervals in the last unit were set by choosing a value called $Z_\alpha$ (or $t_\alpha$) and the alpha value determined the confidence level of the estimate because it was the probability of the interval failing to capture the true mean (or proportion parameter p). This alpha and that one are the same.

The easiest way to see the relationship between the alpha error and the level of confidence is with the following figure.

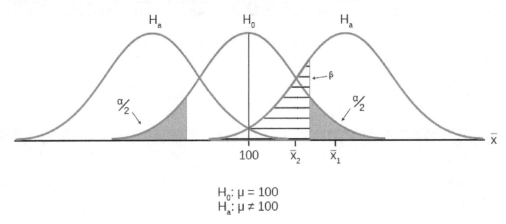

$$H_0: \mu = 100$$
$$H_a: \mu \neq 100$$

**Figure 9.2**

In the center of **Figure 9.2** is a normally distributed sampling distribution marked $H_0$. This is a sampling distribution of $\overline{X}$ and by the Central Limit Theorem it is normally distributed. The distribution in the center is marked $H_0$ and represents the distribution for the null hypotheses $H_0: \mu = 100$. This is the value that is being tested. The formal statements of the null and alternative hypotheses are listed below the figure.

The distributions on either side of the $H_0$ distribution represent distributions that would be true if $H_0$ is false, under the alternative hypothesis listed as $H_a$. We do not know which is true, and will never know. There are, in fact, an infinite number of distributions from which the data could have been drawn if $H_a$ is true, but only two of them are on **Figure 9.2** representing all of the others.

To test a hypothesis we take a sample from the population and determine if it could have come from the hypothesized distribution with an acceptable level of significance. This level of significance is the alpha error and is marked on **Figure 9.2** as the shaded areas in each tail of the $H_0$ distribution. (Each area is actually $\alpha/2$ because the distribution is symmetrical and the alternative hypothesis allows for the possibility for the value to be either greater than or less than the hypothesized value--called a two-tailed test).

If the sample mean marked as $\overline{X}_1$ is in the tail of the distribution of $H_0$, we conclude that the probability that it could have come from the $H_0$ distribution is less than alpha. We consequently state, "the null hypothesis cannot be accepted with ($\alpha$)

level of significance". The truth **may** be that this $\overline{X}_1$ did come from the $H_0$ distribution, but from out in the tail. If this is so then we have falsely rejected a true null hypothesis and have made a Type I error. What statistics has done is provide an estimate about what we know, and what we control, and that is the probability of us being wrong, $\alpha$.

We can also see in **Figure 9.2** that the sample mean could be really from an $H_a$ distribution, but within the boundary set by the alpha level. Such a case is marked as $\overline{X}_2$. There is a probability that $\overline{X}_2$ actually came from $H_a$ but shows up in the range of $H_0$ between the two tails. This probability is the beta error, the probability of accepting a false null.

Our problem is that we can only set the alpha error because there are an infinite number of alternative distributions from which the mean could have come that are not equal to $H_0$. As a result, the statistician places the burden of proof on the alternative hypothesis. That is, we will not reject a null hypothesis unless there is a greater than 90, or 95, or even 99 percent probability that the null is false: the burden of proof lies with the alternative hypothesis. This is why we called this the tyranny of the status quo earlier.

By way of example, the American judicial system begins with the concept that a defendant is "presumed innocent". This is the status quo and is the null hypothesis. The judge will tell the jury that they can not find the defendant guilty unless the evidence indicates guilt beyond a "reasonable doubt" which is usually defined in criminal cases as 95% certainty of guilt. If the jury cannot accept the null, innocent, then action will be taken, jail time. The burden of proof always lies with the alternative hypothesis. (In civil cases, the jury needs only to be more than 50% certain of wrongdoing to find culpability, called "a preponderance of the evidence").

The example above was for a test of a mean, but the same logic applies to tests of hypotheses for all statistical parameters one may wish to test.

The following are examples of Type I and Type II errors.

## Example 9.4

Suppose the null hypothesis, $H_0$, is: Frank's rock climbing equipment is safe.

**Type I error**: Frank thinks that his rock climbing equipment may not be safe when, in fact, it really is safe.

**Type II error**: Frank thinks that his rock climbing equipment may be safe when, in fact, it is not safe.

$\alpha$ = **probability** that Frank thinks his rock climbing equipment may not be safe when, in fact, it really is safe. $\beta$ = **probability** that Frank thinks his rock climbing equipment may be safe when, in fact, it is not safe.

Notice that, in this case, the error with the greater consequence is the Type II error. (If Frank thinks his rock climbing equipment is safe, he will go ahead and use it.)

This is a situation described as "accepting a false null".

## Example 9.5

Suppose the null hypothesis, $H_0$, is: The victim of an automobile accident is alive when he arrives at the emergency room of a hospital. This is the status quo and requires no action if it is true. If the null hypothesis cannot be accepted then action is required and the hospital will begin appropriate procedures.

**Type I error**: The emergency crew thinks that the victim is dead when, in fact, the victim is alive. **Type II error**: The emergency crew does not know if the victim is alive when, in fact, the victim is dead.

**$\alpha$ = probability** that the emergency crew thinks the victim is dead when, in fact, he is really alive = $P$(Type I error). **$\beta$ = probability** that the emergency crew does not know if the victim is alive when, in fact, the victim is dead = $P$(Type II error).

The error with the greater consequence is the Type I error. (If the emergency crew thinks the victim is dead, they will not treat him.)

**9.5** Suppose the null hypothesis, $H_0$, is: a patient is not sick. Which type of error has the greater consequence, Type I or Type II?

## Example 9.6

It's a Boy Genetic Labs claim to be able to increase the likelihood that a pregnancy will result in a boy being born. Statisticians want to test the claim. Suppose that the null hypothesis, $H_0$, is: It's a Boy Genetic Labs has no effect on gender outcome. The status quo is that the claim is false. The burden of proof always falls to the person making the claim, in this case the Genetics Lab.

**Type I error**: This results when a true null hypothesis is rejected. In the context of this scenario, we would state that we believe that It's a Boy Genetic Labs influences the gender outcome, when in fact it has no effect. The probability of this error occurring is denoted by the Greek letter alpha, $\alpha$.

**Type II error**: This results when we fail to reject a false null hypothesis. In context, we would state that It's a Boy Genetic Labs does not influence the gender outcome of a pregnancy when, in fact, it does. The probability of this error occurring is denoted by the Greek letter beta, $\beta$.

The error of greater consequence would be the Type I error since couples would use the It's a Boy Genetic Labs product in hopes of increasing the chances of having a boy.

**9.6** "Red tide" is a bloom of poison-producing algae–a few different species of a class of plankton called dinoflagellates. When the weather and water conditions cause these blooms, shellfish such as clams living in the area develop dangerous levels of a paralysis-inducing toxin. In Massachusetts, the Division of Marine Fisheries (DMF) monitors levels of the toxin in shellfish by regular sampling of shellfish along the coastline. If the mean level of toxin in clams exceeds 800 μg (micrograms) of toxin per kg of clam meat in any area, clam harvesting is banned there until the bloom is over and levels of toxin in clams subside. Describe both a Type I and a Type II error in this context, and state which error has the greater consequence.

## Example 9.7

A certain experimental drug claims a cure rate of at least 75% for males with prostate cancer. Describe both the Type I and Type II errors in context. Which error is the more serious?

**Type I**: A cancer patient believes the cure rate for the drug is less than 75% when it actually is at least 75%.

**Type II**: A cancer patient believes the experimental drug has at least a 75% cure rate when it has a cure rate that is less than 75%.

In this scenario, the Type II error contains the more severe consequence. If a patient believes the drug works at least 75% of the time, this most likely will influence the patient's (and doctor's) choice about whether to use the drug as a treatment option.

# 9.3 | Distribution Needed for Hypothesis Testing

Earlier, we discussed sampling distributions. Particular distributions are associated with hypothesis testing.We will perform hypotheses tests of a population mean using a normal distribution or a Student's $t$-distribution. (Remember, use a Student's $t$-distribution when the population standard deviation is unknown and the sample size is small, where small is considered to be less than 30 observations.) We perform tests of a population proportion using a normal distribution when we can assume that the distribution is normally distributed. We consider this to be true if the sample proportion, $p'$, times the sample size is greater than 5 and $1 - p'$ times the sample size is also greater then 5. This is the same rule of thumb we used when developing the formula for the confidence interval for a population proportion.

## Hypothesis Test for the Mean

Going back to the standardizing formula we can derive the **test statistic** for testing hypotheses concerning means.

$$Z_c = \frac{\bar{x} - \mu_0}{\sigma / \sqrt{n}}$$

The standardizing formula can not be solved as it is because we do not have μ, the population mean. However, if we substitute in the hypothesized value of the mean, $\mu_0$ in the formula as above, we can compute a Z value. This is the test statistic for a test of hypothesis for a mean and is presented in **Figure 9.3**. We interpret this Z value as the associated probability that a sample with a sample mean of $\bar{X}$ could have come from a distribution with a population mean of $H_0$ and we call this Z value $Z_c$ for "calculated". **Figure 9.3** and **Figure 9.4** show this process.

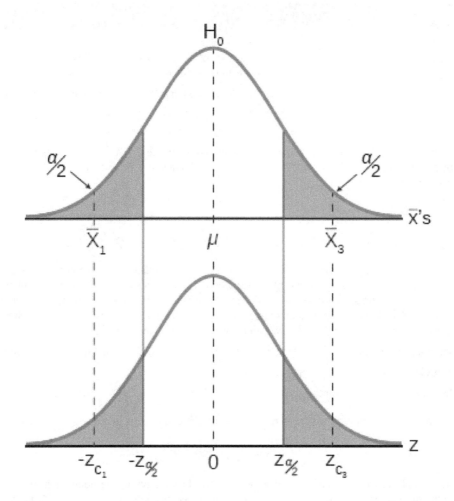

**Figure 9.3**

In **Figure 9.3** two of the three possible outcomes are presented. $\bar{X}_1$ and $\bar{X}_3$ are in the tails of the hypothesized distribution of $H_0$. Notice that the horizontal axis in the top panel is labeled $\bar{X}$'s. This is the same theoretical distribution of $\bar{X}$'s, the sampling distribution, that the Central Limit Theorem tells us is normally distributed. This is why we can draw it with this shape. The horizontal axis of the bottom panel is labeled Z and is the standard normal distribution. $Z_{\frac{\alpha}{2}}$ and $-Z_{\frac{\alpha}{2}}$, called the **critical values**, are marked on the bottom panel as the Z values associated with the probability the analyst has set as the level of significance in the test, ($\alpha$). The probabilities in the tails of both panels are, therefore, the same.

Notice that for each $\bar{X}$ there is an associated $Z_c$, called the calculated Z, that comes from solving the equation above. This calculated Z is nothing more than the number of standard deviations that the **hypothesized** mean is from the sample mean. If the sample mean falls "too many" standard deviations from the hypothesized mean we conclude that the **sample** mean could not have come from the distribution with the hypothesized mean, given our pre-set required level of significance. It **could** have come from $H_0$, but it is deemed just too unlikely. In **Figure 9.3** both $\bar{X}_1$ and $\bar{X}_3$ are in the tails of the distribution. They are deemed "too far" from the hypothesized value of the mean given the chosen level of alpha. If in fact this sample mean it did come from $H_0$, but from in the tail, we have made a Type I error: we have rejected a good null. Our only real comfort is that we know the probability of making such an error, $\alpha$, and we can control the size of $\alpha$.

**Figure 9.4** shows the third possibility for the location of the sample mean, $\bar{x}$. Here the sample mean is within the two critical values. That is, within the probability of $(1-\alpha)$ and we cannot reject the null hypothesis.

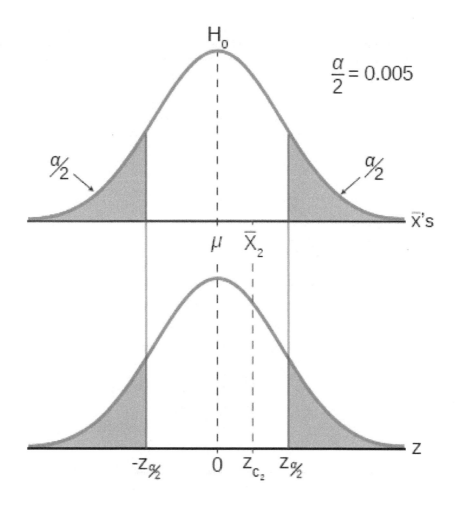

**Figure 9.4**

This gives us the decision rule for testing a hypothesis for a two-tailed test:

| **Decision Rule: Two-tail Test** |
|---|
| If $Z_c < \left\|Z_{\frac{\alpha}{2}}\right\|$ : then cannot REJECT $H_0$ |
| If $Z_c > \left\|Z_{\frac{\alpha}{2}}\right\|$ : then cannot ACCEPT $H_0$ |

**Table 9.3**

This rule will always be the same no matter what hypothesis we are testing or what formulas we are using to make the test. The only change will be to change the $Z_c$ to the appropriate symbol for the test statistic for the parameter being tested. Stating the decision rule another way: if the sample mean is unlikely to have come from the distribution with the hypothesized mean we cannot accept the null hypothesis. Here we define "unlikely" as having a probability less than alpha of occurring.

## P-Value Approach

An alternative decision rule can be developed by calculating the probability that a sample mean could be found that would give a test statistic larger than the test statistic found from the current sample data assuming that the null hypothesis is true. Here the notion of "likely" and "unlikely" is defined by the probability of drawing a sample with a mean from a population with the hypothesized mean that is either larger or smaller than that found in the sample data. Simply stated, the p-value approach compares the desired significance level, $\alpha$, to the p-value which is the probability of drawing a sample mean further from the hypothesized value than the actual sample mean. A large *p*-value calculated from the data indicates that we should not reject the **null hypothesis**. The smaller the *p*-value, the more unlikely the outcome, and the stronger the evidence is against the null hypothesis. We would reject the null hypothesis if the evidence is strongly against it. The relationship between the decision rule of comparing the calculated test statistics, $Z_c$, and the Critical Value, $Z_\alpha$, and using the *p*-value can be seen in **Figure 9.5**.

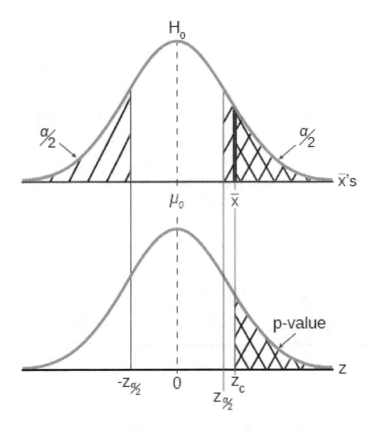

**Figure 9.5**

The calculated value of the test statistic is $Z_c$ in this example and is marked on the bottom graph of the standard normal distribution because it is a Z value. In this case the calculated value is in the tail and thus we cannot accept the null hypothesis, the associated $\overline{X}$ is just too unusually large to believe that it came from the distribution with a mean of $\mu_0$ with a significance level of $\alpha$.

If we use the *p*-value decision rule we need one more step. We need to find in the standard normal table the probability associated with the calculated test statistic, $Z_c$. We then compare that to the $\alpha$ associated with our selected level of confidence. In **Figure 9.5** we see that the *p*-value is less than $\alpha$ and therefore we cannot accept the null. We know that the *p*-value is less than $\alpha$ because the area under the p-value is smaller than $\alpha/2$. It is important to note that two researchers drawing randomly from the same population may find two different P-values from their samples. This occurs because the P-value is calculated as the probability in the tail beyond the sample mean assuming that the null hypothesis is correct. Because the sample means will in all likelihood be different this will create two different P-values. Nevertheless, the conclusions as to the null hypothesis should be different with only the level of probability of $\alpha$.

Here is a systematic way to make a decision of whether you cannot accept or cannot reject a null **hypothesis** if using the **p-value** and a **preset or preconceived $\alpha$** (the " **significance level**"). A preset $\alpha$ is the probability of a **Type I** error (rejecting the null hypothesis when the null hypothesis is true). It may or may not be given to you at the beginning of the problem. In any case, the value of $\alpha$ is the decision of the analyst. When you make a decision to reject or not reject $H_0$, do as follows:

- If $\alpha >$ *p*-value, cannot accept $H_0$. The results of the sample data are significant. There is sufficient evidence to conclude that $H_0$ is an incorrect belief and that the **alternative hypothesis**, $H_a$, may be correct.

- If $\alpha \leq$ *p*-value, cannot reject $H_0$. The results of the sample data are not significant. There is not sufficient evidence to conclude that the alternative hypothesis, $H_a$, may be correct. In this case the status quo stands.

- When you "cannot reject $H_0$", it does not mean that you should believe that $H_0$ is true. It simply means that the sample data have **failed** to provide sufficient evidence to cast serious doubt about the truthfulness of $H_0$. Remember that the null is the status quo and it takes high probability to overthrow the status quo. This bias in favor of the null hypothesis is what gives rise to the statement "tyranny of the status quo" when discussing hypothesis testing and the scientific method.

Both decision rules will result in the same decision and it is a matter of preference which one is used.

## One and Two-tailed Tests

The discussion of Figure 9.3-Figure 9.5 was based on the null and alternative hypothesis presented in Figure 9.3. This was called a two-tailed test because the alternative hypothesis allowed that the mean could have come from a population which was either larger or smaller than the hypothesized mean in the null hypothesis. This could be seen by the statement of the alternative hypothesis as $\mu \neq 100$, in this example.

It may be that the analyst has no concern about the value being "too" high or "too" low from the hypothesized value. If this is the case, it becomes a one-tailed test and all of the alpha probability is placed in just one tail and not split into $\alpha/2$ as in the above case of a two-tailed test. Any test of a claim will be a one-tailed test. For example, a car manufacturer claims that their Model 17B provides gas mileage of greater than 25 miles per gallon. The null and alternative hypothesis would be:

$H_0$: $\mu \leq 25$
$H_a$: $\mu > 25$

The claim would be in the alternative hypothesis. The burden of proof in hypothesis testing is carried in the alternative. This is because failing to reject the null, the status quo, must be accomplished with 90 or 95 percent significance that it cannot be maintained. Said another way, we want to have only a 5 or 10 percent probability of making a Type I error, rejecting a good null; overthrowing the status quo.

This is a one-tailed test and all of the alpha probability is placed in just one tail and not split into $\alpha/2$ as in the above case of a two-tailed test.

Figure 9.6 shows the two possible cases and the form of the null and alternative hypothesis that give rise to them.

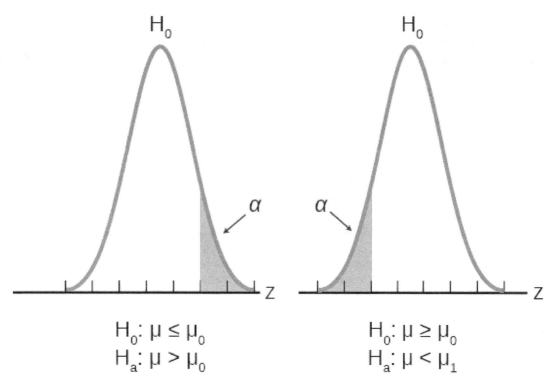

$$H_0: \mu \leq \mu_0$$
$$H_a: \mu > \mu_0$$

$$H_0: \mu \geq \mu_0$$
$$H_a: \mu < \mu_1$$

Figure 9.6

where $\mu_0$ is the hypothesized value of the population mean.

| Sample Size | Test Statistic |
|---|---|
| < 30 (σ unknown) | $t_c = \dfrac{\bar{X} - \mu_0}{s / \sqrt{n}}$ |
| < 30 (σ known) | $Z_c = \dfrac{\bar{X} - \mu_0}{\sigma / \sqrt{n}}$ |
| > 30 (σ unknown) | $Z_c = \dfrac{\bar{X} - \mu_0}{s / \sqrt{n}}$ |
| > 30 (σ known) | $Z_c = \dfrac{\bar{X} - \mu_0}{\sigma / \sqrt{n}}$ |

**Table 9.4 Test Statistics for Test of Means, Varying Sample Size, Population Standard Deviation Known or Unknown**

## Effects of Sample Size on Test Statistic

In developing the confidence intervals for the mean from a sample, we found that most often we would not have the population standard deviation, σ. If the sample size were larger than 30, we could simply substitute the point estimate for σ, the sample standard deviation, s, and use the student's t distribution to correct for this lack of information.

When testing hypotheses we are faced with this same problem and the solution is exactly the same. Namely: If the population standard deviation is unknown, and the sample size is less than 30, substitute s, the point estimate for the population standard deviation, σ, in the formula for the test statistic and use the student's t distribution. All the formulas and figures above are unchanged except for this substitution and changing the Z distribution to the student's t distribution on the graph. Remember that the student's t distribution can only be computed knowing the proper degrees of freedom for the problem. In this case, the degrees of freedom is computed as before with confidence intervals: $df = (n-1)$. The calculated t-value is compared to the t-value associated with the pre-set level of confidence required in the test, $t_{\alpha, \, df}$ found in the student's t tables. If we do not know σ, but the sample size is 30 or more, we simply substitute s for σ and use the normal distribution.

**Table 9.4** summarizes these rules.

## A Systematic Approach for Testing A Hypothesis

A systematic approach to hypothesis testing follows the following steps and in this order. This template will work for all hypotheses that you will ever test.

- Set up the null and alternative hypothesis. This is typically the hardest part of the process. Here the question being asked is reviewed. What parameter is being tested, a mean, a proportion, differences in means, etc. Is this a one-tailed test or two-tailed test? Remember, if someone is making a claim it will always be a one-tailed test.

- Decide the level of significance required for this particular case and determine the critical value. These can be found in the appropriate statistical table. The levels of confidence typical for the social sciences are 90, 95 and 99. However, the level of significance is a policy decision and should be based upon the risk of making a Type I error, rejecting a good null. Consider the consequences of making a Type I error.

  Next, on the basis of the hypotheses and sample size, select the appropriate test statistic and find the relevant critical value: $Z_\alpha$, $t_\alpha$, etc. Drawing the relevant probability distribution and marking the critical value is always big help. Be sure to match the graph with the hypothesis, especially if it is a one-tailed test.

- Take a sample(s) and calculate the relevant parameters: sample mean, standard deviation, or proportion. Using the formula for the test statistic from above in step 2, now calculate the test statistic for this particular case using the parameters you have just calculated.

- Compare the calculated test statistic and the critical value. Marking these on the graph will give a good visual picture of the situation. There are now only two situations:

  a. The test statistic is in the tail: Cannot Accept the null, the probability that this sample mean (proportion) came from the hypothesized distribution is too small to believe that it is the real home of these sample data.

b. The test statistic is not in the tail: Cannot Reject the null, the sample data are compatible with the hypothesized population parameter.

- Reach a conclusion. It is best to articulate the conclusion two different ways. First a formal statistical conclusion such as "With a 95 % level of significance we cannot accept the null hypotheses that the population mean is equal to XX (units of measurement)". The second statement of the conclusion is less formal and states the action, or lack of action, required. If the formal conclusion was that above, then the informal one might be, "The machine is broken and we need to shut it down and call for repairs".

All hypotheses tested will go through this same process. The only changes are the relevant formulas and those are determined by the hypothesis required to answer the original question.

# 9.4 | Full Hypothesis Test Examples
## Tests on Means

## Example 9.8

Jeffrey, as an eight-year old, **established a mean time of 16.43 seconds** for swimming the 25-yard freestyle, with a **standard deviation of 0.8 seconds**. His dad, Frank, thought that Jeffrey could swim the 25-yard freestyle faster using goggles. Frank bought Jeffrey a new pair of expensive goggles and timed Jeffrey for **15 25-yard freestyle swims**. For the 15 swims, **Jeffrey's mean time was 16 seconds. Frank thought that the goggles helped Jeffrey to swim faster than the 16.43 seconds.** Conduct a hypothesis test using a preset $\alpha = 0.05$.

### Solution 9.8

Set up the Hypothesis Test:

Since the problem is about a mean, this is a **test of a single population mean**.

Set the null and alternative hypothesis:

In this case there is an implied challenge or claim. This is that the goggles will reduce the swimming time. The effect of this is to set the hypothesis as a one-tailed test. The claim will always be in the alternative hypothesis because the burden of proof always lies with the alternative. Remember that the status quo must be defeated with a high degree of confidence, in this case 95 % confidence. The null and alternative hypotheses are thus:

$H_0: \mu \geq 16.43$      $H_a: \mu < 16.43$

For Jeffrey to swim faster, his time will be less than 16.43 seconds. The "<" tells you this is left-tailed.

Determine the distribution needed:

**Random variable:** $\bar{X}$ = the mean time to swim the 25-yard freestyle.

**Distribution for the test statistic:**

The sample size is less than 30 and we do not know the population standard deviation so this is a t-test. and the proper formula is: $t_c = \dfrac{\bar{X} - \mu_0}{\sigma / \sqrt{n}}$

$\mu_0 = 16.43$ comes from $H_0$ and not the data. $\bar{X} = 16$. $s = 0.8$, and $n = 15$.

Our step 2, setting the level of significance, has already been determined by the problem, .05 for a 95 % significance level. It is worth thinking about the meaning of this choice. The Type I error is to conclude that Jeffrey swims the 25-yard freestyle, on average, in less than 16.43 seconds when, in fact, he actually swims the 25-yard freestyle, on average, in 16.43 seconds. (Reject the null hypothesis when the null hypothesis is true.) For this case the only concern with a Type I error would seem to be that Jeffery's dad may fail to bet on his son's victory because he does not have appropriate confidence in the effect of the goggles.

To find the critical value we need to select the appropriate test statistic. We have concluded that this is a t-test on the basis of the sample size and that we are interested in a population mean. We can now draw the graph of the t-distribution and mark the critical value. For this problem the degrees of freedom are n-1, or 14. Looking up 14 degrees of freedom at the 0.05 column of the t-table we find 1.761. This is the critical value and we can put this on our graph.

Step 3 is the calculation of the test statistic using the formula we have selected. We find that the calculated test statistic is 2.08, meaning that the sample mean is 2.08 standard deviations away from the hypothesized mean of 16.43.

$$t_c = \frac{\bar{x} - \mu_0}{\frac{s}{\sqrt{n}}} = \frac{16 - 16.43}{\frac{.8}{\sqrt{15}}} = -2.08$$

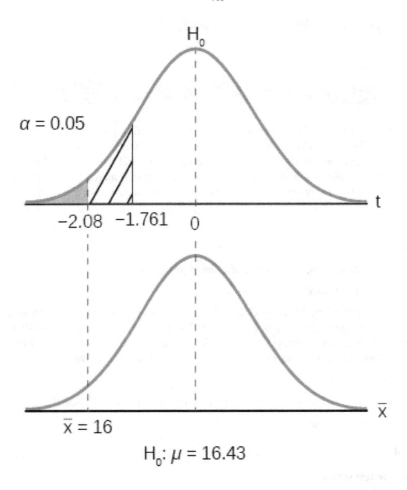

Figure 9.7

Step 4 has us compare the test statistic and the critical value and mark these on the graph. We see that the test statistic is in the tail and thus we move to step 4 and reach a conclusion. The probability that an average time of 16 minutes could come from a distribution with a population mean of 16.43 minutes is too unlikely for us to accept the null hypothesis. We cannot accept the null.

Step 5 has us state our conclusions first formally and then less formally. A formal conclusion would be stated as: "With a 95% level of significance we cannot accept the null hypothesis that the swimming time with goggles comes from a distribution with a population mean time of 16.43 minutes." Less formally, "With 95% significance we believe that the goggles improves swimming speed"

If we wished to use the p-value system of reaching a conclusion we would calculate the statistic and take the additional step to find the probability of being 2.08 standard deviations from the mean on a t-distribution. This value is .0187. Comparing this to the α-level of .05 we see that we cannot accept the null. The p-value has been put on the graph as the shaded area beyond -2.08 and it shows that it is smaller than the hatched area which is the alpha level of 0.05. Both methods reach the same conclusion that we cannot accept the null hypothesis.

**9.8** The mean throwing distance of a football for Marco, a high school freshman quarterback, is 40 yards, with a standard deviation of two yards. The team coach tells Marco to adjust his grip to get more distance. The coach records the distances for 20 throws. For the 20 throws, Marco's mean distance was 45 yards. The coach thought the different grip helped Marco throw farther than 40 yards. Conduct a hypothesis test using a preset $\alpha = 0.05$. Assume the throw distances for footballs are normal.

First, determine what type of test this is, set up the hypothesis test, find the *p*-value, sketch the graph, and state your conclusion.

## Example 9.9

Jane has just begun her new job as on the sales force of a very competitive company. In a sample of 16 sales calls it was found that she closed the contract for an average value of 108 dollars with a standard deviation of 12 dollars. Test at 5% significance that the population mean is at least 100 dollars against the alternative that it is less than 100 dollars. Company policy requires that new members of the sales force must exceed an average of $100 per contract during the trial employment period. Can we conclude that Jane has met this requirement at the significance level of 95%?

### Solution 9.9

1. $H_0$: $\mu \le 100$
   $H_a$: $\mu > 100$
   The null and alternative hypothesis are for the parameter $\mu$ because the number of dollars of the contracts is a continuous random variable. Also, this is a one-tailed test because the company has only an interested if the number of dollars per contact is below a particular number not "too high" a number. This can be thought of as making a claim that the requirement is being met and thus the claim is in the alternative hypothesis.

2. Test statistic: $t_c = \dfrac{\bar{x} - \mu_0}{\frac{s}{\sqrt{n}}} = \dfrac{108 - 100}{\left(\frac{12}{\sqrt{16}}\right)} = 2.67$

3. Critical value: $t_a = 1.753$ with n-1 degrees of freedom= 15

The test statistic is a Student's t because the sample size is below 30; therefore, we cannot use the normal distribution. Comparing the calculated value of the test statistic and the critical value of $t$ $(t_a)$ at a 5% significance level, we see that the calculated value is in the tail of the distribution. Thus, we conclude that 108 dollars per contract is significantly larger than the hypothesized value of 100 and thus we cannot accept the null hypothesis. There is evidence that supports Jane's performance meets company standards.

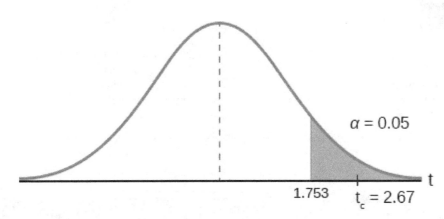

$\alpha = 0.05$

1.753    $t_c = 2.67$

**Figure 9.8**

**9.9** It is believed that a stock price for a particular company will grow at a rate of $5 per week with a standard deviation of $1. An investor believes the stock won't grow as quickly. The changes in stock price is recorded for ten weeks and are as follows: $4, $3, $2, $3, $1, $7, $2, $1, $1, $2. Perform a hypothesis test using a 5% level of significance. State the null and alternative hypotheses, state your conclusion, and identify the Type I errors.

## Example 9.10

A manufacturer of salad dressings uses machines to dispense liquid ingredients into bottles that move along a filling line. The machine that dispenses salad dressings is working properly when 8 ounces are dispensed. Suppose that the average amount dispensed in a particular sample of 35 bottles is 7.91 ounces with a variance of 0.03 ounces squared, $s^2$. Is there evidence that the machine should be stopped and production wait for repairs? The lost production from a shutdown is potentially so great that management feels that the level of significance in the analysis should be 99%.

Again we will follow the steps in our analysis of this problem.

### Solution 9.10

**STEP 1**: Set the Null and Alternative Hypothesis. The random variable is the quantity of fluid placed in the bottles. This is a continuous random variable and the parameter we are interested in is the mean. Our hypothesis therefore is about the mean. In this case we are concerned that the machine is not filling properly. From what we are told it does not matter if the machine is over-filling or under-filling, both seem to be an equally bad error. This tells us that this is a two-tailed test: if the machine is malfunctioning it will be shutdown regardless if it is from over-filling or under-filling. The null and alternative hypotheses are thus:

$$H_0 : \mu = 8$$
$$H_a : \mu \neq 8$$

**STEP 2**: Decide the level of significance and draw the graph showing the critical value.

This problem has already set the level of significance at 99%. The decision seems an appropriate one and shows the thought process when setting the significance level. Management wants to be very certain, as certain as probability will allow, that they are not shutting down a machine that is not in need of repair. To draw the distribution and the critical value, we need to know which distribution to use. Because this is a continuous random variable and we are interested in the mean, and the sample size is greater than 30, the appropriate distribution is the normal distribution and the relevant critical value is 2.575 from the normal table or the t-table at 0.005 column and infinite degrees of freedom. We draw the graph and mark these points.

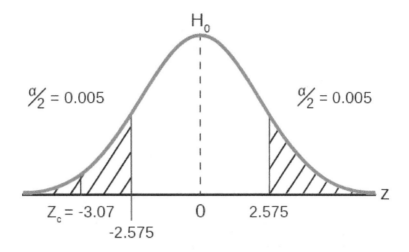

**Figure 9.9**

**STEP 3**: Calculate sample parameters and the test statistic. The sample parameters are provided, the sample mean is 7.91 and the sample variance is .03 and the sample size is 35. We need to note that the sample variance was provided not the sample standard deviation, which is what we need for the formula. Remembering that the standard deviation is simply the square root of the variance, we therefore know the sample standard deviation, s, is 0.173. With this information we calculate the test statistic as -3.07, and mark it on the graph.

$$Z_c = \frac{\bar{x} - \mu_0}{\frac{s}{\sqrt{n}}} = \frac{7.91 - 8}{\frac{.173}{\sqrt{35}}} = -3.07$$

**STEP 4**: Compare test statistic and the critical values Now we compare the test statistic and the critical value by placing the test statistic on the graph. We see that the test statistic is in the tail, decidedly greater than the critical value of 2.575. We note that even the very small difference between the hypothesized value and the sample value is still a large number of standard deviations. The sample mean is only 0.08 ounces different from the required level of 8 ounces, but it is 3 plus standard deviations away and thus we cannot accept the null hypothesis.

**STEP 5**: Reach a Conclusion

Three standard deviations of a test statistic will guarantee that the test will fail. The probability that anything is within three standard deviations is almost zero. Actually it is 0.0026 on the normal distribution, which is certainly almost zero in a practical sense. Our formal conclusion would be " At a 99% level of significance we cannot accept the hypothesis that the sample mean came from a distribution with a mean of 8 ounces" Or less formally, and getting to the point, "At a 99% level of significance we conclude that the machine is under filling the bottles and is in need of repair".

## Hypothesis Test for Proportions

Just as there were confidence intervals for proportions, or more formally, the population parameter $p$ of the binomial distribution, there is the ability to test hypotheses concerning $p$.

The population parameter for the binomial is $p$. The estimated value (point estimate) for $p$ is $p'$ where $p' = x/n$, $x$ is the number of successes in the sample and $n$ is the sample size.

When you perform a hypothesis test of a population proportion **p**, you take a simple random sample from the population. The conditions for a **binomial distribution** must be met, which are: there are a certain number $n$ of independent trials meaning random sampling, the outcomes of any trial are binary, success or failure, and each trial has the same probability of a success $p$. The shape of the binomial distribution needs to be similar to the shape of the normal distribution. To ensure this, the quantities $np'$ and $nq'$ must both be greater than five ($np' > 5$ and $nq' > 5$). In this case the binomial distribution of a sample (estimated) proportion can be approximated by the normal distribution with $\mu = np$ and $\sigma = \sqrt{npq}$. Remember that $q = 1 - p$. There is no distribution that can correct for this small sample bias and thus if these conditions are not met we simply cannot test the hypothesis with the data available at that time. We met this condition when we first were estimating confidence intervals for $p$.

Again, we begin with the standardizing formula modified because this is the distribution of a binomial.

$$Z = \frac{p' - p}{\sqrt{\frac{pq}{n}}}$$

Substituting $p_0$, the hypothesized value of $p$, we have:

$$Z_c = \frac{p' - p_0}{\sqrt{\frac{p_0 q_0}{n}}}$$

This is the test statistic for testing hypothesized values of $p$, where the null and alternative hypotheses take one of the following forms:

| Two-Tailed Test | One-Tailed Test | One-Tailed Test |
|:---:|:---:|:---:|
| $H_0$: $p = p_0$ | $H_0$: $p \leq p_0$ | $H_0$: $p \geq p_0$ |
| $H_a$: $p \neq p_0$ | $H_a$: $p > p_0$ | $H_a$: $p < p_0$ |

Table 9.5

The decision rule stated above applies here also: if the calculated value of $Z_c$ shows that the sample proportion is "too many" standard deviations from the hypothesized proportion, the null hypothesis cannot be accepted. The decision as to what is "too many" is pre-determined by the analyst depending on the level of significance required in the test.

## Example 9.11

The mortgage department of a large bank is interested in the nature of loans of first-time borrowers. This information will be used to tailor their marketing strategy. They believe that 50% of first-time borrowers take out smaller loans than other borrowers. They perform a hypothesis test to determine if the percentage is **the same or different from 50%**. They sample **100 first-time borrowers** and find **53** of these loans are smaller that the other borrowers. For the hypothesis test, they choose a 5% level of significance.

Solution 9.11

STEP 1: Set the null and alternative hypothesis.

$H_0$: $p = 0.50$      $H_a$: $p \neq 0.50$

The words **"is the same or different from"** tell you this is a two-tailed test. The Type I and Type II errors are as follows: The Type I error is to conclude that the proportion of borrowers is different from 50% when, in fact, the proportion is actually 50%. (Reject the null hypothesis when the null hypothesis is true). The Type II error is there is not enough evidence to conclude that the proportion of first time borrowers differs from 50% when, in fact, the proportion does differ from 50%. (You fail to reject the null hypothesis when the null hypothesis is false.)

STEP 2: Decide the level of significance and draw the graph showing the critical value

The level of significance has been set by the problem at the 95% level. Because this is two-tailed test one-half of the alpha value will be in the upper tail and one-half in the lower tail as shown on the graph. The critical value for the normal distribution at the 95% level of confidence is 1.96. This can easily be found on the student's t-table at the very bottom at infinite degrees of freedom remembering that at infinity the t-distribution is the normal distribution. Of course the value can also be found on the normal table but you have go looking for one-half of 95 (0.475) inside the body of the table and then read out to the sides and top for the number of standard deviations.

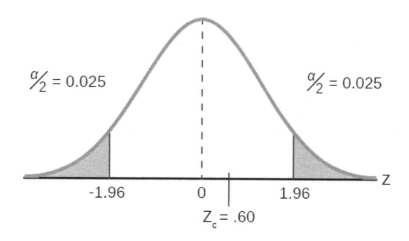

Figure 9.10

**STEP 3**: Calculate the sample parameters and critical value of the test statistic.

The test statistic is a normal distribution, Z, for testing proportions and is:

$$Z = \frac{p' - p_0}{\sqrt{\frac{p_0 q_0}{n}}} = \frac{.53 - .50}{\sqrt{\frac{.5(.5)}{100}}} = 0.60$$

For this case, the sample of 100 found 53 first-time borrowers were different from other borrowers. The sample proportion, $p' = 53/100 = 0.53$ The test question, therefore, is : "Is 0.53 significantly different from .50?" Putting these values into the formula for the test statistic we find that 0.53 is only 0.60 standard deviations away from .50. This is barely off of the mean of the standard normal distribution of zero. There is virtually no difference from the sample proportion and the hypothesized proportion in terms of standard deviations.

**STEP 4**: Compare the test statistic and the critical value.

The calculated value is well within the critical values of ± 1.96 standard deviations and thus we cannot reject the null hypothesis. To reject the null hypothesis we need significant evident of difference between the hypothesized value and the sample value. In this case the sample value is very nearly the same as the hypothesized value measured in terms of standard deviations.

**STEP 5**: Reach a conclusion

The formal conclusion would be "At a 95% level of significance we cannot reject the null hypothesis that 50% of first-time borrowers have the same size loans as other borrowers". Less formally we would say that "There is no evidence that one-half of first-time borrowers are significantly different in loan size from other borrowers". Notice the length to which the conclusion goes to include all of the conditions that are attached to the conclusion. Statisticians for all the criticism they receive, are careful to be very specific even when this seems trivial. Statisticians cannot say more than they know and the data constrain the conclusion to be within the metes and bounds of the data.

**9.11** A teacher believes that 85% of students in the class will want to go on a field trip to the local zoo. She performs a hypothesis test to determine if the percentage is the same or different from 85%. The teacher samples 50 students and 39 reply that they would want to go to the zoo. For the hypothesis test, use a 1% level of significance.

## Example 9.12

Suppose a consumer group suspects that the proportion of households that have three or more cell phones is 30%. A cell phone company has reason to believe that the proportion is not 30%. Before they start a big advertising campaign, they conduct a hypothesis test. Their marketing people survey 150 households with the result that 43 of the households have three or more cell phones.

### Solution 9.12

Here is an abbreviate version of the system to solve hypothesis tests applied to a test on a proportions.

$$H_0 : p = 0.3$$
$$H_a : p \neq 0.3$$
$$n = 150$$
$$p' = \frac{x}{n} = \frac{43}{150} = 0.287$$
$$Z_c = \frac{p' - p_0}{\sqrt{\frac{p_0 q_0}{n}}} = \frac{0.287 - 0.3}{\sqrt{\frac{.3(.7)}{150}}} = 0.347$$

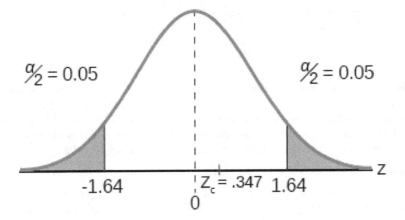

At a significance level of 90%
we cannot reject H₀:
the consumer group is correct.

**Figure 9.11**

## Example 9.13

The National Institute of Standards and Technology provides exact data on conductivity properties of materials. Following are conductivity measurements for 11 randomly selected pieces of a particular type of glass.

1.11; 1.07; 1.11; 1.07; 1.12; 1.08; .98; .98 1.02; .95; .95

Is there convincing evidence that the average conductivity of this type of glass is greater than one? Use a significance level of 0.05.

### Solution 9.13

Let's follow a four-step process to answer this statistical question.

1. **State the Question**: We need to determine if, at a 0.05 significance level, the average conductivity of the

selected glass is greater than one. Our hypotheses will be

    a.  $H_0: \mu \leq 1$

    b.  $H_a: \mu > 1$

2.  **Plan**: We are testing a sample mean without a known population standard deviation with less than 30 observations. Therefore, we need to use a Student's-t distribution. Assume the underlying population is normal.

3.  **Do the calculations and draw the graph**.

4.  **State the Conclusions**: We cannot accept the null hypothesis. It is reasonable to state that the data supports the claim that the average conductivity level is greater than one.

## Example 9.14

In a study of 420,019 cell phone users, 172 of the subjects developed brain cancer. Test the claim that cell phone users developed brain cancer at a greater rate than that for non-cell phone users (the rate of brain cancer for non-cell phone users is 0.0340%). Since this is a critical issue, use a 0.005 significance level. Explain why the significance level should be so low in terms of a Type I error.

Solution 9.14

1.  We need to conduct a hypothesis test on the claimed cancer rate. Our hypotheses will be
    a.  $H_0: p \leq 0.00034$

    b.  $H_a: p > 0.00034$

If we commit a Type I error, we are essentially accepting a false claim. Since the claim describes cancer-causing environments, we want to minimize the chances of incorrectly identifying causes of cancer.

2.  We will be testing a sample proportion with $x = 172$ and $n = 420{,}019$. The sample is sufficiently large because we have $np' = 420{,}019(0.00034) = 142.8$, $nq' = 420{,}019(0.99966) = 419{,}876.2$, two independent outcomes, and a fixed probability of success $p' = 0.00034$. Thus we will be able to generalize our results to the population.

# KEY TERMS

**Binomial Distribution** a discrete random variable (RV) that arises from Bernoulli trials. There are a fixed number, $n$, of independent trials. "Independent" means that the result of any trial (for example, trial 1) does not affect the results of the following trials, and all trials are conducted under the same conditions. Under these circumstances the binomial RV X is defined as the number of successes in $n$ trials. The notation is: $X \sim B(n, p)$ $\mu = np$ and the standard deviation is $\sigma = \sqrt{npq}$. The probability of exactly $x$ successes in $n$ trials is $P(X = x) = \binom{n}{x} p^x q^{n-x}$.

**Central Limit Theorem** Given a random variable (RV) with known mean $\mu$ and known standard deviation σ. We are sampling with size $n$ and we are interested in two new RVs - the sample mean, $\overline{X}$. If the size $n$ of the sample is sufficiently large, then $\overline{X} \sim N\left(\mu, \frac{\sigma}{\sqrt{n}}\right)$. If the size $n$ of the sample is sufficiently large, then the distribution of the sample means will approximate a normal distribution regardless of the shape of the population. The expected value of the mean of the sample means will equal the population mean. The standard deviation of the distribution of the sample means, $\frac{\sigma}{\sqrt{n}}$, is called the standard error of the mean.

**Confidence Interval (CI)** an interval estimate for an unknown population parameter. This depends on:

- The desired confidence level.

- Information that is known about the distribution (for example, known standard deviation).

- The sample and its size.

**Critical Value** The $t$ or $Z$ value set by the researcher that measures the probability of a Type I error, α.

**Hypothesis** a statement about the value of a population parameter, in case of two hypotheses, the statement assumed to be true is called the null hypothesis (notation $H_0$) and the contradictory statement is called the alternative hypothesis (notation $H_a$).

**Hypothesis Testing** Based on sample evidence, a procedure for determining whether the hypothesis stated is a reasonable statement and should not be rejected, or is unreasonable and should be rejected.

**Normal Distribution**

a continuous random variable (RV) with pdf $f(x) = \frac{1}{\sigma\sqrt{2\pi}} e^{\frac{-(x-\mu)^2}{2\sigma^2}}$, where $\mu$ is the mean of the distribution, and $\sigma$ is the standard deviation, notation: $X \sim N(\mu, \sigma)$. If $\mu = 0$ and $\sigma = 1$, the RV is called **the standard normal distribution**.

**Standard Deviation** a number that is equal to the square root of the variance and measures how far data values are from their mean; notation: $s$ for sample standard deviation and $\sigma$ for population standard deviation.

**Student's $t$-Distribution** investigated and reported by William S. Gossett in 1908 and published under the pseudonym Student. The major characteristics of the random variable (RV) are:

- It is continuous and assumes any real values.

- The pdf is symmetrical about its mean of zero. However, it is more spread out and flatter at the apex than the normal distribution.

- It approaches the standard normal distribution as $n$ gets larger.

- There is a "family" of t distributions: every representative of the family is completely defined by the number of degrees of freedom which is one less than the number of data items.

**Test Statistic** The formula that counts the number of standard deviations on the relevant distribution that estimated parameter is away from the hypothesized value.

**Type I Error** The decision is to reject the null hypothesis when, in fact, the null hypothesis is true.

**Type II Error** The decision is not to reject the null hypothesis when, in fact, the null hypothesis is false.

# CHAPTER REVIEW

## 9.1 Null and Alternative Hypotheses

In a **hypothesis test**, sample data is evaluated in order to arrive at a decision about some type of claim. If certain conditions about the sample are satisfied, then the claim can be evaluated for a population. In a hypothesis test, we:

1. Evaluate the **null hypothesis**, typically denoted with $H_0$. The null is not rejected unless the hypothesis test shows otherwise. The null statement must always contain some form of equality ($=$, $\leq$ or $\geq$)

2. Always write the **alternative hypothesis**, typically denoted with $H_a$ or $H_1$, using not equal, less than or greater than symbols, i.e., ($\neq$, $<$, or $>$ ).

3. If we reject the null hypothesis, then we can assume there is enough evidence to support the alternative hypothesis.

4. Never state that a claim is proven true or false. Keep in mind the underlying fact that hypothesis testing is based on probability laws; therefore, we can talk only in terms of non-absolute certainties.

## 9.2 Outcomes and the Type I and Type II Errors

In every hypothesis test, the outcomes are dependent on a correct interpretation of the data. Incorrect calculations or misunderstood summary statistics can yield errors that affect the results. A **Type I** error occurs when a true null hypothesis is rejected. A **Type II error** occurs when a false null hypothesis is not rejected.

The probabilities of these errors are denoted by the Greek letters $\alpha$ and $\beta$, for a Type I and a Type II error respectively. The power of the test, $1 - \beta$, quantifies the likelihood that a test will yield the correct result of a true alternative hypothesis being accepted. A high power is desirable.

## 9.3 Distribution Needed for Hypothesis Testing

In order for a hypothesis test's results to be generalized to a population, certain requirements must be satisfied.

When testing for a single population mean:

1. A Student's $t$-test should be used if the data come from a simple, random sample and the population is approximately normally distributed, or the sample size is large, with an unknown standard deviation.

2. The normal test will work if the data come from a simple, random sample and the population is approximately normally distributed, or the sample size is large.

When testing a single population proportion use a normal test for a single population proportion if the data comes from a simple, random sample, fill the requirements for a binomial distribution, and the mean number of success and the mean number of failures satisfy the conditions: $np > 5$ and $nq > n$ where $n$ is the sample size, $p$ is the probability of a success, and $q$ is the probability of a failure.

## 9.4 Full Hypothesis Test Examples

The **hypothesis test** itself has an established process. This can be summarized as follows:

1. Determine $H_0$ and $H_a$. Remember, they are contradictory.

2. Determine the random variable.

3. Determine the distribution for the test.

4. Draw a graph and calculate the test statistic.

5. Compare the calculated test statistic with the Z critical value determined by the level of significance required by the test and make a decision (cannot reject $H_0$ or cannot accept $H_0$), and write a clear conclusion using English sentences.

# FORMULA REVIEW

## 9.3 Distribution Needed for Hypothesis Testing

| Sample Size | Test Statistic |
|---|---|
| < 30 (σ unknown) | $t_c = \dfrac{\bar{X} - \mu_0}{s / \sqrt{n}}$ |
| < 30 (σ known) | $Z_c = \dfrac{\bar{X} - \mu_0}{\sigma / \sqrt{n}}$ |
| > 30 (σ unknown) | $Z_c = \dfrac{\bar{X} - \mu_0}{s / \sqrt{n}}$ |

**Table 9.6 Test Statistics for Test of Means, Varying Sample Size, Population Known or Unknown**

| Sample Size | Test Statistic |
|---|---|
| > 30 (σ known) | $Z_c = \dfrac{\bar{X} - \mu_0}{\sigma / \sqrt{n}}$ |

**Table 9.6 Test Statistics for Test of Means, Varying Sample Size, Population Known or Unknown**

# PRACTICE

## 9.1 Null and Alternative Hypotheses

**1.** You are testing that the mean speed of your cable Internet connection is more than three Megabits per second. What is the random variable? Describe in words.

**2.** You are testing that the mean speed of your cable Internet connection is more than three Megabits per second. State the null and alternative hypotheses.

**3.** The American family has an average of two children. What is the random variable? Describe in words.

**4.** The mean entry level salary of an employee at a company is $58,000. You believe it is higher for IT professionals in the company. State the null and alternative hypotheses.

**5.** A sociologist claims the probability that a person picked at random in Times Square in New York City is visiting the area is 0.83. You want to test to see if the proportion is actually less. What is the random variable? Describe in words.

**6.** A sociologist claims the probability that a person picked at random in Times Square in New York City is visiting the area is 0.83. You want to test to see if the claim is correct. State the null and alternative hypotheses.

**7.** In a population of fish, approximately 42% are female. A test is conducted to see if, in fact, the proportion is less. State the null and alternative hypotheses.

**8.** Suppose that a recent article stated that the mean time spent in jail by a first–time convicted burglar is 2.5 years. A study was then done to see if the mean time has increased in the new century. A random sample of 26 first-time convicted burglars in a recent year was picked. The mean length of time in jail from the survey was 3 years with a standard deviation of 1.8 years. Suppose that it is somehow known that the population standard deviation is 1.5. If you were conducting a hypothesis test to determine if the mean length of jail time has increased, what would the null and alternative hypotheses be? The distribution of the population is normal.
   a. $H_0$: _____
   b. $H_a$: _____

**9.** A random survey of 75 death row inmates revealed that the mean length of time on death row is 17.4 years with a standard deviation of 6.3 years. If you were conducting a hypothesis test to determine if the population mean time on death row could likely be 15 years, what would the null and alternative hypotheses be?
   a. $H_0$: _____
   b. $H_a$: _____

**10.** The National Institute of Mental Health published an article stating that in any one-year period, approximately 9.5 percent of American adults suffer from depression or a depressive illness. Suppose that in a survey of 100 people in a certain town, seven of them suffered from depression or a depressive illness. If you were conducting a hypothesis test to determine if the true proportion of people in that town suffering from depression or a depressive illness is lower than the percent in the general adult American population, what would the null and alternative hypotheses be?
   a. $H_0$: _____
   b. $H_a$: _____

## 9.2 Outcomes and the Type I and Type II Errors

**11.** The mean price of mid-sized cars in a region is $32,000. A test is conducted to see if the claim is true. State the Type I and Type II errors in complete sentences.

**12.** A sleeping bag is tested to withstand temperatures of –15 °F. You think the bag cannot stand temperatures that low. State the Type I and Type II errors in complete sentences.

**13.** For **Exercise 9.12**, what are $\alpha$ and $\beta$ in words?

**14.** In words, describe $1 - \beta$ For **Exercise 9.12**.

**15.** A group of doctors is deciding whether or not to perform an operation. Suppose the null hypothesis, $H_0$, is: the surgical procedure will go well. State the Type I and Type II errors in complete sentences.

**16.** A group of doctors is deciding whether or not to perform an operation. Suppose the null hypothesis, $H_0$, is: the surgical procedure will go well. Which is the error with the greater consequence?

**17.** The power of a test is 0.981. What is the probability of a Type II error?

**18.** A group of divers is exploring an old sunken ship. Suppose the null hypothesis, $H_0$, is: the sunken ship does not contain buried treasure. State the Type I and Type II errors in complete sentences.

**19.** A microbiologist is testing a water sample for E-coli. Suppose the null hypothesis, $H_0$, is: the sample does not contain E-coli. The probability that the sample does not contain E-coli, but the microbiologist thinks it does is 0.012. The probability that the sample does contain E-coli, but the microbiologist thinks it does not is 0.002. What is the power of this test?

**20.** A microbiologist is testing a water sample for E-coli. Suppose the null hypothesis, $H_0$, is: the sample contains E-coli. Which is the error with the greater consequence?

## 9.3 Distribution Needed for Hypothesis Testing

**21.** Which two distributions can you use for hypothesis testing for this chapter?

**22.** Which distribution do you use when you are testing a population mean and the population standard deviation is known? Assume sample size is large. Assume a normal distribution with n ≥ 30.

**23.** Which distribution do you use when the standard deviation is not known and you are testing one population mean? Assume a normal distribution, with n ≥ 30.

**24.** A population mean is 13. The sample mean is 12.8, and the sample standard deviation is two. The sample size is 20. What distribution should you use to perform a hypothesis test? Assume the underlying population is normal.

**25.** A population has a mean is 25 and a standard deviation of five. The sample mean is 24, and the sample size is 108. What distribution should you use to perform a hypothesis test?

**26.** It is thought that 42% of respondents in a taste test would prefer Brand *A*. In a particular test of 100 people, 39% preferred Brand *A*. What distribution should you use to perform a hypothesis test?

**27.** You are performing a hypothesis test of a single population mean using a Student's *t*-distribution. What must you assume about the distribution of the data?

**28.** You are performing a hypothesis test of a single population mean using a Student's *t*-distribution. The data are not from a simple random sample. Can you accurately perform the hypothesis test?

**29.** You are performing a hypothesis test of a single population proportion. What must be true about the quantities of *np* and *nq*?

**30.** You are performing a hypothesis test of a single population proportion. You find out that *np* is less than five. What must you do to be able to perform a valid hypothesis test?

**31.** You are performing a hypothesis test of a single population proportion. The data come from which distribution?

## 9.4 Full Hypothesis Test Examples

**32.** Assume $H_0$: $\mu = 9$ and $H_a$: $\mu < 9$. Is this a left-tailed, right-tailed, or two-tailed test?

**33.** Assume $H_0$: $\mu \le 6$ and $H_a$: $\mu > 6$. Is this a left-tailed, right-tailed, or two-tailed test?

**34.** Assume $H_0$: $p = 0.25$ and $H_a$: $p \ne 0.25$. Is this a left-tailed, right-tailed, or two-tailed test?

**35.** Draw the general graph of a left-tailed test.

**36.** Draw the graph of a two-tailed test.

**37.** A bottle of water is labeled as containing 16 fluid ounces of water. You believe it is less than that. What type of test would you use?

**38.** Your friend claims that his mean golf score is 63. You want to show that it is higher than that. What type of test would you use?

**39.** A bathroom scale claims to be able to identify correctly any weight within a pound. You think that it cannot be that accurate. What type of test would you use?

**40.** You flip a coin and record whether it shows heads or tails. You know the probability of getting heads is 50%, but you think it is less for this particular coin. What type of test would you use?

**41.** If the alternative hypothesis has a not equals ( ≠ ) symbol, you know to use which type of test?

**42.** Assume the null hypothesis states that the mean is at least 18. Is this a left-tailed, right-tailed, or two-tailed test?

**43.** Assume the null hypothesis states that the mean is at most 12. Is this a left-tailed, right-tailed, or two-tailed test?

**44.** Assume the null hypothesis states that the mean is equal to 88. The alternative hypothesis states that the mean is not equal to 88. Is this a left-tailed, right-tailed, or two-tailed test?

# HOMEWORK

## 9.1 Null and Alternative Hypotheses

**45.** Some of the following statements refer to the null hypothesis, some to the alternate hypothesis.

State the null hypothesis, $H_0$, and the alternative hypothesis. $H_a$, in terms of the appropriate parameter ($\mu$ or $p$).

    a.   The mean number of years Americans work before retiring is 34.
    b.   At most 60% of Americans vote in presidential elections.
    c.   The mean starting salary for San Jose State University graduates is at least $100,000 per year.
    d.   Twenty-nine percent of high school seniors get drunk each month.
    e.   Fewer than 5% of adults ride the bus to work in Los Angeles.
    f.   The mean number of cars a person owns in her lifetime is not more than ten.
    g.   About half of Americans prefer to live away from cities, given the choice.
    h.   Europeans have a mean paid vacation each year of six weeks.
    i.   The chance of developing breast cancer is under 11% for women.
    j.   Private universities' mean tuition cost is more than $20,000 per year.

**46.** Over the past few decades, public health officials have examined the link between weight concerns and teen girls' smoking. Researchers surveyed a group of 273 randomly selected teen girls living in Massachusetts (between 12 and 15 years old). After four years the girls were surveyed again. Sixty-three said they smoked to stay thin. Is there good evidence that more than thirty percent of the teen girls smoke to stay thin? The alternative hypothesis is:
    a.  $p < 0.30$
    b.  $p \le 0.30$
    c.  $p \ge 0.30$
    d.  $p > 0.30$

**47.** A statistics instructor believes that fewer than 20% of Evergreen Valley College (EVC) students attended the opening night midnight showing of the latest Harry Potter movie. She surveys 84 of her students and finds that 11 attended the midnight showing. An appropriate alternative hypothesis is:
    a.  $p = 0.20$
    b.  $p > 0.20$
    c.  $p < 0.20$
    d.  $p \le 0.20$

**48.** Previously, an organization reported that teenagers spent 4.5 hours per week, on average, on the phone. The organization thinks that, currently, the mean is higher. Fifteen randomly chosen teenagers were asked how many hours per week they spend on the phone. The sample mean was 4.75 hours with a sample standard deviation of 2.0. Conduct a hypothesis test. The null and alternative hypotheses are:

    a. $H_o$: $\bar{x} = 4.5, H_a$: $\bar{x} > 4.5$

    b. $H_o$: $\mu \geq 4.5, H_a$: $\mu < 4.5$

    c. $H_o$: $\mu = 4.75, H_a$: $\mu > 4.75$

    d. $H_o$: $\mu = 4.5, H_a$: $\mu > 4.5$

## 9.2 Outcomes and the Type I and Type II Errors

**49.** State the Type I and Type II errors in complete sentences given the following statements.

    a. The mean number of years Americans work before retiring is 34.

    b. At most 60% of Americans vote in presidential elections.

    c. The mean starting salary for San Jose State University graduates is at least $100,000 per year.

    d. Twenty-nine percent of high school seniors get drunk each month.

    e. Fewer than 5% of adults ride the bus to work in Los Angeles.

    f. The mean number of cars a person owns in his or her lifetime is not more than ten.

    g. About half of Americans prefer to live away from cities, given the choice.

    h. Europeans have a mean paid vacation each year of six weeks.

    i. The chance of developing breast cancer is under 11% for women.

    j. Private universities mean tuition cost is more than $20,000 per year.

**50.** For statements a-j in **Exercise 9.109**, answer the following in complete sentences.

    a. State a consequence of committing a Type I error.

    b. State a consequence of committing a Type II error.

**51.** When a new drug is created, the pharmaceutical company must subject it to testing before receiving the necessary permission from the Food and Drug Administration (FDA) to market the drug. Suppose the null hypothesis is "the drug is unsafe." What is the Type II Error?

    a. To conclude the drug is safe when in, fact, it is unsafe.

    b. Not to conclude the drug is safe when, in fact, it is safe.

    c. To conclude the drug is safe when, in fact, it is safe.

    d. Not to conclude the drug is unsafe when, in fact, it is unsafe.

**52.** A statistics instructor believes that fewer than 20% of Evergreen Valley College (EVC) students attended the opening midnight showing of the latest Harry Potter movie. She surveys 84 of her students and finds that 11 of them attended the midnight showing. The Type I error is to conclude that the percent of EVC students who attended is _____.

    a. at least 20%, when in fact, it is less than 20%.

    b. 20%, when in fact, it is 20%.

    c. less than 20%, when in fact, it is at least 20%.

    d. less than 20%, when in fact, it is less than 20%.

**53.** It is believed that Lake Tahoe Community College (LTCC) Intermediate Algebra students get less than seven hours of sleep per night, on average. A survey of 22 LTCC Intermediate Algebra students generated a mean of 7.24 hours with a standard deviation of 1.93 hours. At a level of significance of 5%, do LTCC Intermediate Algebra students get less than seven hours of sleep per night, on average?

The Type II error is not to reject that the mean number of hours of sleep LTCC students get per night is at least seven when, in fact, the mean number of hours

    a. is more than seven hours.

    b. is at most seven hours.

    c. is at least seven hours.

    d. is less than seven hours.

**54.** Previously, an organization reported that teenagers spent 4.5 hours per week, on average, on the phone. The organization thinks that, currently, the mean is higher. Fifteen randomly chosen teenagers were asked how many hours per week they spend on the phone. The sample mean was 4.75 hours with a sample standard deviation of 2.0. Conduct a hypothesis test, the Type I error is:

    a.   to conclude that the current mean hours per week is higher than 4.5, when in fact, it is higher

    b.   to conclude that the current mean hours per week is higher than 4.5, when in fact, it is the same

    c.   to conclude that the mean hours per week currently is 4.5, when in fact, it is higher

    d.   to conclude that the mean hours per week currently is no higher than 4.5, when in fact, it is not higher

## 9.3 Distribution Needed for Hypothesis Testing

**55.** It is believed that Lake Tahoe Community College (LTCC) Intermediate Algebra students get less than seven hours of sleep per night, on average. A survey of 22 LTCC Intermediate Algebra students generated a mean of 7.24 hours with a standard deviation of 1.93 hours. At a level of significance of 5%, do LTCC Intermediate Algebra students get less than seven hours of sleep per night, on average? The distribution to be used for this test is $\overline{X} \sim$ _____

    a.   $N(7.24, \frac{1.93}{\sqrt{22}})$

    b.   $N(7.24, 1.93)$

    c.   $t_{22}$

    d.   $t_{21}$

## 9.4 Full Hypothesis Test Examples

**56.** A particular brand of tires claims that its deluxe tire averages at least 50,000 miles before it needs to be replaced. From past studies of this tire, the standard deviation is known to be 8,000. A survey of owners of that tire design is conducted. From the 28 tires surveyed, the mean lifespan was 46,500 miles with a standard deviation of 9,800 miles. Using alpha = 0.05, is the data highly inconsistent with the claim?

**57.** From generation to generation, the mean age when smokers first start to smoke varies. However, the standard deviation of that age remains constant of around 2.1 years. A survey of 40 smokers of this generation was done to see if the mean starting age is at least 19. The sample mean was 18.1 with a sample standard deviation of 1.3. Do the data support the claim at the 5% level?

**58.** The cost of a daily newspaper varies from city to city. However, the variation among prices remains steady with a standard deviation of 20¢. A study was done to test the claim that the mean cost of a daily newspaper is $1.00. Twelve costs yield a mean cost of 95¢ with a standard deviation of 18¢. Do the data support the claim at the 1% level?

**59.** An article in the *San Jose Mercury News* stated that students in the California state university system take 4.5 years, on average, to finish their undergraduate degrees. Suppose you believe that the mean time is longer. You conduct a survey of 49 students and obtain a sample mean of 5.1 with a sample standard deviation of 1.2. Do the data support your claim at the 1% level?

**60.** The mean number of sick days an employee takes per year is believed to be about ten. Members of a personnel department do not believe this figure. They randomly survey eight employees. The number of sick days they took for the past year are as follows: 12; 4; 15; 3; 11; 8; 6; 8. Let $x$ = the number of sick days they took for the past year. Should the personnel team believe that the mean number is ten?

**61.** In 1955, *Life Magazine* reported that the 25 year-old mother of three worked, on average, an 80 hour week. Recently, many groups have been studying whether or not the women's movement has, in fact, resulted in an increase in the average work week for women (combining employment and at-home work). Suppose a study was done to determine if the mean work week has increased. 81 women were surveyed with the following results. The sample mean was 83; the sample standard deviation was ten. Does it appear that the mean work week has increased for women at the 5% level?

**62.** Your statistics instructor claims that 60 percent of the students who take her Elementary Statistics class go through life feeling more enriched. For some reason that she can't quite figure out, most people don't believe her. You decide to check this out on your own. You randomly survey 64 of her past Elementary Statistics students and find that 34 feel more enriched as a result of her class. Now, what do you think?

**63.** A Nissan Motor Corporation advertisement read, "The average man's I.Q. is 107. The average brown trout's I.Q. is 4. So why can't man catch brown trout?" Suppose you believe that the brown trout's mean I.Q. is greater than four. You catch 12 brown trout. A fish psychologist determines the I.Q.s as follows: 5; 4; 7; 3; 6; 4; 5; 3; 6; 3; 8; 5. Conduct a hypothesis test of your belief.

**64.** Refer to Exercise 9.119. Conduct a hypothesis test to see if your decision and conclusion would change if your belief were that the brown trout's mean I.Q. is **not** four.

**65.** According to an article in *Newsweek*, the natural ratio of girls to boys is 100:105. In China, the birth ratio is 100: 114 (46.7% girls). Suppose you don't believe the reported figures of the percent of girls born in China. You conduct a study. In this study, you count the number of girls and boys born in 150 randomly chosen recent births. There are 60 girls and 90 boys born of the 150. Based on your study, do you believe that the percent of girls born in China is 46.7?

**66.** A poll done for *Newsweek* found that 13% of Americans have seen or sensed the presence of an angel. A contingent doubts that the percent is really that high. It conducts its own survey. Out of 76 Americans surveyed, only two had seen or sensed the presence of an angel. As a result of the contingent's survey, would you agree with the *Newsweek* poll? In complete sentences, also give three reasons why the two polls might give different results.

**67.** The mean work week for engineers in a start-up company is believed to be about 60 hours. A newly hired engineer hopes that it's shorter. She asks ten engineering friends in start-ups for the lengths of their mean work weeks. Based on the results that follow, should she count on the mean work week to be shorter than 60 hours?

Data (length of mean work week): 70; 45; 55; 60; 65; 55; 55; 60; 50; 55.

**68.** Sixty-eight percent of online courses taught at community colleges nationwide were taught by full-time faculty. To test if 68% also represents California's percent for full-time faculty teaching the online classes, Long Beach City College (LBCC) in California, was randomly selected for comparison. In the same year, 34 of the 44 online courses LBCC offered were taught by full-time faculty. Conduct a hypothesis test to determine if 68% represents California. NOTE: For more accurate results, use more California community colleges and this past year's data.

**69.** According to an article in *Bloomberg Businessweek*, New York City's most recent adult smoking rate is 14%. Suppose that a survey is conducted to determine this year's rate. Nine out of 70 randomly chosen N.Y. City residents reply that they smoke. Conduct a hypothesis test to determine if the rate is still 14% or if it has decreased.

**70.** The mean age of De Anza College students in a previous term was 26.6 years old. An instructor thinks the mean age for online students is older than 26.6. She randomly surveys 56 online students and finds that the sample mean is 29.4 with a standard deviation of 2.1. Conduct a hypothesis test.

**71.** Registered nurses earned an average annual salary of $69,110. For that same year, a survey was conducted of 41 California registered nurses to determine if the annual salary is higher than $69,110 for California nurses. The sample average was $71,121 with a sample standard deviation of $7,489. Conduct a hypothesis test.

**72.** La Leche League International reports that the mean age of weaning a child from breastfeeding is age four to five worldwide. In America, most nursing mothers wean their children much earlier. Suppose a random survey is conducted of 21 U.S. mothers who recently weaned their children. The mean weaning age was nine months (3/4 year) with a standard deviation of 4 months. Conduct a hypothesis test to determine if the mean weaning age in the U.S. is less than four years old.

**73.** Over the past few decades, public health officials have examined the link between weight concerns and teen girls' smoking. Researchers surveyed a group of 273 randomly selected teen girls living in Massachusetts (between 12 and 15 years old). After four years the girls were surveyed again. Sixty-three said they smoked to stay thin. Is there good evidence that more than thirty percent of the teen girls smoke to stay thin?
After conducting the test, your decision and conclusion are

    a.  Reject $H_0$: There is sufficient evidence to conclude that more than 30% of teen girls smoke to stay thin.
    b.  Do not reject $H_0$: There is not sufficient evidence to conclude that less than 30% of teen girls smoke to stay thin.
    c.  Do not reject $H_0$: There is not sufficient evidence to conclude that more than 30% of teen girls smoke to stay thin.
    d.  Reject $H_0$: There is sufficient evidence to conclude that less than 30% of teen girls smoke to stay thin.

**74.** A statistics instructor believes that fewer than 20% of Evergreen Valley College (EVC) students attended the opening night midnight showing of the latest Harry Potter movie. She surveys 84 of her students and finds that 11 of them attended the midnight showing.

At a 1% level of significance, an appropriate conclusion is:

    a. There is insufficient evidence to conclude that the percent of EVC students who attended the midnight showing of Harry Potter is less than 20%.

    b. There is sufficient evidence to conclude that the percent of EVC students who attended the midnight showing of Harry Potter is more than 20%.

    c. There is sufficient evidence to conclude that the percent of EVC students who attended the midnight showing of Harry Potter is less than 20%.

    d. There is insufficient evidence to conclude that the percent of EVC students who attended the midnight showing of Harry Potter is at least 20%.

**75.** Previously, an organization reported that teenagers spent 4.5 hours per week, on average, on the phone. The organization thinks that, currently, the mean is higher. Fifteen randomly chosen teenagers were asked how many hours per week they spend on the phone. The sample mean was 4.75 hours with a sample standard deviation of 2.0. Conduct a hypothesis test.

At a significance level of $a = 0.05$, what is the correct conclusion?

    a. There is enough evidence to conclude that the mean number of hours is more than 4.75

    b. There is enough evidence to conclude that the mean number of hours is more than 4.5

    c. There is not enough evidence to conclude that the mean number of hours is more than 4.5

    d. There is not enough evidence to conclude that the mean number of hours is more than 4.75

Instructions: For the following ten exercises,

Hypothesis testing: For the following ten exercises, answer each question.

    a. State the null and alternate hypothesis.

    b. State the *p*-value.

    c. State alpha.

    d. What is your decision?

    e. Write a conclusion.

    f. Answer any other questions asked in the problem.

**76.** According to the Center for Disease Control website, in 2011 at least 18% of high school students have smoked a cigarette. An Introduction to Statistics class in Davies County, KY conducted a hypothesis test at the local high school (a medium sized–approximately 1,200 students–small city demographic) to determine if the local high school's percentage was lower. One hundred fifty students were chosen at random and surveyed. Of the 150 students surveyed, 82 have smoked. Use a significance level of 0.05 and using appropriate statistical evidence, conduct a hypothesis test and state the conclusions.

**77.** A recent survey in the *N.Y. Times Almanac* indicated that 48.8% of families own stock. A broker wanted to determine if this survey could be valid. He surveyed a random sample of 250 families and found that 142 owned some type of stock. At the 0.05 significance level, can the survey be considered to be accurate?

**78.** Driver error can be listed as the cause of approximately 54% of all fatal auto accidents, according to the American Automobile Association. Thirty randomly selected fatal accidents are examined, and it is determined that 14 were caused by driver error. Using $\alpha = 0.05$, is the AAA proportion accurate?

**79.** The US Department of Energy reported that 51.7% of homes were heated by natural gas. A random sample of 221 homes in Kentucky found that 115 were heated by natural gas. Does the evidence support the claim for Kentucky at the $\alpha = 0.05$ level in Kentucky? Are the results applicable across the country? Why?

**80.** For Americans using library services, the American Library Association claims that at most 67% of patrons borrow books. The library director in Owensboro, Kentucky feels this is not true, so she asked a local college statistic class to conduct a survey. The class randomly selected 100 patrons and found that 82 borrowed books. Did the class demonstrate that the percentage was higher in Owensboro, KY? Use $\alpha = 0.01$ level of significance. What is the possible proportion of patrons that do borrow books from the Owensboro Library?

**81.** The Weather Underground reported that the mean amount of summer rainfall for the northeastern US is at least 11.52 inches. Ten cities in the northeast are randomly selected and the mean rainfall amount is calculated to be 7.42 inches with a standard deviation of 1.3 inches. At the $\alpha = 0.05$ level, can it be concluded that the mean rainfall was below the reported average? What if $\alpha = 0.01$? Assume the amount of summer rainfall follows a normal distribution.

**82.** A survey in the *N.Y. Times Almanac* finds the mean commute time (one way) is 25.4 minutes for the 15 largest US cities. The Austin, TX chamber of commerce feels that Austin's commute time is less and wants to publicize this fact. The mean for 25 randomly selected commuters is 22.1 minutes with a standard deviation of 5.3 minutes. At the $\alpha = 0.10$ level, is the Austin, TX commute significantly less than the mean commute time for the 15 largest US cities?

**83.** A report by the Gallup Poll found that a woman visits her doctor, on average, at most 5.8 times each year. A random sample of 20 women results in these yearly visit totals

3; 2; 1; 3; 7; 2; 9; 4; 6; 6; 8; 0; 5; 6; 4; 2; 1; 3; 4; 1

At the $\alpha = 0.05$ level can it be concluded that the sample mean is higher than 5.8 visits per year?

**84.** According to the *N.Y. Times Almanac* the mean family size in the U.S. is 3.18. A sample of a college math class resulted in the following family sizes:
5; 4; 5; 4; 4; 3; 6; 4; 3; 3; 5; 5; 6; 3; 3; 2; 7; 4; 5; 2; 2; 2; 3; 2

At $\alpha = 0.05$ level, is the class' mean family size greater than the national average? Does the Almanac result remain valid? Why?

**85.** The student academic group on a college campus claims that freshman students study at least 2.5 hours per day, on average. One Introduction to Statistics class was skeptical. The class took a random sample of 30 freshman students and found a mean study time of 137 minutes with a standard deviation of 45 minutes. At $\alpha = 0.01$ level, is the student academic group's claim correct?

# REFERENCES

## 9.1 Null and Alternative Hypotheses

Data from the National Institute of Mental Health. Available online at http://www.nimh.nih.gov/publicat/depression.cfm.

## 9.4 Full Hypothesis Test Examples

Data from Amit Schitai. Director of Instructional Technology and Distance Learning. LBCC.

Data from *Bloomberg Businessweek*. Available online at http://www.businessweek.com/news/2011- 09-15/nyc-smoking-rate-falls-to-record-low-of-14-bloomberg-says.html.

Data from energy.gov. Available online at http://energy.gov (accessed June 27. 2013).

Data from Gallup®. Available online at www.gallup.com (accessed June 27, 2013).

Data from *Growing by Degrees* by Allen and Seaman.

Data from La Leche League International. Available online at http://www.lalecheleague.org/Law/BAFeb01.html.

Data from the American Automobile Association. Available online at www.aaa.com (accessed June 27, 2013).

Data from the American Library Association. Available online at www.ala.org (accessed June 27, 2013).

Data from the Bureau of Labor Statistics. Available online at http://www.bls.gov/oes/current/oes291111.htm.

Data from the Centers for Disease Control and Prevention. Available online at www.cdc.gov (accessed June 27, 2013)

Data from the U.S. Census Bureau, available online at http://quickfacts.census.gov/qfd/states/00000.html (accessed June 27, 2013).

Data from the United States Census Bureau. Available online at http://www.census.gov/hhes/socdemo/language/.

Data from Toastmasters International. Available online at http://toastmasters.org/artisan/detail.asp?CategoryID=1&SubCategoryID=10&ArticleID=429&Page=1.

Data from Weather Underground. Available online at www.wunderground.com (accessed June 27, 2013).

Federal Bureau of Investigations. "Uniform Crime Reports and Index of Crime in Daviess in the State of Kentucky enforced by Daviess County from 1985 to 2005." Available online at http://www.disastercenter.com/kentucky/crime/3868.htm (accessed June 27, 2013).

"Foothill-De Anza Community College District." De Anza College, Winter 2006. Available online at http://research.fhda.edu/factbook/DAdemofs/Fact_sheet_da_2006w.pdf.

Johansen, C., J. Boice, Jr., J. McLaughlin, J. Olsen. "Cellular Telephones and Cancer—a Nationwide Cohort Study in Denmark." Institute of Cancer Epidemiology and the Danish Cancer Society, 93(3):203-7. Available online at http://www.ncbi.nlm.nih.gov/pubmed/11158188 (accessed June 27, 2013).

Rape, Abuse & Incest National Network. "How often does sexual assault occur?" RAINN, 2009. Available online at http://www.rainn.org/get-information/statistics/frequency-of-sexual-assault (accessed June 27, 2013).

## SOLUTIONS

**1** The random variable is the mean Internet speed in Megabits per second.

**3** The random variable is the mean number of children an American family has.

**5** The random variable is the proportion of people picked at random in Times Square visiting the city.

**7**

a. $H_0$: $p = 0.42$

b. $H_a$: $p < 0.42$

**9**

a. $H_0$: $\mu = 15$

b. $H_a$: $\mu \neq 15$

**11** Type I: The mean price of mid-sized cars is $32,000, but we conclude that it is not $32,000. Type II: The mean price of mid-sized cars is not $32,000, but we conclude that it is $32,000.

**13** $\alpha$ = the probability that you think the bag cannot withstand -15 degrees F, when in fact it can $\beta$ = the probability that you think the bag can withstand -15 degrees F, when in fact it cannot

**15** Type I: The procedure will go well, but the doctors think it will not. Type II: The procedure will not go well, but the doctors think it will.

**17** 0.019

**19** 0.998

**21** A normal distribution or a Student's $t$-distribution

**23** Use a Student's $t$-distribution

**25** a normal distribution for a single population mean

**27** It must be approximately normally distributed.

**29** They must both be greater than five.

**31** binomial distribution

**32** This is a left-tailed test.

**34** This is a two-tailed test.

**36**

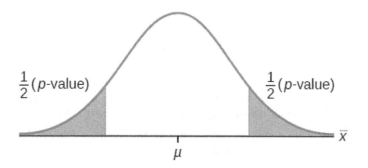

Figure 9.12

**38** a right-tailed test

**40** a left-tailed test

**42** This is a left-tailed test.

**44** This is a two-tailed test.

**45**

   a.  $H_0$: $\mu = 34$; $H_a$: $\mu \neq 34$

   b.  $H_0$: $p \leq 0.60$; $H_a$: $p > 0.60$

   c.  $H_0$: $\mu \geq 100{,}000$; $H_a$: $\mu < 100{,}000$

   d.  $H_0$: $p = 0.29$; $H_a$: $p \neq 0.29$

   e.  $H_0$: $p = 0.05$; $H_a$: $p < 0.05$

   f.  $H_0$: $\mu \leq 10$; $H_a$: $\mu > 10$

   g.  $H_0$: $p = 0.50$; $H_a$: $p \neq 0.50$

   h.  $H_0$: $\mu = 6$; $H_a$: $\mu \neq 6$

   i.  $H_0$: $p \geq 0.11$; $H_a$: $p < 0.11$

   j.  $H_0$: $\mu \leq 20{,}000$; $H_a$: $\mu > 20{,}000$

**47** c

**49**

   a.  Type I error: We conclude that the mean is not 34 years, when it really is 34 years. Type II error: We conclude that the mean is 34 years, when in fact it really is not 34 years.

   b.  Type I error: We conclude that more than 60% of Americans vote in presidential elections, when the actual percentage is at most 60%.Type II error: We conclude that at most 60% of Americans vote in presidential elections when, in fact, more than 60% do.

   c.  Type I error: We conclude that the mean starting salary is less than $100,000, when it really is at least $100,000. Type II error: We conclude that the mean starting salary is at least $100,000 when, in fact, it is less than $100,000.

   d.  Type I error: We conclude that the proportion of high school seniors who get drunk each month is not 29%, when it really is 29%. Type II error: We conclude that the proportion of high school seniors who get drunk each month is 29% when, in fact, it is not 29%.

   e.  Type I error: We conclude that fewer than 5% of adults ride the bus to work in Los Angeles, when the percentage that do is really 5% or more. Type II error: We conclude that 5% or more adults ride the bus to work in Los Angeles when, in fact, fewer that 5% do.

   f.  Type I error: We conclude that the mean number of cars a person owns in his or her lifetime is more than 10, when in reality it is not more than 10. Type II error: We conclude that the mean number of cars a person owns in his or her lifetime is not more than 10 when, in fact, it is more than 10.

g.  Type I error: We conclude that the proportion of Americans who prefer to live away from cities is not about half, though the actual proportion is about half. Type II error: We conclude that the proportion of Americans who prefer to live away from cities is half when, in fact, it is not half.

h.  Type I error: We conclude that the duration of paid vacations each year for Europeans is not six weeks, when in fact it is six weeks. Type II error: We conclude that the duration of paid vacations each year for Europeans is six weeks when, in fact, it is not.

i.  Type I error: We conclude that the proportion is less than 11%, when it is really at least 11%. Type II error: We conclude that the proportion of women who develop breast cancer is at least 11%, when in fact it is less than 11%.

j.  Type I error: We conclude that the average tuition cost at private universities is more than \$20,000, though in reality it is at most \$20,000. Type II error: We conclude that the average tuition cost at private universities is at most \$20,000 when, in fact, it is more than \$20,000.

**51** b

**53** d

**55** d

**56**

a.  $H_0$: $\mu \geq 50{,}000$

b.  $H_a$: $\mu < 50{,}000$

c.  Let $\bar{X}$ = the average lifespan of a brand of tires.

d.  normal distribution

e.  $z = -2.315$

f.  $p$-value = 0.0103

g.  Check student's solution.

h.      i.  alpha: 0.05

     ii.  Decision: Reject the null hypothesis.

     iii.  Reason for decision: The $p$-value is less than 0.05.

     iv.  Conclusion: There is sufficient evidence to conclude that the mean lifespan of the tires is less than 50,000 miles.

i.  (43,537, 49,463)

**58**

a.  $H_0$: $\mu = \$1.00$

b.  $H_a$: $\mu \neq \$1.00$

c.  Let $\bar{X}$ = the average cost of a daily newspaper.

d.  normal distribution

e.  $z = -0.866$

f.  $p$-value = 0.3865

g.  Check student's solution.

h.      i.  Alpha: 0.01

     ii.  Decision: Do not reject the null hypothesis.

     iii.  Reason for decision: The $p$-value is greater than 0.01.

     iv.  Conclusion: There is sufficient evidence to support the claim that the mean cost of daily papers is \$1. The mean cost could be \$1.

i.  (\$0.84, \$1.06)

**60**

a. $H_0: \mu = 10$

b. $H_a: \mu \neq 10$

c. Let $\bar{X}$ the mean number of sick days an employee takes per year.

d. Student's $t$-distribution

e. $t = -1.12$

f. $p$-value = 0.300

g. Check student's solution.

h.  i. Alpha: 0.05

    ii. Decision: Do not reject the null hypothesis.

    iii. Reason for decision: The $p$-value is greater than 0.05.

    iv. Conclusion: At the 5% significance level, there is insufficient evidence to conclude that the mean number of sick days is not ten.

i. (4.9443, 11.806)

**62**

a. $H_0: p \geq 0.6$

b. $H_a: p < 0.6$

c. Let $P'$ = the proportion of students who feel more enriched as a result of taking Elementary Statistics.

d. normal for a single proportion

e. 1.12

f. $p$-value = 0.1308

g. Check student's solution.

h.  i. Alpha: 0.05

    ii. Decision: Do not reject the null hypothesis.

    iii. Reason for decision: The $p$-value is greater than 0.05.

    iv. Conclusion: There is insufficient evidence to conclude that less than 60 percent of her students feel more enriched.

i. Confidence Interval: (0.409, 0.654)
The "plus-4s" confidence interval is (0.411, 0.648)

**64**

a. $H_0: \mu = 4$

b. $H_a: \mu \neq 4$

c. Let $\bar{X}$ the average I.Q. of a set of brown trout.

d. two-tailed Student's t-test

e. $t = 1.95$

f. $p$-value = 0.076

g. Check student's solution.

h.  i. Alpha: 0.05

    ii. Decision: Reject the null hypothesis.

    iii. Reason for decision: The $p$-value is greater than 0.05

    iv.  Conclusion: There is insufficient evidence to conclude that the average IQ of brown trout is not four.

  i.  (3.8865,5.9468)

**66**

a.  *H₀*: $p \geq 0.13$

b.  *Hₐ*: $p < 0.13$

c.  Let $P'$ = the proportion of Americans who have seen or sensed angels

d.  normal for a single proportion

e.  −2.688

f.  *p*-value = 0.0036

g.  Check student's solution.

h.  i.  alpha: 0.05

    ii.  Decision: Reject the null hypothesis.

    iii.  Reason for decision: The *p*-value is less than 0.05.

    iv.  Conclusion: There is sufficient evidence to conclude that the percentage of Americans who have seen or sensed an angel is less than 13%.

  i.  (0, 0.0623).
The"plus-4s" confidence interval is (0.0022, 0.0978)

**69**

a.  *H₀*: $p = 0.14$

b.  *Hₐ*: $p < 0.14$

c.  Let $P'$ = the proportion of NYC residents that smoke.

d.  normal for a single proportion

e.  −0.2756

f.  *p*-value = 0.3914

g.  Check student's solution.

h.  i.  alpha: 0.05

    ii.  Decision: Do not reject the null hypothesis.

    iii.  Reason for decision: The *p*-value is greater than 0.05.

    iv.  At the 5% significance level, there is insufficient evidence to conclude that the proportion of NYC residents who smoke is less than 0.14.

  i.  Confidence Interval: (0.0502, 0.2070): The "plus-4s" confidence interval (see chapter 8) is (0.0676, 0.2297).

**71**

a.  *H₀*: $\mu = 69{,}110$

b.  *Hₐ*: $\mu > 69{,}110$

c.  Let $\overline{X}$ = the mean salary in dollars for California registered nurses.

d.  Student's *t*-distribution

e.  $t = 1.719$

f.  *p*-value: 0.0466

g.  Check student's solution.

h.  i.  Alpha: 0.05

    ii.   Decision: Reject the null hypothesis.

   iii.   Reason for decision: The *p*-value is less than 0.05.

   iv.   Conclusion: At the 5% significance level, there is sufficient evidence to conclude that the mean salary of California registered nurses exceeds $69,110.

  i.   ($68,757, $73,485)

**73** c

**75** c

**77**

a.   $H_0$: $p = 0.488$ $H_a$: $p \neq 0.488$

b.   *p*-value = 0.0114

c.   alpha = 0.05

d.   Reject the null hypothesis.

e.   At the 5% level of significance, there is enough evidence to conclude that 48.8% of families own stocks.

f.   The survey does not appear to be accurate.

**79**

a.   $H_0$: $p = 0.517$ $H_a$: $p \neq 0.517$

b.   *p*-value = 0.9203.

c.   alpha = 0.05.

d.   Do not reject the null hypothesis.

e.   At the 5% significance level, there is not enough evidence to conclude that the proportion of homes in Kentucky that are heated by natural gas is 0.517.

f.   However, we cannot generalize this result to the entire nation. First, the sample's population is only the state of Kentucky. Second, it is reasonable to assume that homes in the extreme north and south will have extreme high usage and low usage, respectively. We would need to expand our sample base to include these possibilities if we wanted to generalize this claim to the entire nation.

**81**

a.   $H_0$: $\mu \geq 11.52$ $H_a$: $\mu < 11.52$

b.   *p*-value = 0.000002 which is almost 0.

c.   alpha = 0.05.

d.   Reject the null hypothesis.

e.   At the 5% significance level, there is enough evidence to conclude that the mean amount of summer rain in the northeaster US is less than 11.52 inches, on average.

f.   We would make the same conclusion if alpha was 1% because the *p*-value is almost 0.

**83**

a.   $H_0$: $\mu \leq 5.8$ $H_a$: $\mu > 5.8$

b.   *p*-value = 0.9987

c.   alpha = 0.05

d.   Do not reject the null hypothesis.

e.   At the 5% level of significance, there is not enough evidence to conclude that a woman visits her doctor, on average, more than 5.8 times a year.

**85**

a.   $H_0$: $\mu \geq 150$ $H_a$: $\mu < 150$

b. *p*-value = 0.0622

c. alpha = 0.01

d. Do not reject the null hypothesis.

e. At the 1% significance level, there is not enough evidence to conclude that freshmen students study less than 2.5 hours per day, on average.

f. The student academic group's claim appears to be correct.

# 10 | HYPOTHESIS TESTING WITH TWO SAMPLES

**Figure 10.1** If you want to test a claim that involves two groups (the types of breakfasts eaten east and west of the Mississippi River) you can use a slightly different technique when conducting a hypothesis test. (credit: Chloe Lim)

## Introduction

Studies often compare two groups. For example, researchers are interested in the effect aspirin has in preventing heart attacks. Over the last few years, newspapers and magazines have reported various aspirin studies involving two groups. Typically, one group is given aspirin and the other group is given a placebo. Then, the heart attack rate is studied over several years.

There are other situations that deal with the comparison of two groups. For example, studies compare various diet and exercise programs. Politicians compare the proportion of individuals from different income brackets who might vote for them. Students are interested in whether SAT or GRE preparatory courses really help raise their scores. Many business applications require comparing two groups. It may be the investment returns of two different investment strategies, or the differences in production efficiency of different management styles.

To compare two means or two proportions, you work with two groups. The groups are classified either as **independent** or **matched pairs**. **Independent groups** consist of two samples that are independent, that is, sample values selected from one population are not related in any way to sample values selected from the other population. **Matched pairs** consist of two samples that are dependent. The parameter tested using matched pairs is the population mean. The parameters tested using independent groups are either population means or population proportions of each group.

# 10.1 | Comparing Two Independent Population Means

The comparison of two independent population means is very common and provides a way to test the hypothesis that the two groups differ from each other. Is the night shift less productive than the day shift, are the rates of return from fixed asset investments different from those from common stock investments, and so on? An observed difference between two sample means depends on both the means and the sample standard deviations. Very different means can occur by chance if there is great variation among the individual samples. The test statistic will have to account for this fact. The test comparing two independent population means with unknown and possibly unequal population standard deviations is called the Aspin-Welch t-test. The degrees of freedom formula we will see later was developed by Aspin-Welch.

When we developed the hypothesis test for the mean and proportions we began with the Central Limit Theorem. We recognized that a sample mean came from a distribution of sample means, and sample proportions came from the sampling distribution of sample proportions. This made our sample parameters, the sample means and sample proportions, into random variables. It was important for us to know the distribution that these random variables came from. The Central Limit Theorem gave us the answer: the normal distribution. Our Z and t statistics came from this theorem. This provided us with the solution to our question of how to measure the probability that a sample mean came from a distribution with a particular hypothesized value of the mean or proportion. In both cases that was the question: what is the probability that the mean (or proportion) from our sample data came from a population distribution with the hypothesized value we are interested in?

Now we are interested in whether or not two samples have the same mean. Our question has not changed: Do these two samples come from the same population distribution? To approach this problem we create a new random variable. We recognize that we have two sample means, one from each set of data, and thus we have two random variables coming from two unknown distributions. To solve the problem we create a new random variable, the difference between the sample means. This new random variable also has a distribution and, again, the Central Limit Theorem tells us that this new distribution is normally distributed, regardless of the underlying distributions of the original data. A graph may help to understand this concept.

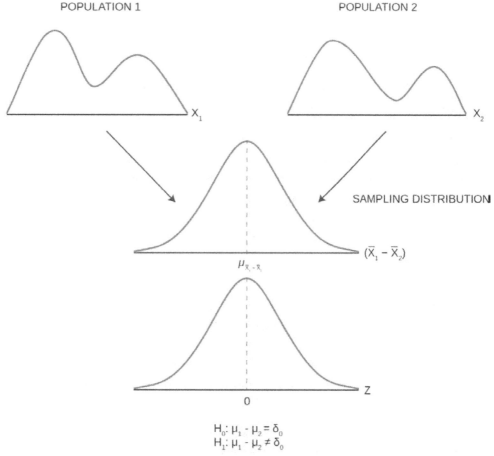

**Figure 10.2**

Pictured are two distributions of data, $X_1$ and $X_2$, with unknown means and standard deviations. The second panel shows the sampling distribution of the newly created random variable ($\bar{X}_1 - \bar{X}_2$). This distribution is the theoretical distribution of many many sample means from population 1 minus sample means from population 2. The Central Limit Theorem tells us that this theoretical sampling distribution of differences in sample means is normally distributed, regardless of the distribution of the actual population data shown in the top panel. Because the sampling distribution is normally distributed, we can develop a standardizing formula and calculate probabilities from the standard normal distribution in the bottom panel, the Z distribution. We have seen this same analysis before in Chapter 7 **Figure 7.2** .

The Central Limit Theorem, as before, provides us with the standard deviation of the sampling distribution, and further, that the expected value of the mean of the distribution of differences in sample means is equal to the differences in the population means. Mathematically this can be stated:

$$E\left(\mu_{\bar{x}_1} - \mu_{\bar{x}_2}\right) = \mu_1 - \mu_2$$

Because we do not know the population standard deviations, we estimate them using the two sample standard deviations from our independent samples. For the hypothesis test, we calculate the estimated standard deviation, or **standard error**, of **the difference in sample means**, $\bar{X}_1 - \bar{X}_2$.

**The standard error is:**

$$\sqrt{\frac{(s_1)^2}{n_1} + \frac{(s_2)^2}{n_2}}$$

We remember that substituting the sample variance for the population variance when we did not have the population variance was the technique we used when building the confidence interval and the test statistic for the test of hypothesis for a single mean back in **Confidence Intervals** and **Hypothesis Testing with One Sample**. **The test statistic (*t*-score)**

**is calculated as follows:**

$$t_c = \frac{(\bar{x}_1 - \bar{x}_2) - \delta_0}{\sqrt{\frac{(s_1)^2}{n_1} + \frac{(s_2)^2}{n_2}}}$$

where:

- $s_1$ and $s_2$, the sample standard deviations, are estimates of $\sigma_1$ and $\sigma_2$, respectively and

- $\sigma_1$ and $\sigma_1$ are the unknown population standard deviations.

- $\bar{x}_1$ and $\bar{x}_2$ are the sample means. $\mu_1$ and $\mu_2$ are the unknown population means.

The number of **degrees of freedom (*df*)** requires a somewhat complicated calculation. The *df* are not always a whole number. The test statistic above is approximated by the Student's *t*-distribution with *df* as follows:

**Degrees of freedom**

$$df = \frac{\left( \frac{(s_1)^2}{n_1} + \frac{(s_2)^2}{n_2} \right)^2}{\left( \frac{1}{n_1 - 1} \right) \left( \frac{(s_1)^2}{n_1} \right)^2 + \left( \frac{1}{n_2 - 1} \right) \left( \frac{(s_2)^2}{n_2} \right)^2}$$

When both sample sizes $n_1$ and $n_2$ are 30 or larger, the Student's *t* approximation is very good. If each sample has more than 30 observations then the degrees of freedom can be calculated as n1 + n2 - 2.

The format of the sampling distribution, differences in sample means, specifies that the format of the null and alternative hypothesis is:

$$H_0 : \mu_1 - \mu_2 = \delta_0$$
$$H_a : \mu_1 - \mu_2 \neq \delta_0$$

where $\delta_0$ is the hypothesized difference between the two means. If the question is simply "is there any difference between the means?" then $\delta_0 = 0$ and the null and alternative hypotheses becomes:

$$H_0 : \mu_1 = \mu_2$$
$$H_a : \mu_1 \neq \mu_2$$

An example of when $\delta_0$ might not be zero is when the comparison of the two groups requires a specific difference for the decision to be meaningful. Imagine that you are making a capital investment. You are considering changing from your current model machine to another. You measure the productivity of your machines by the speed they produce the product. It may be that a contender to replace the old model is faster in terms of product throughput, but is also more expensive. The second machine may also have more maintenance costs, setup costs, etc. The null hypothesis would be set up so that the new machine would have to be better than the old one by enough to cover these extra costs in terms of speed and cost of production. This form of the null and alternative hypothesis shows how valuable this particular hypothesis test can be. For most of our work we will be testing simple hypotheses asking if there is any difference between the two distribution means.

## Example 10.1 Independent groups

The Kona Iki Corporation produces coconut milk. They take coconuts and extract the milk inside by drilling a hole and pouring the milk into a vat for processing. They have both a day shift (called the B shift) and a night shift (called the G shift) to do this part of the process. They would like to know if the day shift and the night shift are equally efficient in processing the coconuts. A study is done sampling 9 shifts of the G shift and 16 shifts of the B shift. The results of the number of hours required to process 100 pounds of coconuts is presented in **Table 10.1**. A study is done and data are collected, resulting in the data in **Table 10.1**.

|  | Sample Size | Average Number of Hours to Process 100 Pounds of Coconuts | Sample Standard Deviation |
|---|---|---|---|
| G Shift | 9 | 2 | 0.866 |
| B Shift | 16 | 3.2 | 1.00 |

Table 10.1

Is there a difference in the mean amount of time for each shift to process 100 pounds of coconuts? Test at the 5% level of significance.

Solution 10.1

**The population standard deviations are not known and cannot be assumed to equal each other.** Let $g$ be the subscript for the G Shift and $b$ be the subscript for the B Shift. Then, $\mu_g$ is the population mean for G Shift and $\mu_b$ is the population mean for B Shift. This is a test of two **independent groups**, two population **means**.

**Random variable:** $\bar{X}_g - \bar{X}_b$ = difference in the sample mean amount of time between the G Shift and the B Shift takes to process the coconuts.

$H_0: \mu_g = \mu_b \qquad H_0: \mu_g - \mu_b = 0$

$H_a: \mu_g \neq \mu_b \qquad H_a: \mu_g - \mu_b \neq 0$

The words **"the same"** tell you $H_0$ has an "=". Since there are no other words to indicate $H_a$, is either faster or slower. This is a two tailed test.

**Distribution for the test:** Use $t_{df}$ where $df$ is calculated using the $df$ formula for independent groups, two population means above. Using a calculator, $df$ is approximately 18.8462.

**Graph:**

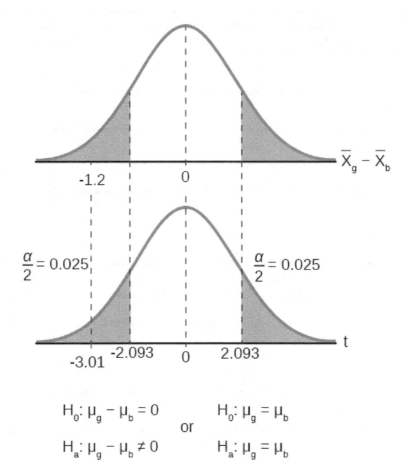

**Figure 10.3**

$$t_c = \frac{\left(\bar{X}_1 - \bar{X}_2\right) - \delta_0}{\sqrt{\frac{s_1^2}{n_1} + \frac{s_2^2}{n_2}}} = -3.01$$

We next find the critical value on the t-table using the degrees of freedom from above. The critical value, 2.093, is found in the .025 column, this is α/2, at 19 degrees of freedom. (The convention is to round up the degrees of freedom to make the conclusion more conservative.) Next we calculate the test statistic and mark this on the t-distribution graph.

**Make a decision:** Since the calculated t-value is in the tail we cannot accept the null hypothesis that there is no difference between the two groups. The means are different.

The graph has included the sampling distribution of the differences in the sample means to show how the t-distribution aligns with the sampling distribution data. We see in the top panel that the calculated difference in the two means is -1.2 and the bottom panel shows that this is 3.01 standard deviations from the mean. Typically we do not need to show the sampling distribution graph and can rely on the graph of the test statistic, the t-distribution in this case, to reach our conclusion.

**Conclusion:** At the 5% level of significance, the sample data show there is sufficient evidence to conclude that the mean number of hours that the G Shift takes to process 100 pounds of coconuts is different from the B Shift (mean number of hours for the B Shift is greater than the mean number of hours for the G Shift).

## NOTE

When the sum of the sample sizes is larger than 30 ($n_1 + n_2 > 30$) you can use the normal distribution to approximate the Student's $t$.

---

## Example 10.2

A study is done to determine if Company A retains its workers longer than Company B. It is believed that Company A has a higher retention than Company B. The study finds that in a sample of 11 workers at Company A their average time with the company is four years with a standard deviation of 1.5 years. A sample of 9 workers at Company B finds that the average time with the company was 3.5 years with a standard deviation of 1 year. Test this proposition at the 1% level of significance.

a. Is this a test of two means or two proportions?

**Solution 10.2**

a. two means because time is a continuous random variable.

b. Are the populations standard deviations known or unknown?

**Solution 10.2**

b. unknown

c. Which distribution do you use to perform the test?

**Solution 10.2**

c. Student's $t$

d. What is the random variable?

**Solution 10.2**

d. $\bar{X}_A - \bar{X}_B$

e. What are the null and alternate hypotheses?

**Solution 10.2**

e.

- $H_o : \mu_A \leq \mu_B$

- $H_a : \mu_A > \mu_B$

f. Is this test right-, left-, or two-tailed?

**Solution 10.2**

f. right one-tailed test

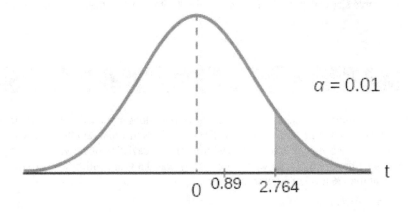

$$H_0: \mu_A \le \mu_B$$

$$H_a: \mu_A > \mu_B$$

**Figure 10.4**

g. What is the value of the test statistic?

**Solution 10.2**

$$t_c = \frac{(\bar{X}_1 - \bar{X}_2) - \delta_0}{\sqrt{\frac{s_1^2}{n_1} + \frac{s_2^2}{n_2}}} = 0.89$$

h. Can you accept/reject the null hypothesis?

**Solution 10.2**
h. Cannot reject the null hypothesis that there is no difference between the two groups. Test statistic is not in the tail. The critical value of the t distribution is 2.764 with 10 degrees of freedom. This example shows how difficult it is to reject a null hypothesis with a very small sample. The critical values require very large test statistics to reach the tail.

i. **Conclusion:**

**Solution 10.2**
i. At the 1% level of significance, from the sample data, there is not sufficient evidence to conclude that the retention of workers at Company A is longer than Company B, on average.

## Example 10.3

An interesting research question is the effect, if any, that different types of teaching formats have on the grade outcomes of students. To investigate this issue one sample of students' grades was taken from a hybrid class and another sample taken from a standard lecture format class. Both classes were for the same subject. The mean course grade in percent for the 35 hybrid students is 74 with a standard deviation of 16. The mean grades of the 40 students form the standard lecture class was 76 percent with a standard deviation of 9. Test at 5% to see if there is any significant difference in the population mean grades between standard lecture course and hybrid class.

### Solution 10.3

We begin by noting that we have two groups, students from a hybrid class and students from a standard lecture format class. We also note that the random variable, what we are interested in, is students' grades, a continuous random variable. We could have asked the research question in a different way and had a binary random variable. For example, we could have studied the percentage of students with a failing grade, or with an A grade. Both of these would be binary and thus a test of proportions and not a test of means as is the case here. Finally, there is no presumption as to which format might lead to higher grades so the hypothesis is stated as a two-tailed test.

$H_0$: $\mu_1 = \mu_2$
$H_a$: $\mu_1 \neq \mu_2$

As would virtually always be the case, we do not know the population variances of the two distributions and thus our test statistic is:

$$t_c = \frac{\left(\bar{x}_1 - \bar{x}_2\right) - \delta_0}{\sqrt{\frac{s_1^2}{n_1} + \frac{s_2^2}{n_2}}} = \frac{(74 - 76) - 0}{\sqrt{\frac{16^2}{35} + \frac{9^2}{40}}} = -0.65$$

To determine the critical value of the Student's t we need the degrees of freedom. For this case we use: df = n1 + n2 - 2 = 35 + 40 -2 = 73. This is large enough to consider it the normal distribution thus $t_{a/2}$ = 1.96. Again as always we determine if the calculated value is in the tail determined by the critical value. In this case we do not even need to look up the critical value: the calculated value of the difference in these two average grades is not even one standard deviation apart. Certainly not in the tail.

**Conclusion: Cannot reject the null at α=5%. Therefore, evidence does not exist to prove that the grades in hybrid and standard classes differ.**

# 10.2 | Cohen's Standards for Small, Medium, and Large Effect Sizes

**Cohen's *d*** is a measure of "effect size" based on the differences between two means. Cohen's *d*, named for United States statistician Jacob Cohen, measures the relative strength of the differences between the means of two populations based on sample data. The calculated value of effect size is then compared to Cohen's standards of small, medium, and large effect sizes.

| Size of effect | d |
|---|---|
| Small | 0.2 |
| medium | 0.5 |
| Large | 0.8 |

Table 10.2 Cohen's Standard Effect Sizes

Cohen's *d* is the measure of the difference between two means divided by the pooled standard deviation: $d = \frac{\bar{x}_1 - \bar{x}_2}{s_{pooled}}$

where $s_{pooled} = \sqrt{\frac{(n_1 - 1)s_1^2 + (n_2 - 1)s_2^2}{n_1 + n_2 - 2}}$

It is important to note that Cohen's d does not provide a level of confidence as to the magnitude of the size of the effect comparable to the other tests of hypothesis we have studied. The sizes of the effects are simply indicative.

## Example 10.4

Calculate Cohen's $d$ for **???**. Is the size of the effect small, medium, or large? Explain what the size of the effect means for this problem.

**Solution 10.4**

$\bar{x}_1 = 4 \; s_1 = 1.5 \; n_1 = 11$

$\bar{x}_2 = 3.5 \; s_2 = 1 \; n_2 = 9$

$d = 0.384$

The effect is small because 0.384 is between Cohen's value of 0.2 for small effect size and 0.5 for medium effect size. The size of the differences of the means for the two companies is small indicating that there is not a significant difference between them.

# 10.3 | Test for Differences in Means: Assuming Equal Population Variances

Typically we can never expect to know any of the population parameters, mean, proportion, or standard deviation. When testing hypotheses concerning differences in means we are faced with the difficulty of two unknown variances that play a critical role in the test statistic. We have been substituting the sample variances just as we did when testing hypotheses for a single mean. And as we did before, we used a Student's t to compensate for this lack of information on the population variance. There may be situations, however, when we do not know the population variances, but we can assume that the two populations have the same variance. If this is true then the pooled sample variance will be smaller than the individual sample variances. This will give more precise estimates and reduce the probability of discarding a good null. The null and alternative hypotheses remain the same, but the test statistic changes to:

$$t_c = \frac{\left(\bar{x}_1 - \bar{x}_2\right) - \delta_0}{\sqrt{S_p^2\left(\frac{1}{n_1} + \frac{1}{n_2}\right)}}$$

where $S_p^2$ is the pooled variance given by the formula:

$$S_p^2 = \frac{\left(n_1 - 1\right)s_1^2 + \left(n_2 - 1\right)s_2^2}{n_1 + n_2 - 2}$$

## Example 10.5

A drug trial is attempted using a real drug and a pill made of just sugar. 18 people are given the real drug in hopes of increasing the production of endorphins. The increase in endorphins is found to be on average 8 micrograms per person, and the sample standard deviation is 5.4 micrograms. 11 people are given the sugar pill, and their average endorphin increase is 4 micrograms with a standard deviation of 2.4. From previous research on endorphins it is determined that it can be assumed that the variances within the two samples can be assumed to be the same. Test at 5% to see if the population mean for the real drug had a significantly greater impact on the endorphins than the population mean with the sugar pill.

**Solution 10.5**

First we begin by designating one of the two groups Group 1 and the other Group 2. This will be needed to keep track of the null and alternative hypotheses. Let's set Group 1 as those who received the actual new medicine being tested and therefore Group 2 is those who received the sugar pill. We can now set up the null and alternative hypothesis as:

$H_0: \mu_1 \leq \mu_2$

$H_1: \mu_1 > \mu_2$

This is set up as a one-tailed test with the claim in the alternative hypothesis that the medicine will produce more endorphins than the sugar pill. We now calculate the test statistic which requires us to calculate the pooled variance, $S_p^2$ using the formula above.

$$t_c = \frac{\left(\bar{x}_1 - \bar{x}_2\right) - \delta_0}{\sqrt{S_p^2\left(\frac{1}{n_1} + \frac{1}{n_2}\right)}} = \frac{(8-4) - 0}{\sqrt{20.4933\left(\frac{1}{18} + \frac{1}{11}\right)}} = 2.31$$

$t_\alpha$, allows us to compare the test statistic and the critical value.

$$t_\alpha = 1.703 \text{ at } df = n_1 + n_2 - 2 = 18 + 11 - 2 = 27$$

The test statistic is clearly in the tail, 2.31 is larger than the critical value of 1.703, and therefore we cannot maintain the null hypothesis. Thus, we conclude that there is significant evidence at the 95% level of confidence that the new medicine produces the effect desired.

# 10.4 | Comparing Two Independent Population Proportions

When conducting a hypothesis test that compares two independent population proportions, the following characteristics should be present:

1. The two independent samples are random samples that are independent.

2. The number of successes is at least five, and the number of failures is at least five, for each of the samples.

3. Growing literature states that the population must be at least ten or even perhaps 20 times the size of the sample. This keeps each population from being over-sampled and causing biased results.

Comparing two proportions, like comparing two means, is common. If two estimated proportions are different, it may be due to a difference in the populations or it may be due to chance in the sampling. A hypothesis test can help determine if a difference in the estimated proportions reflects a difference in the two population proportions.

Like the case of differences in sample means, we construct a sampling distribution for differences in sample proportions: $\left(p'_A - p'_B\right)$ where $p'_A = X_{\frac{A}{n_A}}$ and $p'_B = X_{\frac{B}{n_B}}$ are the sample proportions for the two sets of data in question. $X_A$ and $X_B$ are the number of successes in each sample group respectively, and $n_A$ and $n_B$ are the respective sample sizes from the two groups. Again we go the Central Limit theorem to find the distribution of this sampling distribution for the differences in sample proportions. And again we find that this sampling distribution, like the ones past, are normally distributed as proved by the Central Limit Theorem, as seen in **Figure 10.5** .

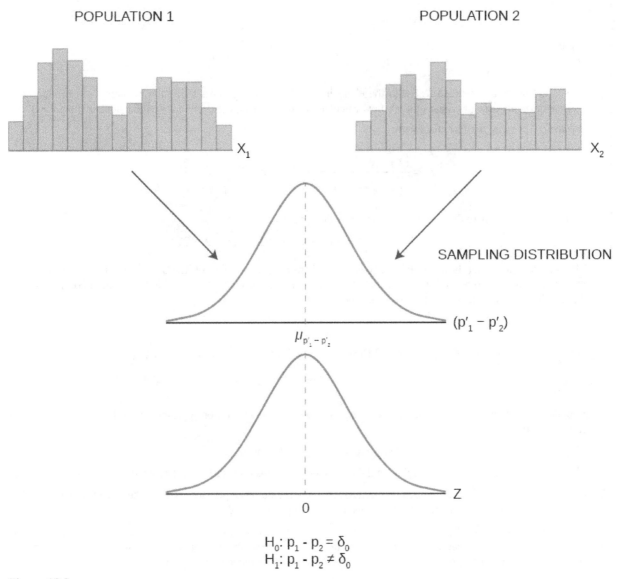

**Figure 10.5**

Generally, the null hypothesis allows for the test of a difference of a particular value, $\delta_0$, just as we did for the case of differences in means.

$$H_0 : p_1 - p_2 = \delta_0$$

$$H_1 : p_1 - p_2 \neq \delta_0$$

Most common, however, is the test that the two proportions are the same. That is,

$$H_0 : p_A = p_B$$

$$H_a : p_A \neq p_B$$

To conduct the test, we use a pooled proportion, $p_c$.

**The pooled proportion is calculated as follows:**

$$p_c = \frac{x_A + x_B}{n_A + n_B}$$

**The test statistic (z-score) is:**

$$Z_c = \frac{(p'_A - p'_B) - \delta_0}{\sqrt{p_c(1 - p_c)(\frac{1}{n_A} + \frac{1}{n_B})}}$$

where $\delta_0$ is the hypothesized differences between the two proportions and $p_c$ is the pooled variance from the formula above.

## Example 10.6

A bank has recently acquired a new branch and thus has customers in this new territory. They are interested in the default rate in their new territory. They wish to test the hypothesis that the default rate is different from their current customer base. They sample 200 files in area A, their current customers, and find that 20 have defaulted. In area B, the new customers, another sample of 200 files shows 12 have defaulted on their loans. At a 10% level of significance can we say that the default rates are the same or different?

### Solution 10.6

This is a test of proportions. We know this because the underlying random variable is binary, default or not default. Further, we know it is a test of differences in proportions because we have two sample groups, the current customer base and the newly acquired customer base. Let A and B be the subscripts for the two customer groups. Then $p_A$ and $p_B$ are the two population proportions we wish to test.

**Random Variable:**

$P'_A - P'_B$ = difference in the proportions of customers who defaulted in the two groups.

$H_0 : p_A = p_B$

$H_a : p_A \neq p_B$

The words **"is a difference"** tell you the test is two-tailed.

**Distribution for the test:** Since this is a test of two binomial population proportions, the distribution is normal:

$$p_c = \frac{x_A + x_B}{n_A + n_B} = \frac{20 + 12}{200 + 200} = 0.08 \quad 1 - p_c = 0.92$$

$(p'_A - p'_B) = 0.04$ follows an approximate normal distribution.

Estimated proportion for group A: $p'_A = \frac{x_A}{n_A} = \frac{20}{200} = 0.1$

Estimated proportion for group B: $p'_B = \frac{x_B}{n_B} = \frac{12}{200} = 0.06$

The estimated difference between the two groups is : $p'_A - p'_B = 0.1 - 0.06 = 0.04$.

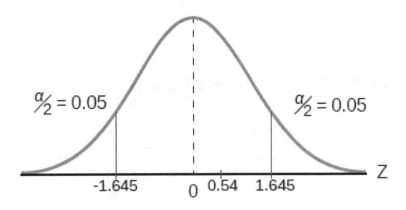

$$H_0: P_A = P_B$$

$$H_a: P_A \neq P_B$$

**Figure 10.6**

$$Z_c = \frac{(P'_A - P'_B) - \delta_0}{P_c(1 - P_c)\left(\frac{1}{n_A} + \frac{1}{n_B}\right)} = 0.54$$

The calculated test statistic is .54 and is not in the tail of the distribution.

Make a decision: Since the calculate test statistic is not in the tail of the distribution we cannot reject $H_0$.

**Conclusion:** At a 1% level of significance, from the sample data, there is not sufficient evidence to conclude that there is a difference between the proportions of customers who defaulted in the two groups.

**10.6** Two types of valves are being tested to determine if there is a difference in pressure tolerances. Fifteen out of a random sample of 100 of Valve $A$ cracked under 4,500 psi. Six out of a random sample of 100 of Valve $B$ cracked under 4,500 psi. Test at a 5% level of significance.

# 10.5 | Two Population Means with Known Standard Deviations

Even though this situation is not likely (knowing the population standard deviations is very unlikely), the following example illustrates hypothesis testing for independent means with known population standard deviations. The sampling distribution for the difference between the means is normal in accordance with the central limit theorem. The random variable is $\bar{X}_1 - \bar{X}_2$. The normal distribution has the following format:

**The standard deviation is:**

$$\sqrt{\frac{(\sigma_1)^2}{n_1} + \frac{(\sigma_2)^2}{n_2}}$$

**The test statistic (z-score) is:**

$$Z_c = \frac{(\bar{x}_1 - \bar{x}_2) - \delta_0}{\sqrt{\frac{(\sigma_1)^2}{n_1} + \frac{(\sigma_2)^2}{n_2}}}$$

## Example 10.7

**Independent groups, population standard deviations known:** The mean lasting time of two competing floor waxes is to be compared. **Twenty floors** are randomly assigned **to test each wax**. Both populations have a normal distributions. The data are recorded in Table 10.3.

| Wax | Sample Mean Number of Months Floor Wax Lasts | Population Standard Deviation |
|-----|-----------------------------------------------|-------------------------------|
| 1 | 3 | 0.33 |
| 2 | 2.9 | 0.36 |

Table 10.3

Does the data indicate that **wax 1 is more effective than wax 2**? Test at a 5% level of significance.

**Solution 10.7**

This is a test of two independent groups, two population means, population standard deviations known.

**Random Variable:** $\bar{X}_1 - \bar{X}_2$ = difference in the mean number of months the competing floor waxes last.

$H_0 : \mu_1 \leq \mu_2$

$H_a : \mu_1 > \mu_2$

The words **"is more effective"** says that **wax 1 lasts longer than wax 2**, on average. "Longer" is a ">" symbol and goes into $H_a$. Therefore, this is a right-tailed test.

**Distribution for the test:** The population standard deviations are known so the distribution is normal. Using the formula for the test statistic we find the calculated value for the problem.

$$Z_c = \frac{(\mu_1 - \mu_2) - \delta_0}{\sqrt{\frac{\sigma_1^2}{n_1} + \frac{\sigma_2^2}{n_2}}} = 0.1$$

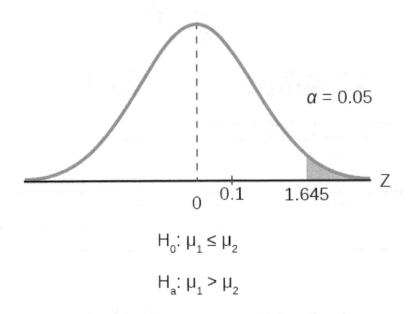

$\alpha = 0.05$

$H_0: \mu_1 \le \mu_2$

$H_a: \mu_1 > \mu_2$

Figure 10.7

The estimated difference between he two means is : $\bar{X}_1 - \bar{X}_2 = 3 - 2.9 = 0.1$

**Compare calculated value and critical value and $Z_\alpha$:** We mark the calculated value on the graph and find the the calculate value is not in the tail therefore we cannot reject the null hypothesis.

**Make a decision:** the calculated value of the test statistic is not in the tail, therefore you cannot reject $H_0$.

**Conclusion:** At the 5% level of significance, from the sample data, there is not sufficient evidence to conclude that the mean time wax 1 lasts is longer (wax 1 is more effective) than the mean time wax 2 lasts.

## Try It Σ

**10.7** The means of the number of revolutions per minute of two competing engines are to be compared. Thirty engines are randomly assigned to be tested. Both populations have normal distributions. Table 10.4 shows the result. Do the data indicate that Engine 2 has higher RPM than Engine 1? Test at a 5% level of significance.

| Engine | Sample Mean Number of RPM | Population Standard Deviation |
|--------|---------------------------|------------------------------|
| 1 | 1,500 | 50 |
| 2 | 1,600 | 60 |

Table 10.4

## Example 10.8

An interested citizen wanted to know if Democratic U. S. senators are older than Republican U.S. senators, on average. On May 26 2013, the mean age of 30 randomly selected Republican Senators was 61 years 247 days old (61.675 years) with a standard deviation of 10.17 years. The mean age of 30 randomly selected Democratic senators was 61 years 257 days old (61.704 years) with a standard deviation of 9.55 years.

Do the data indicate that Democratic senators are older than Republican senators, on average? Test at a 5% level of significance.

### Solution 10.8

This is a test of two independent groups, two population means. The population standard deviations are unknown, but the sum of the sample sizes is 30 + 30 = 60, which is greater than 30, so we can use the normal approximation to the Student's-t distribution. Subscripts: 1: Democratic senators 2: Republican senators

**Random variable:** $\overline{X}_1 - \overline{X}_2$ = difference in the mean age of Democratic and Republican U.S. senators.

$H_0 : \mu_1 \le \mu_2 \quad H_0 : \mu_1 - \mu_2 \le 0$

$H_a : \mu_1 > \mu_2 \quad H_a : \mu_1 - \mu_2 > 0$

The words "older than" translates as a ">" symbol and goes into $H_a$. Therefore, this is a right-tailed test.

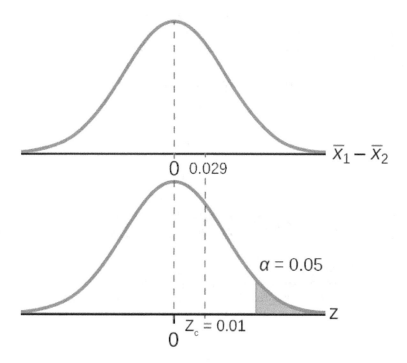

**Figure 10.8**

**Make a decision:** The p-value is larger than 5%, therefore we cannot reject the null hypothesis. By calculating the test statistic we would find that the test statistic does not fall in the tail, therefore we cannot reject the null hypothesis. We reach the same conclusion using either method of a making this statistical decision.

**Conclusion:** At the 5% level of significance, from the sample data, there is not sufficient evidence to conclude that the mean age of Democratic senators is greater than the mean age of the Republican senators.

# 10.6 | Matched or Paired Samples

In most cases of economic or business data we have little or no control over the process of how the data are gathered. In this sense the data are not the result of a planned controlled experiment. In some cases, however, we can develop data that are part of a controlled experiment. This situation occurs frequently in quality control situations. Imagine that the production rates of two machines built to the same design, but at different manufacturing plants, are being tested for differences in some production metric such as speed of output or meeting some production specification such as strength of the product.

The test is the same in format to what we have been testing, but here we can have matched pairs for which we can test if differences exist. Each observation has its matched pair against which differences are calculated. First, the differences in the metric to be tested between the two lists of observations must be calculated, and this is typically labeled with the letter "d." Then, the average of these matched differences, $\bar{X}_d$ is calculated as is its standard deviation, $S_d$. We expect that the standard deviation of the differences of the matched pairs will be smaller than unmatched pairs because presumably fewer differences should exist because of the correlation between the two groups.

When using a hypothesis test for matched or paired samples, the following characteristics may be present:

1.  Simple random sampling is used.
2.  Sample sizes are often small.
3.  Two measurements (samples) are drawn from the same pair of individuals or objects.
4.  Differences are calculated from the matched or paired samples.
5.  The differences form the sample that is used for the hypothesis test.
6.  Either the matched pairs have differences that come from a population that is normal or the number of differences is sufficiently large so that distribution of the sample mean of differences is approximately normal.

In a hypothesis test for matched or paired samples, subjects are matched in pairs and differences are calculated. The differences are the data. The population mean for the differences, $\mu_d$, is then tested using a Student's-t test for a single population mean with $n - 1$ degrees of freedom, where $n$ is the number of differences, that is, the number of pairs not the number of observations.

**The null and alternative hypotheses for this test are:**
$$H_0 : \mu_d = 0$$
$$H_a : \mu_d \neq 0$$

**The test statistic is:**
$$t_c = \frac{\bar{x}_d - \mu_d}{\left(\frac{s_d}{\sqrt{n}}\right)}$$

## Example 10.9

A company has developed a training program for its entering employees because they have become concerned with the results of the six-month employee review. They hope that the training program can result in better six-month reviews. Each trainee constitutes a "pair", the entering score the employee received when first entering the firm and the score given at the six-month review. The difference in the two scores were calculated for each employee and the means for before and after the training program was calculated. The sample mean before the training program was 20.4 and the sample mean after the training program was 23.9. The standard deviation of the differences in the two scores across the 20 employees was 3.8 points. Test at the 10% significance level the null hypothesis that the two population means are equal against the alternative that the training program helps improve the employees' scores.

### Solution 10.9
The first step is to identify this as a two sample case: before the training and after the training. This differentiates this problem from simple one sample issues. Second, we determine that the two samples are "paired." Each observation in the first sample has a paired observation in the second sample. This information tells us that the null and alternative hypotheses should be:
$$H_0 : \mu_d \leq 0$$
$$H_a : \mu_d > 0$$

This form reflects the implied claim that the training course improves scores; the test is one-tailed and the claim is in the alternative hypothesis. Because the experiment was conducted as a matched paired sample rather than simply taking scores from people who took the training course those who didn't, we use the matched pair test statistic:

$$\text{Test Statistic: } t_c = \frac{\bar{X}_d - \mu_d}{\frac{S_d}{\sqrt{n}}} = \frac{(23.9 - 20.4) - 0}{\left(\frac{3.8}{\sqrt{20}}\right)} = 4.12$$

In order to solve this equation, the individual scores, pre-training course and post-training course need to be used to calculate the individual differences. These scores are then averaged and the average difference is calculated:

$$\bar{X}_d = \bar{x}_1 - \bar{x}_2$$

From these differences we can calculate the standard deviation across the individual differences:

$$S_d = \frac{\Sigma\left(d_i - \bar{X}_d\right)^2}{n - 1}\text{where } d_i = x_{1i} - x_{2i}$$

We can now compare the calculated value of the test statistic, 4.12, with the critical value. The critical value is a Student's t with degrees of freedom equal to the number of pairs, not observations, minus 1. In this case 20 pairs and at 90% confidence level $t_{a/2} = \pm 1.729$ at $df = 20 - 1 = 19$. The calculated test statistic is most certainly in the tail of the distribution and thus we cannot accept the null hypothesis that there is no difference from the training program. Evidence seems indicate that the training aids employees in gaining higher scores.

## Example 10.10

A study was conducted to investigate the effectiveness of hypnotism in reducing pain. Results for randomly selected subjects are shown in **Table 10.4**. A lower score indicates less pain. The "before" value is matched to an "after" value and the differences are calculated. Are the sensory measurements, on average, lower after hypnotism? Test at a 5% significance level.

| Subject: | A | B | C | D | E | F | G | H |
|----------|-----|-----|-----|------|------|-----|-----|------|
| Before | 6.6 | 6.5 | 9.0 | 10.3 | 11.3 | 8.1 | 6.3 | 11.6 |
| After | 6.8 | 2.4 | 7.4 | 8.5 | 8.1 | 6.1 | 3.4 | 2.0 |

Table 10.5

Solution 10.10

Corresponding "before" and "after" values form matched pairs. (Calculate "after" – "before.")

| After Data | Before Data | Difference |
|------------|-------------|------------|
| 6.8 | 6.6 | 0.2 |
| 2.4 | 6.5 | -4.1 |
| 7.4 | 9 | -1.6 |
| 8.5 | 10.3 | -1.8 |
| 8.1 | 11.3 | -3.2 |
| 6.1 | 8.1 | -2 |
| 3.4 | 6.3 | -2.9 |
| 2 | 11.6 | -9.6 |

Table 10.6

The data **for the test** are the differences: {0.2, –4.1, –1.6, –1.8, –3.2, –2, –2.9, –9.6}

The sample mean and sample standard deviation of the differences are: $\bar{x}_d = -3.13$ and $s_d = 2.91$ Verify these values.

Let $\mu_d$ be the population mean for the differences. We use the subscript $d$ to denote "differences."

**Random variable:** $\bar{X}_d$ = the mean difference of the sensory measurements

$H_0$: $\mu_d \geq 0$

The null hypothesis is zero or positive, meaning that there is the same or more pain felt after hypnotism. That means the subject shows no improvement. $\mu_d$ is the population mean of the differences.)

$H_a$: $\mu_d < 0$

The alternative hypothesis is negative, meaning there is less pain felt after hypnotism. That means the subject shows improvement. The score should be lower after hypnotism, so the difference ought to be negative to indicate improvement.

**Distribution for the test:** The distribution is a Student's $t$ with $df = n - 1 = 8 - 1 = 7$. Use $t_7$. **(Notice that the test is for a single population mean.)**

**Calculate the test statistic and look up the critical value using the Student's-t distribution:** The calculated value of the test statistic is 3.06 and the critical value of the t distribution with 7 degrees of freedom at the 5% level of confidence is 1.895 with a one-tailed test.

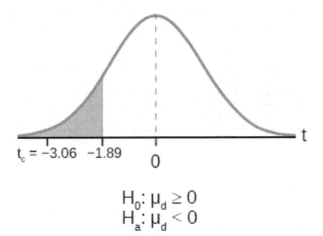

**Figure 10.9**

$\bar{X}_d$ is the random variable for the differences.

The sample mean and sample standard deviation of the differences are:

$\bar{x}_d = -3.13$

$\bar{s}_d = 2.91$

**Compare the critical value for alpha against the calculated test statistic.**

The conclusion from using the comparison of the calculated test statistic and the critical value will gives us the result. In this question the calculated test statistic is 3.06 and the critical value is 1.895. The test statistic is clearly in the tail and thus we cannot accept the null hypotheses that there is no difference between the two situations, hypnotized and not hypnotized.

**Make a decision:** Cannot accept the null hypothesis, $H_0$. This means that $\mu_d < 0$ and there is a statistically significant improvement.

**Conclusion:** At a 5% level of significance, from the sample data, there is sufficient evidence to conclude that the sensory measurements, on average, are lower after hypnotism. Hypnotism appears to be effective in reducing pain.

## Example 10.11

A college football coach was interested in whether the college's strength development class increased his players' maximum lift (in pounds) on the bench press exercise. He asked four of his players to participate in a study. The amount of weight they could each lift was recorded before they took the strength development class. After completing the class, the amount of weight they could each lift was again measured. The data are as follows:

| Weight (in pounds) | Player 1 | Player 2 | Player 3 | Player 4 |
|---|---|---|---|---|
| Amount of weight lifted prior to the class | 205 | 241 | 338 | 368 |
| Amount of weight lifted after the class | 295 | 252 | 330 | 360 |

Table 10.7

**The coach wants to know if the strength development class makes his players stronger, on average.**
Record the **differences** data. Calculate the differences by subtracting the amount of weight lifted prior to the class from the weight lifted after completing the class. The data for the differences are: {90, 11, -8, -8}.

$\overline{x}_d = 21.3$, $s_d = 46.7$

Using the difference data, this becomes a test of a single mean.

**Define the random variable:** $\overline{X}_d$ mean difference in the maximum lift per player.

The distribution for the hypothesis test is a student's t with 3 degrees of freedom.

$H_0$: $\mu_d \leq 0$, $H_a$: $\mu_d > 0$

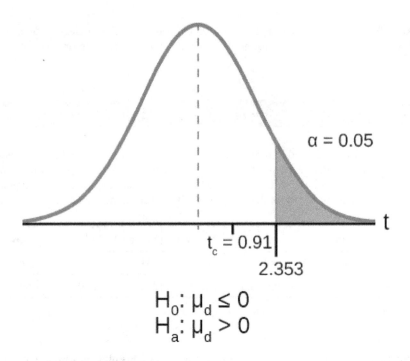

**Figure 10.10**

**Calculate the test statistic look up the critical value:** Critical value of the test statistic is 0.91. The critical value of the student's t at 5% level of significance and 3 degrees of freedom is 2.353.

**Decision:** If the level of significance is 5%, we cannot reject the null hypothesis, because the calculated value of the test statistic is not in the tail.

**What is the conclusion?**

At a 5% level of significance, from the sample data, there is not sufficient evidence to conclude that the strength development class helped to make the players stronger, on average.

# KEY TERMS

**Cohen's _d_** a measure of effect size based on the differences between two means. If _d_ is between 0 and 0.2 then the effect is small. If _d_ approaches is 0.5, then the effect is medium, and if _d_ approaches 0.8, then it is a large effect.

**Independent Groups** two samples that are selected from two populations, and the values from one population are not related in any way to the values from the other population.

**Matched Pairs** two samples that are dependent. Differences between a before and after scenario are tested by testing one population mean of differences.

**Pooled Variance** a weighted average of two variances that can then be used when calculating standard error.

# CHAPTER REVIEW

### 10.1 Comparing Two Independent Population Means

Two population means from independent samples where the population standard deviations are not known

- Random Variable: $\overline{X}_1 - \overline{X}_2$ = the difference of the sampling means

- Distribution: Student's _t_-distribution with degrees of freedom (variances not pooled)

### 10.2 Cohen's Standards for Small, Medium, and Large Effect Sizes

Cohen's _d_ is a measure of "effect size" based on the differences between two means.

It is important to note that Cohen's _d_ does not provide a level of confidence as to the magnitude of the size of the effect comparable to the other tests of hypothesis we have studied. The sizes of the effects are simply indicative.

### 10.3 Test for Differences in Means: Assuming Equal Population Variances

In situations when we do not know the population variances but assume the variances are the same, the pooled sample variance will be smaller than the individual sample variances.

This will give more precise estimates and reduce the probability of discarding a good null.

### 10.4 Comparing Two Independent Population Proportions

Test of two population proportions from independent samples.

- Random variable: $p'_A - p'_B$ = difference between the two estimated proportions

- Distribution: normal distribution

### 10.5 Two Population Means with Known Standard Deviations

A hypothesis test of two population means from independent samples where the population standard deviations are known (typically approximated with the sample standard deviations), will have these characteristics:

- Random variable: $\overline{X}_1 - \overline{X}_2$ = the difference of the means

- Distribution: normal distribution

### 10.6 Matched or Paired Samples

A hypothesis test for matched or paired samples (t-test) has these characteristics:

- Test the differences by subtracting one measurement from the other measurement

- Random Variable: $\overline{x}_d$ = mean of the differences

- Distribution: Student's-t distribution with $n - 1$ degrees of freedom

- If the number of differences is small (less than 30), the differences must follow a normal distribution.

- Two samples are drawn from the same set of objects.
- Samples are dependent.

# FORMULA REVIEW

## 10.1 Comparing Two Independent Population Means

Standard error: $SE = \sqrt{\dfrac{(s_1)^2}{n_1} + \dfrac{(s_2)^2}{n_2}}$

Test statistic ($t$-score): $t_c = \dfrac{(\bar{x}_1 - \bar{x}_2) - \delta_0}{\sqrt{\dfrac{(s_1)^2}{n_1} + \dfrac{(s_2)^2}{n_2}}}$

Degrees of freedom:

$$df = \dfrac{\left(\dfrac{(s_1)^2}{n_1} + \dfrac{(s_2)^2}{n_2}\right)^2}{\left(\dfrac{1}{n_1-1}\right)\left(\dfrac{(s_1)^2}{n_1}\right)^2 + \left(\dfrac{1}{n_2-1}\right)\left(\dfrac{(s_2)^2}{n_2}\right)^2}$$

where:

$s_1$ and $s_2$ are the sample standard deviations, and $n_1$ and $n_2$ are the sample sizes.

$\bar{x}_1$ and $\bar{x}_2$ are the sample means.

## 10.2 Cohen's Standards for Small, Medium, and Large Effect Sizes

Cohen's $d$ is the measure of effect size:

$d = \dfrac{\bar{x}_1 - \bar{x}_2}{s_{pooled}}$

where $s_{pooled} = \sqrt{\dfrac{(n_1-1)s_1^2 + (n_2-1)s_2^2}{n_1+n_2-2}}$

## 10.3 Test for Differences in Means: Assuming Equal Population Variances

$$t_c = \dfrac{(\bar{x}_1 - \bar{x}_2) - \delta_0}{\sqrt{S_p^2\left(\dfrac{1}{n_1} + \dfrac{1}{n_2}\right)}}$$

where $S_p^2$ is the pooled variance given by the formula:

$$S_p^2 = \dfrac{(n_1-1)s_2^1 + (n_2-1)s_2^2}{n_1+n_2-2}$$

## 10.4 Comparing Two Independent Population Proportions

Pooled Proportion: $p_c = \dfrac{x_A + x_B}{n_A + n_B}$

Test Statistic ($z$-score): $Z_c = \dfrac{(p'_A - p'_B)}{\sqrt{p_c(1-p_c)\left(\dfrac{1}{n_A} + \dfrac{1}{n_B}\right)}}$

where

$p'_A$ and $p'_B$ are the sample proportions, $p_A$ and $p_B$ are the population proportions,

$P_c$ is the pooled proportion, and $n_A$ and $n_B$ are the sample sizes.

## 10.5 Two Population Means with Known Standard Deviations

Test Statistic ($z$-score):

$$Z_c = \dfrac{(\bar{x}_1 - \bar{x}_2) - \delta_0}{\sqrt{\dfrac{(\sigma_1)^2}{n_1} + \dfrac{(\sigma_2)^2}{n_2}}}$$

**where:**

$\sigma_1$ and $\sigma_2$ are the known population standard deviations. $n_1$ and $n_2$ are the sample sizes. $\bar{x}_1$ and $\bar{x}_2$ are the sample means. $\mu_1$ and $\mu_2$ are the population means.

## 10.6 Matched or Paired Samples

Test Statistic ($t$-score): $t_c = \dfrac{\bar{x}_d - \mu_d}{\left(\dfrac{s_d}{\sqrt{n}}\right)}$

where:

$\bar{x}_d$ is the mean of the sample differences. $\mu_d$ is the mean of the population differences. $s_d$ is the sample standard deviation of the differences. $n$ is the sample size.

# PRACTICE

## 10.1 Comparing Two Independent Population Means

*Use the following information to answer the next 15 exercises:* Indicate if the hypothesis test is for

a. independent group means, population standard deviations, and/or variances known

b. independent group means, population standard deviations, and/or variances unknown

c. matched or paired samples

d. single mean

e. two proportions

f. single proportion

**1.** It is believed that 70% of males pass their drivers test in the first attempt, while 65% of females pass the test in the first attempt. Of interest is whether the proportions are in fact equal.

**2.** A new laundry detergent is tested on consumers. Of interest is the proportion of consumers who prefer the new brand over the leading competitor. A study is done to test this.

**3.** A new windshield treatment claims to repel water more effectively. Ten windshields are tested by simulating rain without the new treatment. The same windshields are then treated, and the experiment is run again. A hypothesis test is conducted.

**4.** The known standard deviation in salary for all mid-level professionals in the financial industry is $11,000. Company A and Company B are in the financial industry. Suppose samples are taken of mid-level professionals from Company A and from Company B. The sample mean salary for mid-level professionals in Company A is $80,000. The sample mean salary for mid-level professionals in Company B is $96,000. Company A and Company B management want to know if their mid-level professionals are paid differently, on average.

**5.** The average worker in Germany gets eight weeks of paid vacation.

**6.** According to a television commercial, 80% of dentists agree that Ultrafresh toothpaste is the best on the market.

**7.** It is believed that the average grade on an English essay in a particular school system for females is higher than for males. A random sample of 31 females had a mean score of 82 with a standard deviation of three, and a random sample of 25 males had a mean score of 76 with a standard deviation of four.

**8.** The league mean batting average is 0.280 with a known standard deviation of 0.06. The Rattlers and the Vikings belong to the league. The mean batting average for a sample of eight Rattlers is 0.210, and the mean batting average for a sample of eight Vikings is 0.260. There are 24 players on the Rattlers and 19 players on the Vikings. Are the batting averages of the Rattlers and Vikings statistically different?

**9.** In a random sample of 100 forests in the United States, 56 were coniferous or contained conifers. In a random sample of 80 forests in Mexico, 40 were coniferous or contained conifers. Is the proportion of conifers in the United States statistically more than the proportion of conifers in Mexico?

**10.** A new medicine is said to help improve sleep. Eight subjects are picked at random and given the medicine. The means hours slept for each person were recorded before starting the medication and after.

**11.** It is thought that teenagers sleep more than adults on average. A study is done to verify this. A sample of 16 teenagers has a mean of 8.9 hours slept and a standard deviation of 1.2. A sample of 12 adults has a mean of 6.9 hours slept and a standard deviation of 0.6.

**12.** Varsity athletes practice five times a week, on average.

**13.** A sample of 12 in-state graduate school programs at school A has a mean tuition of $64,000 with a standard deviation of $8,000. At school B, a sample of 16 in-state graduate programs has a mean of $80,000 with a standard deviation of $6,000. On average, are the mean tuitions different?

**14.** A new WiFi range booster is being offered to consumers. A researcher tests the native range of 12 different routers under the same conditions. The ranges are recorded. Then the researcher uses the new WiFi range booster and records the new ranges. Does the new WiFi range booster do a better job?

**15.** A high school principal claims that 30% of student athletes drive themselves to school, while 4% of non-athletes drive themselves to school. In a sample of 20 student athletes, 45% drive themselves to school. In a sample of 35 non-athlete students, 6% drive themselves to school. Is the percent of student athletes who drive themselves to school more than the percent of nonathletes?

*Use the following information to answer the next three exercises:* A study is done to determine which of two soft drinks has more sugar. There are 13 cans of Beverage A in a sample and six cans of Beverage B. The mean amount of sugar in Beverage A is 36 grams with a standard deviation of 0.6 grams. The mean amount of sugar in Beverage B is 38 grams with a standard deviation of 0.8 grams. The researchers believe that Beverage B has more sugar than Beverage A, on average. Both populations have normal distributions.

**16.** Are standard deviations known or unknown?

**17.** What is the random variable?

**18.** Is this a one-tailed or two-tailed test?

*Use the following information to answer the next 12 exercises:* The U.S. Center for Disease Control reports that the mean life expectancy was 47.6 years for whites born in 1900 and 33.0 years for nonwhites. Suppose that you randomly survey death records for people born in 1900 in a certain county. Of the 124 whites, the mean life span was 45.3 years with a standard deviation of 12.7 years. Of the 82 nonwhites, the mean life span was 34.1 years with a standard deviation of 15.6 years. Conduct a hypothesis test to see if the mean life spans in the county were the same for whites and nonwhites.

**19.** Is this a test of means or proportions?

**20.** State the null and alternative hypotheses.
   a. $H_0$: _____
   b. $H_a$: _____

**21.** Is this a right-tailed, left-tailed, or two-tailed test?

**22.** In symbols, what is the random variable of interest for this test?

**23.** In words, define the random variable of interest for this test.

**24.** Which distribution (normal or Student's *t*) would you use for this hypothesis test?

**25.** Explain why you chose the distribution you did for **Exercise 10.24**.

**26.** Calculate the test statistic.

**27.** Sketch a graph of the situation. Label the horizontal axis. Mark the hypothesized difference and the sample difference. Shade the area corresponding to the *p*-value.

**28.** At a pre-conceived $\alpha = 0.05$, what is your:
   a. Decision:
   b. Reason for the decision:
   c. Conclusion (write out in a complete sentence):

**29.** Does it appear that the means are the same? Why or why not?

## 10.4 Comparing Two Independent Population Proportions

*Use the following information for the next five exercises.* Two types of phone operating system are being tested to determine if there is a difference in the proportions of system failures (crashes). Fifteen out of a random sample of 150 phones with $OS_1$ had system failures within the first eight hours of operation. Nine out of another random sample of 150 phones with $OS_2$ had system failures within the first eight hours of operation. $OS_2$ is believed to be more stable (have fewer crashes) than $OS_1$.

**30.** Is this a test of means or proportions?

**31.** What is the random variable?

**32.** State the null and alternative hypotheses.

**33.** What can you conclude about the two operating systems?

*Use the following information to answer the next twelve exercises.* In the recent Census, three percent of the U.S. population reported being of two or more races. However, the percent varies tremendously from state to state. Suppose that two random surveys are conducted. In the first random survey, out of 1,000 North Dakotans, only nine people reported being of two or more races. In the second random survey, out of 500 Nevadans, 17 people reported being of two or more races. Conduct a hypothesis test to determine if the population percents are the same for the two states or if the percent for Nevada is statistically higher than for North Dakota.

**34.** Is this a test of means or proportions?

**35.** State the null and alternative hypotheses.
   a.  $H_0$: _____
   b.  $H_a$: _____

**36.** Is this a right-tailed, left-tailed, or two-tailed test? How do you know?

**37.** What is the random variable of interest for this test?

**38.** In words, define the random variable for this test.

**39.** Which distribution (normal or Student's $t$) would you use for this hypothesis test?

**40.** Explain why you chose the distribution you did for the Exercise 10.56.

**41.** Calculate the test statistic.

**42.** At a pre-conceived $\alpha = 0.05$, what is your:
   a.  Decision:
   b.  Reason for the decision:
   c.  Conclusion (write out in a complete sentence):

**43.** Does it appear that the proportion of Nevadans who are two or more races is higher than the proportion of North Dakotans? Why or why not?

## 10.5 Two Population Means with Known Standard Deviations

*Use the following information to answer the next five exercises.* The mean speeds of fastball pitches from two different baseball pitchers are to be compared. A sample of 14 fastball pitches is measured from each pitcher. The populations have normal distributions. Table 10.8 shows the result. Scouters believe that Rodriguez pitches a speedier fastball.

| Pitcher | Sample Mean Speed of Pitches (mph) | Population Standard Deviation |
|---------|-----------------------------------|------------------------------|
| Wesley | 86 | 3 |
| Rodriguez | 91 | 7 |

Table 10.8

**44.** What is the random variable?

**45.** State the null and alternative hypotheses.

**46.** What is the test statistic?

**47.** At the 1% significance level, what is your conclusion?

*Use the following information to answer the next five exercises.* A researcher is testing the effects of plant food on plant growth. Nine plants have been given the plant food. Another nine plants have not been given the plant food. The heights of the plants are recorded after eight weeks. The populations have normal distributions. The following table is the result. The researcher thinks the food makes the plants grow taller.

| Plant Group | Sample Mean Height of Plants (inches) | Population Standard Deviation |
|-------------|---------------------------------------|------------------------------|
| Food | 16 | 2.5 |
| No food | 14 | 1.5 |

Table 10.9

**48.** Is the population standard deviation known or unknown?

**49.** State the null and alternative hypotheses.

**50.** At the 1% significance level, what is your conclusion?

*Use the following information to answer the next five exercises.* Two metal alloys are being considered as material for ball bearings. The mean melting point of the two alloys is to be compared. 15 pieces of each metal are being tested. Both populations have normal distributions. The following table is the result. It is believed that Alloy Zeta has a different melting point.

| | Sample Mean Melting Temperatures (°F) | Population Standard Deviation |
|---|---|---|
| Alloy Gamma | 800 | 95 |
| Alloy Zeta | 900 | 105 |

Table 10.10

**51.** State the null and alternative hypotheses.

**52.** Is this a right-, left-, or two-tailed test?

**53.** At the 1% significance level, what is your conclusion?

## 10.6 Matched or Paired Samples

*Use the following information to answer the next five exercises.* A study was conducted to test the effectiveness of a software patch in reducing system failures over a six-month period. Results for randomly selected installations are shown in Table 10.11. The "before" value is matched to an "after" value, and the differences are calculated. The differences have a normal distribution. Test at the 1% significance level.

| Installation | A | B | C | D | E | F | G | H |
|---|---|---|---|---|---|---|---|---|
| Before | 3 | 6 | 4 | 2 | 5 | 8 | 2 | 6 |
| After | 1 | 5 | 2 | 0 | 1 | 0 | 2 | 2 |

Table 10.11

**54.** What is the random variable?

**55.** State the null and alternative hypotheses.

**56.** What conclusion can you draw about the software patch?

*Use the following information to answer next five exercises.* A study was conducted to test the effectiveness of a juggling class. Before the class started, six subjects juggled as many balls as they could at once. After the class, the same six subjects juggled as many balls as they could. The differences in the number of balls are calculated. The differences have a normal distribution. Test at the 1% significance level.

| Subject | A | B | C | D | E | F |
|---|---|---|---|---|---|---|
| Before | 3 | 4 | 3 | 2 | 4 | 5 |
| After | 4 | 5 | 6 | 4 | 5 | 7 |

Table 10.12

**57.** State the null and alternative hypotheses.

**58.** What is the sample mean difference?

**59.** What conclusion can you draw about the juggling class?

*Use the following information to answer the next five exercises.* A doctor wants to know if a blood pressure medication is effective. Six subjects have their blood pressures recorded. After twelve weeks on the medication, the same six subjects have their blood pressure recorded again. For this test, only systolic pressure is of concern. Test at the 1% significance level.

| Patient | A | B | C | D | E | F |
|---|---|---|---|---|---|---|
| Before | 161 | 162 | 165 | 162 | 166 | 171 |
| After | 158 | 159 | 166 | 160 | 167 | 169 |

Table 10.13

**60.** State the null and alternative hypotheses.

**61.** What is the test statistic?

**62.** What is the sample mean difference?

**63.** What is the conclusion?

# HOMEWORK

## 10.1 Comparing Two Independent Population Means

**64.** The mean number of English courses taken in a two–year time period by male and female college students is believed to be about the same. An experiment is conducted and data are collected from 29 males and 16 females. The males took an average of three English courses with a standard deviation of 0.8. The females took an average of four English courses with a standard deviation of 1.0. Are the means statistically the same?

**65.** A student at a four-year college claims that mean enrollment at four–year colleges is higher than at two–year colleges in the United States. Two surveys are conducted. Of the 35 two–year colleges surveyed, the mean enrollment was 5,068 with a standard deviation of 4,777. Of the 35 four-year colleges surveyed, the mean enrollment was 5,466 with a standard deviation of 8,191.

**66.** At Rachel's 11th birthday party, eight girls were timed to see how long (in seconds) they could hold their breath in a relaxed position. After a two-minute rest, they timed themselves while jumping. The girls thought that the mean difference between their jumping and relaxed times would be zero. Test their hypothesis.

| Relaxed time (seconds) | Jumping time (seconds) |
|---|---|
| 26 | 21 |
| 47 | 40 |
| 30 | 28 |
| 22 | 21 |
| 23 | 25 |
| 45 | 43 |
| 37 | 35 |
| 29 | 32 |

Table 10.14

**67.** Mean entry-level salaries for college graduates with mechanical engineering degrees and electrical engineering degrees are believed to be approximately the same. A recruiting office thinks that the mean mechanical engineering salary is actually lower than the mean electrical engineering salary. The recruiting office randomly surveys 50 entry level mechanical engineers and 60 entry level electrical engineers. Their mean salaries were $46,100 and $46,700, respectively. Their standard deviations were $3,450 and $4,210, respectively. Conduct a hypothesis test to determine if you agree that the mean entry-level mechanical engineering salary is lower than the mean entry-level electrical engineering salary.

**68.** Marketing companies have collected data implying that teenage girls use more ring tones on their cellular phones than teenage boys do. In one particular study of 40 randomly chosen teenage girls and boys (20 of each) with cellular phones, the mean number of ring tones for the girls was 3.2 with a standard deviation of 1.5. The mean for the boys was 1.7 with a standard deviation of 0.8. Conduct a hypothesis test to determine if the means are approximately the same or if the girls' mean is higher than the boys' mean.

*Use the information from Appendix C: Data Sets (http://cnx.org/content/m47873/latest/) to answer the next four exercises.*

**69.** Using the data from Lap 1 only, conduct a hypothesis test to determine if the mean time for completing a lap in races is the same as it is in practices.

**70.** Repeat the test in **Exercise 10.83**, but use Lap 5 data this time.

**71.** Repeat the test in **Exercise 10.83**, but this time combine the data from Laps 1 and 5.

**72.** In two to three complete sentences, explain in detail how you might use Terri Vogel's data to answer the following question. "Does Terri Vogel drive faster in races than she does in practices?"

*Use the following information to answer the next two exercises.* The Eastern and Western Major League Soccer conferences have a new Reserve Division that allows new players to develop their skills. Data for a randomly picked date showed the following annual goals.

| Western | Eastern |
|---|---|
| Los Angeles 9 | D.C. United 9 |
| FC Dallas 3 | Chicago 8 |
| Chivas USA 4 | Columbus 7 |
| Real Salt Lake 3 | New England 6 |
| Colorado 4 | MetroStars 5 |
| San Jose 4 | Kansas City 3 |

Table 10.15

*Conduct a hypothesis test to answer the next two exercises.*

**73.** The **exact** distribution for the hypothesis test is:
   a. the normal distribution
   b. the Student's $t$-distribution
   c. the uniform distribution
   d. the exponential distribution

**74.** If the level of significance is 0.05, the conclusion is:
   a. There is sufficient evidence to conclude that the **W** Division teams score fewer goals, on average, than the **E** teams
   b. There is insufficient evidence to conclude that the **W** Division teams score more goals, on average, than the **E** teams.
   c. There is insufficient evidence to conclude that the **W** teams score fewer goals, on average, than the **E** teams score.
   d. Unable to determine

**75.** Suppose a statistics instructor believes that there is no significant difference between the mean class scores of statistics day students on Exam 2 and statistics night students on Exam 2. She takes random samples from each of the populations. The mean and standard deviation for 35 statistics day students were 75.86 and 16.91. The mean and standard deviation for 37 statistics night students were 75.41 and 19.73. The "day" subscript refers to the statistics day students. The "night" subscript refers to the statistics night students. A concluding statement is:

a. There is sufficient evidence to conclude that statistics night students' mean on Exam 2 is better than the statistics day students' mean on Exam 2.
b. There is insufficient evidence to conclude that the statistics day students' mean on Exam 2 is better than the statistics night students' mean on Exam 2.
c. There is insufficient evidence to conclude that there is a significant difference between the means of the statistics day students and night students on Exam 2.
d. There is sufficient evidence to conclude that there is a significant difference between the means of the statistics day students and night students on Exam 2.

**76.** Researchers interviewed street prostitutes in Canada and the United States. The mean age of the 100 Canadian prostitutes upon entering prostitution was 18 with a standard deviation of six. The mean age of the 130 United States prostitutes upon entering prostitution was 20 with a standard deviation of eight. Is the mean age of entering prostitution in Canada lower than the mean age in the United States? Test at a 1% significance level.

**77.** A powder diet is tested on 49 people, and a liquid diet is tested on 36 different people. Of interest is whether the liquid diet yields a higher mean weight loss than the powder diet. The powder diet group had a mean weight loss of 42 pounds with a standard deviation of 12 pounds. The liquid diet group had a mean weight loss of 45 pounds with a standard deviation of 14 pounds.

**78.** Suppose a statistics instructor believes that there is no significant difference between the mean class scores of statistics day students on Exam 2 and statistics night students on Exam 2. She takes random samples from each of the populations. The mean and standard deviation for 35 statistics day students were 75.86 and 16.91, respectively. The mean and standard deviation for 37 statistics night students were 75.41 and 19.73. The "day" subscript refers to the statistics day students. The "night" subscript refers to the statistics night students. An appropriate alternative hypothesis for the hypothesis test is:

a. $\mu_{day} > \mu_{night}$
b. $\mu_{day} < \mu_{night}$
c. $\mu_{day} = \mu_{night}$
d. $\mu_{day} \neq \mu_{night}$

## 10.4 Comparing Two Independent Population Proportions

**79.** A recent drug survey showed an increase in the use of drugs and alcohol among local high school seniors as compared to the national percent. Suppose that a survey of 100 local seniors and 100 national seniors is conducted to see if the proportion of drug and alcohol use is higher locally than nationally. Locally, 65 seniors reported using drugs or alcohol within the past month, while 60 national seniors reported using them.

**80.** We are interested in whether the proportions of female suicide victims for ages 15 to 24 are the same for the whites and the blacks races in the United States. We randomly pick one year, 1992, to compare the races. The number of suicides estimated in the United States in 1992 for white females is 4,930. Five hundred eighty were aged 15 to 24. The estimate for black females is 330. Forty were aged 15 to 24. We will let female suicide victims be our population.

**81.** Elizabeth Mjelde, an art history professor, was interested in whether the value from the Golden Ratio formula, $\left(\dfrac{\text{larger} + \text{smaller dimension}}{\text{larger dimension}}\right)$ was the same in the Whitney Exhibit for works from 1900 to 1919 as for works from 1920 to 1942. Thirty-seven early works were sampled, averaging 1.74 with a standard deviation of 0.11. Sixty-five of the later works were sampled, averaging 1.746 with a standard deviation of 0.1064. Do you think that there is a significant difference in the Golden Ratio calculation?

**82.** A recent year was randomly picked from 1985 to the present. In that year, there were 2,051 Hispanic students at Cabrillo College out of a total of 12,328 students. At Lake Tahoe College, there were 321 Hispanic students out of a total of 2,441 students. In general, do you think that the percent of Hispanic students at the two colleges is basically the same or different?

*Use the following information to answer the next three exercises.* Neuroinvasive West Nile virus is a severe disease that affects a person's nervous system . It is spread by the Culex species of mosquito. In the United States in 2010 there were 629 reported cases of neuroinvasive West Nile virus out of a total of 1,021 reported cases and there were 486 neuroinvasive reported cases out of a total of 712 cases reported in 2011. Is the 2011 proportion of neuroinvasive West Nile virus cases more than the 2010 proportion of neuroinvasive West Nile virus cases? Using a 1% level of significance, conduct an appropriate hypothesis test.

- "2011" subscript: 2011 group.
- "2010" subscript: 2010 group

**83.** This is:
   a. a test of two proportions
   b. a test of two independent means
   c. a test of a single mean
   d. a test of matched pairs.

**84.** An appropriate null hypothesis is:
   a. $p_{2011} \leq p_{2010}$
   b. $p_{2011} \geq p_{2010}$
   c. $\mu_{2011} \leq \mu_{2010}$
   d. $p_{2011} > p_{2010}$

**85.** Researchers conducted a study to find out if there is a difference in the use of eReaders by different age groups. Randomly selected participants were divided into two age groups. In the 16- to 29-year-old group, 7% of the 628 surveyed use eReaders, while 11% of the 2,309 participants 30 years old and older use eReaders.

**86.** Adults aged 18 years old and older were randomly selected for a survey on obesity. Adults are considered obese if their body mass index (BMI) is at least 30. The researchers wanted to determine if the proportion of women who are obese in the south is less than the proportion of southern men who are obese. The results are shown in **Table 10.16**. Test at the 1% level of significance.

|       | Number who are obese | Sample size |
|-------|----------------------|-------------|
| Men   | 42,769               | 155,525     |
| Women | 67,169               | 248,775     |

Table 10.16

**87.** Two computer users were discussing tablet computers. A higher proportion of people ages 16 to 29 use tablets than the proportion of people age 30 and older. **Table 10.17** details the number of tablet owners for each age group. Test at the 1% level of significance.

|              | 16–29 year olds | 30 years old and older |
|--------------|-----------------|------------------------|
| Own a Tablet | 69              | 231                    |
| Sample Size  | 628             | 2,309                  |

Table 10.17

**88.** A group of friends debated whether more men use smartphones than women. They consulted a research study of smartphone use among adults. The results of the survey indicate that of the 973 men randomly sampled, 379 use smartphones. For women, 404 of the 1,304 who were randomly sampled use smartphones. Test at the 5% level of significance.

**89.** While her husband spent 2½ hours picking out new speakers, a statistician decided to determine whether the percent of men who enjoy shopping for electronic equipment is higher than the percent of women who enjoy shopping for electronic equipment. The population was Saturday afternoon shoppers. Out of 67 men, 24 said they enjoyed the activity. Eight of the 24 women surveyed claimed to enjoy the activity. Interpret the results of the survey.

**90.** We are interested in whether children's educational computer software costs less, on average, than children's entertainment software. Thirty-six educational software titles were randomly picked from a catalog. The mean cost was $31.14 with a standard deviation of $4.69. Thirty-five entertainment software titles were randomly picked from the same catalog. The mean cost was $33.86 with a standard deviation of $10.87. Decide whether children's educational software costs less, on average, than children's entertainment software.

**91.** Joan Nguyen recently claimed that the proportion of college-age males with at least one pierced ear is as high as the proportion of college-age females. She conducted a survey in her classes. Out of 107 males, 20 had at least one pierced ear. Out of 92 females, 47 had at least one pierced ear. Do you believe that the proportion of males has reached the proportion of females?

**92.** "To Breakfast or Not to Breakfast?" by Richard Ayore

In the American society, birthdays are one of those days that everyone looks forward to. People of different ages and peer groups gather to mark the 18th, 20th, ..., birthdays. During this time, one looks back to see what he or she has achieved for the past year and also focuses ahead for more to come.

If, by any chance, I am invited to one of these parties, my experience is always different. Instead of dancing around with my friends while the music is booming, I get carried away by memories of my family back home in Kenya. I remember the good times I had with my brothers and sister while we did our daily routine.

Every morning, I remember we went to the shamba (garden) to weed our crops. I remember one day arguing with my brother as to why he always remained behind just to join us an hour later. In his defense, he said that he preferred waiting for breakfast before he came to weed. He said, "This is why I always work more hours than you guys!"

And so, to prove him wrong or right, we decided to give it a try. One day we went to work as usual without breakfast, and recorded the time we could work before getting tired and stopping. On the next day, we all ate breakfast before going to work. We recorded how long we worked again before getting tired and stopping. Of interest was our mean increase in work time. Though not sure, my brother insisted that it was more than two hours. Using the data in Table 10.18, solve our problem.

| Work hours with breakfast | Work hours without breakfast |
|---|---|
| 8 | 6 |
| 7 | 5 |
| 9 | 5 |
| 5 | 4 |
| 9 | 7 |
| 8 | 7 |
| 10 | 7 |
| 7 | 5 |
| 6 | 6 |
| 9 | 5 |

Table 10.18

## 10.5 Two Population Means with Known Standard Deviations

**NOTE**

If you are using a Student's $t$-distribution for one of the following homework problems, including for paired data, you may assume that the underlying population is normally distributed. (When using these tests in a real situation, you must first prove that assumption, however.)

**93.** A study is done to determine if students in the California state university system take longer to graduate, on average, than students enrolled in private universities. One hundred students from both the California state university system and private universities are surveyed. Suppose that from years of research, it is known that the population standard deviations are 1.5811 years and 1 year, respectively. The following data are collected. The California state university system students took on average 4.5 years with a standard deviation of 0.8. The private university students took on average 4.1 years with a standard deviation of 0.3.

**94.** Parents of teenage boys often complain that auto insurance costs more, on average, for teenage boys than for teenage girls. A group of concerned parents examines a random sample of insurance bills. The mean annual cost for 36 teenage boys was $679. For 23 teenage girls, it was $559. From past years, it is known that the population standard deviation for each group is $180. Determine whether or not you believe that the mean cost for auto insurance for teenage boys is greater than that for teenage girls.

**95.** A group of transfer bound students wondered if they will spend the same mean amount on texts and supplies each year at their four-year university as they have at their community college. They conducted a random survey of 54 students at their community college and 66 students at their local four-year university. The sample means were $947 and $1,011, respectively. The population standard deviations are known to be $254 and $87, respectively. Conduct a hypothesis test to determine if the means are statistically the same.

**96.** Some manufacturers claim that non-hybrid sedan cars have a lower mean miles-per-gallon (mpg) than hybrid ones. Suppose that consumers test 21 hybrid sedans and get a mean of 31 mpg with a standard deviation of seven mpg. Thirty-one non-hybrid sedans get a mean of 22 mpg with a standard deviation of four mpg. Suppose that the population standard deviations are known to be six and three, respectively. Conduct a hypothesis test to evaluate the manufacturers claim.

**97.** A baseball fan wanted to know if there is a difference between the number of games played in a World Series when the American League won the series versus when the National League won the series. From 1922 to 2012, the population standard deviation of games won by the American League was 1.14, and the population standard deviation of games won by the National League was 1.11. Of 19 randomly selected World Series games won by the American League, the mean number of games won was 5.76. The mean number of 17 randomly selected games won by the National League was 5.42. Conduct a hypothesis test.

**98.** One of the questions in a study of marital satisfaction of dual-career couples was to rate the statement "I'm pleased with the way we divide the responsibilities for childcare." The ratings went from one (strongly agree) to five (strongly disagree). Table 10.19 contains ten of the paired responses for husbands and wives. Conduct a hypothesis test to see if the mean difference in the husband's versus the wife's satisfaction level is negative (meaning that, within the partnership, the husband is happier than the wife).

| Wife's Score | 2 | 2 | 3 | 3 | 4 | 2 | 1 | 1 | 2 | 4 |
|---|---|---|---|---|---|---|---|---|---|---|
| Husband's Score | 2 | 2 | 1 | 3 | 2 | 1 | 1 | 1 | 2 | 4 |

Table 10.19

## 10.6 Matched or Paired Samples

**99.** Ten individuals went on a low–fat diet for 12 weeks to lower their cholesterol. The data are recorded in **Table 10.20**. Do you think that their cholesterol levels were significantly lowered?

| Starting cholesterol level | Ending cholesterol level |
|---|---|
| 140 | 140 |
| 220 | 230 |
| 110 | 120 |
| 240 | 220 |
| 200 | 190 |
| 180 | 150 |
| 190 | 200 |
| 360 | 300 |
| 280 | 300 |
| 260 | 240 |

**Table 10.20**

*Use the following information to answer the next two exercises.* A new AIDS prevention drug was tried on a group of 224 HIV positive patients. Forty-five patients developed AIDS after four years. In a control group of 224 HIV positive patients, 68 developed AIDS after four years. We want to test whether the method of treatment reduces the proportion of patients that develop AIDS after four years or if the proportions of the treated group and the untreated group stay the same.

Let the subscript $t$ = treated patient and $ut$ = untreated patient.

**100.** The appropriate hypotheses are:
    a. $H_0$: $p_t < p_{ut}$ and $H_a$: $p_t \geq p_{ut}$
    b. $H_0$: $p_t \leq p_{ut}$ and $H_a$: $p_t > p_{ut}$
    c. $H_0$: $p_t = p_{ut}$ and $H_a$: $p_t \neq p_{ut}$
    d. $H_0$: $p_t = p_{ut}$ and $H_a$: $p_t < p_{ut}$

*Use the following information to answer the next two exercises.* An experiment is conducted to show that blood pressure can be consciously reduced in people trained in a "biofeedback exercise program." Six subjects were randomly selected and blood pressure measurements were recorded before and after the training. The difference between blood pressures was calculated (after - before) producing the following results: $\bar{x}_d = -10.2$ $s_d = 8.4$. Using the data, test the hypothesis that the blood pressure has decreased after the training.

**101.** The distribution for the test is:
    a. $t_5$
    b. $t_6$
    c. $N(-10.2, 8.4)$
    d. $N(-10.2, \frac{8.4}{\sqrt{6}})$

**102.** A golf instructor is interested in determining if her new technique for improving players' golf scores is effective. She takes four new students. She records their 18-hole scores before learning the technique and then after having taken her class. She conducts a hypothesis test. The data are as follows.

|                           | Player 1 | Player 2 | Player 3 | Player 4 |
|---------------------------|----------|----------|----------|----------|
| Mean score before class   | 83       | 78       | 93       | 87       |
| Mean score after class    | 80       | 80       | 86       | 86       |

Table 10.21

The correct decision is:

  a. Reject $H_0$.
  b. Do not reject the $H_0$.

**103.** A local cancer support group believes that the estimate for new female breast cancer cases in the south is higher in 2013 than in 2012. The group compared the estimates of new female breast cancer cases by southern state in 2012 and in 2013. The results are in Table 10.22.

| Southern States | 2012   | 2013   |
|-----------------|--------|--------|
| Alabama         | 3,450  | 3,720  |
| Arkansas        | 2,150  | 2,280  |
| Florida         | 15,540 | 15,710 |
| Georgia         | 6,970  | 7,310  |
| Kentucky        | 3,160  | 3,300  |
| Louisiana       | 3,320  | 3,630  |
| Mississippi     | 1,990  | 2,080  |
| North Carolina  | 7,090  | 7,430  |
| Oklahoma        | 2,630  | 2,690  |
| South Carolina  | 3,570  | 3,580  |
| Tennessee       | 4,680  | 5,070  |
| Texas           | 15,050 | 14,980 |
| Virginia        | 6,190  | 6,280  |

Table 10.22

**104.** A traveler wanted to know if the prices of hotels are different in the ten cities that he visits the most often. The list of the cities with the corresponding hotel prices for his two favorite hotel chains is in Table 10.23. Test at the 1% level of significance.

| Cities | Hyatt Regency prices in dollars | Hilton prices in dollars |
|---|---|---|
| Atlanta | 107 | 169 |
| Boston | 358 | 289 |
| Chicago | 209 | 299 |
| Dallas | 209 | 198 |
| Denver | 167 | 169 |
| Indianapolis | 179 | 214 |
| Los Angeles | 179 | 169 |
| New York City | 625 | 459 |
| Philadelphia | 179 | 159 |
| Washington, DC | 245 | 239 |

Table 10.23

**105.** A politician asked his staff to determine whether the underemployment rate in the northeast decreased from 2011 to 2012. The results are in Table 10.24.

| Northeastern States | 2011 | 2012 |
|---|---|---|
| Connecticut | 17.3 | 16.4 |
| Delaware | 17.4 | 13.7 |
| Maine | 19.3 | 16.1 |
| Maryland | 16.0 | 15.5 |
| Massachusetts | 17.6 | 18.2 |
| New Hampshire | 15.4 | 13.5 |
| New Jersey | 19.2 | 18.7 |
| New York | 18.5 | 18.7 |
| Ohio | 18.2 | 18.8 |
| Pennsylvania | 16.5 | 16.9 |
| Rhode Island | 20.7 | 22.4 |
| Vermont | 14.7 | 12.3 |
| West Virginia | 15.5 | 17.3 |

Table 10.24

# BRINGING IT TOGETHER: HOMEWORK

*Use the following information to answer the next ten exercises.* indicate which of the following choices best identifies the hypothesis test.

a.   independent group means, population standard deviations and/or variances known

b.   independent group means, population standard deviations and/or variances unknown

c.   matched or paired samples

d.   single mean

e.   two proportions

f.   single proportion

**106.** A powder diet is tested on 49 people, and a liquid diet is tested on 36 different people. The population standard deviations are two pounds and three pounds, respectively. Of interest is whether the liquid diet yields a higher mean weight loss than the powder diet.

**107.** A new chocolate bar is taste-tested on consumers. Of interest is whether the proportion of children who like the new chocolate bar is greater than the proportion of adults who like it.

**108.** The mean number of English courses taken in a two–year time period by male and female college students is believed to be about the same. An experiment is conducted and data are collected from nine males and 16 females.

**109.** A football league reported that the mean number of touchdowns per game was five. A study is done to determine if the mean number of touchdowns has decreased.

**110.** A study is done to determine if students in the California state university system take longer to graduate than students enrolled in private universities. One hundred students from both the California state university system and private universities are surveyed. From years of research, it is known that the population standard deviations are 1.5811 years and one year, respectively.

**111.** According to a YWCA Rape Crisis Center newsletter, 75% of rape victims know their attackers. A study is done to verify this.

**112.** According to a recent study, U.S. companies have a mean maternity-leave of six weeks.

**113.** A recent drug survey showed an increase in use of drugs and alcohol among local high school students as compared to the national percent. Suppose that a survey of 100 local youths and 100 national youths is conducted to see if the proportion of drug and alcohol use is higher locally than nationally.

**114.** A new SAT study course is tested on 12 individuals. Pre-course and post-course scores are recorded. Of interest is the mean increase in SAT scores. The following data are collected:

| Pre-course score | Post-course score |
|---|---|
| 1 | 300 |
| 960 | 920 |
| 1010 | 1100 |
| 840 | 880 |
| 1100 | 1070 |
| 1250 | 1320 |
| 860 | 860 |
| 1330 | 1370 |
| 790 | 770 |
| 990 | 1040 |
| 1110 | 1200 |
| 740 | 850 |

Table 10.25

**115.** University of Michigan researchers reported in the *Journal of the National Cancer Institute* that quitting smoking is especially beneficial for those under age 49. In this American Cancer Society study, the risk (probability) of dying of lung cancer was about the same as for those who had never smoked.

**116.** Lesley E. Tan investigated the relationship between left-handedness vs. right-handedness and motor competence in preschool children. Random samples of 41 left-handed preschool children and 41 right-handed preschool children were given several tests of motor skills to determine if there is evidence of a difference between the children based on this experiment. The experiment produced the means and standard deviations shown Table 10.26. Determine the appropriate test and best distribution to use for that test.

|  | Left-handed | Right-handed |
|---|---|---|
| Sample size | 41 | 41 |
| Sample mean | 97.5 | 98.1 |
| Sample standard deviation | 17.5 | 19.2 |

Table 10.26

   a. Two independent means, normal distribution
   b. Two independent means, Student's-t distribution
   c. Matched or paired samples, Student's-t distribution
   d. Two population proportions, normal distribution

**117.** A golf instructor is interested in determining if her new technique for improving players' golf scores is effective. She takes four (4) new students. She records their 18-hole scores before learning the technique and then after having taken her class. She conducts a hypothesis test. The data are as Table 10.27.

|                         | Player 1 | Player 2 | Player 3 | Player 4 |
|-------------------------|----------|----------|----------|----------|
| Mean score before class | 83       | 78       | 93       | 87       |
| Mean score after class  | 80       | 80       | 86       | 86       |

Table 10.27

This is:

a. a test of two independent means.
b. a test of two proportions.
c. a test of a single mean.
d. a test of a single proportion.

# REFERENCES

## 10.1 Comparing Two Independent Population Means

Data from Graduating Engineer + Computer Careers. Available online at http://www.graduatingengineer.com

Data from *Microsoft Bookshelf*.

Data from the United States Senate website, available online at www.Senate.gov (accessed June 17, 2013).

"List of current United States Senators by Age." Wikipedia. Available online at http://en.wikipedia.org/wiki/List_of_current_United_States_Senators_by_age (accessed June 17, 2013).

"Sectoring by Industry Groups." Nasdaq. Available online at http://www.nasdaq.com/markets/barchart-sectors.aspx?page=sectors&base=industry (accessed June 17, 2013).

"Strip Clubs: Where Prostitution and Trafficking Happen." Prostitution Research and Education, 2013. Available online at www.prostitutionresearch.com/ProsViolPosttrauStress.html (accessed June 17, 2013).

"World Series History." Baseball-Almanac, 2013. Available online at http://www.baseball-almanac.com/ws/wsmenu.shtml (accessed June 17, 2013).

## 10.4 Comparing Two Independent Population Proportions

Data from *Educational Resources*, December catalog.

Data from Hilton Hotels. Available online at http://www.hilton.com (accessed June 17, 2013).

Data from Hyatt Hotels. Available online at http://hyatt.com (accessed June 17, 2013).

Data from Statistics, United States Department of Health and Human Services.

Data from Whitney Exhibit on loan to San Jose Museum of Art.

Data from the American Cancer Society. Available online at http://www.cancer.org/index (accessed June 17, 2013).

Data from the Chancellor's Office, California Community Colleges, November 1994.

"State of the States." Gallup, 2013. Available online at http://www.gallup.com/poll/125066/State-States.aspx?ref=interactive (accessed June 17, 2013).

"West Nile Virus." Centers for Disease Control and Prevention. Available online at http://www.cdc.gov/ncidod/dvbid/westnile/index.htm (accessed June 17, 2013).

## 10.5 Two Population Means with Known Standard Deviations

Data from the United States Census Bureau. Available online at http://www.census.gov/prod/cen2010/briefs/c2010br-02.pdf

Hinduja, Sameer. "Sexting Research and Gender Differences." Cyberbulling Research Center, 2013. Available online at http://cyberbullying.us/blog/sexting-research-and-gender-differences/ (accessed June 17, 2013).

"Smart Phone Users, By the Numbers." Visually, 2013. Available online at http://visual.ly/smart-phone-users-numbers (accessed June 17, 2013).

Smith, Aaron. "35% of American adults own a Smartphone." Pew Internet, 2013. Available online at http://www.pewinternet.org/~/media/Files/Reports/2011/PIP_Smartphones.pdf (accessed June 17, 2013).

"State-Specific Prevalence of Obesity AmongAduls—Unites States, 2007." MMWR, CDC. Available online at http://www.cdc.gov/mmwr/preview/mmwrhtml/mm5728a1.htm (accessed June 17, 2013).

"Texas Crime Rates 1960–1012." FBI, Uniform Crime Reports, 2013. Available online at: http://www.disastercenter.com/crime/txcrime.htm (accessed June 17, 2013).

# SOLUTIONS

1 two proportions

3 matched or paired samples

5 single mean

7 independent group means, population standard deviations and/or variances unknown

9 two proportions

11 independent group means, population standard deviations and/or variances unknown

13 independent group means, population standard deviations and/or variances unknown

15 two proportions

17 The random variable is the difference between the mean amounts of sugar in the two soft drinks.

19 means

21 two-tailed

23 the difference between the mean life spans of whites and nonwhites

25 This is a comparison of two population means with unknown population standard deviations.

27 Check student's solution.

28
a. Cannot accept the null hypothesis
b. $p$-value < 0.05
c. There is not enough evidence at the 5% level of significance to support the claim that life expectancy in the 1900s is different between whites and nonwhites.

31 $P'_{OS1} - P'_{OS2}$ = difference in the proportions of phones that had system failures within the first eight hours of operation with $OS_1$ and $OS_2$.

34 proportions

36 right-tailed

38 The random variable is the difference in proportions (percents) of the populations that are of two or more races in Nevada and North Dakota.

40 Our sample sizes are much greater than five each, so we use the normal for two proportions distribution for this hypothesis test.

**42**

a. Cannot accept the null hypothesis.

b. $p$-value < alpha

c. At the 5% significance level, there is sufficient evidence to conclude that the proportion (percent) of the population that is of two or more races in Nevada is statistically higher than that in North Dakota.

**44** The difference in mean speeds of the fastball pitches of the two pitchers

**46** –2.46

**47** At the 1% significance level, we can reject the null hypothesis. There is sufficient data to conclude that the mean speed of Rodriguez's fastball is faster than Wesley's.

**49** Subscripts: 1 = Food, 2 = No Food

$H_0 : \mu_1 \leq \mu_2$

$H_a : \mu_1 > \mu_2$

**51** Subscripts: 1 = Gamma, 2 = Zeta

$H_0 : \mu_1 = \mu_2$

$H_a : \mu_1 \neq \mu_2$

**53** There is sufficient evidence so we cannot accept the null hypothesis. The data support that the melting point for Alloy Zeta is different from the melting point of Alloy Gamma.

**54** the mean difference of the system failures

**56** With a $p$-value 0.0067, we can cannot accept the null hypothesis. There is enough evidence to support that the software patch is effective in reducing the number of system failures.

**60** $H_0: \mu_d \geq 0$ $H_a: \mu_d < 0$

**63** We decline to reject the null hypothesis. There is not sufficient evidence to support that the medication is effective.

**65** Subscripts: 1: two-year colleges; 2: four-year colleges

a. $H_0 : \mu_1 \geq \mu_2$

b. $H_a : \mu_1 < \mu_2$

c. $\bar{X}_1 - \bar{X}_2$ is the difference between the mean enrollments of the two-year colleges and the four-year colleges.

d. Student's-$t$

e. test statistic: -0.2480

f. $p$-value: 0.4019

g. Check student's solution.

h.   i. Alpha: 0.05

   ii. Decision: Cannot reject

   iii. Reason for Decision: $p$-value > alpha

   iv. Conclusion: At the 5% significance level, there is sufficient evidence to conclude that the mean enrollment at four-year colleges is higher than at two-year colleges.

**67** Subscripts: 1: mechanical engineering; 2: electrical engineering

a. $H_0 : \mu_1 \geq \mu_2$

b. $H_a : \mu_1 < \mu_2$

c. $\bar{X}_1 - \bar{X}_2$ is the difference between the mean entry level salaries of mechanical engineers and electrical engineers.

  d. $t_{108}$

  e. test statistic: $t = -0.82$

  f. *p*-value: 0.2061

  g. Check student's solution.

  h.    i. Alpha: 0.05

       ii. Decision: Cannot reject the null hypothesis.

       iii. Reason for Decision: *p*-value > alpha

       iv. Conclusion: At the 5% significance level, there is insufficient evidence to conclude that the mean entry-level salaries of mechanical engineers is lower than that of electrical engineers.

**69**

  a. $H_0 : \mu_1 = \mu_2$

  b. $H_a : \mu_1 \neq \mu_2$

  c. $\bar{X}_1 - \bar{X}_2$ is the difference between the mean times for completing a lap in races and in practices.

  d. $t_{20.32}$

  e. test statistic: $-4.70$

  f. *p*-value: 0.0001

  g. Check student's solution.

  h.    i. Alpha: 0.05

       ii. Decision: Cannot accept the null hypothesis.

       iii. Reason for Decision: *p*-value < alpha

       iv. Conclusion: At the 5% significance level, there is sufficient evidence to conclude that the mean time for completing a lap in races is different from that in practices.

**71**

  a. $H_0 : \mu_1 = \mu_2$

  b. $H_a : \mu_1 \neq \mu_2$

  c. is the difference between the mean times for completing a lap in races and in practices.

  d. $t_{40.94}$

  e. test statistic: $-5.08$

  f. *p*-value: zero

  g. Check student's solution.

  h.    i. Alpha: 0.05

       ii. Decision: Cannot accept the null hypothesis.

       iii. Reason for Decision: *p*-value < alpha

       iv. Conclusion: At the 5% significance level, there is sufficient evidence to conclude that the mean time for completing a lap in races is different from that in practices.

**74** c

**76** Test: two independent sample means, population standard deviations unknown. Random variable: $\bar{X}_1 - \bar{X}_2$ Distribution: $H_0 : \mu_1 = \mu_2$ $H_a : \mu_1 < \mu_2$ $H_0: \mu_1 = \mu_2$ $H_a: \mu_1 < \mu_2$ The mean age of entering prostitution in Canada is lower than the mean age in the United States. Graph: left-tailed *p*-value : 0.0151 Decision: Cannot reject $H_0$. Conclusion: At the

1% level of significance, from the sample data, there is not sufficient evidence to conclude that the mean age of entering prostitution in Canada is lower than the mean age in the United States.

**78** d

**80**

a. $H_0: P_W = P_B$

b. $H_a: P_W \neq P_B$

c. The random variable is the difference in the proportions of white and black suicide victims, aged 15 to 24.

d. normal for two proportions

e. test statistic: –0.1944

f. *p*-value: 0.8458

g. Check student's solution.

h.   i. Alpha: 0.05

    ii. Decision: Cannot accept the null hypothesis.

    iii. Reason for decision: *p*-value > alpha

    iv. Conclusion: At the 5% significance level, there is insufficient evidence to conclude that the proportions of white and black female suicide victims, aged 15 to 24, are different.

**82** Subscripts: 1 = Cabrillo College, 2 = Lake Tahoe College

a. $H_0 : p_1 = p_2$

b. $H_a : p_1 \neq p_2$

c. The random variable is the difference between the proportions of Hispanic students at Cabrillo College and Lake Tahoe College.

d. normal for two proportions

e. test statistic: 4.29

f. *p*-value: 0.00002

g. Check student's solution.

h.   i. Alpha: 0.05

    ii. Decision: Cannot accept the null hypothesis.

    iii. Reason for decision: *p*-value < alpha

    iv. Conclusion: There is sufficient evidence to conclude that the proportions of Hispanic students at Cabrillo College and Lake Tahoe College are different.

**84** a

**85** Test: two independent sample proportions. Random variable: $p'_1 - p'_2$ Distribution:
$H_0 : p_1 = p_2$
$H_a : p_1 \neq p_2$ The proportion of eReader users is different for the 16- to 29-year-old users from that of the 30 and older users. Graph: two-tailed

**87** Test: two independent sample proportions Random variable: $p'_1 - p'_2$ Distribution: $H_0 : p_1 = p_2$

$H_a : p_1 > p_2$ A higher proportion of tablet owners are aged 16 to 29 years old than are 30 years old and older. Graph: right-tailed Do not reject the $H_0$. Conclusion: At the 1% level of significance, from the sample data, there is not sufficient evidence to conclude that a higher proportion of tablet owners are aged 16 to 29 years old than are 30 years old and older.

**89** Subscripts: 1: men; 2: women

a. $H_0 : p_1 \leq p_2$

b. $H_a : p_1 > p_2$

c. $P'_1 - P'_2$ is the difference between the proportions of men and women who enjoy shopping for electronic equipment.

d. normal for two proportions

e. test statistic: 0.22

f. *p*-value: 0.4133

g. Check student's solution.

h. i. Alpha: 0.05

   ii. Decision: Cannot reject the null hypothesis.

   iii. Reason for Decision: *p*-value > alpha

   iv. Conclusion: At the 5% significance level, there is insufficient evidence to conclude that the proportion of men who enjoy shopping for electronic equipment is more than the proportion of women.

**91**

a. $H_0 : p_1 = p_2$

b. $H_a : p_1 \neq p_2$

c. $P'_1 - P'_2$ is the difference between the proportions of men and women that have at least one pierced ear.

d. normal for two proportions

e. test statistic: –4.82

f. *p*-value: zero

g. Check student's solution.

h. i. Alpha: 0.05

   ii. Decision: Cannot accept the null hypothesis.

   iii. Reason for Decision: *p*-value < alpha

   iv. Conclusion: At the 5% significance level, there is sufficient evidence to conclude that the proportions of males and females with at least one pierced ear is different.

**92**

a. $H_0$: $\mu_d = 0$

b. $H_a$: $\mu_d > 0$

c. The random variable $X_d$ is the mean difference in work times on days when eating breakfast and on days when not eating breakfast.

d. $t_9$

e. test statistic: 4.8963

f. *p*-value: 0.0004

g. Check student's solution.

h. i. Alpha: 0.05

   ii. Decision: Cannot accept the null hypothesis.

   iii. Reason for Decision: *p*-value < alpha

   iv. Conclusion: At the 5% level of significance, there is sufficient evidence to conclude that the mean difference in work times on days when eating breakfast and on days when not eating breakfast has increased.

**94** Subscripts: 1 = boys, 2 = girls

a. $H_0 : \mu_1 \le \mu_2$

b. $H_a : \mu_1 > \mu_2$

c. The random variable is the difference in the mean auto insurance costs for boys and girls.

d. normal

e. test statistic: $z = 2.50$

f. $p$-value: 0.0062

g. Check student's solution.

h. i. Alpha: 0.05

   ii. Decision: Cannot accept the null hypothesis.

   iii. Reason for Decision: $p$-value < alpha

   iv. Conclusion: At the 5% significance level, there is sufficient evidence to conclude that the mean cost of auto insurance for teenage boys is greater than that for girls.

**96** Subscripts: 1 = non-hybrid sedans, 2 = hybrid sedans

a. $H_0 : \mu_1 \ge \mu_2$

b. $H_a : \mu_1 < \mu_2$

c. The random variable is the difference in the mean miles per gallon of non-hybrid sedans and hybrid sedans.

d. normal

e. test statistic: 6.36

f. $p$-value: 0

g. Check student's solution.

h. i. Alpha: 0.05

   ii. Decision: Cannot accept the null hypothesis.

   iii. Reason for decision: $p$-value < alpha

   iv. Conclusion: At the 5% significance level, there is sufficient evidence to conclude that the mean miles per gallon of non-hybrid sedans is less than that of hybrid sedans.

**98**

a. $H_0$: $\mu_d = 0$

b. $H_a$: $\mu_d < 0$

c. The random variable $X_d$ is the average difference between husband's and wife's satisfaction level.

d. $t_9$

e. test statistic: $t = -1.86$

f. $p$-value: 0.0479

g. Check student's solution

h. i. Alpha: 0.05

   ii. Decision: Cannot accept the null hypothesis, but run another test.

   iii. Reason for Decision: $p$-value < alpha

   iv. Conclusion: This is a weak test because alpha and the $p$-value are close. However, there is insufficient evidence to conclude that the mean difference is negative.

**99** $p$-value = 0.1494 At the 5% significance level, there is insufficient evidence to conclude that the medication lowered cholesterol levels after 12 weeks.

**103**  Test: two matched pairs or paired samples ($t$-test) Random variable: $\overline{X}_d$ Distribution: $t_{12}$ $H_0$: $\mu_d = 0$ $H_a$: $\mu_d > 0$ The mean of the differences of new female breast cancer cases in the south between 2013 and 2012 is greater than zero. The estimate for new female breast cancer cases in the south is higher in 2013 than in 2012. Graph: right-tailed $p$-value: 0.0004 Decision: Cannot accept $H_0$ Conclusion: At the 5% level of significance, from the sample data, there is sufficient evidence to conclude that there was a higher estimate of new female breast cancer cases in 2013 than in 2012.

**105**  Test: matched or paired samples ($t$-test) Difference data: {–0.9, –3.7, –3.2, –0.5, 0.6, –1.9, –0.5, 0.2, 0.6, 0.4, 1.7, –2.4, 1.8} Random Variable: $\overline{X}_d$ Distribution: $H_0$: $\mu_d = 0$ $H_a$: $\mu_d < 0$ The mean of the differences of the rate of underemployment in the northeastern states between 2012 and 2011 is less than zero. The underemployment rate went down from 2011 to 2012. Graph: left-tailed. Decision: Cannot reject $H_0$. Conclusion: At the 5% level of significance, from the sample data, there is not sufficient evidence to conclude that there was a decrease in the underemployment rates of the northeastern states from 2011 to 2012.

**107**  e

**109**  d

**111**  f

**113**  e

**115**  f

**117**  a

# 11 | THE CHI-SQUARE DISTRIBUTION

**Figure 11.1** The chi-square distribution can be used to find relationships between two things, like grocery prices at different stores. (credit: Pete/flickr)

## Introduction

Have you ever wondered if lottery winning numbers were evenly distributed or if some numbers occurred with a greater frequency? How about if the types of movies people preferred were different across different age groups? What about if a coffee machine was dispensing approximately the same amount of coffee each time? You could answer these questions by conducting a hypothesis test.

You will now study a new distribution, one that is used to determine the answers to such questions. This distribution is called the chi-square distribution.

In this chapter, you will learn the three major applications of the chi-square distribution:

1. the goodness-of-fit test, which determines if data fit a particular distribution, such as in the lottery example

2. the test of independence, which determines if events are independent, such as in the movie example

3. the test of a single variance, which tests variability, such as in the coffee example

# 11.1 | Facts About the Chi-Square Distribution

The notation for the **chi-square distribution** is:

$$\chi \sim \chi^2_{df}$$

where $df$ = degrees of freedom which depends on how chi-square is being used. (If you want to practice calculating chi-square probabilities then use $df = n - 1$. The degrees of freedom for the three major uses are each calculated differently.)

For the $\chi^2$ distribution, the population mean is $\mu = df$ and the population standard deviation is $\sigma = \sqrt{2(df)}$.

The random variable is shown as $\chi^2$.

The random variable for a chi-square distribution with $k$ degrees of freedom is the sum of $k$ independent, squared standard normal variables.

$$\chi^2 = (Z_1)^2 + (Z_2)^2 + ... + (Z_k)^2$$

1.  The curve is nonsymmetrical and skewed to the right.
2.  There is a different chi-square curve for each $df$.

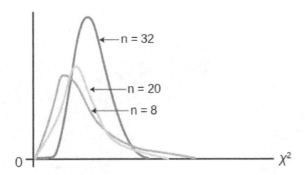

**Figure 11.2**

3.  The test statistic for any test is always greater than or equal to zero.
4.  When $df > 90$, the chi-square curve approximates the normal distribution. For $X \sim \chi^2_{1,000}$ the mean, $\mu = df = 1,000$ and the standard deviation, $\sigma = \sqrt{2(1,000)} = 44.7$. Therefore, $X \sim N(1,000, 44.7)$, approximately.
5.  The mean, $\mu$, is located just to the right of the peak.

# 11.2 | Test of a Single Variance

Thus far our interest has been exclusively on the population parameter μ or it's counterpart in the binomial, p. Surely the mean of a population is the most critical piece of information to have, but in some cases we are interested in the variability of the outcomes of some distribution. In almost all production processes quality is measured not only by how closely the machine matches the target, but also the variability of the process. If one were filling bags with potato chips not only would there be interest in the average weight of the bag, but also how much variation there was in the weights. No one wants to be assured that the average weight is accurate when their bag has no chips. Electricity voltage may meet some average level, but great variability, spikes, can cause serious damage to electrical machines, especially computers. I would not only like to have a high mean grade in my classes, but also low variation about this mean. In short, statistical tests concerning the variance of a distribution have great value and many applications.

A **test of a single variance** assumes that the underlying distribution is **normal**. The null and alternative hypotheses are stated in terms of the **population variance**. The test statistic is:

$$\chi^2_c = \frac{(n-1)s^2}{\sigma_0^2}$$

where:

- $n$ = the total number of observations in the sample data

- $s^2$ = sample variance

- $\sigma_0^2$ = hypothesized value of the population variance

- $H_0 : \sigma^2 = \sigma_0^2$

- $H_a : \sigma^2 \neq \sigma_0^2$

You may think of $s$ as the random variable in this test. The number of degrees of freedom is $df = n - 1$. A test of a single variance may be right-tailed, left-tailed, or two-tailed. **Example 11.1** will show you how to set up the null and alternative hypotheses. The null and alternative hypotheses contain statements about the population variance.

## Example 11.1

Math instructors are not only interested in how their students do on exams, on average, but how the exam scores vary. To many instructors, the variance (or standard deviation) may be more important than the average.

Suppose a math instructor believes that the standard deviation for his final exam is five points. One of his best students thinks otherwise. The student claims that the standard deviation is more than five points. If the student were to conduct a hypothesis test, what would the null and alternative hypotheses be?

### Solution 11.1

Even though we are given the population standard deviation, we can set up the test using the population variance as follows.

- $H_0$: $\sigma^2 \leq 5^2$

- $H_a$: $\sigma^2 > 5^2$

 Try It Σ

**11.1** A SCUBA instructor wants to record the collective depths each of his students' dives during their checkout. He is interested in how the depths vary, even though everyone should have been at the same depth. He believes the standard deviation is three feet. His assistant thinks the standard deviation is less than three feet. If the instructor were to conduct a test, what would the null and alternative hypotheses be?

## Example 11.2

With individual lines at its various windows, a post office finds that the standard deviation for waiting times for customers on Friday afternoon is 7.2 minutes. The post office experiments with a single, main waiting line and finds that for a random sample of 25 customers, the waiting times for customers have a standard deviation of 3.5 minutes on a Friday afternoon.

With a significance level of 5%, test the claim that **a single line causes lower variation among waiting times for customers**.

### Solution 11.2

Since the claim is that a single line causes less variation, this is a test of a single variance. The parameter is the population variance, $\sigma^2$.

**Random Variable:** The sample standard deviation, $s$, is the random variable. Let $s$ = standard deviation for the waiting times.

- $H_0$: $\sigma^2 \geq 7.2^2$

- $H_a$: $\sigma^2 < 7.2^2$

The word **"less"** tells you this is a left-tailed test.

**Distribution for the test:** $\chi^2_{24}$, where:

- $n$ = the number of customers sampled

- $df = n - 1 = 25 - 1 = 24$

**Calculate the test statistic:**

$$\chi^2_c = \frac{(n-1)s^2}{\sigma^2} = \frac{(25-1)(3.5)^2}{7.2^2} = 5.67$$

where $n = 25$, $s = 3.5$, and $\sigma = 7.2$.

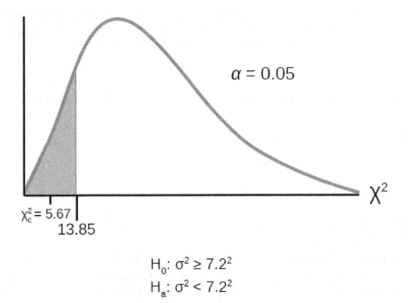

**Figure 11.3**

The graph of the Chi-square shows the distribution and marks the critical value with 24 degrees of freedom at 95% level of confidence, $\alpha = 0.05$, 13.85. The critical value of 13.85 came from the Chi squared table which is read very much like the students t table. The difference is that the students t distribution is symmetrical and the Chi squared distribution is not. At the top of the Chi squared table we see not only the familiar 0.05, 0.10, etc. but also 0.95, 0.975, etc. These are the columns used to find the left hand critical value. The graph also marks the calculated $\chi^2$ test statistic of 5.67. Comparing the test statistic with the critical value, as we have done with all other hypothesis tests, we reach the conclusion.

**Make a decision:** Because the calculated test statistic is in the tail we cannot accept $H_0$. This means that you reject $\sigma^2 \geq 7.2^2$. In other words, you do not think the variation in waiting times is 7.2 minutes or more; you think the variation in waiting times is less.

**Conclusion:** At a 5% level of significance, from the data, there is sufficient evidence to conclude that a single line causes a lower variation among the waiting times **or** with a single line, the customer waiting times vary less than 7.2 minutes.

## Example 11.3

Professor Hadley has a weakness for cream filled donuts, but he believes that some bakeries are not properly filling the donuts. A sample of 24 donuts reveals a mean amount of filling equal to 0.04 cups, and the sample standard deviation is 0.11 cups. Professor Hadley has an interest in the average quantity of filling, of course, but he is particularly distressed if one donut is radically different from another. Professor Hadley does not like surprises.

Test at 95% the null hypothesis that the population variance of donut filling is significantly different from the average amount of filling.

### Solution 11.3

This is clearly a problem dealing with variances. In this case we are testing a single sample rather than comparing two samples from different populations. The null and alternative hypotheses are thus:

$$H_0 : \sigma^2 = 0.04$$

$$H_0 : \sigma^2 \neq 0.04$$

The test is set up as a two-tailed test because Professor Hadley has shown concern with too much variation in filling as well as too little: his dislike of a surprise is any level of filling outside the expected average of 0.04 cups. The test statistic is calculated to be:

$$\chi_c^2 = \frac{(n-1)s^2}{\sigma_o^2} = \frac{(24-1)0.11^2}{0.04^2} = 6.9575$$

The calculated $\chi^2$ test statistic, 6.96, is in the tail therefore at a 0.05 level of significance, we cannot accept the null hypothesis that the variance in the donut filling is equal to 0.04 cups. It seems that Professor Hadley is destined to meet disappointment with each bit.

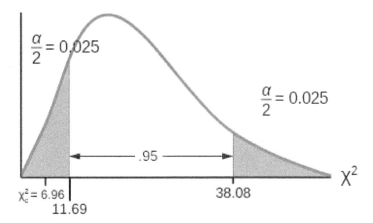

Figure 11.4

**11.3** The FCC conducts broadband speed tests to measure how much data per second passes between a consumer's computer and the internet. As of August of 2012, the standard deviation of Internet speeds across Internet Service

Providers (ISPs) was 12.2 percent. Suppose a sample of 15 ISPs is taken, and the standard deviation is 13.2. An analyst claims that the standard deviation of speeds is more than what was reported. State the null and alternative hypotheses, compute the degrees of freedom, the test statistic, sketch the graph of the distribution and mark the area associated with the level of confidence, and draw a conclusion. Test at the 1% significance level.

# 11.3 | Goodness-of-Fit Test

In this type of hypothesis test, you determine whether the data **"fit"** a particular distribution or not. For example, you may suspect your unknown data fit a binomial distribution. You use a chi-square test (meaning the distribution for the hypothesis test is chi-square) to determine if there is a fit or not. **The null and the alternative hypotheses for this test may be written in sentences or may be stated as equations or inequalities.**

The test statistic for a goodness-of-fit test is:

$$\sum_k \frac{(O-E)^2}{E}$$

where:

- $O$ = **observed values** (data)

- $E$ = **expected values** (from theory)

- $k$ = the number of different data cells or categories

**The observed values are the data values and the expected values are the values you would expect to get if the null hypothesis were true.** There are $n$ terms of the form $\frac{(O-E)^2}{E}$.

The number of degrees of freedom is $df$ = (number of categories – 1).

**The goodness-of-fit test is almost always right-tailed.** If the observed values and the corresponding expected values are not close to each other, then the test statistic can get very large and will be way out in the right tail of the chi-square curve.

### NOTE
---
The number of expected values inside each cell needs to be at least five in order to use this test.

### Example 11.4

Absenteeism of college students from math classes is a major concern to math instructors because missing class appears to increase the drop rate. Suppose that a study was done to determine if the actual student absenteeism rate follows faculty perception. The faculty expected that a group of 100 students would miss class according to **Table 11.1**.

| Number of absences per term | Expected number of students |
|---|---|
| 0–2 | 50 |
| 3–5 | 30 |
| 6–8 | 12 |
| 9–11 | 6 |
| 12+ | 2 |

**Table 11.1**

A random survey across all mathematics courses was then done to determine the actual number **(observed)** of absences in a course. The chart in **Table 11.2** displays the results of that survey.

| Number of absences per term | Actual number of students |
|---|---|
| 0–2 | 35 |
| 3–5 | 40 |
| 6–8 | 20 |
| 9–11 | 1 |
| 12+ | 4 |

Table 11.2

Determine the null and alternative hypotheses needed to conduct a goodness-of-fit test.

$H_0$: Student absenteeism **fits** faculty perception.

The alternative hypothesis is the opposite of the null hypothesis.

$H_a$: Student absenteeism **does not fit** faculty perception.

a. Can you use the information as it appears in the charts to conduct the goodness-of-fit test?

**Solution 11.4**

a. **No.** Notice that the expected number of absences for the "12+" entry is less than five (it is two). Combine that group with the "9–11" group to create new tables where the number of students for each entry are at least five. The new results are in **Table 11.2** and **Table 11.3**.

| Number of absences per term | Expected number of students |
|---|---|
| 0–2 | 50 |
| 3–5 | 30 |
| 6–8 | 12 |
| 9+ | 8 |

Table 11.3

| Number of absences per term | Actual number of students |
|---|---|
| 0–2 | 35 |
| 3–5 | 40 |
| 6–8 | 20 |
| 9+ | 5 |

Table 11.4

b. What is the number of degrees of freedom (*df*)?

**Solution 11.4**

b. There are four "cells" or categories in each of the new tables.

$df$ = number of cells − 1 = 4 − 1 = 3

**11.4** A factory manager needs to understand how many products are defective versus how many are produced. The number of expected defects is listed in Table 11.5.

| Number produced | Number defective |
|-----------------|------------------|
| 0–100           | 5                |
| 101–200         | 6                |
| 201–300         | 7                |
| 301–400         | 8                |
| 401–500         | 10               |

Table 11.5

A random sample was taken to determine the actual number of defects. Table 11.6 shows the results of the survey.

| Number produced | Number defective |
|-----------------|------------------|
| 0–100           | 5                |
| 101–200         | 7                |
| 201–300         | 8                |
| 301–400         | 9                |
| 401–500         | 11               |

Table 11.6

State the null and alternative hypotheses needed to conduct a goodness-of-fit test, and state the degrees of freedom.

## Example 11.5

Employers want to know which days of the week employees are absent in a five-day work week. Most employers would like to believe that employees are absent equally during the week. Suppose a random sample of 60 managers were asked on which day of the week they had the highest number of employee absences. The results were distributed as in Table 11.6. For the population of employees, do the days for the highest number of absences occur with equal frequencies during a five-day work week? Test at a 5% significance level.

|  | Monday | Tuesday | Wednesday | Thursday | Friday |
|---|---|---|---|---|---|
| **Number of Absences** | 15 | 12 | 9 | 9 | 15 |

**Table 11.7 Day of the Week Employees were Most Absent**

### Solution 11.5

The null and alternative hypotheses are:

- $H_0$: The absent days occur with equal frequencies, that is, they fit a uniform distribution.
- $H_a$: The absent days occur with unequal frequencies, that is, they do not fit a uniform distribution.

If the absent days occur with equal frequencies, then, out of 60 absent days (the total in the sample: 15 + 12 + 9 + 9 + 15 = 60), there would be 12 absences on Monday, 12 on Tuesday, 12 on Wednesday, 12 on Thursday, and 12 on Friday. These numbers are the **expected** ($E$) values. The values in the table are the **observed** ($O$) values or data.

This time, calculate the $\chi^2$ test statistic by hand. Make a chart with the following headings and fill in the columns:

- Expected ($E$) values (12, 12, 12, 12, 12)
- Observed ($O$) values (15, 12, 9, 9, 15)
- $(O - E)$
- $(O - E)^2$
- $\dfrac{(O - E)^2}{E}$

Now add (sum) the last column. The sum is three. This is the $\chi^2$ test statistic.

The calculated test statistics is 3 and the critical value of the $\chi^2$ distribution at 4 degrees of freedom the 0.05 level of confidence is 9.48. This value is found in the $\chi^2$ table at the 0.05 column on the degrees of freedom row 4.

The degrees of freedom are the number of cells − 1 = 5 − 1 = 4

Next, complete a graph like the following one with the proper labeling and shading. (You should shade the right tail.)

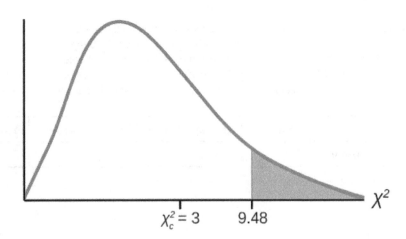

Figure 11.5

$$\chi_c^2 = \sum_k \frac{(O-E)^2}{E} = 3$$

The decision is not to reject the null hypothesis because the calculated value of the test statistic is not in the tail of the distribution.

**Conclusion:** At a 5% level of significance, from the sample data, there is not sufficient evidence to conclude that the absent days do not occur with equal frequencies.

## Try It Σ

**11.5** Teachers want to know which night each week their students are doing most of their homework. Most teachers think that students do homework equally throughout the week. Suppose a random sample of 56 students were asked on which night of the week they did the most homework. The results were distributed as in **Table 11.8**.

|                     | Sunday | Monday | Tuesday | Wednesday | Thursday | Friday | Saturday |
|---------------------|--------|--------|---------|-----------|----------|--------|----------|
| Number of Students  | 11     | 8      | 10      | 7         | 10       | 5      | 5        |

Table 11.8

From the population of students, do the nights for the highest number of students doing the majority of their homework occur with equal frequencies during a week? What type of hypothesis test should you use?

## Example 11.6

One study indicates that the number of televisions that American families have is distributed (this is the **given** distribution for the American population) as in **Table 11.9**.

| Number of Televisions | Percent |
|---|---|
| 0 | 10 |
| 1 | 16 |
| 2 | 55 |
| 3 | 11 |
| 4+ | 8 |

Table 11.9

The table contains expected (*E*) percents.

A random sample of 600 families in the far western United States resulted in the data in **Table 11.10**.

| Number of Televisions | Frequency |
|---|---|
| 0 | 66 |
| 1 | 119 |
| 2 | 340 |
| 3 | 60 |
| 4+ | 15 |
| | **Total = 600** |

Table 11.10

The table contains observed (*O*) frequency values.

At the 1% significance level, does it appear that the distribution "number of televisions" of far western United States families is different from the distribution for the American population as a whole?

**Solution 11.6**

This problem asks you to test whether the far western United States families distribution fits the distribution of the American families. This test is always right-tailed.

The first table contains expected percentages. To get expected (*E*) frequencies, multiply the percentage by 600. The expected frequencies are shown in **Table 11.10**.

| Number of Televisions | Percent | Expected Frequency |
|---|---|---|
| 0 | 10 | (0.10)(600) = 60 |
| 1 | 16 | (0.16)(600) = 96 |
| 2 | 55 | (0.55)(600) = 330 |
| 3 | 11 | (0.11)(600) = 66 |
| over 3 | 8 | (0.08)(600) = 48 |

Table 11.11

Therefore, the expected frequencies are 60, 96, 330, 66, and 48.

$H_0$: The "number of televisions" distribution of far western United States families is the same as the "number of televisions" distribution of the American population.

$H_a$: The "number of televisions" distribution of far western United States families is different from the "number of televisions" distribution of the American population.

Distribution for the test: $\chi_4^2$ where $df$ = (the number of cells) − 1 = 5 − 1 = 4.

**Calculate the test statistic:** $\chi^2$ = 29.65

**Graph:**

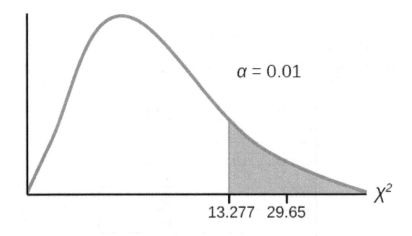

Figure 11.6

The graph of the Chi-square shows the distribution and marks the critical value with four degrees of freedom at 99% level of confidence, $\alpha$ = .01, 13.277. The graph also marks the calculated chi squared test statistic of 29.65. Comparing the test statistic with the critical value, as we have done with all other hypothesis tests, we reach the conclusion.

**Make a decision:** Because the test statistic is in the tail of the distribution we cannot accept the null hypothesis.

This means you reject the belief that the distribution for the far western states is the same as that of the American population as a whole.

**Conclusion:** At the 1% significance level, from the data, there is sufficient evidence to conclude that the "number of televisions" distribution for the far western United States is different from the "number of televisions" distribution for the American population as a whole.

**11.6** The expected percentage of the number of pets students have in their homes is distributed (this is the given distribution for the student population of the United States) as in Table 11.12.

| Number of Pets | Percent |
|---|---|
| 0 | 18 |
| 1 | 25 |
| 2 | 30 |
| 3 | 18 |
| 4+ | 9 |

Table 11.12

A random sample of 1,000 students from the Eastern United States resulted in the data in Table 11.13.

| Number of Pets | Frequency |
|---|---|
| 0 | 210 |
| 1 | 240 |
| 2 | 320 |
| 3 | 140 |
| 4+ | 90 |

Table 11.13

At the 1% significance level, does it appear that the distribution "number of pets" of students in the Eastern United States is different from the distribution for the United States student population as a whole?

## Example 11.7

Suppose you flip two coins 100 times. The results are 20 *HH*, 27 *HT*, 30 *TH*, and 23 *TT*. Are the coins fair? Test at a 5% significance level.

### Solution 11.7

This problem can be set up as a goodness-of-fit problem. The sample space for flipping two fair coins is {*HH*, *HT*, *TH*, *TT*}. Out of 100 flips, you would expect 25 *HH*, 25 *HT*, 25 *TH*, and 25 *TT*. This is the expected distribution from the binomial probability distribution. The question, "Are the coins fair?" is the same as saying, "Does the distribution of the coins (20 *HH*, 27 *HT*, 30 *TH*, 23 *TT*) fit the expected distribution?"

**Random Variable:** Let $X$ = the number of heads in one flip of the two coins. $X$ takes on the values 0, 1, 2. (There are 0, 1, or 2 heads in the flip of two coins.) Therefore, the **number of cells is three**. Since $X$ = the number of heads, the observed frequencies are 20 (for two heads), 57 (for one head), and 23 (for zero heads or both tails). The expected frequencies are 25 (for two heads), 50 (for one head), and 25 (for zero heads or both tails). This test is right-tailed.

$H_0$: The coins are fair.

$H_a$: The coins are not fair.

**Distribution for the test:** $\chi_2^2$ where $df = 3 - 1 = 2$.

**Calculate the test statistic:** $\chi^2 = 2.14$

**Graph:**

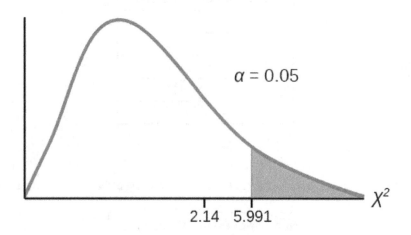

**Figure 11.7**

The graph of the Chi-square shows the distribution and marks the critical value with two degrees of freedom at 95% level of confidence, $\alpha = 0.05$, 5.991. The graph also marks the calculated $\chi^2$ test statistic of 2.14. Comparing the test statistic with the critical value, as we have done with all other hypothesis tests, we reach the conclusion.

**Conclusion:** There is insufficient evidence to conclude that the coins are not fair: we cannot reject the null hypothesis that the coins are fair.

# 11.4 | Test of Independence

Tests of independence involve using a **contingency table** of observed (data) values.

The test statistic for a **test of independence** is similar to that of a goodness-of-fit test:

$$\underset{(i \cdot j)}{\Sigma} \frac{(O - E)^2}{E}$$

where:

- $O$ = observed values
- $E$ = expected values
- $i$ = the number of rows in the table
- $j$ = the number of columns in the table

There are $i \cdot j$ terms of the form $\frac{(O - E)^2}{E}$.

**A test of independence determines whether two factors are independent or not.** You first encountered the term independence in **Section 3.2** earlier. As a review, consider the following example.

**NOTE**

The expected value inside each cell needs to be at least five in order for you to use this test.

## Example 11.8

Suppose $A$ = a speeding violation in the last year and $B$ = a cell phone user while driving. If $A$ and $B$ are independent then $P(A \cap B) = P(A)P(B)$. $A \cap B$ is the event that a driver received a speeding violation last year and also used a cell phone while driving. Suppose, in a study of drivers who received speeding violations in the last year, and who used cell phone while driving, that 755 people were surveyed. Out of the 755, 70 had a speeding violation and 685 did not; 305 used cell phones while driving and 450 did not.

Let $y$ = expected number of drivers who used a cell phone while driving and received speeding violations.

If $A$ and $B$ are independent, then $P(A \cap B) = P(A)P(B)$. By substitution,

$$\frac{y}{755} = \left(\frac{70}{755}\right)\left(\frac{305}{755}\right)$$

Solve for $y$: $y = \dfrac{(70)(305)}{755} = 28.3$

About 28 people from the sample are expected to use cell phones while driving and to receive speeding violations.

In a test of independence, we state the null and alternative hypotheses in words. Since the contingency table consists of **two factors**, the null hypothesis states that the factors are **independent** and the alternative hypothesis states that they are **not independent (dependent)**. If we do a test of independence using the example, then the null hypothesis is:

$H_0$ : Being a cell phone user while driving and receiving a speeding violation are independent events; in other words, they have no effect on each other.

If the null hypothesis were true, we would expect about 28 people to use cell phones while driving and to receive a speeding violation.

**The test of independence is always right-tailed** because of the calculation of the test statistic. If the expected and observed values are not close together, then the test statistic is very large and way out in the right tail of the chi-square curve, as it is in a goodness-of-fit.

The number of degrees of freedom for the test of independence is:

$df$ = (number of columns - 1)(number of rows - 1)

The following formula calculates the **expected number** ($E$):

$$E = \frac{(\text{row total})(\text{column total})}{\text{total number surveyed}}$$

 Try It Σ

**11.8** A sample of 300 students is taken. Of the students surveyed, 50 were music students, while 250 were not. Ninety-seven of the 300 surveyed were on the honor roll, while 203 were not. If we assume being a music student and being on the honor roll are independent events, what is the expected number of music students who are also on the honor roll?

## Example 11.9

A volunteer group, provides from one to nine hours each week with disabled senior citizens. The program recruits among community college students, four-year college students, and nonstudents. In **Table 11.14** is a **sample** of the adult volunteers and the number of hours they volunteer per week.

| Type of Volunteer | 1–3 Hours | 4–6 Hours | 7–9 Hours | Row Total |
|---|---|---|---|---|
| Community College Students | 111 | 96 | 48 | 255 |
| Four-Year College Students | 96 | 133 | 61 | 290 |
| Nonstudents | 91 | 150 | 53 | 294 |
| Column Total | 298 | 379 | 162 | 839 |

**Table 11.14 Number of Hours Worked Per Week by Volunteer Type (Observed)** The table contains **observed (O)** values (data).

Is the number of hours volunteered **independent** of the type of volunteer?

### Solution 11.9

The **observed table** and the question at the end of the problem, "Is the number of hours volunteered independent of the type of volunteer?" tell you this is a test of independence. The two factors are **number of hours volunteered** and **type of volunteer**. This test is always right-tailed.

$H_0$: The number of hours volunteered is **independent** of the type of volunteer.

$H_a$: The number of hours volunteered is **dependent** on the type of volunteer.

The expected result are in **Table 11.14**.

| Type of Volunteer | 1-3 Hours | 4-6 Hours | 7-9 Hours |
|---|---|---|---|
| **Community College Students** | 90.57 | 115.19 | 49.24 |
| **Four-Year College Students** | 103.00 | 131.00 | 56.00 |
| **Nonstudents** | 104.42 | 132.81 | 56.77 |

**Table 11.15 Number of Hours Worked Per Week by Volunteer Type (Expected)** The table contains **expected (E)** values (data).

For example, the calculation for the expected frequency for the top left cell is

$$E = \frac{(\text{row total})(\text{column total})}{\text{total number surveyed}} = \frac{(255)(298)}{839} = 90.57$$

**Calculate the test statistic:** $\chi^2 = 12.99$ (calculator or computer)

**Distribution for the test:** $\chi^2_4$

$df = (3 \text{ columns} - 1)(3 \text{ rows} - 1) = (2)(2) = 4$

**Graph:**

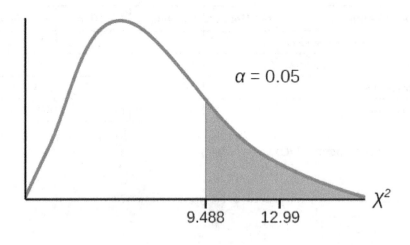

CANNOT ACCEPT H₀

**Figure 11.8**

The graph of the Chi-square shows the distribution and marks the critical value with four degrees of freedom at 95% level of confidence, $\alpha = 0.05$, 9.488. The graph also marks the calculated $\chi_c^2$ test statistic of 12.99.

Comparing the test statistic with the critical value, as we have done with all other hypothesis tests, we reach the conclusion.

**Make a decision:** Because the calculated test statistic is in the tail we cannot accept $H_0$. This means that the factors are not independent.

**Conclusion:** At a 5% level of significance, from the data, there is sufficient evidence to conclude that the number of hours volunteered and the type of volunteer are dependent on one another.

For the example in **Table 11.14**, if there had been another type of volunteer, teenagers, what would the degrees of freedom be?

☞ **11.9** The Bureau of Labor Statistics gathers data about employment in the United States. A sample is taken to calculate the number of U.S. citizens working in one of several industry sectors over time. Table 11.16 shows the results:

| Industry Sector | 2000 | 2010 | 2020 | Total |
|---|---|---|---|---|
| Nonagriculture wage and salary | 13,243 | 13,044 | 15,018 | 41,305 |
| Goods-producing, excluding agriculture | 2,457 | 1,771 | 1,950 | 6,178 |
| Services-providing | 10,786 | 11,273 | 13,068 | 35,127 |
| Agriculture, forestry, fishing, and hunting | 240 | 214 | 201 | 655 |
| Nonagriculture self-employed and unpaid family worker | 931 | 894 | 972 | 2,797 |
| Secondary wage and salary jobs in agriculture and private household industries | 14 | 11 | 11 | 36 |
| Secondary jobs as a self-employed or unpaid family worker | 196 | 144 | 152 | 492 |
| Total | 27,867 | 27,351 | 31,372 | 86,590 |

Table 11.16

We want to know if the change in the number of jobs is independent of the change in years. State the null and alternative hypotheses and the degrees of freedom.

## Example 11.10

De Anza College is interested in the relationship between anxiety level and the need to succeed in school. A random sample of 400 students took a test that measured anxiety level and need to succeed in school. Table 11.17 shows the results. De Anza College wants to know if anxiety level and need to succeed in school are independent events.

| Need to Succeed in School | High Anxiety | Med-high Anxiety | Medium Anxiety | Med-low Anxiety | Low Anxiety | Row Total |
|---|---|---|---|---|---|---|
| **High Need** | 35 | 42 | 53 | 15 | 10 | 155 |
| **Medium Need** | 18 | 48 | 63 | 33 | 31 | 193 |
| **Low Need** | 4 | 5 | 11 | 15 | 17 | 52 |
| **Column Total** | 57 | 95 | 127 | 63 | 58 | 400 |

Table 11.17 Need to Succeed in School vs. Anxiety Level

a. How many high anxiety level students are expected to have a high need to succeed in school?

Solution 11.10

a. The column total for a high anxiety level is 57. The row total for high need to succeed in school is 155. The sample size or total surveyed is 400.

$$E = \frac{(\text{row total})(\text{column total})}{\text{total surveyed}} = \frac{155 \cdot 57}{400} = 22.09$$

The expected number of students who have a high anxiety level and a high need to succeed in school is about 22.

b. If the two variables are independent, how many students do you expect to have a low need to succeed in school and a med-low level of anxiety?

**Solution 11.10**

b. The column total for a med-low anxiety level is 63. The row total for a low need to succeed in school is 52. The sample size or total surveyed is 400.

c. $E = \frac{(\text{row total})(\text{column total})}{\text{total surveyed}} = $ _____

**Solution 11.10**

c. $E = \frac{(\text{row total})(\text{column total})}{\text{total surveyed}} = 8.19$

d. The expected number of students who have a med-low anxiety level and a low need to succeed in school is about _____.

**Solution 11.10**

d. 8

# 11.5 | Test for Homogeneity

The goodness–of–fit test can be used to decide whether a population fits a given distribution, but it will not suffice to decide whether two populations follow the same unknown distribution. A different test, called the **test for homogeneity**, can be used to draw a conclusion about whether two populations have the same distribution. To calculate the test statistic for a test for homogeneity, follow the same procedure as with the test of independence.

## NOTE

The expected value inside each cell needs to be at least five in order for you to use this test.

**Hypotheses**

$H_0$: The distributions of the two populations are the same.

$H_a$: The distributions of the two populations are not the same.

**Test Statistic**

Use a $\chi^2$ test statistic. It is computed in the same way as the test for independence.

**Degrees of Freedom (df)**

$df$ = number of columns - 1

**Requirements**

All values in the table must be greater than or equal to five.

**Common Uses**

Comparing two populations. For example: men vs. women, before vs. after, east vs. west. The variable is categorical with more than two possible response values.

Download for free at https://openstax.org/details/books/introductory-business-statistics

## Example 11.11

Do male and female college students have the same distribution of living arrangements? Use a level of significance of 0.05. Suppose that 250 randomly selected male college students and 300 randomly selected female college students were asked about their living arrangements: dormitory, apartment, with parents, other. The results are shown in Table 11.17. Do male and female college students have the same distribution of living arrangements?

|  | Dormitory | Apartment | With Parents | Other |
|---|---|---|---|---|
| **Males** | 72 | 84 | 49 | 45 |
| **Females** | 91 | 86 | 88 | 35 |

Table 11.18 Distribution of Living Arragements for College Males and College Females

### Solution 11.11

$H_0$: The distribution of living arrangements for male college students is the same as the distribution of living arrangements for female college students.

$H_a$: The distribution of living arrangements for male college students is not the same as the distribution of living arrangements for female college students.

**Degrees of Freedom (df):**
$df$ = number of columns − 1 = 4 − 1 = 3

**Distribution for the test:** $\chi_3^2$

**Calculate the test statistic:** $\chi_c^2 = 10.129$

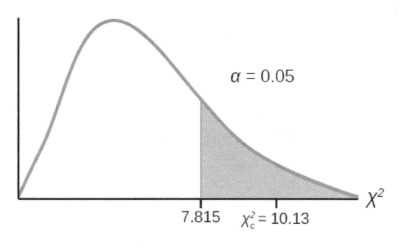

Figure 11.9

The graph of the Chi-square shows the distribution and marks the critical value with three degrees of freedom at 95% level of confidence, $\alpha = 0.05$, 7.815. The graph also marks the calculated $\chi^2$ test statistic of 10.129. Comparing the test statistic with the critical value, as we have done with all other hypothesis tests, we reach the conclusion.

**Make a decision:** Because the calculated test statistic is in the tail we cannot accept $H_0$. This means that the distributions are not the same.

**Conclusion:** At a 5% level of significance, from the data, there is sufficient evidence to conclude that the distributions of living arrangements for male and female college students are not the same.

Notice that the conclusion is only that the distributions are not the same. We cannot use the test for homogeneity to draw any conclusions about how they differ.

## Try It Σ

**11.11** Do families and singles have the same distribution of cars? Use a level of significance of 0.05. Suppose that 100 randomly selected families and 200 randomly selected singles were asked what type of car they drove: sport, sedan, hatchback, truck, van/SUV. The results are shown in **Table 11.19**. Do families and singles have the same distribution of cars? Test at a level of significance of 0.05.

|        | Sport | Sedan | Hatchback | Truck | Van/SUV |
|--------|-------|-------|-----------|-------|---------|
| Family | 5     | 15    | 35        | 17    | 28      |
| Single | 45    | 65    | 37        | 46    | 7       |

Table 11.19

## Try It Σ

☞ **11.11** Ivy League schools receive many applications, but only some can be accepted. At the schools listed in **Table 11.20**, two types of applications are accepted: regular and early decision.

| Application Type Accepted | Brown | Columbia | Cornell | Dartmouth | Penn  | Yale  |
|---------------------------|-------|----------|---------|-----------|-------|-------|
| Regular                   | 2,115 | 1,792    | 5,306   | 1,734     | 2,685 | 1,245 |
| Early Decision            | 577   | 627      | 1,228   | 444       | 1,195 | 761   |

Table 11.20

We want to know if the number of regular applications accepted follows the same distribution as the number of early applications accepted. State the null and alternative hypotheses, the degrees of freedom and the test statistic, sketch the graph of the $\chi^2$ distribution and show the critical value and the calculated value of the test statistic, and draw a conclusion about the test of homogeneity.

# 11.6 | Comparison of the Chi-Square Tests

Above the $\chi^2$ test statistic was used in three different circumstances. The following bulleted list is a summary of which $\chi^2$ test is the appropriate one to use in different circumstances.

- **Goodness-of-Fit:** Use the goodness-of-fit test to decide whether a population with an unknown distribution "fits" a known distribution. In this case there will be a single qualitative survey question or a single outcome of an experiment from a single population. Goodness-of-Fit is typically used to see if the population is uniform (all outcomes occur with equal frequency), the population is normal, or the population is the same as another population with a known distribution. The null and alternative hypotheses are:

  $H_0$: The population fits the given distribution.

  $H_a$: The population does not fit the given distribution.

- **Independence:** Use the test for independence to decide whether two variables (factors) are independent or dependent. In this case there will be two qualitative survey questions or experiments and a contingency table will be constructed. The goal is to see if the two variables are unrelated (independent) or related (dependent). The null and alternative hypotheses are:

  $H_0$: The two variables (factors) are independent.

  $H_a$: The two variables (factors) are dependent.

- **Homogeneity:** Use the test for homogeneity to decide if two populations with unknown distributions have the same distribution as each other. In this case there will be a single qualitative survey question or experiment given to two different populations. The null and alternative hypotheses are:

  $H_0$: The two populations follow the same distribution.

  $H_a$: The two populations have different distributions.

# KEY TERMS

**Contingency Table** a table that displays sample values for two different factors that may be dependent or contingent on one another; it facilitates determining conditional probabilities.

**Goodness-of-Fit** a hypothesis test that compares expected and observed values in order to look for significant differences within one non-parametric variable. The degrees of freedom used equals the (number of categories – 1).

**Test for Homogeneity** a test used to draw a conclusion about whether two populations have the same distribution. The degrees of freedom used equals the (number of columns – 1).

**Test of Independence** a hypothesis test that compares expected and observed values for contingency tables in order to test for independence between two variables. The degrees of freedom used equals the (number of columns – 1) multiplied by the (number of rows – 1).

# CHAPTER REVIEW

## 11.1 Facts About the Chi-Square Distribution

The chi-square distribution is a useful tool for assessment in a series of problem categories. These problem categories include primarily (i) whether a data set fits a particular distribution, (ii) whether the distributions of two populations are the same, (iii) whether two events might be independent, and (iv) whether there is a different variability than expected within a population.

An important parameter in a chi-square distribution is the degrees of freedom $df$ in a given problem. The random variable in the chi-square distribution is the sum of squares of $df$ standard normal variables, which must be independent. The key characteristics of the chi-square distribution also depend directly on the degrees of freedom.

The chi-square distribution curve is skewed to the right, and its shape depends on the degrees of freedom $df$. For $df > 90$, the curve approximates the normal distribution. Test statistics based on the chi-square distribution are always greater than or equal to zero. Such application tests are almost always right-tailed tests.

## 11.2 Test of a Single Variance

To test variability, use the chi-square test of a single variance. The test may be left-, right-, or two-tailed, and its hypotheses are always expressed in terms of the variance (or standard deviation).

## 11.3 Goodness-of-Fit Test

To assess whether a data set fits a specific distribution, you can apply the goodness-of-fit hypothesis test that uses the chi-square distribution. The null hypothesis for this test states that the data come from the assumed distribution. The test compares observed values against the values you would expect to have if your data followed the assumed distribution. The test is almost always right-tailed. Each observation or cell category must have an expected value of at least five.

## 11.4 Test of Independence

To assess whether two factors are independent or not, you can apply the test of independence that uses the chi-square distribution. The null hypothesis for this test states that the two factors are independent. The test compares observed values to expected values. The test is right-tailed. Each observation or cell category must have an expected value of at least 5.

## 11.5 Test for Homogeneity

To assess whether two data sets are derived from the same distribution—which need not be known, you can apply the test for homogeneity that uses the chi-square distribution. The null hypothesis for this test states that the populations of the two data sets come from the same distribution. The test compares the observed values against the expected values if the two populations followed the same distribution. The test is right-tailed. Each observation or cell category must have an expected value of at least five.

## 11.6 Comparison of the Chi-Square Tests

The goodness-of-fit test is typically used to determine if data fits a particular distribution. The test of independence makes use of a contingency table to determine the independence of two factors. The test for homogeneity determines whether two populations come from the same distribution, even if this distribution is unknown.

# FORMULA REVIEW

### 11.1 Facts About the Chi-Square Distribution

$\chi^2 = (Z_1)^2 + (Z_2)^2 + \dots (Z_{df})^2$ chi-square distribution random variable

$\mu_{\chi^2} = df$ chi-square distribution population mean

$\sigma_{\chi^2} = \sqrt{2(df)}$ Chi-Square distribution population standard deviation

### 11.2 Test of a Single Variance

$\chi^2 = \dfrac{(n-1)s^2}{\sigma_0^2}$ Test of a single variance statistic where:

$n$: sample size
$s$: sample standard deviation
$\sigma_0$: hypothesized value of the population standard deviation
$df = n - 1$ Degrees of freedom

### Test of a Single Variance

- Use the test to determine variation.
- The degrees of freedom is the number of samples – 1.
- The test statistic is $\dfrac{(n-1)s^2}{\sigma_0^2}$, where $n$ = sample size, $s^2$ = sample variance, and $\sigma^2$ = population variance.
- The test may be left-, right-, or two-tailed.

### 11.3 Goodness-of-Fit Test

$\sum\limits_{k} \dfrac{(O-E)^2}{E}$ goodness-of-fit test statistic where:

$O$: observed values
$E$: expected values

$k$: number of different data cells or categories

$df = k - 1$ degrees of freedom

### 11.4 Test of Independence

### Test of Independence

- The number of degrees of freedom is equal to (number of columns - 1)(number of rows - 1).
- The test statistic is $\sum\limits_{i \cdot j} \dfrac{(O-E)^2}{E}$ where $O$ = observed values, $E$ = expected values, $i$ = the number of rows in the table, and $j$ = the number of columns in the table.
- If the null hypothesis is true, the expected number $E = \dfrac{(\text{row total})(\text{column total})}{\text{total surveyed}}$.

### 11.5 Test for Homogeneity

$\sum\limits_{i \cdot j} \dfrac{(O-E)^2}{E}$ Homogeneity test statistic where: $O$ = observed values
$E$ = expected values
$i$ = number of rows in data contingency table
$j$ = number of columns in data contingency table
$df = (i-1)(j-1)$ Degrees of freedom

# PRACTICE

### 11.1 Facts About the Chi-Square Distribution

**1.** If the number of degrees of freedom for a chi-square distribution is 25, what is the population mean and standard deviation?

**2.** If $df > 90$, the distribution is _____. If $df = 15$, the distribution is _____.

**3.** When does the chi-square curve approximate a normal distribution?

**4.** Where is $\mu$ located on a chi-square curve?

**5.** Is it more likely the *df* is 90, 20, or two in the graph?

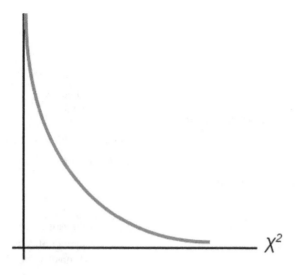

**Figure 11.10**

## 11.2 Test of a Single Variance

*Use the following information to answer the next three exercises:* An archer's standard deviation for his hits is six (data is measured in distance from the center of the target). An observer claims the standard deviation is less.

**6.** What type of test should be used?

**7.** State the null and alternative hypotheses.

**8.** Is this a right-tailed, left-tailed, or two-tailed test?

*Use the following information to answer the next three exercises:* The standard deviation of heights for students in a school is 0.81. A random sample of 50 students is taken, and the standard deviation of heights of the sample is 0.96. A researcher in charge of the study believes the standard deviation of heights for the school is greater than 0.81.

**9.** What type of test should be used?

**10.** State the null and alternative hypotheses.

**11.** *df* = _____

*Use the following information to answer the next four exercises:* The average waiting time in a doctor's office varies. The standard deviation of waiting times in a doctor's office is 3.4 minutes. A random sample of 30 patients in the doctor's office has a standard deviation of waiting times of 4.1 minutes. One doctor believes the variance of waiting times is greater than originally thought.

**12.** What type of test should be used?

**13.** What is the test statistic?

**14.** What can you conclude at the 5% significance level?

## 11.3 Goodness-of-Fit Test

*Determine the appropriate test to be used in the next three exercises.*

**15.** An archeologist is calculating the distribution of the frequency of the number of artifacts she finds in a dig site. Based on previous digs, the archeologist creates an expected distribution broken down by grid sections in the dig site. Once the site has been fully excavated, she compares the actual number of artifacts found in each grid section to see if her expectation was accurate.

**16.** An economist is deriving a model to predict outcomes on the stock market. He creates a list of expected points on the stock market index for the next two weeks. At the close of each day's trading, he records the actual points on the index. He wants to see how well his model matched what actually happened.

**17.** A personal trainer is putting together a weight-lifting program for her clients. For a 90-day program, she expects each client to lift a specific maximum weight each week. As she goes along, she records the actual maximum weights her clients lifted. She wants to know how well her expectations met with what was observed.

*Use the following information to answer the next five exercises:* A teacher predicts that the distribution of grades on the final exam will be and they are recorded in **Table 11.21**.

| Grade | Proportion |
|-------|-----------|
| A | 0.25 |
| B | 0.30 |
| C | 0.35 |
| D | 0.10 |

Table 11.21

The actual distribution for a class of 20 is in **Table 11.22**.

| Grade | Frequency |
|-------|-----------|
| A | 7 |
| B | 7 |
| C | 5 |
| D | 1 |

Table 11.22

**18.** $df =$ _____

**19.** State the null and alternative hypotheses.

**20.** $\chi^2$ test statistic = _____

**21.** At the 5% significance level, what can you conclude?

*Use the following information to answer the next nine exercises:* The following data are real. The cumulative number of AIDS cases reported for Santa Clara County is broken down by ethnicity as in **Table 11.23**.

| Ethnicity | Number of Cases |
|-----------|-----------------|
| White | 2,229 |
| Hispanic | 1,157 |
| Black/African-American | 457 |
| Asian, Pacific Islander | 232 |
| | Total = 4,075 |

Table 11.23

The percentage of each ethnic group in Santa Clara County is as in Table 11.24.

| Ethnicity | Percentage of total county population | Number expected (round to two decimal places) |
|---|---|---|
| White | 42.9% | 1748.18 |
| Hispanic | 26.7% | |
| Black/African-American | 2.6% | |
| Asian, Pacific Islander | 27.8% | |
| | Total = 100% | |

Table 11.24

**22.** If the ethnicities of AIDS victims followed the ethnicities of the total county population, fill in the expected number of cases per ethnic group.
*Perform a goodness-of-fit test to determine whether the occurrence of AIDS cases follows the ethnicities of the general population of Santa Clara County.*

**23.** $H_0$: _____

**24.** $H_a$: _____

**25.** Is this a right-tailed, left-tailed, or two-tailed test?

**26.** degrees of freedom = _____

**27.** $\chi^2$ test statistic = _____

**28.** Graph the situation. Label and scale the horizontal axis. Mark the mean and test statistic. Shade in the region corresponding to the confidence level.

Figure 11.11

Let $\alpha = 0.05$

Decision: _____

Reason for the Decision: _____

Conclusion (write out in complete sentences): _____

**29.** Does it appear that the pattern of AIDS cases in Santa Clara County corresponds to the distribution of ethnic groups in this county? Why or why not?

## 11.4 Test of Independence

*Determine the appropriate test to be used in the next three exercises.*

**30.** A pharmaceutical company is interested in the relationship between age and presentation of symptoms for a common viral infection. A random sample is taken of 500 people with the infection across different age groups.

**31.** The owner of a baseball team is interested in the relationship between player salaries and team winning percentage. He takes a random sample of 100 players from different organizations.

**32.** A marathon runner is interested in the relationship between the brand of shoes runners wear and their run times. She takes a random sample of 50 runners and records their run times as well as the brand of shoes they were wearing.

*Use the following information to answer the next seven exercises:* Transit Railroads is interested in the relationship between travel distance and the ticket class purchased. A random sample of 200 passengers is taken. Table 11.25 shows the results. The railroad wants to know if a passenger's choice in ticket class is independent of the distance they must travel.

| Traveling Distance | Third class | Second class | First class | Total |
|---|---|---|---|---|
| 1–100 miles | 21 | 14 | 6 | 41 |
| 101–200 miles | 18 | 16 | 8 | 42 |
| 201–300 miles | 16 | 17 | 15 | 48 |
| 301–400 miles | 12 | 14 | 21 | 47 |
| 401–500 miles | 6 | 6 | 10 | 22 |
| Total | 73 | 67 | 60 | 200 |

Table 11.25

**33.** State the hypotheses.
$H_0$: _____
$H_a$: _____

**34.** $df =$ _____

**35.** How many passengers are expected to travel between 201 and 300 miles and purchase second-class tickets?

**36.** How many passengers are expected to travel between 401 and 500 miles and purchase first-class tickets?

**37.** What is the test statistic?

**38.** What can you conclude at the 5% level of significance?

*Use the following information to answer the next eight exercises:* An article in the New England Journal of Medicine, discussed a study on smokers in California and Hawaii. In one part of the report, the self-reported ethnicity and smoking levels per day were given. Of the people smoking at most ten cigarettes per day, there were 9,886 African Americans, 2,745 Native Hawaiians, 12,831 Latinos, 8,378 Japanese Americans and 7,650 whites. Of the people smoking 11 to 20 cigarettes per day, there were 6,514 African Americans, 3,062 Native Hawaiians, 4,932 Latinos, 10,680 Japanese Americans, and 9,877 whites. Of the people smoking 21 to 30 cigarettes per day, there were 1,671 African Americans, 1,419 Native Hawaiians, 1,406 Latinos, 4,715 Japanese Americans, and 6,062 whites. Of the people smoking at least 31 cigarettes per day, there were 759 African Americans, 788 Native Hawaiians, 800 Latinos, 2,305 Japanese Americans, and 3,970 whites.

**39.** Complete the table.

| Smoking Level Per Day | African American | Native Hawaiian | Latino | Japanese Americans | White | TOTALS |
|---|---|---|---|---|---|---|
| 1-10 | | | | | | |
| 11-20 | | | | | | |
| 21-30 | | | | | | |
| 31+ | | | | | | |
| TOTALS | | | | | | |

**Table 11.26 Smoking Levels by Ethnicity (Observed)**

**40.** State the hypotheses.
$H_0$: _____
$H_a$: _____

**41.** Enter expected values in Table 11.26. Round to two decimal places.

Calculate the following values:

**42.** $df =$ _____

**43.** $\chi^2$ test statistic = _____

**44.** Is this a right-tailed, left-tailed, or two-tailed test? Explain why.

**45.** Graph the situation. Label and scale the horizontal axis. Mark the mean and test statistic. Shade in the region corresponding to the confidence level.

**Figure 11.12**

State the decision and conclusion (in a complete sentence) for the following preconceived levels of $\alpha$.

**46.** $\alpha = 0.05$
    a. Decision: _____
    b. Reason for the decision: _____
    c. Conclusion (write out in a complete sentence): _____

**47.** $\alpha = 0.01$
    a. Decision: _____
    b. Reason for the decision: _____
    c. Conclusion (write out in a complete sentence): _____

## 11.5 Test for Homogeneity

**48.** A math teacher wants to see if two of her classes have the same distribution of test scores. What test should she use?

**49.** What are the null and alternative hypotheses for **Exercise 11.48**?

**50.** A market researcher wants to see if two different stores have the same distribution of sales throughout the year. What type of test should he use?

**51.** A meteorologist wants to know if East and West Australia have the same distribution of storms. What type of test should she use?

**52.** What condition must be met to use the test for homogeneity?

*Use the following information to answer the next five exercises:* Do private practice doctors and hospital doctors have the same distribution of working hours? Suppose that a sample of 100 private practice doctors and 150 hospital doctors are selected at random and asked about the number of hours a week they work. The results are shown in **Table 11.27**.

| | 20–30 | 30–40 | 40–50 | 50–60 |
|---|---|---|---|---|
| Private Practice | 16 | 40 | 38 | 6 |
| Hospital | 8 | 44 | 59 | 39 |

**Table 11.27**

**53.** State the null and alternative hypotheses.

**54.** $df =$ _____

**55.** What is the test statistic?

**56.** What can you conclude at the 5% significance level?

## 11.6 Comparison of the Chi-Square Tests

**57.** Which test do you use to decide whether an observed distribution is the same as an expected distribution?

**58.** What is the null hypothesis for the type of test from **Exercise 11.57**?

**59.** Which test would you use to decide whether two factors have a relationship?

**60.** Which test would you use to decide if two populations have the same distribution?

**61.** How are tests of independence similar to tests for homogeneity?

**62.** How are tests of independence different from tests for homogeneity?

# HOMEWORK

## 11.1 Facts About the Chi-Square Distribution

*Decide whether the following statements are true or false.*

**63.** As the number of degrees of freedom increases, the graph of the chi-square distribution looks more and more symmetrical.

**64.** The standard deviation of the chi-square distribution is twice the mean.

**65.** The mean and the median of the chi-square distribution are the same if $df = 24$.

## 11.2 Test of a Single Variance

*Use the following information to answer the next twelve exercises:* Suppose an airline claims that its flights are consistently on time with an average delay of at most 15 minutes. It claims that the average delay is so consistent that the variance is no more than 150 minutes. Doubting the consistency part of the claim, a disgruntled traveler calculates the delays for his next 25 flights. The average delay for those 25 flights is 22 minutes with a standard deviation of 15 minutes.

**66.** Is the traveler disputing the claim about the average or about the variance?

**67.** A sample standard deviation of 15 minutes is the same as a sample variance of _____ minutes.

**68.** Is this a right-tailed, left-tailed, or two-tailed test?

**69.** $H_0$: _____

**70.** $df$ = _____

**71.** chi-square test statistic = _____

**72.** Graph the situation. Label and scale the horizontal axis. Mark the mean and test statistic. Shade the area associated with the level of confidence.

**73.** Let $\alpha$ = 0.05
Decision: _____
Conclusion (write out in a complete sentence.): _____

**74.** How did you know to test the variance instead of the mean?

**75.** If an additional test were done on the claim of the average delay, which distribution would you use?

**76.** If an additional test were done on the claim of the average delay, but 45 flights were surveyed, which distribution would you use?

**77.** A plant manager is concerned her equipment may need recalibrating. It seems that the actual weight of the 15 oz. cereal boxes it fills has been fluctuating. The standard deviation should be at most 0.5 oz. In order to determine if the machine needs to be recalibrated, 84 randomly selected boxes of cereal from the next day's production were weighed. The standard deviation of the 84 boxes was 0.54. Does the machine need to be recalibrated?

**78.** Consumers may be interested in whether the cost of a particular calculator varies from store to store. Based on surveying 43 stores, which yielded a sample mean of $84 and a sample standard deviation of $12, test the claim that the standard deviation is greater than $15.

**79.** Isabella, an accomplished **Bay to Breakers** runner, claims that the standard deviation for her time to run the 7.5 mile race is at most three minutes. To test her claim, Rupinder looks up five of her race times. They are 55 minutes, 61 minutes, 58 minutes, 63 minutes, and 57 minutes.

**80.** Airline companies are interested in the consistency of the number of babies on each flight, so that they have adequate safety equipment. They are also interested in the variation of the number of babies. Suppose that an airline executive believes the average number of babies on flights is six with a variance of nine at most. The airline conducts a survey. The results of the 18 flights surveyed give a sample average of 6.4 with a sample standard deviation of 3.9. Conduct a hypothesis test of the airline executive's belief.

**81.** The number of births per woman in China is 1.6 down from 5.91 in 1966. This fertility rate has been attributed to the law passed in 1979 restricting births to one per woman. Suppose that a group of students studied whether or not the standard deviation of births per woman was greater than 0.75. They asked 50 women across China the number of births they had had. The results are shown in **Table 11.28**. Does the students' survey indicate that the standard deviation is greater than 0.75?

| # of births | Frequency |
|-------------|-----------|
| 0 | 5 |
| 1 | 30 |
| 2 | 10 |
| 3 | 5 |

Table 11.28

**82.** According to an avid aquarist, the average number of fish in a 20-gallon tank is 10, with a standard deviation of two. His friend, also an aquarist, does not believe that the standard deviation is two. She counts the number of fish in 15 other 20-gallon tanks. Based on the results that follow, do you think that the standard deviation is different from two? Data: 11; 10; 9; 10; 10; 11; 11; 10; 12; 9; 7; 9; 11; 10; 11

**83.** The manager of "Frenchies" is concerned that patrons are not consistently receiving the same amount of French fries with each order. The chef claims that the standard deviation for a ten-ounce order of fries is at most 1.5 oz., but the manager thinks that it may be higher. He randomly weighs 49 orders of fries, which yields a mean of 11 oz. and a standard deviation of two oz.

**84.** You want to buy a specific computer. A sales representative of the manufacturer claims that retail stores sell this computer at an average price of $1,249 with a very narrow standard deviation of $25. You find a website that has a price comparison for the same computer at a series of stores as follows: $1,299; $1,229.99; $1,193.08; $1,279; $1,224.95; $1,229.99; $1,269.95; $1,249. Can you argue that pricing has a larger standard deviation than claimed by the manufacturer? Use the 5% significance level. As a potential buyer, what would be the practical conclusion from your analysis?

**85.** A company packages apples by weight. One of the weight grades is Class A apples. Class A apples have a mean weight of 150 g, and there is a maximum allowed weight tolerance of 5% above or below the mean for apples in the same consumer package. A batch of apples is selected to be included in a Class A apple package. Given the following apple weights of the batch, does the fruit comply with the Class A grade weight tolerance requirements. Conduct an appropriate hypothesis test.

(a) at the 5% significance level

(b) at the 1% significance level

Weights in selected apple batch (in grams): 158; 167; 149; 169; 164; 139; 154; 150; 157; 171; 152; 161; 141; 166; 172;

## 11.3 Goodness-of-Fit Test

**86.** A six-sided die is rolled 120 times. Fill in the expected frequency column. Then, conduct a hypothesis test to determine if the die is fair. The data in **Table 11.29** are the result of the 120 rolls.

| Face Value | Frequency | Expected Frequency |
|---|---|---|
| 1 | 15 | |
| 2 | 29 | |
| 3 | 16 | |
| 4 | 15 | |
| 5 | 30 | |
| 6 | 15 | |

Table 11.29

**87.** The marital status distribution of the U.S. male population, ages 15 and older, is as shown in Table 11.30.

| Marital Status | Percent | Expected Frequency |
|---|---|---|
| never married | 31.3 | |
| married | 56.1 | |
| widowed | 2.5 | |
| divorced/separated | 10.1 | |

Table 11.30

Suppose that a random sample of 400 U.S. young adult males, 18 to 24 years old, yielded the following frequency distribution. We are interested in whether this age group of males fits the distribution of the U.S. adult population. Calculate the frequency one would expect when surveying 400 people. Fill in Table 11.30, rounding to two decimal places.

| Marital Status | Frequency |
|---|---|
| never married | 140 |
| married | 238 |
| widowed | 2 |
| divorced/separated | 20 |

Table 11.31

*Use the following information to answer the next two exercises:* The columns in Table 11.32 contain the Race/Ethnicity of U.S. Public Schools for a recent year, the percentages for the Advanced Placement Examinee Population for that class, and the Overall Student Population. Suppose the right column contains the result of a survey of 1,000 local students from that year who took an AP Exam.

| Race/Ethnicity | AP Examinee Population | Overall Student Population | Survey Frequency |
|---|---|---|---|
| Asian, Asian American, or Pacific Islander | 10.2% | 5.4% | 113 |
| Black or African-American | 8.2% | 14.5% | 94 |
| Hispanic or Latino | 15.5% | 15.9% | 136 |
| American Indian or Alaska Native | 0.6% | 1.2% | 10 |
| White | 59.4% | 61.6% | 604 |
| Not reported/other | 6.1% | 1.4% | 43 |

Table 11.32

**88.** Perform a goodness-of-fit test to determine whether the local results follow the distribution of the U.S. overall student population based on ethnicity.

**89.** Perform a goodness-of-fit test to determine whether the local results follow the distribution of U.S. AP examinee population, based on ethnicity.

**90.** The City of South Lake Tahoe, CA, has an Asian population of 1,419 people, out of a total population of 23,609. Suppose that a survey of 1,419 self-reported Asians in the Manhattan, NY, area yielded the data in **Table 11.33**. Conduct a goodness-of-fit test to determine if the self-reported sub-groups of Asians in the Manhattan area fit that of the Lake Tahoe area.

| Race | Lake Tahoe Frequency | Manhattan Frequency |
|------|---------------------|---------------------|
| Asian Indian | 131 | 174 |
| Chinese | 118 | 557 |
| Filipino | 1,045 | 518 |
| Japanese | 80 | 54 |
| Korean | 12 | 29 |
| Vietnamese | 9 | 21 |
| Other | 24 | 66 |

Table 11.33

*Use the following information to answer the next two exercises:* UCLA conducted a survey of more than 263,000 college freshmen from 385 colleges in fall 2005. The results of students' expected majors by gender were reported in *The Chronicle of Higher Education (2/2/2006)*. Suppose a survey of 5,000 graduating females and 5,000 graduating males was done as a follow-up last year to determine what their actual majors were. The results are shown in the tables for **Exercise 11.91** and **Exercise 11.92**. The second column in each table does not add to 100% because of rounding.

**91.** Conduct a goodness-of-fit test to determine if the actual college majors of graduating females fit the distribution of their expected majors.

| Major | Women - Expected Major | Women - Actual Major |
|-------|------------------------|----------------------|
| Arts & Humanities | 14.0% | 670 |
| Biological Sciences | 8.4% | 410 |
| Business | 13.1% | 685 |
| Education | 13.0% | 650 |
| Engineering | 2.6% | 145 |
| Physical Sciences | 2.6% | 125 |
| Professional | 18.9% | 975 |
| Social Sciences | 13.0% | 605 |
| Technical | 0.4% | 15 |
| Other | 5.8% | 300 |
| Undecided | 8.0% | 420 |

Table 11.34

**92.** Conduct a goodness-of-fit test to determine if the actual college majors of graduating males fit the distribution of their expected majors.

| Major | Men - Expected Major | Men - Actual Major |
|---|---|---|
| Arts & Humanities | 11.0% | 600 |
| Biological Sciences | 6.7% | 330 |
| Business | 22.7% | 1130 |
| Education | 5.8% | 305 |
| Engineering | 15.6% | 800 |
| Physical Sciences | 3.6% | 175 |
| Professional | 9.3% | 460 |
| Social Sciences | 7.6% | 370 |
| Technical | 1.8% | 90 |
| Other | 8.2% | 400 |
| Undecided | 6.6% | 340 |

Table 11.35

*Read the statement and decide whether it is true or false.*

**93.** In general, if the observed values and expected values of a goodness-of-fit test are not close together, then the test statistic can get very large and on a graph will be way out in the right tail.

**94.** Use a goodness-of-fit test to determine if high school principals believe that students are absent equally during the week or not.

**95.** The test to use to determine if a six-sided die is fair is a goodness-of-fit test.

**96.** In a goodness-of fit test, if the *p*-value is 0.0113, in general, do not reject the null hypothesis.

**97.** A sample of 212 commercial businesses was surveyed for recycling one commodity; a commodity here means any one type of recyclable material such as plastic or aluminum. Table 11.36 shows the business categories in the survey, the sample size of each category, and the number of businesses in each category that recycle one commodity. Based on the study, on average half of the businesses were expected to be recycling one commodity. As a result, the last column shows the expected number of businesses in each category that recycle one commodity. At the 5% significance level, perform a hypothesis test to determine if the observed number of businesses that recycle one commodity follows the uniform distribution of the expected values.

| Business Type | Number in class | Observed Number that recycle one commodity | Expected number that recycle one commodity |
|---|---|---|---|
| Office | 35 | 19 | 17.5 |
| Retail/ Wholesale | 48 | 27 | 24 |
| Food/ Restaurants | 53 | 35 | 26.5 |
| Manufacturing/ Medical | 52 | 21 | 26 |
| Hotel/Mixed | 24 | 9 | 12 |

**98.** Table 11.37 contains information from a survey among 499 participants classified according to their age groups. The second column shows the percentage of obese people per age class among the study participants. The last column comes from a different study at the national level that shows the corresponding percentages of obese people in the same age classes in the USA. Perform a hypothesis test at the 5% significance level to determine whether the survey participants are a representative sample of the USA obese population.

| Age Class (Years) | Obese (Percentage) | Expected USA average (Percentage) |
|---|---|---|
| 20–30 | 75.0 | 32.6 |
| 31–40 | 26.5 | 32.6 |
| 41–50 | 13.6 | 36.6 |
| 51–60 | 21.9 | 36.6 |
| 61–70 | 21.0 | 39.7 |

Table 11.37

## 11.4 Test of Independence

**99.** A recent debate about where in the United States skiers believe the skiing is best prompted the following survey. Test to see if the best ski area is independent of the level of the skier.

| U.S. Ski Area | Beginner | Intermediate | Advanced |
|---|---|---|---|
| Tahoe | 20 | 30 | 40 |
| Utah | 10 | 30 | 60 |
| Colorado | 10 | 40 | 50 |

Table 11.38

**100.** Car manufacturers are interested in whether there is a relationship between the size of car an individual drives and the number of people in the driver's family (that is, whether car size and family size are independent). To test this, suppose that 800 car owners were randomly surveyed with the results in Table 11.39. Conduct a test of independence.

| Family Size | Sub & Compact | Mid-size | Full-size | Van & Truck |
|---|---|---|---|---|
| 1 | 20 | 35 | 40 | 35 |
| 2 | 20 | 50 | 70 | 80 |
| 3–4 | 20 | 50 | 100 | 90 |
| 5+ | 20 | 30 | 70 | 70 |

Table 11.39

**101.** College students may be interested in whether or not their majors have any effect on starting salaries after graduation. Suppose that 300 recent graduates were surveyed as to their majors in college and their starting salaries after graduation. **Table 11.40** shows the data. Conduct a test of independence.

| Major | < $50,000 | $50,000 – $68,999 | $69,000 + |
|-------|-----------|-------------------|-----------|
| English | 5 | 20 | 5 |
| Engineering | 10 | 30 | 60 |
| Nursing | 10 | 15 | 15 |
| Business | 10 | 20 | 30 |
| Psychology | 20 | 30 | 20 |

Table 11.40

**102.** Some travel agents claim that honeymoon hot spots vary according to age of the bride. Suppose that 280 recent brides were interviewed as to where they spent their honeymoons. The information is given in **Table 11.41**. Conduct a test of independence.

| Location | 20–29 | 30–39 | 40–49 | 50 and over |
|----------|-------|-------|-------|-------------|
| Niagara Falls | 15 | 25 | 25 | 20 |
| Poconos | 15 | 25 | 25 | 10 |
| Europe | 10 | 25 | 15 | 5 |
| Virgin Islands | 20 | 25 | 15 | 5 |

Table 11.41

**103.** A manager of a sports club keeps information concerning the main sport in which members participate and their ages. To test whether there is a relationship between the age of a member and his or her choice of sport, 643 members of the sports club are randomly selected. Conduct a test of independence.

| Sport | 18 - 25 | 26 - 30 | 31 - 40 | 41 and over |
|-------|---------|---------|---------|-------------|
| racquetball | 42 | 58 | 30 | 46 |
| tennis | 58 | 76 | 38 | 65 |
| swimming | 72 | 60 | 65 | 33 |

Table 11.42

**104.** A major food manufacturer is concerned that the sales for its skinny french fries have been decreasing. As a part of a feasibility study, the company conducts research into the types of fries sold across the country to determine if the type of fries sold is independent of the area of the country. The results of the study are shown in **Table 11.43**. Conduct a test of independence.

| Type of Fries | Northeast | South | Central | West |
|---|---|---|---|---|
| skinny fries | 70 | 50 | 20 | 25 |
| curly fries | 100 | 60 | 15 | 30 |
| steak fries | 20 | 40 | 10 | 10 |

Table 11.43

**105.** According to Dan Lenard, an independent insurance agent in the Buffalo, N.Y. area, the following is a breakdown of the amount of life insurance purchased by males in the following age groups. He is interested in whether the age of the male and the amount of life insurance purchased are independent events. Conduct a test for independence.

| Age of Males | None | < $200,000 | $200,000–$400,000 | $401,001–$1,000,000 | $1,000,001+ |
|---|---|---|---|---|---|
| 20–29 | 40 | 15 | 40 | 0 | 5 |
| 30–39 | 35 | 5 | 20 | 20 | 10 |
| 40–49 | 20 | 0 | 30 | 0 | 30 |
| 50+ | 40 | 30 | 15 | 15 | 10 |

Table 11.44

**106.** Suppose that 600 thirty-year-olds were surveyed to determine whether or not there is a relationship between the level of education an individual has and salary. Conduct a test of independence.

| Annual Salary | Not a high school graduate | High school graduate | College graduate | Masters or doctorate |
|---|---|---|---|---|
| < $30,000 | 15 | 25 | 10 | 5 |
| $30,000–$40,000 | 20 | 40 | 70 | 30 |
| $40,000–$50,000 | 10 | 20 | 40 | 55 |
| $50,000–$60,000 | 5 | 10 | 20 | 60 |
| $60,000+ | 0 | 5 | 10 | 150 |

Table 11.45

*Read the statement and decide whether it is true or false.*

**107.** The number of degrees of freedom for a test of independence is equal to the sample size minus one.

**108.** The test for independence uses tables of observed and expected data values.

**109.** The test to use when determining if the college or university a student chooses to attend is related to his or her socioeconomic status is a test for independence.

**110.** In a test of independence, the expected number is equal to the row total multiplied by the column total divided by the total surveyed.

**111.** An ice cream maker performs a nationwide survey about favorite flavors of ice cream in different geographic areas of the U.S. Based on Table 11.46, do the numbers suggest that geographic location is independent of favorite ice cream flavors? Test at the 5% significance level.

| U.S. region/ Flavor | Strawberry | Chocolate | Vanilla | Rocky Road | Mint Chocolate Chip | Pistachio | Row total |
|---|---|---|---|---|---|---|---|
| West | 12 | 21 | 22 | 19 | 15 | 8 | 97 |
| Midwest | 10 | 32 | 22 | 11 | 15 | 6 | 96 |
| East | 8 | 31 | 27 | 8 | 15 | 7 | 96 |
| South | 15 | 28 | 30 | 8 | 15 | 6 | 102 |
| Column Total | 45 | 112 | 101 | 46 | 60 | 27 | 391 |

Table 11.46

**112.** Table 11.47 provides a recent survey of the youngest online entrepreneurs whose net worth is estimated at one million dollars or more. Their ages range from 17 to 30. Each cell in the table illustrates the number of entrepreneurs who correspond to the specific age group and their net worth. Are the ages and net worth independent? Perform a test of independence at the 5% significance level.

| Age Group\ Net Worth Value (in millions of US dollars) | 1–5 | 6–24 | ≥25 | Row Total |
|---|---|---|---|---|
| 17–25 | 8 | 7 | 5 | 20 |
| 26–30 | 6 | 5 | 9 | 20 |
| Column Total | 14 | 12 | 14 | 40 |

Table 11.47

**113.** A 2013 poll in California surveyed people about taxing sugar-sweetened beverages. The results are presented in Table 11.48, and are classified by ethnic group and response type. Are the poll responses independent of the participants' ethnic group? Conduct a test of independence at the 5% significance level.

| Opinion/ Ethnicity | Asian- American | White/Non- Hispanic | African- American | Latino | Row Total |
|---|---|---|---|---|---|
| Against tax | 48 | 433 | 41 | 160 | 682 |
| In Favor of tax | 54 | 234 | 24 | 147 | 459 |
| No opinion | 16 | 43 | 16 | 19 | 94 |
| Column Total | 118 | 710 | 81 | 326 | 1235 |

Table 11.48

## 11.5 Test for Homogeneity

**114.** A psychologist is interested in testing whether there is a difference in the distribution of personality types for business majors and social science majors. The results of the study are shown in Table 11.49. Conduct a test of homogeneity. Test at a 5% level of significance.

| | Open | Conscientious | Extrovert | Agreeable | Neurotic |
|---|---|---|---|---|---|
| **Business** | 41 | 52 | 46 | 61 | 58 |
| **Social Science** | 72 | 75 | 63 | 80 | 65 |

Table 11.49

**115.** Do men and women select different breakfasts? The breakfasts ordered by randomly selected men and women at a popular breakfast place is shown in Table 11.50. Conduct a test for homogeneity at a 5% level of significance.

| | French Toast | Pancakes | Waffles | Omelettes |
|---|---|---|---|---|
| **Men** | 47 | 35 | 28 | 53 |
| **Women** | 65 | 59 | 55 | 60 |

Table 11.50

**116.** A fisherman is interested in whether the distribution of fish caught in Green Valley Lake is the same as the distribution of fish caught in Echo Lake. Of the 191 randomly selected fish caught in Green Valley Lake, 105 were rainbow trout, 27 were other trout, 35 were bass, and 24 were catfish. Of the 293 randomly selected fish caught in Echo Lake, 115 were rainbow trout, 58 were other trout, 67 were bass, and 53 were catfish. Perform a test for homogeneity at a 5% level of significance.

**117.** In 2007, the United States had 1.5 million homeschooled students, according to the U.S. National Center for Education Statistics. In Table 11.51 you can see that parents decide to homeschool their children for different reasons, and some reasons are ranked by parents as more important than others. According to the survey results shown in the table, is the distribution of applicable reasons the same as the distribution of the most important reason? Provide your assessment at the 5% significance level. Did you expect the result you obtained?

| Reasons for Homeschooling | Applicable Reason (in thousands of respondents) | Most Important Reason (in thousands of respondents) | Row Total |
|---|---|---|---|
| Concern about the environment of other schools | 1,321 | 309 | 1,630 |
| Dissatisfaction with academic instruction at other schools | 1,096 | 258 | 1,354 |
| To provide religious or moral instruction | 1,257 | 540 | 1,797 |
| Child has special needs, other than physical or mental | 315 | 55 | 370 |
| Nontraditional approach to child's education | 984 | 99 | 1,083 |
| Other reasons (e.g., finances, travel, family time, etc.) | 485 | 216 | 701 |
| Column Total | 5,458 | 1,477 | 6,935 |

**118.** When looking at energy consumption, we are often interested in detecting trends over time and how they correlate among different countries. The information in **Table 11.52** shows the average energy use (in units of kg of oil equivalent per capita) in the USA and the joint European Union countries (EU) for the six-year period 2005 to 2010. Do the energy use values in these two areas come from the same distribution? Perform the analysis at the 5% significance level.

| Year | European Union | United States | Row Total |
|---|---|---|---|
| 2010 | 3,413 | 7,164 | 10,557 |
| 2009 | 3,302 | 7,057 | 10,359 |
| 2008 | 3,505 | 7,488 | 10,993 |
| 2007 | 3,537 | 7,758 | 11,295 |
| 2006 | 3,595 | 7,697 | 11,292 |
| 2005 | 3,613 | 7,847 | 11,460 |
| Column Total | 20,965 | 45,011 | 65,976 |

Table 11.52

**119.** The Insurance Institute for Highway Safety collects safety information about all types of cars every year, and publishes a report of Top Safety Picks among all cars, makes, and models. **Table 11.53** presents the number of Top Safety Picks in six car categories for the two years 2009 and 2013. Analyze the table data to conclude whether the distribution of cars that earned the Top Safety Picks safety award has remained the same between 2009 and 2013. Derive your results at the 5% significance level.

| Year \ Car Type | Small | Mid-Size | Large | Small SUV | Mid-Size SUV | Large SUV | Row Total |
|---|---|---|---|---|---|---|---|
| 2009 | 12 | 22 | 10 | 10 | 27 | 6 | 87 |
| 2013 | 31 | 30 | 19 | 11 | 29 | 4 | 124 |
| Column Total | 43 | 52 | 29 | 21 | 56 | 10 | 211 |

Table 11.53

## 11.6 Comparison of the Chi-Square Tests

**120.** Is there a difference between the distribution of community college statistics students and the distribution of university statistics students in what technology they use on their homework? Of some randomly selected community college students, 43 used a computer, 102 used a calculator with built in statistics functions, and 65 used a table from the textbook. Of some randomly selected university students, 28 used a computer, 33 used a calculator with built in statistics functions, and 40 used a table from the textbook. Conduct an appropriate hypothesis test using a 0.05 level of significance.

Read the statement and decide whether it is true or false.

**121.** If $df = 2$, the chi-square distribution has a shape that reminds us of the exponential.

# BRINGING IT TOGETHER: HOMEWORK

**122.**
   a. Explain why a goodness-of-fit test and a test of independence are generally right-tailed tests.
   b. If you did a left-tailed test, what would you be testing?

# REFERENCES

## 11.1 Facts About the Chi-Square Distribution

Data from *Parade Magazine*.

"HIV/AIDS Epidemiology Santa Clara County."Santa Clara County Public Health Department, May 2011.

## 11.2 Test of a Single Variance

"AppleInsider Price Guides." Apple Insider, 2013. Available online at http://appleinsider.com/mac_price_guide (accessed May 14, 2013).

Data from the World Bank, June 5, 2012.

## 11.3 Goodness-of-Fit Test

Data from the U.S. Census Bureau

Data from the College Board. Available online at http://www.collegeboard.com.

Data from the U.S. Census Bureau, Current Population Reports.

Ma, Y., E.R. Bertone, E.J. Stanek III, G.W. Reed, J.R. Hebert, N.L. Cohen, P.A. Merriam, I.S. Ockene, "Association between Eating Patterns and Obesity in a Free-living US Adult Population." *American Journal of Epidemiology* volume 158, no. 1, pages 85-92.

Ogden, Cynthia L., Margaret D. Carroll, Brian K. Kit, Katherine M. Flegal, "Prevalence of Obesity in the United States, 2009–2010." NCHS Data Brief no. 82, January 2012. Available online at http://www.cdc.gov/nchs/data/databriefs/db82.pdf (accessed May 24, 2013).

Stevens, Barbara J., "Multi-family and Commercial Solid Waste and Recycling Survey." Arlington Count, VA. Available online at http://www.arlingtonva.us/departments/EnvironmentalServices/SW/file84429.pdf (accessed May 24,2013).

## 11.4 Test of Independence

DiCamilo, Mark, Mervin Field, "Most Californians See a Direct Linkage between Obesity and Sugary Sodas. Two in Three Voters Support Taxing Sugar-Sweetened Beverages If Proceeds are Tied to Improving School Nutrition and Physical Activity Programs." The Field Poll, released Feb. 14, 2013. Available online at http://field.com/fieldpollonline/subscribers/Rls2436.pdf (accessed May 24, 2013).

Harris Interactive, "Favorite Flavor of Ice Cream." Available online at http://www.statisticbrain.com/favorite-flavor-of-ice-cream (accessed May 24, 2013)

"Youngest Online Entrepreneurs List." Available online at http://www.statisticbrain.com/youngest-online-entrepreneur-list (accessed May 24, 2013).

## 11.5 Test for Homogeneity

Data from the Insurance Institute for Highway Safety, 2013. Available online at www.iihs.org/iihs/ratings (accessed May 24, 2013).

"Energy use (kg of oil equivalent per capita)." The World Bank, 2013. Available online at http://data.worldbank.org/indicator/EG.USE.PCAP.KG.OE/countries (accessed May 24, 2013).

"Parent and Family Involvement Survey of 2007 National Household Education Survey Program (NHES)," U.S. Department of Education, National Center for Education Statistics. Available online at http://nces.ed.gov/pubsearch/pubsinfo.asp?pubid=2009030 (accessed May 24, 2013).

"Parent and Family Involvement Survey of 2007 National Household Education Survey Program (NHES)," U.S. Department of Education, National Center for Education Statistics. Available online at http://nces.ed.gov/pubs2009/2009030_sup.pdf (accessed May 24, 2013).

# SOLUTIONS

**1** mean = 25 and standard deviation = 7.0711

**3** when the number of degrees of freedom is greater than 90

**5** $df = 2$

**6** a test of a single variance

**8** a left-tailed test

**10** $H_0$: $\sigma^2 = 0.81^2$; $H_a$: $\sigma^2 > 0.81^2$

**12** a test of a single variance

**16** a goodness-of-fit test

**18** 3

**20** 2.04

**21** We decline to reject the null hypothesis. There is not enough evidence to suggest that the observed test scores are significantly different from the expected test scores.

**23** $H_0$: the distribution of AIDS cases follows the ethnicities of the general population of Santa Clara County.

**25** right-tailed

**27** 2016.136

**28** Graph: Check student's solution. Decision: Cannot accept the null hypothesis. Reason for the Decision: Calculated value of test statistics is either in or out of the tail of the distribution. Conclusion (write out in complete sentences): The make-up of AIDS cases does not fit the ethnicities of the general population of Santa Clara County.

**30** a test of independence

**32** a test of independence

**34** 8

**36** 6.6

**39**

| Smoking Level Per Day | African American | Native Hawaiian | Latino | Japanese Americans | White | Totals |
|---|---|---|---|---|---|---|
| **1-10** | 9,886 | 2,745 | 12,831 | 8,378 | 7,650 | 41,490 |
| **11-20** | 6,514 | 3,062 | 4,932 | 10,680 | 9,877 | 35,065 |
| **21-30** | 1,671 | 1,419 | 1,406 | 4,715 | 6,062 | 15,273 |
| **31+** | 759 | 788 | 800 | 2,305 | 3,970 | 8,622 |
| **Totals** | 18,830 | 8,014 | 19,969 | 26,078 | 27,559 | 10,0450 |

Table 11.54

**41**

| Smoking Level Per Day | African American | Native Hawaiian | Latino | Japanese Americans | White |
|---|---|---|---|---|---|
| 1-10 | 7777.57 | 3310.11 | 8248.02 | 10771.29 | 11383.01 |
| 11-20 | 6573.16 | 2797.52 | 6970.76 | 9103.29 | 9620.27 |
| 21-30 | 2863.02 | 1218.49 | 3036.20 | 3965.05 | 4190.23 |
| 31+ | 1616.25 | 687.87 | 1714.01 | 2238.37 | 2365.49 |

Table 11.55

**43** 10,301.8

**44** right

**46**

a. Cannot accept the null hypothesis.

b. Calculated value of test statistics is either in or out of the tail of the distribution.

c. There is sufficient evidence to conclude that smoking level is dependent on ethnic group.

**48** test for homogeneity

**50** test for homogeneity

**52** All values in the table must be greater than or equal to five.

**54** 3

**57** a goodness-of-fit test

**59** a test for independence

**61** Answers will vary. Sample answer: Tests of independence and tests for homogeneity both calculate the test statistic the same way $\sum_{(i,j)} \frac{(O-E)^2}{E}$. In addition, all values must be greater than or equal to five.

**63** true

**65** false

**67** 225

**69** $H_0: \sigma^2 \leq 150$

**71** 36

**72** Check student's solution.

**74** The claim is that the variance is no more than 150 minutes.

**76** a Student's $t$- or normal distribution

**78**

a. $H_0: \sigma = 15$

b. $H_a: \sigma > 15$

c. $df = 42$

d. chi-square with $df = 42$

e. test statistic = 26.88

f. Check student's solution.

g.   i. Alpha = 0.05

    ii.  Decision: Cannot reject null hypothesis.

    iii.  Reason for decision: Calculated value of test statistics is either in or out of the tail of the distribution.

    iv.  Conclusion: There is insufficient evidence to conclude that the standard deviation is greater than 15.

**80**

a.  $H_0: \sigma \leq 3$

b.  $H_a: \sigma > 3$

c.  $df = 17$

d.  chi-square distribution with $df = 17$

e.  test statistic = 28.73

f.  Check student's solution.

g.    i.  Alpha: 0.05

    ii.  Decision: Cannot accept the null hypothesis.

    iii.  Reason for decision: Calculated value of test statistics is either in or out of the tail of the distribution.

    iv.  Conclusion: There is sufficient evidence to conclude that the standard deviation is greater than three.

**82**

a.  $H_0: \sigma = 2$

b.  $H_a: \sigma \neq 2$

c.  $df = 14$

d.  chi-square distiribution with $df = 14$

e.  chi-square test statistic = 5.2094

f.  Check student's solution.

g.    i.  Alpha = 0.05

    ii.  Decision: Cannot accept the null hypothesis

    iii.  Reason for decision: Calculated value of test statistics is either in or out of the tail of the distribution.

    iv.  Conclusion: There is sufficient evidence to conclude that the standard deviation is different than 2.

**84**  The sample standard deviation is \$34.29. $H_0 : \sigma^2 = 25^2$

$H_a : \sigma^2 > 25^2$

$df = n - 1 = 7$.

test statistic: $x^2 = \quad x_7^2 = \quad \dfrac{(n-1)s^2}{25^2} = \quad \dfrac{(8-1)(34.29)^2}{25^2} = 13.169$ ;

Alpha: 0.05

Decision: Cannot reject the null hypothesis.

Reason for decision: Calculated value of test statistics is either in or out of the tail of the distribution.

Conclusion: At the 5% level, there is insufficient evidence to conclude that the variance is more than 625.

87

| Marital Status | Percent | Expected Frequency |
|---|---|---|
| never married | 31.3 | 125.2 |
| married | 56.1 | 224.4 |
| widowed | 2.5 | 10 |
| divorced/separated | 10.1 | 40.4 |

Table 11.56

a.  The data fits the distribution.

b.  The data does not fit the distribution.

c.  3

d.  chi-square distribution with $df = 3$

e.  19.27

f.  0.0002

g.  Check student's solution.

h.  i.  Alpha = 0.05

  ii.  Decision: Cannot accept null hypothesis at the 5% level of significance

  iii.  Reason for decision: Calculated value of test statistics is either in or out of the tail of the distribution.

  iv.  Conclusion: Data does not fit the distribution.

89

a.  $H_0$: The local results follow the distribution of the U.S. AP examinee population

b.  $H_a$: The local results do not follow the distribution of the U.S. AP examinee population

c.  $df = 5$

d.  chi-square distribution with $df = 5$

e.  chi-square test statistic = 13.4

f.  Check student's solution.

g.  i.  Alpha = 0.05

  ii.  Decision: Cannot accept null when $a = 0.05$

  iii.  Reason for Decision: Calculated value of test statistics is either in or out of the tail of the distribution.

  iv.  Conclusion: Local data do not fit the AP Examinee Distribution.

  v.  Decision: Do not reject null when $a = 0.01$

  vi.  Conclusion: There is insufficient evidence to conclude that local data do not follow the distribution of the U.S. AP examinee distribution.

91

a.  $H_0$: The actual college majors of graduating females fit the distribution of their expected majors

b.  $H_a$: The actual college majors of graduating females do not fit the distribution of their expected majors

c.  $df = 10$

d.  chi-square distribution with $df = 10$

e.  test statistic = 11.48

   f.  Check student's solution.

   g.    i.   Alpha = 0.05

         ii.  Decision: Cannot reject null when $a = 0.05$ and $a = 0.01$

         iii.  Reason for decision: Calculated value of test statistics is either in or out of the tail of the distribution.

         iv.  Conclusion: There is insufficient evidence to conclude that the distribution of actual college majors of graduating females fits the distribution of their expected majors.

**94**  true

**96**  false

**98**

   a.  $H_0$: Surveyed obese fit the distribution of expected obese

   b.  $H_a$: Surveyed obese do not fit the distribution of expected obese

   c.  $df = 4$

   d.  chi-square distribution with $df = 4$

   e.  test statistic = 54.01

   f.  Check student's solution.

   g.    i.   Alpha: 0.05

         ii.  Decision: Cannot accept the null hypothesis.

         iii.  Reason for decision: Calculated value of test statistics is either in or out of the tail of the distribution.

         iv.  Conclusion: At the 5% level of significance, from the data, there is sufficient evidence to conclude that the surveyed obese do not fit the distribution of expected obese.

**100**

   a.  $H_0$: Car size is independent of family size.

   b.  $H_a$: Car size is dependent on family size.

   c.  $df = 9$

   d.  chi-square distribution with $df = 9$

   e.  test statistic = 15.8284

   f.  Check student's solution.

   g.    i.   Alpha: 0.05

         ii.  Decision: Cannot reject the null hypothesis.

         iii.  Reason for decision: Calculated value of test statistics is either in or out of the tail of the distribution.

         iv.  Conclusion: At the 5% significance level, there is insufficient evidence to conclude that car size and family size are dependent.

**102**

   a.  $H_0$: Honeymoon locations are independent of bride's age.

   b.  $H_a$: Honeymoon locations are dependent on bride's age.

   c.  $df = 9$

   d.  chi-square distribution with $df = 9$

   e.  test statistic = 15.7027

   f.  Check student's solution.

   g.    i.   Alpha: 0.05

         ii.  Decision: Cannot reject the null hypothesis.

    iii.  Reason for decision: Calculated value of test statistics is either in or out of the tail of the distribution.

    iv.  Conclusion: At the 5% significance level, there is insufficient evidence to conclude that honeymoon location and bride age are dependent.

**104**

a.  $H_0$: The types of fries sold are independent of the location.

b.  $H_a$: The types of fries sold are dependent on the location.

c.  $df = 6$

d.  chi-square distribution with $df = 6$

e.  test statistic =18.8369

f.  Check student's solution.

g.    i.  Alpha: 0.05

    ii.  Decision: Cannot accept the null hypothesis.

    iii.  Reason for decision: Calculated value of test statistics is either in or out of the tail of the distribution.

    iv.  Conclusion: At the 5% significance level, There is sufficient evidence that types of fries and location are dependent.

**106**

a.  $H_0$: Salary is independent of level of education.

b.  $H_a$: Salary is dependent on level of education.

c.  $df = 12$

d.  chi-square distribution with $df = 12$

e.  test statistic = 255.7704

f.  Check student's solution.

g.  Alpha: 0.05

Decision: Cannot accept the null hypothesis.

Reason for decision: Calculated value of test statistics is either in or out of the tail of the distribution.

Conclusion: At the 5% significance level, there is sufficient evidence to conclude that salary and level of education are dependent.

**108**  true

**110**  true

**112**

a.  $H_0$: Age is independent of the youngest online entrepreneurs' net worth.

b.  $H_a$: Age is dependent on the net worth of the youngest online entrepreneurs.

c.  $df = 2$

d.  chi-square distribution with $df = 2$

e.  test statistic = 1.76

f.  Check student's solution.

g.    i.  Alpha: 0.05

    ii.  Decision: Cannot reject the null hypothesis.

    iii.  Reason for decision: Calculated value of test statistics is either in or out of the tail of the distribution.

    iv.  Conclusion: At the 5% significance level, there is insufficient evidence to conclude that age and net worth for the youngest online entrepreneurs are dependent.

**114**

a. *H₀*: The distribution for personality types is the same for both majors

b. *Hₐ*: The distribution for personality types is not the same for both majors

c. *df* = 4

d. chi-square with *df* = 4

e. test statistic = 3.01

f. Check student's solution.

g.   i. Alpha: 0.05

    ii. Decision: Cannot reject the null hypothesis.

    iii. Reason for decision: Calculated value of test statistics is either in or out of the tail of the distribution.

    iv. Conclusion: There is insufficient evidence to conclude that the distribution of personality types is different for business and social science majors.

**116**

a. *H₀*: The distribution for fish caught is the same in Green Valley Lake and in Echo Lake.

b. *Hₐ*: The distribution for fish caught is not the same in Green Valley Lake and in Echo Lake.

c. 3

d. chi-square with *df* = 3

e. 11.75

f. Check student's solution.

g.   i. Alpha: 0.05

    ii. Decision: Cannot accept the null hypothesis.

    iii. Reason for decision: Calculated value of test statistics is either in or out of the tail of the distribution.

    iv. Conclusion: There is evidence to conclude that the distribution of fish caught is different in Green Valley Lake and in Echo Lake

**118**

a. *H₀*: The distribution of average energy use in the USA is the same as in Europe between 2005 and 2010.

b. *Hₐ*: The distribution of average energy use in the USA is not the same as in Europe between 2005 and 2010.

c. *df* = 4

d. chi-square with *df* = 4

e. test statistic = 2.7434

f. Check student's solution.

g.   i. Alpha: 0.05

    ii. Decision: Cannot reject the null hypothesis.

    iii. Reason for decision: Calculated value of test statistics is either in or out of the tail of the distribution.

    iv. Conclusion: At the 5% significance level, there is insufficient evidence to conclude that the average energy use values in the US and EU are not derived from different distributions for the period from 2005 to 2010.

**120**

a. *H₀*: The distribution for technology use is the same for community college students and university students.

b. *Hₐ*: The distribution for technology use is not the same for community college students and university students.

c. 2

d. chi-square with *df* = 2

e. 7.05

f. *p*-value = 0.0294

g. Check student's solution.

h.   i.   Alpha: 0.05

    ii.  Decision: Cannot accept the null hypothesis.

    iii. Reason for decision: *p*-value < alpha

    iv.  Conclusion: There is sufficient evidence to conclude that the distribution of technology use for statistics homework is not the same for statistics students at community colleges and at universities.

**122**

a. The test statistic is always positive and if the expected and observed values are not close together, the test statistic is large and the null hypothesis will be rejected.

b. Testing to see if the data fits the distribution "too well" or is too perfect.

# 12 | F DISTRIBUTION AND ONE-WAY ANOVA

**Figure 12.1** One-way ANOVA is used to measure information from several groups.

## Introduction

Many statistical applications in psychology, social science, business administration, and the natural sciences involve several groups. For example, an environmentalist is interested in knowing if the average amount of pollution varies in several bodies of water. A sociologist is interested in knowing if the amount of income a person earns varies according to his or her upbringing. A consumer looking for a new car might compare the average gas mileage of several models.

For hypothesis tests comparing averages among more than two groups, statisticians have developed a method called "Analysis of Variance" (abbreviated ANOVA). In this chapter, you will study the simplest form of ANOVA called single factor or one-way ANOVA. You will also study the $F$ distribution, used for one-way ANOVA, and the test for differences between two variances. This is just a very brief overview of one-way ANOVA. One-Way ANOVA, as it is presented here, relies heavily on a calculator or computer.

# 12.1 | Test of Two Variances

This chapter introduces a new probability density function, the F distribution. This distribution is used for many applications including ANOVA and for testing equality across multiple means. We begin with the F distribution and the test of hypothesis of differences in variances. It is often desirable to compare two variances rather than two averages. For instance, college administrators would like two college professors grading exams to have the same variation in their grading. In order for a lid to fit a container, the variation in the lid and the container should be approximately the same. A supermarket might be interested in the variability of check-out times for two checkers. In finance, the variance is a measure of risk and thus an interesting question would be to test the hypothesis that two different investment portfolios have the same variance, the volatility.

In order to perform a F test of two variances, it is important that the following are true:

1. The populations from which the two samples are drawn are approximately normally distributed.

2. The two populations are independent of each other.

Unlike most other hypothesis tests in this book, the F test for equality of two variances is very sensitive to deviations from normality. If the two distributions are not normal, or close, the test can give a biased result for the test statistic.

Suppose we sample randomly from two independent normal populations. Let $\sigma_1^2$ and $\sigma_2^2$ be the unknown population variances and $s_1^2$ and $s_2^2$ be the sample variances. Let the sample sizes be $n_1$ and $n_2$. Since we are interested in comparing the two sample variances, we use the F ratio:

$$F = \frac{\left[\frac{s_1^2}{\sigma_1^2}\right]}{\left[\frac{s_2^2}{\sigma_2^2}\right]}$$

$F$ has the distribution $F \sim F(n_1 - 1, n_2 - 1)$

where $n_1 - 1$ are the degrees of freedom for the numerator and $n_2 - 1$ are the degrees of freedom for the denominator.

If the null hypothesis is $\sigma_1^2 = \sigma_2^2$, then the F Ratio, test statistic, becomes $F_c = \frac{\left[\frac{s_1^2}{\sigma_1^2}\right]}{\left[\frac{s_2^2}{\sigma_2^2}\right]} = \frac{s_1^2}{s_2^2}$

The various forms of the hypotheses tested are:

| Two-Tailed Test | One-Tailed Test | One-Tailed Test |
|---|---|---|
| $H_0: \sigma_1^2 = \sigma_2^2$ | $H_0: \sigma_1^2 \leq \sigma_2^2$ | $H_0: \sigma_1^2 \geq \sigma_2^2$ |
| $H_1: \sigma_1^2 \neq \sigma_2^2$ | $H_1: \sigma_1^2 > \sigma_2^2$ | $H_1: \sigma_1^2 < \sigma_2^2$ |

**Table 12.1**

A more general form of the null and alternative hypothesis for a two tailed test would be :

$$H_0 : \frac{\sigma_1^2}{\sigma_2^2} = \delta_0$$

$$H_a : \frac{\sigma_1^2}{\sigma_2^2} \neq \delta_0$$

Where if $\delta_0 = 1$ it is a simple test of the hypothesis that the two variances are equal. This form of the hypothesis does have the benefit of allowing for tests that are more than for simple differences and can accommodate tests for specific differences as we did for differences in means and differences in proportions. This form of the hypothesis also shows the relationship between the F distribution and the $\chi^2$ : the F is a ratio of two chi squared distributions a distribution we saw in the last chapter. This is helpful in determining the degrees of freedom of the resultant F distribution.

If the two populations have equal variances, then $s_1^2$ and $s_2^2$ are close in value and the test statistic, $F_c = \dfrac{s_1^2}{s_2^2}$ is close to one. But if the two population variances are very different, $s_1^2$ and $s_2^2$ tend to be very different, too. Choosing $s_1^2$ as the larger sample variance causes the ratio $\dfrac{s_1^2}{s_2^2}$ to be greater than one. If $s_1^2$ and $s_2^2$ are far apart, then $F_c = \dfrac{s_1^2}{s_2^2}$ is a large number.

Therefore, if $F$ is close to one, the evidence favors the null hypothesis (the two population variances are equal). But if $F$ is much larger than one, then the evidence is against the null hypothesis. In essence, we are asking if the calculated F statistic, test statistic, is significantly different from one.

To determine the critical points we have to find $F_{\alpha, df1, df2}$. See Appendix A for the F table. This F table has values for various levels of significance from 0.1 to 0.001 designated as "p" in the first column. To find the critical value choose the desired significance level and follow down and across to find the critical value at the intersection of the two different degrees of freedom. The F distribution has two different degrees of freedom, one associated with the numerator, df1, and one associated with the denominator, df2 and to complicate matters the F distribution is not symmetrical and changes the degree of skewness as the degrees of freedom change. The degrees of freedom in the numerator is $n_1$-1, where $n_1$ is the sample size for group 1, and the degrees of freedom in the denominator is $n_2$-1, where $n_2$ is the sample size for group 2. $F_{\alpha, df1, df2}$ will give the critical value on the **upper** end of the F distribution.

To find the critical value for the **lower** end of the distribution, reverse the degrees of freedom and divide the F-value from the table into one.

Upper tail critical value : $F_{\alpha, df1, df2}$
Lower tail critical value : $1/F_{\alpha, df2, df1}$

When the calculated value of F is between the critical values, not in the tail, we cannot reject the null hypothesis that the two variances came from a population with the same variance. If the calculated F-value is in either tail we cannot accept the null hypothesis just as we have been doing for all of the previous tests of hypothesis.

An alternative way of finding the critical values of the F distribution makes the use of the F-table easier. We note in the F-table that all the values of F are greater than one therefore the critical F value for the left hand tail will always be less than one because to find the critical value on the left tail we divide an F value into the number one as shown above. We also note that if the sample variance in the numerator of the test statistic is larger than the sample variance in the denominator, the resulting F value will be greater than one. The shorthand method for this test is thus to be sure that the larger of the two sample variances is placed in the numerator to calculate the test statistic. This will mean that only the right hand tail critical value will have to be found in the F-table.

## Example 12.1

Two college instructors are interested in whether or not there is any variation in the way they grade math exams. They each grade the same set of 10 exams. The first instructor's grades have a variance of 52.3. The second instructor's grades have a variance of 89.9. Test the claim that the first instructor's variance is smaller. (In most colleges, it is desirable for the variances of exam grades to be nearly the same among instructors.) The level of significance is 10%.

### Solution 12.1

Let 1 and 2 be the subscripts that indicate the first and second instructor, respectively.

$n_1 = n_2 = 10$.

$H_0$: $\sigma_1^2 \geq \sigma_2^2$ and $H_a$: $\sigma_1^2 < \sigma_2^2$

**Calculate the test statistic:** By the null hypothesis $(\sigma_1^2 \geq \sigma_2^2)$, the $F$ statistic is:

$$F_c = \frac{s_2{}^2}{s_1{}^2} = \frac{89.9}{52.3} = 1.719$$

**Critical value for the test:** $F_{9,9} = 5.35$ where $n_1 - 1 = 9$ and $n_2 - 1 = 9$.

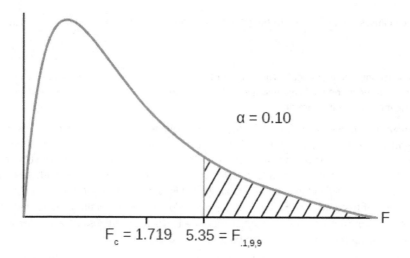

Figure 12.2

**Make a decision:** Since the calculated F value is not in the tail we cannot reject $H_0$.

**Conclusion:** With a 10% level of significance, from the data, there is insufficient evidence to conclude that the variance in grades for the first instructor is smaller.

**12.1** The New York Choral Society divides male singers up into four categories from highest voices to lowest: Tenor1, Tenor2, Bass1, Bass2. In the table are heights of the men in the Tenor1 and Bass2 groups. One suspects that taller men will have lower voices, and that the variance of height may go up with the lower voices as well. Do we have good evidence that the variance of the heights of singers in each of these two groups (Tenor1 and Bass2) are different?

| Tenor1 | Bass2 | Tenor 1 | Bass 2 | Tenor 1 | Bass 2 |
|--------|-------|---------|--------|---------|--------|
| 69 | 72 | 67 | 72 | 68 | 67 |
| 72 | 75 | 70 | 74 | 67 | 70 |
| 71 | 67 | 65 | 70 | 64 | 70 |
| 66 | 75 | 72 | 66 | | 69 |
| 76 | 74 | 70 | 68 | | 72 |
| 74 | 72 | 68 | 75 | | 71 |
| 71 | 72 | 64 | 68 | | 74 |
| 66 | 74 | 73 | 70 | | 75 |
| 68 | 72 | 66 | 72 | | |

Table 12.2

# 12.2 | One-Way ANOVA

The purpose of a one-way ANOVA test is to determine the existence of a statistically significant difference among several group means. The test actually uses **variances** to help determine if the means are equal or not. In order to perform a one-way ANOVA test, there are five basic **assumptions** to be fulfilled:

1. Each population from which a sample is taken is assumed to be normal.

2. All samples are randomly selected and independent.

3. The populations are assumed to have **equal standard deviations (or variances)**.

4. The factor is a categorical variable.

5. The response is a numerical variable.

## The Null and Alternative Hypotheses

The null hypothesis is simply that all the group population means are the same. The alternative hypothesis is that at least one pair of means is different. For example, if there are $k$ groups:

$H_0 : \mu_1 = \mu_2 = \mu_3 = \ldots \mu_k$

$H_a$: At least two of the group means $\mu_1, \mu_2, \mu_3, \ldots, \mu_k$ are not equal. That is, $\mu_i \neq \mu_j$ for some $i \neq j$.

The graphs, a set of box plots representing the distribution of values with the group means indicated by a horizontal line through the box, help in the understanding of the hypothesis test. In the first graph (red box plots), $H_0: \mu_1 = \mu_2 = \mu_3$ and the three populations have the same distribution if the null hypothesis is true. The variance of the combined data is approximately the same as the variance of each of the populations.

If the null hypothesis is false, then the variance of the combined data is larger which is caused by the different means as shown in the second graph (green box plots).

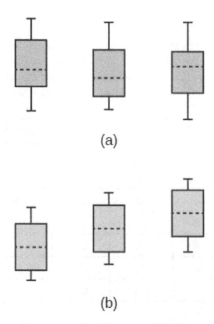

(a)

(b)

**Figure 12.3**   (a) $H_0$ is true. All means are the same; the differences are due to random variation. (b) $H_0$ is not true. All means are not the same; the differences are too large to be due to random variation.

# 12.3 | The F Distribution and the F-Ratio

The distribution used for the hypothesis test is a new one. It is called the **F distribution**, invented by George Snedecor but named in honor of Sir Ronald Fisher, an English statistician. The $F$ statistic is a ratio (a fraction). There are two sets of degrees of freedom; one for the numerator and one for the denominator.

For example, if $F$ follows an $F$ distribution and the number of degrees of freedom for the numerator is four, and the number of degrees of freedom for the denominator is ten, then $F \sim F_{4,10}$.

To calculate the **F ratio**, two estimates of the variance are made.

1. **Variance between samples:** An estimate of $\sigma^2$ that is the variance of the sample means multiplied by $n$ (when the sample sizes are the same.). If the samples are different sizes, the variance between samples is weighted to account for the different sample sizes. The variance is also called **variation due to treatment or explained variation.**

2. **Variance within samples:** An estimate of $\sigma^2$ that is the average of the sample variances (also known as a pooled variance). When the sample sizes are different, the variance within samples is weighted. The variance is also called the **variation due to error or unexplained variation.**

   - $SS_{between}$ = the **sum of squares** that represents the variation among the different samples

   - $SS_{within}$ = the sum of squares that represents the variation within samples that is due to chance.

To find a "sum of squares" means to add together squared quantities that, in some cases, may be weighted. We used sum of squares to calculate the sample variance and the sample standard deviation in **Section 2.**.

$MS$ means " **mean square**." $MS_{between}$ is the variance between groups, and $MS_{within}$ is the variance within groups.

**Calculation of Sum of Squares and Mean Square**

   - $k$ = the number of different groups

   - $n_j$ = the size of the $j^{th}$ group

   - $s_j$ = the sum of the values in the $j^{th}$ group

   - $n$ = total number of all the values combined (total sample size: $\sum n_j$)

   - $x$ = one value: $\sum x = \sum s_j$

- Sum of squares of all values from every group combined: $\sum x^2$

- Between group variability: $SS_{total} = \sum x^2 - \dfrac{\left(\sum x^2\right)}{n}$

- Total sum of squares: $\sum x^2 - \dfrac{(\sum x)^2}{n}$

- Explained variation: sum of squares representing variation among the different samples:
$$SS_{between} = \sum \left[\dfrac{(s_j)^2}{n_j}\right] - \dfrac{(\sum s_j)^2}{n}$$

- Unexplained variation: sum of squares representing variation within samples due to chance: $SS_{within} = SS_{total} - SS_{between}$

- $df$'s for different groups ($df$'s for the numerator): $df = k - 1$

- Equation for errors within samples ($df$'s for the denominator): $df_{within} = n - k$

- Mean square (variance estimate) explained by the different groups: $MS_{between} = \dfrac{SS_{between}}{df_{between}}$

- Mean square (variance estimate) that is due to chance (unexplained): $MS_{within} = \dfrac{SS_{within}}{df_{within}}$

$MS_{between}$ and $MS_{within}$ can be written as follows:

- $MS_{between} = \dfrac{SS_{between}}{df_{between}} = \dfrac{SS_{between}}{k - 1}$

- $MS_{within} = \dfrac{SS_{within}}{df_{within}} = \dfrac{SS_{within}}{n - k}$

The one-way ANOVA test depends on the fact that $MS_{between}$ can be influenced by population differences among means of the several groups. Since $MS_{within}$ compares values of each group to its own group mean, the fact that group means might be different does not affect $MS_{within}$.

The null hypothesis says that all groups are samples from populations having the same normal distribution. The alternate hypothesis says that at least two of the sample groups come from populations with different normal distributions. If the null hypothesis is true, $MS_{between}$ and $MS_{within}$ should both estimate the same value.

### NOTE

The null hypothesis says that all the group population means are equal. The hypothesis of equal means implies that the populations have the same normal distribution, because it is assumed that the populations are normal and that they have equal variances.

### *F*-Ratio or *F* Statistic

$$F = \dfrac{MS_{between}}{MS_{within}}$$

If $MS_{between}$ and $MS_{within}$ estimate the same value (following the belief that $H_0$ is true), then the $F$-ratio should be approximately equal to one. Mostly, just sampling errors would contribute to variations away from one. As it turns out, $MS_{between}$ consists of the population variance plus a variance produced from the differences between the samples. $MS_{within}$ is an estimate of the population variance. Since variances are always positive, if the null hypothesis is false, $MS_{between}$ will generally be larger than $MS_{within}$. Then the $F$-ratio will be larger than one. However, if the population effect is small, it is not unlikely that $MS_{within}$ will be larger in a given sample.

The foregoing calculations were done with groups of different sizes. If the groups are the same size, the calculations simplify somewhat and the $F$-ratio can be written as:

**F-Ratio Formula when the groups are the same size**

$$F = \frac{n \cdot s_{\bar{x}}^2}{s^2_{pooled}}$$

where ...
- $n$ = the sample size
- $df_{numerator} = k - 1$
- $df_{denominator} = n - k$
- $s^2$ pooled = the mean of the sample variances (pooled variance)
- $s_{\bar{x}}^2$ = the variance of the sample means

Data are typically put into a table for easy viewing. One-Way ANOVA results are often displayed in this manner by computer software.

| Source of Variation | Sum of Squares (SS) | Degrees of Freedom (df) | Mean Square (MS) | F |
|---|---|---|---|---|
| Factor (Between) | SS(Factor) | $k-1$ | MS(Factor) = SS(Factor)/(k − 1) | F = MS(Factor)/MS(Error) |
| Error (Within) | SS(Error) | $n-k$ | MS(Error) = SS(Error)/(n − k) | |
| Total | SS(Total) | $n-1$ | | |

Table 12.3

## Example 12.2

Three different diet plans are to be tested for mean weight loss. The entries in the table are the weight losses for the different plans. The one-way ANOVA results are shown in **Table 12.4**.

| Plan 1: $n_1$ = 4 | Plan 2: $n_2$ = 3 | Plan 3: $n_3$ = 3 |
|---|---|---|
| 5 | 3.5 | 8 |
| 4.5 | 7 | 4 |
| 4 | | 3.5 |
| 3 | 4.5 | |

Table 12.4

$s_1 = 16.5$, $s_2 = 15$, $s_3 = 15.5$

Following are the calculations needed to fill in the one-way ANOVA table. The table is used to conduct a hypothesis test.

$$SS(between) = \sum \left[ \frac{(s_j)^2}{n_j} \right] - \frac{\left( \sum s_j \right)^2}{n}$$

$$= \frac{s_1^2}{4} + \frac{s_2^2}{3} + \frac{s_3^2}{3} - \frac{(s_1 + s_2 + s_3)^2}{10}$$

where $n_1 = 4$, $n_2 = 3$, $n_3 = 3$ and $n = n_1 + n_2 + n_3 = 10$

$$= \frac{(16.5)^2}{4} + \frac{(15)^2}{3} + \frac{(15.5)^2}{3} - \frac{(16.5 + 15 + 15.5)^2}{10}$$
$$SS(between) = 2.2458$$

$$S(total) = \sum x^2 - \frac{\left(\sum x\right)^2}{n}$$

$$= \left(5^2 + 4.5^2 + 4^2 + 3^2 + 3.5^2 + 7^2 + 4.5^2 + 8^2 + 4^2 + 3.5^2\right)$$

$$- \frac{(5 + 4.5 + 4 + 3 + 3.5 + 7 + 4.5 + 8 + 4 + 3.5)^2}{10}$$

$$= 244 - \frac{47^2}{10} = 244 - 220.9$$

$$SS(total) = 23.1$$

$$SS(within) = SS(total) - SS(between)$$
$$= \quad 23.1 - 2.2458$$
$$SS(within) = 20.8542$$

| Source of Variation | Sum of Squares (*SS*) | Degrees of Freedom (*df*) | Mean Square (*MS*) | *F* |
|---|---|---|---|---|
| Factor (Between) | $SS$(Factor) = $SS$(Between) = 2.2458 | $k - 1$ = 3 groups – 1 = 2 | $MS$(Factor) = $SS$(Factor)/($k - 1$) = 2.2458/2 = 1.1229 | $F =$ $MS$(Factor)/$MS$(Error) = 1.1229/2.9792 = 0.3769 |
| Error (Within) | $SS$(Error) = $SS$(Within) = 20.8542 | $n - k$ = 10 total data – 3 groups = 7 | $MS$(Error) = $SS$(Error)/($n - k$) = 20.8542/7 = 2.9792 | |
| Total | $SS$(Total) = 2.2458 + 20.8542 = 23.1 | $n - 1$ = 10 total data – 1 = 9 | | |

Table 12.5

# Try It Σ

☞ **12.2** As part of an experiment to see how different types of soil cover would affect slicing tomato production, Marist College students grew tomato plants under different soil cover conditions. Groups of three plants each had one of the following treatments

- bare soil
- a commercial ground cover
- black plastic
- straw
- compost

All plants grew under the same conditions and were the same variety. Students recorded the weight (in grams) of tomatoes produced by each of the $n = 15$ plants:

| Bare: $n_1 = 3$ | Ground Cover: $n_2 = 3$ | Plastic: $n_3 = 3$ | Straw: $n_4 = 3$ | Compost: $n_5 = 3$ |
|---|---|---|---|---|
| 2,625 | 5,348 | 6,583 | 7,285 | 6,277 |
| 2,997 | 5,682 | 8,560 | 6,897 | 7,818 |
| 4,915 | 5,482 | 3,830 | 9,230 | 8,677 |

Table 12.6

Create the one-way ANOVA table.

**The one-way ANOVA hypothesis test is always right-tailed** because larger $F$-values are way out in the right tail of the $F$-distribution curve and tend to make us reject $H_0$.

## Example 12.3

Let's return to the slicing tomato exercise in **Try It**. The means of the tomato yields under the five mulching conditions are represented by $\mu_1$, $\mu_2$, $\mu_3$, $\mu_4$, $\mu_5$. We will conduct a hypothesis test to determine if all means are the same or at least one is different. Using a significance level of 5%, test the null hypothesis that there is no difference in mean yields among the five groups against the alternative hypothesis that at least one mean is different from the rest.

### Solution 12.3

The null and alternative hypotheses are:

$H_0$: $\mu_1 = \mu_2 = \mu_3 = \mu_4 = \mu_5$

$H_a$: $\mu_i \neq \mu_j$ some $i \neq j$

The one-way ANOVA results are shown in **Table 12.6**

| Source of Variation | Sum of Squares ($SS$) | Degrees of Freedom ($df$) | Mean Square ($MS$) | $F$ |
|---|---|---|---|---|
| Factor (Between) | 36,648,561 | $5 - 1 = 4$ | $\dfrac{36,648,561}{4} = 9,162,140$ | $\dfrac{9,162,140}{2,044,672.6} = 4.4810$ |
| Error (Within) | 20,446,726 | $15 - 5 = 10$ | $\dfrac{20,446,726}{10} = 2,044,672.6$ | |
| Total | 57,095,287 | $15 - 1 = 14$ | | |

Table 12.7

**Distribution for the test:** $F_{4,10}$

$df(num) = 5 - 1 = 4$

$df(denom) = 15 - 5 = 10$

**Test statistic:** $F = 4.4810$

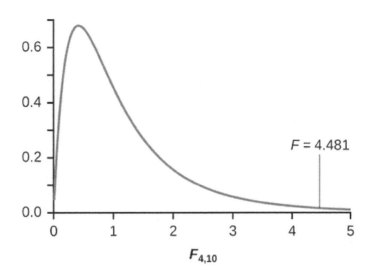

**Figure 12.4**

**Probability Statement:** $p$-value $= P(F > 4.481) = 0.0248$.

**Compare $\alpha$ and the $p$-value:** $\alpha = 0.05$, $p$-value $= 0.0248$

**Make a decision:** Since $\alpha > p$-value, we cannot accept $H_0$.

**Conclusion:** At the 5% significance level, we have reasonably strong evidence that differences in mean yields for slicing tomato plants grown under different mulching conditions are unlikely to be due to chance alone. We may conclude that at least some of mulches led to different mean yields.

**12.3** MRSA, or *Staphylococcus aureus*, can cause a serious bacterial infections in hospital patients. **Table 12.8** shows various colony counts from different patients who may or may not have MRSA. The data from the table is plotted in **Figure 12.5.**

| Conc = 0.6 | Conc = 0.8 | Conc = 1.0 | Conc = 1.2 | Conc = 1.4 |
|---|---|---|---|---|
| 9 | 16 | 22 | 30 | 27 |
| 66 | 93 | 147 | 199 | 168 |
| 98 | 82 | 120 | 148 | 132 |

**Table 12.8**

Plot of the data for the different concentrations:

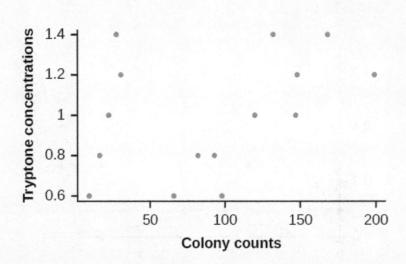

**Figure 12.5**

Test whether the mean number of colonies are the same or are different. Construct the ANOVA table, find the *p*-value, and state your conclusion. Use a 5% significance level.

## Example 12.4

Four sororities took a random sample of sisters regarding their grade means for the past term. The results are shown in **Table 12.9**.

| Sorority 1 | Sorority 2 | Sorority 3 | Sorority 4 |
|------------|------------|------------|------------|
| 2.17 | 2.63 | 2.63 | 3.79 |
| 1.85 | 1.77 | 3.78 | 3.45 |
| 2.83 | 3.25 | 4.00 | 3.08 |
| 1.69 | 1.86 | 2.55 | 2.26 |
| 3.33 | 2.21 | 2.45 | 3.18 |

**Table 12.9 MEAN GRADES FOR FOUR SORORITIES**

Using a significance level of 1%, is there a difference in mean grades among the sororities?

### Solution 12.4

Let $\mu_1$, $\mu_2$, $\mu_3$, $\mu_4$ be the population means of the sororities. Remember that the null hypothesis claims that the sorority groups are from the same normal distribution. The alternate hypothesis says that at least two of the sorority groups come from populations with different normal distributions. Notice that the four sample sizes are each five.

### NOTE

This is an example of a **balanced design**, because each factor (i.e., sorority) has the same number of observations.

$H_0$: $\mu_1 = \mu_2 = \mu_3 = \mu_4$

$H_a$: Not all of the means $\mu_1$, $\mu_2$, $\mu_3$, $\mu_4$ are equal.

**Distribution for the test:** $F_{3,16}$

where $k = 4$ groups and $n = 20$ samples in total

$df(num) = k - 1 = 4 - 1 = 3$

$df(denom) = n - k = 20 - 4 = 16$

**Calculate the test statistic:** $F = 2.23$

**Graph:**

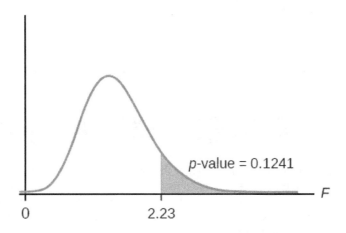

Figure 12.6

**Probability statement:** $p$-value $= P(F > 2.23) = 0.1241$

**Compare $\alpha$ and the $p$-value:** $\alpha = 0.01$
$p$-value $= 0.1241$
$\alpha < p$-value

**Make a decision:** Since $\alpha < p$-value, you cannot reject $H_0$.

**Conclusion:** There is not sufficient evidence to conclude that there is a difference among the mean grades for the sororities.

**12.4** Four sports teams took a random sample of players regarding their GPAs for the last year. The results are shown in **Table 12.10**.

| Basketball | Baseball | Hockey | Lacrosse |
|------------|----------|--------|----------|
| 3.6 | 2.1 | 4.0 | 2.0 |
| 2.9 | 2.6 | 2.0 | 3.6 |
| 2.5 | 3.9 | 2.6 | 3.9 |
| 3.3 | 3.1 | 3.2 | 2.7 |
| 3.8 | 3.4 | 3.2 | 2.5 |

Table 12.10 GPAs FOR FOUR SPORTS TEAMS

Use a significance level of 5%, and determine if there is a difference in GPA among the teams.

## Example 12.5

A fourth grade class is studying the environment. One of the assignments is to grow bean plants in different soils. Tommy chose to grow his bean plants in soil found outside his classroom mixed with dryer lint. Tara chose to grow her bean plants in potting soil bought at the local nursery. Nick chose to grow his bean plants in soil from his mother's garden. No chemicals were used on the plants, only water. They were grown inside the classroom next to a large window. Each child grew five plants. At the end of the growing period, each plant was measured, producing the data (in inches) in **Table 12.11**.

| Tommy's Plants | Tara's Plants | Nick's Plants |
|----------------|---------------|---------------|
| 24 | 25 | 23 |
| 21 | 31 | 27 |
| 23 | 23 | 22 |
| 30 | 20 | 30 |
| 23 | 28 | 20 |

Table 12.11

Does it appear that the three media in which the bean plants were grown produce the same mean height? Test at a 3% level of significance.

### Solution 12.5

This time, we will perform the calculations that lead to the $F'$ statistic. Notice that each group has the same number of plants, so we will use the formula $F' = \dfrac{n \cdot s_{\bar{x}}^2}{s^2_{\text{pooled}}}$ .

First, calculate the sample mean and sample variance of each group.

|  | Tommy's Plants | Tara's Plants | Nick's Plants |
|---|---|---|---|
| **Sample Mean** | 24.2 | 25.4 | 24.4 |
| **Sample Variance** | 11.7 | 18.3 | 16.3 |

Table 12.12

Next, calculate the variance of the three group means (Calculate the variance of 24.2, 25.4, and 24.4). **Variance of the group means = 0.413 =** $s_{\bar{x}}^2$

Then $MS_{between} = ns_{\bar{x}}^2 = (5)(0.413)$ where $n = 5$ is the sample size (number of plants each child grew).

Calculate the mean of the three sample variances (Calculate the mean of 11.7, 18.3, and 16.3). **Mean of the sample variances = 15.433 =** $s^2$ **pooled**

Then $MS_{within} = s^2_{pooled} = 15.433$.

The $F$ statistic (or $F$ ratio) is $F = \dfrac{MS_{between}}{MS_{within}} = \dfrac{ns_{\bar{x}}^2}{s^2_{pooled}} = \dfrac{(5)(0.413)}{15.433} = 0.134$

The $dfs$ for the numerator = the number of groups $- 1 = 3 - 1 = 2$.

The $dfs$ for the denominator = the total number of samples $-$ the number of groups $= 15 - 3 = 12$

The distribution for the test is $F_{2,12}$ and the $F$ statistic is $F = 0.134$

The $p$-value is $P(F > 0.134) = 0.8759$.

**Decision:** Since $\alpha = 0.03$ and the $p$-value $= 0.8759$, then you cannot reject $H_0$. (Why?)

**Conclusion:** With a 3% level of significance, from the sample data, the evidence is not sufficient to conclude that the mean heights of the bean plants are different.

## Notation

The notation for the $F$ distribution is $F \sim F_{df(num), df(denom)}$

where $df(num) = df_{between}$ and $df(denom) = df_{within}$

The mean for the $F$ distribution is $\mu = \dfrac{df(num)}{df(denom) - 2}$

# 12.4 | Facts About the F Distribution

**Here are some facts about the $F$ distribution.**

1.  The curve is not symmetrical but skewed to the right.

2.  There is a different curve for each set of degrees of freedom.

3.  The $F$ statistic is greater than or equal to zero.

4.  As the degrees of freedom for the numerator and for the denominator get larger, the curve approximates the normal as can be seen in the two figures below. Figure (b) with more degrees of freedom is more closely approaching the normal distribution, but remember that the $F$ cannot ever be less than zero so the distribution does not have a tail that goes to infinity on the left as the normal distribution does.

5.  Other uses for the $F$ distribution include comparing two variances and two-way Analysis of Variance. Two-Way Analysis is beyond the scope of this chapter.

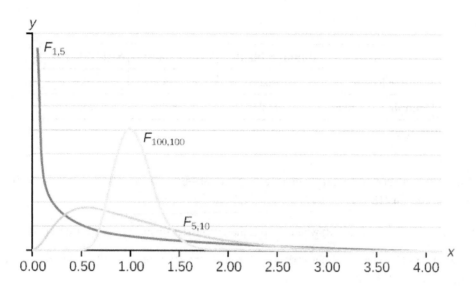

Figure 12.7

# KEY TERMS

**Analysis of Variance** also referred to as ANOVA, is a method of testing whether or not the means of three or more populations are equal. The method is applicable if:

- all populations of interest are normally distributed.
- the populations have equal standard deviations.
- samples (not necessarily of the same size) are randomly and independently selected from each population.
- there is one independent variable and one dependent variable.

The test statistic for analysis of variance is the $F$-ratio.

**One-Way ANOVA** a method of testing whether or not the means of three or more populations are equal; the method is applicable if:

- all populations of interest are normally distributed.
- the populations have equal standard deviations.
- samples (not necessarily of the same size) are randomly and independently selected from each population.

The test statistic for analysis of variance is the $F$-ratio.

**Variance** mean of the squared deviations from the mean; the square of the standard deviation. For a set of data, a deviation can be represented as $x - \bar{x}$ where $x$ is a value of the data and $\bar{x}$ is the sample mean. The sample variance is equal to the sum of the squares of the deviations divided by the difference of the sample size and one.

# CHAPTER REVIEW

### 12.1 Test of Two Variances

The $F$ test for the equality of two variances rests heavily on the assumption of normal distributions. The test is unreliable if this assumption is not met. If both distributions are normal, then the ratio of the two sample variances is distributed as an $F$ statistic, with numerator and denominator degrees of freedom that are one less than the samples sizes of the corresponding two groups. A **test of two variances** hypothesis test determines if two variances are the same. The distribution for the hypothesis test is the $F$ distribution with two different degrees of freedom.

Assumptions:

1. The populations from which the two samples are drawn are normally distributed.
2. The two populations are independent of each other.

### 12.2 One-Way ANOVA

Analysis of variance extends the comparison of two groups to several, each a level of a categorical variable (factor). Samples from each group are independent, and must be randomly selected from normal populations with equal variances. We test the null hypothesis of equal means of the response in every group versus the alternative hypothesis of one or more group means being different from the others. A one-way ANOVA hypothesis test determines if several population means are equal. The distribution for the test is the $F$ distribution with two different degrees of freedom.

Assumptions:

1. Each population from which a sample is taken is assumed to be normal.
2. All samples are randomly selected and independent.
3. The populations are assumed to have equal standard deviations (or variances).

### 12.3 The F Distribution and the F-Ratio

Analysis of variance compares the means of a response variable for several groups. ANOVA compares the variation within each group to the variation of the mean of each group. The ratio of these two is the $F$ statistic from an $F$ distribution with (number of groups − 1) as the numerator degrees of freedom and (number of observations − number of groups) as the denominator degrees of freedom. These statistics are summarized in the ANOVA table.

## 12.4 Facts About the F Distribution

The graph of the $F$ distribution is always positive and skewed right, though the shape can be mounded or exponential depending on the combination of numerator and denominator degrees of freedom. The $F$ statistic is the ratio of a measure of the variation in the group means to a similar measure of the variation within the groups. If the null hypothesis is correct, then the numerator should be small compared to the denominator. A small $F$ statistic will result, and the area under the $F$ curve to the right will be large, representing a large $p$-value. When the null hypothesis of equal group means is incorrect, then the numerator should be large compared to the denominator, giving a large $F$ statistic and a small area (small $p$-value) to the right of the statistic under the $F$ curve.

When the data have unequal group sizes (unbalanced data), then techniques from Section 12.3 need to be used for hand calculations. In the case of balanced data (the groups are the same size) however, simplified calculations based on group means and variances may be used. In practice, of course, software is usually employed in the analysis. As in any analysis, graphs of various sorts should be used in conjunction with numerical techniques. Always look at your data!

# FORMULA REVIEW

## 12.1 Test of Two Variances

$$H_0 : \frac{\sigma_1^2}{\sigma_2^2} = \delta_0$$

$$H_a : \frac{\sigma_1^2}{\sigma_2^2} \neq \delta_0$$

if $\delta_0 = 1$ then

$$H_0 : \sigma_1^2 = \sigma_2^2$$

$$H_a : \sigma_1^2 \neq \sigma_2$$

Test statistic is :

$$F_c = \frac{S_1^2}{S_2^2}$$

## 12.3 The F Distribution and the F-Ratio

$$SS_{between} = \sum \left[ \frac{(s_j)^2}{n_j} \right] - \frac{\left( \sum s_j \right)^2}{n}$$

$$SS_{total} = \sum x^2 - \frac{\left( \sum x \right)^2}{n}$$

$$SS_{within} = SS_{total} - SS_{between}$$

$$df_{between} = df(num) = k - 1$$

$$df_{within} = df(denom) = n - k$$

$$MS_{between} = \frac{SS_{between}}{df_{between}}$$

$$MS_{within} = \frac{SS_{within}}{df_{within}}$$

$$F = \frac{MS_{between}}{MS_{within}}$$

- $k$ = the number of groups
- $n_j$ = the size of the $j^{th}$ group
- $s_j$ = the sum of the values in the $j^{th}$ group
- $n$ = the total number of all values (observations) combined
- $x$ = one value (one observation) from the data
- $s_{\bar{x}}^2$ = the variance of the sample means
- $s^2_{pooled}$ = the mean of the sample variances (pooled variance)

# PRACTICE

## 12.1 Test of Two Variances

*Use the following information to answer the next two exercises.* There are two assumptions that must be true in order to perform an $F$ test of two variances.

**1.** Name one assumption that must be true.

**2.** What is the other assumption that must be true?

*Use the following information to answer the next five exercises.* Two coworkers commute from the same building. They are interested in whether or not there is any variation in the time it takes them to drive to work. They each record their times for 20 commutes. The first worker's times have a variance of 12.1. The second worker's times have a variance of 16.9. The first worker thinks that he is more consistent with his commute times. Test the claim at the 10% level. Assume that commute times are normally distributed.

**3.** State the null and alternative hypotheses.

**4.** What is $s_1$ in this problem?

**5.** What is $s_2$ in this problem?

**6.** What is $n$?

**7.** What is the $F$ statistic?

**8.** What is the critical value?

**9.** Is the claim accurate?

*Use the following information to answer the next four exercises.* Two students are interested in whether or not there is variation in their test scores for math class. There are 15 total math tests they have taken so far. The first student's grades have a standard deviation of 38.1. The second student's grades have a standard deviation of 22.5. The second student thinks his scores are more consistent.

**10.** State the null and alternative hypotheses.

**11.** What is the $F$ Statistic?

**12.** What is the critical value?

**13.** At the 5% significance level, do we reject the null hypothesis?

*Use the following information to answer the next three exercises.* Two cyclists are comparing the variances of their overall paces going uphill. Each cyclist records his or her speeds going up 35 hills. The first cyclist has a variance of 23.8 and the second cyclist has a variance of 32.1. The cyclists want to see if their variances are the same or different. Assume that commute times are normally distributed.

**14.** State the null and alternative hypotheses.

**15.** What is the $F$ Statistic?

**16.** At the 5% significance level, what can we say about the cyclists' variances?

## 12.2 One-Way ANOVA

*Use the following information to answer the next five exercises.* There are five basic assumptions that must be fulfilled in order to perform a one-way ANOVA test. What are they?

**17.** Write one assumption.

**18.** Write another assumption.

**19.** Write a third assumption.

**20.** Write a fourth assumption.

## 12.3 The F Distribution and the F-Ratio

*Use the following information to answer the next eight exercises.* Groups of men from three different areas of the country are to be tested for mean weight. The entries in Table 12.13 are the weights for the different groups.

| Group 1 | Group 2 | Group 3 |
|---------|---------|---------|
| 216 | 202 | 170 |
| 198 | 213 | 165 |
| 240 | 284 | 182 |
| 187 | 228 | 197 |
| 176 | 210 | 201 |

Table 12.13

**21.** What is the Sum of Squares Factor?

**22.** What is the Sum of Squares Error?

**23.** What is the *df* for the numerator?

**24.** What is the *df* for the denominator?

**25.** What is the Mean Square Factor?

**26.** What is the Mean Square Error?

**27.** What is the *F* statistic?

*Use the following information to answer the next eight exercises.* Girls from four different soccer teams are to be tested for mean goals scored per game. The entries in Table 12.14 are the goals per game for the different teams.

| Team 1 | Team 2 | Team 3 | Team 4 |
|--------|--------|--------|--------|
| 1 | 2 | 0 | 3 |
| 2 | 3 | 1 | 4 |
| 0 | 2 | 1 | 4 |
| 3 | 4 | 0 | 3 |
| 2 | 4 | 0 | 2 |

Table 12.14

**28.** What is $SS_{between}$?

**29.** What is the *df* for the numerator?

**30.** What is $MS_{between}$?

**31.** What is $SS_{within}$?

**32.** What is the *df* for the denominator?

**33.** What is $MS_{within}$?

**34.** What is the *F* statistic?

**35.** Judging by the *F* statistic, do you think it is likely or unlikely that you will reject the null hypothesis?

## 12.4 Facts About the F Distribution

**36.** An *F* statistic can have what values?

**37.** What happens to the curves as the degrees of freedom for the numerator and the denominator get larger?

*Use the following information to answer the next seven exercise.* Four basketball teams took a random sample of players regarding how high each player can jump (in inches). The results are shown in Table 12.15.

| Team 1 | Team 2 | Team 3 | Team 4 | Team 5 |
|--------|--------|--------|--------|--------|
| 36 | 32 | 48 | 38 | 41 |
| 42 | 35 | 50 | 44 | 39 |
| 51 | 38 | 39 | 46 | 40 |

Table 12.15

**38.** What is the *df(num)*?

**39.** What is the *df(denom)*?

**40.** What are the Sum of Squares and Mean Squares Factors?

**41.** What are the Sum of Squares and Mean Squares Errors?

**42.** What is the *F* statistic?

**43.** What is the *p*-value?

**44.** At the 5% significance level, is there a difference in the mean jump heights among the teams?

*Use the following information to answer the next seven exercises.* A video game developer is testing a new game on three different groups. Each group represents a different target market for the game. The developer collects scores from a random sample from each group. The results are shown in Table 12.16

| Group A | Group B | Group C |
|---------|---------|---------|
| 101 | 151 | 101 |
| 108 | 149 | 109 |
| 98 | 160 | 198 |
| 107 | 112 | 186 |
| 111 | 126 | 160 |

Table 12.16

**45.** What is the *df(num)*?

**46.** What is the *df(denom)*?

**47.** What are the $SS_{between}$ and $MS_{between}$?

**48.** What are the $SS_{within}$ and $MS_{within}$?

**49.** What is the *F* Statistic?

**50.** What is the *p*-value?

**51.** At the 10% significance level, are the scores among the different groups different?

*Use the following information to answer the next three exercises.* Suppose a group is interested in determining whether teenagers obtain their drivers licenses at approximately the same average age across the country. Suppose that the following data are randomly collected from five teenagers in each region of the country. The numbers represent the age at which teenagers obtained their drivers licenses.

|           | Northeast | South | West | Central | East |
|-----------|-----------|-------|------|---------|------|
|           | 16.3      | 16.9  | 16.4 | 16.2    | 17.1 |
|           | 16.1      | 16.5  | 16.5 | 16.6    | 17.2 |
|           | 16.4      | 16.4  | 16.6 | 16.5    | 16.6 |
|           | 16.5      | 16.2  | 16.1 | 16.4    | 16.8 |
| $\bar{x} =$ | _____ | _____ | _____ | _____ | _____ |
| $s^2 =$   | _____  | _____ | _____ | _____ | _____ |

Table 12.17

Enter the data into your calculator or computer.

**52.** $p$-value = _____

*State the decisions and conclusions (in complete sentences) for the following preconceived levels of $\alpha$.*

**53.** $\alpha = 0.05$

a. Decision: _____

b. Conclusion: _____

**54.** $\alpha = 0.01$

a. Decision: _____

b. Conclusion: _____

# HOMEWORK

### 12.1 Test of Two Variances

**55.** Three students, Linda, Tuan, and Javier, are given five laboratory rats each for a nutritional experiment. Each rat's weight is recorded in grams. Linda feeds her rats Formula A, Tuan feeds his rats Formula B, and Javier feeds his rats Formula C. At the end of a specified time period, each rat is weighed again and the net gain in grams is recorded.

| Linda's rats | Tuan's rats | Javier's rats |
|--------------|-------------|---------------|
| 43.5         | 47.0        | 51.2          |
| 39.4         | 40.5        | 40.9          |
| 41.3         | 38.9        | 37.9          |
| 46.0         | 46.3        | 45.0          |
| 38.2         | 44.2        | 48.6          |

Table 12.18

Determine whether or not the variance in weight gain is statistically the same among Javier's and Linda's rats. Test at a significance level of 10%.

**56.** A grassroots group opposed to a proposed increase in the gas tax claimed that the increase would hurt working-class people the most, since they commute the farthest to work. Suppose that the group randomly surveyed 24 individuals and asked them their daily one-way commuting mileage. The results are as follows.

| working-class | professional (middle incomes) | professional (wealthy) |
|---|---|---|
| 17.8 | 16.5 | 8.5 |
| 26.7 | 17.4 | 6.3 |
| 49.4 | 22.0 | 4.6 |
| 9.4 | 7.4 | 12.6 |
| 65.4 | 9.4 | 11.0 |
| 47.1 | 2.1 | 28.6 |
| 19.5 | 6.4 | 15.4 |
| 51.2 | 13.9 | 9.3 |

Table 12.19

Determine whether or not the variance in mileage driven is statistically the same among the working class and professional (middle income) groups. Use a 5% significance level.

*Use the following information to answer the next two exercises.* The following table lists the number of pages in four different types of magazines.

| home decorating | news | health | computer |
|---|---|---|---|
| 172 | 87 | 82 | 104 |
| 286 | 94 | 153 | 136 |
| 163 | 123 | 87 | 98 |
| 205 | 106 | 103 | 207 |
| 197 | 101 | 96 | 146 |

Table 12.20

**57.** Which two magazine types do you think have the same variance in length?

**58.** Which two magazine types do you think have different variances in length?

**59.** Is the variance for the amount of money, in dollars, that shoppers spend on Saturdays at the mall the same as the variance for the amount of money that shoppers spend on Sundays at the mall? Suppose that the Table 12.21 shows the results of a study.

| Saturday | Sunday | Saturday | Sunday |
|---|---|---|---|
| 75 | 44 | 62 | 137 |
| 18 | 58 | 0 | 82 |
| 150 | 61 | 124 | 39 |
| 94 | 19 | 50 | 127 |
| 62 | 99 | 31 | 141 |
| 73 | 60 | 118 | 73 |
|  | 89 |  |  |

Table 12.21

**60.** Are the variances for incomes on the East Coast and the West Coast the same? Suppose that Table 12.22 shows the results of a study. Income is shown in thousands of dollars. Assume that both distributions are normal. Use a level of significance of 0.05.

| East | West |
|---|---|
| 38 | 71 |
| 47 | 126 |
| 30 | 42 |
| 82 | 51 |
| 75 | 44 |
| 52 | 90 |
| 115 | 88 |
| 67 |  |

Table 12.22

**61.** Thirty men in college were taught a method of finger tapping. They were randomly assigned to three groups of ten, with each receiving one of three doses of caffeine: 0 mg, 100 mg, 200 mg. This is approximately the amount in no, one, or two cups of coffee. Two hours after ingesting the caffeine, the men had the rate of finger tapping per minute recorded. The experiment was double blind, so neither the recorders nor the students knew which group they were in. Does caffeine affect the rate of tapping, and if so how?

Here are the data:

| 0 mg | 100 mg | 200 mg | 0 mg | 100 mg | 200 mg |
|------|--------|--------|------|--------|--------|
| 242 | 248 | 246 | 245 | 246 | 248 |
| 244 | 245 | 250 | 248 | 247 | 252 |
| 247 | 248 | 248 | 248 | 250 | 250 |
| 242 | 247 | 246 | 244 | 246 | 248 |
| 246 | 243 | 245 | 242 | 244 | 250 |

Table 12.23

**62.** King Manuel I, Komnenus ruled the Byzantine Empire from Constantinople (Istanbul) during the years 1145 to 1180 A.D. The empire was very powerful during his reign, but declined significantly afterwards. Coins minted during his era were found in Cyprus, an island in the eastern Mediterranean Sea. Nine coins were from his first coinage, seven from the second, four from the third, and seven from a fourth. These spanned most of his reign. We have data on the silver content of the coins:

| First Coinage | Second Coinage | Third Coinage | Fourth Coinage |
|---------------|----------------|---------------|----------------|
| 5.9 | 6.9 | 4.9 | 5.3 |
| 6.8 | 9.0 | 5.5 | 5.6 |
| 6.4 | 6.6 | 4.6 | 5.5 |
| 7.0 | 8.1 | 4.5 | 5.1 |
| 6.6 | 9.3 | | 6.2 |
| 7.7 | 9.2 | | 5.8 |
| 7.2 | 8.6 | | 5.8 |
| 6.9 | | | |
| 6.2 | | | |

Table 12.24

Did the silver content of the coins change over the course of Manuel's reign?

Here are the means and variances of each coinage. The data are unbalanced.

|  | First | Second | Third | Fourth |
|--|-------|--------|-------|--------|
| Mean | 6.7444 | 8.2429 | 4.875 | 5.6143 |
| Variance | 0.2953 | 1.2095 | 0.2025 | 0.1314 |

Table 12.25

**63.** The American League and the National League of Major League Baseball are each divided into three divisions: East, Central, and West. Many years, fans talk about some divisions being stronger (having better teams) than other divisions. This may have consequences for the postseason. For instance, in 2012 Tampa Bay won 90 games and did not play in the postseason, while Detroit won only 88 and did play in the postseason. This may have been an oddity, but is there good evidence that in the 2012 season, the American League divisions were significantly different in overall records? Use the following data to test whether the mean number of wins per team in the three American League divisions were the same or not. Note that the data are not balanced, as two divisions had five teams, while one had only four.

| Division | Team | Wins |
|---|---|---|
| East | NY Yankees | 95 |
| East | Baltimore | 93 |
| East | Tampa Bay | 90 |
| East | Toronto | 73 |
| East | Boston | 69 |

Table 12.26

| Division | Team | Wins |
|---|---|---|
| Central | Detroit | 88 |
| Central | Chicago Sox | 85 |
| Central | Kansas City | 72 |
| Central | Cleveland | 68 |
| Central | Minnesota | 66 |

Table 12.27

| Division | Team | Wins |
|---|---|---|
| West | Oakland | 94 |
| West | Texas | 93 |
| West | LA Angels | 89 |
| West | Seattle | 75 |

Table 12.28

**12.2 One-Way ANOVA**

**64.** Three different traffic routes are tested for mean driving time. The entries in the **Table 12.29** are the driving times in minutes on the three different routes.

| Route 1 | Route 2 | Route 3 |
|---------|---------|---------|
| 30      | 27      | 16      |
| 32      | 29      | 41      |
| 27      | 28      | 22      |
| 35      | 36      | 31      |

Table 12.29

State $SS_{between}$, $SS_{within}$, and the $F$ statistic.

**65.** Suppose a group is interested in determining whether teenagers obtain their drivers licenses at approximately the same average age across the country. Suppose that the following data are randomly collected from five teenagers in each region of the country. The numbers represent the age at which teenagers obtained their drivers licenses.

|             | Northeast | South | West | Central | East |
|-------------|-----------|-------|------|---------|------|
|             | 16.3      | 16.9  | 16.4 | 16.2    | 17.1 |
|             | 16.1      | 16.5  | 16.5 | 16.6    | 17.2 |
|             | 16.4      | 16.4  | 16.6 | 16.5    | 16.6 |
|             | 16.5      | 16.2  | 16.1 | 16.4    | 16.8 |
| $\overline{x}\ =$ |     |       |      |         |      |
| $s^2\ =$    |           |       |      |         |      |

Table 12.30

State the hypotheses.

$H_0$: _____

$H_a$: _____

## 12.3 The F Distribution and the F-Ratio

*Use the following information to answer the next three exercises.* Suppose a group is interested in determining whether teenagers obtain their drivers licenses at approximately the same average age across the country. Suppose that the following data are randomly collected from five teenagers in each region of the country. The numbers represent the age at which teenagers obtained their drivers licenses.

|   | Northeast | South | West | Central | East |
|---|-----------|-------|------|---------|------|
|   | 16.3      | 16.9  | 16.4 | 16.2    | 17.1 |
|   | 16.1      | 16.5  | 16.5 | 16.6    | 17.2 |
|   | 16.4      | 16.4  | 16.6 | 16.5    | 16.6 |
|   | 16.5      | 16.2  | 16.1 | 16.4    | 16.8 |

|           | Northeast | South | West | Central | East |
|-----------|-----------|-------|------|---------|------|
| $\bar{x} =$ |           |       |      |         |      |
| $s^2 =$     |           |       |      |         |      |

Table 12.31

$H_0$: $\mu_1 = \mu_2 = \mu_3 = \mu_4 = \mu_5$

$H_a$: At least any two of the group means $\mu_1$, $\mu_2$, ..., $\mu_5$ are not equal.

**66.** degrees of freedom – numerator: $df(num) =$ _____

**67.** degrees of freedom – denominator: $df(denom) =$ _____

**68.** $F$ statistic = _____

## 12.4 Facts About the F Distribution

**69.** Three students, Linda, Tuan, and Javier, are given five laboratory rats each for a nutritional experiment. Each rat's weight is recorded in grams. Linda feeds her rats Formula A, Tuan feeds his rats Formula B, and Javier feeds his rats Formula C. At the end of a specified time period, each rat is weighed again, and the net gain in grams is recorded. Using a significance level of 10%, test the hypothesis that the three formulas produce the same mean weight gain.

| Linda's rats | Tuan's rats | Javier's rats |
|--------------|-------------|---------------|
| 43.5         | 47.0        | 51.2          |
| 39.4         | 40.5        | 40.9          |
| 41.3         | 38.9        | 37.9          |
| 46.0         | 46.3        | 45.0          |
| 38.2         | 44.2        | 48.6          |

Table 12.32 Weights of Student Lab Rats

**70.** A grassroots group opposed to a proposed increase in the gas tax claimed that the increase would hurt working-class people the most, since they commute the farthest to work. Suppose that the group randomly surveyed 24 individuals and asked them their daily one-way commuting mileage. The results are in Table 12.33. Using a 5% significance level, test the hypothesis that the three mean commuting mileages are the same.

| working-class | professional (middle incomes) | professional (wealthy) |
|---------------|-------------------------------|------------------------|
| 17.8          | 16.5                          | 8.5                    |
| 26.7          | 17.4                          | 6.3                    |
| 49.4          | 22.0                          | 4.6                    |
| 9.4           | 7.4                           | 12.6                   |
| 65.4          | 9.4                           | 11.0                   |
| 47.1          | 2.1                           | 28.6                   |
| 19.5          | 6.4                           | 15.4                   |
| 51.2          | 13.9                          | 9.3                    |

*Use the following information to answer the next two exercises.* Table 12.34 lists the number of pages in four different types of magazines.

| home decorating | news | health | computer |
|:---:|:---:|:---:|:---:|
| 172 | 87 | 82 | 104 |
| 286 | 94 | 153 | 136 |
| 163 | 123 | 87 | 98 |
| 205 | 106 | 103 | 207 |
| 197 | 101 | 96 | 146 |

Table 12.34

**71.** Using a significance level of 5%, test the hypothesis that the four magazine types have the same mean length.

**72.** Eliminate one magazine type that you now feel has a mean length different from the others. Redo the hypothesis test, testing that the remaining three means are statistically the same. Use a new solution sheet. Based on this test, are the mean lengths for the remaining three magazines statistically the same?

**73.** A researcher wants to know if the mean times (in minutes) that people watch their favorite news station are the same. Suppose that Table 12.35 shows the results of a study.

| CNN | FOX | Local |
|:---:|:---:|:---:|
| 45 | 15 | 72 |
| 12 | 43 | 37 |
| 18 | 68 | 56 |
| 38 | 50 | 60 |
| 23 | 31 | 51 |
| 35 | 22 | |

Table 12.35

Assume that all distributions are normal, the four population standard deviations are approximately the same, and the data were collected independently and randomly. Use a level of significance of 0.05.

**74.** Are the means for the final exams the same for all statistics class delivery types? Table 12.36 shows the scores on final exams from several randomly selected classes that used the different delivery types.

| Online | Hybrid | Face-to-Face |
|--------|--------|--------------|
| 72 | 83 | 80 |
| 84 | 73 | 78 |
| 77 | 84 | 84 |
| 80 | 81 | 81 |
| 81 |    | 86 |
|    |    | 79 |
|    |    | 82 |

Table 12.36

Assume that all distributions are normal, the four population standard deviations are approximately the same, and the data were collected independently and randomly. Use a level of significance of 0.05.

**75.** Are the mean number of times a month a person eats out the same for whites, blacks, Hispanics and Asians? Suppose that Table 12.37 shows the results of a study.

| White | Black | Hispanic | Asian |
|-------|-------|----------|-------|
| 6 | 4 | 7 | 8 |
| 8 | 1 | 3 | 3 |
| 2 | 5 | 5 | 5 |
| 4 | 2 | 4 | 1 |
| 6 |   | 6 | 7 |

Table 12.37

Assume that all distributions are normal, the four population standard deviations are approximately the same, and the data were collected independently and randomly. Use a level of significance of 0.05.

**76.** Are the mean numbers of daily visitors to a ski resort the same for the three types of snow conditions? Suppose that Table 12.38 shows the results of a study.

| Powder | Machine Made | Hard Packed |
|--------|--------------|-------------|
| 1,210  | 2,107        | 2,846       |
| 1,080  | 1,149        | 1,638       |
| 1,537  | 862          | 2,019       |
| 941    | 1,870        | 1,178       |
|        | 1,528        | 2,233       |
|        | 1,382        |             |

Table 12.38

Assume that all distributions are normal, the four population standard deviations are approximately the same, and the data were collected independently and randomly. Use a level of significance of 0.05.

**77.** Sanjay made identical paper airplanes out of three different weights of paper, light, medium and heavy. He made four airplanes from each of the weights, and launched them himself across the room. Here are the distances (in meters) that his planes flew.

| Paper Type/Trial | Trial 1 | Trial 2 | Trial 3 | Trial 4 |
|---|---|---|---|---|
| Heavy | 5.1 meters | 3.1 meters | 4.7 meters | 5.3 meters |
| Medium | 4 meters | 3.5 meters | 4.5 meters | 6.1 meters |
| Light | 3.1 meters | 3.3 meters | 2.1 meters | 1.9 meters |

**Table 12.39**

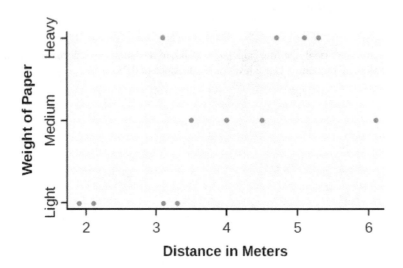

**Figure 12.8**

    a.  Take a look at the data in the graph. Look at the spread of data for each group (light, medium, heavy). Does it seem reasonable to assume a normal distribution with the same variance for each group? Yes or No.

    b.  Why is this a balanced design?

    c.  Calculate the sample mean and sample standard deviation for each group.

    d.  Does the weight of the paper have an effect on how far the plane will travel? Use a 1% level of significance. Complete the test using the method shown in the bean plant example in **Figure 12.8**.

        ◦  variance of the group means _____

        ◦  $MS_{between}=$ _____

        ◦  mean of the three sample variances _____

        ◦  $MS_{within}$ = _____

        ◦  $F$ statistic = _____

        ◦  $df(num)$ = _____, $df(denom)$ = _____

        ◦  number of groups _____

        ◦  number of observations _____

        ◦  $p$-value = _____ $(P(F >$ _____$) =$ _____$)$

        ◦  Graph the $p$-value.

        ◦  decision: _____

        ◦  conclusion: _____

**78.** DDT is a pesticide that has been banned from use in the United States and most other areas of the world. It is quite effective, but persisted in the environment and over time became seen as harmful to higher-level organisms. Famously, egg shells of eagles and other raptors were believed to be thinner and prone to breakage in the nest because of ingestion of DDT in the food chain of the birds.

An experiment was conducted on the number of eggs (fecundity) laid by female fruit flies. There are three groups of flies. One group was bred to be resistant to DDT (the RS group). Another was bred to be especially susceptible to DDT (SS). Finally there was a control line of non-selected or typical fruitflies (NS). Here are the data:

| RS | SS | NS | RS | SS | NS |
|------|------|------|------|------|------|
| 12.8 | 38.4 | 35.4 | 22.4 | 23.1 | 22.6 |
| 21.6 | 32.9 | 27.4 | 27.5 | 29.4 | 40.4 |
| 14.8 | 48.5 | 19.3 | 20.3 | 16 | 34.4 |
| 23.1 | 20.9 | 41.8 | 38.7 | 20.1 | 30.4 |
| 34.6 | 11.6 | 20.3 | 26.4 | 23.3 | 14.9 |
| 19.7 | 22.3 | 37.6 | 23.7 | 22.9 | 51.8 |
| 22.6 | 30.2 | 36.9 | 26.1 | 22.5 | 33.8 |
| 29.6 | 33.4 | 37.3 | 29.5 | 15.1 | 37.9 |
| 16.4 | 26.7 | 28.2 | 38.6 | 31 | 29.5 |
| 20.3 | 39 | 23.4 | 44.4 | 16.9 | 42.4 |
| 29.3 | 12.8 | 33.7 | 23.2 | 16.1 | 36.6 |
| 14.9 | 14.6 | 29.2 | 23.6 | 10.8 | 47.4 |
| 27.3 | 12.2 | 41.7 | | | |

Table 12.40

The values are the average number of eggs laid daily for each of 75 flies (25 in each group) over the first 14 days of their lives. Using a 1% level of significance, are the mean rates of egg selection for the three strains of fruitfly different? If so, in what way? Specifically, the researchers were interested in whether or not the selectively bred strains were different from the nonselected line, and whether the two selected lines were different from each other.

Here is a chart of the three groups:

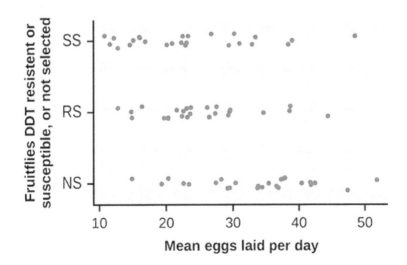

**Figure 12.9**

**79.** The data shown is the recorded body temperatures of 130 subjects as estimated from available histograms.

Traditionally we are taught that the normal human body temperature is 98.6 F. This is not quite correct for everyone. Are the mean temperatures among the four groups different?

Calculate 95% confidence intervals for the mean body temperature in each group and comment about the confidence intervals.

| FL | FH | ML | MH | FL | FH | ML | MH |
|------|------|------|------|------|-------|------|------|
| 96.4 | 96.8 | 96.3 | 96.9 | 98.4 | 98.6 | 98.1 | 98.6 |
| 96.7 | 97.7 | 96.7 | 97   | 98.7 | 98.6 | 98.1 | 98.6 |
| 97.2 | 97.8 | 97.1 | 97.1 | 98.7 | 98.6 | 98.2 | 98.7 |
| 97.2 | 97.9 | 97.2 | 97.1 | 98.7 | 98.7 | 98.2 | 98.8 |
| 97.4 | 98   | 97.3 | 97.4 | 98.7 | 98.7 | 98.2 | 98.8 |
| 97.6 | 98   | 97.4 | 97.5 | 98.8 | 98.8 | 98.2 | 98.8 |
| 97.7 | 98   | 97.4 | 97.6 | 98.8 | 98.8 | 98.3 | 98.9 |
| 97.8 | 98   | 97.4 | 97.7 | 98.8 | 98.8 | 98.4 | 99   |
| 97.8 | 98.1 | 97.5 | 97.8 | 98.8 | 98.9 | 98.4 | 99   |
| 97.9 | 98.3 | 97.6 | 97.9 | 99.2 | 99   | 98.5 | 99   |
| 97.9 | 98.3 | 97.6 | 98   | 99.3 | 99   | 98.5 | 99.2 |
| 98   | 98.3 | 97.8 | 98   |      | 99.1 | 98.6 | 99.5 |
| 98.2 | 98.4 | 97.8 | 98   |      | 99.1 | 98.6 |      |
| 98.2 | 98.4 | 97.8 | 98.3 |      | 99.2 | 98.7 |      |
| 98.2 | 98.4 | 97.9 | 98.4 |      | 99.4 | 99.1 |      |
| 98.2 | 98.4 | 98   | 98.4 |      | 99.9 | 99.3 |      |
| 98.2 | 98.5 | 98   | 98.6 |      | 100  | 99.4 |      |
| 98.2 | 98.6 | 98   | 98.6 |      | 100.8 |     |      |

**Table 12.41**

# REFERENCES

### 12.1 Test of Two Variances

"MLB Vs. Division Standings – 2012." Available online at http://espn.go.com/mlb/standings/_/year/2012/type/vs-division/order/true.

### 12.3 The F Distribution and the F-Ratio

Tomato Data, Marist College School of Science (unpublished student research)

### 12.4 Facts About the F Distribution

Data from a fourth grade classroom in 1994 in a private K – 12 school in San Jose, CA.

Hand, D.J., F. Daly, A.D. Lunn, K.J. McConway, and E. Ostrowski. *A Handbook of Small Datasets: Data for Fruitfly Fecundity.* London: Chapman & Hall, 1994.

Hand, D.J., F. Daly, A.D. Lunn, K.J. McConway, and E. Ostrowski. *A Handbook of Small Datasets.* London: Chapman & Hall, 1994, pg. 50.

Hand, D.J., F. Daly, A.D. Lunn, K.J. McConway, and E. Ostrowski. A Handbook of Small Datasets. London: Chapman & Hall, 1994, pg. 118.

"MLB Standings – 2012." Available online at http://espn.go.com/mlb/standings/_/year/2012.

Mackowiak, P. A., Wasserman, S. S., and Levine, M. M. (1992), "A Critical Appraisal of 98.6 Degrees F, the Upper Limit of the Normal Body Temperature, and Other Legacies of Carl Reinhold August Wunderlich," *Journal of the American Medical Association,* 268, 1578-1580.

## SOLUTIONS

**1** The populations from which the two samples are drawn are normally distributed.

**3** $H_0 : \sigma_1 = \sigma_2$  $H_a : \sigma_1 < \sigma_2$ or $H_0: \sigma_1^2 = \sigma_2^2$ $H_a: \sigma_1^2 < \sigma_2^2$

**5** 4.11

**7** 0.7159

**9** No, at the 10% level of significance, we cannot reject the null hypothesis and state that the data do not show that the variation in drive times for the first worker is less than the variation in drive times for the second worker.

**11** 2.8674

**13** Cannot accept the null hypothesis. There is enough evidence to say that the variance of the grades for the first student is higher than the variance in the grades for the second student.

**15** 0.7414

**17** Each population from which a sample is taken is assumed to be normal.

**19** The populations are assumed to have equal standard deviations (or variances).

**21** 4,939.2

**23** 2

**25** 2,469.6

**27** 3.7416

**29** 3

**31** 13.2

**33** 0.825

**35** Because a one-way ANOVA test is always right-tailed, a high $F$ statistic corresponds to a low $p$-value, so it is likely that we cannot accept the null hypothesis.

**37** The curves approximate the normal distribution.

**39** ten

**41** $SS = 237.33$; $MS = 23.73$

**43** 0.1614

**45** two

**47** $SS = 5,700.4$; $MS = 2,850.2$

**49** 3.6101

**51** Yes, there is enough evidence to show that the scores among the groups are statistically significant at the 10% level.

**55**

a. $H_0: \sigma_1^2 = \sigma_2^2$

b. $H_a: \ \sigma_1^2 \neq \sigma_1^2$

c. $df(num) = 4$; $df(denom) = 4$

d. $F_{4, 4}$

e. 3.00

f. Check student't solution.

g. Decision: Cannot reject the null hypothesis; Conclusion: There is insufficient evidence to conclude that the variances are different.

**58** The answers may vary. Sample answer: Home decorating magazines and news magazines have different variances.

**60**

a. $H_0: = \sigma_1^2 = \sigma_2^2$

b. $H_a: \sigma_1^2 \neq \sigma_1^2$

c. $df(n) = 7$, $df(d) = 6$

d. $F_{7,6}$

e. 0.8117

f. 0.7825

g. Check student's solution.

h.  i. Alpha: 0.05

   ii. Decision: Cannot reject the null hypothesis.

   iii. Reason for decision: calculated test statistics is not in the tail of the distribution

   iv. Conclusion: There is not sufficient evidence to conclude that the variances are different.

**62** Here is a strip chart of the silver content of the coins:

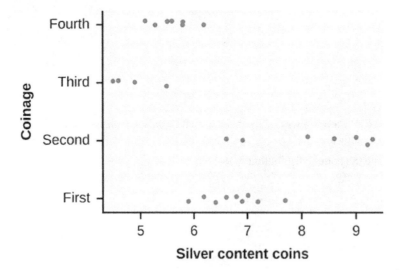

Figure 12.10

While there are differences in spread, it is not unreasonable to use ANOVA techniques. Here is the completed ANOVA table:

| Source of Variation | Sum of Squares (*SS*) | Degrees of Freedom (*df*) | Mean Square (*MS*) | *F* |
|---|---|---|---|---|
| Factor (Between) | 37.748 | 4 − 1 = 3 | 12.5825 | 26.272 |
| Error (Within) | 11.015 | 27 − 4 = 23 | 0.4789 | |
| Total | 48.763 | 27 − 1 = 26 | | |

Table 12.42

$P(F > 26.272) = 0$; Cannot accept the null hypothesis for any alpha. There is sufficient evidence to conclude that the mean silver content among the four coinages are different. From the strip chart, it appears that the first and second coinages had higher silver contents than the third and fourth.

63 Here is a stripchart of the number of wins for the 14 teams in the AL for the 2012 season.

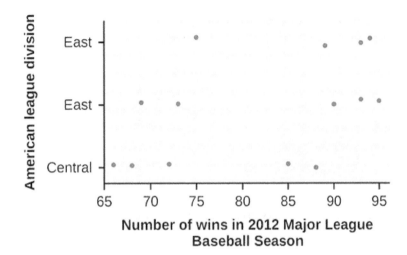

Figure 12.11

While the spread seems similar, there may be some question about the normality of the data, given the wide gaps in the middle near the 0.500 mark of 82 games (teams play 162 games each season in MLB). However, one-way ANOVA is robust. Here is the ANOVA table for the data:

| Source of Variation | Sum of Squares (*SS*) | Degrees of Freedom (*df*) | Mean Square (*MS*) | *F* |
|---|---|---|---|---|
| Factor (Between) | 344.16 | 3 − 1 = 2 | 172.08 | |
| Error (Within) | 1,219.55 | 14 − 3 = 11 | 110.87 | 1.5521 |
| Total | 1,563.71 | 14 − 1 = 13 | | |

Table 12.43

$P(F > 1.5521) = 0.2548$

Since the *p*-value is so large, there is not good evidence against the null hypothesis of equal means. We cannot reject the null hypothesis. Thus, for 2012, there is not any have any good evidence of a significant difference in mean number of wins between the divisions of the American League.

64 $SS_{between} = 26$
$SS_{within} = 441$
$F = 0.2653$

67 $df(denom) = 15$

69

a. $H_0$: $\mu_L = \mu_T = \mu_J$

b. $H_a$: at least any two of the means are different

c. $df(num) = 2$; $df(denom) = 12$

d. $F$ distribution

e. 0.67

f. 0.5305

g. Check student's solution.

h. Decision:Cannot reject null hypothesis; Conclusion: There is insufficient evidence to conclude that the means are different.

**72**

a. $H_a$: $\mu_c = \mu_n = \mu_h$

b. At least any two of the magazines have different mean lengths.

c. $df(num) = 2$, $df(denom) = 12$

d. $F$ distribtuion

e. $F = 15.28$

f. $p$-value = 0.001

g. Check student's solution.

h.  i.  Alpha: 0.05

   ii.  Decision: Cannot accept the null hypothesis.

   iii.  Reason for decision: $p$-value < alpha

   iv.  Conclusion: There is sufficient evidence to conclude that the mean lengths of the magazines are different.

**74**

a. $H_0$: $\mu_o = \mu_h = \mu_f$

b. At least two of the means are different.

c. $df(n) = 2$, $df(d) = 13$

d. $F_{2,13}$

e. 0.64

f. 0.5437

g. Check student's solution.

h.  i.  Alpha: 0.05

   ii.  Decision: Cannot reject the null hypothesis.

   iii.  Reason for decision: $p$-value > alpha

   iv.  Conclusion: The mean scores of different class delivery are not different.

**76**

a. $H_0$: $\mu_p = \mu_m = \mu_h$

b. At least any two of the means are different.

c. $df(n) = 2$, $df(d) = 12$

d. $F_{2,12}$

e. 3.13

f. 0.0807

    g.  Check student's solution.

    h.    i.   Alpha: 0.05

          ii.  Decision: Cannot reject the null hypothesis.

         iii.  Reason for decision: $p$-value > alpha

         iv.  Conclusion: There is not sufficient evidence to conclude that the mean numbers of daily visitors are different.

**78** The data appear normally distributed from the chart and of similar spread. There do not appear to be any serious outliers, so we may proceed with our ANOVA calculations, to see if we have good evidence of a difference between the three groups. $H_0 : \mu_1 = \mu_2 = \mu_3$; $H_a : \mu_i \neq$ ; some $i \neq j$ Define $\mu_1, \mu_2, \mu_3$, as the population mean number of eggs laid by the three groups of fruit flies. $F$ statistic = 8.6657; $p$-value = 0.0004

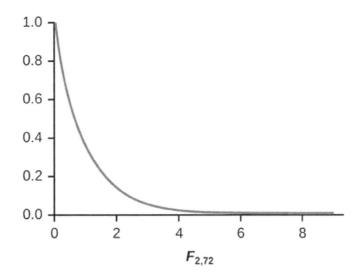

**Figure 12.12**

**Decision:** Since the $p$-value is less than the level of significance of 0.01, we reject the null hypothesis. **Conclusion:** We have good evidence that the average number of eggs laid during the first 14 days of life for these three strains of fruitflies are different. Interestingly, if you perform a two sample $t$-test to compare the RS and NS groups they are significantly different ($p$ = 0.0013). Similarly, SS and NS are significantly different ($p$ = 0.0006). However, the two selected groups, RS and SS are *not* significantly different ($p$ = 0.5176). Thus we appear to have good evidence that selection either for resistance or for susceptibility involves a reduced rate of egg production (for these specific strains) as compared to flies that were not selected for resistance or susceptibility to DDT. Here, genetic selection has apparently involved a loss of fecundity.

# 13 | LINEAR REGRESSION AND CORRELATION

**Figure 13.1** Linear regression and correlation can help you determine if an auto mechanic's salary is related to his work experience. (credit: Joshua Rothhaas)

## Introduction

Professionals often want to know how two or more numeric variables are related. For example, is there a relationship between the grade on the second math exam a student takes and the grade on the final exam? If there is a relationship, what is the relationship and how strong is it?

In another example, your income may be determined by your education, your profession, your years of experience, and your ability, or your gender or color. The amount you pay a repair person for labor is often determined by an initial amount plus an hourly fee.

These examples may or may not be tied to a model, meaning that some theory suggested that a relationship exists. This link between a cause and an effect, often referred to as a model, is the foundation of the scientific method and is the core of how we determine what we believe about how the world works. Beginning with a theory and developing a model of the theoretical relationship should result in a prediction, what we have called a hypothesis earlier. Now the hypothesis concerns a full set of relationships. As an example, in Economics the model of consumer choice is based upon assumptions concerning human behavior: a desire to maximize something called utility, knowledge about the benefits of one product over another, likes and dislikes, referred to generally as preferences, and so on. These combined to give us the demand curve. From that we have the prediction that as prices rise the quantity demanded will fall. Economics has models concerning the relationship between what prices are charged for goods and the market structure in which the firm operates, monopoly verse competition, for example. Models for who would be most likely to be chosen for an on-the-job training position, the impacts of Federal Reserve policy changes and the growth of the economy and on and on.

Models are not unique to Economics, even within the social sciences. In political science, for example, there are models that predict behavior of bureaucrats to various changes in circumstances based upon assumptions of the goals of the bureaucrats. There are models of political behavior dealing with strategic decision making both for international relations and domestic politics.

The so-called hard sciences are, of course, the source of the scientific method as they tried through the centuries to explain the confusing world around us. Some early models today make us laugh; spontaneous generation of life for example. These early models are seen today as not much more than the foundational myths we developed to help us bring some sense of order to what seemed chaos.

The foundation of all model building is the perhaps the arrogant statement that we know what caused the result we see. This is embodied in the simple mathematical statement of the functional form that $y = f(x)$. The response, Y, is caused by the stimulus, X. Every model will eventually come to this final place and it will be here that the theory will live or die. Will the data support this hypothesis? If so then fine, we shall believe this version of the world until a better theory comes to replace it. This is the process by which we moved from flat earth to round earth, from earth-center solar system to sun-center solar system, and on and on.

The scientific method does not confirm a theory for all time: it does not prove "truth". All theories are subject to review and may be overturned. These are lessons we learned as we first developed the concept of the hypothesis test earlier in this book. Here, as we begin this section, these concepts deserve review because the tool we will develop here is the cornerstone of the scientific method and the stakes are higher. Full theories will rise or fall because of this statistical tool; regression and the more advanced versions call econometrics.

In this chapter we will begin with correlation, the investigation of relationships among variables that may or may not be founded on a cause and effect model. The variables simply move in the same, or opposite, direction. That is to say, they do not move randomly. Correlation provides a measure of the degree to which this is true. From there we develop a tool to measure cause and effect relationships; regression analysis. We will be able to formulate models and tests to determine if they are statistically sound. If they are found to be so, then we can use them to make predictions: if as a matter of policy we changed the value of this variable what would happen to this other variable? If we imposed a gasoline tax of 50 cents per gallon how would that effect the carbon emissions, sales of Hummers/Hybrids, use of mass transit, etc.? The ability to provide answers to these types of questions is the value of regression as both a tool to help us understand our world and to make thoughtful policy decisions.

# 13.1 | The Correlation Coefficient r

As we begin this section we note that the type of data we will be working with has changed. Perhaps unnoticed, all the data we have been using is for a single variable. It may be from two samples, but it is still a univariate variable. The type of data described in the examples above and for any model of cause and effect is **bivariate** data — "bi" for two variables. In reality, statisticians use **multivariate** data, meaning many variables.

For our work we can classify data into three broad categories, time series data, cross-section data, and panel data. We met the first two very early on. Time series data measures a single unit of observation; say a person, or a company or a country, as time passes. What are measured will be at least two characteristics, say the person's income, the quantity of a particular good they buy and the price they paid. This would be three pieces of information in one time period, say 1985. If we followed that person across time we would have those same pieces of information for 1985,1986, 1987, etc. This would constitute a times series data set. If we did this for 10 years we would have 30 pieces of information concerning this person's consumption habits of this good for the past decade and we would know their income and the price they paid.

A second type of data set is for cross-section data. Here the variation is not across time for a single unit of observation, but across units of observation during one point in time. For a particular period of time we would gather the price paid, amount purchased, and income of many individual people.

A third type of data set is panel data. Here a panel of units of observation is followed across time. If we take our example from above we might follow 500 people, the unit of observation, through time, ten years, and observe their income, price paid and quantity of the good purchased. If we had 500 people and data for ten years for price, income and quantity purchased we would have 15,000 pieces of information. These types of data sets are very expensive to construct and maintain. They do, however, provide a tremendous amount of information that can be used to answer very important questions. As an example, what is the effect on the labor force participation rate of women as their family of origin, mother and father, age? Or are there differential effects on health outcomes depending upon the age at which a person started smoking? Only panel data can give answers to these and related questions because we must follow multiple people across time. The work we do here however will not be fully appropriate for data sets such as these.

Beginning with a set of data with two independent variables we ask the question: are these related? One way to visually answer this question is to create a scatter plot of the data. We could not do that before when we were doing descriptive statistics because those data were univariate. Now we have bivariate data so we can plot in two dimensions. Three dimensions are possible on a flat piece of paper, but become very hard to fully conceptualize. Of course, more than three dimensions cannot be graphed although the relationships can be measured mathematically.

To provide mathematical precision to the measurement of what we see we use the correlation coefficient. The correlation tells us something about the co-movement of two variables, but **nothing** about why this movement occurred. Formally, correlation analysis assumes that both variables being analyzed are **independent** variables. This means that neither one causes the movement in the other. Further, it means that neither variable is dependent on the other, or for that matter, on any other variable. Even with these limitations, correlation analysis can yield some interesting results.

The correlation coefficient, $\rho$ (pronounced rho), is the mathematical statistic for a population that provides us with a measurement of the strength of a linear relationship between the two variables. For a sample of data, the statistic, r, developed by Karl Pearson in the early 1900s, is an estimate of the population correlation and is defined mathematically as:

$$r = \frac{\frac{1}{n-1} \Sigma \left( X_{1i} - \bar{X}_1 \right)\left( X_{2i} - \bar{X}_2 \right)}{s_{x_1} s_{x_2}}$$

OR

$$r = \frac{\Sigma X_{1i} X_{2i} - n \bar{X}_1 - \bar{X}_2}{\sqrt{\left( \Sigma X_{1i}^2 - n \bar{X}_1^2 \right)\left( \Sigma X_{2i}^2 - n \bar{X}_2^2 \right)}}$$

where $s_{x1}$ and $s_{x2}$ are the standard deviations of the two independent variables $X_1$ and $X_2$, $\bar{X}_1$ and $\bar{X}_2$ are the sample means of the two variables, and $X_{1i}$ and $X_{2i}$ are the individual observations of $X_1$ and $X_2$. The correlation coefficient r ranges in value from -1 to 1. The second equivalent formula is often used because it may be computationally easier. As scary as these formulas look they are really just the ratio of the covariance between the two variables and the product of their two standard deviations. That is to say, it is a measure of relative variances.

In practice all correlation and regression analysis will be provided through computer software designed for these purposes. Anything more than perhaps one-half a dozen observations creates immense computational problems. It was because of this fact that correlation, and even more so, regression, were not widely used research tools until after the advent of "computing machines". Now the computing power required to analyze data using regression packages is deemed almost trivial by comparison to just a decade ago.

To visualize any **linear** relationship that may exist review the plot of a scatter diagrams of the standardized data. **Figure 13.2** presents several scatter diagrams and the calculated value of r. In panels (a) and (b) notice that the data generally trend together, (a) upward and (b) downward. Panel (a) is an example of a positive correlation and panel (b) is an example of a negative correlation, or relationship. The sign of the correlation coefficient tells us if the relationship is a positive or negative (inverse) one. If all the values of $X_1$ and $X_2$ are on a straight line the correlation coefficient will be either 1 or -1 depending on whether the line has a positive or negative slope and the closer to one or negative one the stronger the relationship between the two variables. BUT ALWAYS REMEMBER THAT THE CORRELATION COEFFICIENT DOES NOT TELL US THE SLOPE.

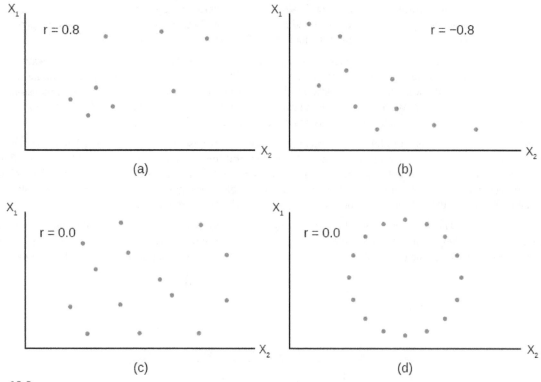

**Figure 13.2**

Remember, all the correlation coefficient tells us is whether or not the data are linearly related. In panel (d) the variables obviously have some type of very specific relationship to each other, but the correlation coefficient is zero, indicating no **linear** relationship exists.

If you suspect a linear relationship between $X_1$ and $X_2$ then $r$ can measure how strong the linear relationship is.

What the VALUE of $r$ tells us:

- The value of $r$ is always between –1 and +1: $-1 \leq r \leq 1$.

- The size of the correlation $r$ indicates the strength of the **linear** relationship between $X_1$ and $X_2$. Values of $r$ close to –1 or to +1 indicate a stronger linear relationship between $X_1$ and $X_2$.

- If $r = 0$ there is absolutely no linear relationship between $X_1$ and $X_2$ **(no linear correlation)**.

- If $r = 1$, there is perfect positive correlation. If $r = -1$, there is perfect negative correlation. In both these cases, all of the original data points lie on a straight line: ANY straight line no matter what the slope. Of course, in the real world, this will not generally happen.

What the SIGN of $r$ tells us

- A positive value of $r$ means that when $X_1$ increases, $X_2$ tends to increase and when $X_1$ decreases, $X_2$ tends to decrease **(positive correlation)**.

- A negative value of $r$ means that when $X_1$ increases, $X_2$ tends to decrease and when $X_1$ decreases, $X_2$ tends to increase **(negative correlation)**.

**NOTE**

 Strong correlation does not suggest that $X_1$ causes $X_2$ or $X_2$ causes $X_1$. We say **"correlation does not imply causation."**

# 13.2 | Testing the Significance of the Correlation Coefficient

The correlation coefficient, $r$, tells us about the strength and direction of the linear relationship between $X_1$ and $X_2$.

The sample data are used to compute $r$, the correlation coefficient for the sample. If we had data for the entire population, we could find the population correlation coefficient. But because we have only sample data, we cannot calculate the population correlation coefficient. The sample correlation coefficient, $r$, is our estimate of the unknown population correlation coefficient.

$\rho$ = population correlation coefficient (unknown)

$r$ = sample correlation coefficient (known; calculated from sample data)

The hypothesis test lets us decide whether the value of the population correlation coefficient $\rho$ is "close to zero" or "significantly different from zero". We decide this based on the sample correlation coefficient $r$ and the sample size $n$.

**If the test concludes that the correlation coefficient is significantly different from zero, we say that the correlation coefficient is "significant."**

- Conclusion: There is sufficient evidence to conclude that there is a significant linear relationship between $X_1$ and $X_2$ because the correlation coefficient is significantly different from zero.

- What the conclusion means: There is a significant linear relationship $X_1$ and $X_2$. If the test concludes that the correlation coefficient is not significantly different from zero (it is close to zero), we say that correlation coefficient is "not significant".

## Performing the Hypothesis Test
- **Null Hypothesis: $H_0$: $\rho = 0$**

- **Alternate Hypothesis: $H_a$: $\rho \neq 0$**

What the Hypotheses Mean in Words
- **Null Hypothesis $H_0$**: The population correlation coefficient IS NOT significantly different from zero. There IS NOT a significant linear relationship (correlation) between $X_1$ and $X_2$ in the population.

- **Alternate Hypothesis $H_a$**: The population correlation coefficient is significantly different from zero. There is a significant linear relationship (correlation) between $X_1$ and $X_2$ in the population.

### Drawing a Conclusion

There are two methods of making the decision concerning the hypothesis. The test statistic to test this hypothesis is:

$$t_c = \frac{r}{\sqrt{\frac{\left(1 - r^2\right)}{(n - 2)}}}$$

$$\text{OR}$$

$$t_c = \frac{r\sqrt{n - 2}}{\sqrt{1 - r^2}}$$

Where the second formula is an equivalent form of the test statistic, n is the sample size and the degrees of freedom are n-2. This is a t-statistic and operates in the same way as other t tests. Calculate the t-value and compare that with the critical value from the t-table at the appropriate degrees of freedom and the level of confidence you wish to maintain. If the calculated value is in the tail then cannot accept the null hypothesis that there is no linear relationship between these two independent random variables. If the calculated t-value is NOT in the tailed then cannot reject the null hypothesis that there is no linear relationship between the two variables.

A quick shorthand way to test correlations is the relationship between the sample size and the correlation. If:

$$|r| \geq \frac{2}{\sqrt{n}}$$

then this implies that the correlation between the two variables demonstrates that a linear relationship exists and is statistically significant at approximately the 0.05 level of significance. As the formula indicates, there is an inverse relationship between the sample size and the required correlation for significance of a linear relationship. With only 10 observations, the required correlation for significance is 0.6325, for 30 observations the required correlation for significance decreases to 0.3651 and at 100 observations the required level is only 0.2000.

Correlations may be helpful in visualizing the data, but are not appropriately used to "explain" a relationship between two variables. Perhaps no single statistic is more misused than the correlation coefficient. Citing correlations between health conditions and everything from place of residence to eye color have the effect of implying a cause and effect relationship. This simply cannot be accomplished with a correlation coefficient. The correlation coefficient is, of course, innocent of this misinterpretation. It is the duty of the analyst to use a statistic that is designed to test for cause and effect relationships and report only those results if they are intending to make such a claim. The problem is that passing this more rigorous test is difficult so lazy and/or unscrupulous "researchers" fall back on correlations when they cannot make their case legitimately.

# 13.3 | Linear Equations

Linear regression for two variables is based on a linear equation with one independent variable. The equation has the form:

$$y = a + bx$$

where $a$ and $b$ are constant numbers.

The variable $x$ **is the independent variable, and $y$ is the dependent variable.** Another way to think about this equation is a statement of cause and effect. The X variable is the cause and the Y variable is the hypothesized effect. Typically, you choose a value to substitute for the independent variable and then solve for the dependent variable.

---

### Example 13.1

The following examples are linear equations.

$$y = 3 + 2x$$
$$y = -0.01 + 1.2x$$

---

The graph of a linear equation of the form $y = a + bx$ is a **straight line**. Any line that is not vertical can be described by this equation.

## Example 13.2

Graph the equation $y = -1 + 2x$.

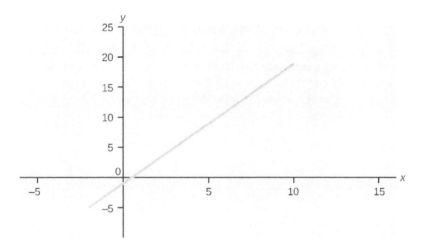

Figure 13.3

## Try It Σ

**13.2** Is the following an example of a linear equation? Why or why not?

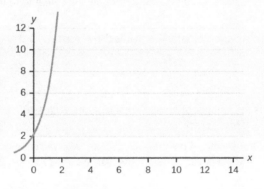

Figure 13.4

## Example 13.3

Aaron's Word Processing Service (AWPS) does word processing. The rate for services is $32 per hour plus a $31.50 one-time charge. The total cost to a customer depends on the number of hours it takes to complete the job.

Find the equation that expresses the **total cost** in terms of the **number of hours** required to complete the job.

### Solution 13.3

Let $x$ = the number of hours it takes to get the job done.
Let $y$ = the total cost to the customer.

The $31.50 is a fixed cost. If it takes $x$ hours to complete the job, then $(32)(x)$ is the cost of the word processing only. The total cost is: $y = 31.50 + 32x$

## Slope and *Y*-Intercept of a Linear Equation

For the linear equation $y = a + bx$, $b$ = slope and $a$ = $y$-intercept. From algebra recall that the slope is a number that describes the steepness of a line, and the $y$-intercept is the $y$ coordinate of the point $(0, a)$ where the line crosses the $y$-axis. From calculus the slope is the first derivative of the function. For a linear function the slope is $dy / dx = b$ where we can read the mathematical expression as "the change in $y$ $(dy)$ that results from a change in $x$ $(dx) = b * dx$".

**Figure 13.5** Three possible graphs of $y = a + bx$. (a) If $b > 0$, the line slopes upward to the right. (b) If $b = 0$, the line is horizontal. (c) If $b < 0$, the line slopes downward to the right.

### Example 13.4

Svetlana tutors to make extra money for college. For each tutoring session, she charges a one-time fee of $25 plus $15 per hour of tutoring. A linear equation that expresses the total amount of money Svetlana earns for each session she tutors is $y = 25 + 15x$.

What are the independent and dependent variables? What is the $y$-intercept and what is the slope? Interpret them using complete sentences.

#### Solution 13.4

The independent variable $(x)$ is the number of hours Svetlana tutors each session. The dependent variable $(y)$ is the amount, in dollars, Svetlana earns for each session.

The $y$-intercept is 25 $(a = 25)$. At the start of the tutoring session, Svetlana charges a one-time fee of $25 (this is when $x = 0$). The slope is 15 $(b = 15)$. For each session, Svetlana earns $15 for each hour she tutors.

## 13.4 | The Regression Equation

Regression analysis is a statistical technique that can test the hypothesis that a variable is dependent upon one or more other variables. Further, regression analysis can provide an estimate of the magnitude of the impact of a change in one variable on another. This last feature, of course, is all important in predicting future values.

Regression analysis is based upon a functional relationship among variables and further, assumes that the relationship is linear. This linearity assumption is required because, for the most part, the theoretical statistical properties of non-linear estimation are not well worked out yet by the mathematicians and econometricians. This presents us with some difficulties in economic analysis because many of our theoretical models are nonlinear. The marginal cost curve, for example, is decidedly nonlinear as is the total cost function, if we are to believe in the effect of specialization of labor and the Law of Diminishing Marginal Product. There are techniques for overcoming some of these difficulties, exponential and logarithmic transformation of the data for example, but at the outset we must recognize that standard ordinary least squares (OLS) regression analysis will always use a linear function to estimate what might be a nonlinear relationship.

The general linear regression model can be stated by the equation:

$$y_i = \beta_0 + \beta_1 X_{1i} + \beta_2 X_{2i} + \cdots + \beta_k X_{ki} + \varepsilon_i$$

where $\beta_0$ is the intercept, $\beta_i$'s are the slope between Y and the appropriate $X_i$, and $\varepsilon$ (pronounced epsilon), is the error term that captures errors in measurement of Y and the effect on Y of any variables missing from the equation that would contribute to explaining variations in Y. This equation is the theoretical population equation and therefore uses Greek letters. The equation we will estimate will have the Roman equivalent symbols. This is parallel to how we kept track of the population parameters and sample parameters before. The symbol for the population mean was $\mu$ and for the sample mean $\overline{X}$ and for the population standard deviation was $\sigma$ and for the sample standard deviation was s. The equation that will be estimated with a sample of data for two independent variables will thus be:

$$y_i = b_0 + b_1 x_{1i} + b_2 x_{2i} + e_i$$

As with our earlier work with probability distributions, this model works only if certain assumptions hold. These are that the Y is normally distributed, the errors are also normally distributed with a mean of zero and a constant standard deviation, and that the error terms are independent of the size of X and independent of each other.

## Assumptions of the Ordinary Least Squares Regression Model

Each of these assumptions needs a bit more explanation. If one of these assumptions fails to be true, then it will have an effect on the quality of the estimates. Some of the failures of these assumptions can be fixed while others result in estimates that quite simply provide no insight into the questions the model is trying to answer or worse, give biased estimates.

1. The independent variables, $x_i$ , are all measured without error, and are fixed numbers that are independent of the error term. This assumption is saying in effect that Y is deterministic, the result of a fixed component "X" and a random error component "$\varepsilon$."

2. The error term is a random variable with a mean of zero and a constant variance. The meaning of this is that the variances of the independent variables are independent of the value of the variable. Consider the relationship between personal income and the quantity of a good purchased as an example of a case where the variance is dependent upon the value of the independent variable, income. It is plausible that as income increases the variation around the amount purchased will also increase simply because of the flexibility provided with higher levels of income. The assumption is for constant variance with respect to the magnitude of the independent variable called homoscedasticity. If the assumption fails, then it is called heteroscedasticity. Figure 13.6 shows the case of homoscedasticity where all three distributions have the same variance around the predicted value of Y regardless of the magnitude of X.

3. While the independent variables are all fixed values they are from a probability distribution that is normally distributed. This can be seen in Figure 13.6 by the shape of the distributions placed on the predicted line at the expected value of the relevant value of Y.

4. The independent variables are independent of Y, but are also assumed to be independent of the other X variables. The model is designed to estimate the effects of independent variables on some dependent variable in accordance with a proposed theory. The case where some or more of the independent variables are correlated is not unusual. There may be no cause and effect relationship among the independent variables, but nevertheless they move together. Take the case of a simple supply curve where quantity supplied is theoretically related to the price of the product and the prices of inputs. There may be multiple inputs that may over time move together from general inflationary pressure. The input prices will therefore violate this assumption of regression analysis. This condition is called multicollinearity, which will be taken up in detail later.

5. The error terms are uncorrelated with each other. This situation arises from an effect on one error term from another error term. While not exclusively a time series problem, it is here that we most often see this case. An X variable in time period one has an effect on the Y variable, but this effect then has an effect in the next time period. This effect gives rise to a relationship among the error terms. This case is called autocorrelation, "self-correlated." The error terms are now not independent of each other, but rather have their own effect on subsequent error terms.

Figure 13.6 shows the case where the assumptions of the regression model are being satisfied. The estimated line is $\hat{y} = a + b$x. Three values of X are shown. A normal distribution is placed at each point where X equals the estimated line and the associated error at each value of Y. Notice that the three distributions are normally distributed around the point on the line, and further, the variation, variance, around the predicted value is constant indicating homoscedasticity from assumption 2. Figure 13.6 does not show all the assumptions of the regression model, but it helps visualize these important ones.

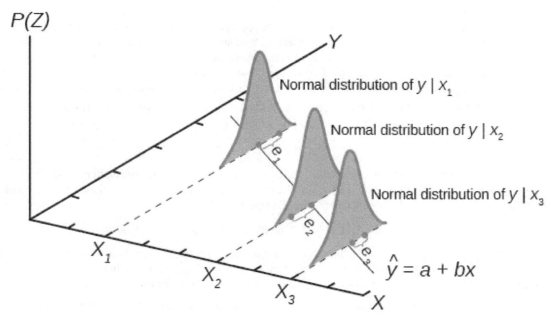

Figure 13.6

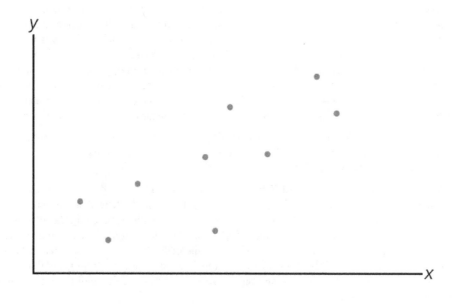

$$y = \beta_0 + \beta_1 X + \varepsilon$$

Figure 13.7

This is the general form that is most often called the multiple regression model. So-called "simple" regression analysis has only one independent (right-hand) variable rather than many independent variables. Simple regression is just a special case of multiple regression. There is some value in beginning with simple regression: it is easy to graph in two dimensions, difficult to graph in three dimensions, and impossible to graph in more than three dimensions. Consequently, our graphs will be for the simple regression case. **Figure 13.7** presents the regression problem in the form of a scatter plot graph of the data set where it is hypothesized that Y is dependent upon the single independent variable X.

A basic relationship from Macroeconomic Principles is the consumption function. This theoretical relationship states that as a person's income rises, their consumption rises, but by a smaller amount than the rise in income. If Y is consumption and X is income in the equation below **Figure 13.7**, the regression problem is, first, to establish that this relationship exists, and second, to determine the impact of a change in income on a person's consumption. The parameter $\beta_1$ was called the Marginal Propensity to Consume in Macroeconomics Principles.

Each "dot" in **Figure 13.7** represents the consumption and income of different individuals at some point in time. This was called cross-section data earlier; observations on variables at one point in time across different people or other units of measurement. This analysis is often done with time series data, which would be the consumption and income of one individual or country at different points in time. For macroeconomic problems it is common to use times series aggregated data for a whole country. For this particular theoretical concept these data are readily available in the annual report of the President's Council of Economic Advisors.

The regression problem comes down to determining which straight line would best represent the data in **Figure 13.8**. Regression analysis is sometimes called "least squares" analysis because the method of determining which line best "fits" the data is to minimize the sum of the squared residuals of a line put through the data.

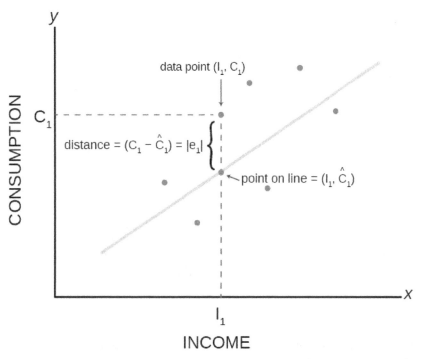

**Figure 13.8**
Population Equation: $C = \beta_0 + \beta_1$ Income $+ \varepsilon$
Estimated Equation: $C = b_0 + b_1$ Income $+ e$

This figure shows the assumed relationship between consumption and income from macroeconomic theory. Here the data are plotted as a scatter plot and an estimated straight line has been drawn. From this graph we can see an error term, $e_1$. Each data point also has an error term. Again, the error term is put into the equation to capture effects on consumption that are not caused by income changes. Such other effects might be a person's savings or wealth, or periods of unemployment. We will see how by minimizing the sum of these errors we can get an estimate for the slope and intercept of this line.

Consider the graph below. The notation has returned to that for the more general model rather than the specific case of the Macroeconomic consumption function in our example.

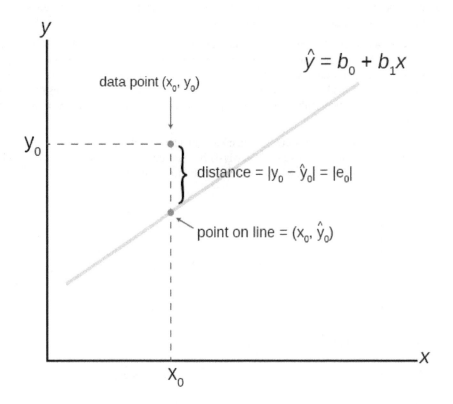

**Figure 13.9**

The $\hat{y}$ is read **"y hat"** and is the **estimated value of y**. (In **Figure 13.8** $\hat{C}$ represents the estimated value of consumption because it is on the estimated line.) It is the value of $y$ obtained using the regression line. $\hat{y}$ is not generally equal to $y$ from the data.

The term $y_0 - \hat{y}_0 = e_0$ is called the **"error" or residual**. It is not an error in the sense of a mistake. The error term was put into the estimating equation to capture missing variables and errors in measurement that may have occurred in the dependent variables. The **absolute value of a residual** measures the vertical distance between the actual value of $y$ and the estimated value of $y$. In other words, it measures the vertical distance between the actual data point and the predicted point on the line as can be seen on the graph at point $X_0$.

If the observed data point lies above the line, the residual is positive, and the line underestimates the actual data value for $y$.

If the observed data point lies below the line, the residual is negative, and the line overestimates that actual data value for $y$.

In the graph, $y_0 - \hat{y}_0 = e_0$ is the residual for the point shown. Here the point lies above the line and the residual is positive.

For each data point the residuals, or errors, are calculated $y_i - \hat{y}_i = e_i$ for i = 1, 2, 3, ..., n where n is the sample size. Each $|e|$ is a vertical distance.

The sum of the errors squared is the term obviously called **Sum of Squared Errors (SSE)**.

Using calculus, you can determine the straight line that has the parameter values of $b_0$ and $b_1$ that minimizes the **SSE**. When you make the **SSE** a minimum, you have determined the points that are on the line of best fit. It turns out that the line of best fit has the equation:

$$\hat{y} = b_0 + b_1 x$$

where $b_0 = \bar{y} - b_1 \bar{x}$ and $b_1 = \dfrac{\Sigma (x - \bar{x})(y - \bar{y})}{\Sigma (x - \bar{x})^2} = \dfrac{\text{cov}(x, y)}{s_x^{\,2}}$

The sample means of the $x$ values and the $y$ values are $\bar{x}$ and $\bar{y}$, respectively. The best fit line always passes through the point ($\bar{x}$, $\bar{y}$) called the points of means.

The slope $b$ can also be written as:

$$b_1 = r_{y,x}\left(\frac{s_y}{s_x}\right)$$

where $s_y$ = the standard deviation of the $y$ values and $s_x$ = the standard deviation of the $x$ values and $r$ is the correlation coefficient between $x$ and $y$.

These equations are called the Normal Equations and come from another very important mathematical finding called the Gauss-Markov Theorem without which we could not do regression analysis. The Gauss-Markov Theorem tells us that the estimates we get from using the ordinary least squares (OLS) regression method will result in estimates that have some very important properties. In the Gauss-Markov Theorem it was proved that a least squares line is BLUE, which is, **B**est, **L**inear, **U**nbiased, **E**stimator. Best is the statistical property that an estimator is the one with the minimum variance. Linear refers to the property of the type of line being estimated. An unbiased estimator is one whose estimating function has an expected mean equal to the mean of the population. (You will remember that the expected value of $\mu_{\bar{x}}$ was equal to the population mean $\mu$ in accordance with the Central Limit Theorem. This is exactly the same concept here).

Both Gauss and Markov were giants in the field of mathematics, and Gauss in physics too, in the $18^{th}$ century and early $19^{th}$ century. They barely overlapped chronologically and never in geography, but Markov's work on this theorem was based extensively on the earlier work of Carl Gauss. The extensive applied value of this theorem had to wait until the middle of this last century.

Using the OLS method we can now find the **estimate of the error variance** which is the variance of the squared errors, $e^2$. This is sometimes called the **standard error of the estimate**. (Grammatically this is probably best said as the estimate of the **error's** variance) The formula for the estimate of the error variance is:

$$s_e^2 = \frac{\Sigma(y_i - \hat{y}_i)^2}{n-k} = \frac{\Sigma e_i^2}{n-k}$$

where $\hat{y}$ is the predicted value of y and y is the observed value, and thus the term $(y_i - \hat{y}_i)^2$ is the squared errors that are to be minimized to find the estimates of the regression line parameters. This is really just the variance of the error terms and follows our regular variance formula. One important note is that here we are dividing by $(n-k)$, which is the degrees of freedom. The degrees of freedom of a regression equation will be the number of observations, n, reduced by the number of estimated parameters, which includes the intercept as a parameter.

The variance of the errors is fundamental in testing hypotheses for a regression. It tells us just how "tight" the dispersion is about the line. As we will see shortly, the greater the dispersion about the line, meaning the larger the variance of the errors, the less probable that the hypothesized independent variable will be found to have a significant effect on the dependent variable. In short, the theory being tested will more likely fail if the variance of the error term is high. Upon reflection this should not be a surprise. As we tested hypotheses about a mean we observed that large variances reduced the calculated test statistic and thus it failed to reach the tail of the distribution. In those cases, the null hypotheses could not be rejected. If we cannot reject the null hypothesis in a regression problem, we must conclude that the hypothesized independent variable has no effect on the dependent variable.

A way to visualize this concept is to draw two scatter plots of x and y data along a predetermined line. The first will have little variance of the errors, meaning that all the data points will move close to the line. Now do the same except the data points will have a large estimate of the error variance, meaning that the data points are scattered widely along the line. Clearly the confidence about a relationship between x and y is effected by this difference between the estimate of the error variance.

## Testing the Parameters of the Line

The whole goal of the regression analysis was to test the hypothesis that the dependent variable, Y, was in fact dependent upon the values of the independent variables as asserted by some foundation theory, such as the consumption function example. Looking at the estimated equation under **Figure 13.8**, we see that this amounts to determining the values of $b_0$ and $b_1$. Notice that again we are using the convention of Greek letters for the population parameters and Roman letters for their estimates.

The regression analysis output provided by the computer software will produce an estimate of $b_0$ and $b_1$, and any other b's for other independent variables that were included in the estimated equation. The issue is how good are these estimates? In order to test a hypothesis concerning any estimate, we have found that we need to know the underlying sampling distribution. It should come as no surprise at his stage in the course that the answer is going to be the normal distribution. This can be seen by remembering the assumption that the error term in the population, $\varepsilon$, is normally distributed. If the error term is normally distributed and the variance of the estimates of the equation parameters, $b_0$ and $b_1$, are determined by the variance of the error term, it follows that the variances of the parameter estimates are also normally distributed. And indeed this is just the case.

We can see this by the creation of the test statistic for the test of hypothesis for the slope parameter, $\beta_1$ in our consumption function equation. To test whether or not Y does indeed depend upon X, or in our example, that consumption depends upon income, we need only test the hypothesis that $\beta_1$ equals zero. This hypothesis would be stated formally as:

$$H_0 : \beta_1 = 0$$
$$H_a : \beta_1 \neq 0$$

If we cannot reject the null hypothesis, we must conclude that our theory has no validity. If we cannot reject the null hypothesis that $\beta_1 = 0$ then $b_1$, the coefficient of Income, is zero and zero times anything is zero. Therefore the effect of Income on Consumption is zero. There is no relationship as our theory had suggested.

Notice that we have set up the presumption, the null hypothesis, as "no relationship". This puts the burden of proof on the alternative hypothesis. In other words, if we are to validate our claim of finding a relationship, we must do so with a level of significance greater than 90, 95, or 99 percent. The *status quo* is ignorance, no relationship exists, and to be able to make the claim that we have actually added to our body of knowledge we must do so with significant probability of being correct. John Maynard Keynes got it right and thus was born Keynesian economics starting with this basic concept in 1936.

The test statistic for this test comes directly from our old friend the standardizing formula:

$$t_c = \frac{b_1 - \beta_1}{S_{b_1}}$$

where $b_1$ is the estimated value of the slope of the regression line, $\beta_1$ is the hypothesized value of beta, in this case zero, and $S_{b_1}$ is the standard deviation of the estimate of $b_1$. In this case we are asking how many standard deviations is the estimated slope away from the hypothesized slope. This is exactly the same question we asked before with respect to a hypothesis about a mean: how many standard deviations is the estimated mean, the sample mean, from the hypothesized mean?

The test statistic is written as a student's t distribution, but if the sample size is larger enough so that the degrees of freedom are greater than 30 we may again use the normal distribution. To see why we can use the student's t or normal distribution we have only to look at $S_{b_1}$ ,the formula for the standard deviation of the estimate of $b_1$:

$$S_{b_1} = \frac{S_e^2}{\sqrt{(x_i - \bar{x})^2}}$$

or

$$S_{b_1} = \frac{S_e^2}{(n-1)S_x^2}$$

Where $S_e$ is the estimate of the error variance and $S^2_x$ is the variance of x values of the coefficient of the independent variable being tested.

We see that $S_e$, the **estimate of the error variance**, is part of the computation. Because the estimate of the error variance is based on the assumption of normality of the error terms, we can conclude that the sampling distribution of the b's, the coefficients of our hypothesized regression line, are also normally distributed.

One last note concerns the degrees of freedom of the test statistic, $\nu = n-k$. Previously we subtracted 1 from the sample size to determine the degrees of freedom in a student's t problem. Here we must subtract one degree of freedom for each parameter estimated in the equation. For the example of the consumption function we lose 2 degrees of freedom, one for $b_0$, the intercept, and one for $b_1$, the slope of the consumption function. The degrees of freedom would be n - k - 1, where k is the number of independent variables and the extra one is lost because of the intercept. If we were estimating an equation with three independent variables, we would lose 4 degrees of freedom: three for the independent variables, k, and one more for the intercept.

The decision rule for acceptance or rejection of the null hypothesis follows exactly the same form as in all our previous test of hypothesis. Namely, if the calculated value of t (or Z) falls into the tails of the distribution, where the tails are defined by $\alpha$ ,the required significance level in the test, we cannot accept the null hypothesis. If on the other hand, the calculated value of the test statistic is within the critical region, we cannot reject the null hypothesis.

If we conclude that we cannot accept the null hypothesis, we are able to state with $(1 - \alpha)$ level of confidence that the slope of the line is given by $b_1$. This is an extremely important conclusion. Regression analysis not only allows us to test if a cause and effect relationship exists, we can also determine the magnitude of that relationship, if one is found to exist. It is this feature of regression analysis that makes it so valuable. If models can be developed that have statistical validity, we are then able to simulate the effects of changes in variables that may be under our control with some degree of probability , of course. For example, if advertising is demonstrated to effect sales, we can determine the effects of changing the advertising budget and decide if the increased sales are worth the added expense.

## Multicollinearity

Our discussion earlier indicated that like all statistical models, the OLS regression model has important assumptions attached. Each assumption, if violated, has an effect on the ability of the model to provide useful and meaningful estimates. The Gauss-Markov Theorem has assured us that the OLS estimates are unbiased and minimum variance, but this is true only under the assumptions of the model. Here we will look at the effects on OLS estimates if the independent variables are correlated. The other assumptions and the methods to mitigate the difficulties they pose if they are found to be violated are examined in Econometrics courses. We take up multicollinearity because it is so often prevalent in Economic models and it often leads to frustrating results.

The OLS model assumes that all the independent variables are independent of each other. This assumption is easy to test for a particular sample of data with simple correlation coefficients. Correlation, like much in statistics, is a matter of degree: a little is not good, and a lot is terrible.

The goal of the regression technique is to tease out the independent impacts of each of a set of independent variables on some hypothesized dependent variable. If two 2 independent variables are interrelated, that is, correlated, then we cannot isolate the effects on Y of one from the other. In an extreme case where $x_1$ is a linear combination of $x_2$, correlation equal to one, both variables move in identical ways with Y. In this case it is impossible to determine the variable that is the true cause of the effect on Y. (If the two variables were actually perfectly correlated, then mathematically no regression results could actually be calculated.)

The normal equations for the coefficients show the effects of multicollinearity on the coefficients.

$$b_1 = \frac{s_y\left(r_{x_1 y} - r_{x_1 x_2} r_{x_2 y}\right)}{s_{x_1}\left(1 - r_{x_1 x_2}^2\right)}$$

$$b_2 = \frac{s_y\left(r_{x_2 y} - r_{x_1 x_2} r_{x_1 y}\right)}{s_{x_2}\left(1 - r_{x_1 x_2}^2\right)}$$

$$b_0 = \bar{y} - b_1 \bar{x}_1 - b_2 \bar{x}_2$$

The correlation between $x_1$ and $x_2$, $r_{x_1 x_2}^2$, appears in the denominator of both the estimating formula for $b_1$ and $b_2$ . If the assumption of independence holds, then this term is zero. This indicates that there is no effect of the correlation on the coefficient. On the other hand, as the correlation between the two independent variables increases the denominator decreases, and thus the estimate of the coefficient increases. The correlation has the same effect on both of the coefficients of these two variables. In essence, each variable is "taking" part of the effect on Y that should be attributed to the collinear variable. This results in biased estimates.

Multicollinearity has a further deleterious impact on the OLS estimates. The correlation between the two independent variables also shows up in the formulas for the estimate of the variance for the coefficients.

$$s_{b_1}^2 = \frac{s_e^2}{(n - 1)s_{x_1}^2\left(1 - r_{x_1 x_2}^2\right)}$$

$$s_{b_2}^2 = \frac{s_e^2}{(n - 1)s_{x_2}^2\left(1 - r_{x_1 x_2}^2\right)}$$

Here again we see the correlation between $x_1$ and $x_2$ in the denominator of the estimates of the variance for the coefficients for both variables. If the correlation is zero as assumed in the regression model, then the formula collapses to the familiar ratio of the variance of the errors to the variance of the relevant independent variable. If however the two independent variables are correlated, then the variance of the estimate of the coefficient increases. This results in a smaller t-value for the test of hypothesis of the coefficient. In short, multicollinearity results in failing to reject the null hypothesis that the X variable has no impact on Y when in fact X does have a statistically significant impact on Y. Said another way, the large standard errors of the estimated coefficient created by multicollinearity suggest statistical insignificance even when the hypothesized relationship is strong.

## How Good is the Equation?

In the last section we concerned ourselves with testing the hypothesis that the dependent variable did indeed depend upon the hypothesized independent variable or variables. It may be that we find an independent variable that has some effect on the dependent variable, but it may not be the only one, and it may not even be the most important one. Remember that the error term was placed in the model to capture the effects of any missing independent variables. It follows that the error term may be used to give a measure of the "goodness of fit" of the equation taken as a whole in explaining the variation of the dependent variable, Y.

The **multiple correlation coefficient**, also called the **coefficient of multiple determination** or the **coefficient of determination**, is given by the formula:

$$R^2 = \frac{SSR}{SST}$$

where SSR is the regression sum of squares, the squared deviation of the predicted value of y from the mean value of y $(\hat{y} - \bar{y})$, and SST is the total sum of squares which is the total squared deviation of the dependent variable, y, from its mean value, including the error term, SSE, the sum of squared errors. **Figure 13.10** shows how the total deviation of the dependent variable, y, is partitioned into these two pieces.

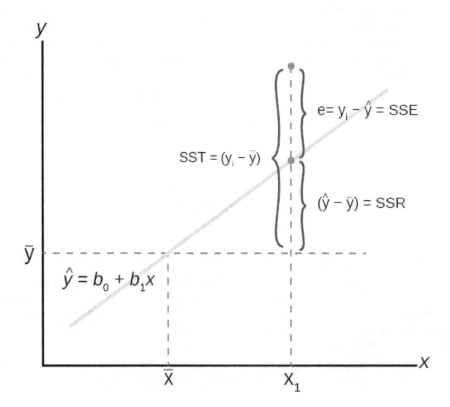

**Figure 13.10**

**Figure 13.10** shows the estimated regression line and a single observation, $x_1$. Regression analysis tries to explain the variation of the data about the mean value of the dependent variable, y. The question is, why do the observations of y vary from the average level of y? The value of y at observation $x_1$ varies from the mean of y by the difference $(y_i - \bar{y})$. The sum of these differences squared is SST, the sum of squares total. The actual value of y at $x_1$ deviates from the estimated value, $\hat{y}$, by the difference between the estimated value and the actual value, $(y_i - \hat{y})$. We recall that this is the error term, e, and the sum of these errors is SSE, sum of squared errors. The deviation of the predicted value of y, $\hat{y}$, from the mean value of y is $(\hat{y} - \bar{y})$ and is the SSR, sum of squares regression. It is called "regression" because it is the deviation explained by the regression. (Sometimes the SSR is called SSM for sum of squares mean because it measures the deviation from the mean value of the dependent variable, y, as shown on the graph.).

Because the SST = SSR + SSE we see that the multiple correlation coefficient is the percent of the variance, or deviation in y from its mean value, that is explained by the equation when taken as a whole. $R^2$ will vary between zero and 1, with zero indicating that none of the variation in y was explained by the equation and a value of 1 indicating that 100% of the variation in y was explained by the equation. For time series studies expect a high $R^2$ and for cross-section data expect low $R^2$.

While a high $R^2$ is desirable, remember that it is the tests of the hypothesis concerning the existence of a relationship between a set of independent variables and a particular dependent variable that was the motivating factor in using the regression model. It is validating a cause and effect relationship developed by some theory that is the true reason that we chose the regression analysis. Increasing the number of independent variables will have the effect of increasing $R^2$. To account for this effect the proper measure of the coefficient of determination is the $\bar{R}^2$, adjusted for degrees of freedom, to keep down mindless addition of independent variables.

There is no statistical test for the $R^2$ and thus little can be said about the model using $R^2$ with our characteristic confidence level. Two models that have the same size of SSE, that is sum of squared errors, may have very different $R^2$ if the competing models have different SST, total sum of squared deviations. The goodness of fit of the two models is the same; they both have the same sum of squares unexplained, errors squared, but because of the larger total sum of squares on one of the models the $R^2$ differs. Again, the real value of regression as a tool is to examine hypotheses developed from a model that predicts certain relationships among the variables. These are tests of hypotheses on the coefficients of the model and not a game of maximizing $R^2$.

Another way to test the general quality of the overall model is to test the coefficients as a group rather than independently. Because this is multiple regression (more than one X), we use the F-test to determine if our coefficients collectively affect Y. The hypothesis is:

$H_o : \beta_1 = \beta_2 = \ldots = \beta_i = 0$

$H_a :$ "at least one of the βi is not equal to 0"

If the null hypothesis cannot be rejected, then we conclude that none of the independent variables contribute to explaining the variation in Y. Reviewing **Figure 13.10** we see that SSR, the explained sum of squares, is a measure of just how much of the variation in Y is explained by all the variables in the model. SSE, the sum of the errors squared, measures just how much is unexplained. It follows that the ratio of these two can provide us with a statistical test of the model as a whole. Remembering that the F distribution is a ratio of Chi squared distributions and that variances are distributed according to Chi Squared, and the sum of squared errors and the sum of squares are both variances, we have the test statistic for this hypothesis as:

$$F_c = \frac{\left(\frac{SSR}{k}\right)}{\left(\frac{SSE}{n-k-1}\right)}$$

where $n$ is the number of observations and $k$ is the number of independent variables. It can be shown that this is equivalent to:

$$F_c = \frac{n-k-1}{k} * \frac{R^2}{1-R^2}$$

building from **Figure 13.10** where $R^2$ is the coefficient of determination which is also a measure of the "goodness" of the model.

As with all our tests of hypothesis, we reach a conclusion by comparing the calculated F statistic with the critical value given our desired level of confidence. If the calculated test statistic, an F statistic in this case, is in the tail of the distribution, then we cannot accept the null hypothesis. By not being able to accept the null hypotheses we conclude that this specification of this model has validity, because at least one of the estimated coefficients is significantly different from zero.

An alternative way to reach this conclusion is to use the p-value comparison rule. The p-value is the area in the tail, given the calculated F statistic. In essence, the computer is finding the F value in the table for us. The computer regression output for the calculated F statistic is typically found in the ANOVA table section labeled "significance F". How to read the output of an Excel regression is presented below. This is the probability of NOT accepting a false null hypothesis. If this probability is less than our pre-determined alpha error, then the conclusion is that we cannot accept the null hypothesis.

## Dummy Variables

Thus far the analysis of the OLS regression technique assumed that the independent variables in the models tested were continuous random variables. There are, however, no restrictions in the regression model against independent variables that are binary. This opens the regression model for testing hypotheses concerning categorical variables such as gender, race, region of the country, before a certain data, after a certain date and innumerable others. These categorical variables take on only two values, 1 and 0, success or failure, from the binomial probability distribution. The form of the equation becomes:

$$\hat{y} = b_0 + b_2 x_2 + b_1 x_1$$

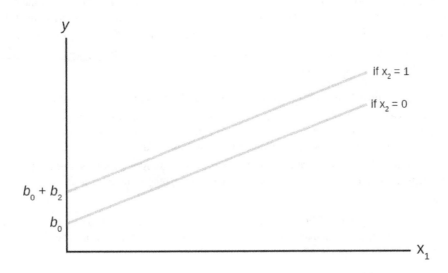

**Figure 13.11**

where $x_2 = 0, 1$. $X_2$ is the dummy variable and $X_1$ is some continuous random variable. The constant, $b_0$, is the y-intercept, the value where the line crosses the y-axis. When the value of $X_2 = 0$, the estimated line crosses at $b_0$. When the value of $X_2 = 1$ then the estimated line crosses at $b_0 + b_2$. In effect the dummy variable causes the estimated line to shift either up or down by the size of the effect of the characteristic captured by the dummy variable. Note that this is a simple parallel shift and does not affect the impact of the other independent variable; $X_1$. This variable is a continuous random variable and predicts different values of y at different values of $X_1$ holding constant the condition of the dummy variable.

An example of the use of a dummy variable is the work estimating the impact of gender on salaries. There is a full body of literature on this topic and dummy variables are used extensively. For this example the salaries of elementary and secondary school teachers for a particular state is examined. Using a homogeneous job category, school teachers, and for a single state reduces many of the variations that naturally effect salaries such as differential physical risk, cost of living in a particular state, and other working conditions. The estimating equation in its simplest form specifies salary as a function of various teacher characteristic that economic theory would suggest could affect salary. These would include education level as a measure of potential productivity, age and/or experience to capture on-the-job training, again as a measure of productivity. Because the data are for school teachers employed in a public school districts rather than workers in a for-profit company, the school district's average revenue per average daily student attendance is included as a measure of ability to pay. The results of the regression analysis using data on 24,916 school teachers are presented below.

| Variable | Regression Coefficients (b) | Standard Errors of the Estimates for Teacher's Earnings Function (s_b) |
|---|---|---|
| Intercept | 4269.9 | |
| Gender (male = 1) | 632.38 | 13.39 |
| Total Years of Experience | 52.32 | 1.10 |
| Years of Experience in Current District | 29.97 | 1.52 |
| Education | 629.33 | 13.16 |
| Total Revenue per ADA | 90.24 | 3.76 |
| $\bar{R}^2$ | .725 | |
| n | 24,916 | |

**Table 13.1 Earnings Estimate for Elementary and Secondary School Teachers**

The coefficients for all the independent variables are significantly different from zero as indicated by the standard errors. Dividing the standard errors of each coefficient results in a t-value greater than 1.96 which is the required level for 95% significance. The binary variable, our dummy variable of interest in this analysis, is gender where male is given a value of 1 and female given a value of 0. The coefficient is significantly different from zero with a dramatic t-statistic of 47 standard deviations. We thus cannot accept the null hypothesis that the coefficient is equal to zero. Therefore we conclude that there is a premium paid male teachers of $632 after holding constant experience, education and the wealth of the school district in which the teacher is employed. It is important to note that these data are from some time ago and the $632 represents a six percent salary premium at that time. A graph of this example of dummy variables is presented below.

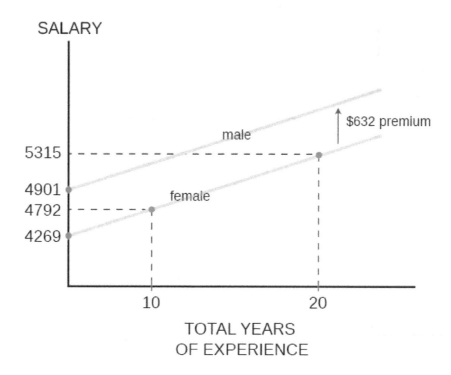

**Figure 13.12**

In two dimensions, salary is the dependent variable on the vertical axis and total years of experience was chosen for the continuous independent variable on horizontal axis. Any of the other independent variables could have been chosen to illustrate the effect of the dummy variable. The relationship between total years of experience has a slope of $52.32 per year of experience and the estimated line has an intercept of $4,269 if the gender variable is equal to zero, for female. If the gender variable is equal to 1, for male, the coefficient for the gender variable is added to the intercept and thus the relationship between total years of experience and salary is shifted upward parallel as indicated on the graph. Also marked on the graph are various points for reference. A female school teacher with 10 years of experience receives a salary of $4,792 on the basis of her experience only, but this is still $109 less than a male teacher with zero years of experience.

A more complex interaction between a dummy variable and the dependent variable can also be estimated. It may be that the dummy variable has more than a simple shift effect on the dependent variable, but also interacts with one or more of the other continuous independent variables. While not tested in the example above, it could be hypothesized that the impact of gender on salary was not a one-time shift, but impacted the value of additional years of experience on salary also. That is, female school teacher's salaries were discounted at the start, and further did not grow at the same rate from the effect of experience as for male school teachers. This would show up as a different slope for the relationship between total years of experience for males than for females. If this is so then females school teachers would not just start behind their male colleagues (as measured by the shift in the estimated regression line), but would fall further and further behind as time and experienced increased.

The graph below shows how this hypothesis can be tested with the use of dummy variables and an interaction variable.

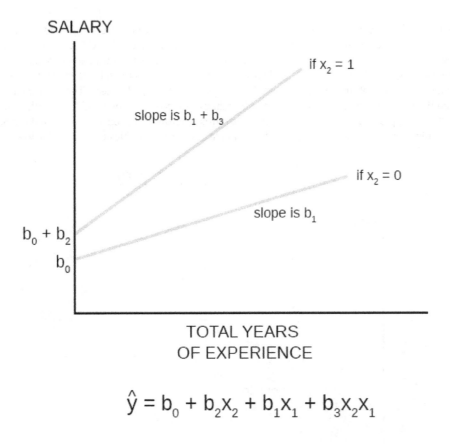

$$\hat{y} = b_0 + b_2 x_2 + b_1 x_1 + b_3 x_2 x_1$$

Figure 13.13

The estimating equation shows how the slope of $X_1$, the continuous random variable experience, contains two parts, $b_1$ and $b_3$. This occurs because of the new variable $X_2 X_1$, called the interaction variable, was created to allow for an effect on the slope of $X_1$ from changes in $X_2$, the binary dummy variable. Note that when the dummy variable, $X_2 = 0$ the interaction variable has a value of 0, but when $X_2 = 1$ the interaction variable has a value of $X_1$. The coefficient $b_3$ is an estimate of the difference in the coefficient of $X_1$ when $X_2 = 1$ compared to when $X_2 = 0$. In the example of teacher's salaries, if there is a premium paid to male teachers that affects the rate of increase in salaries from experience, then the rate at which male teachers' salaries rises would be $b_1 + b_3$ and the rate at which female teachers' salaries rise would be simply $b_1$. This hypothesis can be tested with the hypothesis:

$$H_0 : \beta_3 = 0 | \beta_1 = 0, \; \beta_2 = 0$$
$$H_a : \beta_3 \neq 0 | \beta_1 \neq 0, \; \beta_2 \neq 0$$

This is a t-test using the test statistic for the parameter β3. If we cannot accept the null hypothesis that β3=0 we conclude there is a difference between the rate of increase for the group for whom the value of the binary variable is set to 1, males in this example. This estimating equation can be combined with our earlier one that tested only a parallel shift in the estimated line. The earnings/experience functions in **Figure 13.13** are drawn for this case with a shift in the earnings function and a difference in the slope of the function with respect to total years of experience.

## Example 13.5

A random sample of 11 statistics students produced the following data, where *x* is the third exam score out of 80, and *y* is the final exam score out of 200. Can you predict the final exam score of a randomly selected student if you know the third exam score?

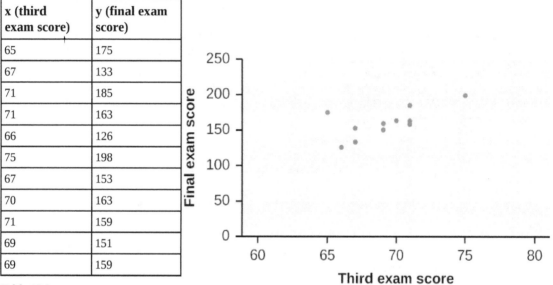

| x (third exam score) | y (final exam score) |
|---|---|
| 65 | 175 |
| 67 | 133 |
| 71 | 185 |
| 71 | 163 |
| 66 | 126 |
| 75 | 198 |
| 67 | 153 |
| 70 | 163 |
| 71 | 159 |
| 69 | 151 |
| 69 | 159 |

Table 13.2

(b) Scatter plot showing the scores on the final exam based on scores from the third exam.

(a) Table showing the scores on the final exam based on scores from the third exam.

Figure 13.14

# 13.5 | Interpretation of Regression Coefficients: Elasticity and Logarithmic Transformation

As we have seen, the coefficient of an equation estimated using OLS regression analysis provides an estimate of the slope of a straight line that is assumed be the relationship between the dependent variable and at least one independent variable. From the calculus, the slope of the line is the first derivative and tells us the magnitude of the impact of a one unit change in the *X* variable upon the value of the *Y* variable measured in the units of the *Y* variable. As we saw in the case of dummy variables, this can show up as a parallel shift in the estimated line or even a change in the slope of the line through an interactive variable. Here we wish to explore the concept of elasticity and how we can use a regression analysis to estimate the various elasticities in which economists have an interest.

The concept of elasticity is borrowed from engineering and physics where it is used to measure a material's responsiveness to a force, typically a physical force such as a stretching/pulling force. It is from here that we get the term an "elastic" band. In economics, the force in question is some market force such as a change in price or income. Elasticity is measured as a percentage change/response in both engineering applications and in economics. The value of measuring in percentage terms is that the units of measurement do not play a role in the value of the measurement and thus allows direct comparison between elasticities. As an example, if the price of gasoline increased say 50 cents from an initial price of $3.00 and generated a decline in monthly consumption for a consumer from 50 gallons to 48 gallons we calculate the elasticity to be 0.25. The price elasticity is the percentage change in quantity resulting from some percentage change in price. A 16 percent increase in price has generated only a 4 percent decrease in demand: 16% price change → 4% quantity change or .04/.16 = .25. This is called an inelastic demand meaning a small response to the price change. This comes about because there are few if any real substitutes for gasoline; perhaps public transportation, a bicycle or walking. Technically, of course, the percentage change in demand from a price increase is a decline in demand thus price elasticity is a negative number. The common convention, however, is to talk about elasticity as the absolute value of the number. Some goods have many substitutes: pears for apples for plums, for grapes, etc. etc. The elasticity for such goods is larger than one and are called elastic in demand. Here a small percentage change in price will induce a large percentage change in quantity demanded. The consumer will easily shift the demand to the close substitute.

While this discussion has been about price changes, any of the independent variables in a demand equation will have an associated elasticity. Thus, there is an income elasticity that measures the sensitivity of demand to changes in income: not much for the demand for food, but very sensitive for yachts. If the demand equation contains a term for substitute goods, say candy bars in a demand equation for cookies, then the responsiveness of demand for cookies from changes in prices of candy bars can be measured. This is called the cross-price elasticity of demand and to an extent can be thought of as brand loyalty from a marketing view. How responsive is the demand for Coca-Cola to changes in the price of Pepsi?

Now imagine the demand for a product that is very expensive. Again, the measure of elasticity is in percentage terms thus the elasticity can be directly compared to that for gasoline: an elasticity of 0.25 for gasoline conveys the same information as an elasticity of 0.25 for $25,000 car. Both goods are considered by the consumer to have few substitutes and thus have inelastic demand curves, elasticities less than one.

The mathematical formulae for various elasticities are:

$$\text{Price elasticity:} \eta_p = \frac{(\%\Delta Q)}{(\%\Delta P)}$$

Where $\eta$ is the Greek small case letter eta used to designate elasticity. $\Delta$ is read as "change".

$$\text{Income elasticity:} \eta_Y = \frac{(\%\Delta Q)}{(\%\Delta Y)}$$

Where Y is used as the symbol for income.

$$\text{Cross-Price elasticity:} \eta_{p1} = \frac{(\%\Delta Q_1)}{(\%\Delta P_2)}$$

Where P2 is the price of the substitute good.

Examining closer the price elasticity we can write the formula as:

$$\eta_p = \frac{(\%\Delta Q)}{(\%\Delta P)} = \frac{dQ}{dP}\left(\frac{P}{Q}\right) = b\left(\frac{P}{Q}\right)$$

Where $b$ is the estimated coefficient for price in the OLS regression.

The first form of the equation demonstrates the principle that elasticities are measured in percentage terms. Of course, the ordinary least squares coefficients provide an estimate of the impact of a unit change in the independent variable, X, on the dependent variable measured in units of Y. These coefficients are not elasticities, however, and are shown in the second way of writing the formula for elasticity as $\left(\frac{dQ}{dP}\right)$, the derivative of the estimated demand function which is simply the slope of the regression line. Multiplying the slope times $\frac{P}{Q}$ provides an elasticity measured in percentage terms.

Along a straight-line demand curve the percentage change, thus elasticity, changes continuously as the scale changes, while the slope, the estimated regression coefficient, remains constant. Going back to the demand for gasoline. A change in price from $3.00 to $3.50 was a 16 percent increase in price. If the beginning price were $5.00 then the same 50¢ increase would be only a 10 percent increase generating a different elasticity. Every straight-line demand curve has a range of elasticities starting at the top left, high prices, with large elasticity numbers, elastic demand, and decreasing as one goes down the demand curve, inelastic demand.

In order to provide a meaningful estimate of the elasticity of demand the convention is to estimate the elasticity at the point of means. Remember that all OLS regression lines will go through the point of means. At this point is the greatest weight of the data used to estimate the coefficient. The formula to estimate an elasticity when an OLS demand curve has been estimated becomes:

$$\eta_p = b\left(\frac{\bar{P}}{\bar{Q}}\right)$$

Where $\bar{P}$ and $\bar{Q}$ are the mean values of these data used to estimate $b$, the price coefficient.

The same method can be used to estimate the other elasticities for the demand function by using the appropriate mean values of the other variables; income and price of substitute goods for example.

## Logarithmic Transformation of the Data

Ordinary least squares estimates typically assume that the population relationship among the variables is linear thus of the form presented in **The Regression Equation**. In this form the interpretation of the coefficients is as discussed above; quite simply the coefficient provides an estimate of the impact of a one **unit** change in X on Y measured in **units** of Y. It does not matter just where along the line one wishes to make the measurement because it is a straight line with a constant slope thus constant estimated level of impact per unit change. It may be, however, that the analyst wishes to estimate not the simple unit measured impact on the Y variable, but the magnitude of the percentage impact on Y of a one unit change in the X variable. Such a case might be how a **unit change** in experience, say one year, effects not the absolute amount of a worker's wage, but the **percentage impact** on the worker's wage. Alternatively, it may be that the question asked is the unit measured impact on Y of a specific percentage increase in X. An example may be "by how many dollars will sales increase if the firm spends X percent more on advertising?" The third possibility is the case of elasticity discussed above. Here we are interested in the percentage impact on quantity demanded for a given percentage change in price, or income or perhaps the price of a substitute good. All three of these cases can be estimated by transforming the data to logarithms before running the regression. The resulting coefficients will then provide a percentage change measurement of the relevant variable.

To summarize, there are four cases:

1. Unit $\Delta X \rightarrow$ Unit $\Delta Y$ (Standard OLS case)

2. Unit $\Delta X \rightarrow \%\Delta Y$

3. $\%\Delta X \rightarrow$ Unit $\Delta Y$

4. $\%\Delta X \rightarrow \%\Delta Y$ (elasticity case)

Case 1: The ordinary least squares case begins with the linear model developed above:

$$Y = a + bX$$

where the coefficient of the independent variable $b = \frac{dY}{dX}$ is the slope of a straight line and thus measures the impact of a unit change in X on Y measured in units of Y.

Case 2: The underlying estimated equation is:

$$\log(Y) = a + bX$$

The equation is estimated by converting the Y values to logarithms and using OLS techniques to estimate the coefficient of the X variable, b. This is called a semi-log estimation. Again, differentiating both sides of the equation allows us to develop the interpretation of the X coefficient b:

$$d(\log_Y) = bdX$$

$$\frac{dY}{Y} = bdX$$

Multiply by 100 to covert to percentages and rearranging terms gives:

$$100b = \frac{\%\Delta Y}{\text{Unit } \Delta X}$$

$100b$ is thus the percentage change in Y resulting from a unit change in X.

Case 3: In this case the question is "what is the unit change in Y resulting from a percentage change in X?" What is the dollar loss in revenues of a five percent increase in price or what is the total dollar cost impact of a five percent increase in labor costs? The estimated equation for this case would be:

$$Y = a + B\log(X)$$

Here the calculus differential of the estimated equation is:

$$dY = bd(\log X)$$

$$dY = b\frac{dX}{X}$$

Divide by 100 to get percentage and rearranging terms gives:

$$\frac{b}{100} = \frac{dY}{100\frac{dX}{X}} = \frac{\text{Unit } \Delta Y}{\%\Delta X}$$

Therefore, $\frac{b}{100}$ is the increase in Y measured in units from a one percent increase in X.

Case 4: This is the elasticity case where both the dependent and independent variables are converted to logs before the OLS estimation. This is known as the log-log case or double log case, and provides us with direct estimates of the elasticities of the independent variables. The estimated equation is:

$$\log Y = a + b\log X$$

Differentiating we have:

$$d(\log Y) = bd(\log X)$$

$$d(\log X) = b\frac{1}{X}dX$$

thus:

$$\frac{1}{Y}dY = b\frac{1}{X}dX \quad \text{OR} \quad \frac{dY}{Y} = b\frac{dX}{X} \quad \text{OR} \quad b = \frac{dY}{dX}\left(\frac{X}{Y}\right)$$

and $b = \frac{\%\Delta Y}{\%\Delta X}$ our definition of elasticity. We conclude that we can directly estimate the elasticity of a variable through double log transformation of the data. The estimated coefficient is the elasticity. It is common to use double log transformation of all variables in the estimation of demand functions to get estimates of all the various elasticities of the demand curve.

# 13.6 | Predicting with a Regression Equation

One important value of an estimated regression equation is its ability to predict the effects on Y of a change in one or more values of the independent variables. The value of this is obvious. Careful policy cannot be made without estimates of the effects that may result. Indeed, it is the desire for particular results that drive the formation of most policy. Regression models can be, and have been, invaluable aids in forming such policies.

The Gauss-Markov theorem assures us that the point estimate of the impact on the dependent variable derived by putting in the equation the hypothetical values of the independent variables one wishes to simulate will result in an estimate of the dependent variable which is minimum variance and unbiased. That is to say that from this equation comes the best unbiased point estimate of y given the values of x.

$$\hat{y} = b_0 + b, X_{1i} + \cdots + b_k X_{ki}$$

Remember that point estimates do not carry a particular level of probability, or level of confidence, because points have no "width" above which there is an area to measure. This was why we developed confidence intervals for the mean and proportion earlier. The same concern arises here also. There are actually two different approaches to the issue of developing estimates of changes in the independent variable, or variables, on the dependent variable. The first approach wishes to measure the **expected mean** value of y from a specific change in the value of x: this specific value implies the expected value. Here the question is: what is the **mean** impact on y that would result from multiple hypothetical experiments on y at this specific value of x. Remember that there is a variance around the estimated parameter of x and thus each experiment will result in a bit of a different estimate of the predicted value of y.

The second approach to estimate the effect of a specific value of x on y treats the event as a single experiment: you choose x and multiply it times the coefficient and that provides a single estimate of y. Because this approach acts as if there were a single experiment the variance that exists in the parameter estimate is larger than the variance associated with the expected value approach.

The conclusion is that we have two different ways to predict the effect of values of the independent variable(s) on the dependent variable and thus we have two different intervals. Both are correct answers to the question being asked, but there are two different questions. To avoid confusion, the first case where we are asking for the **expected value** of the mean of the estimated y, is called a **confidence interval** as we have named this concept before. The second case, where we are asking for the estimate of the impact on the dependent variable y of a single experiment using a value of x, is called the **prediction interval**. The test statistics for these two interval measures within which the estimated value of y will fall are:

### Confidence Interval for Expected Value of Mean Value of y for x=x$_p$

$$\hat{y} = \pm t_{\frac{\alpha}{2}} s_e \left( \sqrt{\frac{1}{n} + \frac{(x_p - \bar{x})^2}{s_x}} \right)$$

### Prediction Interval for an Individual y for x = x$_p$

$$\hat{y} = \pm t_{\frac{\alpha}{2}} s_e \left( \sqrt{1 + \frac{1}{n} + \frac{(x_p - \bar{x})^2}{s_x}} \right)$$

Where $s_e$ is the standard deviation of the error term and $s_x$ is the standard deviation of the x variable.

The mathematical computations of these two test statistics are complex. Various computer regression software packages provide programs within the regression functions to provide answers to inquires of estimated predicted values of y given various values chosen for the x variable(s). It is important to know just which interval is being tested in the computer package because the difference in the size of the standard deviations will change the size of the interval estimated. This is shown in **Figure 13.15**.

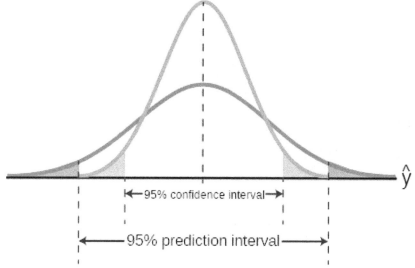

**Figure 13.15** Prediction and confidence intervals for regression equation; 95% confidence level.

**Figure 13.15** shows visually the difference the standard deviation makes in the size of the estimated intervals. The confidence interval, measuring the expected value of the dependent variable, is smaller than the prediction interval for the same level of confidence. The expected value method assumes that the experiment is conducted multiple times rather than just once as in the other method. The logic here is similar, although not identical, to that discussed when developing the relationship between the sample size and the confidence interval using the Central Limit Theorem. There, as the number of experiments increased, the distribution narrowed and the confidence interval became tighter around the expected value of the mean.

It is also important to note that the intervals around a point estimate are highly dependent upon the range of data used to estimate the equation regardless of which approach is being used for prediction. Remember that all regression equations go through the point of means, that is, the mean value of y and the mean values of all independent variables in the equation. As the value of x chosen to estimate the associated value of y is further from the point of means the width of the estimated interval around the point estimate increases. Choosing values of x beyond the range of the data used to estimate the equation possess even greater danger of creating estimates with little use; very large intervals, and risk of error. **Figure 13.16** shows this relationship.

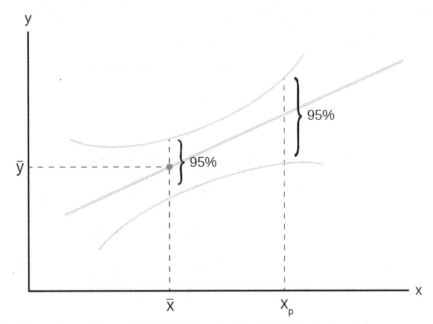

**Figure 13.16**   Confidence interval for an individual value of x, $X_p$, at 95% level of confidence

**Figure 13.16** demonstrates the concern for the quality of the estimated interval whether it is a prediction interval or a confidence interval. As the value chosen to predict y, $X_p$ in the graph, is further from the central weight of the data, $\bar{X}$, we see the interval expand in width even while holding constant the level of confidence. This shows that the precision of any estimate will diminish as one tries to predict beyond the largest weight of the data and most certainly will degrade rapidly for predictions beyond the range of the data. Unfortunately, this is just where most predictions are desired. They can be made, but the width of the confidence interval may be so large as to render the prediction useless. Only actual calculation and the particular application can determine this, however.

## Example 13.6

Recall the **third exam/final exam example** .

We found the equation of the best-fit line for the final exam grade as a function of the grade on the third-exam. We can now use the least-squares regression line for prediction. Assume the coefficient for X was determined to be significantly different from zero.

Suppose you want to estimate, or predict, the mean final exam score of statistics students who received 73 on the third exam. The exam scores (**x-values**) range from 65 to 75. Since 73 is between the x-values 65 and 75, we feel comfortable to substitute x = 73 into the equation. Then:

$$\hat{y} = -173.51 + 4.83(73) = 179.08$$

We predict that statistics students who earn a grade of 73 on the third exam will earn a grade of 179.08 on the final exam, on average.

a. What would you predict the final exam score to be for a student who scored a 66 on the third exam?

**Solution 13.6**

a. 145.27

b. What would you predict the final exam score to be for a student who scored a 90 on the third exam?

**Solution 13.6**

b. The *x* values in the data are between 65 and 75. Ninety is outside of the domain of the observed *x* values in the data (independent variable), so you cannot reliably predict the final exam score for this student. (Even though it is possible to enter 90 into the equation for *x* and calculate a corresponding *y* value, the *y* value that you get will have a confidence interval that may not be meaningful.)

To understand really how unreliable the prediction can be outside of the observed *x* values observed in the data, make the substitution *x* = 90 into the equation.

$$\hat{y} = -173.51 + 4.83(90) = 261.19$$

The final-exam score is predicted to be 261.19. The largest the final-exam score can be is 200.

# 13.7 | How to Use Microsoft Excel® for Regression Analysis

This section of this chapter is here in recognition that what we are now asking requires much more than a quick calculation of a ratio or a square root. Indeed, the use of regression analysis was almost non- existent before the middle of the last century and did not really become a widely used tool until perhaps the late 1960's and early 1970's. Even then the computational ability of even the largest IBM machines is laughable by today's standards. In the early days programs were developed by the researchers and shared. There was no market for something called "software" and certainly nothing called "apps", an entrant into the market only a few years old.

With the advent of the personal computer and the explosion of a vital software market we have a number of regression and statistical analysis packages to choose from. Each has their merits. We have chosen Microsoft Excel because of the wide-spread availability both on college campuses and in the post-college market place. Stata is an alternative and has features that will be important for more advanced econometrics study if you choose to follow this path. Even more advanced packages exist, but typically require the analyst to do some significant amount of programing to conduct their analysis. The goal of this section is to demonstrate how to use Excel to run a regression and then to do so with an example of a simple version of a demand curve.

The first step to doing a regression using Excel is to load the program into your computer. If you have Excel you have the Analysis ToolPak although you may not have it activated. The program calls upon a significant amount of space so is not loaded automatically.

To activate the Analysis ToolPak follow these steps:

Click "File" > "Options" > "Add-ins" to bring up a menu of the add-in "ToolPaks". Select "Analysis ToolPak" and click "GO" next to "Manage: excel add-ins" near the bottom of the window. This will open a new window where you click "Analysis ToolPak" (make sure there is a green check mark in the box) and then click "OK". Now there should be an Analysis tab under the data menu. These steps are presented in the following screen shots.

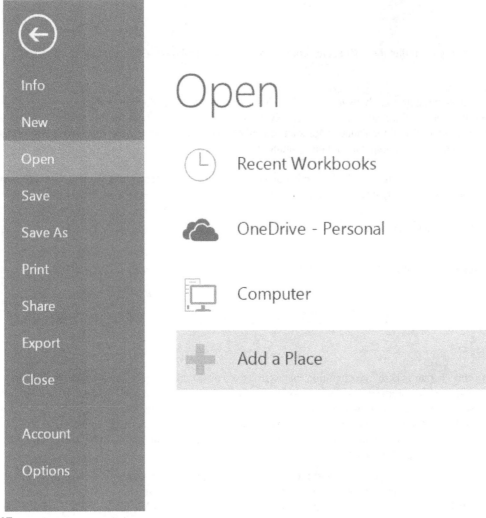

**Figure 13.17**

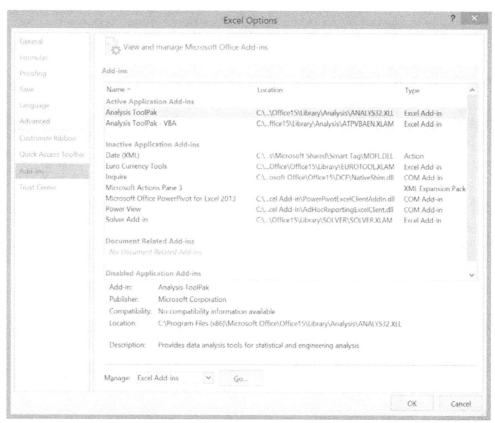

**Figure 13.18**

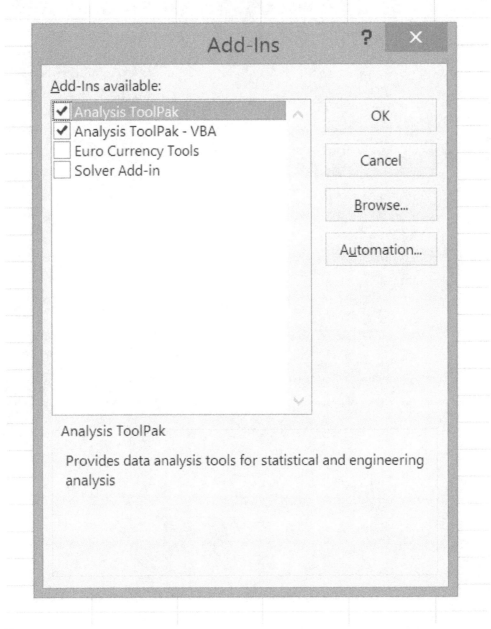

Figure 13.19

Figure 13.20

Click "Data" then "Data Analysis" and then click "Regression" and "OK". Congratulations, you have made it to the regression window. The window asks for your inputs. Clicking the box next to the Y and X ranges will allow you to use the click and drag feature of Excel to select your input ranges. Excel has one odd quirk and that is the click and drop feature requires that the independent variables, the X variables, are all together, meaning that they form a single matrix. If your data are set up with the Y variable between two columns of X variables Excel will not allow you to use click and drag. As an example, say Column A and Column C are independent variables and Column B is the Y variable, the dependent variable.

Excel will not allow you to click and drop the data ranges. The solution is to move the column with the Y variable to column A and then you can click and drag. The same problem arises again if you want to run the regression with only some of the X variables. You will need to set up the matrix so all the X variables you wish to regress are in a tightly formed matrix. These steps are presented in the following scene shots.

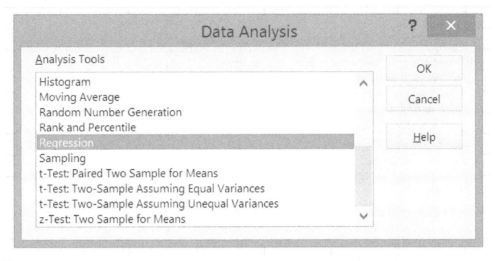

**Figure 13.21**

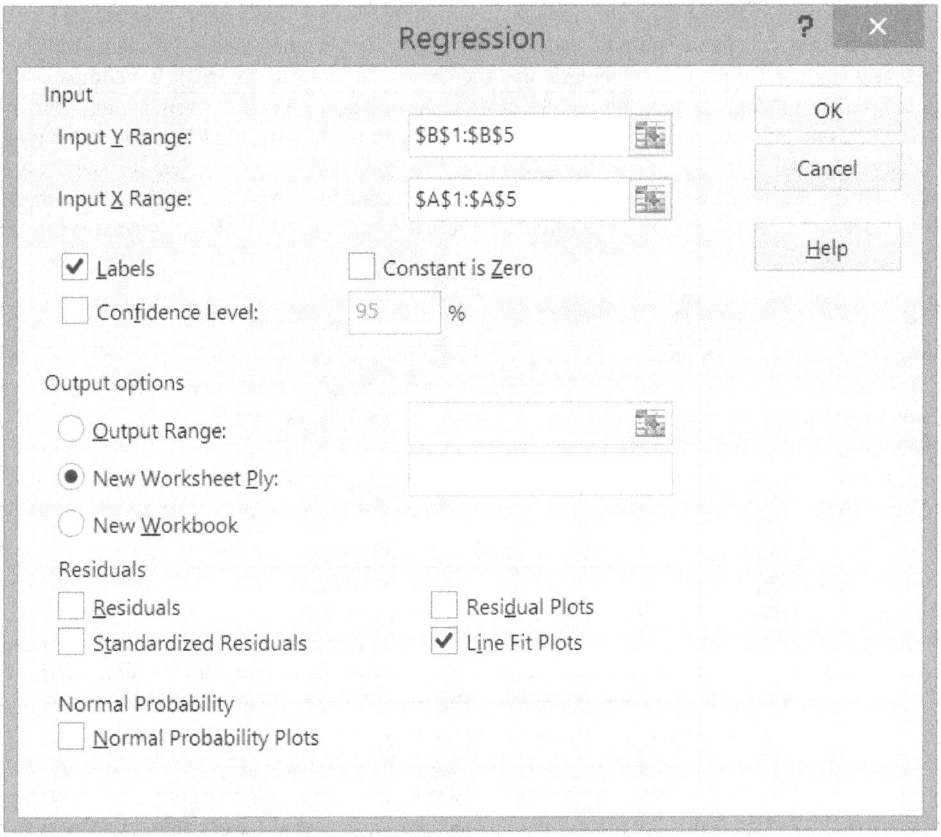

**Figure 13.22**

Once you have selected the data for your regression analysis and told Excel which one is the dependent variable (Y) and which ones are the independent valuables (X's), you have several choices as to the parameters and how the output will be displayed. Refer to screen shot **Figure 13.22** under "Input" section. If you check the "labels" box the program will place the entry in the first column of each variable as its name in the output. You can enter an actual name, such as price or income in a demand analysis, in row one of the Excel spreadsheet for each variable and it will be displayed in the output.

The level of significance can also be set by the analyst. This will not change the calculated t statistic, called t stat, but will alter the p value for the calculated t statistic. It will also alter the boundaries of the confidence intervals for the coefficients. A 95 percent confidence interval is always presented, but with a change in this you will also get other levels of confidence for the intervals.

Excel also will allow you to suppress the intercept. This forces the regression program to minimize the residual sum of squares under the condition that the estimated line must go through the origin. This is done in cases where there is no meaning in the model at some value other than zero, zero for the start of the line. An example is an economic production function that is a relationship between the number of units of an input, say hours of labor, and output. There is no meaning of positive output with zero workers.

Once the data are entered and the choices are made click OK and the results will be sent to a separate new worksheet by default. The output from Excel is presented in a way typical of other regression package programs. The first block of information gives the overall statistics of the regression: Multiple R, R Squared, and the R squared adjusted for degrees of freedom, which is the one you want to report. You also get the Standard error (of the estimate) and the number of observations in the regression.

The second block of information is titled ANOVA which stands for Analysis of Variance. Our interest in this section is the column marked F. This is the calculated F statistics for the null hypothesis that all of the coefficients are equal to zero verse the alternative that at least one of the coefficients are not equal to zero. This hypothesis test was presented in 13.4 under "How Good is the Equation?" The next column gives the p value for this test under the title "Significance F". If the p value is less than say 0.05 (the calculated F statistic is in the tail) we can say with 90 % confidence that we cannot accept the null hypotheses that all the coefficients are equal to zero. This is a good thing: it means that at least one of the coefficients is significantly different from zero thus do have an effect on the value of Y.

The last block of information contains the hypothesis tests for the individual coefficient. The estimated coefficients, the intercept and the slopes, are first listed and then each standard error (of the estimated coefficient) followed by the t stat (calculated student's t statistic for the null hypothesis that the coefficient is equal to zero). We compare the t stat and the critical value of the student's t, dependent on the degrees of freedom, and determine if we have enough evidence to reject the null that the variable has no effect on Y. Remember that we have set up the null hypothesis as the status quo and our claim that we know what caused the Y to change is in the alternative hypothesis. We want to reject the status quo and substitute our version of the world, the alternative hypothesis. The next column contains the p values for this hypothesis test followed by the estimated upper and lower bound of the confidence interval of the estimated slope parameter for various levels of confidence set by us at the beginning.

## Estimating the Demand for Roses

Here is an example of using the Excel program to run a regression for a particular specific case: estimating the demand for roses. We are trying to estimate a demand curve, which from economic theory we expect certain variables affect how much of a good we buy. The relationship between the price of a good and the quantity demanded is the demand curve. Beyond that we have the demand function that includes other relevant variables: a person's income, the price of substitute goods, and perhaps other variables such as season of the year or the price of complimentary goods. Quantity demanded will be our Y variable, and Price of roses, Price of carnations and Income will be our independent variables, the X variables.

For all of these variables theory tells us the expected relationship. For the price of the good in question, roses, theory predicts an inverse relationship, the negatively sloped demand curve. Theory also predicts the relationship between the quantity demanded of one good, here roses, and the price of a substitute, carnations in this example. Theory predicts that this should be a positive or direct relationship; as the price of the substitute falls we substitute away from roses to the cheaper substitute, carnations. A reduction in the price of the substitute generates a reduction in demand for the good being analyzed, roses here. Reduction generates reduction is a positive relationship. For normal goods, theory also predicts a positive relationship; as our incomes rise we buy more of the good, roses. We expect these results because that is what is predicted by a hundred years of economic theory and research. Essentially we are testing these century-old hypotheses. The data gathered was determined by the model that is being tested. This should always be the case. One is not doing inferential statistics by throwing a mountain of data into a computer and asking the machine for a theory. Theory first, test follows.

These data here are national average prices and income is the nation's per capita personal income. Quantity demanded is total national annual sales of roses. These are annual time series data; we are tracking the rose market for the United States from 1984-2017, 33 observations.

Because of the quirky way Excel requires how the data are entered into the regression package it is best to have the independent variables, price of roses, price of carnations and income next to each other on the spreadsheet. Once your data are entered into the spreadsheet it is always good to look at the data. Examine the range, the means and the standard deviations. Use your understanding of descriptive statistics from the very first part of this course. In large data sets you will not be able to "scan" the data. The Analysis ToolPac makes it easy to get the range, mean, standard deviations and other parameters of the distributions. You can also quickly get the correlations among the variables. Examine for outliers. Review the history. Did something happen? Was here a labor strike, change in import fees, something that makes these observations unusual? Do not take the data without question. There may have been a typo somewhere, who knows without review.

Go to the regression window, enter the data and select 95% confidence level and click "OK". You can include the labels in the input range if you have put a title at the top of each column, but be sure to click the "labels" box on the main regression page if you do.

The regression output should show up automatically on a new worksheet.

**SUMMARY OUTPUT**

| Regression Statistics | |
|---|---|
| Multiple R | 0.8560327 |
| R Square | 0.732792 |
| Adjusted R Square | 0.699391 |
| Standard Error | 3629.3427 |
| Observations | 33 |

**ANOVA**

| | df | SS | MS | F | Significance F |
|---|---|---|---|---|---|
| Regression | 3 | 577972629.2 | 2.89E+08 | 21.9392274 | 2.59893E-05 |
| Residual | 29 | 210754050.4 | 13172128 | | |
| Total | 32 | 788726679.5 | | | |

| | Coefficients | Standard Error | t Stat | P-value | Lower 95% | Upper 95% |
|---|---|---|---|---|---|---|
| Intercept | 183475.43 | 16791.81835 | 10.92648 | 7.89854E-09 | 147878.367 | 219072.5 |
| Price of Roses | -1.7607 | 0.2982 | -5.9043 | 5.20E-05 | -2.4049 | -1.1164 |
| Price of Carnations | 1.3397 | 0.5273 | 2.5407 | 0.0246 | 0.208 | 2.4789 |
| Income (per capita) | 3.0338 | 1.2308 | 2.464901 | 0.00886322 | 0.621432 | 5.4446 |

Figure 13.23

The first results presented is the R-Square, a measure of the strength of the correlation between Y and $X_1$, $X_2$, and $X_3$ taken as a group. Our R-square here of 0.699, adjusted for degrees of freedom, means that 70% of the variation in Y, demand for roses, can be explained by variations in $X_1$, $X_2$, and $X_3$, Price of roses, Price of carnations and Income. There is no statistical test to determine the "significance" of an $R^2$. Of course a higher $R^2$ is preferred, but it is really the significance of the coefficients that will determine the value of the theory being tested and which will become part of any policy discussion if they are demonstrated to be significantly different form zero.

Looking at the third panel of output we can write the equation as:

$$Y = b_0 + b_1 X_1 + b_2 X_2 + b_3 X_3 + e$$

where $b_0$ is the intercept, $b_1$ is the estimated coefficient on price of roses, and $b_2$ is the estimated coefficient on price of carnations, $b_3$ is the estimated effect of income and e is the error term. The equation is written in Roman letters indicating that these are the estimated values and not the population parameters, $\beta$'s.

Our estimated equation is:

Quantity of roses sold $= 183,475 - 1.76$ Price of roses $+ 1.33$ Price of carnations $+ 3.03$ Income

We first observe that the signs of the coefficients are as expected from theory. The demand curve is downward sloping with the negative sign for the price of roses. Further the signs of both the price of carnations and income coefficients are positive as would be expected from economic theory.

Interpreting the coefficients can tell us the magnitude of the impact of a change in each variable on the demand for roses. It is the ability to do this which makes regression analysis such a valuable tool. The estimated coefficients tell us that an increase the price of roses by one dollar will lead to a 1.76 reduction in the number roses purchased. The price of carnations seems to play an important role in the demand for roses as we see that increasing the price of carnations by one dollar would increase the demand for roses by 1.33 units as consumers would substitute away from the now more expensive carnations. Similarly, increasing per capita income by one dollar will lead to a 3.03 unit increase in roses purchased.

These results are in line with the predictions of economics theory with respect to all three variables included in this estimate of the demand for roses. It is important to have a theory first that predicts the significance or at least the direction of the coefficients. Without a theory to test, this research tool is not much more helpful than the correlation coefficients we learned about earlier.

We cannot stop there, however. We need to first check whether our coefficients are statistically significant from zero. We set up a hypothesis of:

$$H_0 : \beta_1 = 0$$
$$H_a : \beta_1 \neq 0$$

for all three coefficients in the regression. Recall from earlier that we will not be able to definitively say that our estimated $b_1$ is the actual real population of $\beta_1$, but rather only that with $(1-\alpha)\%$ level of confidence that we cannot reject the null hypothesis that our estimated $\beta_1$ is significantly different from zero. The analyst is making a claim that the price of roses causes an impact on quantity demanded. Indeed, that each of the included variables has an impact on the quantity of roses demanded. The claim is therefore in the alternative hypotheses. It will take a very large probability, 0.95 in this case, to overthrow the null hypothesis, the status quo, that $\beta = 0$. In all regression hypothesis tests the claim is in the alternative and the claim is that the theory has found a variable that has a significant impact on the Y variable.

The test statistic for this hypothesis follows the familiar standardizing formula which counts the number of standard deviations, t, that the estimated value of the parameter, $b_1$, is away from the hypothesized value, $\beta_0$, which is zero in this case:

$$t_c = \frac{b_1 - \beta_0}{S_{b_1}}$$

The computer calculates this test statistic and presents it as "t stat". You can find this value to the right of the standard error of the coefficient estimate. The standard error of the coefficient for $b_1$ is $S_{b_1}$ in the formula. To reach a conclusion we compare this test statistic with the critical value of the student's t at degrees of freedom n-3-1 =29, and alpha = 0.025 (5% significance level for a two-tailed test). Our t stat for $b_1$ is approximately 5.90 which is greater than 1.96 (the critical value we looked up in the t-table), so we cannot accept our null hypotheses of no effect. We conclude that Price has a significant effect because the calculated t value is in the tail. We conduct the same test for $b_2$ and $b_3$. For each variable, we find that we cannot accept the null hypothesis of no relationship because the calculated t-statistics are in the tail for each case, that is, greater than the critical value. All variables in this regression have been determined to have a significant effect on the demand for roses.

These tests tell us whether or not an individual coefficient is significantly different from zero, but does not address the overall quality of the model. We have seen that the R squared adjusted for degrees of freedom indicates this model with these three variables explains 70% of the variation in quantity of roses demanded. We can also conduct a second test of the model taken as a whole. This is the F test presented in section 13.4 of this chapter. Because this is a multiple regression (more than one X), we use the F-test to determine if our coefficients collectively affect Y. The hypothesis is:

$$H_0 : \beta_1 = \beta_2 = ... = \beta_i = 0$$
$$H_a : \text{"at least one of the } \beta_i \text{ is not equal to 0"}$$

Under the ANOVA section of the output we find the calculated F statistic for this hypotheses. For this example the F statistic is 21.9. Again, comparing the calculated F statistic with the critical value given our desired level of significance and the degrees of freedom will allow us to reach a conclusion.

The best way to reach a conclusion for this statistical test is to use the p-value comparison rule. The p-value is the area in the tail, given the calculated F statistic. In essence the computer is finding the F value in the table for us and calculating the p-value. In the Summary Output under "significance F" is this probability. For this example, it is calculated to be $2.6 \times 10^{-5}$, or 2.6 then moving the decimal five places to the left. (.000026) This is an almost infinitesimal level of probability and is certainly less than our alpha level of .05 for a 5 percent level of significance.

By not being able to accept the null hypotheses we conclude that this specification of this model has validity because at least one of the estimated coefficients is significantly different from zero. Since F-calculated is greater than F-critical, we cannot accept $H_0$, meaning that $X_1$, $X_2$ and $X_3$ *together* has a significant effect on Y.

The development of computing machinery and the software useful for academic and business research has made it possible to answer questions that just a few years ago we could not even formulate. Data is available in electronic format and can be moved into place for analysis in ways and at speeds that were unimaginable a decade ago. The sheer magnitude of data sets that can today be used for research and analysis gives us a higher quality of results than in days past. Even with only an Excel spreadsheet we can conduct very high level research. This section gives you the tools to conduct some of this very interesting research with the only limit being your imagination.

# KEY TERMS

**a is the symbol for the Y-Intercept** Sometimes written as $b_0$, because when writing the theoretical linear model $\beta_0$ is used to represent a coefficient for a population.

**b is the symbol for Slope** The word coefficient will be used regularly for the slope, because it is a number that will always be next to the letter "x." It will be written as $b_1$ when a sample is used, and $\beta_1$ will be used with a population or when writing the theoretical linear model.

**Bivariate** two variables are present in the model where one is the "cause" or independent variable and the other is the "effect" of dependent variable.

**Linear** a model that takes data and regresses it into a straight line equation.

**Multivariate** a system or model where more than one independent variable is being used to predict an outcome. There can only ever be one dependent variable, but there is no limit to the number of independent variables.

**$R^2$ – Coefficient of Determination** This is a number between 0 and 1 that represents the percentage variation of the dependent variable that can be explained by the variation in the independent variable. Sometimes calculated by the equation $R^2 = \frac{SSR}{SST}$ where SSR is the "Sum of Squares Regression" and SST is the "Sum of Squares Total." The appropriate coefficient of determination to be reported should always be adjusted for degrees of freedom first.

**$R$ – Correlation Coefficient** A number between −1 and 1 that represents the strength and direction of the relationship between "X" and "Y." The value for "$r$" will equal 1 or −1 only if all the plotted points form a perfectly straight line.

**Residual or "error"** the value calculated from subtracting $y_0 - \hat{y}_0 = e_0$. The absolute value of a residual measures the vertical distance between the actual value of $y$ and the estimated value of $y$ that appears on the best-fit line.

**Sum of Squared Errors (SSE)** the calculated value from adding up all the squared residual terms. The hope is that this value is very small when creating a model.

**X – the independent variable** This will sometimes be referred to as the "predictor" variable, because these values were measured in order to determine what possible outcomes could be predicted.

**Y – the dependent variable** Also, using the letter "y" represents actual values while $\hat{y}$ represents predicted or estimated values. Predicted values will come from plugging in observed "x" values into a linear model.

# CHAPTER REVIEW

## 13.3 Linear Equations

The most basic type of association is a linear association. This type of relationship can be defined algebraically by the equations used, numerically with actual or predicted data values, or graphically from a plotted curve. (Lines are classified as straight curves.) Algebraically, a linear equation typically takes the form $y = mx + b$, where $m$ and $b$ are constants, $x$ is the independent variable, $y$ is the dependent variable. In a statistical context, a linear equation is written in the form $y = a + bx$, where $a$ and $b$ are the constants. This form is used to help readers distinguish the statistical context from the algebraic context. In the equation $y = a + bx$, the constant $b$ that multiplies the $x$ variable ($b$ is called a coefficient) is called as the **slope**. The slope describes the rate of change between the independent and dependent variables; in other words, the rate of change describes the change that occurs in the dependent variable as the independent variable is changed. In the equation $y = a + bx$, the constant a is called as the y-intercept. Graphically, the y-intercept is the $y$ coordinate of the point where the graph of the line crosses the $y$ axis. At this point $x = 0$.

The **slope of a line** is a value that describes the rate of change between the independent and dependent variables. The **slope** tells us how the dependent variable ($y$) changes for every one unit increase in the independent ($x$) variable, on average. The

***y*-intercept** is used to describe the dependent variable when the independent variable equals zero. Graphically, the slope is represented by three line types in elementary statistics.

## 13.4 The Regression Equation

It is hoped that this discussion of regression analysis has demonstrated the tremendous potential value it has as a tool for testing models and helping to better understand the world around us. The regression model has its limitations, especially the requirement that the underlying relationship be approximately linear. To the extent that the true relationship is nonlinear it may be approximated with a linear relationship or nonlinear forms of transformations that can be estimated with linear techniques. Double logarithmic transformation of the data will provide an easy way to test this particular shape of the relationship. A reasonably good quadratic form (the shape of the total cost curve from Microeconomics Principles) can be generated by the equation:

$$Y = a + b_1 X + b_2 X^2$$

where the values of X are simply squared and put into the equation as a separate variable.

There is much more in the way of econometric "tricks" that can bypass some of the more troublesome assumptions of the general regression model. This statistical technique is so valuable that further study would provide any student significant, statistically significant, dividends.

# PRACTICE

## 13.1 The Correlation Coefficient r

**1.** In order to have a correlation coefficient between traits A and B, it is necessary to have:
   a.  one group of subjects, some of whom possess characteristics of trait A, the remainder possessing those of trait B
   b.  measures of trait A on one group of subjects and of trait B on another group
   c.  two groups of subjects, one which could be classified as A or not A, the other as B or not B
   d.  two groups of subjects, one which could be classified as A or not A, the other as B or not B

**2.** Define the Correlation Coefficient and give a unique example of its use.

**3.** If the correlation between age of an auto and money spent for repairs is +.90
   a.  81% of the variation in the money spent for repairs is explained by the age of the auto
   b.  81% of money spent for repairs is unexplained by the age of the auto
   c.  90% of the money spent for repairs is explained by the age of the auto
   d.  none of the above

**4.** Suppose that college grade-point average and verbal portion of an IQ test had a correlation of .40. What percentage of the variance do these two have in common?
   a.  20
   b.  16
   c.  40
   d.  80

**5.** True or false? If false, explain why: The coefficient of determination can have values between -1 and +1.

**6.** True or False: Whenever r is calculated on the basis of a sample, the value which we obtain for r is only an estimate of the true correlation coefficient which we would obtain if we calculated it for the entire population.

**7.** Under a "scatter diagram" there is a notation that the coefficient of correlation is .10. What does this mean?
   a.  plus and minus 10% from the means includes about 68% of the cases
   b.  one-tenth of the variance of one variable is shared with the other variable
   c.  one-tenth of one variable is caused by the other variable
   d.  on a scale from -1 to +1, the degree of linear relationship between the two variables is +.10

**8.** The correlation coefficient for X and Y is known to be zero. We then can conclude that:
   a.  X and Y have standard distributions
   b.  the variances of X and Y are equal
   c.  there exists no relationship between X and Y
   d.  there exists no linear relationship between X and Y
   e.  none of these

**9.** What would you guess the value of the correlation coefficient to be for the pair of variables: "number of man-hours worked" and "number of units of work completed"?
   a.  Approximately 0.9
   b.  Approximately 0.4
   c.  Approximately 0.0
   d.  Approximately -0.4
   e.  Approximately -0.9

**10.** In a given group, the correlation between height measured in feet and weight measured in pounds is +.68. Which of the following would alter the value of r?
   a.  height is expressed centimeters.
   b.  weight is expressed in Kilograms.
   c.  both of the above will affect r.
   d.  neither of the above changes will affect r.

## 13.2 Testing the Significance of the Correlation Coefficient

**11.** Define a t Test of a Regression Coefficient, and give a unique example of its use.

**12.** The correlation between scores on a neuroticism test and scores on an anxiety test is high and positive; therefore

   a.  anxiety causes neuroticism
   b.  those who score low on one test tend to score high on the other.
   c.  those who score low on one test tend to score low on the other.
   d.  no prediction from one test to the other can be meaningfully made.

## 13.3 Linear Equations

**13.** True or False? If False, correct it: Suppose a 95% confidence interval for the slope $\beta$ of the straight line regression of Y on X is given by -3.5 < $\beta$ < -0.5. Then a two-sided test of the hypothesis $H_0 : \beta = -1$ would result in rejection of $H_0$ at the 1% level of significance.

**14.** True or False: It is safer to interpret correlation coefficients as measures of association rather than causation because of the possibility of spurious correlation.

**15.** We are interested in finding the linear relation between the number of widgets purchased at one time and the cost per widget. The following data has been obtained:

X: Number of widgets purchased – 1, 3, 6, 10, 15

Y: Cost per widget(in dollars) – 55, 52, 46, 32, 25

Suppose the regression line is $\hat{y} = -2.5x + 60$. We compute the average price per widget if 30 are purchased and observe which of the following?

   a.  $\hat{y} = 15$ dollars ; obviously, we are mistaken; the prediction $\hat{y}$ is actually +15 dollars.

   b.  $\hat{y} = 15$ dollars , which seems reasonable judging by the data.

   c.  $\hat{y} = -15$ dollars , which is obvious nonsense. The regression line must be incorrect.

   d.  $\hat{y} = -15$ dollars , which is obvious nonsense. This reminds us that predicting Y outside the range of X values in our data is a very poor practice.

**16.** Discuss briefly the distinction between correlation and causality.

**17.** True or False: If r is close to + or -1, we shall say there is a strong correlation, with the tacit understanding that we are referring to a linear relationship and nothing else.

## 13.4 The Regression Equation

**18.** Suppose that you have at your disposal the information below for each of 30 drivers. Propose a model (including a very brief indication of symbols used to represent independent variables) to explain how miles per gallon vary from driver to driver on the basis of the factors measured.          Information:
1.  miles driven per day
2.  weight of car
3.  number of cylinders in car
4.  average speed
5.  miles per gallon
6.  number of passengers

**19.** Consider a sample least squares regression analysis between a dependent variable (Y) and an independent variable (X). A sample correlation coefficient of −1 (minus one) tells us that
a.  there is no relationship between Y and X in the sample
b.  there is no relationship between Y and X in the population
c.  there is a perfect negative relationship between Y and X in the population
d.  there is a perfect negative relationship between Y and X in the sample.

**20.** In correlational analysis, when the points scatter widely about the regression line, this means that the correlation is

a.  negative.
b.  low.
c.  heterogeneous.
d.  between two measures that are unreliable.

## 13.5 Interpretation of Regression Coefficients: Elasticity and Logarithmic Transformation

**21.** In a linear regression, why do we need to be concerned with the range of the independent (X) variable?

**22.** Suppose one collected the following information where X is diameter of tree trunk and Y is tree height.

| X | Y |
|---|---|
| 4 | 8 |
| 2 | 4 |
| 8 | 18 |
| 6 | 22 |
| 10 | 30 |
| 6 | 8 |

Table 13.3

Regression equation: $\hat{y}_i = -3.6 + 3.1 \cdot X_i$

What is your estimate of the average height of all trees having a trunk diameter of 7 inches?

**23.** The manufacturers of a chemical used in flea collars claim that under standard test conditions each additional unit of the chemical will bring about a reduction of 5 fleas (i.e. where $X_j$ = amount of chemical and $Y_J = B_0 + B_1 \cdot X_J + E_J$,

$H_0: B_1 = -5$

Suppose that a test has been conducted and results from a computer include:

Intercept = 60

Slope = −4

Standard error of the regression coefficient = 1.0

Degrees of Freedom for Error = 2000

95% Confidence Interval for the slope −2.04, −5.96

Is this evidence consistent with the claim that the number of fleas is reduced at a rate of 5 fleas per unit chemical?

## 13.6 Predicting with a Regression Equation

**24.** True or False? If False, correct it: Suppose you are performing a simple linear regression of Y on X and you test the hypothesis that the slope $\beta$ is zero against a two-sided alternative. You have $n = 25$ observations and your computed test (t) statistic is 2.6. Then your P-value is given by $.01 < P < .02$, which gives borderline significance (i.e. you would reject $H_0$ at $\alpha = .02$ but fail to reject $H_0$ at $\alpha = .01$).

**25.** An economist is interested in the possible influence of "Miracle Wheat" on the average yield of wheat in a district. To do so he fits a linear regression of average yield per year against year after introduction of "Miracle Wheat" for a ten year period.

The fitted trend line is

$$\hat{y}_j = 80 + 1.5 \cdot X_j$$

( $Y_j$: Average yield in $j$ year after introduction)

( $X_j$: $j$ year after introduction).

　　a. What is the estimated average yield for the fourth year after introduction?
　　b. Do you want to use this trend line to estimate yield for, say, 20 years after introduction? Why? What would your estimate be?

**26.** An interpretation of $r = 0.5$ is that the following part of the Y-variation is associated with which variation in X:

　　a. most
　　b. half
　　c. very little
　　d. one quarter
　　e. none of these

**27.** Which of the following values of $r$ indicates the most accurate prediction of one variable from another?
　　a.　$r = 1.18$
　　b.　$r = -.77$
　　c.　$r = .68$

## 13.7 How to Use Microsoft Excel® for Regression Analysis

**28.** A computer program for multiple regression has been used to fit $\hat{y}_j = b_0 + b_1 \cdot X_{1j} + b_2 \cdot X_{2j} + b_3 \cdot X_{3j}$.

Part of the computer output includes:

| i | $b_i$ | $S_{b_i}$ |
|---|-------|-----------|
| 0 | 8 | 1.6 |
| 1 | 2.2 | .24 |
| 2 | -.72 | .32 |
| 3 | 0.005 | 0.002 |

Table 13.4

   a. Calculation of confidence interval for $b_2$ consists of _____ ± (a student's t value) (_____)

   b. The confidence level for this interval is reflected in the value used for _____.

   c. The degrees of freedom available for estimating the variance are directly concerned with the value used for _____.

**29.** An investigator has used a multiple regression program on 20 data points to obtain a regression equation with 3 variables. Part of the computer output is:

| Variable | Coefficient | Standard Error of $b_i$ |
|----------|-------------|--------------------------|
| 1 | 0.45 | 0.21 |
| 2 | 0.80 | 0.10 |
| 3 | 3.10 | 0.86 |

Table 13.5

   a. 0.80 is an estimate of _____.

   b. 0.10 is an estimate of _____.

   c. Assuming the responses satisfy the normality assumption, we can be 95% confident that the value of $\beta_2$ is in the interval,_____ ± [t.025 · _____], where t.025 is the critical value of the student's t distribution with _____ degrees of freedom.

## SOLUTIONS

1 d

2 A measure of the degree to which variation of one variable is related to variation in one or more other variables. The most commonly used correlation coefficient indicates the degree to which variation in one variable is described by a straight line relation with another variable. Suppose that sample information is available on family income and Years of schooling of the head of the household. A correlation coefficient = 0 would indicate no linear association at all between these two variables. A correlation of 1 would indicate perfect linear association (where all variation in family income could be associated with schooling and vice versa).

3 a. 81% of the variation in the money spent for repairs is explained by the age of the auto

4 b. 16

5 The coefficient of determination is r**2 with $0 \leq$ r**2 $\leq 1$, since $-1 \leq r \leq 1$.

**6** True

**7** d. on a scale from -1 to +1, the degree of linear relationship between the two variables is +.10

**8** d. there exists no linear relationship between X and Y

**9** Approximately 0.9

**10** d. neither of the above changes will affect r.

**11** Definition: A t test is obtained by dividing a regression coefficient by its standard error and then comparing the result to critical values for Students' t with Error *df*. It provides a test of the claim that $\beta_i = 0$ when all other variables have been included in the relevant regression model. Example: Suppose that 4 variables are suspected of influencing some response. Suppose that the results of fitting $Y_i = \beta_0 + \beta_1 X_{1i} + \beta_2 X_{2i} + \beta_3 X_{3i} + \beta_4 X_{4i} + e_i$ include:

| Variable | Regression coefficient | Standard error of regular coefficient |
|----------|------------------------|----------------------------------------|
| .5 | 1 | -3 |
| .4 | 2 | +2 |
| .02 | 3 | +1 |
| .6 | 4 | -.5 |

**Table 13.6**

t calculated for variables 1, 2, and 3 would be 5 or larger in absolute value while that for variable 4 would be less than 1. For most significance levels, the hypothesis $\beta_1 = 0$ would be rejected. But, notice that this is for the case when $X_2$, $X_3$, and $X_4$ have been included in the regression. For most significance levels, the hypothesis $\beta_4 = 0$ would be continued (retained) for the case where $X_1$, $X_2$, and $X_3$ are in the regression. Often this pattern of results will result in computing another regression involving only $X_1$, $X_2$, $X_3$, and examination of the t ratios produced for that case.

**12** c. those who score low on one test tend to score low on the other.

**13** False. Since $H_0: \beta = -1$ would not be rejected at $\alpha = 0.05$, it would not be rejected at $\alpha = 0.01$.

**14** True

**15** d

**16** Some variables seem to be related, so that knowing one variable's status allows us to predict the status of the other. This relationship can be measured and is called correlation. However, a high correlation between two variables in no way proves that a cause-and-effect relation exists between them. It is entirely possible that a third factor causes both variables to vary together.

**17** True

**18** $Y_j = b_0 + b_1 \cdot X_1 + b_2 \cdot X_2 + b_3 \cdot X_3 + b_4 \cdot X_4 + b_5 \cdot X_6 + e_j$

**19** d. there is a perfect negative relationship between Y and X in the sample.

**20** b. low

**21** The precision of the estimate of the Y variable depends on the range of the independent (X) variable explored. If we explore a very small range of the X variable, we won't be able to make much use of the regression. Also, extrapolation is not recommended.

**22** $\hat{y} = -3.6 + (3.1 \cdot 7) = 18.1$

**23** Most simply, since $-5$ is included in the confidence interval for the slope, we can conclude that the evidence is consistent with the claim at the 95% confidence level. Using a t test: $H_0: B_1 = -5 \quad H_A: B_1 \neq -5$

$t_{\text{calculated}} = \dfrac{-5 - (-4)}{1} = -1$  $t_{\text{critical}} = -1.96$ Since $t_{\text{calc}} < t_{\text{crit}}$ we retain the null hypothesis that $B_1 = -5$.

**24** True. $t_{(\text{critical, df} = 23, \text{ two-tailed}, \alpha = .02)} = \pm 2.5$ $t_{\text{critical, df} = 23, \text{ two-tailed}, \alpha = .01} = \pm 2.8$

**25**

a.  $80 + 1.5 \cdot 4 = 86$

b.  No. Most business statisticians would not want to extrapolate that far. If someone did, the estimate would be 110, but some other factors probably come into play with 20 years.

**26** d. one quarter

**27** b. $r = -.77$

**28**

a.  $-.72, .32$

b.  the t value

c.  the t value

**29**

a.  The population value for $\beta_2$, the change that occurs in Y with a unit change in $X_2$, when the other variables are held constant.

b.  The population value for the standard error of the distribution of estimates of $\beta_2$.

c.  $.8, .1, 16 = 20 - 4$.

# APPENDIX A:
# STATISTICAL TABLES

## *F* Distribution

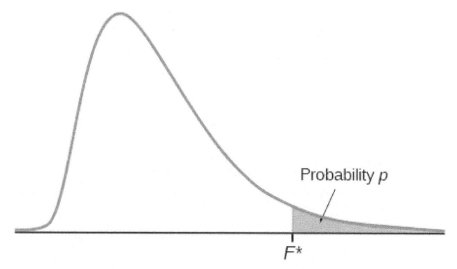

Probability *p*

*F\**

Figure A1  Table entry for *p* is the critical value *F\** with probability *p* lying to its right.

| Degrees of freedom in the denominator | *p* | Degrees of freedom in the numerator | | | | | | | | |
|---|---|---|---|---|---|---|---|---|---|---|
| | | 1 | 2 | 3 | 4 | 5 | 6 | 7 | 8 | 9 |
| 1 | .100 | 39.86 | 49.50 | 53.59 | 55.83 | 57.24 | 58.20 | 58.91 | 59.44 | 59.86 |
| | .050 | 161.45 | 199.50 | 215.71 | 224.58 | 230.16 | 233.99 | 236.77 | 238.88 | 240.54 |
| | .025 | 647.79 | 799.50 | 864.16 | 899.58 | 921.85 | 937.11 | 948.22 | 956.66 | 963.28 |
| | .010 | 4052.2 | 4999.5 | 5403.4 | 5624.6 | 5763.6 | 5859.0 | 5928.4 | 5981.1 | 6022.5 |
| | .001 | 405284 | 500000 | 540379 | 562500 | 576405 | 585937 | 592873 | 598144 | 602284 |
| 2 | .100 | 8.53 | 9.00 | 9.16 | 9.24 | 9.29 | 9.33 | 9.35 | 9.37 | 9.38 |
| | .050 | 18.51 | 19.00 | 19.16 | 19.25 | 19.30 | 19.33 | 19.35 | 19.37 | 19.38 |
| | .025 | 38.51 | 39.00 | 39.17 | 39.25 | 39.30 | 39.33 | 39.36 | 39.37 | 39.39 |
| | .010 | 98.50 | 99.00 | 99.17 | 99.25 | 99.30 | 99.33 | 99.36 | 99.37 | 99.39 |
| | .001 | 998.50 | 999.00 | 999.17 | 999.25 | 999.30 | 999.33 | 999.36 | 999.37 | 999.39 |
| 3 | .100 | 5.54 | 5.46 | 5.39 | 5.34 | 5.31 | 5.28 | 5.27 | 5.25 | 5.24 |
| | .050 | 10.13 | 9.55 | 9.28 | 9.12 | 9.01 | 8.94 | 8.89 | 8.85 | 8.81 |
| | .025 | 17.44 | 16.04 | 15.44 | 15.10 | 14.88 | 14.73 | 14.62 | 14.54 | 14.47 |

Table A1 *F* critical values

| | p | | | | | | | | | |
|---|---|---|---|---|---|---|---|---|---|---|
| **Degrees of freedom in the numerator** | | | | | | | | | | |
| | .010 | 34.12 | 30.82 | 29.46 | 28.71 | 28.24 | 27.91 | 27.67 | 27.49 | 27.35 |
| | .001 | 167.03 | 148.50 | 141.11 | 137.10 | 134.58 | 132.85 | 131.58 | 130.62 | 129.86 |
| 4 | .100 | 4.54 | 4.32 | 4.19 | 4.11 | 4.05 | 4.01 | 3.98 | 3.95 | 3.94 |
| | .050 | 7.71 | 6.94 | 6.59 | 6.39 | 6.26 | 6.16 | 6.09 | 6.04 | 6.00 |
| | .025 | 12.22 | 10.65 | 9.98 | 9.60 | 9.36 | 9.20 | 9.07 | 8.98 | 8.90 |
| | .010 | 21.20 | 18.00 | 16.69 | 15.98 | 15.52 | 15.21 | 14.98 | 14.80 | 14.66 |
| | .001 | 74.14 | 61.25 | 56.18 | 53.44 | 51.71 | 50.53 | 49.66 | 49.00 | 48.47 |
| 5 | .100 | 4.06 | 3.78 | 3.62 | 3.52 | 3.45 | 3.40 | 3.37 | 3.34 | 3.32 |
| | .050 | 6.61 | 5.79 | 5.41 | 5.19 | 5.05 | 4.95 | 4.88 | 4.82 | 4.77 |
| | .025 | 10.01 | 8.43 | 7.76 | 7.39 | 7.15 | 6.98 | 6.85 | 6.76 | 6.68 |
| | .010 | 16.26 | 13.27 | 12.06 | 11.39 | 10.97 | 10.67 | 10.46 | 10.29 | 10.16 |
| | .001 | 47.18 | 37.12 | 33.20 | 31.09 | 29.75 | 28.83 | 28.16 | 27.65 | 27.24 |
| 6 | .100 | 3.78 | 3.46 | 3.29 | 3.18 | 3.11 | 3.05 | 3.01 | 2.98 | 2.96 |
| | .050 | 5.99 | 5.14 | 4.76 | 4.53 | 4.39 | 4.28 | 4.21 | 4.15 | 4.10 |
| | .025 | 8.81 | 7.26 | 6.60 | 6.23 | 5.99 | 5.82 | 5.70 | 5.60 | 5.52 |
| | .010 | 13.75 | 10.92 | 9.78 | 9.15 | 8.75 | 8.47 | 8.26 | 8.10 | 7.98 |
| | .001 | 35.51 | 27.00 | 23.70 | 21.92 | 20.80 | 20.03 | 19.46 | 19.03 | 18.69 |
| 7 | .100 | 3.59 | 3.26 | 3.07 | 2.96 | 2.88 | 2.83 | 2.78 | 2.75 | 2.72 |
| | .050 | 5.59 | 4.74 | 4.35 | 4.12 | 3.97 | 3.87 | 3.79 | 3.73 | 3.68 |
| | .025 | 8.07 | 6.54 | 5.89 | 5.52 | 5.29 | 5.12 | 4.99 | 4.90 | 4.82 |
| | .010 | 12.25 | 9.55 | 8.45 | 7.85 | 7.46 | 7.19 | 6.99 | 6.84 | 6.72 |
| | .001 | 29.25 | 21.69 | 18.77 | 17.20 | 16.21 | 15.52 | 15.02 | 14.63 | 14.33 |

Table A1 *F* critical values

| Degrees of freedom in the denominator | p | Degrees of freedom in the numerator | | | | | | | | | | |
|---|---|---|---|---|---|---|---|---|---|---|---|---|
| | | 10 | 12 | 15 | 20 | 25 | 30 | 40 | 50 | 60 | 120 | 1000 |
| 1 | .100 | 60.19 | 60.71 | 61.22 | 61.74 | 62.05 | 62.26 | 62.53 | 62.69 | 62.79 | 63.06 | 63.30 |
| | .050 | 241.88 | 243.91 | 245.95 | 248.01 | 249.26 | 250.10 | 251.14 | 251.77 | 252.20 | 253.25 | 254.19 |
| | .025 | 968.63 | 976.71 | 984.87 | 993.10 | 998.08 | 1001.4 | 1005.6 | 1008.1 | 1009.8 | 1014.0 | 1017.7 |
| | .010 | 6055.8 | 6106.3 | 6157.3 | 6208.7 | 6239.8 | 6260.6 | 6286.8 | 6302.5 | 6313.0 | 6339.4 | 6362.7 |
| | .001 | 605621 | 610668 | 615764 | 620908 | 624017 | 626099 | 628712 | 630285 | 631337 | 633972 | 636301 |
| 2 | .100 | 9.39 | 9.41 | 9.42 | 9.44 | 9.45 | 9.46 | 9.47 | 9.47 | 9.47 | 9.48 | 9.49 |
| | .050 | 19.40 | 19.41 | 19.43 | 19.45 | 19.46 | 19.46 | 19.47 | 19.48 | 19.48 | 19.49 | 19.49 |
| | .025 | 39.40 | 39.41 | 39.43 | 39.45 | 39.46 | 39.46 | 39.47 | 39.48 | 39.48 | 39.49 | 39.50 |

Table A2 *F* critical values (continued)

| | | Degrees of freedom in the numerator | | | | | | | | | | |
|---|---|---|---|---|---|---|---|---|---|---|---|---|
| | .010 | 99.40 | 99.42 | 99.43 | 99.45 | 99.46 | 99.47 | 99.47 | 99.48 | 99.48 | 99.49 | 99.50 |
| | .001 | 999.40 | 999.42 | 999.43 | 999.45 | 999.46 | 999.47 | 999.47 | 999.48 | 999.48 | 999.49 | 999.50 |
| 3 | .100 | 5.23 | 5.22 | 5.20 | 5.18 | 5.17 | 5.17 | 5.16 | 5.15 | 5.15 | 5.14 | 5.13 |
| | .050 | 8.79 | 8.74 | 8.70 | 8.66 | 8.63 | 8.62 | 8.59 | 8.58 | 8.57 | 8.55 | 8.53 |
| | .025 | 14.42 | 14.34 | 14.25 | 14.17 | 14.12 | 14.08 | 14.04 | 14.01 | 13.99 | 13.95 | 13.91 |
| | .010 | 27.23 | 27.05 | 26.87 | 26.69 | 26.58 | 26.50 | 26.41 | 26.35 | 26.32 | 26.22 | 26.14 |
| | .001 | 129.25 | 128.32 | 127.37 | 126.42 | 125.84 | 125.45 | 124.96 | 124.66 | 124.47 | 123.97 | 123.53 |
| 4 | .100 | 3.92 | 3.90 | 3.87 | 3.84 | 3.83 | 3.82 | 3.80 | 3.80 | 3.79 | 3.78 | 3.76 |
| | .050 | 5.96 | 5.91 | 5.86 | 5.80 | 5.77 | 5.75 | 5.72 | 5.70 | 5.69 | 5.66 | 5.63 |
| | .025 | 8.84 | 8.75 | 8.66 | 8.56 | 8.50 | 8.46 | 8.41 | 8.38 | 8.36 | 8.31 | 8.26 |
| | .010 | 14.55 | 14.37 | 14.20 | 14.02 | 13.91 | 13.84 | 13.75 | 13.69 | 13.65 | 13.56 | 13.47 |
| | .001 | 48.05 | 47.41 | 46.76 | 46.10 | 45.70 | 45.43 | 45.09 | 44.88 | 44.75 | 44.40 | 44.09 |
| 5 | .100 | 3.30 | 3.27 | 3.24 | 3.21 | 3.19 | 3.17 | 3.16 | 3.15 | 3.14 | 3.12 | 3.11 |
| | .050 | 4.74 | 4.68 | 4.62 | 4.56 | 4.52 | 4.50 | 4.46 | 4.44 | 4.43 | 4.40 | 4.37 |
| | .025 | 6.62 | 6.52 | 6.43 | 6.33 | 6.27 | 6.23 | 6.18 | 6.14 | 6.12 | 6.07 | 6.02 |
| | .010 | 10.05 | 9.89 | 9.72 | 9.55 | 9.45 | 9.38 | 9.29 | 9.24 | 9.20 | 9.11 | 9.03 |
| | .001 | 26.92 | 26.42 | 25.91 | 25.39 | 25.08 | 24.87 | 24.60 | 24.44 | 24.33 | 24.06 | 23.82 |
| 6 | .100 | 2.94 | 2.90 | 2.87 | 2.84 | 2.81 | 2.80 | 2.78 | 2.77 | 2.76 | 2.74 | 2.72 |
| | .050 | 4.06 | 4.00 | 3.94 | 3.87 | 3.83 | 3.81 | 3.77 | 3.75 | 3.74 | 3.70 | 3.67 |
| | .025 | 5.46 | 5.37 | 5.27 | 5.17 | 5.11 | 5.07 | 5.01 | 4.98 | 4.96 | 4.90 | 4.86 |
| | .010 | 7.87 | 7.72 | 7.56 | 7.40 | 7.30 | 7.23 | 7.14 | 7.09 | 7.06 | 6.97 | 6.89 |
| | .001 | 18.41 | 17.99 | 17.56 | 17.12 | 16.85 | 16.67 | 16.44 | 16.31 | 16.21 | 15.98 | 15.77 |
| 7 | .100 | 2.70 | 2.67 | 2.63 | 2.59 | 2.57 | 2.56 | 2.54 | 2.52 | 2.51 | 2.49 | 2.47 |
| | .050 | 3.64 | 3.57 | 3.51 | 3.44 | 3.40 | 3.38 | 3.34 | 3.32 | 3.30 | 3.27 | 3.23 |
| | .025 | 4.76 | 4.67 | 4.57 | 4.47 | 4.40 | 4.36 | 4.31 | 4.28 | 4.25 | 4.20 | 4.15 |
| | .010 | 6.62 | 6.47 | 6.31 | 6.16 | 6.06 | 5.99 | 5.91 | 5.86 | 5.82 | 5.74 | 5.66 |
| | .001 | 14.08 | 13.71 | 13.32 | 12.93 | 12.69 | 12.53 | 12.33 | 12.20 | 12.12 | 11.91 | 11.72 |

Table A2 *F* critical values (continued)

| Degrees of freedom in the denominator | *p* | Degrees of freedom in the numerator | | | | | | | | |
|---|---|---|---|---|---|---|---|---|---|---|
| | | 1 | 2 | 3 | 4 | 5 | 6 | 7 | 8 | 9 |
| 8 | .100 | 3.46 | 3.11 | 2.92 | 2.81 | 2.73 | 2.67 | 2.62 | 2.59 | 2.56 |
| | .050 | 5.32 | 4.46 | 4.07 | 3.84 | 3.69 | 3.58 | 3.50 | 3.44 | 3.39 |
| | .025 | 7.57 | 6.06 | 5.42 | 5.05 | 4.82 | 4.65 | 4.53 | 4.43 | 4.36 |
| | .010 | 11.26 | 8.65 | 7.59 | 7.01 | 6.63 | 6.37 | 6.18 | 6.03 | 5.91 |
| | .001 | 25.41 | 18.49 | 15.83 | 14.39 | 13.48 | 12.86 | 12.40 | 12.05 | 11.77 |

Table A3 *F* critical values (continued)

|  |  | Degrees of freedom in the numerator |  |  |  |  |  |  |  |  |
|---|---|---|---|---|---|---|---|---|---|---|---|
| 9 | .100 | 3.36 | 3.01 | 2.81 | 2.69 | 2.61 | 2.55 | 2.51 | 2.47 | 2.44 |
|  | .050 | 5.12 | 4.26 | 3.86 | 3.63 | 3.48 | 3.37 | 3.29 | 3.23 | 3.18 |
|  | .025 | 7.21 | 5.71 | 5.08 | 4.72 | 4.48 | 4.32 | 4.20 | 4.10 | 4.03 |
|  | .010 | 10.56 | 8.02 | 6.99 | 6.42 | 6.06 | 5.80 | 5.61 | 5.47 | 5.35 |
|  | .001 | 22.86 | 16.39 | 13.90 | 12.56 | 11.71 | 11.13 | 10.70 | 10.37 | 10.11 |
| 10 | .100 | 3.29 | 2.92 | 2.73 | 2.61 | 2.52 | 2.46 | 2.41 | 2.38 | 2.35 |
|  | .050 | 4.96 | 4.10 | 3.71 | 3.48 | 3.33 | 3.22 | 3.14 | 3.07 | 3.02 |
|  | .025 | 6.94 | 5.46 | 4.83 | 4.47 | 4.24 | 4.07 | 3.95 | 3.85 | 3.78 |
|  | .010 | 10.04 | 7.56 | 6.55 | 5.99 | 5.64 | 5.39 | 5.20 | 5.06 | 4.94 |
|  | .001 | 21.04 | 14.91 | 12.55 | 11.28 | 10.48 | 9.93 | 9.52 | 9.20 | 8.96 |
| 11 | .100 | 3.23 | 2.86 | 2.66 | 2.54 | 2.45 | 2.39 | 2.34 | 2.30 | 2.27 |
|  | .050 | 4.84 | 3.98 | 3.59 | 3.36 | 3.20 | 3.09 | 3.01 | 2.95 | 2.90 |
|  | .025 | 6.72 | 5.26 | 4.63 | 4.28 | 4.04 | 3.88 | 3.76 | 3.66 | 3.59 |
|  | .010 | 9.65 | 7.21 | 6.22 | 5.67 | 5.32 | 5.07 | 4.89 | 4.74 | 4.63 |
|  | .001 | 19.69 | 13.81 | 11.56 | 10.35 | 9.58 | 9.05 | 8.66 | 8.35 | 8.12 |
| 12 | .100 | 3.18 | 2.81 | 2.61 | 2.48 | 2.39 | 2.33 | 2.28 | 2.24 | 2.21 |
|  | .050 | 4.75 | 3.89 | 3.49 | 3.26 | 3.11 | 3.00 | 2.91 | 2.85 | 2.80 |
|  | .025 | 6.55 | 5.10 | 4.47 | 4.12 | 3.89 | 3.73 | 3.61 | 3.51 | 3.44 |
|  | .010 | 9.33 | 6.93 | 5.95 | 5.41 | 5.06 | 4.82 | 4.64 | 4.50 | 4.39 |
|  | .001 | 18.64 | 12.97 | 10.80 | 9.63 | 8.89 | 8.38 | 8.00 | 7.71 | 7.48 |
| 13 | .100 | 3.14 | 2.76 | 2.56 | 2.43 | 2.35 | 2.28 | 2.23 | 2.20 | 2.16 |
|  | .050 | 4.67 | 3.81 | 3.41 | 3.18 | 3.03 | 2.92 | 2.83 | 2.77 | 2.71 |
|  | .025 | 6.41 | 4.97 | 4.35 | 4.00 | 3.77 | 3.60 | 3.48 | 3.39 | 3.31 |
|  | .010 | 9.07 | 6.70 | 5.74 | 5.21 | 4.86 | 4.62 | 4.44 | 4.30 | 4.19 |
|  | .001 | 17.82 | 12.31 | 10.21 | 9.07 | 8.35 | 7.86 | 7.49 | 7.21 | 6.98 |
| 14 | .100 | 3.10 | 2.73 | 2.52 | 2.39 | 2.31 | 2.24 | 2.19 | 2.15 | 2.12 |
|  | .050 | 4.60 | 3.74 | 3.34 | 3.11 | 2.96 | 2.85 | 2.76 | 2.70 | 2.65 |
|  | .025 | 6.30 | 4.86 | 4.24 | 3.89 | 3.66 | 3.50 | 3.38 | 3.29 | 3.21 |
|  | .010 | 8.86 | 6.51 | 5.56 | 5.04 | 4.69 | 4.46 | 4.28 | 4.14 | 4.03 |
|  | .001 | 17.14 | 11.78 | 9.73 | 8.62 | 7.92 | 7.44 | 7.08 | 6.80 | 6.58 |
| 15 | .100 | 3.07 | 2.70 | 2.49 | 2.36 | 2.27 | 2.21 | 2.16 | 2.12 | 2.09 |
|  | .050 | 4.54 | 3.68 | 3.29 | 3.06 | 2.90 | 2.79 | 2.71 | 2.64 | 2.59 |
|  | .025 | 6.20 | 4.77 | 4.15 | 3.80 | 3.58 | 3.41 | 3.29 | 3.20 | 3.12 |
|  | .010 | 8.68 | 6.36 | 5.42 | 4.89 | 4.56 | 4.32 | 4.14 | 4.00 | 3.89 |
|  | .001 | 16.59 | 11.34 | 9.34 | 8.25 | 7.57 | 7.09 | 6.74 | 6.47 | 6.26 |

Table A3 *F* critical values (continued)

| Degrees of freedom in the denominator | p | Degrees of freedom in the numerator | | | | | | | | | | |
|---|---|---|---|---|---|---|---|---|---|---|---|---|
| | | 10 | 12 | 15 | 20 | 25 | 30 | 40 | 50 | 60 | 120 | 1000 |
| 8 | .100 | 2.54 | 2.50 | 2.46 | 2.42 | 2.40 | 2.38 | 2.36 | 2.35 | 2.34 | 2.32 | 2.30 |
| | .050 | 3.35 | 3.28 | 3.22 | 3.15 | 3.11 | 3.08 | 3.04 | 3.02 | 3.01 | 2.97 | 2.93 |
| | .025 | 4.30 | 4.20 | 4.10 | 4.00 | 3.94 | 3.89 | 3.84 | 3.81 | 3.78 | 3.73 | 3.68 |
| | .010 | 5.81 | 5.67 | 5.52 | 5.36 | 5.26 | 5.20 | 5.12 | 5.07 | 5.03 | 4.95 | 4.87 |
| | .001 | 11.54 | 11.19 | 10.84 | 10.48 | 10.26 | 10.11 | 9.92 | 9.80 | 9.73 | 9.53 | 9.36 |
| 9 | .100 | 2.42 | 2.38 | 2.34 | 2.30 | 2.27 | 2.25 | 2.23 | 2.22 | 2.21 | 2.18 | 2.16 |
| | .050 | 3.14 | 3.07 | 3.01 | 2.94 | 2.89 | 2.86 | 2.83 | 2.80 | 2.79 | 2.75 | 2.71 |
| | .025 | 3.96 | 3.87 | 3.77 | 3.67 | 3.60 | 3.56 | 3.51 | 3.47 | 3.45 | 3.39 | 3.34 |
| | .010 | 5.26 | 5.11 | 4.96 | 4.81 | 4.71 | 4.65 | 4.57 | 4.52 | 4.48 | 4.40 | 4.32 |
| | .001 | 9.89 | 9.57 | 9.24 | 8.90 | 8.69 | 8.55 | 8.37 | 8.26 | 8.19 | 8.00 | 7.84 |
| 10 | .100 | 2.32 | 2.28 | 2.24 | 2.20 | 2.17 | 2.16 | 2.13 | 2.12 | 2.11 | 2.08 | 2.06 |
| | .050 | 2.98 | 2.91 | 2.85 | 2.77 | 2.73 | 2.70 | 2.66 | 2.64 | 2.62 | 2.58 | 2.54 |
| | .025 | 3.72 | 3.62 | 3.52 | 3.42 | 3.35 | 3.31 | 3.26 | 3.22 | 3.20 | 3.14 | 3.09 |
| | .010 | 4.85 | 4.71 | 4.56 | 4.41 | 4.31 | 4.25 | 4.17 | 4.12 | 4.08 | 4.00 | 3.92 |
| | .001 | 8.75 | 8.45 | 8.13 | 7.80 | 7.60 | 7.47 | 7.30 | 7.19 | 7.12 | 6.94 | 6.78 |
| 11 | .100 | 2.25 | 2.21 | 2.17 | 2.12 | 2.10 | 2.08 | 2.05 | 2.04 | 2.03 | 2.00 | 1.98 |
| | .050 | 2.85 | 2.79 | 2.72 | 2.65 | 2.60 | 2.57 | 2.53 | 2.51 | 2.49 | 2.45 | 2.41 |
| | .025 | 3.53 | 3.43 | 3.33 | 3.23 | 3.16 | 3.12 | 3.06 | 3.03 | 3.00 | 2.94 | 2.89 |
| | .010 | 4.54 | 4.40 | 4.25 | 4.10 | 4.01 | 3.94 | 3.86 | 3.81 | 3.78 | 3.69 | 3.61 |
| | .001 | 7.92 | 7.63 | 7.32 | 7.01 | 6.81 | 6.68 | 6.52 | 6.42 | 6.35 | 6.18 | 6.02 |
| 12 | .100 | 2.19 | 2.15 | 2.10 | 2.06 | 2.03 | 2.01 | 1.99 | 1.97 | 1.96 | 1.93 | 1.91 |
| | .050 | 2.75 | 2.69 | 2.62 | 2.54 | 2.50 | 2.47 | 2.43 | 2.40 | 2.38 | 2.34 | 2.30 |
| | .025 | 3.37 | 3.28 | 3.18 | 3.07 | 3.01 | 2.96 | 2.91 | 2.87 | 2.85 | 2.79 | 2.73 |
| | .010 | 4.30 | 4.16 | 4.01 | 3.86 | 3.76 | 3.70 | 3.62 | 3.57 | 3.54 | 3.45 | 3.37 |
| | .001 | 7.29 | 7.00 | 6.71 | 6.40 | 6.22 | 6.09 | 5.93 | 5.83 | 5.76 | 5.59 | 5.44 |
| 13 | .100 | 2.14 | 2.10 | 2.05 | 2.01 | 1.98 | 1.96 | 1.93 | 1.92 | 1.90 | 1.88 | 1.85 |
| | .050 | 2.67 | 2.60 | 2.53 | 2.46 | 2.41 | 2.38 | 2.34 | 2.31 | 2.30 | 2.25 | 2.21 |
| | .025 | 3.25 | 3.15 | 3.05 | 2.95 | 2.88 | 2.84 | 2.78 | 2.74 | 2.72 | 2.66 | 2.60 |
| | .010 | 4.10 | 3.96 | 3.82 | 3.66 | 3.57 | 3.51 | 3.43 | 3.38 | 3.34 | 3.25 | 3.18 |
| | .001 | 6.80 | 6.52 | 6.23 | 5.93 | 5.75 | 5.63 | 5.47 | 5.37 | 5.30 | 5.14 | 4.99 |
| 14 | .100 | 2.10 | 2.05 | 2.01 | 1.96 | 1.93 | 1.91 | 1.89 | 1.87 | 1.86 | 1.83 | 1.80 |
| | .050 | 2.60 | 2.53 | 2.46 | 2.39 | 2.34 | 2.31 | 2.27 | 2.24 | 2.22 | 2.18 | 2.14 |
| | .025 | 3.15 | 3.05 | 2.95 | 2.84 | 2.78 | 2.73 | 2.67 | 2.64 | 2.61 | 2.55 | 2.50 |
| | .010 | 3.94 | 3.80 | 3.66 | 3.51 | 3.41 | 3.35 | 3.27 | 3.22 | 3.18 | 3.09 | 3.02 |
| | .001 | 6.40 | 6.13 | 5.85 | 5.56 | 5.38 | 5.25 | 5.10 | 5.00 | 4.94 | 4.77 | 4.62 |

Table A4 *F* critical values (continued)

| | | Degrees of freedom in the numerator | | | | | | | | | |
|---|---|---|---|---|---|---|---|---|---|---|---|---|
| 15 | .100 | 2.06 | 2.02 | 1.97 | 1.92 | 1.89 | 1.87 | 1.85 | 1.83 | 1.82 | 1.79 | 1.76 |
| | .050 | 2.54 | 2.48 | 2.40 | 2.33 | 2.28 | 2.25 | 2.20 | 2.18 | 2.16 | 2.11 | 2.07 |
| | .025 | 3.06 | 2.96 | 2.86 | 2.76 | 2.69 | 2.64 | 2.59 | 2.55 | 2.52 | 2.46 | 2.40 |
| | .010 | 3.80 | 3.67 | 3.52 | 3.37 | 3.28 | 3.21 | 3.13 | 3.08 | 3.05 | 2.96 | 2.88 |
| | .001 | 6.08 | 5.81 | 5.54 | 5.25 | 5.07 | 4.95 | 4.80 | 4.70 | 4.64 | 4.47 | 4.33 |

Table A4 $F$ critical values (continued)

| Degrees of freedom in the denominator | $p$ | Degrees of freedom in the numerator | | | | | | | | |
|---|---|---|---|---|---|---|---|---|---|---|
| | | 1 | 2 | 3 | 4 | 5 | 6 | 7 | 8 | 9 |
| 16 | .100 | 3.05 | 2.67 | 2.46 | 2.33 | 2.24 | 2.18 | 2.13 | 2.09 | 2.06 |
| | .050 | 4.49 | 3.63 | 3.24 | 3.01 | 2.85 | 2.74 | 2.66 | 2.59 | 2.54 |
| | .025 | 6.12 | 4.69 | 4.08 | 3.73 | 3.50 | 3.34 | 3.22 | 3.12 | 3.05 |
| | .010 | 8.53 | 6.23 | 5.29 | 4.77 | 4.44 | 4.20 | 4.03 | 3.89 | 3.78 |
| | .001 | 16.12 | 10.97 | 9.01 | 7.94 | 7.27 | 6.80 | 6.46 | 6.19 | 5.98 |
| 17 | .100 | 3.03 | 2.64 | 2.44 | 2.31 | 2.22 | 2.15 | 2.10 | 2.06 | 2.03 |
| | .050 | 4.45 | 3.59 | 3.20 | 2.96 | 2.81 | 2.70 | 2.61 | 2.55 | 2.49 |
| | .025 | 6.04 | 4.62 | 4.01 | 3.66 | 3.44 | 3.28 | 3.16 | 3.06 | 2.98 |
| | .010 | 8.40 | 6.11 | 5.19 | 4.67 | 4.34 | 4.10 | 3.93 | 3.79 | 3.68 |
| | .001 | 15.72 | 10.66 | 8.73 | 7.68 | 7.02 | 6.56 | 6.22 | 5.96 | 5.75 |
| 18 | .100 | 3.01 | 2.62 | 2.42 | 2.29 | 2.20 | 2.13 | 2.08 | 2.04 | 2.00 |
| | .050 | 4.41 | 3.55 | 3.16 | 2.93 | 2.77 | 2.66 | 2.58 | 2.51 | 2.46 |
| | .025 | 5.98 | 4.56 | 3.95 | 3.61 | 3.38 | 3.22 | 3.10 | 3.01 | 2.93 |
| | .010 | 8.29 | 6.01 | 5.09 | 4.58 | 4.25 | 4.01 | 3.84 | 3.71 | 3.60 |
| | .001 | 15.38 | 10.39 | 8.49 | 7.46 | 6.81 | 6.35 | 6.02 | 5.76 | 5.56 |
| 19 | .100 | 3.36 | 3.01 | 2.81 | 2.69 | 2.61 | 2.55 | 2.51 | 2.47 | 2.44 |
| | .050 | 5.12 | 4.26 | 3.86 | 3.63 | 3.48 | 3.37 | 3.29 | 3.23 | 3.18 |
| | .025 | 7.21 | 5.71 | 5.08 | 4.72 | 4.48 | 4.32 | 4.20 | 4.10 | 4.03 |
| | .010 | 10.56 | 8.02 | 6.99 | 6.42 | 6.06 | 5.80 | 5.61 | 5.47 | 5.35 |
| | .001 | 22.86 | 16.39 | 13.90 | 12.56 | 11.71 | 11.13 | 10.70 | 10.37 | 10.11 |
| 20 | .100 | 2.97 | 2.59 | 2.38 | 2.25 | 2.16 | 2.09 | 2.04 | 2.00 | 1.96 |
| | .050 | 4.35 | 3.49 | 3.10 | 2.87 | 2.71 | 2.60 | 2.51 | 2.45 | 2.39 |
| | .025 | 5.87 | 4.46 | 3.86 | 3.51 | 3.29 | 3.13 | 3.01 | 2.91 | 2.84 |
| | .010 | 8.10 | 5.85 | 4.94 | 4.43 | 4.10 | 3.87 | 3.70 | 3.56 | 3.46 |
| | .001 | 14.82 | 9.95 | 8.10 | 7.10 | 6.46 | 6.02 | 5.69 | 5.44 | 5.24 |
| 21 | .100 | 2.96 | 2.57 | 2.36 | 2.23 | 2.14 | 2.08 | 2.02 | 1.98 | 1.95 |
| | .050 | 4.32 | 3.47 | 3.07 | 2.84 | 2.68 | 2.57 | 2.49 | 2.42 | 2.37 |

Table A5 $F$ critical values (continued)

| | | Degrees of freedom in the numerator | | | | | | | | |
|---|---|---|---|---|---|---|---|---|---|---|
| | .025 | 5.83 | 4.42 | 3.82 | 3.48 | 3.25 | 3.09 | 2.97 | 2.87 | 2.80 |
| | .010 | 8.02 | 5.78 | 4.87 | 4.37 | 4.04 | 3.81 | 3.64 | 3.51 | 3.40 |
| | .001 | 14.59 | 9.77 | 7.94 | 6.95 | 6.32 | 5.88 | 5.56 | 5.31 | 5.11 |
| | .100 | 2.95 | 2.56 | 2.35 | 2.22 | 2.13 | 2.06 | 2.01 | 1.97 | 1.93 |
| | .050 | 4.30 | 3.44 | 3.05 | 2.82 | 2.66 | 2.55 | 2.46 | 2.40 | 2.34 |
| 22 | .025 | 5.79 | 4.38 | 3.78 | 3.44 | 3.22 | 3.05 | 2.93 | 2.84 | 2.76 |
| | .010 | 7.95 | 5.72 | 4.82 | 4.31 | 3.99 | 3.76 | 3.59 | 3.45 | 3.35 |
| | .001 | 14.38 | 9.61 | 7.80 | 6.81 | 6.19 | 5.76 | 5.44 | 5.19 | 4.99 |
| | .100 | 2.94 | 2.55 | 2.34 | 2.21 | 2.11 | 2.05 | 1.99 | 1.95 | 1.92 |
| | .050 | 4.28 | 3.42 | 3.03 | 2.80 | 2.64 | 2.53 | 2.44 | 2.37 | 2.32 |
| 23 | .025 | 5.75 | 4.35 | 3.75 | 3.41 | 3.18 | 3.02 | 2.90 | 2.81 | 2.73 |
| | .010 | 7.88 | 5.66 | 4.76 | 4.26 | 3.94 | 3.71 | 3.54 | 3.41 | 3.30 |
| | .001 | 14.20 | 9.47 | 7.67 | 6.70 | 6.08 | 5.65 | 5.33 | 5.09 | 4.89 |

Table A5 *F* critical values (continued)

| | | Degrees of freedom in the numerator | | | | | | | | | | |
|---|---|---|---|---|---|---|---|---|---|---|---|---|
| **Degrees of freedom in the denominator** | *p* | 10 | 12 | 15 | 20 | 25 | 30 | 40 | 50 | 60 | 120 | 1000 |
| | .100 | 2.03 | 1.99 | 1.94 | 1.89 | 1.86 | 1.84 | 1.81 | 1.79 | 1.78 | 1.75 | 1.72 |
| | .050 | 2.49 | 2.42 | 2.35 | 2.28 | 2.23 | 2.19 | 2.15 | 2.12 | 2.11 | 2.06 | 2.02 |
| 16 | .025 | 2.99 | 2.89 | 2.79 | 2.68 | 2.61 | 2.57 | 2.51 | 2.47 | 2.45 | 2.38 | 2.32 |
| | .010 | 3.69 | 3.55 | 3.41 | 3.26 | 3.16 | 3.10 | 3.02 | 2.97 | 2.93 | 2.84 | 2.76 |
| | .001 | 5.81 | 5.55 | 5.27 | 4.99 | 4.82 | 4.70 | 4.54 | 4.45 | 4.39 | 4.23 | 4.08 |
| | .100 | 2.00 | 1.96 | 1.91 | 1.86 | 1.83 | 1.81 | 1.78 | 1.76 | 1.75 | 1.72 | 1.69 |
| | .050 | 2.45 | 2.38 | 2.31 | 2.23 | 2.18 | 2.15 | 2.10 | 2.08 | 2.06 | 2.01 | 1.97 |
| 17 | .025 | 2.92 | 2.82 | 2.72 | 2.62 | 2.55 | 2.50 | 2.44 | 2.41 | 2.38 | 2.32 | 2.26 |
| | .010 | 3.59 | 3.46 | 3.31 | 3.16 | 3.07 | 3.00 | 2.92 | 2.87 | 2.83 | 2.75 | 2.66 |
| | .001 | 5.58 | 5.32 | 5.05 | 4.78 | 4.60 | 4.48 | 4.33 | 4.24 | 4.18 | 4.02 | 3.87 |
| | .100 | 1.98 | 1.93 | 1.89 | 1.84 | 1.80 | 1.78 | 1.75 | 1.74 | 1.72 | 1.69 | 1.66 |
| | .050 | 2.41 | 2.34 | 2.27 | 2.19 | 2.14 | 2.11 | 2.06 | 2.04 | 2.02 | 1.97 | 1.92 |
| 18 | .025 | 2.87 | 2.77 | 2.67 | 2.56 | 2.49 | 2.44 | 2.38 | 2.35 | 2.32 | 2.26 | 2.20 |
| | .010 | 3.51 | 3.37 | 3.23 | 3.08 | 2.98 | 2.92 | 2.84 | 2.78 | 2.75 | 2.66 | 2.58 |
| | .001 | 5.39 | 5.13 | 4.87 | 4.59 | 4.42 | 4.30 | 4.15 | 4.06 | 4.00 | 3.84 | 3.69 |
| | .100 | 1.96 | 1.91 | 1.86 | 1.81 | 1.78 | 1.76 | 1.73 | 1.71 | 1.70 | 1.67 | 1.64 |
| | .050 | 2.38 | 2.31 | 2.23 | 2.16 | 2.11 | 2.07 | 2.03 | 2.00 | 1.98 | 1.93 | 1.88 |
| 19 | .025 | 2.82 | 2.72 | 2.62 | 2.51 | 2.44 | 2.39 | 2.33 | 2.30 | 2.27 | 2.20 | 2.14 |
| | .010 | 3.43 | 3.30 | 3.15 | 3.00 | 2.91 | 2.84 | 2.76 | 2.71 | 2.67 | 2.58 | 2.50 |

Table A6 *F* critical values (continued)

| | | Degrees of freedom in the numerator | | | | | | | | | | |
|---|---|---|---|---|---|---|---|---|---|---|---|---|
| | .001 | 5.22 | 4.97 | 4.70 | 4.43 | 4.26 | 4.14 | 3.99 | 3.90 | 3.84 | 3.68 | 3.53 |
| 20 | .100 | 1.94 | 1.89 | 1.84 | 1.79 | 1.76 | 1.74 | 1.71 | 1.69 | 1.68 | 1.64 | 1.61 |
| | .050 | 2.35 | 2.28 | 2.20 | 2.12 | 2.07 | 2.04 | 1.99 | 1.97 | 1.95 | 1.90 | 1.85 |
| | .025 | 2.77 | 2.68 | 2.57 | 2.46 | 2.40 | 2.35 | 2.29 | 2.25 | 2.22 | 2.16 | 2.09 |
| | .010 | 3.37 | 3.23 | 3.09 | 2.94 | 2.84 | 2.78 | 2.69 | 2.64 | 2.61 | 2.52 | 2.43 |
| | .001 | 5.08 | 4.82 | 4.56 | 4.29 | 4.12 | 4.00 | 3.86 | 3.77 | 3.70 | 3.54 | 3.40 |
| 21 | .100 | 1.92 | 1.87 | 1.83 | 1.78 | 1.74 | 1.72 | 1.69 | 1.67 | 1.66 | 1.62 | 1.59 |
| | .050 | 2.32 | 2.25 | 2.18 | 2.10 | 2.05 | 2.01 | 1.96 | 1.94 | 1.92 | 1.87 | 1.82 |
| | .025 | 2.73 | 2.64 | 2.53 | 2.42 | 2.36 | 2.31 | 2.25 | 2.21 | 2.18 | 2.11 | 2.05 |
| | .010 | 3.31 | 3.17 | 3.03 | 2.88 | 2.79 | 2.72 | 2.64 | 2.58 | 2.55 | 2.46 | 2.37 |
| | .001 | 4.95 | 4.70 | 4.44 | 4.17 | 4.00 | 3.88 | 3.74 | 3.64 | 3.58 | 3.42 | 3.28 |
| 22 | .100 | 1.90 | 1.86 | 1.81 | 1.76 | 1.73 | 1.70 | 1.67 | 1.65 | 1.64 | 1.60 | 1.57 |
| | .050 | 2.30 | 2.23 | 2.15 | 2.07 | 2.02 | 1.98 | 1.94 | 1.91 | 1.89 | 1.84 | 1.79 |
| | .025 | 2.70 | 2.60 | 2.50 | 2.39 | 2.32 | 2.27 | 2.21 | 2.17 | 2.14 | 2.08 | 2.01 |
| | .010 | 3.26 | 3.12 | 2.98 | 2.83 | 2.73 | 2.67 | 2.58 | 2.53 | 2.50 | 2.40 | 2.32 |
| | .001 | 4.83 | 4.58 | 4.33 | 4.06 | 3.89 | 3.78 | 3.63 | 3.54 | 3.48 | 3.32 | 3.17 |
| 23 | .100 | 1.89 | 1.84 | 1.80 | 1.74 | 1.71 | 1.69 | 1.66 | 1.64 | 1.62 | 1.59 | 1.55 |
| | .050 | 2.27 | 2.20 | 2.13 | 2.05 | 2.00 | 1.96 | 1.91 | 1.88 | 1.86 | 1.81 | 1.76 |
| | .025 | 2.67 | 2.57 | 2.47 | 2.36 | 2.29 | 2.24 | 2.18 | 2.14 | 2.11 | 2.04 | 1.98 |
| | .010 | 3.21 | 3.07 | 2.93 | 2.78 | 2.69 | 2.62 | 2.54 | 2.48 | 2.45 | 2.35 | 2.27 |
| | .001 | 4.73 | 4.48 | 4.23 | 3.96 | 3.79 | 3.68 | 3.53 | 3.44 | 3.38 | 3.22 | 3.08 |

Table A6 *F* critical values (continued)

| Degrees of freedom in the denominator | $p$ | Degrees of freedom in the numerator | | | | | | | | |
|---|---|---|---|---|---|---|---|---|---|---|
| | | 1 | 2 | 3 | 4 | 5 | 6 | 7 | 8 | 9 |
| 24 | .100 | 2.93 | 2.54 | 2.33 | 2.19 | 2.10 | 2.04 | 1.98 | 1.94 | 1.91 |
| | .050 | 4.26 | 3.40 | 3.01 | 2.78 | 2.62 | 2.51 | 2.42 | 2.36 | 2.30 |
| | .025 | 5.72 | 4.32 | 3.72 | 3.38 | 3.15 | 2.99 | 2.87 | 2.78 | 2.70 |
| | .010 | 7.82 | 5.61 | 4.72 | 4.22 | 3.90 | 3.67 | 3.50 | 3.36 | 3.26 |
| | .001 | 14.03 | 9.34 | 7.55 | 6.59 | 5.98 | 5.55 | 5.23 | 4.99 | 4.80 |
| 25 | .100 | 2.92 | 2.53 | 2.32 | 2.18 | 2.09 | 2.02 | 1.97 | 1.93 | 1.89 |
| | .050 | 4.24 | 3.39 | 2.99 | 2.76 | 2.60 | 2.49 | 2.40 | 2.34 | 2.28 |
| | .025 | 5.69 | 4.29 | 3.69 | 3.35 | 3.13 | 2.97 | 2.85 | 2.75 | 2.68 |
| | .010 | 7.77 | 5.57 | 4.68 | 4.18 | 3.85 | 3.63 | 3.46 | 3.32 | 3.22 |
| | .001 | 13.88 | 9.22 | 7.45 | 6.49 | 5.89 | 5.46 | 5.15 | 4.91 | 4.71 |
| 26 | .100 | 2.91 | 2.52 | 2.31 | 2.17 | 2.08 | 2.01 | 1.96 | 1.92 | 1.88 |

Table A7 *F* critical values (continued)

| | | Degrees of freedom in the numerator | | | | | | | | |
|---|---|---|---|---|---|---|---|---|---|---|
| | .050 | 4.23 | 3.37 | 2.98 | 2.74 | 2.59 | 2.47 | 2.39 | 2.32 | 2.27 |
| | .025 | 5.66 | 4.27 | 3.67 | 3.33 | 3.10 | 2.94 | 2.82 | 2.73 | 2.65 |
| | .010 | 7.72 | 5.53 | 4.64 | 4.14 | 3.82 | 3.59 | 3.42 | 3.29 | 3.18 |
| | .001 | 13.74 | 9.12 | 7.36 | 6.41 | 5.80 | 5.38 | 5.07 | 4.83 | 4.64 |
| | .100 | 2.90 | 2.51 | 2.30 | 2.17 | 2.07 | 2.00 | 1.95 | 1.91 | 1.87 |
| | .050 | 4.21 | 3.35 | 2.96 | 2.73 | 2.57 | 2.46 | 2.37 | 2.31 | 2.25 |
| 27 | .025 | 5.63 | 4.24 | 3.65 | 3.31 | 3.08 | 2.92 | 2.80 | 2.71 | 2.63 |
| | .010 | 7.68 | 5.49 | 4.60 | 4.11 | 3.78 | 3.56 | 3.39 | 3.26 | 3.15 |
| | .001 | 13.61 | 9.02 | 7.27 | 6.33 | 5.73 | 5.31 | 5.00 | 4.76 | 4.57 |
| | .100 | 2.89 | 2.50 | 2.29 | 2.16 | 2.06 | 2.00 | 1.94 | 1.90 | 1.87 |
| | .050 | 4.20 | 3.34 | 2.95 | 2.71 | 2.56 | 2.45 | 2.36 | 2.29 | 2.24 |
| 28 | .025 | 5.61 | 4.22 | 3.63 | 3.29 | 3.06 | 2.90 | 2.78 | 2.69 | 2.61 |
| | .010 | 7.64 | 5.45 | 4.57 | 4.07 | 3.75 | 3.53 | 3.36 | 3.23 | 3.12 |
| | .001 | 13.50 | 8.93 | 7.19 | 6.25 | 5.66 | 5.24 | 4.93 | 4.69 | 4.50 |
| | .100 | 2.89 | 2.50 | 2.28 | 2.15 | 2.06 | 1.99 | 1.93 | 1.89 | 1.86 |
| | .050 | 4.18 | 3.33 | 2.93 | 2.70 | 2.55 | 2.43 | 2.35 | 2.28 | 2.22 |
| 29 | .025 | 5.59 | 4.20 | 3.61 | 3.27 | 3.04 | 2.88 | 2.76 | 2.67 | 2.59 |
| | .010 | 7.60 | 5.42 | 4.54 | 4.04 | 3.73 | 3.50 | 3.33 | 3.20 | 3.09 |
| | .001 | 13.39 | 8.85 | 7.12 | 6.19 | 5.59 | 5.18 | 4.87 | 4.64 | 4.45 |
| | .100 | 2.88 | 2.49 | 2.28 | 2.14 | 2.05 | 1.98 | 1.93 | 1.88 | 1.85 |
| | .050 | 4.17 | 3.32 | 2.92 | 2.69 | 2.53 | 2.42 | 2.33 | 2.27 | 2.21 |
| 30 | .025 | 5.57 | 4.18 | 3.59 | 3.25 | 3.03 | 2.87 | 2.75 | 2.65 | 2.57 |
| | .010 | 7.56 | 5.39 | 4.51 | 4.02 | 3.70 | 3.47 | 3.30 | 3.17 | 3.07 |
| | .001 | 13.29 | 8.77 | 7.05 | 6.12 | 5.53 | 5.12 | 4.82 | 4.58 | 4.39 |
| | .100 | 2.84 | 2.44 | 2.23 | 2.09 | 2.00 | 1.93 | 1.87 | 1.83 | 1.79 |
| | .050 | 4.08 | 3.23 | 2.84 | 2.61 | 2.45 | 2.34 | 2.25 | 2.18 | 2.12 |
| 40 | .025 | 5.42 | 4.05 | 3.46 | 3.13 | 2.90 | 2.74 | 2.62 | 2.53 | 2.45 |
| | .010 | 7.31 | 5.18 | 4.31 | 3.83 | 3.51 | 3.29 | 3.12 | 2.99 | 2.89 |
| | .001 | 12.61 | 8.25 | 6.59 | 5.70 | 5.13 | 4.73 | 4.44 | 4.21 | 4.02 |

Table A7 *F* critical values (continued)

| Degrees of freedom in the numerator | | | | | | | | | | | |
|---|---|---|---|---|---|---|---|---|---|---|---|
| Degrees of freedom in the denominator | *p* | 10 | 12 | 15 | 20 | 25 | 30 | 40 | 50 | 60 | 120 | 1000 |
| | .100 | 1.88 | 1.83 | 1.78 | 1.73 | 1.70 | 1.67 | 1.64 | 1.62 | 1.61 | 1.57 | 1.54 |
| 24 | .050 | 2.25 | 2.18 | 2.11 | 2.03 | 1.97 | 1.94 | 1.89 | 1.86 | 1.84 | 1.79 | 1.74 |
| | .025 | 2.64 | 2.54 | 2.44 | 2.33 | 2.26 | 2.21 | 2.15 | 2.11 | 2.08 | 2.01 | 1.94 |

Table A8 *F* critical values (continued)

| Degrees of freedom in the numerator | | | | | | | | | | | | |
|---|---|---|---|---|---|---|---|---|---|---|---|---|
| | .010 | 3.17 | 3.03 | 2.89 | 2.74 | 2.64 | 2.58 | 2.49 | 2.44 | 2.40 | 2.31 | 2.22 |
| | .001 | 4.64 | 4.39 | 4.14 | 3.87 | 3.71 | 3.59 | 3.45 | 3.36 | 3.29 | 3.14 | 2.99 |
| 25 | .100 | 1.87 | 1.82 | 1.77 | 1.72 | 1.68 | 1.66 | 1.63 | 1.61 | 1.59 | 1.56 | 1.52 |
| | .050 | 2.24 | 2.16 | 2.09 | 2.01 | 1.96 | 1.92 | 1.87 | 1.84 | 1.82 | 1.77 | 1.72 |
| | .025 | 2.61 | 2.51 | 2.41 | 2.30 | 2.23 | 2.18 | 2.12 | 2.08 | 2.05 | 1.98 | 1.91 |
| | .010 | 3.13 | 2.99 | 2.85 | 2.70 | 2.60 | 2.54 | 2.45 | 2.40 | 2.36 | 2.27 | 2.18 |
| | .001 | 4.56 | 4.31 | 4.06 | 3.79 | 3.63 | 3.52 | 3.37 | 3.28 | 3.22 | 3.06 | 2.91 |
| 26 | .100 | 1.86 | 1.81 | 1.76 | 1.71 | 1.67 | 1.65 | 1.61 | 1.59 | 1.58 | 1.54 | 1.51 |
| | .050 | 2.22 | 2.15 | 2.07 | 1.99 | 1.94 | 1.90 | 1.85 | 1.82 | 1.80 | 1.75 | 1.70 |
| | .025 | 2.59 | 2.49 | 2.39 | 2.28 | 2.21 | 2.16 | 2.09 | 2.05 | 2.03 | 1.95 | 1.89 |
| | .010 | 3.09 | 2.96 | 2.81 | 2.66 | 2.57 | 2.50 | 2.42 | 2.36 | 2.33 | 2.23 | 2.14 |
| | .001 | 4.48 | 4.24 | 3.99 | 3.72 | 3.56 | 3.44 | 3.30 | 3.21 | 3.15 | 2.99 | 2.84 |
| 27 | .100 | 1.85 | 1.80 | 1.75 | 1.70 | 1.66 | 1.64 | 1.60 | 1.58 | 1.57 | 1.53 | 1.50 |
| | .050 | 2.20 | 2.13 | 2.06 | 1.97 | 1.92 | 1.88 | 1.84 | 1.81 | 1.79 | 1.73 | 1.68 |
| | .025 | 2.57 | 2.47 | 2.36 | 2.25 | 2.18 | 2.13 | 2.07 | 2.03 | 2.00 | 1.93 | 1.86 |
| | .010 | 3.06 | 2.93 | 2.78 | 2.63 | 2.54 | 2.47 | 2.38 | 2.33 | 2.29 | 2.20 | 2.11 |
| | .001 | 4.41 | 4.17 | 3.92 | 3.66 | 3.49 | 3.38 | 3.23 | 3.14 | 3.08 | 2.92 | 2.78 |
| 28 | .100 | 1.84 | 1.79 | 1.74 | 1.69 | 1.65 | 1.63 | 1.59 | 1.57 | 1.56 | 1.52 | 1.48 |
| | .050 | 2.19 | 2.12 | 2.04 | 1.96 | 1.91 | 1.87 | 1.82 | 1.79 | 1.77 | 1.71 | 1.66 |
| | .025 | 2.55 | 2.45 | 2.34 | 2.23 | 2.16 | 2.11 | 2.05 | 2.01 | 1.98 | 1.91 | 1.84 |
| | .010 | 3.03 | 2.90 | 2.75 | 2.60 | 2.51 | 2.44 | 2.35 | 2.30 | 2.26 | 2.17 | 2.08 |
| | .001 | 4.35 | 4.11 | 3.86 | 3.60 | 3.43 | 3.32 | 3.18 | 3.09 | 3.02 | 2.86 | 2.72 |
| 29 | .100 | 1.83 | 1.78 | 1.73 | 1.68 | 1.64 | 1.62 | 1.58 | 1.56 | 1.55 | 1.51 | 1.47 |
| | .050 | 2.18 | 2.10 | 2.03 | 1.94 | 1.89 | 1.85 | 1.81 | 1.77 | 1.75 | 1.70 | 1.65 |
| | .025 | 2.53 | 2.43 | 2.32 | 2.21 | 2.14 | 2.09 | 2.03 | 1.99 | 1.96 | 1.89 | 1.82 |
| | .010 | 3.00 | 2.87 | 2.73 | 2.57 | 2.48 | 2.41 | 2.33 | 2.27 | 2.23 | 2.14 | 2.05 |
| | .001 | 4.29 | 4.05 | 3.80 | 3.54 | 3.38 | 3.27 | 3.12 | 3.03 | 2.97 | 2.81 | 2.66 |
| 30 | .100 | 1.82 | 1.77 | 1.72 | 1.67 | 1.63 | 1.61 | 1.57 | 1.55 | 1.54 | 1.50 | 1.46 |
| | .050 | 2.16 | 2.09 | 2.01 | 1.93 | 1.88 | 1.84 | 1.79 | 1.76 | 1.74 | 1.68 | 1.63 |
| | .025 | 2.51 | 2.41 | 2.31 | 2.20 | 2.12 | 2.07 | 2.01 | 1.97 | 1.94 | 1.87 | 1.80 |
| | .010 | 2.98 | 2.84 | 2.70 | 2.55 | 2.45 | 2.39 | 2.30 | 2.25 | 2.21 | 2.11 | 2.02 |
| | .001 | 4.24 | 4.00 | 3.75 | 3.49 | 3.33 | 3.22 | 3.07 | 2.98 | 2.92 | 2.76 | 2.61 |
| 40 | .100 | 1.76 | 1.71 | 1.66 | 1.61 | 1.57 | 1.54 | 1.51 | 1.48 | 1.47 | 1.42 | 1.38 |
| | .050 | 2.08 | 2.00 | 1.92 | 1.84 | 1.78 | 1.74 | 1.69 | 1.66 | 1.64 | 1.58 | 1.52 |
| | .025 | 2.39 | 2.29 | 2.18 | 2.07 | 1.99 | 1.94 | 1.88 | 1.83 | 1.80 | 1.72 | 1.65 |
| | .010 | 2.80 | 2.66 | 2.52 | 2.37 | 2.27 | 2.20 | 2.11 | 2.06 | 2.02 | 1.92 | 1.82 |
| | .001 | 3.87 | 3.64 | 3.40 | 3.14 | 2.98 | 2.87 | 2.73 | 2.64 | 2.57 | 2.41 | 2.25 |

**Table A8** *F* critical values (continued)

| | Degrees of freedom in the numerator | | | | | | | | | |
|---|---|---|---|---|---|---|---|---|---|---|
| Degrees of freedom in the denominator | p | 1 | 2 | 3 | 4 | 5 | 6 | 7 | 8 | 9 |
| 50 | .100 | 2.81 | 2.41 | 2.20 | 2.06 | 1.97 | 1.90 | 1.84 | 1.80 | 1.76 |
| | .050 | 4.03 | 3.18 | 2.79 | 2.56 | 2.40 | 2.29 | 2.20 | 2.13 | 2.07 |
| | .025 | 5.34 | 3.97 | 3.39 | 3.05 | 2.83 | 2.67 | 2.55 | 2.46 | 2.38 |
| | .010 | 7.17 | 5.06 | 4.20 | 3.72 | 3.41 | 3.19 | 3.02 | 2.89 | 2.78 |
| | .001 | 12.22 | 7.96 | 6.34 | 5.46 | 4.90 | 4.51 | 4.22 | 4.00 | 3.82 |
| 60 | .100 | 2.79 | 2.39 | 2.18 | 2.04 | 1.95 | 1.87 | 1.82 | 1.77 | 1.74 |
| | .050 | 4.00 | 3.15 | 2.76 | 2.53 | 2.37 | 2.25 | 2.17 | 2.10 | 2.04 |
| | .025 | 5.29 | 3.93 | 3.34 | 3.01 | 2.79 | 2.63 | 2.51 | 2.41 | 2.33 |
| | .010 | 7.08 | 4.98 | 4.13 | 3.65 | 3.34 | 3.12 | 2.95 | 2.82 | 2.72 |
| | .001 | 11.97 | 7.77 | 6.17 | 5.31 | 4.76 | 4.37 | 4.09 | 3.86 | 3.69 |
| 100 | .100 | 2.76 | 2.36 | 2.14 | 2.00 | 1.91 | 1.83 | 1.78 | 1.73 | 1.69 |
| | .050 | 3.94 | 3.09 | 2.70 | 2.46 | 2.31 | 2.19 | 2.10 | 2.03 | 1.97 |
| | .025 | 5.18 | 3.83 | 3.25 | 2.92 | 2.70 | 2.54 | 2.42 | 2.32 | 2.24 |
| | .010 | 6.90 | 4.82 | 3.98 | 3.51 | 3.21 | 2.99 | 2.82 | 2.69 | 2.59 |
| | .001 | 11.50 | 7.41 | 5.86 | 5.02 | 4.48 | 4.11 | 3.83 | 3.61 | 3.44 |
| 200 | .100 | 2.73 | 2.33 | 2.11 | 1.97 | 1.88 | 1.80 | 1.75 | 1.70 | 1.66 |
| | .050 | 3.89 | 3.04 | 2.65 | 2.42 | 2.26 | 2.14 | 2.06 | 1.98 | 1.93 |
| | .025 | 5.10 | 3.76 | 3.18 | 2.85 | 2.63 | 2.47 | 2.35 | 2.26 | 2.18 |
| | .010 | 6.76 | 4.71 | 3.88 | 3.41 | 3.11 | 2.89 | 2.73 | 2.60 | 2.50 |
| | .001 | 11.15 | 7.15 | 5.63 | 4.81 | 4.29 | 3.92 | 3.65 | 3.43 | 3.26 |
| 1000 | .100 | 2.71 | 2.31 | 2.09 | 1.95 | 1.85 | 1.78 | 1.72 | 1.68 | 1.64 |
| | .050 | 3.85 | 3.00 | 2.61 | 2.38 | 2.22 | 2.11 | 2.02 | 1.95 | 1.89 |
| | .025 | 5.04 | 3.70 | 3.13 | 2.80 | 2.58 | 2.42 | 2.30 | 2.20 | 2.13 |
| | .010 | 6.66 | 4.63 | 3.80 | 3.34 | 3.04 | 2.82 | 2.66 | 2.53 | 2.43 |
| | .001 | 10.89 | 6.96 | 5.46 | 4.65 | 4.14 | 3.78 | 3.51 | 3.30 | 3.13 |

Table A9 *F* critical values (continued)

| | Degrees of freedom in the numerator | | | | | | | | | | |
|---|---|---|---|---|---|---|---|---|---|---|---|
| Degrees of freedom in the denominator | p | 10 | 12 | 15 | 20 | 25 | 30 | 40 | 50 | 60 | 120 | 1000 |
| 50 | .100 | 1.73 | 1.68 | 1.63 | 1.57 | 1.53 | 1.50 | 1.46 | 1.44 | 1.42 | 1.38 | 1.33 |
| | .050 | 2.03 | 1.95 | 1.87 | 1.78 | 1.73 | 1.69 | 1.63 | 1.60 | 1.58 | 1.51 | 1.45 |
| | .025 | 2.32 | 2.22 | 2.11 | 1.99 | 1.92 | 1.87 | 1.80 | 1.75 | 1.72 | 1.64 | 1.56 |
| | .010 | 2.70 | 2.56 | 2.42 | 2.27 | 2.17 | 2.10 | 2.01 | 1.95 | 1.91 | 1.80 | 1.70 |
| | .001 | 3.67 | 3.44 | 3.20 | 2.95 | 2.79 | 2.68 | 2.53 | 2.44 | 2.38 | 2.21 | 2.05 |

Table A10 *F* critical values (continued)

| | | Degrees of freedom in the numerator | | | | | | | | | | |
|---|---|---|---|---|---|---|---|---|---|---|---|---|---|
| 60 | .100 | 1.71 | 1.66 | 1.60 | 1.54 | 1.50 | 1.48 | 1.44 | 1.41 | 1.40 | 1.35 | 1.30 |
| | .050 | 1.99 | 1.92 | 1.84 | 1.75 | 1.69 | 1.65 | 1.59 | 1.56 | 1.53 | 1.47 | 1.40 |
| | .025 | 2.27 | 2.17 | 2.06 | 1.94 | 1.87 | 1.82 | 1.74 | 1.70 | 1.67 | 1.58 | 1.49 |
| | .010 | 2.63 | 2.50 | 2.35 | 2.20 | 2.10 | 2.03 | 1.94 | 1.88 | 1.84 | 1.73 | 1.62 |
| | .001 | 3.54 | 3.32 | 3.08 | 2.83 | 2.67 | 2.55 | 2.41 | 2.32 | 2.25 | 2.08 | 1.92 |
| 100 | .100 | 1.66 | 1.61 | 1.56 | 1.49 | 1.45 | 1.42 | 1.38 | 1.35 | 1.34 | 1.28 | 1.22 |
| | .050 | 1.93 | 1.85 | 1.77 | 1.68 | 1.62 | 1.57 | 1.52 | 1.48 | 1.45 | 1.38 | 1.30 |
| | .025 | 2.18 | 2.08 | 1.97 | 1.85 | 1.77 | 1.71 | 1.64 | 1.59 | 1.56 | 1.46 | 1.36 |
| | .010 | 2.50 | 2.37 | 2.22 | 2.07 | 1.97 | 1.89 | 1.80 | 1.74 | 1.69 | 1.57 | 1.45 |
| | .001 | 3.30 | 3.07 | 2.84 | 2.59 | 2.43 | 2.32 | 2.17 | 2.08 | 2.01 | 1.83 | 1.64 |
| 200 | .100 | 1.63 | 1.58 | 1.52 | 1.46 | 1.41 | 1.38 | 1.34 | 1.31 | 1.29 | 1.23 | 1.16 |
| | .050 | 1.88 | 1.80 | 1.72 | 1.62 | 1.56 | 1.52 | 1.46 | 1.41 | 1.39 | 1.30 | 1.21 |
| | .025 | 2.11 | 2.01 | 1.90 | 1.78 | 1.70 | 1.64 | 1.56 | 1.51 | 1.47 | 1.37 | 1.25 |
| | .010 | 2.41 | 2.27 | 2.13 | 1.97 | 1.87 | 1.79 | 1.69 | 1.63 | 1.58 | 1.45 | 1.30 |
| | .001 | 3.12 | 2.90 | 2.67 | 2.42 | 2.26 | 2.15 | 2.00 | 1.90 | 1.83 | 1.64 | 1.43 |
| 1000 | .100 | 1.61 | 1.55 | 1.49 | 1.43 | 1.38 | 1.35 | 1.30 | 1.27 | 1.25 | 1.18 | 1.08 |
| | .050 | 1.84 | 1.76 | 1.68 | 1.58 | 1.52 | 1.47 | 1.41 | 1.36 | 1.33 | 1.24 | 1.11 |
| | .025 | 2.06 | 1.96 | 1.85 | 1.72 | 1.64 | 1.58 | 1.50 | 1.45 | 1.41 | 1.29 | 1.13 |
| | .010 | 2.34 | 2.20 | 2.06 | 1.90 | 1.79 | 1.72 | 1.61 | 1.54 | 1.50 | 1.35 | 1.16 |
| | .001 | 2.99 | 2.77 | 2.54 | 2.30 | 2.14 | 2.02 | 1.87 | 1.77 | 1.69 | 1.49 | 1.22 |

**Table A10 *F* critical values (continued)**

Numerical entries represent the probability that a standard normal random variable is between $0$ and $z$ where $z = \frac{x - \mu}{\sigma}$.

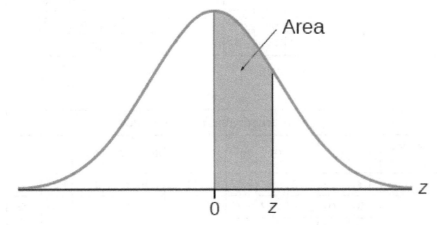

**Figure A2**

# Standard Normal Probability Distribution: Z Table

| z | 0.00 | 0.01 | 0.02 | 0.03 | 0.04 | 0.05 | 0.06 | 0.07 | 0.08 | 0.09 |
|-----|--------|--------|--------|--------|--------|--------|--------|--------|--------|--------|
| 0.0 | 0.0000 | 0.0040 | 0.0080 | 0.0120 | 0.0160 | 0.0199 | 0.0239 | 0.0279 | 0.0319 | 0.0359 |
| 0.1 | 0.0398 | 0.0438 | 0.0478 | 0.0517 | 0.0557 | 0.0596 | 0.0636 | 0.0675 | 0.0714 | 0.0753 |
| 0.2 | 0.0793 | 0.0832 | 0.0871 | 0.0910 | 0.0948 | 0.0987 | 0.1026 | 0.1064 | 0.1103 | 0.1141 |
| 0.3 | 0.1179 | 0.1217 | 0.1255 | 0.1293 | 0.1331 | 0.1368 | 0.1406 | 0.1443 | 0.1480 | 0.1517 |
| 0.4 | 0.1554 | 0.1591 | 0.1628 | 0.1664 | 0.1700 | 0.1736 | 0.1772 | 0.1808 | 0.1844 | 0.1879 |
| 0.5 | 0.1915 | 0.1950 | 0.1985 | 0.2019 | 0.2054 | 0.2088 | 0.2123 | 0.2157 | 0.2190 | 0.2224 |
| 0.6 | 0.2257 | 0.2291 | 0.2324 | 0.2357 | 0.2389 | 0.2422 | 0.2454 | 0.2486 | 0.2517 | 0.2549 |
| 0.7 | 0.2580 | 0.2611 | 0.2642 | 0.2673 | 0.2704 | 0.2734 | 0.2764 | 0.2794 | 0.2823 | 0.2852 |
| 0.8 | 0.2881 | 0.2910 | 0.2939 | 0.2967 | 0.2995 | 0.3023 | 0.3051 | 0.3078 | 0.3106 | 0.3133 |
| 0.9 | 0.3159 | 0.3186 | 0.3212 | 0.3238 | 0.3264 | 0.3289 | 0.3315 | 0.3340 | 0.3365 | 0.3389 |
| 1.0 | 0.3413 | 0.3438 | 0.3461 | 0.3485 | 0.3508 | 0.3531 | 0.3554 | 0.3577 | 0.3599 | 0.3621 |
| 1.1 | 0.3643 | 0.3665 | 0.3686 | 0.3708 | 0.3729 | 0.3749 | 0.3770 | 0.3790 | 0.3810 | 0.3830 |
| 1.2 | 0.3849 | 0.3869 | 0.3888 | 0.3907 | 0.3925 | 0.3944 | 0.3962 | 0.3980 | 0.3997 | 0.4015 |
| 1.3 | 0.4032 | 0.4049 | 0.4066 | 0.4082 | 0.4099 | 0.4115 | 0.4131 | 0.4147 | 0.4162 | 0.4177 |
| 1.4 | 0.4192 | 0.4207 | 0.4222 | 0.4236 | 0.4251 | 0.4265 | 0.4279 | 0.4292 | 0.4306 | 0.4319 |
| 1.5 | 0.4332 | 0.4345 | 0.4357 | 0.4370 | 0.4382 | 0.4394 | 0.4406 | 0.4418 | 0.4429 | 0.4441 |
| 1.6 | 0.4452 | 0.4463 | 0.4474 | 0.4484 | 0.4495 | 0.4505 | 0.4515 | 0.4525 | 0.4535 | 0.4545 |
| 1.7 | 0.4554 | 0.4564 | 0.4573 | 0.4582 | 0.4591 | 0.4599 | 0.4608 | 0.4616 | 0.4625 | 0.4633 |
| 1.8 | 0.4641 | 0.4649 | 0.4656 | 0.4664 | 0.4671 | 0.4678 | 0.4686 | 0.4693 | 0.4699 | 0.4706 |
| 1.9 | 0.4713 | 0.4719 | 0.4726 | 0.4732 | 0.4738 | 0.4744 | 0.4750 | 0.4756 | 0.4761 | 0.4767 |
| 2.0 | 0.4772 | 0.4778 | 0.4783 | 0.4788 | 0.4793 | 0.4798 | 0.4803 | 0.4808 | 0.4812 | 0.4817 |
| 2.1 | 0.4821 | 0.4826 | 0.4830 | 0.4834 | 0.4838 | 0.4842 | 0.4846 | 0.4850 | 0.4854 | 0.4857 |
| 2.2 | 0.4861 | 0.4864 | 0.4868 | 0.4871 | 0.4875 | 0.4878 | 0.4881 | 0.4884 | 0.4887 | 0.4890 |
| 2.3 | 0.4893 | 0.4896 | 0.4898 | 0.4901 | 0.4904 | 0.4906 | 0.4909 | 0.4911 | 0.4913 | 0.4916 |
| 2.4 | 0.4918 | 0.4920 | 0.4922 | 0.4925 | 0.4927 | 0.4929 | 0.4931 | 0.4932 | 0.4934 | 0.4936 |
| 2.5 | 0.4938 | 0.4940 | 0.4941 | 0.4943 | 0.4945 | 0.4946 | 0.4948 | 0.4949 | 0.4951 | 0.4952 |
| 2.6 | 0.4953 | 0.4955 | 0.4956 | 0.4957 | 0.4959 | 0.4960 | 0.4961 | 0.4962 | 0.4963 | 0.4964 |
| 2.7 | 0.4965 | 0.4966 | 0.4967 | 0.4968 | 0.4969 | 0.4970 | 0.4971 | 0.4972 | 0.4973 | 0.4974 |
| 2.8 | 0.4974 | 0.4975 | 0.4976 | 0.4977 | 0.4977 | 0.4978 | 0.4979 | 0.4979 | 0.4980 | 0.4981 |
| 2.9 | 0.4981 | 0.4982 | 0.4982 | 0.4983 | 0.4984 | 0.4984 | 0.4985 | 0.4985 | 0.4986 | 0.4986 |
| 3.0 | 0.4987 | 0.4987 | 0.4987 | 0.4988 | 0.4988 | 0.4989 | 0.4989 | 0.4989 | 0.4990 | 0.4990 |
| 3.1 | 0.4990 | 0.4991 | 0.4991 | 0.4991 | 0.4992 | 0.4992 | 0.4992 | 0.4992 | 0.4993 | 0.4993 |
| 3.2 | 0.4993 | 0.4993 | 0.4994 | 0.4994 | 0.4994 | 0.4994 | 0.4994 | 0.4995 | 0.4995 | 0.4995 |
| 3.3 | 0.4995 | 0.4995 | 0.4995 | 0.4996 | 0.4996 | 0.4996 | 0.4996 | 0.4996 | 0.4996 | 0.4997 |
| 3.4 | 0.4997 | 0.4997 | 0.4997 | 0.4997 | 0.4997 | 0.4997 | 0.4997 | 0.4997 | 0.4997 | 0.4998 |

Table A11 Standard Normal Distribution

# Student's *t* Distribution

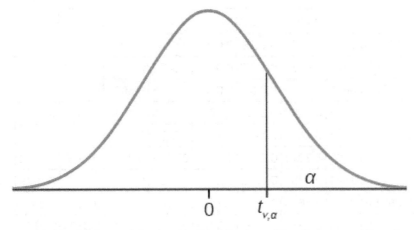

**Figure A3 Upper critical values of Student's *t* Distribution with *v* Degrees of Freedom**

For selected probabilities, *a*, the table shows the values $t_{v,a}$ such that $P(t_v > t_{v,a}) = a$, where $t_v$ is a Student's *t* random variable with *v* degrees of freedom. For example, the probability is .10 that a Student's *t* random variable with 10 degrees of freedom exceeds 1.372.

| v | 0.10 | 0.05 | 0.025 | 0.01 | 0.005 | 0.001 |
|---|------|------|-------|------|-------|-------|
| 1 | 3.078 | 6.314 | 12.706 | 31.821 | 63.657 | 318.313 |
| 2 | 1.886 | 2.920 | 4.303 | 6.965 | 9.925 | 22.327 |
| 3 | 1.638 | 2.353 | 3.182 | 4.541 | 5.841 | 10.215 |
| 4 | 1.533 | 2.132 | 2.776 | 3.747 | 4.604 | 7.173 |
| 5 | 1.476 | 2.015 | 2.571 | 3.365 | 4.032 | 5.893 |
| 6 | 1.440 | 1.943 | 2.447 | 3.143 | 3.707 | 5.208 |
| 7 | 1.415 | 1.895 | 2.365 | 2.998 | 3.499 | 4.782 |
| 8 | 1.397 | 1.860 | 2.306 | 2.896 | 3.355 | 4.499 |
| 9 | 1.383 | 1.833 | 2.262 | 2.821 | 3.250 | 4.296 |
| 10 | 1.372 | 1.812 | 2.228 | 2.764 | 3.169 | 4.143 |
| 11 | 1.363 | 1.796 | 2.201 | 2.718 | 3.106 | 4.024 |
| 12 | 1.356 | 1.782 | 2.179 | 2.681 | 3.055 | 3.929 |
| 13 | 1.350 | 1.771 | 2.160 | 2.650 | 3.012 | 3.852 |
| 14 | 1.345 | 1.761 | 2.145 | 2.624 | 2.977 | 3.787 |
| 15 | 1.341 | 1.753 | 2.131 | 2.602 | 2.947 | 3.733 |
| 16 | 1.337 | 1.746 | 2.120 | 2.583 | 2.921 | 3.686 |
| 17 | 1.333 | 1.740 | 2.110 | 2.567 | 2.898 | 3.646 |
| 18 | 1.330 | 1.734 | 2.101 | 2.552 | 2.878 | 3.610 |

**Table A12 Probability of Exceeding the Critical Value** NIST/SEMATECH e-Handbook of Statistical Methods, http://www.itl.nist.gov/div898/handbook/, September 2011.

| $v$ | 0.10 | 0.05 | 0.025 | 0.01 | 0.005 | 0.001 |
|---|---|---|---|---|---|---|
| 19 | 1.328 | 1.729 | 2.093 | 2.539 | 2.861 | 3.579 |
| 20 | 1.325 | 1.725 | 2.086 | 2.528 | 2.845 | 3.552 |
| 21 | 1.323 | 1.721 | 2.080 | 2.518 | 2.831 | 3.527 |
| 22 | 1.321 | 1.717 | 2.074 | 2.508 | 2.819 | 3.505 |
| 23 | 1.319 | 1.714 | 2.069 | 2.500 | 2.807 | 3.485 |
| 24 | 1.318 | 1.711 | 2.064 | 2.492 | 2.797 | 3.467 |
| 25 | 1.316 | 1.708 | 2.060 | 2.485 | 2.787 | 3.450 |
| 26 | 1.315 | 1.706* | 2.056 | 2.479 | 2.779 | 3.435 |
| 27 | 1.314 | 1.703 | 2.052 | 2.473 | 2.771 | 3.421 |
| 28 | 1.313 | 1.701 | 2.048 | 2.467 | 2.763 | 3.408 |
| 29 | 1.311 | 1.699 | 2.045 | 2.462 | 2.756 | 3.396 |
| 30 | 1.310 | 1.697 | 2.042 | 2.457 | 2.750 | 3.385 |
| 40 | 1.303 | 1.684 | 2.021 | 2.423 | 2.704 | 3.307 |
| 60 | 1.296 | 1.671 | 2.000 | 2.390 | 2.660 | 3.232 |
| 100 | 1.290 | 1.660 | 1.984 | 2.364 | 2.626 | 3.174 |
| $\infty$ | 1.282 | 1.645 | 1.960 | 2.326 | 2.576 | 3.090 |

**Table A12 Probability of Exceeding the Critical Value** NIST/SEMATECH e-Handbook of Statistical Methods, http://www.itl.nist.gov/div898/handbook/, September 2011.

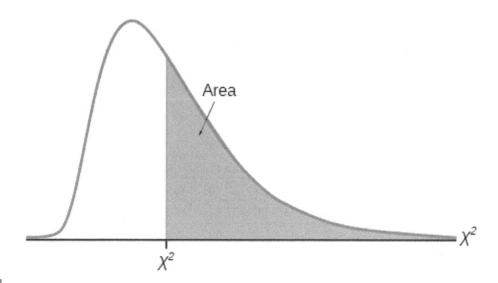

Figure A4

# $\chi^2$ Probability Distribution

| df | 0.995 | 0.990 | 0.975 | 0.950 | 0.900 | 0.100 | 0.050 | 0.025 | 0.010 | 0.005 |
|---|---|---|---|---|---|---|---|---|---|---|
| 1 | 0.000 | 0.000 | 0.001 | 0.004 | 0.016 | 2.706 | 3.841 | 5.024 | 6.635 | 7.879 |
| 2 | 0.010 | 0.020 | 0.051 | 0.103 | 0.211 | 4.605 | 5.991 | 7.378 | 9.210 | 10.597 |
| 3 | 0.072 | 0.115 | 0.216 | 0.352 | 0.584 | 6.251 | 7.815 | 9.348 | 11.345 | 12.838 |
| 4 | 0.207 | 0.297 | 0.484 | 0.711 | 1.064 | 7.779 | 9.488 | 11.143 | 13.277 | 14.860 |
| 5 | 0.412 | 0.554 | 0.831 | 1.145 | 1.610 | 9.236 | 11.070 | 12.833 | 15.086 | 16.750 |
| 6 | 0.676 | 0.872 | 1.237 | 1.635 | 2.204 | 10.645 | 12.592 | 14.449 | 16.812 | 18.548 |
| 7 | 0.989 | 1.239 | 1.690 | 2.167 | 2.833 | 12.017 | 14.067 | 16.013 | 18.475 | 20.278 |
| 8 | 1.344 | 1.646 | 2.180 | 2.733 | 3.490 | 13.362 | 15.507 | 17.535 | 20.090 | 21.955 |
| 9 | 1.735 | 2.088 | 2.700 | 3.325 | 4.168 | 14.684 | 16.919 | 19.023 | 21.666 | 23.589 |
| 10 | 2.156 | 2.558 | 3.247 | 3.940 | 4.865 | 15.987 | 18.307 | 20.483 | 23.209 | 25.188 |
| 11 | 2.603 | 3.053 | 3.816 | 4.575 | 5.578 | 17.275 | 19.675 | 21.920 | 24.725 | 26.757 |
| 12 | 3.074 | 3.571 | 4.404 | 5.226 | 6.304 | 18.549 | 21.026 | 23.337 | 26.217 | 28.300 |
| 13 | 3.565 | 4.107 | 5.009 | 5.892 | 7.042 | 19.812 | 22.362 | 24.736 | 27.688 | 29.819 |
| 14 | 4.075 | 4.660 | 5.629 | 6.571 | 7.790 | 21.064 | 23.685 | 26.119 | 29.141 | 31.319 |
| 15 | 4.601 | 5.229 | 6.262 | 7.261 | 8.547 | 22.307 | 24.996 | 27.488 | 30.578 | 32.801 |
| 16 | 5.142 | 5.812 | 6.908 | 7.962 | 9.312 | 23.542 | 26.296 | 28.845 | 32.000 | 34.267 |
| 17 | 5.697 | 6.408 | 7.564 | 8.672 | 10.085 | 24.769 | 27.587 | 30.191 | 33.409 | 35.718 |
| 18 | 6.265 | 7.015 | 8.231 | 9.390 | 10.865 | 25.989 | 28.869 | 31.526 | 34.805 | 37.156 |
| 19 | 6.844 | 7.633 | 8.907 | 10.117 | 11.651 | 27.204 | 30.144 | 32.852 | 36.191 | 38.582 |
| 20 | 7.434 | 8.260 | 9.591 | 10.851 | 12.443 | 28.412 | 31.410 | 34.170 | 37.566 | 39.997 |
| 21 | 8.034 | 8.897 | 10.283 | 11.591 | 13.240 | 29.615 | 32.671 | 35.479 | 38.932 | 41.401 |
| 22 | 8.643 | 9.542 | 10.982 | 12.338 | 14.041 | 30.813 | 33.924 | 36.781 | 40.289 | 42.796 |
| 23 | 9.260 | 10.196 | 11.689 | 13.091 | 14.848 | 32.007 | 35.172 | 38.076 | 41.638 | 44.181 |
| 24 | 9.886 | 10.856 | 12.401 | 13.848 | 15.659 | 33.196 | 36.415 | 39.364 | 42.980 | 45.559 |
| 25 | 10.520 | 11.524 | 13.120 | 14.611 | 16.473 | 34.382 | 37.652 | 40.646 | 44.314 | 46.928 |
| 26 | 11.160 | 12.198 | 13.844 | 15.379 | 17.292 | 35.563 | 38.885 | 41.923 | 45.642 | 48.290 |
| 27 | 11.808 | 12.879 | 14.573 | 16.151 | 18.114 | 36.741 | 40.113 | 43.195 | 46.963 | 49.645 |
| 28 | 12.461 | 13.565 | 15.308 | 16.928 | 18.939 | 37.916 | 41.337 | 44.461 | 48.278 | 50.993 |
| 29 | 13.121 | 14.256 | 16.047 | 17.708 | 19.768 | 39.087 | 42.557 | 45.722 | 49.588 | 52.336 |
| 30 | 13.787 | 14.953 | 16.791 | 18.493 | 20.599 | 40.256 | 43.773 | 46.979 | 50.892 | 53.672 |
| 40 | 20.707 | 22.164 | 24.433 | 26.509 | 29.051 | 51.805 | 55.758 | 59.342 | 63.691 | 66.766 |
| 50 | 27.991 | 29.707 | 32.357 | 34.764 | 37.689 | 63.167 | 67.505 | 71.420 | 76.154 | 79.490 |
| 60 | 35.534 | 37.485 | 40.482 | 43.188 | 46.459 | 74.397 | 79.082 | 83.298 | 88.379 | 91.952 |
| 70 | 43.275 | 45.442 | 48.758 | 51.739 | 55.329 | 85.527 | 90.531 | 95.023 | 100.425 | 104.215 |

Table A13 Area to the Right of the Critical Value of $\chi^2$

| df | 0.995 | 0.990 | 0.975 | 0.950 | 0.900 | 0.100 | 0.050 | 0.025 | 0.010 | 0.005 |
|---|---|---|---|---|---|---|---|---|---|---|
| 80 | 51.172 | 53.540 | 57.153 | 60.391 | 64.278 | 96.578 | 101.879 | 106.629 | 112.329 | 116.321 |
| 90 | 59.196 | 61.754 | 65.647 | 69.126 | 73.291 | 107.565 | 113.145 | 118.136 | 124.116 | 128.299 |
| 100 | 67.328 | 70.065 | 74.222 | 77.929 | 82.358 | 118.498 | 124.342 | 129.561 | 135.807 | 140.169 |

Table A13 Area to the Right of the Critical Value of $\chi^2$

.

# APPENDIX B: MATHEMATICAL PHRASES, SYMBOLS, AND FORMULAS

## English Phrases Written Mathematically

| When the English says: | Interpret this as: |
|---|---|
| $X$ is at least 4. | $X \geq 4$ |
| The minimum of $X$ is 4. | $X \geq 4$ |
| $X$ is no less than 4. | $X \geq 4$ |
| $X$ is greater than or equal to 4. | $X \geq 4$ |
| $X$ is at most 4. | $X \leq 4$ |
| The maximum of $X$ is 4. | $X \leq 4$ |
| $X$ is no more than 4. | $X \leq 4$ |
| $X$ is less than or equal to 4. | $X \leq 4$ |
| $X$ does not exceed 4. | $X \leq 4$ |
| $X$ is greater than 4. | $X > 4$ |
| $X$ is more than 4. | $X > 4$ |
| $X$ exceeds 4. | $X > 4$ |
| $X$ is less than 4. | $X < 4$ |
| There are fewer $X$ than 4. | $X < 4$ |
| $X$ is 4. | $X = 4$ |
| $X$ is equal to 4. | $X = 4$ |
| $X$ is the same as 4. | $X = 4$ |
| $X$ is not 4. | $X \neq 4$ |
| $X$ is not equal to 4. | $X \neq 4$ |
| $X$ is not the same as 4. | $X \neq 4$ |
| $X$ is different than 4. | $X \neq 4$ |

Table B1

# Symbols and Their Meanings

| Chapter (1st used) | Symbol | Spoken | Meaning |
|---|---|---|---|
| Sampling and Data | $\sqrt{\phantom{x}}$ | The square root of | same |
| Sampling and Data | $\pi$ | Pi | 3.14159… (a specific number) |
| Descriptive Statistics | $Q_1$ | Quartile one | the first quartile |
| Descriptive Statistics | $Q_2$ | Quartile two | the second quartile |
| Descriptive Statistics | $Q_3$ | Quartile three | the third quartile |
| Descriptive Statistics | $IQR$ | interquartile range | $Q_3 - Q_1 = IQR$ |
| Descriptive Statistics | $\bar{x}$ | x-bar | sample mean |
| Descriptive Statistics | $\mu$ | mu | population mean |
| Descriptive Statistics | $s$ | s | sample standard deviation |
| Descriptive Statistics | $s^2$ | s squared | sample variance |
| Descriptive Statistics | $\sigma$ | sigma | population standard deviation |
| Descriptive Statistics | $\sigma^2$ | sigma squared | population variance |
| Descriptive Statistics | $\Sigma$ | capital sigma | sum |
| Probability Topics | $\{\}$ | brackets | set notation |
| Probability Topics | $S$ | S | sample space |
| Probability Topics | $A$ | Event A | event A |
| Probability Topics | $P(A)$ | probability of A | probability of A occurring |
| Probability Topics | $P(A|B)$ | probability of A given B | prob. of A occurring given B has occurred |
| Probability Topics | $P(A \cup B)$ | prob. of A or B | prob. of A or B or both occurring |
| Probability Topics | $P(A \cap B)$ | prob. of A and B | prob. of both A and B occurring (same time) |
| Probability Topics | $A'$ | A-prime, complement of A | complement of A, not A |
| Probability Topics | $P(A')$ | prob. of complement of A | same |
| Probability Topics | $G_1$ | green on first pick | same |
| Probability Topics | $P(G_1)$ | prob. of green on first pick | same |
| Discrete Random Variables | $PDF$ | prob. density function | same |
| Discrete Random Variables | $X$ | X | the random variable X |
| Discrete Random Variables | $X \sim$ | the distribution of X | same |
| Discrete Random Variables | $\geq$ | greater than or equal to | same |
| Discrete Random Variables | $\leq$ | less than or equal to | same |
| Discrete Random Variables | $=$ | equal to | same |
| Discrete Random Variables | $\neq$ | not equal to | same |

**Table B2 Symbols and their Meanings**

| Chapter (1st used) | Symbol | Spoken | Meaning |
|---|---|---|---|
| Continuous Random Variables | $f(x)$ | $f$ of $x$ | function of $x$ |
| Continuous Random Variables | $pdf$ | prob. density function | same |
| Continuous Random Variables | $U$ | uniform distribution | same |
| Continuous Random Variables | $Exp$ | exponential distribution | same |
| Continuous Random Variables | $f(x) =$ | $f$ of $x$ equals | same |
| Continuous Random Variables | $m$ | $m$ | decay rate (for exp. dist.) |
| The Normal Distribution | $N$ | normal distribution | same |
| The Normal Distribution | $z$ | $z$-score | same |
| The Normal Distribution | $Z$ | standard normal dist. | same |
| The Central Limit Theorem | $\bar{X}$ | $X$-bar | the random variable $X$-bar |
| The Central Limit Theorem | $\mu_{\bar{x}}$ | mean of $X$-bars | the average of $X$-bars |
| The Central Limit Theorem | $\sigma_{\bar{x}}$ | standard deviation of $X$-bars | same |
| Confidence Intervals | $CL$ | confidence level | same |
| Confidence Intervals | $CI$ | confidence interval | same |
| Confidence Intervals | $EBM$ | error bound for a mean | same |
| Confidence Intervals | $EBP$ | error bound for a proportion | same |
| Confidence Intervals | $t$ | Student's $t$-distribution | same |
| Confidence Intervals | $df$ | degrees of freedom | same |
| Confidence Intervals | $t_{\frac{\alpha}{2}}$ | student t with $\alpha/2$ area in right tail | same |
| Confidence Intervals | $p'$ | $p$-prime | sample proportion of success |
| Confidence Intervals | $q'$ | $q$-prime | sample proportion of failure |
| Hypothesis Testing | $H_0$ | $H$-naught, $H$-sub 0 | null hypothesis |
| Hypothesis Testing | $H_a$ | $H$-a, $H$-sub a | alternate hypothesis |
| Hypothesis Testing | $H_1$ | $H$-1, $H$-sub 1 | alternate hypothesis |
| Hypothesis Testing | $\alpha$ | alpha | probability of Type I error |
| Hypothesis Testing | $\beta$ | beta | probability of Type II error |
| Hypothesis Testing | $\bar{X1} - \bar{X2}$ | $X$1-bar minus $X$2-bar | difference in sample means |
| Hypothesis Testing | $\mu_1 - \mu_2$ | $mu$-1 minus $mu$-2 | difference in population means |
| Hypothesis Testing | $P'_1 - P'_2$ | $P$1-prime minus $P$2-prime | difference in sample proportions |

Table B2 Symbols and their Meanings

| Chapter (1st used) | Symbol | Spoken | Meaning |
|---|---|---|---|
| Hypothesis Testing | $p_1 - p_2$ | p1 minus p2 | difference in population proportions |
| Chi-Square Distribution | $X^2$ | Ky-square | Chi-square |
| Chi-Square Distribution | $O$ | Observed | Observed frequency |
| Chi-Square Distribution | $E$ | Expected | Expected frequency |
| Linear Regression and Correlation | $y = a + bx$ | y equals a plus b-x | equation of a straight line |
| Linear Regression and Correlation | $\hat{y}$ | y-hat | estimated value of y |
| Linear Regression and Correlation | $r$ | sample correlation coefficient | same |
| Linear Regression and Correlation | $\varepsilon$ | error term for a regression line | same |
| Linear Regression and Correlation | $SSE$ | Sum of Squared Errors | same |
| F-Distribution and ANOVA | $F$ | F-ratio | F-ratio |

**Table B2 Symbols and their Meanings**

# Formulas

| Symbols You Must Know | | |
|---|---|---|
| **Population** | | **Sample** |
| $N$ | Size | $n$ |
| $\mu$ | Mean | $\bar{x}$ |
| $\sigma^2$ | Variance | $s^2$ |
| $\sigma$ | Standard Deviation | $s$ |
| $p$ | Proportion | $p'$ |
| **Single Data Set Formulae** | | |
| **Population** | | **Sample** |
| $\mu = E(x) = \frac{1}{N}\sum_{i=1}^{N}(x_i)$ | Arithmetic Mean | $\bar{x} = \frac{1}{n}\sum_{i=1}^{n}(x_i)$ |
| | Geometric Mean | $\tilde{x} = \left(\prod_{i=1}^{n}X_i\right)^{\frac{1}{n}}$ |
| $Q_3 = \frac{3(n+1)}{4},\ Q_1 = \frac{(n+1)}{4}$ | Inter-Quartile Range $IQR = Q_3 - Q_1$ | $Q_3 = \frac{3(n+1)}{4},\ Q_1 = \frac{(n+1)}{4}$ |

**Table B3**

| $\sigma^2 = \frac{1}{N}\sum_{i=1}^{N}(x_i - \mu)^2$ | Variance | $s^2 = \frac{1}{n}\sum_{i=1}^{n}(x_i - \bar{x})^2$ |
|---|---|---|

### Single Data Set Formulae

| Population | | Sample |
|---|---|---|
| $\mu = E(x) = \frac{1}{N}\sum_{i=1}^{N}(m_i * f_i)$ | Arithmetic Mean | $\bar{x} = \frac{1}{n}\sum_{i=1}^{n}(m_i * f_i)$ |
| | Geometric Mean | $\tilde{x} = \left(\prod_{i=1}^{n}X_i\right)^{\frac{1}{n}}$ |
| $\sigma^2 = \frac{1}{N}\sum_{i=1}^{N}(m_i - \mu)^2 * f_i$ | Variance | $s^2 = \frac{1}{n}\sum_{i=1}^{n}(m_i - \bar{x})^2 * f_i$ |
| $CV = \frac{\sigma}{\mu} * 100$ | Coefficient of Variation | $CV = \frac{s}{\bar{x}} * 100$ |

Table B3

| Basic Probability Rules | |
|---|---|
| $P(A \cap B) = P(A|B) * P(B)$ | **Multiplication Rule** |
| $P(A \cup B) = P(A) + P(B) - P(A \cap B)$ | **Addition Rule** |
| $P(A \cap B) = P(A) * P(B)$ or $P(A|B) = P(A)$ | **Independence Test** |
| **Hypergeometric Distribution Formulae** | |
| $nCx = \binom{n}{x} = \frac{n!}{x!(n-x)!}$ | **Combinatorial Equation** |
| $P(x) = \frac{\binom{A}{x}\binom{N-A}{n-x}}{\binom{N}{n}}$ | **Probability Equation** |
| $E(X) = \mu = np$ | **Mean** |
| $\sigma^2 = \left(\frac{N-n}{N-1}\right)np(q)$ | **Variance** |
| **Binomial Distribution Formulae** | |
| $P(x) = \frac{n!}{x!(n-x)!}p^x(q)^{n-x}$ | **Probability Density Function** |
| $E(X) = \mu = np$ | **Arithmetic Mean** |
| $\sigma^2 = np(q)$ | **Variance** |
| **Geometric Distribution Formulae** | |

| $P(X = x) = (1-p)^{x-1}(p)$ | **Probability when $x$ is the first success.** | **Probability when $x$ is the number of failures before first success** | $P(X = x) = (1-p)^x(p)$ |
|---|---|---|---|

Table B4

| $\mu = \frac{1}{p}$ | Mean | Mean | $\mu = \frac{1-p}{p}$ |
|---|---|---|---|
| $\sigma^2 = \frac{(1-p)}{p^2}$ | Variance | Variance | $\sigma^2 = \frac{(1-p)}{p^2}$ |

| Poisson Distribution Formulae | |
|---|---|
| $P(x) = \frac{e^{-\mu}\mu^x}{x!}$ | **Probability Equation** |
| $E(X) = \mu$ | **Mean** |
| $\sigma^2 = \mu$ | **Variance** |
| **Uniform Distribution Formulae** | |
| $f(x) = \frac{1}{b-a}$ for $a \le x \le b$ | **PDF** |
| $E(X) = \mu = \frac{a+b}{2}$ | **Mean** |
| $\sigma^2 = \frac{(b-a)^2}{12}$ | **Variance** |
| **Exponential Distribution Formulae** | |
| $P(X \le x) = 1 - e^{-mx}$ | **Cumulative Probability** |
| $E(X) = \mu = \frac{1}{m}$ or $m = \frac{1}{\mu}$ | **Mean and Decay Factor** |
| $\sigma^2 = \frac{1}{m^2} = \mu^2$ | **Variance** |

Table B4

| The following page of formulae requires the use of the " $Z$ ", " $t$ ", " $\chi^2$ " or " $F$ " tables. | |
|---|---|
| $Z = \frac{x-\mu}{\sigma}$ | **Z-transformation for Normal Distribution** |
| $Z = \frac{x-np'}{\sqrt{np'(q')}}$ | **Normal Approximation to the Binomial** |
| **Probability** (ignores subscripts) <br> **Hypothesis Testing** | **Confidence Intervals** <br> [bracketed symbols equal margin of error] <br> (subscripts denote locations on respective distribution tables) |
| $Z_c = \frac{\bar{x} - \mu_0}{\frac{\sigma}{\sqrt{n}}}$ | *Interval for the population mean when sigma is known* <br> $\bar{x} \pm \left[ Z_{(\alpha/\ 2)} \frac{\sigma}{\sqrt{n}} \right]$ |
| $Z_c = \frac{\bar{x} - \mu_0}{\frac{s}{\sqrt{n}}}$ | *Interval for the population mean when sigma is unknown but $n > 30$* <br> $\bar{x} \pm \left[ Z_{(\alpha/\ 2)} \frac{s}{\sqrt{n}} \right]$ |
| $t_c = \frac{\bar{x} - \mu_0}{\frac{s}{\sqrt{n}}}$ | *Interval for the population mean when sigma is unknown but $n < 30$* <br> $\bar{x} \pm \left[ t_{(n-1),\ (\alpha/\ 2)} \frac{s}{\sqrt{n}} \right]$ |

Table B5

| | |
|---|---|
| $Z_c = \dfrac{p' - p_0}{\sqrt{\dfrac{p_0 q_0}{n}}}$ | *Interval for the population proportion*<br><br>$p' \pm \left[ Z_{(\alpha/2)} \sqrt{\dfrac{p'q'}{n}} \right]$ |
| $t_c = \dfrac{\bar{d} - \delta_0}{s_d}$ | *Interval for difference between two means with matched pairs*<br><br>$\bar{d} \pm \left[ t_{(n-1),\,(\alpha/2)} \dfrac{s_d}{\sqrt{n}} \right]$ where $s_d$ is the deviation of the differences |
| $Z_c = \dfrac{(\bar{x}_1 - \bar{x}_2) - \delta_0}{\sqrt{\dfrac{\sigma_1^2}{n_1} + \dfrac{\sigma_2^2}{n_2}}}$ | *Interval for difference between two means when sigmas are known*<br><br>$(\bar{x}_1 - \bar{x}_2) \pm \left[ Z_{(\alpha/2)} \sqrt{\dfrac{\sigma_1^2}{n_1} + \dfrac{\sigma_2^2}{n_2}} \right]$ |
| $t_c = \dfrac{(\bar{x}_1 - \bar{x}_2) - \delta_0}{\sqrt{\left( \dfrac{(s_1)^2}{n_1} + \dfrac{(s_2)^2}{n_2} \right)}}$ | *Interval for difference between two means with equal variances when sigmas are unknown*<br><br>$(\bar{x}_1 - \bar{x}_2) \pm \left[ t_{df,\,(\alpha/2)} \sqrt{\left( \dfrac{(s_1)^2}{n_1} + \dfrac{(s_2)^2}{n_2} \right)} \right]$ where<br><br>$df = \dfrac{\left( \dfrac{(s_1)^2}{n_1} + \dfrac{(s_2)^2}{n_2} \right)^2}{\left( \dfrac{1}{n_1 - 1} \right)\left( \dfrac{(s_1)^2}{n_1} \right) + \left( \dfrac{1}{n_2 - 1} \right)\left( \dfrac{(s_2)^2}{n_2} \right)}$ |
| $Z_c = \dfrac{(p'_1 - p'_2) - \delta_0}{\sqrt{\dfrac{p'_1(q'_1)}{n_1} + \dfrac{p'_2(q'_2)}{n_2}}}$ | *Interval for difference between two population proportions*<br><br>$(p'_1 - p'_2) \pm \left[ Z_{(\alpha/2)} \sqrt{\dfrac{p'_1(q'_1)}{n_1} + \dfrac{p'_2(q'_2)}{n_2}} \right]$ |
| $\chi_c^2 = \dfrac{(n-1)s^2}{\sigma_0^2}$ | *Tests for GOF, Independence, and Homogeneity*<br><br>$\chi_c^2 = \Sigma \dfrac{(O - E)^2}{E}$ where $O$ = observed values and $E$ = expected values |
| $F_c = \dfrac{s_1^2}{s_2^2}$ | *Where $s_1^2$ is the sample variance which is the larger of the two sample variances* |

| **The Next 3 Formulae are for Determining Sample Size with Confidence Intervals**<br>(note: E represents the margin of error) | | |
|---|---|---|
| $n = \dfrac{Z_{\left(\frac{a}{2}\right)}^2 \sigma^2}{E^2}$<br><br>*Use when sigma is known*<br>$E = \bar{x} - \mu$ | $n = \dfrac{Z_{\left(\frac{a}{2}\right)}^2 (0.25)}{E^2}$<br><br>*Use when $p\prime$ is unknown*<br>$E = p' - p$ | $n = \dfrac{Z_{\left(\frac{a}{2}\right)}^2 [p'(q')]}{E^2}$<br><br>*Use when $p\prime$ is uknown*<br>$E = p' - p$ |

Table B5

| **Simple Linear Regression Formulae for $y = a + b(x)$** | |
|---|---|
| $r = \dfrac{\Sigma \left[ (x - \bar{x})(y - \bar{y}) \right]}{\sqrt{\Sigma (x - \bar{x})^2 * \Sigma (y - \bar{y})^2}} = \dfrac{S_{xy}}{S_x S_y} = \sqrt{\dfrac{SSR}{SST}}$ | **Correlation Coefficient** |

Table B6

| | |
|---|---|
| $b = \dfrac{\Sigma\left[\left(x - \bar{x}\right)\left(y - \bar{y}\right)\right]}{\Sigma\left(x - \bar{x}\right)^2} = \dfrac{S_{xy}}{SS_x} = r_{y,\,x}\left(\dfrac{s_y}{s_x}\right)$ | **Coefficient $b$ (slope)** |
| $a = \bar{y} - b\left(\bar{x}\right)$ | **y-intercept** |
| $s_e^2 = \dfrac{\Sigma\left(y_i - \hat{y}_i\right)^2}{n - k} = \dfrac{\sum\limits_{i=1}^{n} e_i^2}{n - k}$ | **Estimate of the Error Variance** |
| $S_b = \dfrac{s_e^2}{\sqrt{\left(x_i - \bar{x}\right)^2}} = \dfrac{s_e^2}{(n-1)s_x^2}$ | **Standard Error for Coefficient $b$** |
| $t_c = \dfrac{b - \beta_0}{s_b}$ | **Hypothesis Test for Coefficient $\beta$** |
| $b \pm \left[t_{n-2,\,\alpha/2}\, S_b\right]$ | **Interval for Coefficient $\beta$** |
| $\hat{y} \pm \left[t_{\alpha/2} * s_e\left(\sqrt{\dfrac{1}{n} + \dfrac{\left(x_p - \bar{x}\right)^2}{s_x}}\right)\right]$ | **Interval for Expected value of $y$** |
| $\hat{y} \pm \left[t_{\alpha/2} * s_e\left(\sqrt{1 + \dfrac{1}{n} + \dfrac{\left(x_p - \bar{x}\right)^2}{s_x}}\right)\right]$ | **Prediction Interval for an Individual $y$** |
| **ANOVA Formulae** | |
| $SSR = \sum\limits_{i=1}^{n} (\hat{y}_i - \bar{y})^2$ | **Sum of Squares Regression** |
| $SSE = \sum\limits_{i=1}^{n} (\hat{y}_i - \bar{y}_i)^2$ | **Sum of Squares Error** |
| $SST = \sum\limits_{i=1}^{n} (y_i - \bar{y})^2$ | **Sum of Squares Total** |
| $R^2 = \dfrac{SSR}{SST}$ | **Coefficient of Determination** |

Table B6

| The following is the breakdown of a one-way ANOVA table for linear regression. | | | | |
|---|---|---|---|---|
| *Source of Variation* | *Sum of Squares* | *Degrees of Freedom* | *Mean Squares* | *F − Ratio* |
| Regression | SSR | *1 or k − 1* | $MSR = \dfrac{SSR}{df_R}$ | $F = \dfrac{MSR}{MSE}$ |
| Error | SSE | $n - k$ | $MSE = \dfrac{SSE}{df_E}$ | |
| Total | SST | $n - 1$ | | |

Table B7

# INDEX

CPSIA information can be obtained
at www.ICGtesting.com
Printed in the USA
BVHW062320291220
596438BV00006B/147